D1379409

CORPORATE TAXATION

CORPORATE TAXATION

Charlotte Crane
Professor of Law
Northwestern University School of Law

Linda McKissack Beale
Associate Professor of Law
Wayne State University Law School

Library of Congress Cataloging-in-Publication Data

Crane, Charlotte.
  Corporate taxation / Charlotte Crane, Linda McKissack Beale.
    p. cm. -- (Lexisnexis graduate tax series)
  Includes index.
  ISBN 978-1-4224-1999-1
  1. Corporations--Taxation--Law and legislation--United States. I. Beale, Linda McKissack. II. Title.
  KF6464.C73 2012
  343.7306'7--dc23
                                                                    2011046881

This publication is designed to provide authoritative information in regard to the subject matter covered. It is sold with the understanding that the publisher is not engaged in rendering legal, accounting, or other professional services. If legal advice or other expert assistance is required, the services of a competent professional should be sought.

NOTE TO USERS
To ensure that you are using the latest materials available in this area, please be sure to periodically check the LexisNexis Law School web site for downloadable updates and supplements at www.lexisnexis.com/lawschool.

Editorial Offices
121 Chanlon Rd., New Providence, NJ 07974 (908) 464-6800
201 Mission St., San Francisco, CA 94105-1831 (415) 908-3200
www.lexisnexis.com

MATTHEW◆BENDER

(2012–Pub.3253)

PREFACE

This First Edition of *Taxation of Corporations* comes out on roughly the twenty-fifth anniversary of the "repeal of *General Utilities*." Many at the time saw that development as a high-water mark in the commitment to the corporate tax and to the body of law traditionally associated with a law school course in corporate tax.

Much has changed since then. There is currently enormous pressure on the corporate tax. Although any entity with publicly traded equity is still subject to subchapter C, the percentage of new equity being invested domestically in such entities continues to dwindle. In addition, ever increasing percentages of the equity subject to subchapter C is held by shareholders, including charitable institutions, pension plans and other tax-preferred savings vehicles, which are relatively indifferent to many of the traditional aspects of shareholder taxation. These trends may have made the basic structure of subchapter C seem less important. But the details about its implementation in previously obscure areas — like the use of subchapter C corporations as "blockers" or the special rules applicable when corporations are partners — have become increasingly important, and cannot be understood without understanding the basic structure.

There is much discussion about substantial corporate tax reform ongoing in Congress, but the direction of that reform remains to be seen. The last decade saw changes that reduced both the taxes on shareholder income and the taxes on corporate income. In 2003, Congress enacted a temporary preferential rate for corporate dividends, significantly impacting (at least temporarily) the primary rationale for many of the corporate tax provisions that attempt to prevent a bailout of earnings at capital gains rates rather than the ordinary rates that have typically applied to corporate dividends. The 2004 "American Jobs Creation Act" provided another round of tax breaks for C corporations, along with more anti-abuse rules. The codification of the economic substance doctrine, considered in Congress since at least 1995 and finally enacted in 2010, will likely have an ongoing impact on corporate transactions, but the exact nature of that impact remains unclear. Proposals to remove the disparity between the tax burden on income earned by subchapter C corporations and that earned by other business entities by expanding the scope of the tax to unincorporated enterprises continue to be made, with increasing likelihood that they will be taken seriously.

Even without such politically-charged moves by Congress, the law of subchapter C is no longer the law that was put in place in 1986. The legislative and regulatory responses to the "corporate tax shelters" devised in the decades immediately following *General Utilities*' repeal have introduced significant complexity in even the most basic provisions. Other regulatory developments, including the "check-the-box" regulations and the streamlining of many aspects of the law surrounding reorganizations, may have provided solutions to the problems perceived by practitioners intent on reducing taxes in connection with transactional planning, but they have done little to make the law as a whole more comprehensible.

Newer pressures have been created by the effort to improve the income tax compliance of shareholders through basis information reporting. At the corporate level, this change has put new emphasis on the concept of the share as the basic unit of property, a concept which if implemented to the fullest has the possibility of producing unexpected results in many transactions and perhaps highly questionable alterations in the reorganization provisions. New pressures have also been created by the "globalization" of subchapter C. Its provisions are often used (in the quest for the maximization of foreign tax credits) to calculate the US income of entities not currently subject to US tax. It is safe to say that the drafters of many provisions, especially sections 304, 351(g) and 338, could not have foreseen the role these provisions would come to play.

These developments have clearly made the corporate taxation more of a challenge to teach. This text was therefore developed with the underlying rationale of helping the student establish a solid background in the basic principles of subchapter C, not just as it exists today but as it will evolve in the near future.

Both authors believe that problem solving is critical to learning corporate tax. The text therefore provides relatively simple practice problems for each chapter designed to ensure that students grasp the fundamental operations of those provisions. The text also includes discussion problems that require students to synthesize the materials and consider planning alternatives. In these problems — and sometimes even in the text — the issues raised go beyond issues for which there is clear authority.

Student course materials all too often are prepared so that they address only what can be said is definitely the law, and use only the regulations and the decided cases as the sources both for the questions that are raised and the answers that are provided. This approach leaves both the instructor and the student with a high level of confidence about having mastered the material. But it ultimately shortchanges the student because first, there is a lot of gloss on the statute that doesn't reveal itself easily in either regulations or decided cases, and, second, this approach does not prepare the student to analyze transactions that are even slightly unusual, much less to understand the pressures that drive the evolution of the law. An appreciation of why there is no authority on a point can be as important as understanding the authorities that do exist.

The result, we both hope and fear, is a set of problems that are somewhat challenging. Those instructors who have limited time may prefer to rely on the Practice Problems as the vehicles used for presenting the materials and assign the discussion problems sparingly. In order not to render the material too intimidating, the teacher's manual provides answers for both types of problems and explores a number of issues that can be raised in the discussion problems at the discretion of the instructor.

On the other hand, we have omitted from the student text many details revealed by decided authorities that sometimes clutter the "notes" sections of traditional casebooks. Our view is that these items tend to overwhelm both the student and the instructor, and all too frequently highlight relatively insignificant parts of the law. Discussion of many such items is nevertheless included in the teacher's manual. The manual also develops a number of other advanced topics that were not included in the text because they raise difficult conceptual issues or are perhaps too advanced for most J.D. tax courses: the instructor may choose to discuss these topics or not depending on the level of preparation of the students and the intended coverage of the course. The manual also offers suggestions for additional reading, with both more theoretical articles and articles selected from practice that will be of particular interest to those who are teaching the course as a skills-oriented course.

Because the corporate provisions are so dense and changes are frequent and substantial, the authors designed the text to be used flexibly. We do not begin with section 351 and the formation of corporations but rather with operating distributions. This approach grounds the student in the aspects of subchapter C that distinguish it from the other regimes under which business income may be taxed, and reduces the chance that the student will associate section 351 only with corporate formation. Nonetheless, for those who wish to continue using the "life cycle" order of introducing topics, the text is set up in free-standing chapters that can be used in whatever order the instructor chooses. An instructor may also opt for in-depth coverage of some areas and less detailed coverage of others.

The text includes almost no original materials from court cases or administrative guidance. We indicate for each chapter the most relevant Code sections and authoritative materials. It is our assumption that students will read relevant materials online before class, and that the instructor will highlight those items that are particularly important for the course as it develops. Our view is that students should encounter these authorities in their full, unedited state, rather than reading a carefully edited excerpt that points them directly to the relevant phrases. We believe that it is important for students to develop an ability to read and understand tax statutes, revenue rulings, regulation preambles and amendments on their own, without being "spoonfed" by text and teacher.

Part I of the text covers the fundamentals of corporate taxation. In Subpart A dealing with the general taxation of corporations, the text begins with a discussion of the corporate tax base (Chapter 1) and distributions from corporations (Chapter 2). It then covers shareholder transfers of property to corporations under section 351 (Chapter 3) and deals separately with liability assumptions in connection with those transactions (Chapter 4). (We hope that this separation will result in more focused attention on the conceptual difficulties inherent in dealing with liabilities that may not be associated with any particular asset or that may not be easily quantified.) The last chapters in Subpart A deal with corporate liquidations and their effects on the corporation and minority shareholders (Chapter 5) and the DRD and liquidations of controlled subsidiaries (Chapter 6). Subpart B covers other building block transactions: redemptions under section 302 (Chapter 7), redemptions through related corporation sales under section 304 (Chapter 8), and stock distributions and similar transactions such as recapitalizations (Chapter 9).

Once these basic building block transactions are introduced, students are prepared to explore choice of entity issues and the pass-through corporate tax entity. Subpart C introduces subchapter S concepts (Chapter 10) and discusses choice of entity and capital structure issues (Chapter 11). Subpart D deals with taxable asset and stock acquisitions (Chapter 12), section 338 recharacterization of stock acquisitions as asset acquisitions (Chapter 13), and the rules for carryovers of tax attributes and limitations on losses after corporate acquisitions and restructurings (Chapter 14).

Subpart E concludes Part I with nontaxable reorganizations. It begins with an overview discussing the sources of rules, basic patterns and consequences to the parties in acquisitive reorganizations, with special emphasis here on A reorgs (Chapter 15). There follows an intensive discussion of boot in reorganizations (Chapter 16); B reorgs (Chapter 17); C reorgs (Chapter 18); and triangular mergers and a discussion of drop-downs and push-ups of acquired stock or assets and multi-step reorganizations generally (Chapter 19). The remaining chapters in this Subpart deal with other acquisitive and nondivisive transactions including acquisitive section 351 transactions, double dummies, and nondivisive D reorgs (Chapter 20); the complications in the implementation of subchapter C resulting from the presence of disregarded entities (Chapter 21); F reorgs

PREFACE

(Chapter 22); and an extensive discussion of section 355, including the post-General Utilities anti-abuse rules (Chapters 23 – 25).

Part II provides a discussion of advanced topics that some instructors may wish to incorporate along with one of the earlier chapters or pick and choose for a few advanced topics at the end of the course. Subpart A deals with debt and equity issues of particular interest in the corporate context, including section 1032 and the use of a corporation's own stock, options, or tracking stock (Chapter 26) and transactions involving debt of related parties (Chapter 27). Subpart B provides a brief introduction to consolidated returns, as a means of exploring advanced topics in entity organization (Chapter 28).

TABLE OF CONTENTS

TABLE OF CONTENTS

TABLE OF CONTENTS

TABLE OF CONTENTS

TABLE OF CONTENTS

TABLE OF CONTENTS

TABLE OF CONTENTS

TABLE OF CONTENTS

TABLE OF CONTENTS

TABLE OF CONTENTS

TABLE OF CONTENTS

TABLE OF CONTENTS

TABLE OF CONTENTS

Part I

FUNDAMENTALS OF CORPORATE TAXATION

TAXATION OF CORPORATIONS GENERALLY

Chapter 1

THE CORPORATE TAX BASE

Statutes and Regulations	IRC §§ 1(h)(11); 11; 55–59; 59A; 162(m); 163(e)(5), (i), (j), (l); 170(b)(2); 280G; 291; 301; 448; 482; 531–537; 541–547; 269A; 1201; 1211–1212; 1222–1223; 1501–1504; 1561(a)(1); 1563
Other Primary Authorities	Estate of Jelke v. Commissioner, T.C. Memo 2005-131 (2005), *vacated and remanded by* 507 F.3d 1317 (11th Cir. 2007)
	Exacto Spring Corp. v. Commissioner, 196 F.3d 833 (7th Cir. 1999)
	Boler v. Commissioner, T.C. Memo 2002-155
	Roman Systems, Ltd. v. Commissioner, T.C. Memo 1981-273 (1981)

Corporations in the United States are subject to what is sometimes referred to as the classic regime of corporate taxation. Corporations are for the most part regarded as entirely separate legal entities, subject to tax on their income, and shareholders are considered to be receiving income fully subject to tax when they receive distributions from corporations out of corporate earnings.

Subchapter C sets out the rules for implementing this classical regime. It applies to entities that have charters as "corporations" and to certain other entities that are treated as corporations for tax purposes (due to an election or due to an applicable Code provision that specifies that status).

Subchapter C does not, however, apply to all legal entities or even to all legal entities that can provide limited liability to their owners. There are several choices of entities available in most states for doing business with limited liability that may be accorded federal income tax treatment as "pass-through" entities. (Owners of interests in pass-through entities report their share of the pass-through entity's earnings on their individual tax returns as the income is earned, and the entity itself is not subject to tax on the earnings.) Pass-through entities include those organized under state law as limited partnerships which must have at least one general partner who is liable for the entity's debts or, in some states, "limited liability limited partnerships" in which no partner is liable for the entity's debts. They also include limited liability companies (LLCs), a type of entity that has been available only since the mid-1990s that does not need to have any member that is personally liable for the entity's debts: unless they elect otherwise, multiple-member LLCs are treated as pass-through entities subject to the partnership tax rules in subchapter

K. Reg. § 301.7701-2(c)(1).

Pass-through treatment is not available for entities, however, if a market exists in their interests, except in certain partnerships with mostly passive income. § 7704 (publicly traded partnership rules). Thus, although the United States came to this result almost by accident, the ordinary cost of access to public capital markets is the subjection of the business to corporate-level taxation.

The legal form of the entity does not entirely determine the tax regime to which the entity will be subject. Entities that would normally be taxed as pass-through entities may elect to be subject to subchapter C. Reg. § 301.7701-3(a). Single-member entities of the type for which pass-through treatment is normally available will be disregarded for tax purposes, unless they elect to be treated as corporations. Reg. § 301.7701-2(c)(2). Finally, entities organized under ordinary state corporate law or otherwise treated as a corporation may elect to be treated as pass-throughs under subchapter S, but only if they have 100 or fewer shareholders and very simple capital structures. § 1361 *et seq.*

All gains on stock held by shareholders who are otherwise taxable will be taxed on the sale of the stock, regardless of the reasons for holding the stock. A significant amount of publicly traded stock, however, is held by entities that are not subject to U.S. federal income tax on most or all of their income, including corporate pension plans, tax-preferred retirement accounts held by individuals, and tax-exempt entities such as educational institutions.

Since 2003, the maximum tax rate on qualifying dividends received by individuals has been set at 15%, the same as the maximum rate for most capital gains recognized by individuals. § 1(h)(11). This special rate for dividends was originally set to expire at the end of 2008 but has since been extended through 2012. At the time of publication of this book, it is unclear whether the special rate on dividends received by individuals will be extended again or made permanent and, if extended, whether it will remain tied to the capital gains rate or will be a slightly higher rate.

What may be perceived by some as the potential harshness of the classical tax regime (that is, the potential for tax at the corporate tax rate on corporate earnings and tax at the individual's rate on dividend distributions) is mitigated in various ways. First, the burden imposed on the corporation itself may well be far less than the statutory rate suggests. Although the statutory corporate tax rate is a flat 35% for the largest corporations, a substantial number of publicly held corporations that report significant business profits actually pay current federal income tax at substantially lower effective rates. Many large corporations, in fact, may pay no corporate tax at all for long periods of time. One study estimated that more than 46 corporations with combined reported profits of more than $42.6 billion reported no or negative income tax liabilities in 2003.[1] A 2008 GAO study confirmed that during the years 1996 to 2005, more than half of the domestic corporations with sales over

---

[1] Robert S. McIntyre & T.D. Coo Nguyen, *Corporate Income Taxes in the Bush Years*, Citizens for Tax Justice (Sept. 2004), available at http://www.ctj.org/corpfed04an.pdf (finding that while pretax profits of 275 of America's top 500 corporations jumped 26% from 2001 to 2003, their effective tax rate fell by a fifth; 46 companies with profits of $42.6 billion paid a negative effective rate of -12.8% in 2003).

$50 million filed a tax return showing no tax liability; almost 3% filed returns in each of those years showing no liability.[2]

What explains these results? Is it the porousness of the base itself, with the plethora of corporate tax incentives aimed at encouraging particular types of investments and, in more recent years, at reducing effective rates overall in the name of economic growth and international competitiveness? How much of these differences between reported profits and reported taxable income can be accounted for by the discrepancy between tax and book accounting for offshore investments? The ability to carry losses forward to profitable years is also a factor. These issues are a matter of significant political debate and cannot be resolved here. Nonetheless, the reality is that the more visible aspects of the statute, including the stated rate and the full taxation of dividends, do not accurately reflect the burdens actually borne.

Second, the burden on shareholders as corporate earnings are withdrawn is also often less than the burden on other income received by individuals. When corporate income is distributed to shareholders, it generally will be taxed at preferential capital gains rates for qualifying dividends (currently 0% in the lowest income brackets and 15% for the rest). In addition, many shareholders who own significant holdings of corporate stock have retained their interests long term and passed them to their heirs at death with a step-up in basis under section 1014 and those interests have historically been subject to a relatively generous estate tax regime as well. (As of the finalization of this text, it is uncertain what rules will apply in these cases in the future; the estate tax has been temporarily reinstated with a $5 million exemption and a top rate of 35%, but is slated to spring back at 2001 levels in 2011.) Under the historical regime, those shareholders who need not consume values held through corporate shares before death can avoid the individual-level tax completely by simply refraining from selling those shares until death. Finally, those who must consume values held in corporations can nonetheless sometimes avoid taxation by properly "monetizing" their interest: for instance, they may borrow without repayment during life and at death transfer their stock to their heirs, who will receive it (again, under the historical regime) with a stepped-up basis for sales without gains from which to repay the loan.

---

[2] GAO, Tax Administration: Comparison of the Reported Tax Liabilities of Foreign- and U.S.-Controlled Corporations, 1998–2005 (GAO-08-957, July 2008), available at http://www.gao.gov/new.items/d08957.pdf. *See, e.g.,* Chye-Ching Huang, *Putting U.S. Corporate Taxes in Perspective*, Center for Budget and Policy Priorities (Oct. 27, 2008), available at http://www.cbpp.org/files/10-27-08tax.pdf.

Monetizing Shares

Estee Lauder's estate planning took these monetizing transactions to such a level that Congress took notice. She and her son Ronald hoped to avoid $95 million in taxes by borrowing shares of Estee Lauder Co. from acquaintances and selling those borrowed shares in the company's initial public offering in 1995, thereby accomplishing a "short against the box" transaction. Because the shares were borrowed, the open transaction rules applied and no gain was taken into account. If the transaction were not closed prior to Ms. Lauder's death, then the heirs could sell shares received from the estate with a stepped-up basis to repay the borrowed shares, thus avoiding any income tax on the monetization or the sale of inherited shares. Congress restricted the tax advantages of "shorts against the box" with the enactment of section 1259, in the Tax Reform Act of 1997 (and deprived the Lauders of their hoped-for tax benefit on positions already in place by tinkering with the rules that would have made the basis step-up under section 1014 available). Section 1259 is a constructive sale provision, which taxes certain transactions as though the taxpayer had sold an appreciated financial position to a third party for its fair market value. The transactions covered include shorts against the box, swaps, and forwards. The limitation isn't absolute: a taxpayer can do a short, close the position within a month of the year end, and then put the short back on after 60 days without causing a constructive sale. § 1259.

The classical regime has both vigorous opponents and strong supporters. Opponents view the regime as normatively inappropriate, on the grounds that only individuals bear the burden of tax. They also point out the somewhat haphazard way in which the classical regime developed in the U.S. Proponents support separate taxation of corporations on various grounds, ranging from "benefits received" by corporations as actors that have been granted "personhood" in today's global society (including corporations' ability to lobby for laws beneficial to their interests and to rely on free speech, due process, and other constitutional protections) to a means of ensuring some progressivity in the tax system (given the substantial ability of both wealthy corporations and wealthy shareholders to engage in tax sheltering activities) to an important factor in sustaining democratic institutions (by restraining, in some small degree, the power of multinational corporate entities).

Two general normative principles that apply to transactions between corporations and their shareholders help define the corporate tax base under the classical regime. First, in general, only values earned by a corporation above and beyond the values shareholders contribute to it as capital are included in income. Second, an additional corporate tax will not always be applied to income that a corporation receives from its stockholdings in other corporations. Thus, there are many provisions that either allow a corporation that receives value from another corporation to eliminate all or part of that value from income (for instance, the dividends-received deduction under section 243 and the treatment of complete liquidations of subsidiaries under section 332) or allow nonrecognition for a transaction that would appear to be a realization event (for instance, the nonrecognition on the transfer of value to a corporate parent upon liquidation of a corporation under section 337). There are, however, many places in which the details in the statute deviate from both these general principles.

Since 1986, the Code has in effect provided that all values earned by a corporation (including appreciation of its assets) be taxed to that corporation no later than upon distribution to individual shareholders. This was a substantial change in the law that is still referred to as "the repeal of *General Utilities*" because it reversed the result of a Supreme Court decision of that name. Thus all of the gain on assets held by corporations will be taxed if those assets are ever withdrawn from corporate solution. Moving assets among related corporations may also trigger this gain and therefore requires careful planning. The technical aspects of the provisions enforcing the repeal of *General Utilities* are a substantial part of this course.

1.1. THE CORPORATE RATE STRUCTURE

Section 11(b) sets out the rates applicable to corporate income. The rates are graduated from 15% to 35%, but the benefits of this graduated system are eliminated for corporations with incomes higher than certain threshold amounts by two surcharge provisions in the flush language of paragraph (1). The surcharge provision begins to eliminate the benefit of the 15% and 25% rates once a corporation's income exceeds $100,000, and begins to eliminate the benefit of the 34% rate once a corporation's income exceeds $15,000,000. The average and stated marginal rates level out at 35% for corporations earning more than $18,333,333.

2010 stated corporate rates:

Up to $50,000	15%
Over 50,000 but not over $75,000	25%
Over 75,000 but not over $10,000,000	34%
Over $10,000,000	35%

2010 corporate rates including the two surcharges:

Up to $50,000	15%
Over $50,000 but not over $75,000	25%
Over $75,000 but not over $100,000	34%
Over $100,000 but not over $335,000	39%
Over $335,000 but not over $10,000,000	34%
Over $10,000,000 but not over $15,000,000	35%
Over $15,000,000 but not over $18,333,333	38%
Over $18,333,333	35%

Since corporations with smaller incomes enjoy the lower bracket rates, but corporations with higher incomes are essentially taxed at either a 34% or a 35% rate, one might think that it would be advantageous to replace a single large corporation with multiple smaller corporations each earning less than $75,000 in profits. That potential benefit is eliminated by section 1561(a)(1), which provides that the aggregate income of a controlled group of corporations filing separately that is taxed in each bracket cannot exceed the maximum for that bracket that a single unaffiliated corporation would be entitled to. A group of corporations is a "controlled group of corporations" under section 1563 if, under a special set of attribution rules and various rules for excluding certain stock from the determination, five or fewer individuals (or estates or trusts) own more than 50% by vote or value of each corporation, taking into account only that part of the stock ownership of each that is held in identical proportions in each such corporation, or if they share a common parent corporation that owns 80% by vote or value.

The graduated rates are not available for "personal service corporations as defined in section 448." The section covers those corporations "substantially all of the activities of which involve the performance of services in the fields of health, law, engineering, architecture, accounting, actuarial science, performing arts or consulting" and are owned by the service providers.

Despite the fact that section 1201 suggests otherwise, there is currently no general special rate for corporate capital gains, since section 1201 directs that the maximum rate on capital gains is 35%, the same rate as the top corporate rate on regular income. The capital losses of corporations are nevertheless subject to the "basketing" limitation of section 1211 that disallows losses in excess of gains. (There is nothing equivalent to the $3,000 of excess capital loss annually allowed to individuals against ordinary income.) The limitations on carrybacks and carryforwards applicable to corporations are found in section 1212: capital losses generally may be carried back 3 years and forward 5 years.

Congress has in the past imposed additional taxes on corporate income. See, for instance, section 59A, which imposed a 0.12% tax on the difference between regular corporate income and a modified alternative minimum tax base between 1986 and 1996.

The fact that corporate rates are graduated and can be lower than individual rates creates, at least for relatively small businesses, an incentive to do business as corporations despite the entity-level tax to which corporations are subject.

Table 1. The Combined Burden of the Corporate and Individual Tax on Currently Distributed Corporate Earnings

Total amount available after tax to a corporation and to shareholders on current distribution								
		Ind'l rate ⇒	0	0.15	0.25	0.28	0.33	0.35
	Corp. rate ↓							
Before distribution	0		100	100	100	100	100	100
After distribution			100	0.85	75	72	67	65
Before distribution	0.15		85	85	85	85	85	85
After distribution			85	72.25	63.75	61.2	56.95	55.25
Before distribution	0.25		75	75	75	75	75	75
After distribution			75	63.75	56.25	54	50.25	48.75
Before distribution	0.34		66	66	66	66	66	66
After distribution			66	56.1	49.5	47.52	44.22	42.9
Before distribution	0.35		65	65	65	65	65	65
After distribution			66	55.25	48.75	46.8	43.55	42.25
Before distribution	0.38		62	62	62	62	62	62
After distribution			62	56.1	46.5	44.64	41.54	40.3

If all corporate income were currently distributed (which it typically is not), the above figures would reflect the interaction of typical corporate and individual rates. For a taxpayer subject to tax at the lower individual rates who receives a distribution from a corporation subject to the lowest corporate rates, the aggregate corporate and individual tax (for instance, 27.75% when the shareholder rate is 15% and the corporate rate is 15%) is still less than the individual tax due for an individual subject to tax at the highest rates on income that is earned in a pass-through entity or is earned in a sole proprietorship (for instance, if the individual's other income renders the entity income subject to the 33% rate).

Is this of any consequence, given that any corporate tax will always produce a higher combined tax on any given income stream than would be faced if the entire income stream were earned by the individual directly? Perhaps, if income splitting can be accomplished more effectively through the use of a corporation than through the use of a pass-through entity. If a high-bracket taxpayer can incorporate the income stream and give stock to low-bracket taxpayers, the aggregate tax paid by the corporation and the low-bracket taxpayer on the income stream can be less than the tax the high-bracket taxpayer would have faced on that same income stream without incorporation. However, the superiority of the corporate form for this kind of income splitting is greatly reduced by the "repeal of General Utilities" (which means that all gain arising at the corporate level must eventually be subject to tax, at least theoretically, upon distribution or other disposition, though possibly with indefinite deferral) and the rise of the limited liability company (which means that there is more choice among types of pass-through entities that will be acceptable as business vehicles). Note that the 15% rate for individuals' dividend income is currently set to expire in 2012.

Because corporations can control the timing of distributions to shareholders, the full impact of the entity and shareholder levels of tax is rarely felt. Corporate managers often prefer to, and can, retain rather than distribute earnings. When corporate rates generally are lower than individual rates (or when tax preferences are available for corporations that are not available for individuals), there can be significant tax advantages in using the corporate form.

Table 2. The Effect of Entity and Shareholder Taxation with Deferred Imposition of Individual-Level Tax

year of distribution	1	2	3	4	5	6	7	8
tax-free accumulation on investment of 100, with return of 10%								
	100	110	121	133	146	161	177	195	214
accumulation at individual tax rates, currently taxable at 35%								
	100.00	106.50	113.42	120.79	128.65	137.01	145.91	155.40	165.50
accumulation at 15% corporate rates, currently taxable; shareholder 15% tax on liquidation or distribution								
	100.00	108.50	117.72	127.73	138.59	150.37	163.15	177.01	192.06
SH tax		1.28	2.66	4.16	5.79	7.55	9.47	11.55	13.81
		107.23	115.06	123.57	132.80	142.81	153.67	165.46	178.25
accumulation at 25% corporate rates, currently taxable; shareholder 15% tax on liquidation or distribution								
	100.00	107.50	115.56	124.23	133.55	143.56	154.33	165.90	178.35
SH tax		1.13	2.33	3.63	5.03	6.53	8.15	9.89	11.75
		106.38	113.23	120.60	128.51	137.03	146.18	156.02	166.60
accumulation at 35% corporate rates, currently taxable; shareholder 15% tax on liquidation or distribution								
	100.00	106.50	113.42	120.79	128.65	137.01	145.91	155.40	165.50
SH tax		0.98	2.01	3.12	4.30	5.55	6.89	8.31	9.82
		105.53	111.41	117.68	124.35	131.46	139.03	147.09	155.67

accumulation on investment of 100, with untaxed return of 10%, and 15% capital gain on sale at year 8									
		100	110	121	133	146	161	177	195	214
								tax on sale		17
										197

This table illustrates how the burden to the shareholder (SH) of the entity-level tax is affected by the ability to control the timing of the individual shareholder-level tax. When the corporate-level tax is less than the individual-level tax on the same income stream would be, accumulations within the corporation can be more advantageous than accumulations outside, if the shareholder tax can be deferred long enough.

This table does not capture an additional benefit inherent in accumulation <u>outside</u> the corporate form. If the accumulation occurring outside corporate solution is not subject to tax without a realization event (for instance, appreciation in raw land), the accumulation can either be enjoyed as consumption value through borrowing or by heirs at death without ever being subjected to tax. Because the corporate entity is considered separate from its shareholders, shareholders do not "look through" the corporate entity to the assets — and thus there is no similar step-up in basis in the assets of a corporation upon the death of a shareholder (though there is a step-up in basis of the corporate stock).

The possibility that a corporation might hold assets yielding income that is not currently taxed creates further complications in determining the relative advantage or disadvantage of using a corporate form subject to subchapter C.

The availability of a 15% rate on dividends effectively requires the corporation and its shareholders to consider their positions with respect to the above calculation every year, since this rate means that a shareholder can now "cash in" the portion of his holding that represents corporate earnings at only a slightly greater tax cost than selling his stock, and need not give up his percentage of participation in the corporation at all. (The slightly higher tax cost associated with distributing earnings results from the fact that no offset for basis is allowed in computing the amount of a dividend distributed from corporate earnings.)

1.2.　COMPUTING CORPORATE INCOME

Apart from transactions between corporations and their shareholders, corporate income is computed under the same general rules applicable to individuals, except that the issues involving personal items of individuals are not directly relevant for corporations. There is, accordingly, nothing equivalent to the personal exemptions or standard deductions allowed to individuals. There are some provisions which require deductions to be computed differently for corporations.

Corporate income does not include amounts expended by the corporation for the factors used to generate corporate income. Interest paid on capital, salary and wages paid on labor, and rent on property used in the business but not owned by the corporation are all deductible to the corporation under regular tax accounting rules. Thus the returns on factors not held by the corporation are not subject to the corporate tax. This is true in most cases even when those factors are owned by shareholders, and may result in an incentive to make those factors available without contributing them to the corporation, for instance, by leasing real estate and licensing intellectual property. Although in some eras rate differentials have been great enough such that the tax cost of contributing assets to corporations and subjecting the return to them to the entity and then to shareholder taxation has been beneficial, in recent years the differentials have been much less.

Most corporations are required to use an accrual method of accounting. Limited exceptions are set out in section 448, and include corporations involved in farming, corporations that provide the services of their professional owners, and corporations whose gross receipts average less than $5 million. Most corporations can choose a non-calendar taxable year, but again there are limitations imposed on the ability of personal service corporations to do so.

Section 291 requires the inclusion in corporate income of certain "corporate preference items," including recapture as ordinary income of 20% of the gain on section 1250 real property attributable to cost recovery (preventing nonrecognition to the extent of this gain), and recapture of 20% of the cost of pollution control facilities deducted under section 169. Other items affect only corporations in certain specialized industries such as real estate investment, mineral exploration, and lending.

The rules for computing income for tax purposes vary in some substantial ways from the rules that apply for financial accounting or "book" purposes under Generally Accepted Accounting Principles (GAAP). Many of these disparities result from the fact that income tax rules tend to err in ways that result in the reporting of higher incomes sooner, while GAAP rules tend to err in ways that reduce income, so that lenders and investors will not be misled. Some disparities, however, run the other way: Congress frequently allows accelerated deductions for depreciation (or even expensing), purportedly as an incentive for investment, while GAAP requires much slower allowances for depreciation. Interest on municipal bonds is excluded from taxable income, but included in GAAP income.

Corporations are required to file a schedule reconciling the differences between book and tax income, called a schedule M. For much of the recent history of the corporate tax, these schedules have been of limited use to the Internal Revenue Service (referred to herein as the Service or the IRS) because various entries could be aggregated in ways that were difficult to unravel. In 2004, however, the Service introduced a new Schedule M-3, which requires substantially more reporting of specific, unaggregated items for large corporations with total assets of $10 million or more.

1.3. PROVISIONS FOR CALCULATING TAXABLE INCOME APPLICABLE ONLY TO CORPORATIONS

1.3.1. Limitations for "Non-Business" Expenditures

There is no general provision limiting corporate deductions comparable to the provisions of section 262 denying deductions for personal expenses, or section 165(c), limiting the deductibility of the losses of individuals. There is an analogous concept, however, in the idea that expenditures that benefit shareholders in their capacity as shareholders should not be deductible. Otherwise, there appears to be a general presumption that corporate expenditures serve a business purpose. Thus, the Service only rarely — and controversially — denies deductions for business expenses that neither should properly be capitalized nor treated as the equivalent of dividends. Congress has introduced a few specific limits — including the caps on compensation in section 162(m).

Note that when an amount is paid under the guise of a corporate expense that benefits not the corporation but one of its employees, the expense is likely to nevertheless be deductible as a compensation expense. Thus paying an employee (who is not also a shareholder) too much for the use of a messenger service the employee owns will not render the payment nondeductible. This treatment may not avoid all problems for the corporation, however, because compensation payments bring with them liabilities for withholding and payroll taxes that are not likely to be involved in the payment of other business expenses.

1.3.2.   Limitations on Interest

Because interest paid on capital made available in the form of loans is deductible, while dividends paid on capital made available in the form of equity is not, there is an incentive to create claims upon corporations that can be characterized as debt for purposes of the interest deduction, but that may resemble equity for other purposes. Rather than attempting to police this line by defining "debt," Congress has in recent years simply denied the interest deduction for corporate interest in certain circumstances. *See, e.g.*, §§ 163(e)(5), 163(i) (partial disallowance of the original issue discount deduction on applicable high yield discount obligations, sometimes called the "AHYDO Rule"), § 163(j) (excess interest expense of thinly capitalized corporations, sometimes called the "Earnings Stripping Rule"), § 163(l) (disallowance of interest deduction on certain debt that is payable in equity, sometimes called the "Equity-Linked Debt Rule").

1.3.3.   Limitations to Enforce Public Policy Relating to Governance

Although Congress has never attempted to take the regulation of corporate governance out of the hands of the states, throughout the history of the corporate income tax it has used the corporate income tax to effect changes in corporate governance. Among the devices currently in effect include sections 162(m) and 280G, which deny corporate deductions for, respectively, excessive compensation and certain "golden parachute" payments.

1.3.4.   Limitations on Charitable Contributions

Corporations may deduct only 10% of taxable income as deductions for contributions to charities under section 170(b)(2).

1.4. COMPUTING THE INCOME OF RELATED CORPORATIONS

Corporations, no matter how closely related by ownership or how integrally related their businesses may be, are each entitled to compute and pay federal taxes on their own income. This is in stark contrast to the method used by states in imposing corporate income taxes, which frequently require "combined" or "unitary" reporting by related corporations, and then allocate a portion of that income to the taxing state.

Under section 482, however, the Service is entitled to adjust items of income and deduction to properly reflect the income of certain related entities. Thus if A Corp sells goods to related B Corp at a price $2 lower than B Corp could buy from others, the Service has the authority to increase A Corp's income and decrease B Corp's income by $2. These transfer pricing issues are often both complex and difficult, because of the difficulty in establishing the appropriate market price for a transaction and the ability of corporate groups to move assets and money around.

Corporations seeking to combine their incomes may, provided there is adequate common ownership under the rules set out in section 1504, elect to file a consolidated return under section 1501. The development of the (rather elaborate) rules for computing income in consolidation has been delegated to the Service under section 1502.

1.5. MISCELLANEOUS CORPORATE LEVEL TAXES

1.5.1. The Alternative Minimum Tax

Congressional concern over the possibility that a corporation could be highly profitable and yet pay little or no income tax because of excessive availability of preferential tax provisions led to the enactment of a corporate alternative minimum tax (AMT) under section 55. A tax of 20% is assessed on a corporation's "alternative minimum taxable income" for corporations with gross receipts greater than $7.5 million, if this tax exceeds the regularly computed tax. (Technically, under the version of the AMT currently in effect, only the portion of this liability that exceeds the regular tax is actually the "alternative minimum tax" and both the AMT and the regular tax are due.)

"Alternative minimum taxable income" (AMTI) is computed from taxable income, making the adjustments outlined in sections 56 and 57. It may be convenient to think of these adjustments as computing three separate tax bases: (1) the regular tax base, (2) a tentative alternative minimum tax base (tentative AMTI), and (3) "adjusted current earnings" (or "ACE"), as defined in section 56(g) and more fully specified in Reg. section 1.56(g)-1. Each of the second and third are expansions of the regular tax base, with adjustments to include some items that are excluded from the regular income tax base, and to reduce some deductions that are allowed for regular tax purposes. 75% of the amount by which the third and most inclusive tax base, ACE, exceeds the second (tentative AMTI), is added to the second to derive AMTI. The AMT is computed by multiplying this base by 20% and then subtracting the regular income tax.

The tentative AMTI is computed by making the adjustments to taxable income outlined in sections 56 and 57, including limitations on accelerated cost recovery, depletion and mineral extraction costs, on deferrals allowed for income from long-term contracts, and some types of exempt municipal bond interest.

ACE is computed under the rules set out in Reg. section 1.56(g)-1, which generally requires adjustments similar to those made in computing the corporation's earnings and profits (a concept relevant to the taxation of distributions to shareholders). Many of the adjustments made in computing ACE affect items related to those included in the computation of tentative AMTI. Because ultimately ACE has an effect only to the extent that it is greater than the tentative AMTI, only when the adjustment for ACE purposes is greater than that required for tentative AMTI will the inclusion of an item seemingly already considered for tentative AMTI purposes have an effect on ACE and on ultimate AMT liability.

Because the items affected by the AMT calculation include many types of recovery of capitalized costs, the AMT calculations must be done for every year even when there is no AMT liability, so that the appropriate basis for AMT purposes can be maintained.

1.5.2. The Accumulated Earnings Tax

For most of the history of the corporate income tax, two features of the income tax have operated so that there is incentive to retain rather than distribute corporate earnings. First, earnings are not taxed to shareholders until they are actually distributed, except in the case of certain earnings of controlled foreign corporations. Second, the rates for individuals have usually been far in excess of the rates for corporations. In order, apparently, to prevent corporations from accumulating their income, rather than distributing it, simply to avoid payment of taxes on the distributions, Congress enacted the tax outlined in sections 531 to 537, the "accumulated earnings tax."

The tax is technically imposed on "every corporation . . . formed or availed of for the purpose of avoiding the income tax with respect to its shareholders . . . by permitting earnings and profits to accumulate instead of being divided or distributed." § 532. Section 533 creates an apparently irrebuttable presumption that such a purpose exists whenever "the earnings and profits of a corporation are permitted to accumulate beyond the reasonable needs of the business."

The "reasonable needs of the business" is not defined in the statute. Reg. section 1.537-1 directs that "the corporation must have specific definite and feasible plans for the use of [any] accumulation" that it seeks to justify as reasonable.

The tax is 15% of the corporation's "accumulated taxable income." Note that the tax is imposed on the entire accumulation, not just the excess.

"Accumulated taxable income" is computed starting with taxable income, but allowing deductions for nondeductible taxes and dividends paid, as well as some other deductions subject to limitation under the regular tax. A reduction (called a credit) is further allowed, which for most corporations is $250,000.

1.5.3. The Personal Holding Company Tax

The accumulated earnings tax requires a corporation to satisfy a subjective test regarding the "reasonable needs" of the corporation for capital in the future. This test seemed unlikely to be adequate to prevent the use of "corporate pocketbooks" created to take advantage of lower corporate rates. The personal holding company tax was introduced to provide a more objective weapon against corporate accumulations to avoid shareholder taxes. The test has two parts — an ownership requirement and an income requirement. The tax is only imposed on corporations that (i) are closely held as defined under the provisions of section 542(a)(2) (applying various exceptions in section 542(b),(c)), and (ii) which have at least 60% of their income from certain relatively passive sources, as computed under section 543. When the tax is imposed, it is imposed only on this relatively passive income, called "personal holding company income," and only to the extent that it has not been distributed.

Section 543 defines "personal holding company income" to include dividends, interest, royalties, and annuities. The complexity in the provisions stems from the acknowledgment that some activities that are more properly viewed as businesses than as investments nevertheless only generate rent, interest, and royalties. Thus, for instance, a special rule is provided for categorizing rent when it is more than 50% of the income of the corporation.

Although the stakes have changed substantially under the current rate structure, the personal holding company tax, like the accumulated earnings tax, remains on the books. Like the accumulated earnings tax, the rate of the personal holding company tax was reduced to 15% when the special 15% rate for dividends was introduced in 2003.

1.5.4. The Effect of Stock Ownership on Shareholders

If a corporation is taxed under subchapter C, its shareholders generally will not be taxed unless they receive something of value from the corporation, either as a distribution from an ongoing corporation or a distribution in liquidation. Taxable income earned by the corporation but not distributed to shareholders will have no effect on the shareholder's income and no effect on the shareholder's basis in her stock. The results when an entity is not subject to subchapter C are very different — if an entity is taxed under subchapter S or as a partnership under subchapter K, the income will be passed through to the owners of the entity, and their bases will be increased to the extent that income is passed through but not actually distributed in cash and/or property.

The sale of corporate stock by shareholders is ordinarily treated the same as the sale of any capital asset. (Indeed, corporate stock is the quintessential capital asset.) Under the rather intricate netting rules outlined in sections 1222, 1223 and 1(h), to the extent that long-term capital gains (that is, gain on capital assets held more than 1 year) exceed capital losses, they are subject to a special low rate, currently a maximum of 15%. (Note that dividends that qualify for the preferential capital gains rate are not included in the netting process, but are merely treated as a net capital gain in the section 1(h) bracketing.)

In certain circumstances, however, the tax consequences can be very different, depending upon who the purchaser is (if the purchaser of the stock is the corporation that issued the stock, the transaction is not always honored as a sale of the stock) and what the consideration is (if the consideration is the stock of a corporation that is acquiring a controlling interest in the subject corporation, nonrecognition treatment may be available). These two special circumstances, redemptions and reorganizations, respectively, are of considerable importance in the overall logic of subchapter C. Indeed, many provisions and doctrines are "anti-bail-out provisions" aimed at preventing shareholders from claiming the treatment available for sales (preferential capital gains rates and use of basis) when the transaction essentially involves only the distribution of corporate earnings. The need for these provisions is substantially reduced as long as dividends are taxed at the same rate as capital gains, and the primary difference is only the ability to use basis.

1.6. SPECIAL RATES ON SALE OF CERTAIN CORPORATE STOCK

Congress has provided several special rates applicable to investors who sell stock in certain (generally smaller) corporations. Section 1202 allows an exclusion from an individual's income for 50% of the gain (up to a cumulative $10 million) on stock of corporations that are engaged in certain (generally non-service) businesses and that have aggregate gross assets of less than $50 million, if such stock is acquired at original issuance (subject to certain exceptions for conversions and transfers by gift, death, and other events) and has been held more than 5 years at the time of the sale. The purported rationale for this generous exclusion is to encourage investment in small ventures. Section 1244 allows an individual an ordinary loss treatment for losses up to $50,000 per year on stock of corporations to which less than $1 million of contributions to capital were made.

PRACTICE PROBLEMS

1. Which of the following statements is false?

    (a) Shareholders ordinarily do not take account of increases in the value of corporate stock they own until the stock is sold.

    (b) If a shareholder holds stock that has declined in value since it was purchased, the dividends this shareholder receives will not be income to the shareholder until the total of dividends and the then current value of the stock received exceeds the shareholder's basis.

    (c) A corporation is not allowed a deduction from income for distributions made to shareholders with respect to their stock.

    (d) If $100 is earned by a corporation and the after-tax amount is distributed to shareholders, the amount remaining in the shareholders' hands after federal income tax at the current rates can be less than $45, assuming taxation at the maximum rates.

2.   X Corporation has been profitable for its entire 100-year existence. Al bought 500 shares in June for $200 a share, or a total of $10,000. He received a dividend distribution of $.50 a share or $250 several months later. The most likely result of this distribution to Al is

    (a)   Deduction to the corporation of $50 and income to Al of $50.

    (b)   No deduction to the corporation and income to Al of $250.

    (c)   Deduction to the corporation of $50 and basis reduction to Al of $50.

    (d)   No deduction to corporation and basis reduction to Al of $50.

3.   Under current law, which of the following would not be true for the 3 individual owners of a currently unincorporated business?

    (a)   If they incorporate, earnings they withdraw as distributions on their stock will not be deductible by the corporation.

    (b)   If they incorporate, amounts paid to them as interest on capital lent to the corporation will generally be deductible by the corporation, if the terms of the debt are generally what would have been available to the corporation from a third-party lender.

    (c)   If they incorporate, amounts that are paid to them as salary will under all circumstances be deductible to the corporation.

    (d)   If they incorporate, the corporation will be able to deduct against its income at least a portion of the amounts it incurs as business expenses, for expenditures such as meals to entertain customers, even when the shareholders themselves may enjoy a personal benefit from the expenditure.

4.   Given the same amount of income in any given year, the highest combined income tax on earnings of the business reinvested in the business will be paid if the business is conducted as a

    (a)   Corporation subject to subchapter C.

    (b)   Partnership taxed as a pass-through.

    (c)   Sole proprietorship.

    (d)   Limited liability company that has not elected corporate status.

    (e)   The answer will depend upon the amount of income of the entity and the other income of its owners.

5.   A rough general description of the corporate tax base under current law might be:

    (a)   Includes earnings from operations, but not most gain on assets.

    (b)   Includes all income, including gains from assets, made available above and beyond shareholder contributions.

(c)   Includes almost all net values received by the corporation.

(d)   Includes almost all net values received by the corporation other than loan proceeds.

6.   Which of the following statements is true?

(a)   Both corporate and individual shareholders will ordinarily prefer dividends to sale or exchange treatment when the resulting gain is short term.

(b)   Corporate shareholders will prefer dividend treatment only if they own more than 20% of the stock of the distributing corporation.

(c)   Individual shareholders will always prefer sale or exchange treatment to dividend treatment.

7.   Which of the following is not designed to reduce the benefit corporations can enjoy from various tax preference items?

(a)   The corporate alternative minimum tax imposed by section 55 and following.

(b)   The reduction of certain deductions provided in section 291.

(c)   The accumulated earnings tax imposed by section 531.

(d)   The passive activity loss limits in section 469.

DISCUSSION PROBLEMS

1.   Fred has owned an auto body shop in his own name for several years. The rather casual income statements he has prepared in prior years suggest that he has, if accounted for on the cash basis, profits of about $80,000 per year, before paying himself at all.

In a typical prior year, Fred withdrew about $65,000 in each year to meet his current living expenses, and set aside $15,000 for future investments in the business. How should these profits and withdrawals have been reported for income tax purposes? How should they have been reported if he had had an informal partner with whom the withdrawals of $65,000 were equally shared?

Fred's suppliers have said they are giving him better credit terms because of the presence of the reserve fund he has kept in a bank account separate from his personal accounts, but he is not sure how much difference the separation of these funds actually makes. He has accumulated about $90,000 in these accounts, which are invested in CDs. He currently thinks that he will look for a location at which to expand his business and will use most of the reserved funds for that.

For non-tax reasons suggested by his insurance agent and his banker, Fred is contemplating changing the form in which he does business. Fred understands the simple corporate form, since his brother-in-law operates his business through a corporation. (He has heard that he ought to also be considering using a limited liability company or a partnership, but he wants first to understand completely the tax consequences of the form he knows best.) He knows, for instance, that distributions of dividends will trigger an income tax on the recipient, but he has watched his brother-in-law pay himself a salary without paying much of a dividend now for years.

What are the consequences if Fred chooses to incorporate under his state's general corporation law? If Fred has no income other than the auto body shop income, could using this standard state corporate form offer any possible tax advantage? Would anything be different if Fred were a lawyer involved in a solo practice?

Fred may soon inherit a parcel of rental real estate property from a great aunt, which will generate about $200,000 per year in income. Under these changed personal circumstances would the corporate form offer any advantage to Fred?

2.   Without regard for the answers above, Fred went ahead and incorporated his business, including the bank accounts his suppliers say they rely on for his credit with them. He thinks he is ready to expand the business, and is now considering his options regarding the funding of the expansion.

(a)   He could liquidate the inheritance and use the funds to obtain a new location in his own name. He could also use the funds set aside within the incorporated business to develop the new location. What are the potential advantages and disadvantages of each approach? What are Fred's creditors likely to prefer? What is likely to be best for Fred?

(b)   What advantage might there be in lending part of the inheritance to the corporation to meet its working capital needs? In building and maintaining a new location, but leaving this building and land outside of the corporation?

(c)   What other taxes besides the regular income tax (on the corporate earnings) and the payroll taxes (payable on the return to his labor that Fred pays himself) might Fred want to take into account?

(d)   Fred is also considering expanding his business to include sponsoring entrants in demolition derbies. His buddies have convinced him that he should be concerned about the tort exposure this might entail. What tax considerations should be taken into account in the decision (i) whether to have a separately incorporated entity, and (ii) what the relationship between the two corporations should be? (Others are worrying about the business and legal consequences of this proposal.)

Chapter 2

DISTRIBUTIONS FROM CORPORATIONS

Statutes and Regulations	IRC §§ 61(a)(7); 301(a), (b), (c); 312(a), (b), (c), (f)(1) (omitting (1)(A)), (k) (1)–(3), (l), (n)(4), (5), (7); 316(a); 317(a)
	Reg. §§ 1.301-1(a)–(c); 1.312-6(a), (b), (d); 1.312-7(b)(1); 1.316-1(a)(1), (e) Ex. (1); 1.316-2(a)–(c)
Other Primary Authorities	General Utils. & Operating Co. v. Helvering, 296 U.S. 200 (1935)
	Eisenberg v. Commissioner, 155 F.3d 50 (2d Cir. 1998)
	Exacto Spring Corp. v. Commissioner, 196 F.3d 833 (7th Cir. 1999)
	Boler v. Commissioner, T.C. Memo. 2002-155
	Roman Systems, Ltd. v. Commissioner, T.C. Memo. 1981–273
	Rev. Rul. 74-164, 1974-1 C.B. 74

Under the Code, corporations and shareholders are treated as separate taxpayers, so that corporations pay tax on their operational earnings and shareholders pay tax when they receive a distribution out of those earnings. But there is much in the structure of Subchapter C that suggests that shareholders are not to be taxed on amounts received from a corporation unless they represent earnings. In more technical terms, therefore, distributions by a corporation to its shareholders are taxed as "dividends" under sections 301 and 316 only to the extent that they are paid out of the corporation's "earnings and profits." Although the tax concept of "earnings and profits" is similar to the state law concepts of "retained earnings" or "earned surplus," the income tax uses its own rules for determining corporate earnings, many of which are found in section 312. (This awkwardly constructed section does not *define* actual earnings and profits, but rather sets forth various rules for the effect of certain transactions on earnings and profits.) Similarly, although the term "dividend" is frequently used outside of tax law to refer to any amount paid by a corporation to its shareholders with respect to their stock, for tax purposes the term applies only to those distributions to shareholders that are made from a corporation's earnings and profits.

2.1. FUNDAMENTAL DISTRIBUTION CONSIDERATIONS: DIVIDENDS AND EARNINGS AND PROFITS

If a distribution is made out of earnings and profits and thus is a "dividend," it is income in the hands of the shareholder without regard to the shareholder's basis in the stock. § 301(c)(1). This treatment rests on the presumption that the dividend is distributed only out of earnings and does not impair the capital of the corporation or the shareholder's ability to receive future dividends. Indeed, a distribution out of earnings and profits as defined for tax purposes will be treated as a dividend even if it impairs capital under applicable state law.

On the other hand, if the corporation has no earnings and profits (or if the distribution exceeds the corporation's earnings and profits), the shareholder will be allowed to treat the distribution (or the excess, in the latter case) as a return of capital, to the extent of the shareholder's basis in the stock the shareholder owns of that class. § 301(c)(2).

Application of Non-Dividend Portions of Distributions to Different Blocks of Stock

If a shareholder holds blocks of stock acquired at different times and therefore with different bases, should the shareholder be treated as receiving a separate distribution in respect of each block of stock for purposes of applying subsection 301(c)?

Consider a shareholder with 100x shares of CorpX acquired for $10 a share in 2000 and 100x shares of CorpX acquired for $15 a share in 2005. The shareholder receives a distribution of $4000x at the end of the third quarter 2006, of which $1500x was paid out of earnings and profits. The shares' aggregate bases in the hands of the shareholder is $2500x. If the shareholder may aggregate bases against the $2500x non-dividend portion of the distribution, there is no realized gain in excess of basis. If the shareholder must allocate $1250x of the non-dividend portion to the first block of shares and the remaining $1250x to the second block of shares, however, the shareholder realizes $250x gain in excess of basis.

The Fourth Circuit concluded that a shareholder must treat a distribution as made proportionally with respect to each block of shares. Johnson v. United States, 435 F.2d 1257 (4th Cir. 1971). *The government has adopted this approach in regulations proposed in 2009 which apply a block-by-block approach throughout subchapter C.*

Any distribution in excess of basis will be treated as gain from the sale or exchange of the stock. § 301(c)(3).

Under current law in effect through 2012, dividends from domestic and qualifying foreign corporations received by individuals are treated as net capital gains. § 1(h)(11). Thus, the same maximum 15% rate applies to any portion of a distribution to an individual shareholder that is not used to reduce basis, whether or not the corporation has earnings and profits. For individuals, the primary difference between a distribution that is treated as a dividend and one that is treated as a sale or exchange (for instance, a distribution in redemption of stock) is the allowance of basis recovery. Cf. § 302(a). As is considered in greater detail elsewhere, there are different (and frequently more important) stakes involved in characterizing distributions to corporate shareholders as "dividends," given the special provisions in section 243 allowing deductions from income for the dividends received by corporations. These "dividend-received deductions" for corporate shareholders substantially reduce, but do not eliminate, the corporate tax on dividends received from domestic corporations (unless the dividend-paying corporation is controlled by the dividend-receiving corporation).

2.1.1. Determining Whether a Distribution is a Dividend

The determination whether a distribution to a shareholder is out of earnings and profits is ordinarily made strictly from the distributing corporation's point of view. If a shareholder pays $5000 for stock in a corporation with a substantial history of earnings, and subsequently the stock value falls to $3000 because of rumors of scandal, and the corporation then distributes a dividend of $20 supported by earnings and profits, the shareholder has dividend income of $20, even though she holds her stock at a loss. Shareholders are treated as fungible — there is ordinarily no linking of the undistributed earnings of the corporation to any particular shareholder.

The provisions of section 316 identify two separate pools of earnings and profits for sourcing distributions. The two pools are "current earnings and profits" in section 316(a)(2) and "accumulated earnings and profits" in section 316(a)(1). The Code provides that distributions are treated as made out of current earnings and profits first, and then out of accumulated earnings and profits.

The determination of *current* earnings and profits is made at the close of the taxable year, without taking into account any distributions that are made during the year. If current earnings and profits are sufficient, a distribution will be treated as a dividend without consideration of a pre-existing deficit in accumulated earnings and profits. Reg. § 1.316-1(a)(1) (flush language); Reg. § 1.316-2(a) (second sentence), (b) (first sentence); Rev. Rul. 74-164, 1974-1 C.B. 74. In other words, a corporate distribution can be treated as a dividend if the corporation has *current* earnings and profits, even if it has a long history of prior operating losses. This is frequently referred to as the "nimble dividend" rule. For example, if a corporation with losses of $10,000 per year for five years has earnings and profits of $8,000 in the sixth year and in that year distributes $5,000 to its shareholders, the $5,000 will be deemed to have been distributed out of the $8,000 current earnings and profits. At the end of the year, the remaining current earnings and profits of $3,000 are folded into the accumulated earnings and profits deficit of $50,000 to produce an accumulated deficit account of $47,000 as of the beginning of the next year.

To the extent of current earnings and profits, all distributions made during the year share equally, without regard either to the timing of the distribution ("computed as of the close of the taxable year without diminution by reason of any distributions made during the taxable year") or to the timing of the earnings ("without regard to the amount of the earnings and profits at the time the distribution was made"). § 316(a)(2), Reg. § 1.316-2(b) (second sentence). Thus, if there are $100,000 in current earnings and profits after taking into account the entire year's performance and a distribution of $50,000 in March that is followed by a distribution of $25,000 in October, it does not matter that there were only $10,000 of earnings through March — both of the distributions will be dividends paid out of current earnings and profits.

To the extent that distributions exceed the current earnings and profits, however, distributions to shareholders are treated as being made out of accumulated earnings and profits computed as of the time each distribution is made. Reg. § 1.316-2(b) (third sentence). Thus, after current earnings and profits have been exhausted, distributions are treated as coming from accumulated earnings and profits as of the beginning of the year, reduced by any distribution occurring earlier in the year. (This difference is the result of the fact that section 316(a)(1) does not include the "without diminution" language.) Thus, suppose that there are $30,000 in accumulated earnings and profits as of the beginning of the year, and $100,000 in current earnings and profits after taking into account the entire year's performance and that a distribution of $50,000 in March is followed by a distribution of $150,000 in October. These distributions will share pro rata in current earnings and profits ($25,000 of current earnings and profits will be allocated to the March distribution and $75,000 to the October distribution). They will then share in order of time in the accumulated earnings and profits as of the beginning of the year ($25,000 to the March distribution and $5,000 to the October distribution).

Finally, if there are no current earnings and profits, distributions will be treated as coming only from accumulated earnings and profits (if any). Because section 316(a)(1) does not contain the "without regard to . . . time" language, the determination of accumulated earnings and profits as of the time of a distribution will take into account the actual interim performance of the corporation during the current year. In other words, if there is an overall loss for the current year, the interim performance of the corporation as of the time of each distribution must be taken into account in determining the amount of accumulated earnings and profits available at that time. This is done either on a prorated basis or, if the corporation can establish the actual timing of losses, as the losses actually occur. Reg. § 1.316-2(b) (fourth sentence).

Ordered Rules for Utilizing Earnings and Profits

The rules described in this section can be thought of as a set of ordered rules with certain reiterative steps, where CEP = current earnings and profits, AEP = accumulated earnings and profits, and D = a distribution in a series of n distributions.

If $CEP \geq \Sigma_1^n D$, D = dividend.

If $CEP < \Sigma_1^n D$, then:

if $CEP \geq 0$,

(i) allocate to each D an amount of $CEP = [D / \Sigma_1^n D] * CEP$;

(ii) allocate AEP to the remaining amount of each D in chronological order until AEP is exhausted;

(iii) each D will be treated as a dividend to the extent that CEP and AEP, if any, is allocated to it.

if $CEP < 0$,

(i) reduce AEP by the amount of the CEP deficit incurred as of the time of the first distribution (determined by pro-rating the annual CEP deficit to each period of the current year or by actual timing of current losses);

(ii) allocate AEP to the first distribution to the extent available;

(iii) continue applying steps (i) and (ii) to each distribution in chronological order until AEP is exhausted;

(iv) each D will be treated as a dividend to the extent that AEP is allocated to it.

Example: Assume that Corporation enters the current taxable year with accumulated earnings and profits of 200x. Corporation expects to have a profitable year. At the end of the first quarter, Corporation distributes 100x to its shareholders. At the end of the second quarter, Corporation distributes another 100x to its shareholders. During the current year, Corporation incurs operating losses totaling 100x but it cannot relate the loss to particular periods.

	AEP	CEP	D_1	D_2	
Current Year	200x	<100x>	100x	100x	
1st QTR	-25x	-<25x>			*Reduction of AEP by CEP deficit incurred as of first distribution (assumes that the remaining 75x of the current loss was incurred after the first distribution)*
	175x	<75x>			
	-100x		-100x		*Allocation of AEP to first distribution, with result that all of the distribution is a dividend out of AEP and 75x AEP remains at the end of the first quarter*
	75x		0		

2nd QTR	-25x	-<25x>			Reduction of AEP by CEP deficit incurred as of second distribution (assumes that 50x of the current losses were incurred after the second distribution)
	50x	<50x>			
	-50x			-50x	Allocation of AEP to second distribution, with result that half of the distribution is a dividend out of AEP (the remainder is return of capital or gain) and no AEP remains at the end of the second quarter
	0			50x	
Next Year	<50x>				The remaining current year losses incurred after the second distribution create a deficit in AEP going into the next year.

For example, a corporation with accumulated earnings and profits of $50,000 may expect to have a profitable year and thus make a distribution of $50,000 to its shareholders at the end of the first quarter, in spite of having incurred a loss of $35,000 in that quarter. If the losses continue throughout the year, so that it has an annual operating loss of $100,000, it has no current earnings and profits, as determined at the end of the year, to fund the distribution. Accordingly, only $15,000 of the first quarter distribution will be a dividend, considered to be made out of the accumulated earnings and profits available at the time of the distribution (i.e., $50,000 accumulated earnings and profits minus $35,000 loss incurred during the first quarter). The corporation will have a $65,000 deficit in accumulated earnings and profits going into the next year (that is, $50,000 prior year accumulated earnings and profits minus $35,000 deficit incurred by the end of the first quarter minus $15,000 distribution treated as a dividend out of accumulated earnings and profits minus $65,000 losses incurred in the remaining three quarters of the current year).

Allocation of Earnings and Profits Among Different Classes of Stock

If a corporation has classes of stock that do not all have the same priority as to dividends, the priority may affect the allocation of earnings and profits. Suppose a corporation has two classes of common stock, Class A and Class B, that differ only in voting rights. If the corporation makes distributions in respect of both classes of shares, the allocation of earnings and profits to the distributions will be as discussed in the text.

But suppose the corporation has two classes of stock, one of which is preferred as to dividends. It makes a required distribution on the preferred and also makes a distribution on the common stock. The sum of the distributions exceeds the current and accumulated earnings and profits of the corporation. The earnings and profits are treated as distributed on the preferred stock before any earnings and profits are treated as distributed on the common stock. Rev. Rul. 69-440, 1969-2 C.B. 46.

Note that the interim performance during the current year is taken into account in determining available accumulated earnings and profits at the time of a distribution *only when a corporation incurs a current-year loss.* When there are current earnings and profits, all current year's performance has already been taken into account in deriving that amount. For example, suppose a corporation begins a year with $2 million of accumulated earnings and profits and its current-year performance results in a net $200,000 addition to earnings and profits. Suppose further that the $200,000 represents sales of two assets, one in February that produced a $1.5 million loss and one in October that produced a $1.7 million gain. A distribution of $600,000 at the end of the first quarter would be treated as $200,000 out of current earnings and profits and $400,000 out of accumulated earnings and profits, leaving $1.6 million in accumulated earnings and profits at the beginning of the next year. If, on the other hand, the gain in October had been only $1 million, the corporation would have incurred a $500,000 loss for the year. It would have no positive current earnings and profits for the year. The corporation now can determine its *actual* earnings and profits by taking into account the interim performance up to the date of the March distribution (the $1.5 million loss), so it has only $500,000 in accumulated earnings and profits "available" after the February sale. Accordingly, only $500,000 of the March distribution is a dividend.

Actual Performance or Ratable Loss?

Is there a choice whether to use the actual timing of current performance when there are no current earnings and profits, and the effect of current performance on accumulated earnings and profits must be determined? If so, who gets to choose, the IRS or the taxpayer? Reg. § 1.316-2(b) (fourth sentence) says that when the actual amount of accumulated e&p available at the time of a distribution during the year has to be determined (when there is a current year deficit), you do so either by looking at "the actual earnings and profits to the date of a distribution within any taxable year" or, if that cannot be shown, by looking at the "earnings and profits for the year . . . in which the distribution was made . . . prorated to the date of the distribution not counting the date on which the distribution was made."

> *The use of actual e&p would seem to be the required default rule under the regulations. But it would also require a more detailed closing of the tax books than most corporations would ordinarily do. It appears that the IRS has interpreted the regulations as allowing the taxpayer to choose between actual timing (where it can be shown) and prorating the overall loss over the year. See Rev. Rul. 74-164; G.C.M. 35307 (1973); FSA 200225014.*

If a distribution is paid from a parent corporation that has one or more subsidiaries with earnings and profits, the earnings and profits of the parent corporation generally are not consolidated with the earnings and profits of its subsidiary corporations for purposes of determining whether the parent's distribution is a dividend. If the affiliated group of corporations files a consolidated return, however, the group's earnings and profits are combined for these determinations.

2.1.2. Determining the Amount of Earnings and Profits

There is no statutory definition of "earnings and profits." The starting point is the taxable income of the corporation. For many reasons, taxable income does not adequately capture the amount that the corporation has earned that is available for distribution to shareholders, and therefore many adjustments are required. Some, but not all, are outlined in section 312. For instance, upwards adjustments are required for cost recovery faster than straight line under section 312(k), for discharge of indebtedness income excluded because of insolvency to the extent not accounted for through an adjustment to basis under section 312(l), and for gain deferred under the installment method under section 312(n)(5). Other adjustments in translating taxable income into earnings and profits are mentioned only in regulations, such as the upward adjustment for exempt income, including interest on municipal bonds. Reg. § 1.312-6(b). Still others are not mentioned at all in the Code or regulations but are clearly required to measure accurately the amount of economic earnings available to a corporation for distribution, such as the downward adjustment for federal income taxes paid and the upward adjustment for the portion of dividends received that is entitled to a dividends-received deduction under section 243.

> **What Values Should Be Reflected in E&P?**
>
> *A number of items that are excluded from income in computing taxable income are included for determining e&p, such as tax-exempt interest on municipal bonds excluded under section 103. These values are clearly amounts available for distribution to shareholders and are above and beyond any original contributions to the corporation. Gains that have been realized and not recognized, however, are not treated as increasing earnings and profits. The court in* Bangor & A.R. Co. v. Commissioner, *193 F.2d 827 (1st Cir. 1951), offered the following explanation why it is appropriate not to treat realized gains as upward adjustments in earnings and profits for the year realized:*
>
> It is important to observe the distinction between (1) income which is exempt from tax and (2) income which, though "realized" in a constitutional sense and thus within the power of Congress to tax, is not at the outset "recognized," the incidence of the tax being merely postponed.

> As to (1), exempt income, such for instance as interest on tax-free bonds, if income
> of this sort is to be taken into "earnings and profits," the only logical time to do so
> is when the income is realized. It is so provided by regulation. . . .
>
> But as to (2), income which, though "realized," is not at the outset "recognized," the
> problem is quite different. . . . Congress has determined that in certain types of
> transaction the economic changes are not definitive enough to be given tax
> consequences, and has clearly provided that gains and losses on such transactions
> shall not be recognized for income-tax liability but shall be taken account of
> later. . . . It is sensible to carry through the theory in determining the tax effect of
> such transactions on earnings and profits.

Some deductions, such as the dividends-received deduction, that are permitted in computing taxable income are simply not taken into account in determining earnings and profits (i.e., must be restored to arrive at earnings and profits). Others, such as construction period carrying charges and intangible drilling costs, are required to be capitalized for earnings and profits purposes rather than deducted immediately.

On the other hand, most deductions that are disallowed under particular provisions of the Code are nonetheless deducted in determining earnings and profits. Rev. Rul. 75-515, 1975-2 C.B. 117 (holding cancellation of indebtedness income in excess of amounts that reduce basis under section 1017 must increase earnings and profits), explains that this general rule applies because the earnings and profits are intended to provide an economic measure of the amount available for distribution.

In general, the computation of earnings and profits of a corporation for dividend purposes is based upon reasonable accounting concepts that take into account the economic realities of corporate transactions as well as those resulting from the application of tax law. Thus, losses and expenses that are disallowed as a deduction for federal income tax purposes, charitable contributions in excess of the limitations provided therefor, and other items that have actually depleted the assets of the corporation, even though not reflected in the income computation, are allowable as deductions in computing earnings and profits.

The earnings and profits determinations under section 312 also include timing adjustments. Because earnings and profits are adjusted to reflect slower depreciation and amortization deductions for most properties (adjusting from 200% or 150% declining balance method to straight line or to the alternative depreciation system in § 168(g)), most properties will have a different basis for earnings and profits purposes than they have for computing gain or loss on a sale or exchange for taxable income purposes. Accordingly, the gain or loss that is reflected in earnings and profits will be determined using the earnings and profits basis and may be different from the gain or loss used in determining taxable income. Since depreciation on plant and equipment is capitalized as an inventory cost under section 263A rather than deducted, determinations of inventories will also differ for earnings and profits purposes for this reason.

Because the concept of earnings and profits is tied to income tax concepts, neither loan proceeds nor unrecognized appreciation of assets is included. Thus, a corporation with appreciated assets can borrow against those assets before they produce taxable income (and thus before there are earnings and profits) and distribute the loan proceeds to its shareholders without causing its shareholders to recognize income (to the extent the shareholders have basis in their stock).

Authority for Adjustments to Taxable Income to Determine E&P

Item	Relevant Authority	Treatment for e&p purposes: included/excluded (income); deducted/not deducted (expenses); adjusted
Accelerated depreciation deductions or amortizations under §§ 168, 169, 184, 187, 188 or any similar provision, for property other than tangible property depreciated under § 168 or property eligible for the unit-of-production depreciation method under § 167(a)	§ 312(k)(1); Reg. § 1.312-15(a)(1)	Adjusted to a straight-line deduction
Accelerated depreciation deductions for tangible property under § 168	§ 312(k)(3)	Adjusted to alternative depreciation system deduction under § 168(g)
Amortizable bond premium paid on tax-exempt bonds	Rev. Rul. 71-165	Deducted
Borrowings against appreciated assets	Falkoff v. Commissioner, 604 F.2d 1045 (7th Cir. 1979)	Excluded
Cancellation of indebtedness income excluded under § 108 and resulting in reduction of basis under § 1017	§ 312(l)	Excluded
Capital losses disallowed under § 1211	Cf. Rev. Rul. 75-515	Deducted (but no carryovers for e&p purposes)[1]
Charitable contribution deduction for fair market value under § 170	Rev. Rul 78-123.[2] But see Kaplan v. Commissioner, 43 T.C. 580 (1965) (non-acq.)	Adjusted to basis deduction

---

[1] Note that recognized but disallowed losses would also include related party losses under section 267 and similar losses. The regulations promulgated under section 312 make clear the importance of the distinction between recognized and "recognized though not allowed as a deduction." Treas. Reg. § 1.312-7(b) (third sentence).

[2] The Revenue Ruling predates *General Utilities'* repeal, and thus predates the addition to the Code of section 312(b)(2), which now reduces earnings and profits upon a distribution of appreciated property by the full fair market value, because the corporation will have included that gain in income under section 311(b), resulting in a corresponding increase in its earnings and profits. However, the Revenue Ruling's discussion of the rationale for not reducing earnings and profits for the appreciation in respect of charitable contributions of appreciated property that are fully deducted remains current.

When a corporation makes a disposition of property with respect to stock, such as a dividend paid in property, earnings and profits must be reduced by the adjusted basis of the distributed property rather than its fair market value because it is the adjusted basis that is reflected in

Item	Relevant Authority	Treatment for e&p purposes: included/excluded (income); deducted/not deducted (expenses); adjusted
Compensation that is not reasonable under § 162(a)(1)	Rev. Rul 75-515	Deducted
Compensation for injuries or sicknesses excluded under § 104(a)	Castner Garage, Ltd. v. Commissioner, 43 B.T.A. 1 (1940) (*acq.*)	Included
Contributions to capital under § 118	Rev. Rul. 66-353	Excluded[3]
Deductions disallowed on public policy grounds under § 162(c), (e), (f), and (g)	Rev. Rul. 77-442; *cf.* Rev. Rul. 75-515	Deducted
Dividends-received deduction under § 243		Not deducted
Excess Charitable Contributions under § 170	Rev. Rul. 75-515	Deducted
Expensing of costs of tangible property under § 179	§ 312(k)(3)	Adjusted to a ratable deduction over 5 years
Federal income tax liabilities and tax penalties (such as additions to tax for tax fraud)	Deutsch v. Commissioner, 38 T.C. 118 (1962); Rev. Rul. 57-332; Rev. Rul. 70-609	Deducted[4]
Federal income tax refund due to a net operating loss carryback	Rev. Rul. 64-146; Deutsch v. Commissioner, 38 T.C. 118 (1962)	Included in year in which the loss permitting the refund is sustained
Gains deferred in a like-kind exchange under § 1031	§ 312(f)(1) (flush language)	Excluded

the earnings and profits of the taxpayer. The unrealized appreciation in the value of the property distributed is not reflected in the earnings and profits and therefore does not constitute a reduction of earnings and profits available for the payment of dividends. See section 312(a)(3) of the Code and section 1.312-1(b) of the regulations.

[3] Gifts or bequests to a corporation should probably be treated as contributions to capital under section 118 and excluded from determinations of earnings and profits. *See* A.J. Diebold, TC Memo ¶ 53,052 (1953).

[4] The correct year for the deduction is somewhat uncertain. For accrual taxpayers, the *Deutsch* case holds that taxes are taken into account in the earnings and profits of the year to which the return relates, and Rev. Rul. 57-332, 1957-2 C.B. 231, provides that penalties for tax fraud are taken into account in the earnings and profits of the year that the fraudulent return is filed. For cash-method taxpayers, the tax administrator position is that a cash-method corporation cannot reduce earnings and profits for federal income taxes until the year that the taxes are actually paid. This appears to follow from the regulation that requires taxpayers to use the same accounting method for determining earnings and profits that is "properly employed in computing taxable income." Reg. § 1.312-6(a). Several courts follow that position. *See, e.g.*, Helvering v. Alworth Trust, 136 F.2d 812 (8th Cir. 1943); Webb v. Commissioner, 67 T.C. 1008 (1977), *aff'd per curiam*, 572 F.2d 135 (5th Cir. 1978); Mazzocchi Bus Co. v. Commissioner, 14 F.3d 923 (3d Cir. 1994). There are, however, several court of appeals opinions that allow a cash-method corporation to reduce its earnings and profits in respect of accrued but unpaid tax liabilities. *See, e.g.*, Demmon v. United States, 321 F.2d 203, 204–206 (7th Cir. 1956); Drybrough v. Commissioner, 238 F.2d 735, 738–740 (6th Cir. 1956).

Item	Relevant Authority	Treatment for e&p purposes: included/excluded (income); deducted/not deducted (expenses); adjusted
Gains deferred in an installment sale under § 453	§ 312(n)(5)	Included
Gains recognized in computing taxable income	§ 312(f)(1) (flush language)	Included
Interest expense disallowed under § 265(a)(2)	*Cf.* Rev. Rul. 71-165	Deducted
Life insurance proceeds	Rev. Rul. 54-230	Included[5]
LIFO inventory accounting	§ 312(n)(4)	Adjusted to FIFO accounting
Original issue discount accrued during the taxable year	Rev. Rul. 66-35	Deducted
Other cancellation of indebtedness income	Schweppe v. Commissioner, 168 F.2d 284 (9th Cir. 1948); Rev. Rul. 75-515; Rev. Rul. 58-546	Included (even if other tax attributes are reduced under § 108(b))
Percentage depletion deduction	Reg. § 1.312-6(c)	Adjusted to cost depletion method
Receipts on issuance of corporation's own stock or options under § 1032	§ 312(f)(1) (flush language)	Excluded
Recovery of amount for which a bad debt deduction was taken	Rev. Rul. 58-546	Included
Reduction of stated capital under state law to facilitate payment of dividends		Not deducted (state law change does not affect earnings and profits)
State and local taxes	Rev. Rul. 60-123	Deducted (in same manner and year as deductible in computing taxable income)
Stock dividends under § 305	§ 312(d)	Not Deducted (not treated as a distribution of earnings and profits)
Stock option bargain element	Luckman v. Commissioner, 418 F.2d 381 (7th Cir. 1969); Divine v. Commissioner, 500 F.2d 1041 (2d Cir. 1974)	Deducted (economic expense in year that employees exercise option)

---

[5] Premiums that are disallowed as deductions for computing taxable income would nevertheless reduce earnings and profits, to the extent they exceed the policy's cash-surrender value. IRS Form 5452 (line 6b of worksheet).

Item	Relevant Authority	Treatment for e&p purposes: included/excluded (income); deducted/not deducted (expenses); adjusted
Tax Benefit Rule Exclusion under § 111	Rev. Rul. 58-546; *but see* Lasater's Estate v. Scofield, 74 F. Supp. 458 (W.D. Tex. 1947)	Included (if the related deduction reduced earnings and profits in an earlier year)

2.1.3. Adjustments to Earnings and Profits for Distributions of Cash

Earnings and profits must also be adjusted downwards to take into account distributions made by the corporation. When distributions are made from current earnings and profits, these downward adjustments are made as of the end of the year in which the distribution is made, after current earnings and profits have been prorated among all of the distributions made during that year but before they are folded into accumulated earnings and profits. When distributions are made from accumulated earnings and profits, the downward adjustment is made as of the time of the distribution.

Relevant Dates for Determinations

For purposes of determining its effect on a corporation's earnings and profits, a distribution is treated as made on the date of the payment of the distribution to the shareholder, rather than on the date of the declaration of a dividend or the record date for the determination of which shareholders will receive the dividend (the ex-dividend date). Rev. Rul. 62-131, 1962-2 C.B. 94. For a shareholder, a dividend is included in income when received, without regard to the shareholder's method of accounting, regardless of the earlier declaration and record date for the dividend. See Commissioner v. American Light & Traction Co., 156 F.2d 398 (7th Cir. 1946); Caruth Corp. v. United States, 865 F.2d 644 (5th Cir. 1989). Accordingly, if a corporation pays a dividend by check at the end of its taxable year, the distribution will be treated as made out of earnings and profits available for that taxable year. Rev. Rul. 65-23, 1965-1 C.B. 520. If the shareholder receives the check in the next year, the shareholder includes the dividend in income in that later year. Rev. Rul. 64-290, 1964-2 C.B. 465.

Neither current nor accumulated earnings and profits will be adjusted below zero by distributions. Only operating losses can produce deficits in earnings and profits. If distributions exceed current earnings and profits, the excess is treated as paid out of accumulated earnings and profits to the extent thereof. If distributions exceed both current and accumulated earnings and profits, they are treated, on the shareholder side, as a return of capital. What is the source of those distributions from the corporation's perspective? The answer is irrelevant for tax purposes, but such distributions will be funded by borrowings against unrecognized appreciation or from the capital contributions made to the corporation by shareholders over its life.

2.2. DISTRIBUTIONS OF PROPERTY

Dividends, especially of publicly traded corporations, are normally paid in cash. They can, however, be paid in other forms, either in the debt of the corporation or in property held by the corporation. § 317. The stock of the distributing corporation is not considered property for these purposes, and distributions of stock are treated under a separate provision. § 305.

The amount of the distribution to the shareholder is the fair market value of the property distributed. § 301(b)(1). The fair market value is determined for this purpose as of the date of the distribution. § 301(b)(3).

2.2.1. Distributions of Appreciated and Depreciated Property

A current distribution of property by a corporation to its shareholders will trigger gain but not loss on the distribution. § 311. Note the peculiar structure of section 311 — in (a), it appears to state a general rule that "no gain or loss shall be recognized . . . on the distribution (not in complete liquidation) with respect to its stock of . . . property." But in (b), a significant exception is made to that general rule providing that gain shall be recognized.

This peculiar structure is the result of the historical development of the provision. Prior to 1986, section 311(a) was the general rule for all distributions, whether of gain or loss property. It codified the holding in *General Utils. & Operating Co. v. Helvering*, 296 U.S. 200 (1935), a case in which a corporation distributed property in satisfaction of a declared dividend. The government had initially argued that the declaration of a cash dividend created an enforceable debt, so that the corporation's use of property to satisfy the debt triggered gain under general tax law principles. The Court's holding that the corporation could distribute property in satisfaction of the obligation to pay a cash dividend *without* triggering gain on the distributed property implied that it did not consider the corporate property distribution to be a realization event. The case came to stand for the proposition that gain or loss will not be recognized by a corporation on a distribution of corporate property unless there is an explicit statutory provision so providing. Section 311(b) was enacted in 1986 to provide for gain recognition to the distributing corporation in such cases. The amendment of section 311 by the addition of subsection (b) is commonly referred to as "the repeal of *General Utilities*."

Although section 311(a) says that "no . . . loss shall be recognized," section 311 does not operate as a typical nonrecognition provision. If a corporation distributes loss property, neither the distributing corporation nor the distributee shareholders can later use the unused basis. The distributing corporation's loss is disallowed by section 311(b) and nothing in the Code allocates the unused basis to other corporate property. The distributee shareholder does not benefit from the corporation's excess basis: it is required to take a fair market value basis in the distributed property under section 301(d).

2.2.2. Effect of the Distribution of Property on Earnings and Profits

a. Gain Property

Distributions of cash can by their nature have only one effect on earnings and profits — namely, the decrease in earnings and profits in respect of the loss of the cash to the corporation. In contrast, distributions of appreciated property affect the earnings and profits in two ways. First, the distribution itself is treated as a hypothetical sale of the distributed property to the shareholder, triggering gain at the corporate level that increases current earnings and profits by the amount of the gain less any tax thereon. §§ 311(b), 312(b)(1). Second, the property distribution represents economic value transferred to shareholders that is no longer available for future distribution, so the amount of the distribution reduces earnings and profits to the extent thereof. §§ 312(a)(3), 312(b)(2). Section 312(a)(3), originally written to accommodate the rules applicable under the *General Utilities* doctrine providing for nonrecognition of gain or loss, provides that distributions of property will reduce earnings and profits only by the adjusted basis of the property. This is modified by section 312(b)(2), which substitutes fair market value for adjusted basis. As a result, the earnings and profits are reduced for the full fair market value of the appreciated property.

It takes a bit of creative reading to get the appropriate result in respect of the hypothetical sale from section 312(b) and the regulations thereunder, given that section 312(b) was only clumsily amended to respond to the repeal of the *General Utilities* doctrine, and the regulations were not amended at all. Among the mysteries of section 312 is why there should be a section 312(b)(1) at all, since section 311(b) gain would seem to be included in earnings and profits as a matter of course under section 312(f)(1). Section 312(b)(1) is best viewed as merely clarifying that the section 311(b) gain does have the effect on earnings and profits of increasing them separately from (and prior to) the reductions on account of the distribution itself. The language also directs that the upward adjustment to earnings and profits is based on the adjusted basis for earnings and profits purposes, which will for most depreciable assets differ from the adjusted basis for computing taxable income because of the slower cost recovery reductions. Accordingly, the current earnings and profits of the distributing corporation will be increased to reflect the taxable gain on the distribution (as determined for earnings and profits purposes), and decreased to reflect the increase in taxes due to the section 311(b) gain. That increase in current earnings and profits due to the section 311(b) gain may result in dividend treatment for a portion of the distribution even if there are no accumulated earnings and profits in the corporation, under the nimble dividend rule. At the end of the year, the earnings and profits account will be reduced (but not below zero) by the full fair market value of the distribution, since that economic amount is no longer available for future distributions to shareholders.

b. Loss Property

The effect of the distribution of loss property on earnings and profits is even more complex. If section 311 were symmetric, the recognition of a loss on a distribution of depreciated property would be taken into account in taxable income and, under section 312(f)(1), the full amount of the recognized loss would reduce earnings and profits. The distribution would then reduce earnings and profits by its amount, which should be its fair market value, as it would be measured for purposes of determining the amount of the distribution to the distributee shareholder.

Under section 311(a), however, losses are not recognized to a distributing corporation on a distribution property. Accordingly, there is no disposition-equivalent transaction to affect earnings and profits to match the hypothetical disposition of section 311(b) in the case of appreciated property. The only effect of a distribution of loss property is the reduction in earnings and profits to account for the distribution to a shareholder that is no longer available for future distributions. The statute, however, provides that earnings and profits shall be reduced by the *full adjusted basis of the property* (again, as determined for earnings and profits purposes). § 312(a)(3). Since the adjusted basis of loss property equals its fair market value plus the realized loss on the distribution, this rule effectively provides for earnings and profits to be reduced by the loss incurred by the corporation on the distribution plus the amount of the distribution (the fair market value of the property). As a result, a distribution of loss property reduces earnings and profits of the distributing corporation by an amount in excess of the amount of the distribution to the distributee shareholder as determined under section 301(b).

To illustrate, assume a distributing corporation has accumulated earnings and profits of $200x and no current earnings and profits. It makes only one distribution during the current year, an in-kind distribution of loss property having a fair market value of $150x and a basis of $200x. This distribution (unlike distributions of appreciated property) does not result in recognition. Under section 301(a), the distribution to the shareholder is $150x and the entire amount of that distribution is a dividend out of accumulated earnings and profits. Under section 312(a)(3), the distribution reduces the corporation's earnings and profits by $200x, wiping out the entire accumulated earnings and profits account. Assuming that the corporation continues to have no current earnings and profits the next year, a corporate distribution of cash will be treated as a return of capital rather than a dividend because there is no accumulated earnings and profits.

**Application of Ordering Rules When There Are Both
Cash and Property Distributions During the Taxable Year**

Neither the Code nor the regulations explicitly provide that the ordering rules for sourcing distributions out of e&p apply when a corporation makes a distribution of property rather than cash. Property distributions can occur in the same year as cash distributions, however, and thus it is necessary to determine how the ordering rules apply in the case of property distributions. Coherent interpretation of the rules requires consistency in their application, except to the extent that property distributions require special provisions not reasonably accommodated. See G.C.M. 36, 138 (Jan. 15, 1975).

Accordingly, if a corporation makes a distribution of a loss property and an ordinary cash distribution later in the year, the current e&p, determined at the end of the year without regard to the distributions, would be allocated between the two distributions pro rata in accordance with their fair market values. The accumulated e&p would be absorbed by the distributions on a first-come, first-served basis. If the property distribution occurs prior to the cash distribution, and there is some accumulated e&p remaining after accounting for the fair market value of the distribution to the shareholder, should the decrease for the full adjusted basis (i.e., the additional decrease for the excess of the adjusted basis over the fair market value, representing the unrecognized loss) nevertheless be treated as occurring immediately upon the distribution of the loss property or should it be taken into account only after e&p are allotted to the cash distribution? If the latter, it is more likely that the cash distribution will be treated as a dividend. If the former, it is possible that the reduction of e&p in respect of the loss amount will result in none of the cash distribution being treated as a dividend. The statute is silent, but the legislative history indicates that the required additional reduction in e&p to take into account the unrecognized loss should be treated as occurring immediately after the distribution of the property. See H.R. Rep. No. 99-426 at 897 (1985).

Example: *Assume that the distributing corporation has $35,000 of accumulated e&p and $10,000 of current e&p. The corporation distributes to its shareholder loss property with a basis of $25,000 and fair market value of $10,000 at the end of the second quarter. It makes a $30,000 cash distribution on December 31.*

Ordering Rules					
AEP	CEP	CORP	D1 (property FMV 10,000)	D2 cash $30,000	
35,000	10,000				
		No L recognized			No hypothetical sale for corporation under § 311(a)
	-10,000 / 0		-2,500 / 7,500	-7,500 / 22,500	Allocate CEP pro rata to all distributions; these amounts are dividends
-7,500 / 27,500			-7,500 / 0		Allocate AEP as available at time of distributions — $7,500 of AEP is used to make remainder of property distribution; this amount is a dividend

-15,000 12,500					And $15,000 more of AEP is used under § 312(a)(3) (basis reduction for full $25,000); the reduction of EP for the corporation ($25,000) is greater than the amount of the dividend to the shareholder ($10,000)
-12,500 0				-12,500 10,000	Allocate AEP as available at time of distribution — remaining $12,500 of AEP is used for cash distribution, the rest of the distribution ($10,000) is return of basis (to extent thereof) or gain, under § 301(c)(2), (3).

2.2.3. Effect of Liabilities Associated with Distributed Property

a. On the Amount Distributed

A shareholder's net worth is increased only by the net fair market value of property distributed when a distributing corporation distributes property and the distributee shareholder assumes a liability secured by the property. Section 301(b) therefore provides that the amount of the distribution will be reduced by the amount of the liability assumed or by "the amount of any liability to which the property received by the shareholder is subject immediately before, and immediately after the distribution." This language assumes that it will be the shareholder, not the corporation, that ultimately pays the liability.

Note that the statute distinguishes between the case in which the debt is actually assumed by the shareholder and the case in which the property distributed is subject to a liability, but ultimately includes both situations. Some abusive tax shelter schemes purported to take advantage of (imagined?) ambiguity in this statute through transactions in which it was claimed both (i) that a liability reduced the amount of a distribution and (ii) that no additional benefit was made available to the shareholder when the corporation paid the liability rather than the shareholder. Reg. section 1.301-1(g), incorporating the standards in section 357(d) for determining when a liability is assumed, was promulgated in response to these schemes. Under section 357(d), a recourse liability is treated as assumed if the transferee actually agrees to and is expected to repay the liability. A nonrecourse liability (that is, a liability for which the creditor has remedies only against the property in question, and cannot sue the debtor for any shortfall on foreclosure) is treated as having been assumed when it is transferred, but only to the extent of the amount of the liability not secured by other property and only to the extent of the fair market value of the encumbered property.

b. On Earnings and Profits

Loan proceeds are not included in a corporation's income, and are therefore not included in a corporation's earnings and profits except in very limited situations covered by section 312(i). What should be the treatment of those funds when a shareholder assumes an obligation of a corporation in connection with a distribution? From one perspective, it seems that the shareholder's assumption of the obligation might be treated as merely a contribution to capital that is excluded in the computation of the corporation's taxable income and disregarded for purposes of determining the corporation's earnings and profits. If a shareholder borrows funds and contributes those loan proceeds to a corporation, the funds are treated as a shareholder contribution to capital and do not increase earnings and profits.

That perspective is not adopted in the regulations implementing section 312(c)'s direction that "proper adjustment" be made for liabilities assumed. Instead, a shareholder's assumption of a corporation's liabilities is viewed as resulting in an increase in the corporation's assets available for distribution to shareholders, to the extent of the amount of the liability (which, in general will be the amount of loan proceeds that the corporation received when it made the original borrowing). Since earnings and profits are intended to reflect the amount economically available to the corporation for distribution, the reduction in earnings and profits under section 312 on account of the distribution is limited ("reduced by the amount of the liability") in order to reflect this freeing up of assets to the corporation. Reg. § 1.312-3. For example, if a corporation distributes property with a basis and fair market value of $50 subject to a liability of $15, the reduction in earnings and profits in respect of the distribution will be $35 and not $50. This reflects the presumption that the corporation has benefited from $15 of loan proceeds that it need not now repay and has $50 less in assets that have been distributed to its shareholders, for a net change of $35.

PRACTICE PROBLEMS

1. M Corp had taxable income and earnings and profits of over $20 million per year when Ed bought 100 shares for $1000. It has since had losses of more than $1 million per year ($.50 per share) for two years, and the value of Ed's stock has dropped to $950. Despite this rocky situation, M Corp distributed a dividend of $1 per share. The most likely result of this $100 distribution to Ed is

(a)   loss of $50, basis in stock of $850.

(b)   no income, reduction of basis in stock to $900.

(c)   dividend income of $100, no effect on basis.

(d)   dividend income of $50, no effect on stock basis.

2. Z Corp operated at no profit or loss for tax purposes in its first year of operation. It nevertheless distributed $20,000 to its shareholders, as a result of a loan taken out by pledging property that had been contributed to it. The effect of

this distribution on the shareholders will be

    (a)   dividend of $20,000.

    (b)   capital gain of $20,000.

    (c)   reduction in stock basis of up to $20,000, with ordinary income to the extent $20,000 exceeds basis.

    (d)   reduction in stock basis of up to $20,000, with capital gain to the extent $20,000 exceeds basis.

3.   Z Corp, in its first year of operation, has income of $50,000, subject to estimated federal income tax payments of $7,500. It distributes $50,000 to its shareholders. At the beginning of the next taxable year, its e&p is

    (a)   zero.

    (b)   a deficit of $7,500.

    (c) $50,000.

    (d) $42,500.

4.   Z Corp has $100,000 of accumulated e&p at the beginning of the taxable year. It has a projected taxable income of $50,000 this year, on which $7,500 in federal income taxes is expected to be paid. It declares and pays a dividend of $.50 per share on each of its 45,000 shares. The income projections prove correct. What is the result of the distribution to the shareholders, and what is the corporation's accumulated e&p as of the beginning of the next year? Assume that Z Corp's shareholders all have substantial basis in their shares.

    (a)   Dividend distribution of a total of $50,000 ($1 of income per share), and accumulated e&p increased to $150,000.

    (b)   Dividend distribution of a total of $22,500 ($.50 per share), and accumulated e&p decreased to $77,500.

    (c)   Dividend distribution of a total of $15,000 ($.50 per share, reduced by $.16 2/3 per share to 33 1/3 per share), and accumulated e&p increased to $135,000.

    (d)   Dividend distribution of a total of $22,500 ($.50 per share), and accumulated e&p increased to $120,000.

5.   Z Corp has $100,000 of accumulated e&p at the beginning of the taxable year. It has a projected taxable income of $50,000 this year, on which $7,500 in federal income taxes is expected to be paid. It declares and pays a dividend of $1 per share on each of its 45,000 shares. The income projections prove correct. What is the result of the distribution to the shareholders, and what is the corporation's accumulated e&p as of the beginning of the next year? Assume that Z Corp's shareholders all have substantial basis in their shares.

    (a)   Dividend distribution of a total of $50,000, and no change in accumulated e&p.

(b)   Dividend distribution of a total of $42,500, and no change in accumulated e&p.

(c)   Dividend distribution of a total of $45,000, and accumulated e&p of $97,500.

(d)   Dividend distribution of a total of $45,000, and accumulated e&p increased to $105,000.

6.   Z Corp has $100,000 of accumulated e&p at the beginning of the taxable year. It has a projected taxable income of $50,000 this year, on which $7,500 in federal income taxes is expected to be paid. It declares and pays a dividend of $5 per share on each of its 30,000 shares. The income projections prove correct. What is the result of the distribution to the shareholders and the corporation? What is the corporation's accumulated e&p as of the beginning of the next year? Assume that Z Corp's shareholders all have substantial basis in their shares.

(a)   Total dividend distribution of $150,000, and accumulated e&p reduced to -$15,000.

(b)   Total dividend distribution of $142,500, return of capital distribution of 7,500, and accumulated e&p reduced to zero.

(c)   Total dividend distribution of $142,500 and a return of capital distribution of 7,500, and accumulated e&p reduced to -$15,000.

(d)   Total dividend distribution of $150,000 and accumulated earnings reduced to zero.

7.   In the previous question, if a shareholder held a single share with a basis of $100 before the distribution, what is the shareholder's basis in the stock after the distribution?

(a) $95 ($100 less $5 of distribution).

(b) $96.41 ($100 plus $1.66 share of income less $0.25 share of taxes less $5 of distribution).

(c) $100 (basis is not adjusted for distributions).

(d) $99.75 ($100-$0.25).

8.   Same as previous two questions: Z Corp has $100,000 of accumulated e&p at the beginning of the taxable year. It has a projected taxable income of $50,000 this year, on which $7,500 in federal income taxes are expected to be paid. It declares and pays a dividend of $5 per share on each of its 30,000 shares. The income projections prove correct. This time, however, there are two distributions: $100,000 is paid on March 31, and $50,000 is paid on September 30. What is the aggregate result of the distribution to the shareholders who are holding on March 31 and on September 30? Assume that Z Corp's shareholders all have substantial basis in their shares.

(a)   March 31 — total dividend of $95,000 and return of capital of $5,000, and September 30 — total dividend of $47,500 and return of capital of $2,500.

(b)   March 31 — total dividend of $100,000, September 30 — total dividend of $42,500 and $7,500 return of capital.

(c) March 31 — total dividend of $96,000 and $4,000 return of capital; September 30 — total dividend of $36,600 and $13,400 return of capital.

(d) March 31 — total dividend of $100,000 and September 30 — total dividend of $50,000.

9. Same as previous two questions: Z Corp has $100,000 of accumulated e&p at the beginning of the taxable year. It has a projected taxable income of $50,000 this year, on which $7,500 in federal income taxes are expected to be paid. It declares and pays a dividend of $5 per share on each of its 30,000 shares. The income projections prove correct. This time, however, there are two classes of stock. 10,000 of the shares are common stock on which dividends are regularly declared only after dividends have been paid on the preferred stock. Thus a distribution of $100,000 was made on the 20,000 shares of preferred stock, and a distribution of $50,000 was made on the common stock, at the end of the fiscal year. What is the result of the distributions to the shareholders? Assume that Z Corp's shareholders all have substantial basis in their shares.

(a) Preferred stock — total dividend of $95,000 and return of capital of $5,000; common stock — total dividend of $47,500 and return of capital of $2,500.

(b) Preferred stock — total dividend of $100,000; common stock — total dividend of $42,500 and $7,500 return of capital.

(c) Preferred stock — total dividend of $96,000 and $4,000 return of capital; common stock — total dividend of $36,600 and $13,400 return of capital.

(d) Preferred stock — total dividend of $100,000; common stock — total dividend of $50,000.

10. Z Corp has $100,000 of accumulated e&p at the beginning of the taxable year. It has a projected taxable income of $50,000 this year. It declares and pays a dividend of $5 per share on each of its 30,000 shares at the end of the first quarter of its fiscal year.

But this time, the income projections prove incorrect, and the corporation earns $100,000 in the year of the distribution, and pays $20,000 in federal income taxes. All of the earnings are attributable to specific events occurring after the distribution. What is the result of the distribution to the shareholders and the corporation? Assume that Z Corp's shareholders all have substantial basis in their shares. What is the corporation's accumulated e&p as of the beginning of the next year?

(a) Total dividend of $150,000; accumulated e&p of $100,000.

(b) Total dividend of $80,000; accumulated e&p of $100,000.

(c) Total dividend of $150,000; accumulated e&p of $30,000.

(d) Total dividend of $100,000 return of capital of $50,000; accumulated e&p of $100,000.

11. Z Corp has $140,000 of accumulated e&p at the beginning of the taxable year. It has a projected taxable income of $50,000 this year. It declares and pays a dividend of $5 per share on its 20,000 class A common shares midway through its taxable year. Its other 10,000 shares are in class B common stock on which

dividends are regularly declared only after dividends have been declared and paid on the other, class A, common stock and certain performance goals are met. This later stock received its $5 dividend at the end of the corporation's fourth quarter.

But this time, the income projections prove incorrect, and the corporation loses $30,000 in the year of the distribution, mostly attributable to specific events occurring after the first distribution on the class A shares but before the distribution to the class B shares. What is the result of the distribution to the shareholders and the corporation? Assume that Z Corp's shareholders all have substantial basis in their shares. What is the corporation's accumulated e&p as of the beginning of the next year?

(a)   Total dividend distribution of $100,000 to class A; total dividend distribution of $10,000 and return of capital of $40,000 to class B; no accumulated e&p.

(b)   Total dividend distribution of $93,333 to the class A shareholders and $6,777 return of capital; total dividend distribution of $46,777 to the class B shareholders, with $3,333 return of capital; no accumulated e&p.

(c)   Total dividend distribution of $110,000, distributed proportionately to the class A and class B shareholders; with a deficit in e&p of $30,000.

(d)   Total dividend distribution of $150,000, distributed proportionately to the class A and B shareholders, with a deficit in e&p of $40,000.

12.   Z Corp has accumulated e&p of $100,000 and, without taking into account the distribution in question here, current e&p of $500,000. It distributes to shareholders property that it holds with a basis of $10,000 and a fair market value of $110,000. What is the result to the shareholders and to Z Corp of this distribution? Assume a 35% tax rate unless otherwise indicated.

(a)   Total dividend of $100,000 and no net effect on e&p ($600,000 accumulated as of beginning of next year).

(b)   Total dividend of $100,000; $65,000 increase in current e&p on gain ($100,000–$35,000 in taxes) to $565,000, reduced by distribution to $455,000; accumulated e&p $555,000 at beginning of next year.

(c)   Total dividend of $110,000; $65,000 increase in current e&p on gain ($100,000–$35,000 in taxes) to $565,000, reduced by distribution to $455,000; accumulated e&p of $555,000 at beginning of next year.

(d)   Total dividend of $75,000 ($110,000–$35,000 in taxes); accumulated e&p of $525,000.

13.   Z Corp has accumulated e&p of $100,000 and, without taking into account the distribution in question here, current e&p of $50,000. It distributes to shareholders property that it holds with a basis of $120,000 and a fair market value of $40,000. What is the result to the shareholders and to Z Corp of this distribution? Assume that Z Corp's shareholders all have substantial basis in their shares.

(a)   Loss of $80,000; dividend of $120,000; accumulated e&p deficit of $50,000 as of beginning of next year.

(b)   No loss, dividend of $40,000; accumulated e&p of $30,000 as of beginning of next year.

(c)   Loss of $80,000; dividend of $70,000 with return of capital of $50,000; zero e&p as of beginning of next year.

(d)   No loss, dividend of $120,000; accumulated e&p of $30,000 as of beginning of next year.

14.   Z Corp has accumulated e&p of $100,00, and distributed property that, unencumbered, would sell for $100,000, for which it paid $100,000. It was subject to a liability of $30,000. What is the effect of this distribution on the shareholders and on Z Corp?

(a)   Dividend distribution of $70,000; reduction in e&p by $70,000.

(b)   Dividend distribution of $70,000; income of $30,000 to Z Corp, net reduction in e&p of $40,000.

(c)   Dividend distribution of $100,000; reduction in e&p of $100,000.

(d)   Dividend distribution of $100,000; reduction in e&p of $70,000.

15.   What is the basis of the properties distributed to shareholders in problems 12 and 13 above, respectively?

(a) $110,000 and $120,000.

(b) $110,000 and $40,000.

(c) $10,000 and $120,000.

(d) $10,000 and $40,000.

DISCUSSION PROBLEMS

1.   Small Corp has a single shareholder, Sam, who holds 1000 shares with a total basis of $50,000. Small Corp has been existence for 50 years and is a calendar year taxpayer.

In July of Year 51, Small Corp made distributions of $80,000 to Sam. No other distributions were made in Year 51. As of December 31 of Year 50, Small Corp had no earnings and profits. In Year 51, Small Corp had before-tax earnings of $50,000 as of July 1.

It is now mid-December, and Sam has come to you asking for assurances about how this distribution will be taxed. The facts outlined above have been offered by Sam as the critical information about his company.

(You may assume for the purposes of answering these questions that no federal income tax will be owed on the current income of Small Corp, and therefore that changes in "income" will be directly reflected in "earnings and profits.")

(a)   What else do you need to know before you can determine how Sam will be taxed on this distribution? What are the most likely possibilities, and upon what are they contingent?

(b)   As you talk further, you learn that Sam bought all of the stock of Small Corp for $50,000 on January 1 of Year 51. How is a distribution of $80,000 possible from a corporation worth $50,000 at the end of Year 50, which had no accumulated earnings and profits at that date and which does not know its current e&p for the year?

(c)   You can tell from Sam's demeanor that the business did not go very well for the second half of the year, so you realize that the answer to Sam's question may not be as simple as he would like. He indicates that there might be an additional $10,000 of income in the second half of the year, at most. If this turns out to be true, how will the $80,000 distributed to Sam in July be taxed?

(d)   What if Sam sold half his stock for $50,000 shortly before the July 1 distribution (and therefore received only half the distribution)?

(e)   What if Sam purchased 300 shares of stock in Year 40 for $5000 and the remaining 700 shares in Year 48 for $45,000?

(f)   What if Small Corp actually lost $60,000 in the second half of Year 51?

(g)   What if, in part (c) above (current earnings of $50,000 in the first six months plus $10,000 in the second six months), Small Corp had had $20,000 of accumulated e&p?

(h)   What if, in part (f) above (current earnings of 50,000 in the first six months less 60,000 of losses in the second six months) above, Small Corp had had $20,000 of accumulated e&p?

(i)   Toward the end of the conversation, Sam lets it slip that there is a second class of common stock in Small Corp, title to which is in his son's name (with a basis of $30,000), and which is entitled to a dividend totaling $30,000, which Sam plans to have the corporation pay in December. How will this distribution affect the tax treatment of Sam's distribution, under all of the earnings scenarios above (i.e., $10,000 of additional income or $60,000 of loss in the second half of the year; no accumulated earnings or $20,000 of accumulated earnings)?

(j)   What would be the result if the second class of stock were preferred stock — that is, no dividend could be paid to the holders of the common stock until the dividend were paid on the preferred stock?

(k)   What would be the result if the second class of stock were tracking stock — that is, the stock is entitled to a dividend that depends upon the performance of a particular part of Small Corp's business? Assume that the relevant part of Small Corp's business had separate income of $40,000, while the rest of the business had results that, when netted, yielded $10,000 of income (thus $30,000 of losses in the rest of the business) or, alternatively $60,000 of loss (that is, $100,000 of losses in the rest of the business).

2.   Central Corp is owned by three equal shareholders and runs a small but highly profitable manufacturing business. But it also holds a piece of land which it purchased 20 years ago for $100,000, when it was planning to build a new factory

made unnecessary by outsourcing overseas. Its shareholders cannot agree either about its best use or its fair market value. Finally, to avoid an impasse, the corporation and its shareholders agree that the land will be distributed to Sue, the shareholder who believes it will be most valuable, at the same time that cash is distributed to the other shareholders.

(a) What are the tax effects (both on e&p and income) to the corporation and to the shareholders if the cash distributions to the other two shareholders are equal to $250,000 each?

(b) As in part a, except what are the tax effects to the corporation and to the shareholders if the cash distributions are $75,000 each?

(c) As in part a, except that the property is subject to a $35,000 mortgage?

(d) As in part a, except what if the land is sold two years later for $325,000?

(e) What if, instead of an immediate distribution of the land, the corporation had given Sue the option to buy the land for $50,000 and the other shareholders received distributions of $200,000 each. Two years later, on hearing that there might be a buyer for the land, Sue exercised her option to buy the land and then sold it for $325,000.

(f) As in problem 2-a, except that Sue is in the middle of a messy divorce. In the state in which they live, the rights of a divorcing couple to property owned during the marriage are so confused that buyers regularly offer only 75% of what they would have offered had they not feared that they were buying a lawsuit when they buy from a seller going through a divorce.

Chapter 3

SHAREHOLDER TRANSFERS OF PROPERTY TO CORPORATIONS UNDER SECTION 351

Statutes and Regulations	IRC §§ 118(a), 351; 358; 362(a), (e); 368(c), 1032
	Reg. § 1.351-1; Prop. Reg. § 1.351-1
	Reg. § 1.362-1(a); Prop. Reg. § 1.362-4 (as needed)
Other Primary Authorities	Rev. Proc. 77-37, 1977-2 C.B. 568
	Rev. Rul. 59-259, 1959-2 C.B. 115
	Intermountain Lumber Co. v. Commissioner, 65 T.C. 1025 (1976)
	Rev. Rul. 2003-51, 2003-1 C.B. 938
	West Coast Marketing Corp. v. Commissioner, 46 T.C. 32 (1966)

Even though a corporation is treated as a separate taxable entity and transfers of property from a corporation to its shareholders are generally taxable for both shareholders and corporation, transfers of property from new or existing shareholders to corporations in exchange for stock may be nonrecognition transactions if the conditions of section 351 are satisfied. A property transfer will be governed by section 351 if the group of transferring shareholders has "control" of the transferee corporation, within the meaning of section 368(c), immediately after the transaction.

Why should controlling shareholder transfers of property be eligible for nonrecognition? Underlying most of Subchapter C's nonrecognition provisions is the economic rationale that owners should be able to rearrange their enterprises: the Code accordingly recognizes, in appropriate cases, the similarity of a substantial continuing equity interest in property when a taxpayer changes from a direct ownership interest to an indirect ownership interest through an entity. A taxpayer may own equipment directly (for instance, earth-moving equipment owned through a sole proprietorship) that generates a stream of income over time or the taxpayer may transfer the equipment to a corporate entity at the same time that another taxpayer transfers complementary property, permitting each of the taxpayers to continue to reap economic benefits, indirectly through a corporate enterprise running an expanded excavating business, from the stream of income generated by their equipment. The economic interest is not substantially changed. Of course, not all corporate formations will evidence so clear a similarity between the property interest owned prior to and after the transfer, but clearly Congress has thought it appropriate to permit corporate formations like this to be undertaken without imposing a substantial tax burden on the transfer that would tend to discourage such rearrangements of economic interests.

There are limitations to the types of enterprises intended to be protected by the nonrecognition provision. Section 351(e), for example, removes from nonrecognition the formation of an investment company. Permitting passive investors to combine their investments by using the corporate formation nonrecognition provisions would not further the goal of removing transactional barriers to formation of new enterprises; instead, it would merely provide a tax-free means for investors to diversify their investments as they would otherwise do in regular sales subject to section 1001. There are threshold conditions on nonrecognition for transfers to corporations, which are treated as separate taxable entities that make payments out of their net earnings to their shareholders/owners, whereas there are no such conditions on formation of partnerships, which are treated as conduit entities that pass through their tax items to their partners/owners whether or not the income is actually distributed. The difference can be attributed to the extent to which a shareholder's connection to contributed property is treated as severed in the corporate context, compared to a partner's more direct interest in the partnership context.

3.1. IN EXCHANGE FOR STOCK

When the conditions of section 351 are satisfied, the transferring shareholders do not recognize gain or loss, and have a basis in their corporate shares that reflects their basis in the transferred property under section 358(a). The corporation recognizes no gain or loss on its issuance of corporate shares in exchange for the transferred property under section 1032, and the corporation ordinarily has a basis equal to the transferor shareholder's basis in the transferred property under section 362(a)(1).

3.1.1. The Threshold Condition: Control under Section 368(c)

Not all contributions to corporations will enjoy nonrecognition: only those that involve transfers by a shareholder or group of shareholders that represent a controlling interest will be eligible. This "control group" may be one shareholder or one thousand shareholders acting together, so long as they represent the requisite interest in the corporation.

Control under section 368(c) means ownership of at least 80% of "the *total combined voting power* of all classes of stock entitled to vote and at least 80% of the *total number of shares* of all other classes of stock of the corporation." The statutory language setting forth the first 80% test, involving voting power, is clear: it can be satisfied regardless of the total number of shares or the total market value of the stock involved, and without requiring proportionate ownership of each *class* of voting stock. The second test involving ownership of nonvoting stock is ambiguous. It could be intended to permit nonrecognition transactions so long as the control group owns 80% of the total number of nonvoting shares, independent of the classes of shares established, or it could be intended to cover only those transactions in which the control group acquires 80% of the total shares issued in each class of nonvoting shares. The IRS has ruled that the control group must own

80% of the shares of each class of stock to satisfy the test. Rev. Rul. 59-259, 1959-2 C.B. 115 (citing the legislative history indicating that Congress intended that the control group own a controlling interest of all other classes of stock). There is no attribution of share ownership under section 368(c), and the test is not the same as that used in section 1504(a)(4), the section which determines, for instance, qualification to file a consolidated return.

The control test is one that focuses on the situation *after* the transaction. Significantly, not only need the corporation not be formed as a result of the transaction in question, control need not be established as a result of the transaction. All that is required is that the requisite control exist immediately after the transaction is completed. Thus, section 351 is satisfied when two shareholders, each of whom owns half of the 100 shares outstanding in a corporation, contribute appreciated property and take back stock. Similarly, section 351 is satisfied when two shareholders who own 90% and 10% of the corporate stock, respectively, contribute property in similar proportions to their ownership in exchange for additional stock.

What if the transaction is one in which the 10% shareholder is to become a 50% shareholder as a result of the transfer? If only he participates in the transfer, there will have been transfers made by transferors whose ownership totals only 50% after the transaction. Obviously, the other shareholder must participate by making a transfer in order for the control group requirement for nonrecognition to be satisfied. But how much must this second shareholder transfer to make him count as a "transferor" and thereby provide the first shareholder with nonrecognition — would only a nominal amount be adequate? The regulations provide an explicit answer to this question. If the "primary purpose of the transfer was to afford nonrecognition to some other transferor," a transfer can count as part of the transferring control group only if the transfer is of an amount such that the stock issued in exchange "is not of relatively small value in comparison to the value of the stock . . . already owned." Reg. § 1.351-1(a)(1)(ii). For ruling purposes, the IRS requires that an existing shareholder must transfer in exchange for an additional equity interest property worth at least 10% of the value of the stock already owned, to count as part of the transferring control group. Rev. Proc. 77-37. Thus, if the majority shareholder held stock worth $90 before the transaction, under the ruling standard he must transfer property resulting in the receipt of stock worth at least $9.

> **Private Ruling Practice**
>
> *Practitioners historically have been able to ask the IRS to rule in advance on the transactions they propose. The IRS issues guidelines (as Revenue Procedures) that set out the representations that must be made in these ruling requests. Frequently, the IRS will ask that the representations include assurances consistent with a standard somewhat stricter than a court might require in order to satisfy one of the conditions. These ruling requests usually may be withdrawn without adverse consequences, but an adverse ruling cannot be appealed to the courts directly. As a consequence, the ruling process has added a gloss on the statute.*

3.1.2. "Immediately After"

The regulations make clear that the phrase "immediately after" does not require that all property transfers be simultaneous, "but comprehends a situation where the rights of the parties have been previously defined and the execution of the agreement proceeds with an expedition consistent with orderly procedure." Reg. § 1.351-1(a)(1). This is a necessary concession to the realities of property transfers, which in some cases may require months to finalize due to state law transfer requirements. This is particularly true in the case of real estate, where the property being transferred to the corporation must be adequately severed from any property retained.

Several authorities have given more meaning than might be expected to the phrase "immediately after" in the control requirement, applying some version of the step transaction doctrine to integrate a subsequent sale or other transaction that causes the transferring group to fail the control test. *See, e.g.*, Intermountain Lumber Co. & Subsidiaries, etc. v. Commissioner, 65 T.C. 1025 (1976) (recasting a transaction because of a pre-arranged sale of shares by the sole transferring shareholder). In general, there can be no binding obligation to transfer the stock received to another party. This additional limitation, however, need not be an obstacle in those cases in which the ultimate holder of the stock can be treated as part of the transferring control group. Thus the regulations provide that there is no problem with "control" "immediately after" when an underwriter transfers the stock on initial issue to the party actually funding the corporation. Reg. § 1.351-1(3). Nor is it a problem if there is a pre-existing agreement to transfer the shares received as property in another section 351 transaction. *See* Rev. Rul. 2003-51, 2003-1 C.B. 938.

> **Judicial Doctrines in the Interpretation of Subchapter C**
>
> *The law of corporate transactions is in large part determined by the detailed provisions of the Code and the regulations interpreting it. But there is also a significant body of "common law" in this area, as courts have developed judicial doctrines to expand upon and clarify the vague or ambiguous language in the Code as applied to particular transactions. The primary judicial doctrines, discussed in every corporate tax text and essential considerations in the context of preparing a tax opinion on any uncertain position, are:*
>
> *(i) business purpose, see, e.g., Gregory v. Helvering, 293 U.S. 465 (1935) (considered elsewhere in this text in connection with spinoff transactions);*

(ii) sham transaction/economic substance requirement, see, e.g., *Kirchman v. Commissioner, 862 F.2d 1486, 1490 (11th Cir. 1989)* (stating that a transaction ceases to merit respect for tax purposes when it has "no economic effects other than the creation of tax benefits"); and

(iii) step transaction, see, e.g., *Falconwood Corp. v. United States, 422 F.3d 1339 (Fed. Cir. 2005).*

All of these doctrines are closely related, and are sometimes collapsed under a fourth doctrine that runs throughout the jurisprudence of the federal income tax — the principle that substance determines the tax consequences (often referred to as the "substance over form" doctrine).

The Step Transaction Doctrine

The step transaction doctrine is particularly important in analyzing corporate transactions, in particular multi-step acquisitions or other restructurings that involve nonrecognition transactions such as section 351. If the doctrine applies, two or more distinct transactional steps — ones that would otherwise be assessed independently of each other in determining their appropriate tax consequences — will be collapsed into a single integrated transaction and the tax consequences will be determined by considering the integrated transaction rather than its component parts. For example, two transferors may transfer some property to a newly formed corporation on January 1 of year 1, and a third transferor may transfer additional property to the corporation on July 1. If those transfers were planned together and the third transfer took place as expeditiously as possible under the circumstances, the three will be stepped together and the "immediately after" test for control to determine whether section 351 applies will be based on the three transfers.

The courts have not settled on a single statement of the step transaction doctrine. There are three predominant versions. Some jurisdictions have adopted a single version that must be satisfied before transactional steps can be integrated, while other jurisdictions may consider the effect of all of the versions before determining whether to integrate the steps.

The three versions, listed in increasing order of a result in which steps will be combined, are:

(i) binding commitment, see, e.g., *Commissioner v. Gordon, 391 U.S. 83, 96 (1968);*

(ii) mutual interdependence, see, e.g., *Penrod v. Commissioner, 88 T.C. 1415, 1428 (1987); and*

(iii) end result, see, e.g., *King Enterprises v. United States, 418 F.2d 511, 516-518 (Ct. Cl. 1969).*

Although taxpayers cannot count on using the step transaction doctrine to recast a transaction as they would choose, see Commissioner v. Danielson, 378 F.2d 771, 778 (3d Cir. 1967), there are many transactions in which the government has so consistently applied it that its application has become an accepted part of the interpretation of subchapter C.

Section 351 requires the transferors to have control of the transferee corporation "immediately after" the protected transfer. What kind of post-incorporation transfers can safely be accomplished without violating the "immediately after" control requirement? The section makes clear that the "control immediately after" requirement will not be violated if a corporate transferor distributes part or all of the stock it receives in the section 351 exchange to its shareholders. § 351(c). (Such distribution may be taxable under ordinary distribution rules to the corporation under section 311 and to shareholders under section 301, or may be part of a section 355 spin that is eligible for nonrecognition.)

Similarly, what authority there is seems to agree that non-commercial, voluntary transfers of stock, even if planned in connection with transaction formation of the corporation, should not be stepped together with the section 351 transaction to cause it to fail the "control immediately after" test. *See, e.g.*, Intermountain Lumber Co. v. Commissioner, 65 T.C. 1025 (1976) (in dictum); Wilgard Realty Co. v. Commissioner, 127 F.2d 514 (2d Cir. 1942) (transfer of 20% to children immediately after incorporation). This acceptance of donative transfers immediately after or simultaneous with incorporation relates to the concept of tax ownership — the right to dispose of the benefits and burdens of holding an asset. Note that the alternative would be to give the property itself to those to whom stock would otherwise be donated, with the result that there would possibly be considerable transaction costs in the replication of transfers (from donor to donees, and from donees to corporation).

What if assets are transferred to a transferee corporation, and then either the assets so transferred, or the stock of the transferee, are further dropped? The transfer of the assets to a second-tier subsidiary controlled by the first-tier transferee does not seem to create issues under the statute, even though there is no explicit provision comparable to section 351(c). The Service has clearly accepted that a series of section 351 dropdowns of assets will not cause the control-immediately-after requirement to fail. *See, e.g.*, Rev. Rul. 77-449, 1977-2 C.B. 110; Rev. Rul. 83-34, 1983-1 C.B. 79 (series of dropdowns analyzed as separate section 351 transactions). A dropdown of the stock — i.e., the transfer of the stock by the original transferor group to another corporation controlled by it — is more troublesome, since the transferor group must maintain control "immediately after," and there is no attribution applicable in determining such control, nor does section 368(c) use the phrase "directly or indirectly" that would facilitate an interpretation permitting such dropdowns. Nevertheless, the IRS has ruled that such dropdowns of stock will not always spoil a section 351 transfer, even when there is a binding commitment to participate in that drop at the time of the initial transfer. *See* Rev. Rul. 2003-51, 2003-1 C.B. 938. Section 351 would be spoiled if the transferor group transferred the stock of the transferee corporation to an acquiring corporation over which there was no control, even in a nonrecognition transaction.

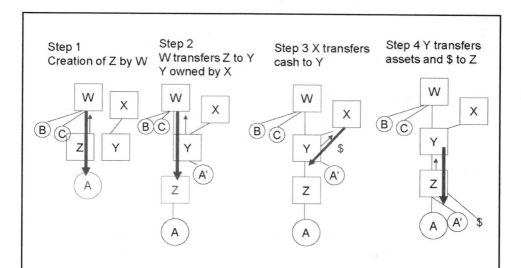

Post-incorporation transfers: Rev. Rul. 2003-51

Two unrelated corporations, W and X, sought to combine portions of their business operations. Toward that end, (1) W created a new Z corporation; (2) two transfers were then made to Y, a corporation at that point wholly owned by W: W transferred cash and the stock of the newly created Z and X transferred operating assets; and (3) a final transfer was then made by Y to Z of the capital it had received from W and its operating assets. The ruling states that each of transfers (1), (2), and (3) would qualify under section 351. The ruling holds that transfer (1) (by which Z was created by W) is not spoiled by the re-transfer by W to Y of the stock received in a transaction that met the requirements of section 351, or by the loss of indirect control of Z as a result of X's participation in Y. The ruling relied on the fact that the same result could have been reached had W merely contributed assets to Y, and then Y created Z corporation.

3.1.3. Contributions of Services in Connection with Section 351 Transfers

Section 351 provides nonrecognition only for property transfers, not for performance of services in exchange for stock. § 351(d)(1). This is consistent with the general bias in the Code against deferral of service income and also comports with the underlying premise that a formation transaction continues an equity interest in the property transferred.

A service provider may, however, transfer property to the corporation in exchange for stock in addition to receiving stock as payment for services. If the primary purpose for a service provider's property transfer is to ensure that the service provider's stock will be counted towards the control requirement and thereby qualify other property transfers for nonrecognition treatment, the regulations require that the service provider transfer property that is not "of relatively small value in comparison to the value of the stock . . . to be received for services." Reg. § 1.351-1(a)(1)(ii). Again, this means that the stock received for property must be at least 10% of the stock received for services. (Note that this is the same proportion that applies in the case of an existing shareholder's additional transfer of property to qualify a transaction under the control requirement.) If the additional property transfer is made and is deemed not to be relatively small, the service provider is treated as a "transferor," and therefore all of the stock she holds after the transaction counts in determining whether the transferring group satisfies the control requirement. *See, e.g.*, Reg. § 1.351-1(a)(2), Ex. 3 (400 shares with value of $20,000, received for $2000 of services and $18,000 of property, constituted control, where corporation had 100 shares outstanding prior to the transaction).

3.1.4. Basis in Stock to Shareholders and Transferred Property to Corporations Potential Abuses

A transferring shareholder's basis in the stock received will be the same as the basis in the property and cash given up, as provided in section 358's exchanged basis rule. This will preserve any unrecognized gain or loss on the contributed assets in the shareholder's stock. The transferor shareholder's basis in the transferred properties also becomes the corporation's basis in the transferred assets under section 362(b)(1)'s transferred basis rule. These determinations are made on a transferor by transferor basis. If more than one class of stock is received, the shareholder allocates the aggregate basis among them by fair market value. Reg. § 1.358-2(b)(2). These results are justified both by the nonrecognition model on which the provisions are based, and by the fact that any other result would exacerbate unduly the tax disadvantages of incorporating. Transferring potential income streams to corporations taxable under subchapter C subjects that income to tax at the corporate level and then subjects the net profits to tax to the extent they are distributed to shareholders as dividends. Limiting either the shareholder's basis or the corporation's basis to something less than the shareholder's old basis would generally tend to increase the overall income in the system.

By the same token, the cloning of a taxpayer's basis when property is transferred to a corporation could be advantageous in permitting duplication of losses, if the property transferred is a loss property. The corporation would have a high basis, possibly permitting depreciation deductions that reduce its tax liability, while a shareholder could sell some of the shares as desired to recognize part of the realized loss on the property transfer. In the recent focus on corporate tax shelters, Congress has been concerned that the rules of sections 358 and 362 can result in an inappropriate replication of losses and the generation of artificial losses through manipulation of the basis rules. It has therefore limited the availability of replicated basis or replicated losses resulting from section 351 transactions in various ways. Specifically, section 336(d) limits the deductibility of losses contributed in section 351 transactions when it is likely that those losses were "stuffed" into the corporation in order to shelter gain on liquidation; section 362(e) limits the replication of losses when a transferor shareholder transfers property with an aggregate built-in loss; and section 358(h), considered further in connection with the corporation's assumption of shareholder liabilities in section 351 transactions, reduces a shareholder's basis in certain circumstances when the overall value of the corporation after the section 351 transaction is less than the shareholder's basis in the stock.

3.2.   IN EXCHANGE FOR STOCK AND OTHER CONSIDERATION

3.2.1.   Boot Generally

Sometimes a corporation will find it appropriate to transfer to its shareholders cash or property (that is, something other than "the stock permitted to be received") in addition to stock in transactions that would otherwise qualify under section 351. It may be necessary to transfer cash to some shareholders, for instance, to obtain the intended proportion of stock ownership on formation, or to transfer some property held by the corporation, for instance, when as the result of the transaction there is a new shareholder who will not share in the risks involved in owning a particular asset. Such additional property received by shareholders, referred to in subchapter C as "money or other property", is commonly called "boot."

Despite the use of "solely" in the basic nonrecognition provision of section 351(a), the transfer of boot as well as stock will not entirely defeat nonrecognition. If a shareholder has realized any gain on the transfer of an asset to the corporation, however, that gain will be recognized to the extent of the boot received in respect of that asset. Receipt of boot nonetheless will not permit a transferring shareholder to recognize any realized loss on a transferred asset. § 351(b). (Note that in the appropriate case, section 1239 can apply to require the transferor shareholder to recognize ordinary income on the transfer of property that will be subject to cost recovery in the corporation's hands.)

If a shareholder transfers multiple assets and receives some boot, how does she determine the amount and character of any gain to be recognized — on an aggregate basis (recognizing the net built-in gain, to the extent of the aggregate boot received), or on an asset-by-asset basis? If on an asset-by-asset basis, how is the boot allocated to the assets — first to gain properties, in proportion to the gain in the asset, and only if there is excess boot would any be allocated to loss properties, or in proportion to the properties' fair market values? The Service takes the position that the determination of gain is made on an asset- by-asset basis by allocating the boot received to the properties in proportion to their fair market values. Rev. Rul. 68-55, 1968-1 C.B. 140. This rule has at least two important consequences. First, the basis of loss assets is not available to limit the gain recognized on gain assets, so that a transfer of properties with an aggregate net loss can still result in gain recognition. Second, the allocation of boot to loss properties reduces the total amount of gain that would be recognized if all of the boot were allocated first to gain properties. In other words, the IRS position increases tax liabilities compared to a situation where the taxpayer could choose to allocate boot first to loss properties, but it does not maximize tax liabilities as would result if boot were allocated first to gain properties. There is no clear authority on whether these results can be avoided by specifying that particular loss assets are transferred in exchange for boot consideration or by attempting to transfer loss property for boot consideration in a transaction that is separate from the section 351 transaction. It seems highly likely that a court would integrate such tax-avoiding "side transactions" with the section 351 transaction, given the clear statutory prohibition on recognition of losses in this context.

Specified Allocation of Boot to Transferred Property

There is some authority on specified allocation, though it does not appear to include situations in which there is a loss asset, the situation discussed in the main text. Cohen and Whitney, for example, first illustrate the way in which specific allocation could be advantageous (discussing an example in which $20 of stock and $80 of boot is allocated to an asset with no realized gain or loss, and the $100 balance of the stock is allocated to an asset with $100 of realized gain, resulting in no gain recognition in respect of any of the boot) but then go on to show that administrative determinations interpret Rev. Rul. 68-55, 1968-1 C.B. 140, as mandating ratable allocation of boot, regardless of attempted designation of specific consideration, citing GCM 39418 (Oct. 14, 1983); PLR 8012036 (Dec. 27, 1979). Benjamin J. Cohen & Ronald E. Whitney, Revisiting the Allocation of Boot in Section 351 Exchanges, 48 Tax Law. 959 (1995). Even so, they point out some authority that does permit an exception "where the transfer of inventory to a foreign corporation is a section 351 exchange that is taxable under section 367." See P.L.R. 8550037 (Sept. 16, 1985) (transfer of inventory to foreign corporation with section 351 taxable under section 367 allows specific allocation of cash boot to inventory). There are also a few cases permitting specific allocation, though in no case with loss properties where allocation could avoid gain recognition. Furthermore, these cases should likely be confined to their facts. See Lovell & Hart, 29 T.C.M. 1599 (1970) (in which the Service conceded capital gain characterization without providing a rationale); Wham Construction Co., No. 72-689 (D.S.C. Feb. 16, 1976), aff'd on other grounds, 600 F.2d 1052 (4th Cir. 1979) (in which the government claimed that accounts receivable should be treated as boot).

Under section 358, the transferor receiving boot will always receive a fair market value basis in that boot. (The statutory language is cumbersome, primarily because of the reluctance of the drafter to view money as "property" to which basis must be allocated.) The shareholder's basis in the stock received will be computed, using the formula in section 358(a), by starting with the shareholder's basis in the property given up, reducing it by the fair market value of the boot properties and the amount of boot cash received, and increasing it by any gain recognized on the exchange. This is the same formula used in computing basis after transactions granted nonrecognition under section 1031. Note that when all boot triggers gain, the shareholder's basis in stock will be the same as the shareholder's old basis in the property (i.e., none of the boot has been treated as basis recovery).

The shareholder also tacks the holding period of capital assets transferred to the stock's holding period. Section 1223(1) (tacked holding period for exchanged basis property that is capital or section 1231 asset). In the case of multiple assets, that tacking creates a problem: if the shareholder is not treated as receiving separate blocks of stock in respect of each asset transferred, how can the holding period tack for some assets and start fresh for others? The Service's solution is to treat the stock received as a single block of stock, but fragment each stock into segments representing basis and holding period related to particular properties. To illustrate, assume that, in exchange for 100 shares worth $400, Max, a transferor/shareholder in a section 351 transaction, transfers two properties, each worth $200: Property 1 is a capital asset with a long-term holding period and a basis of $160. Property 2 is an ordinary asset with a basis of $40. The 100 shares Max receives in exchange will be fragmented so that each share reflects the holding period and basis of each type of property Max has transferred. This can be solved mechanically by (i) assuming a hypothetical allocation of shares to each property so that 50 of the shares will be received for property 1, with a basis of $160 ($3.20 a share) and a long-term holding period; 50 of the shares will be received for property 2, with a basis of $40 ($0.80 a share) and a fresh-start holding period; and (ii) collapsing that hypothetical allocation into each share. Since half the shares are received for each property in this example, that means that, upon the collapse, Max will be treated as holding 100 shares, with ½ of each share representing property 1 and so having $1.60 (i.e., ½ * $3.20) basis and long-term holding period and ½ of each share representing property 2 and so having $0.40 (i.e., ½ * $0.80) basis and a fresh-start holding period. This fragmentation approach is set out in Rev. Rul. 85-164, 1985-2 C.B. 117. (Note that fragmentation is no longer necessary once the stock has been held for the long-term holding period.)

3.2.2. Consequences to Corporate Transferees

a. Gain or Loss with Respect to the Stock Used

Ordinarily, when appreciated or depreciated property is transferred, the transferor will recognize any gain or loss unless there is a specific nonrecognition rule that applies. Is issuer's stock "property" for the purposes of this rule? Although section 317 says that "property" does not include stock, this section applies by its terms only to distributions under part I of subchapter C and not to exchanges outside of that Part. Nevertheless, section 1032 provides that no gain or loss will be recognized when a corporation uses its own stock in exchange for "money or other property."

This no-gain-or-loss rule finesses the question of whether a corporation has basis in its own stock for most, but not quite all, purposes. It was not always the rule, however, and occasionally one encounters older authorities that treat newly issued stock differently. The extension of section 1032 to reacquired stock was determined to be appropriate, because issuers could too easily "manage" the losses inherent in reacquired stock (while avoiding recognition of any gains).

The regulations clarify that this nonrecognition rule applies to transfers of stock in exchange for services as well. Reg. 1.1032-1(a) (last sentence). Regulations issued in 2000 further expand the scope of section 1032 to include certain very limited uses of the stock of related corporations. Some frequently suggested limitations on the applicability of section 1032 (e.g., to tracking stock, through which the shareholders have an interest in the profits of only a portion of the issuing corporation's activities) have not been adopted.

b.   Gain or Loss With Respect to Property Received by the Corporation and Boot Given Up by the Corporation

Section 351 provides for nonrecognition only to transferring shareholders and not to the corporate transferee. There are two provisions that ensure that corporations will not be taxed on transfers from shareholders: section 118, which provides nonrecognition for a corporation that receives "contributions to capital"; and section 1032, which provides nonrecognition with respect to a corporation's receipt of money or other property in exchange for its own stock.

Nothing prevents a corporation from recognizing gain when it uses its property as boot in a transaction governed by section 351. Section 351(f) provides that section 311 applies, and thus that the corporation recognizes gain but cannot recognize loss.

c.   Basis and Holding Period for the Stock

The fact that the corporation does not recognize any gain or loss in its stock when the stock is used in a transaction (e.g., as consideration in an exchange or as compensation to an employee) says nothing about whether the corporation can take this value paid out into account for tax purposes. In general, if a corporation uses its stock in a transfer that is fully taxed to the recipient, the corporation will have a deduction or will have basis in an asset, depending upon the nature of the expenditure involved. Thus, when a corporation uses stock as compensation for services of managers, the corporation deducts the compensation expense. If it should use its stock in fully taxable transactions to acquire assets, it records a basis in those assets equal to the fair market value of the stock transferred.

Note that this is one of the very, very rare situations in which a taxpayer will get basis for transferring property which is not clearly after-tax, that is, in which it has not earned that basis by taking an amount into income.

Consistent with the nonrecognition nature of a transfer of property in exchange for stock that qualifies under section 351, the corporation ordinarily takes a basis equal to the transferring shareholder's basis in the property under section 362(a). Section 362(a) provides that the total basis transferred to the corporation will be determined by the transferor. It is also fairly well settled (and comports with the Service's ruling position on determination of gain by shareholders) that the aggregate basis transferred by a single transferor is allocated among the items transferred by that shareholder in accordance with the original basis of the individual assets transferred: it is not reassigned pro rata among the assets received. Thus, as is consistent with the nonrecognition nature of the transaction, the corporation can take property with a basis greater than its fair market value. There are limitations, however, in section 362(d) (no basis increase above the fair market value of property by virtue of gain recognition as a result of liability assumption) and section 362(e) (limitation on transfer of built-in losses).

To What Extent Is the § 351 Transferee Treated as Successor to the Transferor?

In the other transactions granted nonrecognition under the provisions of subchapter C, those covered by sections 332 and 368, the transferee inherits much of the tax history of the transferor under section 381(a). Consistent with this overall approach, transferors in those transactions rarely are required to take amounts into income under doctrines that might override the general statutory nonrecognition, including the tax benefit rule and the assignment of income doctrine. The transferee corporation is truly treated as the successor of the transferor.

Transactions under section 351 are not covered by section 381. As a result, the authorities dealing with the extent to which other doctrines might override section 351, and the extent to which a transferee "steps into the shoes" of the transferor for various tax purposes are somewhat inconsistent. When there is a single transferor, and the assets amount to a trade or business, it is possible — although not inevitable — that the transferee corporation will simply continue the accounting methods, including special reserve methods, of the transferor. See, e.g., Rev. Rul. 95-74, 1995-2 C.B. 36; Philadelphia & Reading Corp. v. United States, 221 Ct. Cl. 148 (1979). Furthermore, the government was unsuccessful in its attempt to apply the tax benefit rule to trigger gain on the bad debt reserves of a section 351 transferor, Nash v. United States, 398 U.S. 1 (1970); and a section 351 transferee was unsuccessful in arguing that collection on the receivables of a cash-basis transferor should result in income to the transferor rather than the transferee under general assignment of income principles, Hempt Bros., Inc. v. United States, 490 F.2d 1172 (3d Cir. 1974). Even for a section 351 transaction involving many transferors, a section 351 transaction is not treated as an appropriate moment for triggering recapture under sections 1245, 1250, 1254, and similar provisions.

However, a section 351 transferee will not always be treated as the successor of its transferor(s). The reason should be obvious in situations in which the transferor continues its own business or when there are many transferors — since on such facts it would be difficult to determine which history ended up where.

Even when there is only a single transferor, the transferee may not be treated as a successor taxpayer. For instance, after a section 351 transfer, a transferee corporation need not comply with section 481 in order to use a different inventory accounting method, Ezo Products Co. v. Commissioner, 37 T.C. 385 (1961); by the same token, the transferee corporation is not entitled to continue an erroneous accounting method, TAM 9446003.

If the corporation transfers other property, including cash, to a shareholder as part of a section 351 transaction, the corporation does not directly receive basis credit for this boot consideration. Under section 362(a)(1), the corporation receives an increase in its overall basis in the items the shareholder transferred equal to the amount of gain recognized by the shareholder. Thus, although unrecognized gain in appreciated property that is transferred to a corporation in a section 351 transaction will potentially be taxed twice — both to the shareholder (if she sells her corporate stock) and to the corporation (if it sells the transferred property), the gain that is recognized as a result of the section 351 transaction itself will not be. Consistent with the Service's asset-by-asset approach to the allocation of boot and the computation of gain, the basis created as a result of the gain recognition from the use of boot appears to be added to the basis of the assets that resulted in the gain. Note that if boot does not trigger gain to the recipient shareholder, the corporation gets no basis credit for that use of boot. Thus boot that is allocated to the acquisition of a shareholder's loss property will not result in an increase in the corporation's basis. This is true even when the corporation uses appreciated property as boot and recognizes gain thereon under section 351(f).

The corporation will have a tacked holding period in the transferred properties. § 1223(2).

3.2.3.   Special Limitations on Built-In Losses

Several notorious corporate tax shelters prompted Congress to alter the rule embedded in the general rule of section 362(a) that a section 351 transfer to a corporation will replicate basis — and thus replicate gains and losses. There are in effect two special rules that limit the ability to "import" "built-in losses." Both apply only when the bases of the properties transferred by a single shareholder/transferor, in the aggregate, are greater than the fair market values of the properties transferred, again in the aggregate.

Section 362(e)(2) applies to the more typical case to require a reduction in the basis of the loss properties transferred so there is no longer an excess of basis over fair market value, in the aggregate, in respect of that particular shareholder-corporation exchange. Thus if a transferor transfers four properties, each with a fair market value of $100 and with bases respectively of $180, $120, $90, and $50, there is an aggregate built-in loss of $40. Accordingly, the bases of the two loss properties must be reduced, in the aggregate, by that amount. Put another way, the basis of each loss property must be reduced so that there is no more than $60 of aggregate loss remaining, since there is $60 of aggregate gain in the gain properties, requiring a total basis reduction of $40. The basis reduction is allocated to the loss properties in proportion to their built-in losses before the transaction. Accordingly, 8/10 of the $40 reduction must be allocated to the first loss property and 2/10 to the second, resulting in the corporation holding the four properties with a basis, respectively, of $148 (180-32), $112 (120-8), $90, and $50. Proposed regulations promulgated under this section confirm that these rules will apply individually to each transferor, and that adjustments to basis attributable to gain triggered by boot should be taken into account *before* making the adjustments required by section 362(e)(2). Prop. Reg. § 1.362-4. If the transferor/shareholder and transferee/corporation agree, they may jointly elect to let the corporation enjoy the full section 362(a) basis without reduction under section 362(e) and instead the shareholder's basis in the stock received is limited to its fair market value.

Section 362(e)(1) applies to the more limited cases of transfers of properties where there is an aggregate built-in loss when the transferor would not have been subject to tax on any gain or loss on the property immediately before the transfer (for instance, because the transferor is a foreign taxpayer not subject to U.S. taxation or is a domestic entity exempt from U.S. tax), but the transferee corporation is subject to tax. In this situation, the basis of each loss asset will be reduced to fair market value, regardless of the presence of gain assets.

3.2.4.   Securities Received by Shareholders

Section 351 does not currently provide nonrecognition for the receipt of a corporate issuer's securities in exchange for issuer's securities given up, or for the receipt of securities in exchange for other property. Prior to 1989, however, any receipt of securities in connection with a section 351 transaction was granted nonrecognition.

3.2.5.   Certain Preferred Stock

The nonrecognition treatment provided in section 351 is premised, even if loosely, on a continuing economic interest in the property transferred. This continuing interest is less comfortably treated as an interest involving the same economic risks the more limited the transferor's participation is and the more guaranteed the transferor's return is. In 1989, Congress eliminated a provision permitting the receipt of securities in a section 351 transaction without recognition. And in 1997, to more effectively limit the applicability of section 351 to situations in which the transferor's continuing interest was adequate, Congress enacted section 351(g). Under this section, "nonqualified preferred stock" is treated as stock for the purposes of satisfying the transferor/control group standard. When a transferor receives nonqualified preferred and other stock as well, the nonqualified preferred is treated as boot for the purpose of computing the transferor's recognized gain, and no loss may be recognized. If a transferor receives *only* nonqualified preferred stock and no other stock in the transferee corporation, however, the tax consequences to the transferor will be governed by section 1001 and not section 351, so any gains or losses will be recognized.

Section 351(g)(3) defines "preferred stock" as "stock which is limited and preferred as to dividends and does not participate in corporate growth to any significant extent." "Preferred stock" is nonqualifying if it has any one of the following characteristics:

- Its holder can put the stock to the issuer or a party related to the issuer;

- The issuer or a related party is required to redeem it;

- The issuer has the right to redeem it, and this right is likely to be exercised; or

- The dividends to be paid fluctuate with an index.

The statute provides for a number of exceptions to the put/redemption rights criteria. Preferred stock will not be section 351(g) stock, for instance, if it is convertible to common or if its holder has no redemption rights other than at her death or disability.

3.2.6.   Other Rights in Stock of the Issuer

In general, warrants and rights to acquire additional stock of the transferee corporation are treated as boot. Reg. § 1.351-1(a)(1). A right to receive additional stock that is contingent upon some future event (for instance, the profits generated by a particular asset or business) will not be treated as boot. See Rev. Proc. 84-42,

1984-1 C.B. 521, for the conditions under which the Service will allow such rights. In the older cases considering the question, courts have not required all of these conditions to grant nonrecognition treatment.

3.2.7.   Constructive Exchanges

In some cases, a corporation need not actually issue stock for the transaction to be treated as a section 351 exchange. For example, if a sole shareholder transfers additional property to his corporation, the issuance of additional stock would be essentially a "meaningless gesture." In that case, the corporation will be deemed to have issued stock for purposes of satisfying section 351, and the shareholder will enjoy section 351 nonrecognition on the transfer, with additional basis in the existing shares. *See, e.g.*, Lessinger v. Commissioner, 872 F.2d 519 (2d Cir. 1989); Rev. Rul 64-155, 1964-1 C.B. 138. The same logic would apply to transfers from multiple shareholders in proportion to their interests.

3.2.8.   Installment Notes of Transferee Corporation

The proposed regulations under section 453 contemplate that a shareholder may use the installment method to defer inclusion of gain when notes otherwise qualifying for installment sale treatment are received in connection with a section 351 transaction. Prop. Reg. § 1.453-1(f)(ii).

These regulations, however, suggest results that may not be intuitive. When boot is received, the ordinary basis rules of section 358 provide that a shareholder takes a fair market value basis in the boot property, and any leftover basis is allocated to the stock received. When the boot is an installment note, however, basis is allocated first to the stock, up to its fair market value, and any excess is allocated to the installment note. This ordinarily will have the effect of accelerating the recognition of gain, since in most cases the shareholder is likely to be paid on the installment note before she sells the stock.

Under the proposed regulations, the corporation does not earn basis in the assets received until the shareholder actually takes the installment gain into income. Prop. Reg. § 1.453-1(f)(ii) (last two sentences). This is a deviation from the ordinary rules with respect to installment sales outside of section 351 transactions in which the taxpayer has basis to the extent of its promise to pay. The rule is apparently justified by the general rule of section 362 limiting corporate basis to shareholder gain recognized.

3.3.   NONTAXABLE CONTRIBUTIONS UNDER SECTION 118

Section 118 provides that a corporation does not have income when it receives property from shareholders as a capital contribution, whether or not it gives stock in return. This may happen when there is a single shareholder (where the issuance of new stock might be a meaningless gesture), but it may also happen when the contribution changes economic rights. For instance, a shareholder may contribute to capital, without getting stock in return, when a corporation is experiencing difficulties and the shareholder believes that the additional investment will ultimately be more beneficial than allowing the corporate difficulties to fester. In effect, this amounts to a transfer of value to the other shareholders, but those shareholders have no realization event until they sell their stock. The corporation has no income, and the shareholder making the contribution to capital has no taxable event but will have an increased basis in the existing shares. Reg. § 1.118-1 (noting that payments are treated as an additional price paid for shares).

What if the form of the contribution is a transfer of stock of the corporation back to the corporation? That is also treated as a contribution and not a disposition subject to the recognition rules of section 1001. Commissioner v. Fink, 483 U.S. 89 (1987) (stating that the non-taxation of a contributing shareholder is "settled" law, and disallowing the shareholder's claim for a loss in respect of the shares).

3.4. TAX CONSEQUENCES OF A FAILED SECTION 351 TRANSACTION

What happens if a group of transferors plans a section 351 transaction but the transaction fails because one of the requirements is not satisfied, such as a pre-arranged transaction that results in a lack of control immediately after the transfer? In that case, the transfers will be treated under the otherwise applicable rules that would apply to the exchange (including, for instance, section 267) given their economic substance. In most cases, that means that the transferors will have simply engaged in a taxable exchange and both gains and losses will be recognized, and they will take a fair market value basis in their stock with a newly begun holding period.

PRACTICE PROBLEMS

1.   A transfers $100 to a newly created corporation in exchange for all of its stock. What is the result to A and to the corporation?

(a)   A holds stock with basis of $100; corporation has income of $100.

(b)   A holds stock with basis of $100; corporation has no income.

(c)   A holds stock with basis of $0; corporation has no income.

(d)   A can deduct $100, holds stock with no basis; corporation has no income.

2.   A transfers property with a fair market value of $500, which she purchased 5 years ago for $100, to a newly created corporation in exchange for all of its stock. What results?

(a)   Gain of $400 to A, stock held with basis of $400; income of $400 to corporation, corporate basis of 5$00 in property.

(b)   Gain of $400 to A, stock held with a basis of $500; no income to corporation, basis of $400 in asset.

(c)   No gain to A; basis of $100 in stock; no income to corporation, basis of $100 in property.

(d)   No gain to A, basis of $100 in stock; no income to corporation, basis of $500 in property.

3.   A transfers property with a fair market value of $500, which she purchased 5 years ago for $100, to a newly created corporation in exchange for all of its stock and $125. What results?

(a)   Gain of $125 to A, basis of $100 in stock; no income to corporation, basis of $225 in property.

(b)   Gain of 125 to A, basis of $225 in stock; no income to corporation, basis of $225 in property.

(c)   Gain of $25 to A, basis of $100 in stock; no income to corporation, basis of $125 in property.

(d)   Gain of $25 to A, basis of $100 in stock; no income to corporation, basis of $225 in property.

4.   A transfers property with a fair market value of $500, which she purchased 5 years ago for $100, to a newly created corporation in exchange for all of its stock and $425. What results?

(a)   A recognized $400 of gain and holds stock with basis of $100; corporation holds property with a basis of $500.

(b)   A recognized $425 of gain and holds stock with basis of $100; corporation holds property with a basis of $525.

(c)   A recognized $425 of gain and holds stock with basis of $100; corporation holds property with a basis of $500.

(d)   A recognizes $400 of gain and holds stock with basis of $75; corporation holds property with basis of $500.

5.   A transfers property with a fair market value of $500, which she purchased 5 years ago for $700, to a newly created corporation in exchange for all of its stock. What results?

(a)   A recognizes a loss of $200, holds stock with basis of $500; corporation holds property with basis of $500.

(b)   A recognizes no loss, holds stock with basis of $700; corporation holds property with basis of $700.

(c)   A recognizes no loss, holds stock with basis of $700; corporation holds property with basis of $500.

(d)   A recognizes no loss, holds stock with basis of $500; corporation holds property with basis of $700.

6.   A transfers one asset with a fair market value of $500, which she purchased 5 years ago for $700, and another asset with a fair market value of $350 and a basis of zero to a newly created corporation in exchange for all of its stock. What results?

(a)   A holds stock with a basis of $700; corporation holds assets with a basis of $700 and zero.

(b)   A holds stock with a basis of $850; corporation holds assets with a basis of $500 and zero.

(c)   A holds stock with basis of $1050; corporation holds assets with basis of $500 and zero.

(d)   A holds stock with a basis of $850; corporation holds assets with basis of $700 and zero.

7.   A transfers property with a fair market value of $500, which she purchased 5 years ago for $700, to a newly created corporation in exchange for all of its stock and cash of $200. What results?

(a)   A recognizes loss of $100 (boot is ½ of value, triggering ½ of loss), holds stock worth $300 with $600 basis; corporation holds property with $600 basis.

(b)   A recognizes no loss, holds stock worth $300 with basis of $500; corporation holds property with basis of $900.

(c)   A recognizes no loss, holds stock worth $300 with basis of $500; corporation holds property with basis of $500.

(d)   A recognizes loss of $200, holds stock worth $300 with $500 basis; corporation holds property with $500 basis.

DISCUSSION PROBLEMS

1.   Al wants your assistance in his plans to incorporate his small manufacturing operation. It has netted roughly $100,000 a year lately, not taking into account compensation to Al. He plans to contribute the following assets in exchange for stock in the newly formed corporation:

	FMV	basis
Land	500,000	300,000
Building	400,000	0
Machinery	200,000	0
Raw materials inventory	100,000	200,000
Finished goods inventory	200,000	200,000
Patent (on Al's own invention)	100,000 (?)	0

(a)   What concerns do you have about Al's plans?

(b)   Assuming that your concerns have been satisfied, and Al goes ahead with his plans, what will be the tax consequences to Al of the transfers? What will be his basis in his stock?

What will be the tax consequences to the corporation? What is its basis in the assets transferred to it? What will be the corporation's earnings and profits?

(c)   As in part b, except that Al took back two classes of common stock with essentially the same economic rights except that one class, worth only half as much as the other class, was nonvoting? What if Al purported to engage in two transactions, in which he exchanged the land for the nonvoting stock, and all of the other assets for the voting stock?

(d)   As in part b, except that the basis of the land in Al's hands was $1,050,000? $1.4 million?

2.   (a) In addition to the facts in 1, assume that Al will be bringing in a "partner," Ed. In exchange for his future services, Ed will receive 25% of the stock of the corporation. What will the consequences of the combined transactions be?

(i)   What if Ed contributes $5,000 of cash, in addition to his future services? (Hint: what is the presumed value of Ed's services if he is still to receive 25% of the stock?)

(ii)   What if Ed contributes $100,000 (instead of the $5,000 in part (i)) in addition to his future services in exchange for 25% of the stock?

(b)   What are the consequences to Al and the corporation in respect of Al's transfer if the facts are as in Problem 2(a)(ii), except that — in order to properly adjust the values contributed and the shares to be owned — the cash Ed is contributing will be distributed to Al in addition to the stock he is to receive? (Assume the percentage of stock each is receiving is the same.)

(i)   How does this result change for Al and the corporation if Al's basis in the land is $1.05 million? $1.4 million?

(c)   As in Problem 2a, except that, instead of Ed joining the group, the building is contributed by Art, who is Al's brother. Art takes back both preferred stock worth $300,000 and common stock worth $100,000. This preferred stock has the right to vote equivalent to 25% of the overall vote in the corporation and will pay a fixed dividend indefinitely, and Art can either wait until the corporation is liquidated and receive $500,000 or require the corporation to redeem it after 10 years for $400,000.

(i)   As above, except that Art received only $400,000 worth of the same preferred stock, with the same voting rights? What if Art had a basis of $600,000 in the building?

(d)   As in Problem 2a, except that Al takes back an interest-bearing note from the corporation, payable in two installments over the next two years.

3.   As in Problem 2, but adding that two years later, the bank insists that another patent worth about $100,000 and owned individually by Ed be contributed to the corporation. Ed, not wanting to share all of the value of this patent with Al, takes back all of a new class of preferred stock, the dividends on which are to be determined with reference to the sales related to the patent. What are the consequences of this change?

(i)   What if Ed makes the transfer at the same time as Al, but has only a license to use someone else's patent, which is nevertheless worth $100,000?

4.   What if, instead of immediately bringing Ed in as a "partner" with an immediate equity interest, Al had, upon the formation of the corporation with his contributions and receiving all of the stock, entered into an agreement with Ed to sell Ed 50% of the stock if Ed was still working for the corporation in 3 years?

5.   After having successfully run his business for 15 years after incorporating Alco, Al wants to retire. The nature of the business is such that most of the value of Alco not reflected in its hard assets will dissipate quickly after he leaves, but several of those assets are highly appreciated, and Al's basis in Alco stock is far less than the value of these assets. Al has found an entity, Swapco, which may be interested in acquiring Al's corporation. Swapco was formed several years ago to act as an investment vehicle for a number of other retiring entrepreneurs like Al. Swapco now holds a variety of the assets from the businesses run by those entrepreneurs but is rapidly moving toward owning only blue chip stock and bonds. It has proposed that it acquire the stock of Al's corporation in exchange for its stock. It will then systematically dispose of the assets of Al's corporation and use the resulting funds to build its stock portfolio. What more does Al need to know about Swapco before he can determine what the tax consequences of his transfer of Alco stock to Swapco will be?

Chapter 4

THE EFFECT OF LIABILITY ASSUMPTIONS IN SECTION 351 TRANSACTIONS

Statutes and Regulations	IRC §§ 357(c); 358(h)
	Reg. § 1.357-1, -2
Other Primary Authorities	Peracchi v. Commissioner, 143 F.3d 487 (9th Cir. 1998)
	Lessinger v. Commissioner, 872 F.2d 519 (2d Cir. 1989)
	Alderman v. Commissioner, 55 T.C. 662 (1971)
	Rev. Rul. 95-74, 1995-2 C.B. 36
	Coltec Indus. v. United States, 454 F.3d 1340 (Fed. Cir. 2006)
	Black & Decker Corp. v. United States, 436 F.3d 431 (4th Cir. 2006)

4.1. TAX CONSEQUENCES TO THE SHAREHOLDER OF CORPORATE ASSUMPTION OF SHAREHOLDER DEBT

Under ordinary circumstances, when an individual incurs debt, she receives loan proceeds without taking an amount into income, but nevertheless is allowed basis when those loan proceeds are used. (These steps are conflated when the seller is also the creditor — that is, when the buyer agrees to pay over time in a seller-financed deal.) This treatment reflects the view that the receipt of the loan proceeds did not add to the wealth of the taxpayer, because the benefit of the loan proceeds is (by definition when the parties are dealing at arm's length) offset by the burden of the loan repayment (even though that repayment may be considerably deferred). When the debt is repaid, the debtor gets no deduction for the payment of loan principal because she is in effect paying back an amount that our tax accounting rules never treated as hers.

Therefore, when a transferee assumes a liability in connection with a transfer of property in a way that means the transferor/debtor will no longer repay the liability, adjustments must be made to reflect the fact that the original presumption about repayment turned out to be wrong. In general, the transferor will include the liability shed in her amount realized, and the transferee includes the amount of the assumed liability in its basis. This treatment reflects the fact that the transferor at some earlier point in time received some benefit as a result of the liability (either from having received loan proceeds without including the amount in income, or from having basis made available to her despite the fact that no payment had been made). It also gives the transferee credit in advance for the amount that must be paid on the liability, just as ordinarily happens in the case of any taxpayer taking on a debt.

4.1.1. The Foundational Rules in Subsections 357(a), (b), and (c)

In a section 351 transfer in which a shareholder's/transferor's liabilities are assumed by the corporation, the transferor is similarly relieved of the obligation to repay the debt. A similar adjustment to undo the tax treatment of the original receipt of the loan proceeds is necessary. Section 357 provides two approaches to the treatment of transferors whose liabilities are assumed. One, set out in section 357(b), is aimed at those who overtly try to separate the use of loan proceeds from their repayment. It produces somewhat harsh results. A transferor who is shown to have "a purpose to avoid federal income taxation" or to have a purpose that "was not a bona fide business purpose" will be treated as having received boot to the extent of "the total amount of the liability assumed." This provision anticipates, for instance, the circumstance in which an individual owns appreciated property, pledges that property in connection with the receipt of loan proceeds when he knows that the property will be transferred to a corporation, and then shortly thereafter contributes the property to a corporation controlled by him with the corporation assuming the loan or taking the property subject to the loan. In this situation, the transferor has managed to separate the enjoyment of the loan proceeds (which he as an individual retains) from the repayment of the liability (which his corporation, perhaps facing a lower tax bracket, will repay with its own after-tax dollars). Section 357(b), sometimes called the "tainted debt" rule, will require the transferor to treat the amount of *all* of the liabilities associated with the transfer as if cash had been received, not just any particular liability that may have been assumed with a tax-avoidance purpose. *See* Reg. § 1.357-1(c) (second sentence). All of the assumed debt, in these circumstances, is thus treated just like any other boot property received by the transferor/shareholder.

The other approach to liability assumptions, set out in section 357(a), applies when no tax avoidance purpose is present. This more gentle provision applies generally when there are longstanding liabilities associated with the property transferred. Under this provision, the income that might otherwise be generated as a result of debt relief as value received by the transferor is not recognized, but instead is deferred through the mechanism of a reduction in the transferor's basis in the stock received in the exchange. *See* §§ 357(a) (providing that a liability assumption is not to be treated as money received for the purposes of calculating gain on the transfer); 358(d) (treating the assumption as money received, but only for the purpose of computing the transferor's basis under § 358(a)(1)(A)). Thus, if property held with a basis of $500 is transferred subject to a liability of $400 and only stock is received in exchange, the transferor recognizes no gain and holds the stock with a basis of $100 (i.e., $500 exchanged basis - $400 liability shed + zero gain recognized). This "debt goes to basis first" rule furthers the underlying reason for nonrecognition under section 351, that is, nonrecognition on incorporation and other significant transfers from shareholders. It is highly likely that many assets that a transferor might consider transferring to a corporation will be subject to liabilities. If the debt rule followed in fully taxable transactions and in section 357(b) applied to most ordinary incorporations, the resulting tax liability might well discourage potential transferors from incorporating.

Even in this context, however, there is a potential for gain recognition on account of liabilities shed. If the aggregate amount of the liabilities assumed exceeds the aggregate amount of basis in the properties transferred so that there is insufficient basis to account for the liabilities shed, the transferor recognizes that excess liability gain under section 357(c)(1) (sometimes called the "excess liability" rule). Thus, under section 357(c) and subsections 358(a) and (d)(1), if property held with a basis of $500 is transferred subject to a liability of $650 in exchange for stock, $150 of gain will be recognized attributable to the excess liability, and the stock will be held with a basis of zero (i.e., $500 exchanged basis - $650 liability shed + $150 gain recognized). Consistent with the wording of section 357(c), this determination is made in the aggregate for each transferor in respect of all of the assets and liabilities transferred by that transferor. Accordingly, if a transferor transfers two properties with aggregate bases of $1000 and a liability of $1100 is assumed in respect of one of the properties, the excess liability rule in section 357(c) results in $100 of gain recognition and zero basis in the stock. Reg. § 1.357-2(a) (last sentence) makes clear that if the "tainted debt" rule in section 357(b) has resulted in all liabilities assumed being treated as boot, the excess liability rule in section 357(c) will not apply.

Reg. § 1.357-2 directs that the character and holding period of this excess liability gain will be determined by reference to the relative fair market values of the assets transferred. This regulation seems to direct that the fair market value of loss assets as well as gain assets be considered, and leaves unanswered many questions about this gain calculation (such as whether it is appropriate to use gross or net fair market values in allocating the gain, and in the latter case, whether there is a distinction made between liabilities that are secured by particular assets and those that are unsecured or effectively secured by all of the assets). As discussed further below, neither these regulations nor the regulations under section 362 address the approach to be used in determining the effect of the resulting shareholder gain on the corporation's basis in each of the assets transferred.

When section 357(c) has applied, the shareholder will by definition hold the stock received with a zero basis; under section 358(d), this result is reached under the same language that applies to liabilities not in excess of transferor's basis, that is, that the stock will have a basis equal to the basis of the property transferred, less money (here including liability relief as money) received plus gain recognized.

4.1.2. Liabilities That Will "Give Rise to a Deduction"

The language of section 357(c)(1) simply refers to "liabilities." This language seems not to distinguish liabilities such as the accounts payable of cash basis taxpayers from the typical bank loan (which represents loan proceeds received without tax). The accounts payable of cash basis taxpayers are different from bank loans because by definition they have not yet been deducted and thus have not produced a tax benefit. In a series of notorious cases, the government nevertheless asserted that the accounts payable of cash basis taxpayers should be treated as "liabilities" for the purposes of section 357(c). (Note that this approach in effect treated these accounts payable as accrued for tax purposes; most cash basis taxpayers caught by this approach would have had no problem under section 357(c) if they had similarly been allowed, for the purpose of this computation, to accrue their accounts receivable, and thus have basis in them adequate to soak up the accrued liability.)

After a number of such cases in which the government asserted that the payables of cash basis taxpayers should be treated as "liabilities," Congress added section 357(c)(3), which provides that those liabilities "the payment of which would give rise to a deduction" would not be counted as liabilities for the purpose of determining the amount of liabilities assumed under section 357. This language was perfectly adequate for solving the problem to which it was addressed, but created problems of its own. First, the statute seems to have accepted the proposition that obligations to make payments that will give rise to deductions when paid must be considered "liabilities," a proposition that was not self-evident. (There are hints elsewhere in the Code that the term "obligation" was appropriate for this larger class of anticipated payments and that "liability" should have been limited to those obligations that had accrued for tax purposes and thus had given rise to a tax benefit. Confusion about these terms still plagues subchapter C and subchapter K. *Cf.* Reg. § 1.752-1(a)(4) (dealing with "liabilities," defined as having already given rise to deduction or basis) and Reg. § 1.752-7 (dealing with "obligations," defined as those commitments that have not already given rise to basis or deduction).

Second, the section 357(c) drafters seem to have had a very limited notion of the range of problems that might arise under section 357(c) when unaccrued liabilities are involved. For instance, some liabilities not yet deducted by the transferor would be capitalized, rather than deducted, when paid by the transferor. Should transferors relieved of such liabilities avoid the application of section 357(a), when section 357(c)(3) refers only to liabilities that "will give rise to a deduction"? Furthermore, are there circumstances in which payment would give rise to a deduction to a transferor, but not to a transferee, who should be treated as having given consideration for assets when the liability was assumed, and may therefore not be entitled to any additional basis or deduction on payment? Several types of liabilities faced by accrual taxpayers can have these characteristics, such as: those liabilities (like those arising from tort judgments) that may not be taken into account, even by accrual basis taxpayers, until payment or other economic performance under section 461(h); liabilities for nonqualifying deferred compensation that are similarly suspended under section 404; and contingent liabilities. In Rev. Rul. 95-74, 1995-2 C.B. 36, the Service confirmed that it would interpret section 357(c)(3) broadly to include not just those liabilities the payment on which literally would give rise to a deduction, but also those liabilities on which payment would give rise to basis, both judged from the transferor's point of view.

Section 358(d)(2) ensures that no reduction to the shareholder's stock basis need ordinarily be taken as a result of this type of liability, but in certain cases the special rule in section 358(h), discussed further below, may apply to reduce a shareholder's basis when the presence of these liabilities results in an overall built-in loss in the shareholder's stock under the regular application of section 358.

4.1.3.   The Determination of Excess Liabilities under Section 357(c)

Section 357(c) unambiguously states that excess liabilities are to be determined by comparing "the sum of the amount of the liabilities" with "the total of the adjusted basis of the property transferred." This comparison is made by looking at each transferring shareholder's transfers in the aggregate, but separately from those of other transferors. Rev. Rul. 66-142, 1966-1 C.B. 66. Thus, unlike the determination of gain to be recognized on a section 351 transfer by a shareholder in return for cash in addition to stock that requires an asset-by-asset calculation so that basis of loss assets is not inappropriately used to offset gain, the aggregate basis of all of the assets transferred by that transferor, both encumbered and unencumbered, must be taken into account in determining whether there are excess liabilities.

Because of this aggregated approach, transferors can in many cases avoid a section 357(c) problem simply by contributing to the corporation additional property in which they have sufficient basis. (Note that the deal might have to be adjusted to make sure that such additional property contributions are satisfactory to other incorporating transferors, since additional property would ordinarily entitle a transferor to a larger interest in the corporation). Such additional property may include cash, since cash, which is deemed to have a basis equal to its face value, represents an after-tax asset being used by the transferor. Even if the transferor shareholder borrows to obtain the cash to contribute, there is no problem, since he will have to use his own after-tax dollars to repay the loan.

In some situations, however, taxpayers may not have the liquidity necessary to borrow and contribute the proceeds or may simply prefer not to do so. Some such taxpayers, like the taxpayer in *Peracchi v. Commissioner*, 143 F.3d 487 (9th Cir. 1998), have attempted to avoid gain recognition under section 357(c) by contributing their own promissory note to the corporation. Should this work? Is a promise by the transferor/shareholder to provide cash in the future to the corporation different from a promise by the transferor/shareholder to pay a third party for the purposes of determining whether there should be gain under section 357(c)? Given the conventional approach to basis in one's own note and the literal language in section 357(c) for determining when excess liabilities will trigger gain, it appears that the answer under the statute is that the situations should indeed be treated differently. Unhappy with this conclusion, however, the court in *Peracchi* reasoned backward from the premise that the corporation should not have income when the transferor/shareholder pays on the note to conclude that the corporation itself must be treated as having basis in the note and that therefore the transferor must be treated as having basis in the note upon the transfer.

Aside from the court's questionable approach to the interpretation of the statute, and the resulting undermining of the statutory scheme, the desirability of the result in *Peracchi* depends in part upon how likely it actually is, under the facts in any particular case, that the shareholder will pay on the note. When there is only one shareholder, who controls the corporation, how likely is it that that such a note will ever be paid? Would the fact that the corporation has other creditors who may insist on the presence of a certain amount of equity in the corporation — and therefore may insist that the note be paid — make a difference? The court in *Peracchi* made much of the fact that the corporation's creditors would be able to pursue the corporation's right to payment in bankruptcy. But is that enough, when that bankruptcy might not occur, if ever, until years after the shareholder deferred gain recognition by separating the use of the loan proceeds from the obligation to repay them? How much difference should it make that the shareholder actually pays or accrues a market rate of interest on the note — and does that in turn depend upon how much reliance can be placed on the provisions of tax law that govern the taxation of the note more generally?

On the other hand, what if the transferor of the note is one of several unrelated transferors, and these other transferors have every interest in forcing the transferor to pay? In that case, the statutory provision (and hence the government's position in *Peracchi*) could be viewed as having a harsh result. Notwithstanding the harsh result, is it appropriate for a court to provide relief to taxpayers, as the *Peracchi* court did, by reasoning backwards from the result it deemed advisable for the corporation to arrive at the conclusion that the taxpayer should be treated as having a basis in his own promissory note that permits avoidance of the section 357(c) gain?

Distinguishing the cases in which the note is likely to be paid from the situations in which it is not would be a highly fact-specific exercise. Such an investigation does not seem to have been anticipated by the statute as written, and statutory language that would provide a determinative formula for deciding such questions would be very difficult to draft. On balance, therefore, the irrebuttable presumption embedded in section 357(c) as interpreted by the government, that no payment will be made on the note, is likely the sounder position when the shareholder has insufficient liquidity to correct a problem under section 357(c) at the time of the property transfer.

Inconsistent Analyses in Three Cases Dealing
with Transferor's Promissory Note

In Alderman v. Commissioner, *55 T.C. 662 (1971), the Tax Court reasoned that a promissory note has no basis in the hands of its maker. Accordingly, the transferor of such a promissory note recognizes section 357(c) gain. The corporation's aggregate basis is determined under section 362(a), which includes the section 357(c) gain recognized to the transferor.*

In Peracchi v. Commissioner, *143 F.3d 487 (9th Cir. 1998), the Ninth Circuit affirmed the district court's determination that the taxpayer would be treated as having basis in its own promissory note transferred to a corporation in a section 351 transaction, and no section 357(c) gain, by analogy with a similar transaction in which a taxpayer borrows from a bank, transfers the proceeds to a corporation which uses them to purchase the taxpayer's note from the bank. Even though the note was written at no current cost to the taxpayer, the judges considered that the note represented a "new and substantial increase in Peracchi's investment in the corporation." The judges also based their decision on their concern that a corporation would have zero basis in the promissory note and thus would recognize a "phantom" gain if it sold the note. The Ninth Circuit gave "little weight" to the Service's position, as expressed in Rev. Rul. 68-629, 1968-2 C.B. 154, 155 (ruling that a transferor has no basis in a promissory note). The opinion failed to address the increase in the corporation's basis because of the section 357(c) gain or the possibility of allocating that increase to the note.*

In Lessinger v. Commissioner, *872 F.2d 519 (2d Cir. 1989), the Second Circuit held that a taxpayer who contributes a promissory note should not have section 357(c) gain because no gain would be recognized if a third party held the note, the cash was contributed to the corporation, and the corporation purchased the note with the cash. Even though it agreed with the Service that a taxpayer has no basis in his own promissory note, the court considered the following points persuasive: (i) the note would be a corporate asset that should have a basis equal to its face amount (or at least not have income when payment is made on the note); (ii) if the corporation declared bankruptcy, the transferor would have to make payment on the note; (iii) the transaction is economically equivalent to the transferor's borrowing from a bank, contributing the proceeds, and having its note purchased by the corporation with those proceeds. Accordingly, the court considered that it would be appropriate to read the reference to "adjusted basis" in section 357(c) in this context to refer to the corporate transferee's basis in the note rather than the shareholder/transferor's basis in the transferred property, resulting in no gain under section 357(c) to the shareholder/transferor.*

A fourth case of relevance in this context is Seggerman Farms Inc. v. Commissioner, *308 F.3d 803 (7th Cir. 2002), in which taxpayers who incorporated their farming business with excess liabilities claimed that remaining secondarily liable as guarantors on all the transferred debt should relieve them of gain recognition under section 357(c). Without embracing or disavowing the* Peracchi *and* Lessinger *decisions, the Seventh Circuit held that section 357(c)'s plain language mandating gain recognition clearly controlled, in spite of the harsh tax consequences for the taxpayers.*

4.1.4. The Nature of Assumptions for the Purpose of Section 357

When most of the provisions dealing with liabilities in subchapter C were written, there was built into them a general presumption that creditors with remedies against property would pursue those remedies first, even if they had remedies against other parties, including the original debtor who had subsequently transferred the property. Thus under the original statutory language, "assumes a liability or acquires property subject to a liability," liabilities would be treated as if the transferor were relieved of the liability, even when the transferring debtor remained liable on the debt. This standard within subchapter C resulted in more situations in which debt relief to the transferor is deemed to occur than under the standards of Reg. § 1.1001-2 governing debt relief in taxable property transactions.

This language relating to "property subject to a liability" proved to be too easily manipulated. In one common tax shelter scheme, a tax-indifferent transferor (frequently a foreign corporation) would pledge more than one property to secure debt, then transfer a low-basis property subject to the debt to a corporation in a section 351 transaction. The transferor would theoretically recognize gain as a result of the excess liability, but this gain would not be subject to tax in the United States, while the basis increase under section 362 would be available to offset corporate income taxable in the United States. Enacted in 1999 in response to such schemes, section 357(d) now cuts back on the circumstances in which liabilities will be treated as assumed. A *recourse* debt will be treated as assumed only if "the transferee has agreed to, and is expected to, satisfy such liability (or portion) whether or not the transferor has been relieved of such liability." Under subsections 357(d)(1)(B) and (d)(2), a *nonrecourse* liability will be presumed to be assumed, except that the amount assumed will be reduced to the extent that there are other assets that are encumbered by the same liability. (Note that Reg. § 1.357-2 (third sentence) has not been amended to reflect this change.) Thus if a transferor holds two assets, each with a fair market value of $50, and both subject to the same nonrecourse liability of $60, and the transferor transfers one of these assets in a section 351 transaction, there will be only $10 of liability assumption for the purposes of applying section 357.

4.2. TAX CONSEQUENCES TO THE CORPORATION OF THE ASSUMPTION OF SHAREHOLDER LIABILITIES

4.2.1. Corporate Transferee's Basis in Assets

Under section 362(a), a corporation takes the property transferred by the shareholder with a transferred basis, increased only by gain recognized by the shareholder. The corporation gets no additional basis credit or deduction for payment of those liabilities that reduce shareholder basis under sections 357(a) and 358(d).

If, however, a transferor/shareholder recognizes gain on the transfer under the excess liability or tainted debt rules (subsections (c) and (b) of section 357, respectively), that gain will be taken into account in determining the corporate transferee's basis under section 362(a). The corporation's step-up in basis for this liability gain is, however, limited under section 362(d), which was enacted in 1999 in reaction to the tax shelter transactions discussed in 4.1.4 above. Section 362(d)(1) provides that the basis of property cannot be increased above its fair market value as a result of gain attributable to the assumption of a liability (which would include both section 357(c) gain and gain from treating liabilities as boot under the tainted debt rule). There is considerable tension between this rule and the provisions of Reg. § 1.357-2 for determining the character of shareholder gain; the combination of these two rules virtually guarantees that the basis increase cannot be assigned to the asset that determined the character of the gain. Suppose a shareholder contributes two assets, both worth $50, one ordinary and held with a basis of $10 and the other capital and held with a basis of $60, and the corporation assumes a liability of $80. There is clearly $10 of gain under section 357(c), and under Reg. § 1.357-2, $5 of this gain will be characterized as ordinary and $5 as capital. Although our instincts might suggest that gain should increase the basis of each of these assets by five, this result is forbidden under section 362(d)(1), because it would increase a loss. It is unclear whether all ten of the basis increase can be assigned to the gain asset. Section 362(d)(2) limits the amount of basis step-up available when multiple assets secure a nonrecourse liability.

4.2.2. Payments by the Corporation on Section 357(c)(3) Assumed Liabilities

Because transactions covered by section 351 can involve so many different fact patterns, there has never been a single understanding of the extent to which such transactions should be treated as a continuation of prior business operations for tax purposes. In many cases, the Service has taken the position that, at least as far as the tax consequences to the corporation are concerned, only those consequences specifically mentioned in the statute (primarily, shareholder basis) should be treated as continuing. This position was buttressed by the fact that section 381, which directs the extent to which transactions afforded nonrecognition under other parts of subchapter C will be treated as continuations of businesses for many tax purposes, does not mention section 351. Therefore, after a section 351 transaction, accounting methods may not continue, investment credits may be subject to recapture, and various suspended accounts may not survive.

Two rulings in the early 1980s established a different approach to some transactions described in section 351. In Rev. Rul. 80-198, 1980-2 C.B. 113, the Service held that when an individual transferred all of the assets and liabilities of a sole proprietorship to a new corporation in exchange for all of its stock, the transferee corporation could report in its income the accounts receivable as collected and would be allowed deductions under section 162 for the payments it makes to satisfy the accounts payable. In Rev. Rul. 83-155, 1983-2 C.B. 38, the Service similarly held that guaranteed payments to a retired partner made pursuant to a partnership agreement by a corporation to which the partnership had transferred all of its assets and liabilities in a section 351 exchange were deductible by the corporation as ordinary and necessary business expenses under section 162(a). Both of these rulings were premised on the idea that in certain circumstances, the transferee corporation could "step into the shoes" of its transferor(s) for more than simply basis in assets and could, for instance, "inherit" accounting methods and other aspects of the tax history associated with the business prior to the section 351 transaction, including deferred amortization accounts and installment reporting of gain. Both rulings, however, were premised on the fact that the assets transferred constituted an ongoing business before the transfer.

According to Rev. Rul. 95-74, liabilities that are excluded from the section 357(c) determination under section 357(c)(3) are similarly taken into account as deductible expenses or capitalized expenditures (i.e., additions to basis) under the rules that would have applied to the transferor had no transfer occurred, at least when the section 351 transfer involved the transfer of assets constituting a business.

a.   Contingent Liability Shelters

The rule adopted in Rev. Rul. 95-74 tempted many taxpayers, faced with liabilities that would not be deductible until paid under section 461(h) or section 401 (or which were not deductible when they were taken into account for financial purposes because they were contingent), to "accelerate" a deduction for such liabilities in a transaction of the sort described in Notice 2001-17, 2001-1 C.B. 730. The strategy involved the transfer to a corporation of liquid high-basis assets with a value just in excess of the burden of a liability that had not yet been deducted. Because the value of the assets was almost fully offset by the burden of the liabilities (which nonetheless would not be taken into account as a reduction to basis under sections 357 and 358 because it was a liability that would give rise to a deduction upon payment deductible to the transferor), the value of the resulting corporation would be far less than the basis of its stock in the transferor's hands. A sale of the stock shortly thereafter would generate a loss, while the payment of the liability by the subsidiary would generate a deduction on payment. (In the most aggressive of these schemes, the loss and the deduction would show up on the same consolidated return and the deal would involve a number of accommodation parties.)

In reaction to this scheme, Congress enacted section 358(h) in 2000, which in certain circumstances limits the basis of the transferor shareholder to the net fair market value of the assets (including stock) received. This step-down of basis does not apply, however, if the section 351 transaction involved the transfer of the trade or business with which the liability is associated. (Treasury has exercised the authority granted in the statute to make unavailable an additional exception for a transfer of all of the assets with which the liability is associated. Reg. § 1.358-5(a).) Note that section 358(h), like section 362(e), results in the denial of replicated losses despite the overall effect of replicated gains and losses in section 351 transactions generally.

> **Contingent Liability Shelter Cases**
>
> *Two cases tested similar fact patterns under the economic substance doctrine and the statutory scheme before the enactment of section 358(h):* Black & Decker Corp. v. United States, *436 F.3d 431 (4th Cir. 2006) and* Coltec Indus. v. United States, *454 F.3d 1340 (Fed. Cir. 2006). The authors' view is that the courts failed to comprehend the way the provisions in subchapter C work together to ensure the correct gain recognition and basis for transferor and corporation. In these cases involving convoluted transactions in which the same taxpayer not only tried to claim a loss on subsidiary stock basis but also retained substantial interests in the stock of the subsidiary claiming the deduction on payment of the losses, the courts struggled to reach results that should have been fairly easy to reach had the courts had a better understanding of the operation of subchapter C generally. The decisions thus put considerable weight on the judicial doctrine of economic substance, and led to a renewed concern about the scope of the doctrine and renewed discussion in Congress of codification. The doctrine was codified in 2010 as section 7701(o), along with the introduction of a new penalty in section 6662(b). Codification of the doctrine could result in a narrower scope limit, a needed tool in the arsenal of weapons to fight tax shelters.*

OPTIONAL PRACTICE PROBLEMS

This exercise is designed to help recall the general principles regarding the assumption of liabilities in connection with property transactions. It is necessary to understand these general principles in order to understand the ways in which section 357 alters their application in section 351 transactions.

Unless otherwise stated in the problem, assume that interest at a fair market rate must be paid on all liabilities. Also assume, unless otherwise stated, that the fair market value of all property transferred is greater than any liability to which it is subject.

1. Al purchases a piece of land by paying $50,000 in cash and promising the seller he will pay an additional $60,000 at the end of 6 years. Al's basis in the land is:

    (a) $50,000, with no increase for amounts paid by Al to the seller, if any, during the next 2 years.

    (b) $50,000, with an increase to $110,000 only when Al pays off the debt completely.

    (c) $110,000.

    (d) $110,000, but this basis will be reduced if the property declines in value in the time before Al pays.

2. Al purchases a piece of land by paying $50,000 in cash and promising the seller he will pay an additional $60,000 at the end of 6 years. The seller took a mortgage on the property, but is likely to allow Al to transfer the property to a third party so long as the third party is willing to expressly assume the debt. In the third year when the property has a value of $150,000 without regard to the liability, Al finds such a buyer, Bev. How much cash can Al expect to receive from Bev if he sells

the property and it remains subject to the debt owed to the original purchaser?

    (a) $90,000 ($150,000-$60,000).

    (b) $150,000 (because $150,000 is the fair market value).

    (c) $40,000 ($150,000-$110,000).

    (d) $100,000 ($150,000-$50,000).

    3.   What is Al's gain and what is Bev's basis, in Question 2?

    (a) $40,000 gain to Al and $90,000 basis to Bev.

    (b) $100,000 gain to Al and $150,000 basis to Bev.

    (c) $40,000 gain to Al and $150,000 basis to Bev.

    (d) $90,000 gain to Al and $150,000 basis to Bev.

    4.   If the property were worth only $85,000 at the time Al transferred it to Bev, and all other facts are the same, what is the effect on Al? (Hints: How much cash will Bev pay? How much will Al's amount realized be?)

    (a)   Loss of $25,000.

    (b)   Loss of $50,000.

    (c)   Income or gain of $35,000.

    (d)   Income or gain of $25,000.

PRACTICE PROBLEMS

    1.   In a transaction that otherwise qualifies as a section 351 transaction, A transfers property with a fair market value of $100, a basis of $30, subject to a debt of $20, and takes back only stock with a fair market value of $80. The debt was an ordinary purchase money debt, incurred 10 years ago when A acquired the property. The corporation assumes the debt, and is expected to pay on it, as anticipated by section 357(d). How much gain will A recognize?

    (a) $80.

    (b)   None.

    (c) $20.

    (d) $10.

    2.   In Question 1, above, what will be A's basis in the stock she receives?

    (a) $30.

    (b) $20.

    (c)   zero.

    (d) $10.

    3.   In Question 1 above, what will be the corporation's basis in the transferred asset?

(a) $10.

(b) $50.

(c) $20.

(d) $30.

4.   In Question 1, what will be the tax consequence to A and to the corporation when the corporation makes a payment of $5 principal on the assumed debt?

(a)   No income to A; no basis increase or deduction to the corporation.

(b)   Deemed distribution of $5 to A; no basis increase or deduction to the corporation.

(c)   No income to A; basis increase of $5 for the corporation.

(d)   No income to A; deduction of $5 for the corporation.

5.   In Question 1, what if the debt to which the property was subject had been $45?

(a)   A would have gain of $15; corporation would take with basis of $30.

(b)   A would have no gain; corporation would have basis of $15.

(c)   A would have gain of $15; corporation would have basis of $45.

(d)   A would have gain of $45; corporation would have basis of $45.

6.   What if the debt in Question 5 had been an account payable, and A were a cash basis taxpayer?

(a)   Same answer as Question 5.

(b)   Same answer as Questions 1-3, but the corporation can deduct when it pays.

(c)   A has $15 of gain, corporation takes with a basis of $30, and corporation can deduct when it pays.

(d)   No gain to A, no basis reduction on A's stock, and a corporate deduction when the debt is paid.

7.   Max has a small business that produces high quality prints of PowerPoint® and other presentation papers. He is a cash method taxpayer. At the end of the year, his balance sheet shows the following:

• Computer system (AB 0, FMV 6),

• Accounts receivable (AB 0 FMV 10),

• Accounts payable (4).

Max decides to incorporate and transfers all the assets, with the corporation assuming the obligation to pay the trade creditors. Which statement most accurately describes the result for Max?

(a)   Liabilities exceed basis, so Max recognizes a section 357(c) gain of 4.

(b)   The general default rule of section 357(a) applies whenever there is an incorporation.

(c)   The debt will cause all gain of 16 to be recognized, under section 357(b).

(d)   Max will not recognize any section 357(c) gain, and his basis will not be reduced on account of the assumption of the accounts payable obligation.

DISCUSSION PROBLEMS

1.   A transfers a piece of property worth $500 subject to a liability of $200 and held with a basis of $450 in exchange for stock in a corporation in which he owns all of the stock. Suppose the property has been subject to the $200 liability for 10 years. What tax result?

2.   A starts out with a parcel of land held for investment worth $900 with an adjusted basis of $600 and ends up a 50% interest in X Corp., a newly formed corporation that obtains the property. B starts out with $500, which he transfers to X Corp and ends up with a 50% interest in X Corp. Consider the tax consequences of the incorporation, under the following fact scenarios.

(a)   What if, immediately before the transfer of the property to X Corp, A borrows $400 from a lender, using his property as security?

(b)   What if A's property had a basis of $300 and was subject to a liability of $400 incurred when A purchased the property?

(c)   What if A's property had a basis of $1250, a fair market value of $900 and was subject to a liability of $400 incurred when A purchased the property?

(d)   What if A had contributed two parcels of land, one subject to a $400 liability with a basis of $200 and fair market value of $700, and another with a basis of $100 and a fair market value of $200?

(e)   What if A and B each contributes his own note for $400 in addition to the other consideration, under the facts as described in subpart b?

(f)   A (who is a cash basis taxpayer) transfers to the corporation property worth $900 and a trade payable of $400 that A incurred in connection with his prior use of the property.

(g)   What if the $400 liability is a contractor's lien for work done on the land at A's instance, and A is a cash basis taxpayer? An accrual basis taxpayer?

(h)   What if the $400 liability in subpart g is A's best guess about the amount of a fine that is likely to be imposed for a minor breach of environmental regulations, and by statute is likely to be recovered against the owner of the property at the time it is imposed?

(i)   What if the property is not land but stock, and the liability, which is clearly assumed by the corporation, is for a tort A committed?

Chapter 5

SECTION 336 LIQUIDATIONS

Statutes and Regulations	IRC §§ 331; 334; 346; 336; 453(h); 1504(a)
	Reg. §§ 1.331-1; 1.332-2
Other Primary Authorities	Rev. Rul. 70-106, 1970-1 C.B. 70

When a corporation terminates its existence and distributes all of its assets remaining after any sale of its assets to a third party, the transaction, referred to as a "complete liquidation," generally is a recognition event for both the corporation (section 336) and the shareholders (section 331). When another corporation owns a controlling interest (as defined in section 1504(a)(2)) in the liquidating corporation and the transaction otherwise meets the requirements of sections 332 and 337, however, the distribution to the controlling corporate parent will be a nonrecognition transaction for the liquidating subsidiary corporation, and the shareholder corporation will own the assets of the liquidated subsidiary corporation with tax characteristics almost as if the latter had never had a separate existence. This chapter will address the first type of liquidation transaction, and the following chapter will address various rules that accommodate corporate shareholders, including liquidations into a controlling corporate parent.

The changes made in 1986 to the provisions governing complete liquidations are the most significant part of the "repeal of *General Utilities*." Because the operating rules stated in several of the relevant code sections were changed to produce results essentially the opposite of former law and because the incentives of the parties are very likely to be different from those of **parties** in seemingly similar transactions under prior law, older authorities — that are still good law for many purposes — can be confusing.

5.1. WHEN IS A CORPORATION IN LIQUIDATION?

There can be a surprising amount of ambiguity regarding when a corporation is in fact engaged in a complete liquidation, and exactly when the transaction should be considered to have begun and ended. Although there is nothing in the statute that requires that a formal plan of liquidation be adopted as a condition to the applicability of sections 336 and 331, there are circumstances in which the presence of such a plan will ensure that a series of distributions or redemptions, or both, will be treated as part of the same overall transaction. See section 346, confirming that a liquidation need not be completed in one single transfer but requiring a plan if all of a series of redemption transactions are to be treated as a liquidation. The regulations under section 332, although not directly applicable, provide some guidance about the nature of a complete liquidation: they indicate that "it is essential that a status of liquidation exist at the time the first distribution is made under the plan and that such status continue until the liquidation is complete." By "status of liquidation," the regulations make clear that the corporation must be winding down ("winding up its affairs, paying its debts and distributing any remaining balance to its shareholders"). And the retention of a "nominal amount of assets for the sole purpose of preserving the corporation's legal existence" will not prevent a complete liquidation. Reg. § 1.332-2(c).

Shareholders need not actually receive title in the individual assets of the corporation in order for the transaction to be treated as a complete liquidation. The corporation's assets can, for instance, be held by a liquidating trust on behalf of the shareholders while the winding down of the corporation's business is completed. If such a trust continues to operate the business, however, the Service might claim that the corporation has not in fact been liquidated and continues as an entity taxable under subchapter C. (This old IRS position may have been complicated slightly by the entity classification "check-the-box" rules, under which many legal entities with multiple owners that are not chartered under corporate law by default will avoid subchapter C and be taxed as partnerships, unless there are interests that are publicly traded.)

5.2. TAX CONSEQUENCES OF LIQUIDATIONS

5.2.1. Effect on Individual and Minority Corporate Shareholders

Under section 331, individual and noncontrolling corporate shareholders will compute gain or loss on their stock holding as if the assets they receive were received "in full payment in exchange for" their stock. Section 331(b) rather redundantly indicates that section 301 will not apply. Thus, earnings and profits will not be a factor in determining the shareholders' treatment, which may be a disadvantage to noncontrolling corporate shareholders. Given the reduction in the tax rate applicable to dividends, this exchange treatment frequently will have only a small influence on the overall tax difference between a receipt in liquidation and a receipt of earnings and profits from an ongoing corporation. A more significant difference between operating and liquidating distributions is the ability of the shareholder to offset the value received by his basis in his stock. He will recognize gain or loss (generally capital) on the distribution. Note that section 267 contains an explicit exception from its nonrecognition rules for losses of shareholders in complete liquidations.

Even though the rate at which income/gain is taxed may be the same in the case of a dividend distribution as in a liquidating distribution, the timing of use of basis may be very different depending upon whether a transfer to shareholders is treated as a distribution from an ongoing corporation, a redemption of a particular block of stock, or as the first step of a liquidation. In Rev. Rul. 68-348, 1968-2 C.B. 141, and Rev. Rul. 85-48, 1985-1 C.B. 126, the IRS adopted a "basis first, then gain" rule, permitting a shareholder to apply all basis against the first proceeds received without trying to predict the total amount to be received and thus to calculate gain on something like the installment method. This open transaction rule for gain recognition in complete liquidations is ordinarily taxpayer friendly, but it will defer the recognition of loss until it is clear that only de minimis value remains to be received. Rev. Rul. 69-334, 1969-1 C.B. 98.

If a shareholder has different blocks of shares in the liquidating corporation, gain or loss is determined separately on each block. *Cf.* Reg. § 1.331-1(e), Ex. What are the consequences then if there are distributions in liquidation over two taxable years in respect of different blocks of shares? Can the shareholder treat the first year's distribution as being received on the higher-basis block of shares and the second year's distribution as being received on the lower-basis block? The existence of the taxpayer-friendly open transaction rule would appear to support such treatment, even though recent regulatory developments emphasize tracing of basis in certain nonrecognition transactions between corporations and their shareholders.

In some situations, there may be very different results, depending upon whether future amounts to be received by shareholders are treated as continuing distributions by the liquidating corporation, or whether such receipts are treated as made with respect to property the shareholders should be treated as having received previously in a closed transaction. Assume, for example, that shareholders of a liquidating corporation actually receive intellectual property rights from the corporation. Payments after the initial distribution will be treated as ordinary income arising from the ownership of that property, rather than further distributions from the corporation. In other cases — for instance, if it is impossible to value the rights received by shareholders — it may be appropriate to treat later receipts as part of the continuing liquidation. *See, e.g.*, Burnet v. Logan, 283 U.S. 404 (1931) (characterizing later payments as made in continuation of the liquidation and with respect to the shareholder's stock).

If a corporation that is not publicly traded has sold assets on the installment basis within twelve months of its adoption of a plan of liquidation and then distributed the related notes to its shareholders within that same twelve-month period, the shareholders will step into the shoes of the corporation with respect to the notes. They will report their gain on the installment basis essentially as if they had sold their stock directly to the issuer of the installment note, and use a portion of their basis in their stock as their basis in the installment notes. § 453(h). Thus the shareholder need not value the note and take the entire gain into account immediately.

> **Did Open Transaction Reporting for Liquidations**
> **Survive *General Utilities'* Repeal?**
>
> *Before the repeal of* General Utilities *in 1986, there was still considerable ambiguity about whether a complete liquidation of a corporation to individual shareholders should be considered a realization and recognition event under general tax principles. After 1986, these arguments seem hard to sustain.*
>
> *If a complete liquidation is a realization and recognition event under general tax principles, there seems to be no reason why the installment method as prescribed by section 453 should not apply. Under this approach, ratable basis recovery rather than open transaction treatment should prevail.*
>
> *Although it would appear that the Service has the authority under either section 336 or section 453 to issue rulings obsoleting the old rulings allowing open transaction treatment, it has not done so.*

Under section 334(a), shareholders will have a basis in distributed property equal to the property's fair market value.

Perhaps surprisingly, there is no separate Code language indicating the result — either in terms of amount of the distribution or basis — when shareholders receive property subject to a liability in a complete liquidation. Nevertheless, under general tax principles, they will be treated as having received an amount equal only to the net value of their stock, and they will take a (gross) fair market value basis in the assets under section 334(a). This is consistent with the statutory scheme set out in section 301 for distributions from ongoing corporations involving liabilities. Remember that the apparently "unearned" basis will be "earned" when the shareholders are required to pay on the liability without being entitled to a deduction.

Liabilities that relate back to the corporation's preliquidation activities but that could not be accounted for at the time of the liquidation may give rise to a different treatment. In such cases, as the Supreme Court held in *Arrowsmith v. Commissioner*, 334 U.S. 6 (1952), payments should be treated as relating back to the original liquidation, and therefore produce only a capital loss. Note, however, that most payments relating to operations involving, and sales of property received in, a liquidation will ordinarily not relate back, but instead will be characterized by the nature of the shareholder's holding and use of the property after the liquidation.

Distributions in complete liquidation of a corporation are ordinarily made pro rata to all the shareholders. What should be the consequences of a non-pro rata distribution? The shareholder who receives an excess amount in exchange for his shares would be treated as having received a pro rata distribution and then, in a separate transaction, having received from other shareholders the excess payment, which would be characterized according to the context as a gift, compensation or satisfaction of an obligation, with appropriate tax consequences. *See* Rev. Rul. 79-10, 1979-1 C.B. 140.

a. Special Shareholder Level Consequences

Gain recognized by shareholders under section 331 is treated as gain with respect to the stock deemed given up for all purposes. Therefore, any special treatment of stock sales, including section 1202 (providing a special rate for gain on certain qualified small business stock) and section 1045 (providing for rollover of gain on such qualified small business stock) will be available.

5.2.2. Effect on the Liquidating Corporation

Under section 336, corporations are fully taxed on the difference between the fair market value of the assets distributed and their bases in these assets. Unlike operating distributions of property or liquidations into controlling corporate shareholders, losses are allowed (subject to a variety of anti-abuse rules) in complete liquidations unrelated to reorganizations. Compare § 336(a) with §§ 336(d), 337(a).

a.   Prior Law

This was not always the case. Before 1986, there was considerable tension in the Code about the extent to which the liquidation of a corporation should be treated as a taxable event. These transactions, like the distributions from continuing corporations described in section 311 and contributions to corporations, were granted nonrecognition under the particular statutory provisions of subchapter C. In the case of section 331 liquidations and section 311 distributions, however, changes in statutory provisions and judicial doctrines created an ever-increasing number of circumstances in which nonrecognition was not available. Pre-1986 amendments to section 311, for instance, required gain recognition when a corporation used property to redeem shareholders. And the tax benefit rule required that under some circumstances corporations would recognize gain if assets the basis of which had already been deducted had value at the time of a liquidation. *See* Hillsboro Nat'l Bank v. Commissioner, 460 U.S. 370 (1983) (apparently rejecting the need for an actual "recovery" or "repayment" in order for the tax benefit rule to apply, and requiring recapture in the context of a corporate liquidation when other gain would not be recognized).

b.   Problems in the Determination of Corporate Gain

i.   Asset-By-Asset Constructive Sale

The statute requires that "gain or loss be recognized . . . as if such property were sold to the distributee at its fair market value." In the section 311 constructive sale context, the IRS has long been committed to the idea that this computation must be made on an asset-by-asset basis, not on an aggregate basis, so that losses are not effectively recognized by permitting the basis in loss assets to offset the gain in gain assets. Thus, if a corporation makes an operating distribution of two assets, each with a basis of $50 and one worth $65 and the other worth $40, there is gain of $15 ($65-$50), not a gain of $5 (($65+$40)-($50+$50)). It appears that the language in section 331 contemplates a similar asset-by-asset constructive sale, whether or not the sum of the values of individual assets can be reconciled with what a buyer would have paid, in the aggregate, for all of the assets.

Why might the sum of the values of the individual assets be different from the total value of the assets combined? The most likely situation is the one in which the combination is worth more than the sum of the values of individual assets because there is goodwill associated with the business. Indeed, some would define "goodwill" as an asset, and acknowledge that it is precisely the difference between the sum of individual assets and the value in the aggregate. It is relatively easy in this situation to simply treat this goodwill as an additional asset of the corporation, at least until you think about whether this goodwill is likely to survive a liquidation, and whether it should be included in the final measure of corporate income if it cannot.

But the value of the combined assets can also be worth less than the sum of the individual values. Why? Because in some circumstances, potential liabilities for tort damages, regulatory fines, and taxes can follow the combined assets, even when the corporation is dissolved. (For the shareholders, there is less potential that liabilities will follow the assets than there would be if the shareholders had simply sold all of the stock, but it nevertheless exists.) Thus, the buyer of the assets of a business that is known to have flaunted environmental laws is likely to pay less for these assets than for the sum of the value of the individual assets used in the business. It is not clear how gain is to be computed under section 336 in such circumstances.

ii.   Destroyed Values

It is also possible that some assets, including various components of goodwill, will be destroyed by virtue of the liquidation, even when they would have survived had the shareholders sold stock. This is especially likely for some corporate expenditures, like the cost of raising equity capital, that are not allowed as expenses to the corporation and thus remain on the corporation's tax books as "assets" at the time of liquidation.

iii.   Liabilities and Valuation Difficulties

As section 336 is written, "gain" is to be recognized . . . as if . . . [the corporation's property] were sold . . . at fair market value." This language puts considerable pressure on a proper determination of "fair market value" in the absence of any market transaction, and frequently in the absence of any facts from which the values of the assets might be imputed. The required computation does, however, seem fairly straightforward.

Liabilities to which assets are subject — which would ordinarily reduce the cash consideration a purchaser might pay and thus must be taken into account in determining the amount realized — can ordinarily be ignored in making this computation. Section 336(b), however, directs that they not always be entirely ignored because "the fair market value" of "property subject to a liability shall be treated as not less than the amount of such liability." Although this may look like merely a harmless invocation of the familiar rule found in section 7701(g) and the doctrine relied on in the *Tufts* case, it is a considerably stronger rule. It appears that it is not limited to nonrecourse liabilities, but will apply even when the recipient shareholders will be liable on the debt. It would appear that this element of gain can be avoided, however, if the shareholders who would become liable on the debt borrow a sufficient amount to eliminate the excess debt immediately before the liquidation, and then contribute the proceeds to the corporation, which then can pay down on the liability. It is unclear why the statute assumes that the corporation should have no income when the shareholders have sufficient liquidity to make these arrangements before the liquidation, while the corporation should have income when they cannot.

The statute does make some sense, however, if you assume that the liabilities are nonrecourse liabilities and that the reason why the basis of the property is lower than the amount of the liability is because cost recovery deductions have been claimed.

iv.   **Stuffed Losses Disallowance Rules**

When section 336 was amended to trigger gains and losses, there were fears that the anticipated gain could all be sheltered by the contribution of loss property. Remember that in their ordinary operation, sections 351, 358 and 362 replicate the shareholders' basis in the assets transferred to the corporation. Section 336(d) contains several provisions aimed at preventing that result, especially when a liquidation might have been contemplated at the time of the contribution.

Section 336(d)(1), the "related shareholder loss disallowance rule," applies to disallow corporate losses when and to the extent that a party related under section 267 (that is, a shareholder directly or indirectly owning more than 50% in value of the outstanding stock, applying the constructive ownership rules of section 267(c)) either receives property in a distribution that "is not pro rata," section 336(d)(1)(a)(i), or receives property that was contributed to the corporation during the five-year period ending on the date of the distribution, section 336(d)(1)(a)(ii) (whether or not the property was a loss property at the time of contribution). The meaning of "is not pro rata" is not entirely clear in this context. It perhaps could be read to refer to a distribution of loss property to a shareholder who receives thereby more than the total share of asset value represented by his stock, as if he were being compensated by the other shareholders for some reason. More likely it refers to a distribution in which a shareholder receives more than his share of the loss asset itself, as if it were being selectively distributed to him rather than shared ratably among all the shareholders. The provision will apply whether or not the related shareholder was the original contributor of the loss property.

Section 336(d)(2), the "anti-stuffing rule," penalizes stuffing liquidating corporations with loss properties by limiting losses that would otherwise be recognized to amounts in excess of the built-in loss that existed at the time of the corporation's acquisition of the asset. It applies not only to liquidating distributions but also to other transactions such as sales that are deemed to be, along with the corporation's acquisition of the property and ultimate liquidation, "part of a plan a principal purpose of which was to recognize loss . . . in connection with the liquidation." The statutory mechanism reduces basis in applicable cases down to the fair market value of the property at the time it was contributed. There is a statutory presumption that "any property . . . acquired within two years before the date of the adoption of the plan of complete liquidation" was acquired with a loss-creating purpose. Although the statute authorizes the Treasury to create grounds for avoiding the presumption, and the committee reports suggest that leniency in favor of the taxpayer would be appropriate, this authority has not been used.

Note that since shareholders are taxed on the distribution and receive a fair market value basis in the distributed assets, the loss that is disallowed is *not* preserved in basis (and merely deferred). Instead, it simply vanishes.

When there is overlap between the anti-stuffing rule in (d)(2) and the related shareholder rule in (d)(1), the related shareholder rule's more severe result — disallowance of the entire loss rather than just the pre-incorporation loss — applies, according to the legislative history.

c. Equivalence of Corporate-Sale-And-Liquidation and Liquidation-And-Shareholder-Sale

A quick reading of the language of section 336 suggests that the drafters thought that the gain and loss to be recognized by a corporation on the sale of its assets to a third party would, or at least should, be the same as the gain and loss to the corporation to be recognized on liquidation. The statutory resolution of the various problems (the presence of assets that do not survive the liquidation but might have survived a transfer, "negative goodwill" in the form of anticipated but unaccrued liabilities, and stuffed losses subject to 336(d)(2)) all suggest that this will not always be the case.

Applying the Step Transaction Doctrine: Distribution Followed by Sale, or Sale Followed by a Distribution?

Although the stakes are far lower since the repeal of General Utilities, *there are still some substantial differences between the results that will apply when a corporation sells its assets and distributes the proceeds and the results that will apply when a corporation distributes its assets and the shareholders then sell them. For instance, if a corporation were to sell assets, and then use the proceeds in a self-tender to be tested under section 302, a corporation can recognize a corporate level loss; if, however, the corporate assets were used as the consideration in the self-tender, followed by a sale of the assets by the shareholders, the corporation could not recognize the loss and the excess basis will be destroyed. Similarly, if a corporation sold and then liquidated, it would not have to worry about an excess liability on an individual asset, whereas if it liquidated and then sold, it would have to worry about avoiding gain under section 336(b); and if a corporation contemplating liquidation holds a loss asset, section 336(d)(1) might prohibit the use of the loss if the corporation liquidated and then the shareholder sold the asset, whereas if the corporation sold the asset, the loss would be allowed. What should we look at to determine which treatment should apply?*

The leading cases indicate that there is no single answer to the question. The appropriate treatment will depend on what the substance of the transaction ultimately was. If the sale was clearly pre-arranged by the corporation, a transitory holding by the shareholders might be ignored, under general assignment of income principles and the decision in Commissioner v. Court Holding Co., *324 U.S. 331 (1945) (holding that a corporation had in fact sold assets before the purported distribution of those assets to its shareholders).* United States v. Cumberland Pub. Serv. Co., *338 U.S. 451 (1950). The Tax Court has summarized the subsequent cases in* Martin Ice Cream Co. v. Commissioner, *110 T.C. 189, 212 (1998):*

> Where shareholders are found to have negotiated the sale of corporate assets independently, on their own behalf, the form of the transaction is respected, and the corporation is not recast as the seller, notwithstanding that some negotiations were carried on by the shareholders before the liquidation. *See, e.g.*, Bolker v. Commissioner, 81 T.C. 782 (1983), *aff'd*, 760 F.2d 1039 (9th Cir. 1985); Doyle Hosiery Corp. v. Commissioner, 17 T.C. 641 (1951); Amos L. Beaty & Co. v. Commissioner, 14 T.C. 52 (1950). Where a corporation is found to have negotiated a transaction, and at the last minute, the shareholders are substituted for the corporation as sellers, *Court Holding* has been applied to regard the corporation as the seller for federal income tax purposes. *See, e.g.*, Waltham Netoco Theatres, Inc. v. Commissioner, 401 F.2d 333 (1st Cir. 1968), *aff'g* 49 T.C. 399, 405 (1968); Kaufmann v. Commissioner, 175 F.2d 28 (3d Cir. 1949), *aff'g* 11 T.C. 483 (1948).

Note that if a corporation sells its assets to a third party in contemplation of a liquidation and receives in exchange installment notes with respect to which it may report gain on the installment method, the distribution of those notes to shareholders in the liquidation will trigger all corporate level gain inherent in the notes. *See* § 453B. As noted above, the shareholders receiving such notes report the payments on the notes as received in respect of their stock, if the timing and other requirements of the statute are satisfied. *See* § 453(h).

d.   Other Corporate Level Consequences

When a complete liquidation occurs, the corporation's existence for tax purposes ceases. Its tax attributes, including any grandfathered accounting methods, net operating loss carryovers, capital loss carryovers, and credit carryovers, are destroyed.

PRACTICE PROBLEMS

1.   Bob owns all of the stock of Small Corporation, which he bought five years ago with a basis of $5,000. He causes the corporation to liquidate, that is, to distribute to him its only assets not needed to pay expenses and taxes, a piece of vacant land worth $7,000 and cash of $11,000. The result of the liquidation transaction to Bob is

    (a)   Cannot tell without knowing more about the corporation's earnings and profits.

    (b)   Gain of $7,000.

    (c)   Gain of $13,000.

    (d)   Gain of $11,000.

2.   After the liquidation of Small Corporation, Bob's basis in the land he receives is

    (a) $19,000.

    (b) $7,000.

    (c) $12,000.

    (d) $5,000.

    3.   If Small Corporation paid $1,500 for the land, what result on liquidation?

    (a)   Gain of $5,500.

    (b)   No gain or loss in respect of Small's assets on the liquidation of Small.

    (c)   Small's gain calculation will not be made until Bob sells the land.

    (d)   Insufficient information to determine.

    4.   If the land was purchased for $1,500 and was worth $7,000 but was subject to a liability of $2,000 at the time of the liquidation, what result to Bob on the liquidation described above?

    (a)   Gain of $12,500.

    (b)   Gain of $11,000.

    (c)   Gain of $20,000.

    (d)   Gain of $13,500.

    5.   If the land was purchased for $1,500 and was worth $7,000 but was subject to a liability of $2,000 at the time of the liquidation, what result to Small Corporation on the liquidation described above?

    (a)   Gain of $3,500 and debt discharge income of $2,000.

    (b)   Gain of $7,500.

    (c)   Gain of $5,500.

    (d)   Gain of $3,500.

    6.   If the land was purchased for $1,500 and was worth $7,000 but was subject to a liability of $8,300 at the time of the liquidation, what result to Small Corporation on the liquidation described above?

    (a)   Gain of $6,800.

    (b)   Gain of $1,300.

    (c)   Gain of $5,500.

    (d)   Cannot compute without knowing whether debt is recourse or nonrecourse.

    7.   If the land was purchased for $1,500 and was worth $7,000 but was subject to a liability of $8,300 at the time of the liquidation, what result to Bob when he receives the land and the cash in the liquidation described above?

    (a)   Gain of $11,000.

    (b)   Gain of $13,000.

    (c)   Cannot determine from the facts given, but may be gain of $4,700 or of $6,000.

8.   If the corporation paid $10,000 in cash for the land, what is the result of the liquidation to the corporation?

(a)   Loss would be recognized but for section 267.

(b)   Gain of $8,000.

(c)   Loss of $3,000.

(d)   No gain or loss to Small Corporation on Small Corporation's assets on its liquidation.

9.   If Bob had contributed the property to Small Corporation after having paid $10,000 in cash for it and because it had been designated as a good site for Small Corporation's next venture, what result to the corporation on liquidation?

(a)   Loss would be recognized but for section 267.

(b)   Gain of $8,000.

(c)   Loss of $3,000.

(d)   Depends upon when the contribution was made.

DISCUSSION PROBLEMS

1.   X Corp holds only cash and assets it acquired with cash; it received no other property as contributions from its shareholders. It has earnings and profits of well over $2 million. Its stock is held by two individuals, Sue and Tom, each of whom own 50% of the stock with a basis of $10,000. Its books show the following assets:

	tax basis	fair market value
Unimproved real estate A	100,000	500,000
Unimproved real estate B	1,000,000	500,000
Cash and other liquid assets	500,000	500,000

(a)   What are the tax consequences of a transfer of the real estate and other assets to all of the parties?

(b)   What if both shareholders held their stock with a basis of $800,000?

(c)   What if Tom had purchased one quarter of the stock of X Corp for $5,000 ten years ago, but had only just bought the other quarter of the corporation's stock for $400,000, ten months prior to the liquidation?

(d)   What are the consequences in (a) if the liquid assets are distributed 9 months before, and in a different tax year from, the real estate assets?

(e)   What if parcel B is subject to a $300,000 mortgage?

(f)   What if parcel B is subject to a $600,000 mortgage or a $1.1 million mortgage? Does it matter if the mortgage is recourse and is expressly assumed by A and B at the closing? What steps might A and B take to ameliorate the situation? What happens if they later make payments on this mortgage?

(g) Prior to but in anticipation of the liquidation (and after the date that the corporation adopted a plan of liquidation), X Corp sold the two parcels of real estate to an unrelated third party, who paid $400,000 down and agreed to pay $100,000 per year for 6 years, with market interest, and gave X Corp a note therefore. What are the consequences of the transfer of this note in the liquidation?

(h) Over the course of its life, X Corp spent $50,000 raising capital in ways that were not eligible for deduction under section 248 and were therefore capitalized for tax purposes. The assets of a smaller business were acquired several years ago, resulting in goodwill on the corporation's books of $50,000. How will these items affect the corporation's income?

(i) The same as part (a), except parcel B was contributed by Tom, rather than purchased with cash contributed by the shareholders, and Tom receives the entire interest on liquidation. How would this change the result?

2. Y Corp is held by its two founding shareholders and only employees, M and N, and has been engaged in the software development business. Its most significant asset, security software developed by M and N for the corporation, was recently sold to a company that was identified as a good broker to handle the resale of the software, and which will pay M and N a total price contingent on the amount for which the software can be resold. That buyer is now receiving bids far greater than M and N anticipated. After paying off Y Corp's considerable debt, M and N plan to pay themselves bonuses that amount to the remaining sale proceeds, to liquidate Y Corp and then to part company.

Before the formal liquidation, they have come to you to help them negotiate a contract between themselves over rights to the computer code reflected by projects not covered by the sale agreement.

Are there any issues or alternative approaches to the situation that they might not have anticipated that you might want to raise with them? *Cf.* Martin Ice Cream v. Commissioner, 110 T.C. 189 (1998).

Chapter 6

DISTRIBUTIONS TO CORPORATE SHAREHOLDERS

6.1. DIVIDENDS-RECEIVED DEDUCTION

Statutes and Regulations   IRC §§ 243(a), (b), (c); 246(b), (c); 1059
Other Primary Authorities   Rev. Rul. 82-11, 1982-1 C.B. 51

Litton Indus. v. Commissioner, 89 T.C. 1086 (1987)

Special deductions for dividends received (sections 243 and following) allow corporate shareholders to avoid (or reduce) the burden of more than one level of tax on earnings while they remain within corporate solution — i.e., as the earnings are distributed upstream from domestic subsidiaries to domestic parents. Under section 243, a corporation can generally deduct the entire amount of any dividends received from subsidiaries in which it owns at least 80% of the stock under subsections 243(a)(3) and 243(b); 80% of any dividend it receives from corporations in which it owns 20% or more of the stock under section 243(c); and 70% of all other dividends received under section 243(a)(1). Thus, the maximum tax to a corporate shareholder on dividends will be 10.5% (35% rate times 100% minus 70%), unless a special rule applies.

6.1.1. Overview

The dividends-received deduction (commonly referred to by its acronym as the DRD) is premised on the idea that income that has been subject to U.S. corporate taxation at the level of the distributing corporation should not again be subject to the full force of corporate taxation when it is distributed to corporate shareholders. (There is, however, no requirement that distributing corporations establish that they have actually paid a corporate-level tax on any of their income. As with all dividends, the corporate distributor must merely have earnings and profits, which will provide an approximation of income that has been taxed.) It is therefore not available in general for dividends received from foreign corporations, except to the extent that those foreign corporations had income effectively connected with a U.S. trade or business or received dividends from a domestic subsidiary. (The rules for tracking such foreign earnings will not be considered here.)

The stock ownership tests for the DRD are derived from the affiliated-group definitions and are based on a required percentage interest of the vote and value of the distributing corporation. To receive a 100% DRD, two requirements must be satisfied:

(i) the recipient corporation must own at least 80% of the vote and value of the distributing corporation (not counting plain vanilla preferred stock) and thus be a member of the same affiliated group (defined under section 1504) as the distributing corporation when the dividend is distributed, and

(ii) the dividend must be distributed out of earnings and profits that was accumulated in taxable years when the two corporations were members of the same affiliated group. § 243(b)(1)(B). The 80% DRD similarly requires that the recipient corporation own 20% or more of the vote and value of the distributing corporation, not counting plain vanilla preferred; but there is no corresponding earnings and profits requirement.

Strategic Preferences of Corporate Shareholders

Because the dividend-received deduction effectively eliminates taxation of dividends from controlled subsidiaries and substantially reduces the tax imposed on dividends from other corporations, a corporate shareholder's preference regarding the way in which it receives its return on stock is frequently the opposite of the preference of individual shareholders. Corporate shareholders will frequently prefer to receive distributions that will be treated as dividends so that they can take the DRD into account, rather than to sell shares or have stock redeemed in transactions that are honored as sales.

This same incentive will tempt a corporate shareholder to reduce the value of its stock holdings in a subsidiary by withdrawing earnings from the subsidiary before selling the subsidiary. Will this strategy work?

In several cases, the corporate parent succeeded in causing distributions from the subsidiary to be sold, thereby lessening the amount of sale proceeds and resulting capital gains. In Litton Indus. v. Commissioner, 89 T.C. 1086 (1987), acq. (1988), *the distribution occurred before the parent had determined whether it would sell shares in the subsidiary in a public offering or attempt to find a single buyer; there was a business purpose for the distribution in that the extra cash would have adversely affected the price of a public offering, and (perhaps most important) the subsidiary could have financed the distribution entirely on its own even though the distribution was actually only of the subsidiary's note and not of cash. On these grounds the* Litton *court was able to distinguish* Waterman S.S. Corp. v. Commissioner, 430 F.2d 1185 (5th Cir. 1970), *in which the appellate court had held that the distribution should be treated as if it were part of the consideration paid by the buyer.*

The usefulness of the Waterman Steamship *strategy has, however, been severely limited by the fact that section 1059 will frequently result in a basis reduction, decreasing dollar-for-dollar the tax benefit of the DRD.*

6.1.2. Limitations

It is easy to see that the availability of a DRD creates arbitrage opportunities. A corporation may be able to engineer an artificial loss if it can take a DRD into account at the same time that it takes another type of deduction in respect of the same amount, such as a deduction for explicit interest, or a deduction for making a payment to a creditor in lieu of a dividend that has been paid on the stock (that is, in connection with a securities lending transaction), or even a simple loss on the sale of the stock with respect to which the dividend was received. Similarly, the purpose of the DRD would not be served by permitting a DRD in respect of dividend income from a distributing corporation that is itself exempt from tax. Over time, Congress has enacted a variety of anti-abuse provisions in sections 246 and 246A to counter such manipulations of the DRD.

a.　Holding Period Requirements

Section 246(c)(1)(A) limits the DRD to stock that is held for more than 45 days during the 91-day period that surrounds the ex-dividend date. The requirement is increased to more than 90 days out of 181 days in the case of certain preferred stock dividends. Days on which the shareholder is protected against loss with respect to the stock reduce the shareholder's holding period. § 246(c)(4).

The theory here is that a longer holding period increases the exposure of the corporate shareholder to the economic risk of loss. This increased economic risk makes it less likely that the DRD claimant has put itself in the position of a shareholder for only a very brief period of time solely to engage in the tax arbitrage that the DRD would make possible if the DRD were too easily available. This arbitrage could be easily accomplished: buy the stock after the dividend is declared but before the ex-dividend date (and therefore the price paid includes the dividend), receive the dividend, and then sell immediately for a loss (that is, at a lower price that reflects the value withdrawn from the corporation through the dividend). Although the IRS might take the position that there was no substance in some such transactions in which the purported shareholder never took on any of the risk involved in holding the stock of the dividend-paying corporation, the holding period requirement establishes a bright-line test for the amount of economic risk a corporate shareholder must have taken on. *Cf.* Rev. Rul. 82-11, 1982-1 C.B. 51 (a pre-section 246 ruling denying the DRD to a corporation that purchased stock before the ex-dividend date (i.e., "with" a dividend for exchange purposes), claiming a DRD, then sold the stock "without" the dividend, claiming a capital loss).

b.　In-Lieu-Of Payments

A shareholder that is obligated to make dividend-equivalent payments in respect of stock (or "substantially similar or related property") is not entitled to a DRD with respect to dividends received on that stock. § 246(c)(1)(B). Such payments would be made by a taxpayer to a securities lender, for instance, when the taxpayer has borrowed stock to sell to another party, (e.g., a "short sale" of stock). This provision substantially eliminated the advantages under the DRD of entering into a short-sale-against-the-box, in which a shareholder would borrow stock equivalent to stock already held, make a short sale of that stock, and make payments to the lender "equivalent" to the dividend payments received on the stock. Without section 246(c)(1)(B), this taxpayer might claim both a DRD with respect to the dividend it actually received and a deduction (or basis) for the payment of the dividend-equivalent amount to the lender.

c.　Aggregate DRD Limitation

In very general terms (and disregarding the application of this provision in the context of dividends from foreign corporations), under section 246(b) the 70% DRD cannot exceed 70% of a corporation's taxable income otherwise computed. A preliminary determination about the applicability of section 246(b) is made by computing taxable income with the full DRD but without any NOL carryover, capital loss carryback or section 199 deduction. If the DRD causes the corporation's taxable income (thus computed) to go negative, creating or increasing a net operating loss, the limit will not apply. But if there is still zero or positive taxable income (again computed without the specially treated items) even when taking the DRD into account, the limit in section 246(b) may apply. If there are specially treated items, the limit will begin to apply whenever taxable income (with the dividends but before the DRD) falls below the dividends, implying a negative other income, but it will not apply again once, as income falls, the level of income other than dividends falls just below the amount of the normally allowed DRD.

d. Dividends From Tax Exempt Corporations

Although there is no provision ensuring that taxable domestic C corporations that pay dividends have actually paid a corporate income tax on the profits out of which the dividend is being paid, there are other sections that reinforce the idea that the DRD is related to cascading corporate-level taxation. Section 246(a) thus disallows the DRD for dividends received from organizations that are exempt from tax under sections 501 and 521.

e. Debt-Financed Portfolio Stock

Except for certain distributing corporations with concentrated stock ownership, section 246A reduces the 70% and 80% DRD when the receiving corporation has "debt-financed portfolio stock." The provision is rather detailed, but in gist it reduces the DRD by a percentage that reflects the "average indebtedness percentage," determined by dividing the average amount of portfolio debt by the average amount of the adjusted basis of the stock during the base period (generally, between dividends or in some cases up to one year). The statute provides for regulations to limit the reduction to the "allocable interest" and to disallow a related interest deduction instead of reducing the DRD in certain cases.

6.1.3. Special Rules Regarding Earnings and Profits

When a shareholder that is a corporation owns more than 20% of the distributing corporation, section 301(e) provides that most of the rules in subsections 312(k) and (n) do not apply. Since these rules all adjust earnings and profits to maximize the possibility that there are earnings and profits to support the characterization of distributions as dividends, this provision reduces the chances that shareholders that are corporations that would enjoy the 80% or the 100% DRD will be able to characterize their distributions as dividends.

6.1.4. Extraordinary Dividends under Section 1059

For corporate shareholders, the DRD results in exclusion or light taxation of corporate dividends. The "extraordinary dividend" provision in section 1059 is designed to prevent the arbitrage otherwise possible if a corporation purchased stock, received a lightly taxed dividend, and then (after having held the stock long enough to satisfy the DRD holding period) sold the stock for a loss. The mechanism used is to permanently reduce the receiving corporation's basis in the stock upon which the extraordinary dividend is paid by the amount that the corresponding DRD has reduced corporate income, resulting in a deferral of gain so long as there is sufficient basis. Gain is triggered to the extent the DRD exceeds the recipient corporation's basis in the stock.

Section 1059 is not designed to transform all of the benefit of the DRD into a deferral — it only applies under certain circumstances. The section applies only if the dividend in question satisfies a two-pronged "amount and holding period" test: it is extraordinary relative to the shareholder's basis and it is paid on stock that has not been held for more than 2 years before the dividend announcement date. (This date — meant to be the date upon which the shareholders might first count on the distribution and including any contract right to be paid a dividend — is determined by tax law standards: it may be well before the corporate law dividend declaration date.) A dividend will be considered extraordinary under section 1059(c) if it is more than 10% of the shareholder's basis in the stock (5% for preferred stock). In making this determination, all dividends within an 85-day window are aggregated; and, if they would total 20% of basis, all dividends within one year are aggregated. The fair market value of the stock at the time of the dividend may be used instead of basis in applying these rules for determining the relative size, and therefore the "extraordinary" nature, of the dividend.

Three types of shareholdings are excluded from section 1059's mechanism:

- original shareholdings under section 1059(d)(6) (to the extent the earnings and profits are not attributable to earnings or transfers of property from corporations that were not owned in the same percentage by the taxpayer);

- affiliated shareholdings under section 1059(e)(2) (those eligible for a 100% DRD under section 243, to the extent the earnings and profits are not attributable to earnings or gains when the distributing corporation was not a member of the affiliated group); and

- qualified preferred shareholdings under section 1059(e)(3) (to the extent the stock is not purchased in arrears, is held more than five years, pays fixed annual dividends, and has an actual rate of return (as defined in section 1059(e)(3)(B)(i)) not in excess of 15%). If there is a disposition within five years, the extraordinary dividend reduction on such preferred stock is limited to the amount that exceeds the stated rate of return on the stock (as defined in section 1059(e)(3)(B)(ii)).

Section 1059(f) sets out an anti-abuse rule that addresses a type of "stepped down preferred" issued in the 1990s and similar abusive issuances. Any dividend on such "disqualified" preferred stock will be treated as an extraordinary dividend, without regard to the holding period requirement. Disqualified preferred is any preferred that has a declining dividend rate or for which the issue price exceeds the liquidation rights or is otherwise structured to avoid the provisions of section 1059.

Finally, section 1059(e) expands the operation of the general mechanism described above for many transactions that are not simple distributions with respect to stock. It applies the basis reduction and gain recognition mechanism of section 1059(a) to specified redemption transactions in contexts in which section 1059(a) might not have applied — that is, regardless of the relative size of the distribution or holding period for the underlying stock. The covered transactions include partial liquidations, non-pro rata redemptions, and redemptions that would not have been characterized as dividends except for that fact that options were taken into account under the attribution rules or section 304 applied. In addition, whenever boot in a reorganization exchange is characterized as a dividend, it will be treated as an extraordinary dividend regardless of the holding period under section 1059(e).

PRACTICE PROBLEMS

1.   X Corp owns 1% of the common stock of one of its suppliers, with a total basis of $1 million and a fair market value of $10 million. It receives a dividend of $50,000 with respect to the stock. What are the tax consequences of this dividend?

(a) $50,000 in income, $35,000 DRD, no change in basis.

(b) $50,000 in income, $40,000 DRD, basis reduction of $40,000.

(c) $50,000 in income, $35,000 DRD, basis reduction of $35,000.

(d) $5,000 in income, no basis reduction.

2.   What if, in question 1, X Corp's holding had been of 25% of the stock?

(a) $50,000 in income, $35,000 DRD, no basis reduction.

(b) $50,000 in income, $50,000 DRD, no basis reduction.

(c) $50,000 in income, $40,000 DRD, no basis reduction.

3.   In question 1, what would the result be if the stock had been preferred stock, and the dividend paid was $200,000?

(a)   Dividend income of $200,000; DRD of $160,000, basis reduction of $160,000.

(b)   Dividend income of $200,000, DRD of $140,000; basis reduction of $140,000.

(c)   Cannot tell on the facts given.

4.   In question 1, what if X Corp had owned 85% of the distributing corporation?

(a)   No dividend income.

(b)   Dividend income of $50,000, DRD of $50,000, basis reduction of $50,000.

(c)   Dividend income of $50,000, DRD of $50,000, no basis reduction.

5.   What if Corp X in question 1 had had a $9,000 taxable loss (before taking into account any dividend income, DRD or net operating loss carryforward) and also had a net operating loss carryforward to that year of $15,000 and received a dividend of $30,000?

(a)   Dividend income of $30,000; DRD of $30,000; no basis reduction.

(b)   Dividend income of $30,000; DRD of $24,000; no basis reduction.

    (c)   Dividend income of $30,000; DRD of $21,000; no basis reduction.

    (d)   Dividend income of $30,000, DRD of $14,700; no basis reduction.

    6.   In question 5, what if X Corp had $50,000 of other taxable income (before taking into account the dividend, any available DRD, or any available net operating loss carryover) and had a net operating loss carryover to the year of the distribution of $15,000 and received a dividend of $30,000?

    (a)   Dividend income of $30,000; DRD of $30,000; no basis reduction.

    (b)   Dividend income of $30,000; DRD of $24,000; no basis reduction.

    (c)   Dividend income of $30,000; DRD of $21,000; no basis reduction.

    (d)   Dividend income of $30,000, DRD of $14,700; no basis reduction.

    7.   In question 1, what if Corp X had borrowed $900,000 to buy the stock, and had paid $45,000 in interest on this debt in this year?

    (a)   Dividend income of $50,000; DRD of $35,000; no basis reduction.

    (b)   Dividend income of $50,000; DRD of $3,500; no basis reduction.

    (c)   Dividend income of $50,000; DRD of $5,000; no basis reduction.

DISCUSSION PROBLEMS

    1.   Fragile Corp has suffered many years of operating losses and has a large deficit in e&p. Despite these deficits, it is still in business because it has intangible assets believed to be of substantial value. It has contracts on which it should begin to realize profits (and improve its cash flow) in the next few years. In order to continue in business, it needs a capital infusion. Fragile has several large corporate customers who rely on it for their supplies and therefore need it to remain in business. These customers therefore are willing to provide financing, but only if they can receive a return that is taxed as a dividend (and consequently taxed relatively lightly). How can Fragile take advantage of the financing these customers seem willing to provide?

    2.   Slick Corp has come to you for advice on a tax scheme. It is temporarily holding a considerable amount of cash, waiting for its next big investment. Meanwhile, it would like to make the most of that cash. It plans to buy, from individual shareholders who prefer capital gains rather than dividends, stock in corporations for which dividends have already been declared but have not yet been paid. (Before the special dividend rate in section 1(h), potential interested sellers included most individual shareholders; while the special dividend rate remains in effect, most shareholders are almost indifferent between dividend receipts and sales receipts unless either (i) they have capital losses from other transactions that are likely to go unused unless they recognize gains from selling the stock or (ii) they have a high basis in their stock that they want to take into account.)

    Slick Corp plans to make its money on the fact that the price it must pay for the stock will reflect the preference of individual shareholders for capital gains, who will in effect share their tax savings with it. It does not plan on making a profit simply from having chosen stock that is likely to appreciate in the time it holds it. Thus it plans to sell the stock shortly after the dividend receipt, and if it then sells the stock for no more than the amount it paid for the stock less the dividend it received, it will be content.

Slick Corp is obviously assuming that individual shareholders will be willing to reduce the price they are willing to accept for their stock (because of the tax they can avoid on a dividend — e.g., $15 for every $100 in basis individual shareholders are able to use because their return on the stock comes as a sale rather than a dividend) by an amount that will be greater than the tax Slick will owe on the dividend it receives, reduced by the dividend-received deduction (e.g.,.35 $.30 or $10.5 on every $100). In order for this scheme to work, what limits are there on Slick's ability to finance, buy and sell the stock?

(Assume that Slick's assumptions about the price effect of the timing of the dividend and the sale are correct.)

3.   Slick Corp.'s financial officer has returned to you with another scheme. This time, he plans to have Slick accommodate another corporation's need to generate capital losses to offset its capital gains. The plan is for Slick to issue preferred stock to other corporations. The preferred will bear a relatively high dividend rate, perhaps as high as 20% per year. After the dividend is paid, the other corporations will sell their Slick preferred stock to Slick's accommodating investment banker at a loss. The financial officer believes that the tax benefit of the loss (35% on each dollar of loss available) should more than offset the tax on the dividend (10.5% on each dollar of dividend paid and reduction in stock value). Assuming an arrangement can be set up so that the purchasing corporation never loses so much on the sale of the preferred stock that it actually suffers an after-tax loss, will this scheme work?

4.   Cash Corp holds two blocks of the common stock of Earnings Co., a publicly traded corporation with a long history of substantial profits. One block of 1000 shares was purchased for $10 per share in 1990; one block of 1000 shares was purchased for $50 per share on February 1. In response to a temporary reduction in the rate at which dividends are taxed to individual shareholders, on March 1, when its stock was selling for $51 per share, Earnings Co announced a dividend of $5 per share, which it paid on March 5. The ex dividend date was March 4.

What are the likely consequences of the receipt of this distribution by Cash Corp?

5.   Parent Corp has owned Sub Corp since its initial incorporation. Sub Corp has been very profitable and has accumulated a considerable amount of cash, but its business is moving further and further away from that which Parent Corp's management understands. A buyer has made overtures to Parent Corp, suggesting that it would be willing to pay up to $50 million for all of the stock of Sub Corp. Parent Corp has come to you looking for advice about how to structure such a sale transaction. Any suggestions?

6.2.   LIQUIDATIONS OF CONTROLLED SUBSIDIARIES

Statutes and Regulations   IRC §§ 332 (omit (c) and (d)); 334(b); 337;
                                    381; 1504(a)(2) and (4)
                                    Reg. § 1.332-1, -2, -5, -7
Other Primary Authorities   George L. Riggs, 64 T.C. 474 (1975), *acq.*

The general rule for complete liquidations provides for taxation at both the corporate and shareholder levels — the corporation is treated as constructively selling its assets, and the shareholders are treated as receiving those assets in exchange for their corporate stock.

An entirely different approach is taken, however, when there is a controlling corporate shareholder. Sections 332 and 337 apply a nonrecognition rule to complete liquidations of corporations that are controlled (under the definition in section 1502(a)(2)) by another corporation, to the extent that assets are received by the controlling parent corporation: neither parent nor subsidiary recognizes gain or loss on a liquidating distribution to the parent. In addition, the subsidiary may not recognize any losses that would otherwise be recognized on liquidating distributions to minority shareholders, under section 336(d)(3). The parent corporation receives the assets with a basis equal to the liquidating subsidiary's basis in those assets under section 334(b) and a tacked holding period under section 1223(2). The parent's basis in its stock holding in the subsidiary simply disappears, but the parent succeeds to the subsidiary corporation's tax attributes under section 381(a)(1).

Definition of Control

Although most of the building block provisions in subchapter C rely on the test for control in section 368(c), since 1986 section 332 treatment has been conditioned on the presence of control within the meaning of section 1504(a)(2). The test in section 368(c), requiring 80% of vote and 80% of the total number of shares of all other classes of stock, can usually be applied in a relatively straightforward way simply by looking at stock ownership. The test in section 1504(a)(2), on the other hand, requires 80% of vote and 80% of value. "Value" is not always easy to ascertain when there are multiple classes of stock.

In many situations, including section 332, "plain vanilla preferred" stock (that is, nonvoting, nonconvertible preferred with no rights to participation in corporate growth) is ignored. Thus, if Y Corp is worth $10 million and has two classes of stock outstanding, voting common stock and plain vanilla preferred with a liquidation preference of $9 million, X Corp will have control of Y Corp within the meaning of section 1504(a)(2) so long as it owns at least 80% of the common stock, even though that represents only $800,000 out of the apparent $10 million value of Y Corp. In contrast, control under section 368(c) would not be satisfied unless X Corp also owned 80% of the preferred.

Note that although control of an affiliated group as defined in section 1504(a)(2) is the prerequisite to filing a consolidated return, the filing of a consolidated return is not a prerequisite to the application of section 332. Indeed, if a consolidated return has been filed, many of the results discussed here will be displaced by those contained in the consolidated return regulations promulgated under section 1502.

These rules, which implement the general aversion to cascading corporate-level taxes on profits that have not been distributed out of corporate solution, produce an overall result very close to that which would have obtained if the subsidiary structure had never existed, as far as the parent-subsidiary transactions are concerned. There are, however, several technical differences. For instance, if either parent or subsidiary has a deficit in earnings and profits, the deficit in that corporation's account may only reduce the combined earnings and profits accumulated after the liquidation date and not the previously accumulated earnings and profits of the other corporation. § 381(c)(2)(B). Similarly, if the parent has a carryover loss, it may not be carried back to reduce the subsidiary's income in years prior to the liquidation. § 381(b)(3). Any carryover loss of the subsidiary may only be carried forward. § 381(c)(1).

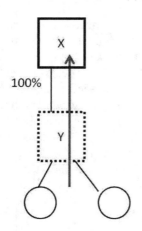

100% ownership no gain or loss

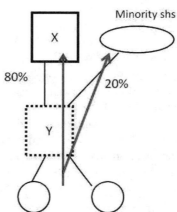

gain but not loss on distribution
to minority shs
Section 336(d)

332 liquidation to minority shs when 332 applies

Moreover, the tax consequences for the part of the transaction involving minority shareholders are still determined under sections 331 and 336. Nonrecognition is available to the liquidating subsidiary only to the extent that transfers are made to the controlling corporation. Under section 336(d)(3), however, no losses will be recognized, even on distributions to minority shareholders.

**Operation of Section 381 in Section 332
Liquidations with Minority Shareholders**

Sections 381 and 337 seem to strongly indicate that the controlling parent succeeds to all of the tax attributes of the 100% controlled subsidiary when the latter is liquidated. Thus all of the subsidiary's earnings and profits and all of its carryover items are inherited by the parent.

But what should happen when there has been a distribution to minority shareholders? There is nothing in the language of section 381(c), where one would normally look for the special rules that apply to the succession to tax attributes, that suggests that the parent should inherit less than 100% of the carryovers. Nor is there anything that indicates that the parent should inherit less than 100% of the earnings and profits.

But these provisions need to be understood in the context of the normal operation of section 312, which provides for determinations of e&p in connection with "a distribution of property by a corporation with respect to its stock." The core operative provisions in sections 312(a)–(c) are not restricted to ordinary operating distributions on stock — they can apply by their terms to dividend distributions, distributions in redemption and, apparently, distributions in liquidation. (While at first glance section 312(d)(1) might appear to carve out an exception for section 332 distributions by stating that property distributions are not treated as distributions of e&p if no gain is recognized to the distributee, it would not appear to prevent reduction of e&p for distributions to minority shareholders in the section 332 context, since there is gain recognition to the corporation on its distributions to minority shareholders. It appears that it would be appropriate to treat the liquidation transaction with respect to the minority shareholders as if it were a redemption of their interests. This redemption would have two effects, an increase in earnings and profits to the extent of the gain recognized with respect to the distribution to the minority interest, and a reduction of the earnings and profits by the adjusted basis of distributed property (or fair market value in the case of appreciated property) under section 312(a)(3), (b)(2) (or, alternatively, by analogy with section 312(n)(7), by the lesser amount representing the minority interest's proportionate share of those earnings). The language in the regulations under section 381 suggests that this is the correct result. Reg. section 1.381(c)(2)-1(c)(2) provides that the earnings and profits of the controlled subsidiary at the time of the liquidating distribution are computed by "taking into account the amount of earnings and profits properly applicable to distributions to minority stockholders, regardless of whether such distributions actually occur before or after the close of the date of distribution," that is, before or after transfers to the controlling parent.

6.2.1.   Conditions Prerequisite to Sections 332 and 337

Section 332 is not an expressly elective provision, but taxpayers can essentially elect into or out of the provision by satisfying, or failing to satisfy, the specific requirements over which they have control before the liquidation. The statute dictates that there must be a plan to completely liquidate within three years of the adoption of the plan, so presumably if there were no actions that could be construed as creating such a plan, the section would not apply. Section 332(b)(2) nevertheless provides that if all liquidating distributions occur within a taxable year, the resolution of the shareholders (or presumably of the Board, when no additional shareholder action is required under the corporate charter for dissolution) to distribute the assets constitutes a plan. *See also* Burnside Veneer Co. v. Commissioner, 167 F.2d 214 (6th Cir. 1948) (no formal plan necessary if completed in one year).

Second, there must be "control" within the meaning of the statute. The real significance of the plan requirement is the establishment of the date on which this key element in a section 332 transaction, the presence of "control," is to be initially determined. Purchases of stock that result in the acquisition of control preceding a liquidation will be honored and nonrecognition under section 332 will be allowed. So it is crucial that, if such adjustments to the stock holdings or corporate equity structure are to be made in order to qualify the transaction under section 332, they be made at a point before the adoption of the "plan" under which the assets are to be distributed. *Compare* Rev. Rul. 70-106, 1970-1 C.B. 70 (the prior agreement between minority and majority shareholders, whereby parent acquired 80% control to achieve section 332 liquidation, constituted the plan; thus the liquidation was not within section 332) *and* Estate of Glass v. Commissioner, 55 T.C. 543 (1970), *aff'd per curiam*, 453 F.2d 1375 (5th Cir. 1972) (corporation that acquired control after plan to liquidate 75%-owned subsidiary could not use step transaction doctrine to integrate and satisfy the section 332 requirements), *with* George L. Riggs, Inc. v. Commissioner, 64 T.C. 474 (1975) *acq.* 1976-2 C.B. 2 (notification to shareholders of intent to sell all assets, redemption of all preferred, tender offer for minority shares and liquidation of subsidiaries did not constitute plan of liquidation of corporation since a "mere general intention to liquidate" is not a plan) *and* Rev. Rul. 75-521, 1975-2 C.B. 120 (honoring acquisition of 50% of stock necessary to acquire control when "immediately after" this acquisition a plan was adopted).

Finally, the statute indicates that control must be maintained until the liquidation of the subsidiary is completed. Presumably sales of stock that resulted in a loss of control would prevent the application of the statute. *See* Granite Trust Co. v. United States, 238 F.2d 670 (1st Cir. 1956) (sales after adoption of plan of liquidation destroyed section 1504(a) control and rendered liquidation taxable); Commissioner v. Day & Zimmermann, Inc., 151 F.2d 517 (3d Cir. 1945) (selling some shares before adopting plan of liquidation permits opting out of section 332).

Although the statute requires that there be a plan to liquidate, there is no requirement that any particular state law procedure be used. Thus, distributions of assets to controlling shareholders accomplished through merger transactions have long been held to qualify as liquidations. *See* Reg. § 1.332-2(d).

Generally, retention of assets by a "liquidating" subsidiary will disqualify the liquidation, if the assets are used to continue the subsidiary's trade or business. *See* Rev. Rul. 76-525, 1976-2 C.B. 98. However, there may be some possibility of retaining assets for corporate law purposes merely to keep the corporate name alive. *See* Rev. Rul. 84-2, 1984-1 C.B. 92 (nominal part of liquidated subsidiary's assets transferred to new subsidiary to retain corporate name).

The last steps of some corporate acquisition transactions will sometimes include the liquidation of a Target whose assets have been transferred to an Acquirer in a reorganization under section 368. Although frequently referred to either as "liquidations" or as "distributions," these transactions will be governed by the special rules of section 361(c), and not by the rules of either section 311 or section 332.

What Is Section 337(c) All About?

In many situations under subchapter C, it may be possible to aggregate the stock owned by affiliated corporations for the purposes of applying rules that define "ownership" of stock and whether there is sufficient ownership to amount to "control." Such an approach is rarely taken unless the statue clearly allows it, and the statute usually provides operating rules to determine exactly how this indirect control can be established. Within affiliated groups filing a consolidated return, however, the presumption is the other way around, that is, the ownership of all members of the group can ordinarily be aggregated.

Section 337(c) contains a clear rule to the contrary, that prevents aggregation for section 337 purposes even for consolidated groups. This provision was added in 1987 to block "mirror" transactions. These mirror transactions would have defeated the spirit of General Utilities repeal because they would have allowed the separation of assets held by a corporation to occur under circumstances in which the Acquirer could choose whether to hold the assets acquired with Target's old basis or with a fair market value basis (or, more precisely, in a subsidiary that it held with a fair market value basis).

In its simplest form, the Acquirer would create new subsidiaries and fund them with the cash to be used to buy a portion of the Target stock. Target would then be liquidated into these subsidiaries. If Acquirer wanted to use Target's basis in assets, it would then liquidate the appropriate subsidiary. But if it wanted to dispose of Target's low basis assets without recognizing gain on them, Acquirer would sell the stock of its new subsidiary.

X is parent of consolidated group

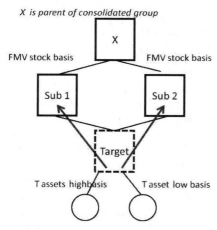

Step 1: X creates Sub1 and Sub2
Funds with cash used to buy T stock

Step 2 liquidate Target into Sub 1 and Sub 2

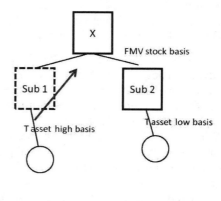

X now could choose to use T's old asset basis (by liquidating Sub 1) for some assets, while disposing of others with no gain by selling the stock of Sub 2 held with a fmv basis.

"Mirror" transactions not possible

Section 337(c) provides that an 80% distributee must hold sub stock directly

6.2.2. Debt in Connection With Liquidations

a. Distributions on Subsidiary Debt Held by Parent

Section 337(b) provides that if the controlling parent also holds debt of the liquidating subsidiary, the liquidating transfer to the parent in respect of the debt will nevertheless be treated as a nonrecognition distribution under section 332 (assuming that the section applies generally). This avoids the possibility of requiring recognition of gain (or allowing recognition of loss) to the liquidating corporation that would ordinarily be associated with the transfer of property in satisfaction of debt.

While the subsidiary is protected by this explicit rule from gain or loss recognition on transfers to satisfy its debt held by the parent, the parent is not. The section 332 regulations make clear that the parent will recognize any gain or loss realized on the debt satisfaction at the time of the liquidation, should it hold the debt with a basis different from the amount received. Reg. § 1.332-7 (parent subject to tax where amount received in payment exceeds parent's basis in the debt).

The existence of subsidiary debt also raises the possibility of application of the "no net value" principles in connection with purported section 332 liquidations. If the subsidiary has only enough assets to pay off the debt (or can pay off only a portion of the debt), the parent will not receive any distribution of property in respect of its subsidiary stock and the liquidation will fail section 332's requirement of property distributions in respect of stock. Instead, the "liquidation" (which it turns out is only the payment of property to satisfy the debt) will in many situations be subject to the general principles of tax law that apply when property is transferred in satisfaction of debt. *See* Rev. Rul. 59-296, 1959-2 C.B. 87; Rev. Rul 68-602, 1968-2 C.B. 135, both superseded by Rev. Rul. 2003–125, 2003–2 C.B. 1243.

The application of section 332 is also complicated in those situations in which a parent corporation with multiple stock interests in the liquidating subsidiary does not receive some property in respect of each class of stock. *See* Prop. Reg. § 1.332-2(b) (adopting the position in Spaulding Bakeries, Inc. v. Commissioner, 27 T.C. 684 (1957), *aff'd* 252 F.2d 693 (2d Cir. 1958)); H. K. Porter Co. v. Commissioner, 87 T.C. 689 (1986) (section 332 nonrecognition is inapplicable unless the parent corporation receives "at least partial payment for each class of stock"). Accordingly, if there are only enough funds to make required distributions on the preferred stock but not on the common stock, section 332 will not apply. In such cases, the purported subsidiary liquidation might be governed by section 331 or perhaps section 368 (depending on the other circumstances of the transaction). The parent corporation may be eligible for a worthless security deduction under section 165(g).

Whether a parent can gratuitously cancel subsidiary debt prior to a liquidation has been addressed in a number of revenue rulings, with no clear answer emerging. *Compare* Rev. Rul. 68-602, 1968-2 C.B. 135 (ruling that cancellation of debt between parent and wholly owned insolvent subsidiary immediately prior to liquidation will be disregarded and liquidation will not qualify under section 332), *with* Rev. Rul. 78-330, 1978-2 C.B. 147 (suggesting that in some cases gratuitous cancellation of subsidiary debt that has independent economic substance could be respected in analysis of solvency of subsidiary prior to a merger) *and* CCA 200818005 (ruling that deemed transactions in a section 338(h)(10) election must have the consequences that the actual transactions would have, and finding that the deemed liquidation would not qualify as a section 332 liquidation because no property was received in respect of the stock interest, even after debt cancellation).

b.   Parent Debt Distributed by Subsidiary

A parent corporation may also be indebted to its controlled subsidiary. What happens when the subsidiary distributes the parent's debt back to the parent in the liquidation and the subsidiary's basis in the debt is less than the amount due? An older revenue ruling, Rev. Rul. 74-54, 1974-1 C.B. 76, indicates that section 332 trumps the ordinary cancellation of debt rules and provides nonrecognition to the parent, even though the debt is extinguished when the parent receives it in the liquidating distribution. Changes to the rules for original issue discount and cancellation of debt income under section 108 cast doubt on this result. *See* Notice 90-90, 1991-1 C.B. 774 (indicating that Treasury considers it appropriate for a parent to take into account its cancellation of indebtedness income in such a situation).

PRACTICE PROBLEMS

1.   Parent Co. owns all of the stock of Sub Co., and has a basis of $20 in that stock. Sub Co. owns only one asset, which has a fair market value of $100 and a basis of $50. If Sub Co. is liquidated, what are the results to Parent?

(a)   Parent recognizes loss of $20 on stock of Sub and has basis of $50 in asset.

(b)   Parent recognizes gain of $80 on stock and has basis of $50 in asset.

(c)   Parent recognizes no gain and has basis of $50 in asset.

(d)   Parent recognizes gain of $80 and has basis of $130 in asset.

2.   Parent Co. owns all of the stock of Sub Co., and has a basis of $20 in that stock. Sub Co. owns only one asset, which has a fair market value of $100 and a basis of $50. If Sub Co. is liquidated, what are the results to Sub Co.?

(a)   Sub has gain of $50.

(b)   Sub has no gain.

(c)   Cannot tell until Parent sells.

3.   Parent Co. owns all of the stock of Sub Co., and has a basis of $20 in that stock. Sub Co. owns only one asset, which has a fair market value of $100 and a basis of $130. If Sub Co. is liquidated, what are the results to Sub Co.?

(a)   No loss recognized.

(b)   Loss of $30 recognized.

(c)   No loss to Sub, but Parent's basis in Sub stock is increased by $30.

4.   Parent Co. owns 80% of the stock of Sub Co., and has a basis of $20 in that stock. The other 20% is owned by an individual.

Sub Co. owns only one asset, which has a fair market value of $100 and a basis of $50.

If Sub Co. is liquidated in kind, what are the results to Sub Co.?

(a) No gain.

(b) Gain of $10.

(c) Gain of $50.

5.   Parent Co. owns 80% of the stock of Sub Co., and has a basis of $20 in that stock. The other 20% is owned by an individual.

Sub Co. owns only one asset, which has a fair market value of $100 and a basis of $130. If Sub Co is liquidated in kind, what are the results to Sub?

(a) No loss.

(b) Loss of $30.

(c) Loss of $6.

6.   Parent Co. owns 100% of the stock of Sub Co., and has a basis of $20 in that stock. Parent Co. also holds a note of Sub Co., reflecting debt owed by Sub Co. to Parent Co. of $60.

Sub Co. owns only one asset, which has a fair market value of $100 and a basis of $50. If Sub Co. is liquidated, what are the results to Sub Co.?

(a) Gain of $60.

(b) Gain of $30.

(c) No gain.

DISCUSSION PROBLEMS

1.   X Corp owns all of the stock of Y Corp and holds bonds of Y Corp in the face amount of $500,000. Y Corp holds two assets, one with a basis of $1.5 million and a fair market value of $2 million, and one with a basis of $1.7 million and a fair market value of $.4 million.

(a) What are the tax consequences of the liquidation of Y Corp?

(b) What are the tax consequences of the liquidation of Y Corp if it also has minority shareholders who own 20% of its stock?

(c) Y Corp had accumulated earnings and profits of $800,000 before it was liquidated. What is the effect of the liquidation on the earnings and profits of X Corp? Assume that the loss assets are distributed to X Corp and gain assets to minority shareholders.

(d) What if Y Corp had minority shareholders who owned only 20% of its common stock, and it issued preferred stock worth $100,000 to a friendly bank before the liquidation?

2.   As in problem 1 above, X Corp owns all of the stock of Y Corp, and holds bonds of Y Corp in the face amount of $500,000. Y Corp owns only one asset, with a basis of $100,000 and a fair market value of $350,000.

(a)   What is the consequence of a complete liquidation of Y Corp?

(b)   On the above facts, what if instead of bonds with a face amount of $500,000, X Corp held bonds of $200,000 and preferred stock with a liquidation preference of $300,000?

(c)   What if the asset had a basis of $600,000 and a fair market value of $350,000?

OTHER BUILDING BLOCK TRANSACTIONS

Chapter 7

REDEMPTIONS UNDER SECTION 302

Statutes and Regulations	IRC §§ 302(a); 302(c); 317; note § 303; 302(b)(1), (2), (5), (d); 318; 312(n) (7)
Other Primary Authorities	United States v. Davis, 397 U.S. 301 (1970) Cerone v. Commissioner, 87 T.C. 1 (1986) Rev. Rul. 75-502, 1975-2 C.B. 111 Rev. Rul. 77-226, 1977-2 C.B. 90 Rev. Rul. 75-447, 1975-2 C.B. 113 Notice 2001-45, 2001-2 C.B. 129

The sale of the stock of a corporation is the quintessential "sale or exchange of a capital asset," according to which the selling shareholder has no gain or other income unless the sale proceeds exceed her basis, and for which a preferential rate is likely to be applicable. This treatment stands in stark contrast to the tax treatment of dividends, which are generally taxed without basis offset and for which a preferential rate has not been applicable historically (although one currently applies under section 1(h)(11)). This contrast produces significant tension when the buying taxpayer is the issuing corporation. Should the transaction be treated as if the buyer were a third party, or as if the sale proceeds had merely been distributed without the shareholder's having relinquished any shares? Rather than adopt a single answer for all redemptions, the Code tests for dividend equivalence: distributions in redemption that are more like third-party sales are given exchange treatment, whereas those that do not sufficiently change the essential relationship between the shareholder and the corporation are treated as regular distributions.

The dividend-equivalence test is made more difficult by the fact that, as is the case throughout subchapter C, the same statutory rules are generally expected to suffice for closely held corporations in which even relatively small shareholders frequently may be able to influence the corporation, and for publicly held corporations in which only substantial shareholders and managers or directors can do so. Redemption transactions include some in which shareholders clearly have little control over the terms at which they may sell (including public tender offers by the issuer in which the shareholders can elect to participate), others in which shareholders have an enormous degree of control over the terms (redemptions of significant shareholders in closely held corporations), and still others in which it may not be so easy to assess the degree of shareholder control (including transactions to alter the relationships among shareholders in anticipation of infusions of additional capital).

7.1. THE APPLICABLE STATUTORY PROVISIONS

Section 317(b) indicates that stock is redeemed when a "corporation acquires its stock from a shareholder in exchange for property, whether or not the stock so acquired is cancelled, retired, or held as treasury stock." Section 317(a) indicates that property is to be broadly understood, but does not include the distributing company's stock (or stock rights). Thus, redemption encompasses stock buybacks or repurchases but not recapitalizations or other stock-for-stock exchanges.

The provisions of section 302 provide the guidelines for determining dividend equivalence for stock buybacks. Section 302 is one of several provisions in subchapter C designed to reinforce the separate entity and shareholder tax regimes by ensuring that corporate earnings that find their way into shareholders' hands are taxed as dividends (even though no transaction actually structured as a dividend distribution has occurred) when the shareholders receiving these earnings are in the same position as they would have been in had they simply received a dividend distribution. The "same position" for the purposes of this analysis involves both voting rights and the right to participate in the future earnings and growth of the corporation; and in most situations it includes not just rights that the shareholder directly holds, but also rights over which the shareholder can be presumed to have significant control, including those associated with stock owned by family members and controlled entities.

Section 302(a) confirms that a shareholder's sale of stock back to an issuing corporation will be honored as an exchange transaction taxed under the normal rules of section 1001 if one of the specific tests set out in section 302(b) is satisfied, while section 302(d) makes clear that the provisions in section 301 governing operating distributions will otherwise apply to distributions in redemption.

Why does it matter whether the transaction is honored as a sale or exchange? The reasons for corporate shareholders will be different than those for individual shareholders. First, any gain on a sale will usually be a capital gain, often taxed at a preferential rate for individuals but not for corporations and subject in both cases to the capital gains netting rules. Second, if the redemption is treated as an exchange, any basis in the redeemed shares will be used to offset some or all of the sale proceeds. The ability to take basis into account means that sale treatment is still usually desirable for individual shareholders, even though dividends are taxed at the lowest capital gain rate under still-temporary provisions originally enacted in 2003. Sale treatment will frequently be undesirable for corporations, however, since there is no special preferential rate for corporate capital gains and the dividends-received deduction (which reduces the taxable amount by at least 70%) is not applicable to sales proceeds. Only if the corporation has a high basis in the stock will it be more desirable for a corporation to have a redemption honored as a sale or exchange.

The "All or Nothing" Nature of the Section 302 Paradigm

Assume Ellen and Fred each own 1000 shares of ELFRED Inc and there are no other shareholders; the company has assets valued at $4 million with $3,500,000 of accumulated earnings and profits at the time of the transactions in question; and its shares are worth $2000 apiece.

If Ellen sells 750 shares to Sam, there is a taxable disposition with no effect on the corporation other than the fact that it now has three shareholders instead of two (its earnings and profits are the same and its assets are unchanged).

If instead ELFRED makes a cash distribution of $1.5 million ($750,000 to each shareholder), then it will be a dividend to Fred and Ellen. ELFRED's earnings and profits will be reduced to $2 million, and its net worth will be reduced to $2.5 million. Fred's and Ellen's relationship to the corporation and to each other remains unchanged.

What if ELFRED instead buys back half of each of its shareholders' shares? The pro rata redemption looks very much like the dividend distribution. Fred and Ellen continue in the same ownership relationship as before (though there are fewer shares, there is no difference in their respective ownership and control). The corporation's net worth has decreased just as it would in a dividend distribution (and its earnings and profits are decreased also).

What if, instead, ELFRED makes a non pro rata redemption, buying back 750 of Ellen's shares for $1.5 million but none of Fred's? Then the value of ELFRED has been reduced to $2.5 million and Ellen's ownership has been reduced from 50% to 20% while Fred's ownership has increased from 50% to 80%.

Potential approaches to taxation of Ellen's redemption include:

(1) ***Bifurcation option (hypothetical):*** *treat as in part a sale by Ellen to Fred (to account for Ellen's decreased interest and Fred's increased interest in ownership of the corporation) and in part a distribution to Ellen from the corporation (to account for the remaining amount received by Ellen).*

From Ellen's perspective, Ellen can be viewed as selling to Fred 30% of the corporation (her interest declined to 20%, his increased to 80%). That 30% interest amounts to 3/5 of her 1000 shares or 600 shares. Since each share prior to the transaction is worth $2,000, that means that Ellen would be viewed as having sold 600 shares to Fred for $1.2 million in an exchange governed by section 1001. Ellen would then be treated as receiving the remaining $300,000 of the repurchase price in a distribution of earnings that is subject to the rules for distributions by corporations under section 301 (accounting for the value received in respect of the remaining 150 shares).

(One can also consider Fred's side of Ellen's deemed exchange with Fred under this bifurcation hypothesis. Fred would be treated as purchasing 600 of Ellen's shares, accounting for his increased interest in the corporation after the redemption. Since Fred holds only 1000 shares after the entire transaction is complete, Fred must also have sold 600 shares back to the corporation for their fair market value, resulting in Fred's receipt of the $1.2 million he is deemed to have used to purchase the stock from Ellen. Fred's deemed redemption is one that will also need to be analyzed under section 302 to determine the tax consequences to Fred.)

After all is said and done, the corporation has $1.5 million less than it had before the redemption, Ellen has 750 fewer shares and $1.5 million more cash, and Fred owns 30% more of the corporation than he did prior to the transaction.

> *(2) All or nothing option (section 302):* treat according to its dominant characteristics as either a sale *(if it materially alters the redeeming shareholder's position relative to the other shareholders, like the taxable disposition to Sam)* or a section 301 distribution *(if it leaves the shareholders in essentially the same position relative to other shareholders as before the buyback, like the taxable dividend).*
>
> The Code in section 302 adopts the "all or nothing" option, treating redemptions that are "not essentially equivalent to a dividend" as exchanges but those that are "essentially equivalent to a dividend" as dividends.

Section 302 makes the most sense when one considers its application to closely-held corporations, in which shareholders have enough control, either individually or collectively, to avoid direct payment of dividends by arranging to have their stock redeemed. Its provisions nevertheless apply to all corporations and all shareholders, whether such a level of control is likely to exist or not.

Section 302(b) contains four provisions that at first reading seem to offer mutually exclusive routes to sale-or-exchange treatment. One of those provisions, section 302(b)(4) covering partial liquidations, is quite different. It is tested from the corporation's perspective and relates to significant contractions or discontinuations of a corporate business. That provision will be considered in section 7.5. The remaining three provisions focus on what has happened to the shareholder. They set out two safe harbors that provide objective criteria for determining whether a shareholder's interest is sufficiently reduced to warrant exchange treatment and one general economic substance provision that may apply even when neither of the safe harbors is applicable. Section 302(b)(2) provides a formulaic safe harbor, applicable only to those who hold a voting interest in a corporation, that measures a shareholder's loss of participation in the corporation that results in a "substantially disproportionate" redemption. Section 302(b)(3) provides a safe harbor that is available when a shareholder no longer actually owns any stock. Although many such "complete terminations" would also satisfy the "substantially disproportionate" test, some might fail because of attributed ownership. Section 302(b)(3) therefore sets out the conditions under which some of the attribution rules will not apply. Finally, section 302(b)(1) provides the overarching standard for determining whether a redemption should be treated as an exchange from the shareholder's point of view: it will be so treated when it is "not essentially equivalent to a dividend."

For the purposes of section 302, the measure of a shareholder's participation includes not just the stock actually owned by that shareholder, but also stock owned by taxpayers over which the shareholder can be presumed to have some control. Section 318 operates in specified contexts to attribute ownership from one owner to another owner, and will be discussed in this chapter. (A note of caution: attribution rules are complex, and there are several versions in the Code. Each only applies for the purposes of the specific Code sections that explicitly reference the attribution provision. Application is complicated by the fact that a Code section that incorporates an attribution rule may modify its operation within that particular section.)

Finally, there are rules treating redemptions to pay death taxes as per se exchanges, governed by section 303, and for treating stock acquisitions between related corporations as redemptions that must be tested under section 302, governed by section 304. Those provisions will be dealt with in later chapters.

7.2. ATTRIBUTION OF STOCK OWNERSHIP UNDER SECTION 318

The application of section 302(b) is complicated by section 302(c), which directs that stock owned by parties related to a shareholder must be treated as owned by the shareholder when evaluating the effect of a redemption. The attribution rules are provided in section 318. Perhaps a shortcut way of grasping section 318 is to appreciate that it sets up presumptions about when various parties can appropriately be deemed to control the actions of other parties and thus to be in effective control of their stock. The statute has in general been treated as creating irrebuttable presumptions — the few taxpayers who have attempted to argue that these presumptions should not apply because of the reality of their personal situations have in most cases failed to convince the deciding authority that the attribution rules do not apply.

Section 318(a) provides four main types of attribution rules in paragraphs (1) through (4), governing family attribution, entity attribution (often referred to as "upstream" attribution from entities to owners), owner attribution (often referred to as "downstream" attribution from owners to entities), and option attribution.

Paragraph (5) provides "operating rules" for reattributing ownership that has already been attributed under the basic four rules, and that reattributed ownership can be reattributed yet again to another owner, so long as the reattribution does not violate the operating rules. This possibility of cascading reattribution engenders considerable complexity, since a particular redeeming shareholder may be both grandparent of another shareholder, holder of an option on stock that is held by a person whose ownership would be attributed to her, and owner of partnership or corporate interests that also own stock in the relevant corporation, resulting in various ways that ownership might be attributed to the shareholder through these other relationships. The operation of the attribution rules is intended to attribute the actual outstanding stock (or, in some cases, to treat options as though they were also outstanding stock); it should not result in multiple counting of the same share of stock. Thus, although if one applied the rules to all of the shareholders and totaled the interests so attributed, the total would exceed 100% if any of the relevant relationships were found, the ownership attributed to any one shareholder should never be greater than 100%.

The regulations provide three additional very important attribution rules. First, a corporation is not considered as owning its own stock under downstream attribution. Reg. § 1.318-1(b)(1). Second, in attempting to determine how much a person owns altogether under the attribution rules, the pathway that results in the largest stock ownership is applied (but including any one block of stock only once along that entire pathway). Reg. § 1.318-1(b)(2). Finally, in the rules for which there is a threshold ownership requirement before ownership can be attributed to a corporation from a shareholder or to that shareholder from the corporation, the attribution rules are also applied to determine whether the shareholder satisfies the threshold requirement — i.e., both actual and constructive ownership is taken into consideration for the threshold requirement. Reg. § 1.318-1(b)(3).

7.2.1. Attribution from Family Members (The "Family Attribution Rule")

Under section 318(a)(1), a person is deemed to own whatever stock in the relevant corporation is owned by his spouse, parents, children, and grandchildren — i.e., looking down from the relevant person two generations (children or grandchildren) but up only one generation (parents). He is not deemed to own stock owned by his siblings, his grandparents, or his great-grandchildren. (Note that this rule is significantly less broad than the family attribution rule under section 267, which can attribute ownership from any linear ancestor or descendant, as well as spouse and siblings.) Accordingly, if Mary owns 10% of May Corp and Mary's mother and grandmother each own 45% of May Corp, Mary will be treated as owning a total of 55% of May Corp — 10% directly and 45% by family attribution from her mother.

7.2.2. Attribution from Entities (The "Upstream Attribution Rule")

Under subsections 318(a)(2)(A) and (B), a partner or trust beneficiary is deemed to own stock owned by a pass-through entity in which he has an interest, according to his proportionate interest in the pass-through entity. There is less likely to be attribution from corporations because the provision includes a threshold ownership requirement: under section 318(a)(2)(C), a shareholder of a corporation is deemed to own stock in a second corporation that is owned by the first corporation only if he owns 50% or more of the *value* of the stock of the first corporation, and then the attribution is in proportion by value. An example may be helpful. If Max owns 56% of Max Corp and Max Corp owns 10% of Sub Corp, then Max satisfies the threshold ownership for upstream attribution (he owns at least 50% of the value of Max Corp), so Max Corp's ownership of Sub Corp will be attributed "upstream" proportionately to Max. Max will be treated as owning 5.6% of Sub Corp.

7.2.3. Attribution to Entities (The "Downstream Attribution Rule")

Under subsections 318(a)(3)(A) and (B), a pass-through entity is deemed to own all of the stock owned by its owners (unless, in the case of trusts, the beneficiary's interest is "a remote contingent interest," defined in the statute as representing 5% or less of the value of the entity under an actuarial calculation). Again, there is less likely to be attribution to corporations: a corporation is only deemed to own all of the stock owned by those shareholders who own 50% or more of the value of its stock. If Max owns 10% of May Corp and 52% of Max Corp, Max Corp will be treated as owning 10% of May Corp through downstream attribution from Max, but May Corp will not be treated as owning any of Max Corp, since Max lacks the requisite threshold ownership of May Corp to permit downstream attribution to May Corp of other stocks owned by Max.

7.2.4.   Attribution of Options

If a taxpayer owns an option to purchase stock, or an option to acquire an option in stock, he is treated as owning the stock.

7.2.5.   Reattribution

Under section 318(a)(5), once stock is treated as owned by a particular person under section 318(a), it can be reattributed to another person by applying the rules again, subject to the limitations set out in subparagraphs (A) through (E).

Significantly, there is no successive reattribution under the family rules; otherwise, siblings would own each other's stock by reattribution from parents. Section 318(a)(5)(B).

Section 318(a)(5)(C) does not permit stock that has been attributed from one owner to an entity under section 318(a)(3) to be reattributed from the entity to another owner under section 318(a)(2): such "downstream-upstream" (sometimes called "sideways" or "in and out") reattribution would otherwise result in all partners being treated as owners of each other's stock.

These limitations do not prevent other combinations of applications of the attribution rules. Thus, if a taxpayer is deemed to own stock both through the family attribution rule and through the option attribution rule, the latter stock can be reattributed under the family rule even if the former cannot. Nor do the limitations block option attribution when the taxpayer has an option on stock owned by a family member.

For example, suppose Greatgrandad actually owns only 10% of a corporation after a repurchase is complete, Dad owns 35% and Son owns 20%. Dad's 35% is attributable to Greatgrandad under the family rules (from two generations down) but Son's 20% is not. Son's 20% can be attributed to Dad, making Dad a 55% owner, but it cannot be reattributed from Dad to Greatgrandad, since that would violate the prohibition against successive applications of the family attribution rule in section 318(a)(5)(B). However, if Dad also owns an option on half of Son's interest, that 10% is attributed to Dad under the option attribution rule, and will be re-attributed to Greatgrandad, resulting in Greatgrandad's owning directly 10% and by attribution both Dad's 35% and Dad's 10% owned under the option rule.

7.3.   REDEMPTIONS TESTED FROM THE SHAREHOLDER'S PERSPECTIVE

7.3.1.   The "Not Essentially Equivalent to a Dividend" Standard

When a shareholder sells stock back to the issuing corporation, the transaction will be honored as a sale if it is "not essentially equivalent to a dividend" under section 301(b)(1). The statute says nothing more about what dividend equivalence means, and what is known comes generally from a small number of sources: the legislative history, the decision in *United States v. Davis*, 397 U.S. 301 (1970), and the Service's rulings (and of course, the safe harbors provided in subsections 302(b)(2) and (3)).

The legislative history is generally accepted as accurately explaining the provision: it was intended to ensure that those taxpayers who could not satisfy the objective standard of subsection 302(b)(2), but who were unlikely to have been in a position to choose a redemption rather than a dividend, would not be treated as receiving a dividend distribution. The *Davis* decision is consistent with the legislative history. There, Bradley and his family owned all the shares of a corporation at the time that the corporation redeemed Bradley's preferred stock. The Court held that the attribution rules applied to each of the section 302(b) redemption tests: in the *Davis* case, the result was a redemption of some stock by a sole shareholder. To qualify for exchange treatment, the *Davis* Court concluded that "a redemption must result in a meaningful reduction of the shareholder's proportionate interest in the corporation." Such a reduction is simply not possible for a sole shareholder without a complete termination of the interest, since even one share remaining would represent 100% of the stock.

It is unclear how much of a loss of voting control should be sufficient to satisfy section 302(b)(1). The courts have sometimes found adequate loss of control even when a redeemed shareholder continues to hold more than 50%, if the redemption caused the shareholder to hold less than necessary for some significant corporate events. *See, e.g.*, Wright v. United States, 482 F.2d 600 (8th Cir. 1973). The Treasury Department and Service have rejected such arguments. *See* Rev. Rul. 78-401, 1978-2 C.B. 127. On the other hand, the Service has ruled that when shareholders whose voting rights represent an insignificant part of the governance, rights of the corporation are redeemed, the transaction will be treated as "not essentially equivalent to a dividend." Because of the Supreme Court's language in *Davis*, however, the Service has insisted that the redemption actually results in a decline in the percentage ownership of the shareholder in question. For even the smallest shareholder, participation in a redemption that is pro rata will result in dividend treatment. *See* Reg. § 1.302-2(b).

What Constitutes a "Meaningful Reduction"?

Majority Shareholders:

Rev. Rul. 78-401, 1978-2 C.B. 127 (reduction from 90% to 60% is not meaningful, because shareholder still had control of corporation even though shareholder could no longer control extraordinary transactions because of state law supermajority requirement, at least where there is no indication that any such transactions were likely to occur).

Rev. Rul. 75-502, 1975-2 C.B. 111 (reduction from 57% to deadlock with 50% of the voting stock (and proportionate reduction in earnings and liquidation rights) is meaningful, because reduced from majority control to deadlock with the other owner).

Minority Shareholders:

Rev. Rul. 76-364, 1976-2 C.B. 91 (losing influence as a swing voter can be meaningful, where prior to redemption shareholder could combine with any one other shareholder to control decisions, but after redemption any two of the other shareholders could control decisions.

> *Rev. Rul. 76-385, 1976-2 C.B. 92 (any reduction in holding by minority shareholder with very few shares in large publicly traded corporation is meaningful, since shareholder never had any degree of control).*
>
> *Rev. Rul. 81-289, 1981-2 C.B. 82 (proportionate reduction of all shareholders who participate in tender offer is not meaningful and treated as a dividend).*
>
> Nonvoting Shareholders:
>
> *Rev. Rul. 77-426, 1977-2 CB 87 (redemption of 5% of preferred by shareholder who owns only nonvoting preferred is an exchange, even though shareholder continues to own 100% of the nonvoting preferred outstanding — this results because common shareholders increase their economic rights at the cost of the preferred shareholder).*
>
> *Rev. Rul. 85-106, 1985-2 C.B. 116 (redemption of preferred by shareholder who owns both preferred and common is not a meaningful reduction, because control remains unaffected).*

Another question that arises in this context is whether family hostilities in a family-owned corporation are relevant to determining whether a reduction is meaningful. It seems clear that the family attribution rules would apply, even when there are hostilities among the various owners, to make each owner a sole shareholder for purposes of testing the redemption under the safe harbors. But should animosity between the family members be taken into consideration nonetheless in applying the *Davis* interpretation of section 302(b)(1)? A Tax Court case, *Cerone v. Commissioner*, 87 T.C. 1 (1986), suggests that it may be.

Under section 302(b)(5), the failure of a transaction to meet the standards of the other provisions of section 302(b) is not to be taken into account in determining whether section 302(b)(1) should apply.

7.3.2. The "Substantially Disproportionate" Standard

Section 302(b)(2) provides a safe harbor, assuring shareholders that they will receive exchange treatment if its standards are met. The "substantially disproportionate" standard in section 302(b)(2) has three critical components: a threshold test, an ownership reduction requirement, and an anti-abuse provision.

The threshold test, set out in section 302(b)(2)(B), denies the safe harbor to a shareholder who retains 50% of the voting power.

If the threshold test is satisfied, the ownership reduction test requires a "substantially disproportionate" redemption, which requires a reduction in both voting stock and common stock ownership to less than 80% of the percentage of each such type of stock owned immediately before the transaction. This can be expressed as:

$$\frac{\text{stock owned after}}{\text{stock outstanding after}} \quad < \quad .8 \quad * \quad \frac{\text{stock owned before}}{\text{stock outstanding before}}$$

The anti-abuse provision makes the safe harbor inapplicable if the redemption is made under a plan with a purpose or effect of a series of redemptions that result in a distribution (in the aggregate) that is not substantially disproportionate.

These tests are fairly easy to apply as long as the redeeming shareholder owns only common stock. Suppose he owned 1000 shares of common stock, representing 10% of the only class of stock in the corporation before the corporation purchased 600 of his shares from him. After the redemption, he clearly owns less than 50% of the voting power, so he satisfies the threshold test. Before the transaction, he owned 10% of the stock (1000 out of 10,000); after the transaction he owned 4.25% (400 out of 9400). Since his retained ownership (4.25%) is less than 80% of his prior ownership (10%), this is a substantially disproportionate reduction. The provision anticipates that only outstanding stock will be included in the calculation, see Reg. § 1.302-3(a)(3), so a redemption reduces not only the shareholder's holding, but also the total amount of stock outstanding. Thus in this example, the shareholder would be able to satisfy the statutory standard so long as *more* than 200 shares were redeemed.

Things are considerably murkier when more than one class of stock is involved. Section 302(b)(2) seems primarily aimed at redemptions of voting common stock, although it includes a somewhat cryptic reference to situations in which there is also nonvoting common involved. How should section 302(b)(2) apply if a shareholder who owns both voting common and nonvoting preferred redeems both types of stock? Reg. § 1.302-3 answers the question with what has been called the "preferred piggyback rule": so long as a shareholder is redeeming both voting and nonvoting stock and satisfies the ownership reduction tests as to the voting stock, the nonvoting stock can "piggyback" on the test and get exchange treatment as well. (Sales of preferred stock can bring with them a different set of complications under section 306, discussed in Chapter 9.)

What if a shareholder redeems only *non*voting stock or stock rights? The regulations conclude that the safe harbor cannot apply at all. *See* Reg. §§ 1.302-3(a)(3), 1.302-2(a).

These answers perhaps can be explained with the notion that the provision is intended to be an objective test looking for a substantial reduction in the shareholder's ability to control, for which the primary characteristic is the ability to vote on shareholder decisions. *See, e.g.*, Benjamin v. Commissioner, 66 T.C. 1084 (1976), *aff'd* 592 F.2d 1259 (5th Cir. 1979) (indicating that the right to vote is the most significant of the rights associated with a proprietary interest in a corporation). But it would appear that a shareholder who owns only *voting* preferred stock *can* rely on section 302(b)(2) if some of that voting preferred stock is redeemed, even though the test for reduction in common stock ownership cannot be applied. Rev. Rul. 81-41, 1981-1 C.B. 121. Other issues are resolved similarly to their resolution elsewhere: stock with contingent voting rights, for example, will not count as voting stock until the contingency occurs and the rights are vested. Reg. § 1.302-3(a)(3).

The anti-abuse provision in section 302(b)(2)(D) aggregates all the distributions to each shareholder in a series of related redemptions and tests to see if the substantially disproportionate result has been reversed by the later redemptions, so that, for instance, a shareholder whose shares are repurchased shortly before another shareholder has shares repurchased gives up majority control only temporarily. For example, if shareholders A and B are the only shareholders of a corporation, each owning 500 shares of the voting common stock, and A plans to have the corporation redeem 250 of her shares in two months, B could have the corporation redeem 250 of B's shares this month and claim a substantially disproportionate reduction (from 50% to 25% of the voting and common stock is substantially disproportionate, since 25% is less than 80% of 50%). But after both A's and B's redemptions take place, the proportionate ownership would be the same as before either redemption. Thus, B's redemption should not qualify as an exchange under the test. *See* Rev. Rul. 85-14, 1985-1 C.B. 92 (noting that a "plan" does not require joint planning by the two shareholders, but merely one shareholder's decision to piggyback on another shareholder's redemption). The provision directs a result that would likely be reached in any event, if the step transaction doctrine were applied.

7.3.3. Complete Terminations

On a quick reading, section 302(b)(3) seems to be setting out a completely different standard governing when shareholders sell all of their stock. Actually, such a redemption would in most cases automatically meet the tests of substantial disproportion in section 302(b)(2), if the attribution rules did not apply, and would certainly satisfy the "not essentially equivalent to a dividend" test in section 302(b)(1). Thus the most important effect of sections 302(b)(3) and 302(c)(2) is to establish the conditions which must be satisfied in order for the government to waive the application of the family attribution rule.

In general, the shareholder seeking to avoid family attribution must:

- relinquish all relationships with the corporation, including those as employee or director (creditor relationships are allowed, perhaps so that the consideration for the redemption can be debt);

- refrain from acquiring any interest for ten years; and

- file an agreement to notify the IRS of any change in status that would affect eligibility under section 302(c)(2).

The waiver provision in section 302(c)(2)(A)(i) requires that a shareholder have "no interest (including an interest as officer, director, or employee), other than an interest as a creditor." This raises questions about what will constitute a prohibited "interest" in the corporation and what constitutes an acceptable "creditor" interest. The Ninth Circuit interpreted this language in *Lynch v. Commissioner*, 801 F.2d 1176 (9th Cir. 1986), as a bright-line rule intended to provide "definite standards" rather than to require a factual analysis. Rev. Rul. 59-119, 1959-1 C.B. 68, provides additional insight on the kinds of continuing relationships that might be problematic, such as having a nominee who sits on the board of directors as the retiring shareholder's representative. Even acquisition of an interest in a parent or subsidiary of the redeemed corporation violates the requirement. Reg. § 1.302-4(c). The regulations also flesh out the characteristics of a genuine creditor relationship that is acceptable, including a prohibition against actually receiving stock in the corporation as a remedy for a default. Reg. § 1.302-4(d), (e). Accordingly, as in other contexts, the federal tax characterization of an interest will depend on its substance and not merely its form as debt.

The prohibition against re-acquiring an interest in the corporation looks ahead 10 years, but a special anti-abuse provision set out in section 302(c)(2)(B) looks back 10 years from the redemption to prevent a shareholder from first splitting up her interests among related parties, and then having only one of the separated interests terminated, if tax avoidance is the principal purpose motivating the transaction.

The Anti-abuse Provision in Section 302(c)(2)(B)

The ten-year look-back rule includes both an "acquire and redeem" provision, section 302(c)(2)(B)(i), and a "dispose of some and redeem the rest" provision, section 302(c)(2)(B)(ii). In either case the flush language requires that the relevant transaction — the acquisition in (i) or the disposition in (ii) — have tax avoidance as one of its principal purposes.

What tax avoidance gimmicks are these provisions attempting to prevent? Consider a family corporation in which the founding matriarch owns 100% of the stock. At her retirement, she may well want to gift some of the stock to her daughter, who will take over the corporation, while having the corporation repurchase the remainder of her stock, to provide a nest egg for her retirement. This is the typical scenario in which the complete termination and family attribution rule waiver provisions should apply to provide exchange treatment: there is clearly no tax avoidance purpose in the mother's disposition of the stock to her daughter.

But now assume that the daughter is only 16, and the mother makes the gift and redeems the rest of her shares because she wishes to take advantage of the complete termination provision to monetize some of her shares, which have a very high basis, while still retaining control. The corporation has considerable earnings and profits, so a simple dividend is undesirable. In this case, the waiver of family attribution would not be available and the redemption would be treated as a section 301 distribution.

Similarly, assume that the mother decides to give her daughter some liquidity because she learns that her daughter plans to marry a ne'er-do-well upon graduation from college. She gifts a block of stock to the daughter and arranges to have the corporation repurchase it upon her daughter's graduation. Without this provision, the daughter would be able to get exchange treatment when the corporation buys all of the stock back upon her graduation and marriage, even though this is in substance a distribution to the mother and gift of the cash from the mother to the daughter.

There is no provision for waiving attribution from or to entities. There is a rather intricate provision, section 318(a)(2)(C), which allows an entity to avoid the application of the family rules to produce deemed ownership in one of its owners and thus, by reattribution, deemed ownership to it. It only applies, however, when the owner of the entity has terminated all of her actual interest. Under this provision, for instance, all of the stock held by Mother's testamentary trust, in which Father has a substantial beneficial interest, may be redeemed and treated as a complete termination even though the children still actually own stock. Without the invocation of section 318(a)(2)(C), Father would be deemed to own the children's stock, and the Trust would be deemed to own what Father was deemed to own, potentially spoiling redemption treatment for the Trust.

7.4. SERIAL REDEMPTIONS, STEP TRANSACTIONS, AND *ZENZ*

In determining the effects of redemption transactions, there is considerable authority that the overall results of related transactions should be considered when characterizing the redemption. Sometimes this works to the detriment of shareholders; for instance, when, as section 302(b)(2)(D) specifically directs, a series of redemptions can be treated as a single transaction for the purposes of applying the disproportionate redemption rules.

Sometimes, however, this approach works to the advantage of the shareholders. In *Zenz v. Quinlivan*, 213 F.2d 914 (6th Cir. 1954), a sole taxpayer who sold a block of stock and then had the remainder redeemed was allowed sale-or-exchange treatment under pre-1954 law. (Why sell and redeem, rather than just sell? The smaller, post-redemption corporation will be worth less, and the acquisition will therefore be easier to finance.) In *Zenz* itself, it appears that the buyer also wanted earnings and profits to be reduced before he purchased, and without section 312(n)(7), earnings and profits would arguably be reduced by the full amount of the redemption proceeds. In Rev. Rul. 54-458, 1954-2 C.B. 167, the Service held that this same treatment would obtain even if the redemption occurred before the sale, eliminating the need to postpone the redemption until after the selling shareholder has lost control of the corporation. In Rev. Rul. 75-447, 1975-2 C.B. 113, the Service made it clear that the application of the step transaction and the irrelevance of order of the transactions applied equally in the context of transactions in which the interests of the redeemed shareholder were not completely terminated.

7.5. REDEMPTIONS TESTED FROM THE CORPORATION'S PERSPECTIVE — PARTIAL LIQUIDATIONS

Non-corporate shareholders can receive exchange treatment on a redemption of stock in the case of a partial liquidation of the corporation, under section 302(b)(4). This redemption category is tested from the corporation's perspective and historically was part of the liquidation rules (provisions for winding up a corporation's business) rather than part of the redemption provisions. That history is helpful in understanding the nature of corporate contractions that are treated as partial liquidations. Regulations originally promulgated under section 346 are still applicable to partial liquidations.

Section 302(e) defines partial liquidations, providing a facts-and-circumstances general rule for determining whether a partial liquidation has occurred under section 302(e)(1) and a more objective safe harbor when the corporation has terminated one of its lines of business under section 302(e)(2).

The safe harbor provided within section 302(e) invokes an active trade or business requirement very similar in operation to that used in testing spinoff transactions under section 355, in that a qualifying business must be "active" and conducted for five years and not acquired in a taxable transaction within that five-year period. (If a corporation could buy and then liquidate the new business, it would provide a way to bail out earnings and profits through an exchange transaction rather than as an operating distribution.) For example, if a corporation has conducted two businesses for a decade and abandons one of them while continuing to operate the other, its individual shareholders will receive exchange treatment under section 302(a) when it distributes to them either the business assets or the proceeds of the sale of the assets. This could occur, for example, if a company that operated two related businesses, such as a manufacturing and a distributing business, decided to sell the distributing business assets to focus solely on manufacturing. The provision also covers the situation in which the corporation suffered a fire that so damaged the manufacturing plant that the company distributed the insurance proceeds to shareholders and narrowed its enterprise to the distributing business.

Note that the partial liquidation provision applies whether the corporation liquidates a business and distributes its proceeds to a single shareholder or distributes them pro rata among all the shareholders, even though the latter context superficially resembles a typical operating distribution. § 302(e)(4). If a partial liquidation distribution is pro rata, the shareholders need not even actually surrender stock in the corporation. Fowler Hosiery Co. v. Comm'r, 301 F.2d 394 (7th Cir. 1962).

If the liquidation of an actively conducted business is not involved, a corporate distribution may still represent a partial liquidation if it represents a genuine contraction of the corporate business. The Service's ruling policy provides a safe harbor for a contraction of a corporate business if the distribution results in a 20% or greater reduction in gross revenues, net fair market value of assets, and employees.

Genuine Contraction of a Corporate Business

There are a number of revenue rulings and other authorities that provide guidance on the kind of contraction that satisfies the partial liquidation requirements.

— Rev. Rul. 75-223, 1975-1 C.B. 109 (a parent corporation's liquidation of a subsidiary and distribution of the assets received to its shareholders is a partial liquidation), clarified by Rev. Rul. 77-376, 1977-2 C.B. 107 (size of subsidiary irrelevant).

— Rev. Rul. 79-184, 1979-1 C.B. 143 (a parent corporation's sale of a subsidiary's stock and distribution of the proceeds to its shareholders is the sale of an investment and not a partial liquidation of parent's business).

— Rev. Rul. 74-296, 1974-1 C.B. 80 (a department store's contraction to a discount apparel store involving elimination of departments, reduction of merchandise types, reduction in floor space, employees, inventory and fixed assets, qualifies as a partial liquidation).

— Rev. Rul. 67-16, 1967-1 C.B. 77 (distribution of condemnation proceeds does not qualify as a partial liquidation, where the company continued to operate the business essentially the same as before the condemnation).

— Rev. Rul. 67-299, 1967-2 C.B. 138 (distribution of an amount equal to the proceeds from sale of a parcel by a real estate company not a partial liquidation, because proceeds were used to renovate another parcel and only later was an equivalent amount distributed).

> — *Rev. Rul. 58-565, 1958-2 C.B. 140 (distribution of an amount equal to the proceeds from sale of a building does not qualify as a partial liquidation, because the proceeds were used to pay off existing debt and a plan of partial liquidation was not adopted until 3 years later when an equivalent payment was made to shareholders).*
>
> — *Rev. Rul. 71-250, 1971-1 C.B. 112 (temporary investment of sales proceeds while expansion considered, followed by distribution when expansion rejected, doesn't prevent partial liquidation).*
>
> — *Rev. Rul. 60-322, 1960-2 C.B. 118 (corporation's distribution of cash from sale of portfolio bonds and excess inventory is not a contraction of the business).*

Because section 302(c)(4) applies only to individual shareholders, a corporate shareholder that receives a distribution that is part of a partial liquidation under section 302(e) will be treated as receiving a dividend, which will be treated as an extraordinary dividend under section 1059 without regard to the holding period of the stock.

7.6. TAX CONSEQUENCES OF SECTION 302

7.6.1. Tax Consequences to the Shareholder

When a sale of stock to the issuing corporation is treated as an exchange under section 302(a), the shareholder does not treat any part of the sale proceeds as a dividend. Rather, the basis in the redeemed shares is taken into account under section 1001 to determine the gain (or loss) on the exchange, which will ordinarily be a capital gain or loss.

In contrast, when the buyback fails all of the section 302(b) tests and is therefore treated under section 302(d) as a distribution, the regular rules for operating distributions with respect to the corporation's stock apply.

Prior to the temporary application of the preferential capital gains rate to dividends, individual shareholders anticipating that any given amount would be distributed by a corporation almost always preferred to receive that amount as a redemption that was treated as an exchange rather than as a distribution with respect to stock. There was, however, one circumstance in which arranging the transaction as a redemption that would be honored as a sale or exchange was less advantageous. Remember that when a shareholder redeems a block of stock, only the basis of the stock actually redeemed is available to offset the proceeds, whereas when a shareholder receives a return of capital distribution under section 301(c)(2) outside the context of a redemption, her entire basis in the class of stock on which the operating distribution is made is available. Assuming that the latter approach (i.e., that the aggregate basis of the shareholder's entire block of stock is available, rather than just the basis in the shares actually redeemed) also applies under section 301(c)(2) when there has been an actual redemption that falls under section 302(d) and therefore under section 301(c), a redemption treated as a section 301 distribution would be preferable when the corporation has little or no earnings and profits.

To illustrate this, suppose a shareholder owns 100 shares of stock, with a basis of $4 and value of $20 for each share. This shareholder is to receive $40 from the corporation, and the corporation has no earnings and profits.

If the shareholder gives up 2 shares of stock and the transaction is honored as a redemption that is a section 302(a) sale (for instance, because there are 1,000,000 shares outstanding), the shareholder will offset the $40 of proceeds with $8 of basis, resulting in $32 of taxable gain. The shareholder will have different economic and governance rights in the corporation after the redemption.

In contrast, if the shareholder gives up 2 shares of stock and the transaction is nonetheless treated as a section 302(d)/section 301 distribution (for instance, because the redemption is pro rata), the tax consequences for the shareholder will arguably be different. There will be no dividend distribution under section 301(c)(1), and the shareholder will be treated as receiving the distribution as recovery of basis under section 301(c)(2). The shareholder would then be able to use the entire $40 of his aggregate basis in the 100 shares to offset the dividend receipt, leaving $160 basis in the 100 shares still owned. After the distribution, the shareholders will have the same economic and governance rights as before.

The Service is aware of, and a bit uneasy about, the advantage to taxpayers of being able to use all of their basis in a redemption that is treated as a dividend. *See* Ann. 2006-30, 2006-19 IRB 879 (discussed below in connection with other problems involving shareholder basis after redemptions).

a. The Effect on Shareholder Basis of a "Redemption" Taxed as a Dividend

When a shareholder actually gives up stock to the issuing corporation, but is nevertheless taxed as if she had not, the shareholder has been denied the use of the basis related to that stock. All is not lost, however. The regulations provide that in such cases "proper adjustment" will be made to the stock remaining in the shareholder's hands. Reg. § 1.302-2(c). The examples given in that regulation indicate that the basis of the redeemed stock will shift over to the shareholder's remaining stock. If the redeeming shareholder owns no more stock, the basis shifts to stock of the related party whose attributed ownership caused the taxpayer to fail section 302(b). *See* example 2 (wife's basis in her stock in the corporation increased by the basis of husband's redeemed stock).

These pro-taxpayer basis-shifting provisions provided the mechanism for a slightly intricate shelter scheme. Two taxpayers, A and B Corp, would own stock in a third, C Corp. A (the taxpayer standing to benefit from the scheme) would also own an option to buy what would be 50% of the stock of B Corp, making A and B Corp related parties under section 318. B Corp's interest in C Corp would be redeemed, but the redemption would be treated as a dividend because of the interest still owned by A. B Corp's basis in its C stock would shift to A, which might now own stock in C that was worth less than its new basis in that stock. A could then recognize a loss on the C stock.

All this transaction does is shift basis from B to A, and it does so at the tax cost of the dividend received by B Corp. Why would this be worth doing? In some of the shelters, B Corp was an offshore corporation not subject to US tax on the redemption/deemed dividend at all or was a tax-exempt entity indifferent to the tax consequences of the transaction. Thus if A was an individual, the benefit of a short-term capital loss could easily be worth more than B Corp's tax cost as a result of the dividend. The IRS and Treasury responded to these transactions in two ways. First, the IRS issued Notice 2001-45, and indicated that the transaction would be a "listed transaction" (triggering various reporting requirements and making IRS audit of the transaction almost inevitable) and outlined its reasons why the shelter would not work (based largely on the transitory nature of A's holdings). Second, Treasury is contemplating new regulations that would alter the basis-shifting rules so that only the originally redeemed shareholder would be able to benefit from the unused basis. A first attempt at such regulations was widely criticized (in large part because they required the redeemed shareholder to have access to information about the continued holdings of too many other shareholders) and has been withdrawn. Ann. 2006-30, 2006-19 IRB 879. In January 2009, proposed regulations were promulgated that include a slightly simpler scheme. Notice of Proposed Regulations, REG-143686-07, 74 FR 3509 (Jan. 21, 2009), 2009–1 C.B. 579. The lack of final regulations should not, however, affect the (il)legitimacy of the transactions to which Notice 2001-45 was addressed.

b.   Redemptions as Extraordinary Dividends for the Corporate Shareholder

Under section 1059(e)(1), many transactions that are tested as redemptions and taxed under section 302(d) as dividends are treated as extraordinary dividends to distributee corporations to which section 1059(a) applies without regard to holding period.

The Seagram Transaction: Attribution and Section 1059

The apparent inevitability of the section 318 attribution rules and more specifically the option rule formed the basis for an infamous transaction whereby Seagram sold its almost 25% stock interest in DuPont back to DuPont in exchange for cash and warrants that gave it limited rights to buy a large block of DuPont stock. (Seagram had acquired the DuPont stock in another infamous transaction involving competing tender offers that amounted to a fight for the right to acquire a DuPont subsidiary.)

Why would a shareholder give up stock in exchange for rights to buy stock? Because when it took back these rights, Seagram was not treated as having reduced its interest in DuPont under the attribution rules of section 318 and the redemption-characterizing rules of section 302. Thus the entire amount it received from DuPont was a dividend eligible for the 80% dividends-received deduction.

The transaction did produce an extraordinary dividend, but at the time section 1059 deferred gain recognition to any later sale, rather than requiring immediate gain recognition. The Seagram transaction prompted a change in the way section 1059(a) works, so that now such "excess reductions" trigger gain.

All non-pro rata distributions in redemption, all distributions where section 302(d) treatment is the result of the application of the option attribution rule, and all distributions that are part of a partial liquidation of the redeeming corporation (as well as those section 304 sales between affiliated corporations that are treated as section 301 distributions in redemption under the complex mechanisms of that provision) come under the special rule for extraordinary dividend treatment. § 1059(e)(1).

The cost to the distributee corporation of dividend treatment, and the availability of the DRD, is the reduction of basis in the stock held by the distributee corporation. The nontaxed portion (the amount for which a DRD is available) reduces the distributee corporation's basis and any amount in excess of basis is treated as exchange gain.

The generally available exceptions to the application of section 1059 to regular distribution transactions under section 301 do not apply to these redemption transactions. Thus, the ordinarily available exceptions for original shareholder's stock under subsection 1059(d)(6) and for affiliated stock under subsection 1059(e)(2) cannot be used. See Reg. § 1.1059(e)-1(a). The exception for qualified preferred dividends when the stock is held more than 5 years is similarly inapplicable in this context, but the limitation on the reduction set out in section 1059(e)(3)(A)(ii) remains applicable.

Accordingly, a corporation that receives a distribution in redemption in a transaction that constitutes a partial liquidation under section 302(b)(4) for individual shareholders may get dividend treatment and a DRD, but will also be required to reduce its basis in the stock and take any gain in excess of basis into account.

7.6.2. Tax Consequences to the Redeeming Corporation

A redemption can have two effects on a corporation's earnings and profits: an increase in earnings and profit on account of any constructive sale of distributed properties and a reduction for the values distributed.

If a corporation makes an in-kind distribution in redemption of its stock, the regular rules of section 311 apply. Gain, but not loss, on a constructive sale is recognized to the corporation on the distribution, which increases the corporation's earnings and profits under section 312(f)(1). Recall that this increase will be net of federal income taxes so that, if there were no other earnings and profits, the earnings and profits created by the transfer of the appreciated property will in most cases not be enough to support full dividend characterization (if otherwise appropriate) for the entire amount distributed.

When a distribution in redemption is treated as a section 302(d)/section 301 distribution, the redeeming corporation will reduce its earnings and profits under the ordinary rules of subsections 312(a)–(c).

When a redemption transaction is honored as a section 1001 sale for the shareholder, the corporation also reduces its earnings and profits, in this case by the amount of earnings and profits represented by the redeemed stock. Because such transactions were sometimes used to wipe-out earnings and profits as a preliminary to an operating distribution that would therefore be treated as a return of capital under section 301(c), section 312(n)(7) provides for a "ratable share" reduction in accumulated earnings and profits for these exchange redemptions. If the ratable share allocable to a block of redeemed stock exceeds the repurchase price paid by the corporation for the stock, the earnings and profits reduction is limited to the repurchase price (i.e., limited to the actual value that has left the corporation).

The ratable share determination is complicated if there are multiple classes of stock. The legislative history of the 1984 Act suggests that earnings and profits must be allocated among the classes, with attention to the legal priorities as to earnings (but no earnings are allocated to preferred stock that is not convertible and does not otherwise participate in future earnings). Conference Report, H.R. Rep. No. 98-681, at 840, 98th Cong. 2d Sess. (1984).

The determination of "accumulated" earnings and profits for this purpose should take into account current earnings and profits remaining available at the time of the redemption. That is, in determining the accumulated earnings and profits available at the time of the redemption distribution, the following should occur: (i) current earnings and profits should be reduced by any section 301 distributions out of those earnings and profits for the taxable year, (ii) the available amount of those remaining current earnings and profits should be determined based on the timing of the distribution, and (iii) that amount should be added to the accumulated earnings otherwise available at the time of the distribution. The redemption would be treated as distributing the stock's proportionate share of that amount. *Cf.* Rev. Rul. 74-338 and 74-339, 1974-2 C.B. 101 and 103.

What about expenses that the corporation incurs in a buyback? Those expenses are nondeductible and nonamortizable capital expenditures, under section 162(k)(1), except for interest payments and certain others excepted in section 162(k)(2). This provision should not deny deductions that have no nexus other than timing to the redemption, such as a payment of a compensation item to a departing employee at the same time that the corporation repurchases the employee's stock.

7.7. REDEMPTIONS UNDER SECTION 303

Section 303 is a separate provision benefiting heirs of estates of shareholders holding significant amounts of stock. The death of a shareholder may require liquidation of stock to pay related expenses, and Congress apparently concluded that such a liquidation should be granted exchange treatment even if it doesn't fall within the ordinary section 302(b) provisions for such treatment, if the stock is a substantial portion of the decedent's estate. Accordingly, subject to certain limitations outlined in section 303(b), redemptions of stock that is included in the gross estate of a decedent (or substituted basis stock under section 303(c)) are treated as per se exchanges to the extent of the various taxes (and interest) imposed because of the death and any funeral and administration expenses allowable as deductions to the estate. § 303(a).

The limitations are generally related to the timing of the distributions, see § 303(b)(1) and (4) (limiting the benefit to distributions that occur within a reasonable period after the death of the decedent — usually within 90 days of the expiration of the statutory limitation period for assessing federal estate taxes); the requirement that a shareholder's interest must be reduced by payment of the section 303(a) amounts, see § 303(b)(3) (extending the benefit beyond the decedent's estate only to shareholder-beneficiaries whose interests are actually reduced by paying the specified amounts, making the provision ordinarily applicable only to residuary beneficiaries); and the requirement that a significant proportion of the decedent's estate be represented by the stock, see § 303(b)(2)(A) (requiring that the value of the stock included in the estate must exceed 35% of the value of the gross estate minus certain deductions). A special rule aggregates the stock of multiple corporations and treats all of the stock as though it were one corporation for the latter limitation, if 20% of the value of the stock of each is included in the decedent's estate (taking account of stock owned by a surviving spouse as though it were included in determining the value of the decedent's estate). § 303(b)(2)(B).

Most of these redemptions are in the context of closely held corporations, but the benefit of the provision is not limited to such corporate stock. And while the goal of Congress to remove any tax impediments to payment of estate taxes and other decedent expenses in connection with ownership of stock may be laudable, note that the provision doesn't require that there have been an impediment — section 303 applies whether or not the redemption is necessary to pay the estate taxes and other expenses. It would apply to redemptions of Microsoft shares upon Bill Gates' death the same as it applies to the redemption of stock in a closely held corporation owned by the NoName family, on the death of the family matriarch and founder of the corporation. Furthermore, the benefit results in costless extraction of corporate earnings for the decedent's heirs: since basis is stepped up (or down) at death under section 1014 (assuming that the estate tax will continue to include such a provision), section 303 redemptions generally will be tax-free.

There is a special rule for application of the generation-skipping transfer rules under section 2611(a). § 303(d).

The tax consequences of a section 303 redemption treated as an exchange are the same, to the shareholder/estate and to the corporation, as with ordinary redemptions governed by section 302(a). In particular, an in-kind redemption would generate section 311 gain to the redeeming corporation, and the redemption would reduce earnings and profits by the section 312(n)(7) amount.

PRACTICE PROBLEMS

1.   A and B each owns 500 of the 1,000 outstanding shares of X Corp, now worth $7 per share, or $3,500 for a block of 500 shares. A bought 500 shares 5 years ago for $5 per share, paying a total of $2,500. X Corp has accumulated e&p of $5000. If A sells 100 shares to B for fair market value, what are the consequences?

   (a)   A has capital loss of $2,800 ($3,500-$700); B holds two blocks of stock, 500 shares with basis unknown and 100 shares with basis of $700; no effect on X Corp.

   (b)   A has dividend income $200 (he has not gone below 80% of his prior holding); B holds two blocks of stock, 500 shares with basis unknown and 100 shares with basis of 700; reduction in X Corp. e&p of 200.

(c)   A has long term capital gain of $200 ($700-$500); B holds two blocks of stock, 500 shares with basis unknown and 100 shares with basis of $700; no effect on X Corp.

(d)   None of the above.

2.   A and B each owns 500 of the 1,000 outstanding shares of X Corp, now worth $7 per share, or $3,500. A bought 500 shares 5 years ago for $5 per share, for a total of $2,500. X Corp has accumulated e&p of $5,000. A sells 100 shares of X Corp back to X Corp for $700. What is the most likely result to A? Assume that A and B are not related.

(a)   Gain of $200.

(b)   No gain; A holds 400 shares with basis of $1,700.

(c)   Dividend of $700.

3.   A owns 1,000 of the outstanding shares of X Corp, and B, C, D, and E each owns 250 of the 2,000 outstanding shares of X Corp, now worth $7 per share. A bought her 1,000 shares 5 years ago for $5 per share, for a total of $5,000. X Corp has accumulated e&p of $10,000. A sells 200 shares of X Corp back to X Corp for $1,400. What is the most likely result to A? Assume that A, B, C, D, and E are not related.

(a)   Gain of $400.

(b)   No gain; A holds 800 shares with basis of $3,600.

(c)   Dividend of $1,400.

4.   A and B each owns 500 of the 1,000 outstanding shares of X Corp, now worth $7 per share, or $3,500. A bought 500 shares 5 years ago for $5 per share, for a total of $2,500. X Corp has accumulated e&p of $5,000. A sells 400 shares to X Corp at their market value. What is the effect on A assuming A and B are not related?

(a)   Dividend of $2,800.

(b)   Capital gain of $2,800.

(c)   Capital gain of $800.

(d)   Insufficient information to answer.

5.   A and B each owns 500 of the 1000 outstanding shares of X Corp, now worth $7 per share, or $3,500. A bought 500 shares 5 years ago for $5 per share, for a total of $2,500. A is B's mother. X Corp has accumulated e&p of $5,000. A sells 400 shares to X Corp at their market value. What is the effect on A?

(a)   Dividend of $2,800.

(b)   Capital gain of $2,800.

(c)   Capital gain of $800.

(d)   Insufficient information to answer.

6.   A and B each owns 500 of the 1,000 outstanding shares of X Corp, now worth $7 per share, or $3,500. A bought 500 shares 5 years ago for $5 per share, for a total of $2,500. A is B's mother. X Corp has accumulated e&p of $5,000. A sells 400 shares to X Corp at their market value. What is A's basis in her remaining shares?

(a)   Basis of $500.

(b)   Basis of $5,300.

(c)   Basis of $2,500.

(d)   Incomplete information without knowing B's basis.

7.   A, B, C, and D each owns 25% of Middle Entity, a partnership. Middle Entity owns 100% of the stock of Corp Co. Applying the constructive receipt rules of section 318, and assuming no other relationships among the shareholders, how much stock in Corp Co. is A deemed to own?

(a)   100%.

(b)   25%.

(c)   None.

(d)   Not enough information.

8.   A, B, C, and D each own 25% of Middle Co, a subchapter C corporation. Middle Co. owns 100% of the stock of Corp Co. Applying the constructive ownership rules of section 318, and assuming no other relationships among the shareholders, how much stock in Corp Co. is A deemed to own?

(a)   100%.

(b)   25%.

(c)   None.

(d)   50%.

9.   A, B, C, and D each owns 25% of Middle Co, a subchapter C corporation. Middle Co owns 100% of the stock of Corp Co. A is the child of C. Applying the section 318 attribution rules and assuming no other relationships among the shareholders, how much stock in Corp Co. is A treated as owning for the purposes of the application of section 302?

(a)   100%.

(b)   25%.

(c)   50%.

(d)   None.

10.   A, B, C, and D each owns 25% of Middle Co, a subchapter C corporation. Middle Co owns 100% of the stock of Corp Co. A and B are the children of C. Applying the section 318 attribution rules and assuming no other relationships among the shareholders, how much stock in Corp Co. is C deemed to own?

(a)   100%.

(b)   75%.

(c)   50%.

(d)   25%.

11.   A, B, C, and D each owns 25% of Middle Co, a subchapter C corporation. Middle Co owns 100% of the stock of Corp Co. A and B are the children of C. Applying the section 318 attribution rules and assuming no other relationships among the shareholders, how much stock in Corp Co. is A deemed to own?

(a)   75%.

(b)   25%.

(c)   50%.

(d)   None.

12.   A owns 30% of Corp Y. A is also a 60% partner in a partnership that owns 80% of Corp Z, and Corp Z owns 25% (by value) of Corp X. A owns 50% of the common stock of Corp X, which amounts to 40% of its value. A's grandmother owns 10% of Corp Y and A's mother owns 15% of Corp Y. Corp X owns 10% of Corp Y. A redeems half of her shares in Corp Y. How much of Corp Y is A treated as owning before the redemption, and consequently, what are the most likely tax consequences of this redemption to A under section 302?

(a)   A will be treated as owning 64.6% of Corp Y before the redemption, and the redemption will not be treated as an dividend.

(b)   A will be treated as owning 50.2% of Corp Y before the redemption, and the redemption will be treated as an exchange.

(c)   A will be treated as owning 45% of Corp Y before the redemption, and the redemption will be treated as an exchange.

(d)   Insufficient information.

13.   D owns 100 shares of Publico, a publicly traded corporation, with 100,000,000 shares of common stock outstanding. D purchased the shares for $3 per share. Publico has been profitable since its founding in 1920, with average annual earnings in excess of $2,000,000 for the last 5 years. Publico makes a tender offer for its shares, offering to buy up to 15% of each shareholder's holdings, for $6 per share. D participates in the transaction but not to the full extent of the offer; he only tenders 10%, or 10 shares, but almost every other shareholder of Publico tenders the full 15%. What is the most likely result of the transaction to D?

(a)   Dividend of $60.

(b)   Dividend of $30.

(c)   Gain of $30.

14.   Ben owns 50 of the 100 shares of Smallco; the other 50 shares are owned 5 shares each by 10 unrelated shareholders. What is the smallest number of full shares that Ben can sell to Smallco and be assured of obtaining sale or exchange treatment under section 302(b)(2)?

(a)   17 (must own less than 40% of remaining shares).

(b)   10 (must sell 20% of holding before the transaction).

(c)   25 (must own half of the number owned before).

(d)   46 (must own less than any other shareholder).

DISCUSSION PROBLEMS

X is a corporation owned entirely by two individuals, A and B (who are unrelated unless otherwise stated). A owns 60 shares of X common stock (bought in one transaction three years ago for $600 or $10 per share). B owns 40 shares of X common stock (with a basis of $30 per share). The stock's fair market value is $20 per share. X's accumulated e&p is $500 and there is no current e&p. X uses the accrual method of accounting.

What are the results to the parties from the alternative transactions in parts (1) through (9) below (i.e., what are the amount and character of shareholder income or loss and the impact on the corporation's e&p account, if any)?

1.   A sells 10 X shares to B for $200. What might A want to do if 50 of A's shares have $10 per share basis and the other 10 shares have $20 per share basis?

2.   A sells 30 shares back to X for $600.

3.   A sells 20 shares back to X for $400.

4.   X Corp proposes to redeem 10 of B's shares for $200. What is the minimum number of shares that B must redeem to ensure sale or exchange treatment?

5.   A sells 10 shares back to X for $200.

6.   A sells 30 shares back to X for $600. Shortly thereafter, B sells 10 shares back to X for $200 in an exchange that had been agreed to in the year prior to the year of A's redemption. What would result to A and B?

(a)   What if A's redemption was carried out under an agreement that gave A additional voting rights in her retained shares, so that she retained voting control of the Corporation, even after B's redemption?

(b)   What if, in the second scenario (in which A retains voting rights in spite of the redemption), the earnings are current e&p instead of accumulated e&p?

If A's redemptions were treated as a section 301 distribution (as in the alternative scenario in this problem) and B's redemption were nonetheless treated as a section 302(a) distribution (because in essence B has reduced a minority shareholding even further when A retains voting control), which type of distribution is considered made first out of current e&p — the ordinary distribution or the ratable share reduction?

7.   In one transaction, A sells 20 X shares to B for $400 and 10 shares back to X for $200.

8. A sells 30 shares back to X for $600. What would result if A and B are "related" in the following ways:

(a)   B is A's brother, and their father is living.

(b)   B is A's equal partner in a two-person partnership.

(c)   B is a corporation in which A owns one half of the stock.

(d)   A has an option to buy B's shares.

9. As in (8) above, if A and B each own 50 shares, rather than 60 shares and 40 shares, respectively, how many shares will A and B each own by attribution? Assume no relationships other than as shareholders except as specified in each subpart?

(a)   B is A's brother, and their father is living.

(b)   B is A's equal partner in a two-person partnership.

(c)   B is a corporation in which A owns one half of the stock.

(d)   A has an option to buy B's shares.

10. What if, in the facts of Problem (5) above, A was a corporate shareholder?

11. What if, in Problem (2) above, B had been obligated to buy the 30 shares that A instead sold to the corporation?

12. What if, in Problem (5), A had then sold her remaining stock to an unrelated party, D?

Chapter 8

SECTION 304 REDEMPTIONS THROUGH SALES TO RELATED CORPORATIONS

Statutes and Regulations	IRC §§ 304(a)–(c); 1059(a) and (e)
	Prop. Reg. § 1.304-2
	Review §§ 302(b), 301 and 318
Other Primary Authorities	Bhada v. Commissioner, 892 F.2d 39 (6th Cir. 1989)
	Combrink v. Comm'r, 117 T.C. 82 (2001)

Caution: the existing section 304 regulations have not been revised since amendments were enacted in 1997. Although the results in the examples in that regulation are generally not affected, the regulation refers to the old "contribution to capital" fiction rather than the newer "section 351 transaction" fiction. Proposed regulations were issued in January 2009 that incorporate the 1997 changes, and probably can be relied on as the government's position with respect to section 304 itself. Other portions of these proposed regulations, which touch on significant issues under sections 301, 302, and other provisions relating to stock exchanged in reorganizations, are more controversial and may well not be reflected in any final version of these regulations.

8.1. THE RATIONALE OF SECTION 304

Some Code sections, perhaps most of the older ones in subchapter C, are written to provide a roadmap for taxpayers seeking a favorable tax treatment that is openly offered but is subject to certain conditions. For example, section 332 offers certain corporations the ability to liquidate with results close to those applicable if the corporation had never been formed, conditioned on 80% ownership; section 351 offers nonrecognition on certain transfers to corporations in exchange for corporate stock, conditioned on 80% transferor control; and section 368 offers nonrecognition to corporations and shareholders undergoing certain restructurings, conditioned on satisfying one of the rather arcane category definitions.

Section 304 is not such a Code section. It was written to impose results its drafters viewed as undesirable, in order to discourage taxpayers from entering into transactions that were viewed as potentially abusive and to lay down relatively harsh consequences when such transactions were attempted. Section 304 was enacted with the straightforward purpose of preventing circumvention of the normal tax treatment of dividends received by shareholders under sections 302 and 301. Like section 302 (upon which the approach of and analysis under section 304 builds) and sections 305 and 306, section 304 prevents a shareholder from obtaining sale or exchange treatment when the shareholder has not given up enough of her interest in the corporation whose stock is transferred. Here, the "not giving up enough" targeted by the statute occurs when a shareholder sells stock of one corporation to another corporation that the shareholder controls. Without this provision, a shareholder could avoid dividend treatment simply by creating two corporations, each of which had earnings, and then transferring one corporation's stock to the other corporation in a transaction that would be treated as a sale.

Although it has served its intended role in discouraging these "bail-out" transactions, section 304 has significance in several other contexts. Because of the potential breadth of its application, it can serve as a trap for unwary managers who plan sales between related corporations without an abusive tax purpose. As is sometimes the case with anti-abuse provisions, it also has become a provision which some taxpayers can use to their advantage. Of most interest is the fact that in its basic operation, section 304 transforms what might otherwise be characterized as a receipt on a sale of stock into a dividend received with respect to stock. Here is where interesting planning possibilities emerge. What kind of taxpayer might prefer dividend to sale receipt? What might be the stakes involved when there is a Code section that you can rely upon to transform a sale to a related corporation into a dividend? Some of the more notorious possibilities for pro-taxpayer uses of section 304, *e.g.*, Merrill Lynch & Co. v. Comm'r, 386 F.3d 464 (2d Cir. 2004), *aff'g and remanding*, 120 T.C. 12 (2003), *aff'd on remand*, 131 T.C. No. 19 (2008), have not been possible for a number of years, since section 304 was made inapplicable to transactions entirely within consolidated groups under Reg. section 1.1502-80(b). Other possibilities, especially involving foreign corporations, remain.

8.2. THE MECHANICS OF SECTION 304

The section 304 statute is most easily grasped if broken into three components: the provisions of section 304(a) and (c) that characterize the transactions that are covered and make them subject to redemption analysis; those provisions in section 304(b)(1) that determine whether the deemed redemption transaction will be treated as a section 1001 exchange or as a section 301 distribution; and those provisions in section 304(a) that recharacterize the transaction for the purpose of determining the other tax consequences of the transaction, given that the economic position of the transferring shareholder and the acquiring corporation did actually change. There are also ancillary provisions, in sections 304(b)(3) and (4), that determine the consequences when there is an overlap of section 304 with section 351 transactions and in some other situations.

A brief note on terminology. The section 304 provisions are written in terms of the "Issuing" and "Acquiring" corporations and persons "in control." The Issuing corporation is the corporation whose shares are transferred in the transaction (even though the shares in question are not ordinarily issued in the course of the transaction under discussion), and the Acquiring corporation is the corporation that acquires stock in Issuing. The persons in control who transfer Issuing stock to Acquiring are generally referred to herein as "transferor(s)".

8.2.1. Covered Transactions

Section 304(a), among other things, sets forth the conditions under which the sale under consideration will be covered by the special provisions in section 304. If a taxpayer that controls one corporation transfers stock in exchange for property to another corporation that the taxpayer controls after the transaction, the transaction is within the purview of the section.

There are two subcategories of covered transactions: section 304(a)(1) (first sentence) describes a transaction in which a corporation buys its sibling's stock from the transferor (often called a "brother-sister section 304"); and section 304(a)(2) describes a transaction in which a subsidiary corporation buys its parent corporation's stock from the parent's shareholder (usually called a "parent-subsidiary section 304"). Brother-sister transactions are probably the more commonly encountered of the two, in spite of the parenthetical in section 304(a)(1) that applies paragraph (1) only when paragraph (2) is not otherwise applicable.

Section 304(c) defines control for purposes of applying these coverage provisions. It modifies the section 318 attribution rules in ways that make control more likely to exist. Under section 304(c)(1), control is defined as ownership of 50% of the vote *or* value in the tested corporation. Rev. Rul. 89-57, 1989-1 C.B. 90, clarifies that this value test is applied by looking to the total value of the stock in the aggregate, not to the value of each class. Under section 304(c)(3), the section 318 rules are relaxed to provide broader attribution in determining whether a transaction is covered by section 304: the 50% thresholds for upstream and downstream attribution are reduced to 5%. Downstream attribution from shareholders is made proportional to value owned where this modified percentage applies, and upstream attribution to shareholders remains proportional when less than 50% is owned, as in the ordinary application of section 318(a)(3)(C).

Furthermore, under the second sentence of section 304(c)(1), a person considered in control of one corporation under the first sentence, with the relaxed attribution rules, will also be considered to control any corporation of which the first corporation "owns" (presumably, directly) at least 50% of vote or value. An example may help understand how this attribution provision expands the potential application of the section. Assume Max owns 50% of Corp 1, 30% of Corp 2, and none of Corp 3. Corp 1 owns 20% of Corp 2 and none of Corp 3. Corp 2 owns 50% of Corp 3. Even with the attribution rules of section 304(c) (but without the second sentence), Max is treated as owning only 20% of Corp 3, and Corp 1 is treated as owning only 25% of Corp 3. With the special rule, however, Corp 1 will be treated as controlling Corp 3, because Corp 2 owns 50% of Corp 3 directly, and Corp 1 "controls" Corp 2 under the regular attribution rules of section 304(c). Accordingly, a sale of Corp 1 stock to Corp 3 may be treated as a parent-subsidiary section 304 transaction.

For determining whether two or more persons control Acquiring, the actual or constructive ownership of Acquiring stock *after* the transaction is taken into account under section 304(c)(2)(A) when the transferors receive Acquiring stock as consideration for Issuing stock. Thus, control of Acquiring may not be acquired until the transaction occurs and yet be counted to determine if section 304 applies to the transaction.

8.2.2. Will the Transaction Be Honored as a Sale Under Section 302?

Remember that the statute presumes that a shareholder may attempt to get corporate earnings out while enjoying sale or exchange treatment. Perhaps not surprisingly, the statute therefore treats covered transactions as subject to the redemption rules in section 302 for determining whether distribution or exchange treatment is appropriate. The way the statute does this is not entirely straightforward, however. It creates one set of fictions for determining whether the transferring shareholder should be treated as having sold his stock or as having received a section 301 distribution under the tests in section 302, and it provides another set of fictions for determining most of the other consequences of the transactions.

Section 304(a)(1) and (a)(2) both provide that the property received shall be treated as "a distribution in redemption of stock." The provisions in section 304(b)(1) direct how the fictional redemption will be tested and thus determine whether it will be characterized as a section 302(a)/section 1001 sale or a section 302(d)/section 301 distribution.

Subsections 304(a)(1) and (a)(2) provide further fictions for these redemptions (section 304(a)(1) as a redemption by Acquiring, and section 304(a)(2) as a redemption by Issuing), but these particular fictions do not enter into the section 302 analysis of sale/exchange or distribution treatment; they are only invoked after the section 302 analysis, to reconcile the recast treatment of the transaction with the reality about which corporation actually owns which stock afterward.

For both types of transactions, the first sentence of section 304(b)(1) directs that the hypothetical redemption will be tested for dividend equivalence under section 302 as if it were a redemption of the Issuing corporation's stock by the Issuing corporation. Thus the transferor's "before and after" ownership of the Issuing corporation is tested under section 302 in both categories of section 304 transactions. Note that the section 318 rules are also adjusted for the purpose of applying the section 302(b) tests to the changes in ownership of Issuing stock: there is no threshold ownership requirement at all for either upstream or downstream entity attribution, making it even more likely that a sale between related corporations will result in dividend treatment. *See* section 304(b)(1) (second sentence) (removing the threshold requirement for upstream and downstream attribution and, unlike the somewhat similar modification in section 304(c), *not* providing proportional downstream attribution when the lower threshold applies).

a. Consequences of Section 302(a) Exchange Treatment

The application of these rules to transactions that must be tested under section 304 will not always mean that the receipt will be treated as a dividend. It is possible, though perhaps somewhat unusual, to satisfy section 302(b) and obtain sale or exchange treatment, if the transferor has really given up significant ownership in the Issuing corporation. This will only be possible if there are other shareholders of the Acquiring corporation. For instance, suppose A owns 50% of Issuing and 100% of Acquiring before the transaction, and A transfers half of his stock in Issuing to Acquiring. After the transaction, A will actually own only 25% of Issuing, but after the application of section 318(a)(2)(C), he will be treated as still owning all of his original 50% holding in Issuing, he will fail to satisfy section 302(b), and thus his receipt will be treated as a section 301 distribution. On the other hand, if A only owned 50% of Acquiring, he would be treated as only owning 37.5% of Issuing after the transaction (the 25% he still actually owns, plus half the 25% Acquiring owns). In such a case, he would satisfy the safe harbor of section 302(b)(2), and the transaction would be honored as a sale of stock.

If a section 302(b) test is satisfied, then the transaction is honored as a sale or exchange for all purposes. In both the parent-subsidiary transaction and the brother-sister transaction, the transferor can offset the sales proceeds by his actual basis in the transferred Issuing stock. Because the transferor is allowed to use his basis in the Issuing stock to offset the receipt, his basis in any of the Issuing corporation stock he may still own is unchanged. There is no change to the transferor's Acquiring corporation stock basis. Because the transaction has been honored as a sale, the Acquiring corporation takes a cost basis in the Issuing stock received. *See* Prop. Reg. § 1.304-2(a)(5) and (c), ex. 1.

It is unclear whether there will be any effect of the section 304 transaction that is in fact treated as a sale on Acquiring's (or Issuing's) earnings and profits. A corporation ordinarily does not adjust its earnings and profits when it buys property or when a shareholder sells its stock to another party. Does either the fact that the property acquired here is stock in a related party (which may in many cases represent little more than an interest in Acquiring itself), or the fact that section 304(a)(1) and (2) both treat covered transactions as redemptions change this result? The latter seems directly relevant. If the transaction had actually been a redemption, there would have been a reduction in earnings and profits for the distribution under section 312, as limited by the ratable-share provision in section 312(n)(7).

If a reduction in earnings and profits is appropriate, however, there is some question about whose earnings and profits are reduced: (i) Issuing's, because the section 304(b)(1) test is in terms of Issuing; or (ii) Issuing's in a parent-subsidiary transaction but Acquiring's in a brother-sister transaction, because of the language in subsections 304(a)(1) and 304(a)(2) characterizing the two types of transactions differently as redemptions of Issuing (for parent-subsidiary) or Acquiring (for brother-sister)? Again, because subsections 304(a)(1) (first sentence) and (a)(2) function to treat these sales among related parties as redemptions, the indication in section 304(a) that the redemptions are treated as redemptions of Acquiring and Issuing stock, respectively, seems to provide an answer in favor of a reduction in earnings and profits of Acquiring and Issuing, respectively.

b.   Consequences of Section 302(d) Distribution Treatment

If none of the section 302(b) tests is satisfied when the transaction is tested as required under section 304(b)(1), the property receipt is treated under section 302(d) as a distribution under section 301. There are, however, a few complications to the normal operation of section 301 in the section 304 context that must be considered.

i.   Whose Earnings and Profits are Considered?

Section 304(b)(2) provides that the amount of the distribution constituting a dividend will be determined by looking to the earnings and profits of Acquiring (the corporation that is actually paying the purchase price for Issuing stock and losing equivalent value) and, if those are insufficient, the earnings and profits of Issuing (even though Issuing has not actually transferred any value to the transferors). Why did Congress enact this provision? Without it, in either of the two categories of covered transactions, the final structure would permit a controlling shareholder to move earnings and profits around to support dividend treatment or not, as desired. For example, in the brother-sister structure, Issuing could make a distribution to Acquiring after the transaction to reimburse Acquiring for the purchase of Issuing. It would be inappropriate to permit the mere fact that the earnings are in Issuing rather than Acquiring to prevent the treatment of the transaction as a dividend.

ii.   What is Transferor's Basis in Any Retained Stock?

If the entire transaction is treated as a dividend, what happens to the basis in the transferor's Issuing stock that he no longer holds? If there are insufficient earnings and profits to support the characterization of the transaction as a dividend, how will subsections 301(c)(2) and 301(c)(3) be applied to the return of capital distribution? If the transferring controlling shareholder is a corporation, how will the basis reduction (and possible gain) dictated by the section 1059 extraordinary dividend provision be implemented? If there is anything left of the basis of the transferring shareholder in the stock of the Issuing corporation transferred, where does it end up?

When the earnings and profits are sufficient to render the entire sales proceeds a dividend. In a parent-subsidiary section 304 transaction that is treated as a dividend distribution, the transaction is treated as a redemption of Issuing. It would seem that the transferor's unused basis in the transferred Issuing stock would jump to the transferor's remaining Issuing stock, if any, under the regular section 302 rules, resulting in the transferor having an aggregate basis in its Issuing stock that is the same as its aggregate basis in Issuing stock before the transaction. As discussed in the treatment of section 302(d) transactions elsewhere, questions remain about how this basis shift will be implemented. In regulations proposed in January 2009, the government proposes to allocate the basis shifted among the blocks of stock of the same class held by the transferor.

For a brother-sister section 304 transaction that is treated in its entirety as a dividend distribution, the first sentence of section 304(a)(1) provides that the property receipt is to be treated as a distribution in redemption of Acquiring stock. But of which Acquiring stock? The flush language in the second sentence of section 304(a)(1) comes into play here. In a brother-sister section 304 transaction that is treated as a section 301 distribution, the statute provides a special mechanism for determining the other tax consequences to the transferor and to the Acquiring corporation. The transfer of Issuing stock is treated as if it were a section 351 transaction in which new Acquiring stock is deemed issued to the transferor, after which this deemed issued Acquiring stock is treated as redeemed by the Acquiring corporation. The transferor is therefore deemed to briefly own new stock in Acquiring with a basis (determined under section 358) equal to the stock in Issuing he has actually transferred. The deemed issued Acquiring stock is then deemed to be redeemed.

As a result of these fictions, the transferor has a basis in the deemed issued Acquiring shares equal to his old basis in the transferred Issuing shares under section 358. When those Acquiring shares are "redeemed" in a transaction that is entirely treated as a section 301 distribution that is a dividend, the transferor's basis "jumps" to the transferor's remaining *Acquiring* shares, leaving the transferor with a reduced aggregate basis in his Issuing shares and a corresponding increase in aggregate basis in the Acquiring shares. (If the transferor does not actually own any stock in Acquiring, the basis in the transferred shares may jump back to transferor's other shares in Issuing. If transferor actually owns neither Acquiring nor Issuing shares, the Service is likely to adhere to its old position that the stock basis simply disappears. *See* Rev. Rul. 70-496, 1970-2 C.B. 745, obsoleted by Rev. Rul. 2003-99, 2003-2 C.B. 388.)

When earnings and profits are insufficient. When a sale of stock to a related corporation is treated as a section 301 distribution, but there are inadequate earnings and profits, the transferring shareholder will be able to offset some of the distribution by his basis under section 301(c)(2).

In a parent-subsidiary section 304 transaction, the treatment should be relatively straightforward. The parent (Issuing) is treated as having redeemed its own stock. Under the regulations proposed in January 2009 (and generally consistent with prior understandings), if there is insufficient earnings and profits, section 301(c)(2) applies and the transferring shareholder treats the excess redemption proceeds as a return of his basis in holdings in the same class of Issuing corporation stock, to the extent thereof, on a share-by-share basis.

In a brother-sister section 304 transaction, regulations proposed in January 2009 clarified the government's position and provided specific guidance for the section 304 context. Under the general rules for section 301(c)(2) and their application under section 304, the transferor shareholder will be able to use all of his basis in the common stock of Acquiring to offset the distribution. He is likely, however, to have two or more blocks of stock (for instance, if he actually owned Acquiring stock before the transaction): one or more blocks of stock actually held prior to the transaction (having whatever basis the transferor had in such stock) and the block deemed to be held because of the section 351 fiction (the deemed held stock having a basis equal to the Issuing stock actually transferred to Acquiring). The basis of all such blocks of stock (but not the basis of other *classes* of Acquiring stock) will be available to offset the receipt of the section 301 distribution in excess of e&p, but this offset will be made on a share-by-share basis. Thus there can be basis left over with respect to some blocks of stock and gain under section 301(c)(3) with respect to other blocks of stock. The aggregate remaining basis in all such blocks of stock will be the Transferor's post-transaction basis in his Acquiring stock. *See* Prop. Reg. § 1.304-2(a)(4) and (c), ex. 2.

In both transactions, questions remain when there is unused basis and the transferring shareholder actually owns no stock of the same class of Acquiring (in the brother-sister transaction) or Issuing (in the parent-subsidiary transaction) after the sale is completed. The regulation currently in force, Reg. § 1.302-2(c), provides only that in such cases "proper adjustment" will be made to the stock remaining in the shareholder's hands. Regulations proposed in January 2009 under section 302, and clearly applicable when that section is invoked as a result of section 304, treat such unused basis as a recognized but deferred loss. Such a loss can be taken into account when the circumstances are such that, had they been present at the time of the original section 304 transaction, the redemption would not have been considered dividend equivalent.

iii.   How Does Section 1059 Apply?

If the transferor in a section 304 transaction is a corporation, then it will be eligible for a DRD to the extent that the deemed section 301 distribution is treated as a dividend. But section 1059 will also come into play. Section 1059(e)(1)(A)(iii)(II) and sentence one of the flush language apply the section 1059 basis reduction rule to the section 304 hypothetical section 301 distribution in redemption without regard to whether the amount of the dividend would otherwise be considered "extraordinary" or whether the holding period is short or long. As a result, basis is reduced by the amount of the DRD and any excess over that basis amount is treated as gain.

Again, the question arises as to which basis is reduced. Here, the second sentence of the flush language under section 1059(e)(1) provides the answer — only the basis in the stock "redeemed" is taken into account.

Brother-sister transaction. In a brother-sister transaction, the "stock redeemed" is the Acquiring stock that is deemed issued in the section 351 transaction and deemed redeemed in the section 302 transaction (that is treated as a section 301 distribution). For example, if a corporate transferor transfers stock of Issuing with a basis of $50,000 to Acquiring, in which the corporate transferor owns 50% of the common stock and vote when the common stock of Acquiring represents 40% of its value, then the corporate transfer owns 20% by value of Acquiring and receives an 80% DRD under section 243. Assume the sales proceeds are $100,000. The DRD is $80,000, leaving $20,000 in taxable income (ordinary). After the section 351 transaction and before the hypothetical redemption, the corporate transferor will have a basis of $50,000 in the deemed issued Acquiring shares (a section 358 exchanged basis). Section 1059(a) reduces that basis and triggers gain; that is, $50,000 - $80,000 leaves a zero basis and $30,000 of taxable gain. The overall result is a $100,000 distribution with $50,000 of gross income ($20,000 ordinary income and $30,000 gain) and $50,000 of basis recovery. Note that (ignoring character) this is the same as the result from a sale: $100,000 amount realized minus $50,000 basis in the Issuing stock sold equals $50,000 of gross income. Thus, section 1059 removes the benefit of the DRD for the corporation in this context.

Parent-subsidiary transaction. In a parent-subsidiary transaction, the limitation in section 1059 to the "stock redeemed" that is taken into account would apparently be, again, only the stock of Issuing that was actually transferred to Acquiring and treated as redeemed. Thus, the corporate transferor would have a DRD in respect of the dividend from Issuing, but will then reduce the basis in the redeemed Issuing stock by the DRD and recognize gain for the excess.

If there is unused basis after the application of section 1059, it is allocated to the transferring shareholder's remaining Issuing stock of the same class in the parent-subsidiary transaction, or to the transferring shareholder's remaining Acquiring stock of the same class, as above.

iv.   What Is Acquiring's Basis in the Issuing Shares?

Another question that matters to participants is the Acquiring corporation's basis in the Issuing shares. Again, the two types of transactions have different results.

Parent-subsidiary transaction. The Service appears to have taken the position that the Acquiring subsidiary's basis in Issuing would be a cost basis. *See* Rev. Rul. 80-189, 1980-2 C.B. 106. An argument can be made, however, that section 362(a) should apply to produce a transferred basis in respect of a contribution to capital.

Brother-sister transaction. The hypothetical section 351/301 redemption provides a definitive answer for the Acquiring corporation's basis in the transferred Issuing stock in a brother-sister transaction: it will be determined under the ordinary rule in section 362(a) applicable to section 351 transactions. Accordingly, Acquiring's basis will be the transferor's basis in the Issuing stock transferred, as if there had actually been a section 351 transfer of that stock, rather than the purchase price paid for the stock. (Note that there will never be exchange gain to the transferor to increase the basis of the stock in Acquiring's hands, since the section 351 is a hypothetical "boot-free" transaction, prior to and separate from the transaction in which Acquiring transfers property to the transferor.)

8.2.3.   Section 304 Transactions in Which Acquiring Stock Is Received

Section 304 has several interesting aspects, in addition to its potential wholesale transformation of a sale transaction into a dividend transaction. First, section 304 generally produces unwelcome results for individual shareholders only to the extent that the consideration used by the Acquiring corporation is not stock of the Acquiring corporation. Acquiring stock is not "property" under section 317(a). *See* Bhada v. Commissioner, 892 F.2d 39 (6th Cir. 1989). Thus if the Acquiring corporation receives stock of a properly related party from shareholders who do not control it and gives back solely preferred stock in the exchange, neither section 304 nor section 351 apply. Under *Bhada*, the shareholder should have sale or exchange treatment, and recognize gain computed by the difference between her basis in the Issuing stock and the value of the Acquiring stock she receives. (The treatment of such transactions in which the preferred stock would have been non-qualified preferred under section 351(g), however, is not entirely clear.)

Second, when a transferor transfers Issuing stock to Acquiring for both Acquiring stock and other property, section 304 will overlap with section 351 if the transferor actually owns 80% or more of Acquiring after the transfer and thus satisfies the section 368(c) control test. For instance, suppose A owned 100% of Acquiring and 100% of Issuing. If A transfers Issuing stock to Acquiring, and takes back more stock of Acquiring and cash, A has participated in a transaction described in both sections 351 and 304. Without section 304, the transaction would have triggered recognition of the realized gain on the Issuing stock, if any, to the extent of the cash received. Under section 304, A should have a dividend to the extent of the full amount of the cash (assuming sufficient earnings and profits). Section 304(b)(3) directs that in such overlap cases, section 304 and not section 351 will control. This greatly limits the cases in which non-stock consideration can be taken back without dividend treatment. In sum, boot in a section 351 transaction triggers gain only to the extent thereof; but the entire amount of "boot" in a section 304 transaction that fails the section 302 tests will be a section 301 distribution and therefore a dividend, if there are sufficient earnings and profits.

Once again, there are questions about the treatment of nonqualified preferred stock in this context. In a regular section 351 transaction, section 351(g) stock is "counted" as stock for control purposes but is treated as boot to a transferor that receives both other stock and nonqualified preferred. If a transferor receives section 351(g) stock as well as other Acquiring stock in a transaction that otherwise appears to be covered by section 304(a), is that nonqualified preferred treated as boot subject to section 304 or is this merely a section 351 transaction? If no stock other than section 351(g) stock is used? In either case, would such stock escape the taint of section 306 (*see* section 306(c)(3))?

When section 304 applies to the "boot" in a transaction that overlaps section 304 and section 351, some of the benefits of section 351 are lost — in particular, the pro-taxpayer treatment of liability assumptions generally provided in section 357. Under section 304(b)(3), most liability assumptions will be treated as property given by Acquiring in exchange for the Issuing stock. There is an exception for liabilities used to acquire the transferred stock in section 304(b)(3)(B)(i), but it is not always easy to apply this provision, especially in the closely held context because the exception is inapplicable where the stock is acquired from a related person (with certain exceptions). Because liability assumptions will be counted as property for the purposes of section 304, and because section 304 will trump section 351, section 304 may apply to produce unexpected results even in relatively simple corporate restructuring transactions. *See* Combrink v. Comm'r, 117 T.C. 82 (2001) (holding that the contribution by a transferor of a sister corporation to a corporation from which the transferor had borrowed resulted under section 304 in a distribution taxed as a dividend).

PRACTICE PROBLEMS

1. Assume that A owns 100% of X Corp and 50% of Y Corp. Which of the following transactions will not be subject to recharacterization under section 304?

(a) A transfers 10 shares of X Corp stock to Y Corp in exchange for $500.

(b) A transfers 10 shares of X Corp stock to Y Corp in exchange for 20 shares of Y Corp stock.

2.   Assume that A owns all of the 100 outstanding shares of X Corp with a basis of $10 in each share. A also owns 50 of 100 outstanding shares of Y Corp with a basis of $3 in each share. X Corp and Y Corp each have $50,000 of earnings and profits. Assume there is no relationship among any of the other shareholders of X and Y. If A sells 10 shares of Y Corp to X Corp for $5000, what is the result to A?

(a)   Gain of $4,970.

(b)   Dividend of $5,000.

3.   What result if X Corp had e&p of only $1000, but Y Corp had e&p of $50,000?

(a)   Dividend of $1,000, basis recovery of $30, and gain of $3,970.

(b)   Dividend of $5,000.

4.   Assume that A owns 75 of the 100 outstanding shares of X Corp with a basis of $10 in each share. A also owns 50 of the 100 outstanding shares of Y Corp with a basis of $3 in each share. Both X Corp and Y Corp have $50,000 of earnings and profits. Assume there is no relationship among any of the other shareholders of X and Y. If A sells 44 shares of Y Corp to X Corp for $4400, what is the result to A?

(a)   Gain of $4,268.

(b)   Dividend of $5,000.

(c)   Dividend of $1,000, basis recovery of $132, and gain of $3,268.

5.   What if, in Question 4, 20 shares of Y Corp are owned by A's mother?

(a)   Gain of $4,400.

(b)   Dividend of $4,400.

DISCUSSION PROBLEM

Al owns 100% of Old Corp, currently worth $4 million, with earnings and profits of $6 million, with a total basis of $10,000. He also owns stock, held with a basis of $1.5 million, representing one-third of the economic interests and all of the voting rights in New Corp, a corporation worth $9 million with earnings and profits of $1.5 million. All shares of the other class of stock in New Corp are equally owned by his children, Bev and Cyd. In order to consolidate the businesses, and to provide Al with some liquidity in anticipation of his retirement, Al wants to sell 50% of the stock of Old Corp to New Corp.

1.   What result to Al if Al takes back $2 million in cash?

2.   What result to Al if he had owned no New Corp stock, and Bev and Cyd had owned it all?

3.   What result in Question 1, above (Al owns stock representing 1/3 of the value and 100% of the vote of New Corp and a transfer of 50% of Old Corp) if Old Corp and New Corp each had earnings and profits of only $500,000?

4.   What result if in Question 1, above (stock representing 1/3 of the value and 100% of the vote of New Corp is held by the transferring shareholder), if the transferring shareholder is TR Corp, and the other shareholders of

New Corp are wholly owned subsidiaries of TR Corp?

5. What result in Question 1, above (Al owns stock representing 1/3 of the value and 100% of the vote of New Corp), if Al had transferred all of the stock of Old Corp to New Corp?

6. What result in Question 2, above (Al actually owns no stock in New Corp), if Al had transferred all of the stock of Old Corp to New Corp?

7. What if, in Question 1, Al had taken back preferred stock in New Corp, with a value based on its dividend rights, roughly equal to $2 million?

8. What if, in Question 1, Al had borrowed $2 million from New Corp and contributed half of his Old Corp stock to New Corp in satisfaction of that liability?

Chapter 9

STOCK DISTRIBUTIONS AND SIMILAR TRANSACTIONS

Statutes and Regulations	IRC §§ 305, 306, 317
	Reg. §§ 1.305-1 through -7, especially -2(b)
	and -4(b) and -7(a); 1.306-3
Other Primary Authorities	Eisner v. Macomber, 252 U.S. 189 (1920)
	Rev. Rul. 90-11, 1990-1 C.B. 6
	Rev. Rul. 83-42, 1983-1 C.B. 76

9.1. STOCK DIVIDENDS

The general rule in section 305 provides that distributions of a corporation's own stock will not result in income. Section 305(b) provides a list of exceptions that are treated as distributions taxable under section 301, all of which have in common the fact that the distribution has changed the relative economic claims of the shareholders to the corporation's assets and future earnings. The stakes involved in taxable stock dividends have been substantially reduced, but not eliminated, by the fact that dividends to individual shareholders are currently entitled to the preferential rate applicable to capital gains, under section 1(h)(11).

The parallel pattern of nontaxable stock distributions and taxable stock dividends was established in some of the earliest cases involving the taxation of corporations and their shareholders, including the case most often associated with establishing the realization doctrine within the income tax, *Eisner v. Macomber*, 252 U.S. 189 (1920). In *Macomber*, the Court held that a stock dividend (which clearly involved a change on the balance sheet from retained earnings available for distribution to paid-in capital, but had no other effect except dividing shares into smaller units and therefore probably making them more liquid) was not taxable because there was no gain "severed" from the shareholder's capital adequate to meet the Court's notion of what was required before "income" would be present. *Macomber* was actually one of a series of cases in which the Court first held that Congress did not intend to tax stock distributions and then, faced with subsequent congressional language that seemed to indicate an intent to treat stock distributions as dividends taxable to the full extent consistent with an "income tax" under the Sixteenth Amendment, determined that a constitutional limit in fact existed.

Most read *Macomber* and the subsequent cases that tested Congress' power to tax stock dividends, to have held, at most, that a stock distribution cannot be income when it does not change the underlying economic rights of the shareholders but merely changes the way those rights are recorded on the distributing corporation's books. In section 305(b), Congress has provided that any distributions that do in fact change a shareholder's rights vis-à-vis other shareholders will be taxable. Thus, while pro rata stock distributions generally are not taxable, other stock distributions — and other transactions that have the effect of a non-pro rata stock distribution — will be taxable.

A cautionary note is necessary. In considering stock distributions, it must be determined that the distribution is a distribution to a shareholder as a shareholder and not a disguised payment of compensation or other transaction not covered in section 305.

9.1.1.   Categories of Taxable Stock Distributions

a.   Taxable Transactions in Section 305(b)

Section 305(b), which directs which stock dividends will be taxable, is perhaps best understood by considering an example. Suppose individual shareholders Max and Sally each own 500 shares of MaSaco, a corporation that is worth $100,000 and has $80,000 of e&p. Sally's stock is worth $50,000, as is Max's. MaSaco distributes $25,000 to Sally and 500 shares to Max. After the distribution of $25,000 to Sally, the corporation is worth only $75,000, but the distribution of additional shares to Max doesn't reduce the corporation's worth. Sally's net worth is the same as before the transaction: she had stock worth $50,000, and now she has cash of $25,000 and stock worth $25,000 (one-third of the corporation). Sally's entitlement to future profits, however, is reduced while Max's is increased, even though Max's stock in the aggregate may still appear to have the same value immediately after the transaction. It seems that both Sally and Max should be taxable on their distributions in this case, since both their economic interests have changed considerably, with Sally receiving cash out of the corporation, and Max having a greater interest in the corporation that could be described as a constructive receipt of an equivalent dividend followed by its reinvestment in the corporation.

In fact, that will be the case under section 305(b)(2), which sets out the general rule that provides the concept underlying each of the taxable stock distribution provisions: any time some shareholders receive "property" and other shareholders receive an "increase in the[ir] proportionate interests . . . in the assets or earnings and profits" of the corporation, both sets of shareholders will be taxed. The statute assumes that such distributions will appear in tandem, since the rights under state corporate law of one group of shareholders will be encroached upon if they do not. Reg. section 1.305-3(b)(4) sets out a presumption that distributions within 36 months of each other are appropriately "matched" for this purpose. Indeed, the provision may apply if there is a deemed distribution (e.g., a section 302(d)/301 redemption by one shareholder that (i) is not an "isolated redemption" and (ii) results in an increased interest (to another shareholder) that is deemed to be a stock distribution). *See* Reg. § 1.305-3(b)(2), (3).

The other paragraphs of section 305(b) merely confirm the situations in which such tandem distributions will be presumed to exist. Section 305(b)(1) provides that if any shareholder can elect to receive cash, all shareholders will be treated as having received a taxable dividend. The shareholders' ability to choose between cash or stock suggests that those who receive stock again should be treated as having a constructive receipt of cash that is used to purchase the additional stock (resulting in the "increased interest" that is the focus of the taxable distribution provisions). Perhaps not surprisingly, then, this result applies even if no shareholder in fact elects to receive cash (since the constructive receipt by all shareholders would clearly amount to a section 301 distribution).

There is an exception, however, that makes stock distributions administratively feasible. Most cash distributions in lieu of fractional shares will not cause the stock distribution to be taxable. *See* Reg. § 1.305-3(c).

What Constitutes an Election to Receive Cash or Stock?

Reg. § 1.305-2(a)(3): *§ 305(b)(1) applicable where declaration of stock dividend provides default distribution of stock unless shareholder specifically requests cash.*

Reg. § 1.305-2(a)(4): *§ 305(b)(1) applicable where resolution provides for stock distributions but corporate charter permits any majority shareholder to receive any part of such a stock distribution as a cash distribution upon request.*

Rev. Rul. 76-53, 1976-1 C.B. 87: *§ 305(b)(1) applicable where corporation has a formal dividend reinvestment plan that regularly permits shareholders to elect to reinvest declared dividends as new stock purchases at a discount (95% of fair market value).*

Rev. Rul. 78-375, 1978-2 C.B. 130: *§ 305(b)(1) applicable where dividend reinvestment plan permits purchases at discounts by some shareholders as well as purchases of additional stock at the discounted price.*

Compare Rev. Rul. 77-149, 1977-1 C.B. 82: *§ 301, and not § 305(b)(1), applicable where corporation makes only cash distributions but has a dividend reinvestment plan that permits shareholders to pay local bank as agent to purchase stock at fair market value on the open market.*

Rev. Rul. 76-258, 1976-2 C.B. 95: *§ 305(b)(1) applicable where corporation distributes preferred stock that is immediately redeemable for cash at the option of the shareholder.*

Rev. Rul. 83-68, 1983-1 C.B. 75, modified by Rev. Rul. 90-98, 1990-2 C.B. 56: *§ 305(b)(1) applicable where corporation has an informal policy of redeeming stock from shareholders upon request, after a stock distribution, but Federal Home Loan Bank (FHLB) members will not be treated as having an election to redeem for these purposes.*

Cf. Frontier Sav. Ass'n v. Commissioner, 87 T.C. 665 (1986), **aff'd sub nom.** *Colonial Sav. Ass'n v. Commissioner, 854 F.2d 1001 (7th Cir. 1988),* **cert. denied,** *489 U.S. 1090 (1989),* **acq.,** *1990-1 C.B. 1: § 305(b)(1) not applicable for FHLB stock distributions, rejecting the conclusion of Rev. Rul. 83-68 based on view that FHLB retained discretion not to approve redemption requests.*

Section 305(b)(3) provides that a distribution will be taxed if some common shareholders receive preferred stock and other shareholders receive common stock. This provision is necessary because under section 317, the issuer's own stock is not "property" (so the basic provision in paragraph (b)(2) would not apply by its terms), yet because the preferred stock represents an upgrade in the common shareholder's interests, it seems appropriate to treat it as if it were property.

There is much in the background of section 305, and in the language of the section itself, that relies on there being a clear definition of "preferred stock." Despite this fact, the Code contains no single definition of "preferred stock." Section 351(g)(3)(B) and section 305(e) (which effectively transforms some preferred stock into bonds) both contain language defining "preferred stock" as "stock which is limited and preferred as to dividends and does not participate in corporate growth," but both of these definitions are expressly limited to the specific sections in question. Reg. section 1.305-5(a) confirms that the most important feature for the purposes of section 305 is not the dividend preference, but the limitation on the ability to share in corporate earnings and growth.

Note that when section 305(b) effectively treats a distribution of stock as if it were a distribution of property, it does so only for the purpose of determining the shareholder's treatment. The provision does not affect the tax consequences to the distributing corporation. *See* § 311(a) (providing nonrecognition for non-liquidating distributions of a corporation's own stock, or rights, in respect of its stock).

Section 305(b)(4) provides that almost any stock distribution with respect to preferred stock will be taxable. This one may not seem an exact fit with the analysis set forth above, but it might help to appreciate that this statutory language does away with the need to find the "matching" distribution of property to the other shareholders. It is in the nature of preferred stock that it be limited, so if the rights of preferred shareholders are expanded, the common shareholders must somehow be receiving compensation. The statute simply creates an irrebuttable presumption that they have been so compensated. This section confirmed an early court case that held that distributions on preferred were taxable. *See* Koshland v. Helvering, 298 U.S. 441 (1936).

Section 305(b)(5) makes distributions of convertible preferred stock taxable unless a showing can be made that the effect stated in paragraph (b)(2) is not present. In most cases this effect will be present, since if there is any chance that some recipients will convert and some will not, there will be an increase in the relative interests of some shareholders and a distribution of quasi-property (preferred stock) to others. *See* Reg. § 1.305-6(a)(2).

The section reaches even more broadly because of the definitional expansion in section 305(d), which treats "rights to acquire stock" as stock and "holders of rights or of convertible securities" as shareholders. As a result, a payment of interest on debt instruments that convert to equity can be a property distribution to a shareholder and can result in a disproportionate distribution if there is a stock distribution on actual shares that is not outside the 36-month window of Reg. section 1.305-3(b)(4).

A distribution of stock on common when there is an outstanding issue of stock that is convertible into common and on which dividends are regularly paid will be taxable under section 305 unless there is an appropriate adjustment in the conversion ratio of the convertible stock. *See* Reg. § 1.305-3(d).

b. Deemed Distributions under Section 305(c)

The concept of a disproportionate distribution applies to transactions other than those that take the actual form of a stock distribution. In section 305(c), Congress directed that regulations identify the transactions that will be treated as if they were stock distributions. Changes in conversion ratios that do more than simply adjust for dilution, changes in redemption prices, large redemption premiums, and redemptions that were taxed under section 301 because they failed under section 302(b) to be treated as exchanges may all be treated as "a distribution with respect to any shareholder whose proportionate interest in the earnings and profits or assets of the corporation is increased" thereby.

Although the language of the statute appears mandatory, the Treasury (acting in response to cues in the legislative history) has exercised its regulatory authority under section 305(c) with some restraint in the case of recapitalization transactions, listing only those transactions that are clearly abusive, such as use of stock to pay dividend arrearages on preferred shares. For other transactions, the regulations indicate that an increase in a shareholder's proportionate interest that accompanies one of the types of specified transactions that has a result described in any of paragraphs (2)–(5) of section 305(b) will result in a deemed distribution of stock to that shareholder that will be taxable under section 301, with certain exceptions. Accordingly, in the case of section 302 redemptions that are treated as section 301 distributions, nonredeeming shareholders will be treated as receiving a distribution of shares that will also be treated as a section 301 distribution, unless the redeeming shareholder's redemption is an "isolated" redemption. The Service treats many buybacks as isolated redemptions, avoiding the constructive dividend distribution issue. *See, e.g.*, Rev. Rul. 77-19, 1977-1 C.B. 83 (twenty isolated redemptions over three years from shareholders upon death or retirement, together with redemptions from public minority group, held not to constitute a periodic redemption plan).

i.   Excess Redemption Premium

The last sentence of section 305(c) (added in 1990) serves a slightly different purpose from the rest of section 305, as it is part of the battle to hold the debt/equity line. It directs that Treasury write regulations that treat the excess redemption price of stock not only as a distribution with respect to that stock, but as a distribution that will be taken into account over the time during which the stock to be redeemed is outstanding. Under Reg. section 1.305-5(b), promulgated under this authority, holders of preferred stock that may be called at a price higher than its issue price (sometimes called "OID preferred") will be required to accrue this premium as if it were interest. The rule in section 305(c) alters the tax treatment of the holder, by accelerating the inclusion of the premium as if it were actually interest, but it appears not to change the treatment to the corporation issuing the interest nor the availability of a dividends-received deduction to a shareholder corporation.

9.1.2. Tax Consequences of Taxable Stock Distributions

The statute provides that stock distributions that fall under subsections (b) and (c) of section 305 are included in income by the shareholder as distributions of property to which section 301 applies. Under section 301(c), the distribution will be a dividend to the extent of the corporation's allocable earnings and profits, with any excess first treated as a recovery of capital (the basis in the stock on which the distribution is made) and then as gain. The new stock will have a fair market value basis under section 301(d), determined as of the date of the distribution. Reg. § 1.301-1(h).

a. Amount of the Distribution

The regulations establish that the amount of the distribution will generally be the fair market value of the stock received. Reg. § 1.305-1(b)(1). In the ordinary case, this will seem like the obvious and only possible result. There may be circumstances, however, when this rule is not so obvious, such as when the value of the property distributed to other shareholders clearly differs from the value of the stock distributed, or when, as a part of the same transaction, some shareholders can purchase stock at a discount.

Exceptions set out in the regulations provide that when a corporation (such as a mutual fund) regularly distributes its earnings and profits and offers shareholders a choice of stock or money, the amount of the distribution of stock will be treated as the amount of cash that the shareholder could otherwise have received. There are special OID-like rules for determining the amount of a distribution in certain transactions that are taxable under section 305(c). *See* Reg. § 1.305-3(e) Exs. (6), (8), (9), and (15).

How Many Shares Is a Nonredeeming Shareholder Treated as Receiving in a Constructive Stock Distribution Under Section 305(c)?

Reg. section 1.305-3(e) Ex. 8 provides an illustration of the calculation:

X has 1000 shares outstanding with 10 shareholders and a periodic plan of redemption. X redeems 5 shares from each of 9 shareholders (for 45 total) but does not redeem any of C's shares. As a result, C's interest has increased. Cash to the 9 shareholders is taxable under section 301. C is deemed to have received a distribution of additional X shares under sections 305(b)(2) and 305(c).

Amount of C's distribution equals the fair market value (FMV) of the shares which would have been distributed to C if the increase in ownership had been represented by additional issuance of a number of shares (#) to C (rather than by reduction in other shareholders' shares).

    C's % ownership before redemption: *100/1000 = 10%*

    C's % ownership after redemption: *100/955 = 10.47%*

    Number of shares providing that percentage is #.

*Using numbers **prior** to redemption:*

    (100 + #) / (1000 + #) = 10.47%

    # = 5.25

    FMV/share = FMV of 955 actual shares / 1005.25 deemed shares

    FMV distribution = FMV/share * number of shares distributed

b. Effect of Taxable Stock Dividends on the Corporation

The corporation will have no gain or loss on the distribution under section 311(a)(1), and thus its earnings and profits will not be increased under subsections 312(b)(1) and (f)(1) in respect of the distribution, even if it uses appreciated treasury stock. Its earnings and profits will be reduced by the portion of the fair market value of the stock that is includible in income by the shareholders. Reg. § 1.312-1(d).

9.1.3. Tax Consequences of Nontaxable Stock Distributions

Obviously, if a stock distribution is not taxable under section 305(a), the recipient will need to determine its basis in the new stock issued. Section 307 and Reg. section 1.307-1(a) provide that the basis of new stock distributed on old stock will be determined by allocating the basis of the old stock between the two, in proportion to their respective fair market values. (Note that this rule will be applied together with the block-by-block approach to stockholding generally, so that for each block of stock with respect to which a stock dividend is received, basis will be spread between the new stock and the old. But a stock dividend will not present the opportunity to spread basis across blocks of stock.) Under section 1223(5), the holding period of the new stock will tack that of the old. If there was a single block of old stock, and the new and old shares are of the same class, these rules effectively treat the entire group of shares as a single block of stock acquired at the same time for the same price.

There is an elective exception to the allocation of basis when the distribution is of stock rights that have de minimis value compared to the old stock held by the shareholder. Under section 307(b), if the stock rights are worth less than 15% of the old stock's fair market value at the time of the distribution, the basis is not allocated unless the shareholder so elects. The election must be made in the return for the taxable year in which the rights are received. The regulations, however, prevent shareholders from claiming an artificial loss if the rights subsequently lapse: the allocation is treated as made only if the rights are exercised or sold. *See* Reg. § 1.307-1(a).

The distributing corporation again has no gain or loss on the distribution, even if it uses treasury stock, under section 311(a)(1), and no reduction in its earnings and profits, under section 312(d)(1)(B).

a. The Section 306 Taint

Much of the stock that is received without tax under section 305 is subject to a "taint" imposed by section 306. The section 306 taint kicks in to treat transactions that would otherwise be entitled to sale treatment as dividends whenever stock previously received tax-free is sold without the underlying stock also being sold. The idea here is that dividends of preferred stock allow a corporation to encapsulate value that can easily be sold by the shareholders without substantially affecting their economic interests, as long as they continue to hold their common stock.

This provision was in large part a reaction to an early corporate tax shelter, the "preferred stock bailout," according to which insurance companies assisted small corporations in issuing preferred stock that would pay very reliable dividends and have very certain redemption terms. The insurance companies bought the preferred stock from the shareholders, collected the interest-like dividend payments, and then sold the stock back to the corporation. The result was essentially the same as if the shareholders had received a lump sum distribution directly from the corporation, since the price that the insurance companies paid for the preferred stock was based strictly on the present value of the anticipated dividend payments and the redemption price. *See* Chamberlin v. Commissioner, 207 F.2d 462 (6th Cir. 1953) (upholding the "bailout" tax treatment claimed by the shareholders). Congress addressed the preferred stock bailout by treating the taxable disposition of the preferred as the appropriate time for treatment of the transaction as a distribution from the corporation.

Section 306(c)(1)(A) treats as section 306 stock any stock that is distributed and not subject to tax under section 305, except common stock issued on common. Most commentators simply summarize the effect of this language as limiting the scope of section 306 to stock that is "not common," and therefore as limiting the scope of section 306 to preferred stock. While this generalization is an easy rule of thumb, it overlooks the several ways in which common stock can in fact carry the section 306 taint. While the section 306(c)(1)(B) test for stock received in reorganizations seems to be limited to "not common stock," there are several routes by which common stock could be rendered section 306 stock. First, the regulations make the point that *any* stock received in a distribution and not taxed under section 305 can be treated as section 306 stock under section 306(c)(1)(A). *See* Reg. § 1.306-3(a) and (c). More importantly (and with real consequences), section 306(c)(1)(C) can cause any stock received in exchange for section 306 stock to be treated as section 306 stock if the stock received takes its basis from the section 306 stock. Reg. § 1.306-3(e). *But see* Reg. § 1.306-3(f).

The taint only attaches to stock, however, if the initial stock distribution would have been taxed at least in part as a dividend if it had been made in cash. § 306(c)(2).

The taint comes into play differently depending upon how the shareholder disposes of the section 306 stock. If the tainted stock is sold to anyone other than the distributing corporation, the amount realized is treated as "ordinary income," to the extent the fair market value would have been a dividend on the date of the stock distribution if it had been distributed in cash. (After Congress changed the characterization of dividends from ordinary income to net capital gain under section 1(h)(11) as part of the 2003 rate changes, it also amended this provision to treat these "ordinary income" amounts as dividends for purposes of section 1(h)(11). *See* section 306(a)(1)(D).) Amounts beyond that treated as "ordinary income" are treated as return of basis of the disposed shares and then gain from sale, but no loss can be recognized. This provision in essence applies the section 301(c) rules upon the sale of the tainted stock, but unambiguously limits the basis taken into consideration to the basis of the disposed stock. Any unrecovered basis would presumably "snap back" to the remaining stock (including the underlying stock, if all of the section 306 stock is disposed of). Reg. § 1.306-1(b)(2), Ex. 2 and 3. A corporate shareholder, however, will not be eligible for the dividends-received deduction, and the distributing corporation has no earnings and profit reduction on account of the treatment of the sales proceeds as a dividend. Reg. § 1.312-1(e).

If, on the other hand, the tainted stock is redeemed by the distributing corporation, the entire amount paid is treated as a section 301 distribution *made at the time of the redemption* (i.e., the determinations of earnings and profits are those that would be made if an actual distribution had been made). The regular section 301 and 316 rules apply, and a corporate shareholder is eligible for a dividends-received deduction. In this case, the distributing corporation does reduce its earnings and profits account for the amount treated as a dividend. Finally, if boot is received in exchange for section 306 stock in a reorganization, section 356(f) provides that the entire amount will be treated as a distribution to which section 301 applies.

In either case when the "distribution" is from earnings and profits, the income is eligible for the special rate for dividends. *See* section 306(a)(1)(D). Again, the temporarily reduced rate on dividends makes the inability to use basis (in most cases) almost the only penalty ultimately imposed under the section 306 regime. The fact that the corporation's earnings and profits are not reduced when the section 306 stock is sold to a third party may also be seen as having considerable deterrent effect.

The taint can be avoided if the shareholder sells all of its stock of the distributing corporation in the same transaction, or if, as provided in section 306(b)(4), it can be established that the distribution and disposition were "not in pursuance of a plan having as one of its principal purposes the avoidance of Federal income tax." There is no taint if there were no earnings and profits to support a cash dividend at the time of the stock distribution, under section 306(c)(2).

i.   From Nontaxable Receipts of and Exchanges of Section 306 Stock

The section 306 taint can apply to more than just the stock received in a simple stock distribution. It can apply to *any* stock received in any nontaxable transaction in which section 306 stock is surrendered or otherwise transferred, including nonrecognition exchanges in which a "substituted basis" or a "transferred basis" rule is used, as described in section 306(c)(1)(C). Indeed, this provision's language is broad enough to cover the receipt of section 306 stock as a gift, the basis of which is the donor's basis under section 1015. Reg. § 1.306-3(e) (fifth sentence).

Section 306(c)(1)(C) encompasses certain situations in which section 306 stock is given up in section 351 transactions in exchange for stock under circumstances in which one might not expect the stock received to be section 306 stock, either because it is common stock or because the transferee corporation has no earnings and profits. The regulations provide the example of a person exchanging preferred stock previously distributed by his controlled corporation A for common stock of his controlled corporation B in a section 351 transaction. The *common* stock of B will be treated as section 306 stock on its disposition by the shareholder, just as the preferred stock in corporation A now held by corporation B will also be treated as section 306 stock. Reg. § 1.306-3(e). This rule prevents the shareholder with the section 306 stock from "encapsulating" this tainted stock in another corporation holding little else than the tainted stock, and selling the newly issued stock. Note that the carryover of the section 306 taint to stock that is received in exchange for section 306 stock in this example was applied to common stock. Furthermore, Rev. Rul. 77-108, 1977-1 C.B. 86, held that the test in section 306(c)(2) requiring that earnings and profits be present at the time of the receipt of the potentially tainted stock does not apply to the re-transfers of section 306 stock covered by section 306(c)(1)(C).

The reach of section 306(c)(1)(C) is not as broad as it might first appear, however, since most authorities read section 306(c)(1)(B) (discussed below) as excluding the application of section 306(c)(1)(C) at all in transactions that are reorganizations.

ii.   From the Receipt of Stock "Other Than Common Stock" in Other Exchange Transactions

The section 306 taint will also apply to stock "which is not common stock" received in nonrecognition transactions that are not simple distributions of stock, if the result of the transaction is something that resembles a dividend.

Section 306(c)(1)(B) provides the standards under which stock received in a reorganization will be section 306 stock. (It is, furthermore, generally read to exclude the application of other subsections of 306(c) to stock received in reorganizations.) Stock "other than common stock" received in a reorganization will be subject to the section 306 taint if "the effect of the transaction was substantially the same as the receipt of a stock dividend." § 306(c)(1)(B)(ii) (first condition). Reg. section 1.306-3(d) further provides that "ordinarily, section 306 stock includes stock which is not common stock received in pursuance of a plan of reorganization . . . if cash received in lieu of such stock would have been treated as a dividend under section 356(a)(2)." This language suggests that not all preferred stock received in a reorganization will be section 306 stock, even though it is received without tax. There is surprisingly little law on how this provision should be interpreted after the amplification of the operation of section 356 in *Commissioner v. Clark*, 489 U.S. 726 (1989).

Section 306(c)(1)(B)(ii) (second condition) also provides that "not common" stock received in exchange for stock that was section 306 stock will automatically be section 306 stock — whether or not it is a dividend-equivalent transaction. (This result is the same result that would be reached if section 306(c)(1)(C) were applicable, but section 306(c)(1)(B) is generally read as displacing section 306(c)(1)(C) entirely when the transaction in question is a reorganization.)

Under section 306(c)(3) stock "other than common stock" received in section 351 transactions can also be subject to the section 306 taint in certain circumstances if its receipt would have been taxed as a dividend — to any extent — had the same value been distributed in cash. Note that the discussion above regarding the application of section 306 to stock received in section 351 transactions was limited to those circumstances in which the "property" contributed to the issuing corporation was itself section 306 stock. Section 306(c)(3), enacted long after the rest of section 306 was in place, covers additional situations in which the stock received by the shareholder in the section 351 transaction itself represents a limited interest and therefore presents a potential for a "stock bailout."

The literal language of the test in section 306(c)(3) would seem to apply to any section 351 transaction involving a transferee corporation that had earnings and profits, but the provision has always been interpreted narrowly as targeting only those transactions in which preferred stock is received as the result of the transfer of the *stock* of one corporation to a second corporation when the transferor shareholder has control of both corporations as described in section 304. Perhaps this narrow reading results from the fact that the second sentence of the provision invokes "rules similar to the rules of section 304(b)(2) (according to which the earnings and profits of both corporations are pooled for the purpose of determining dividend equivalence)," a provision that makes limited sense except in the case of common control. The modified attribution rules under section 304(c)(3)(B) are also applicable. *See* § 306(c)(4).

There are, however, other circumstances in which the receipt of preferred stock in section 351 transactions may result in stock with a section 306 taint even without reference to section 306(c)(3). Such transactions (and any other transaction between a corporation and its shareholders) will always be scrutinized under Reg. section 1.301-1(*l*) to determine whether they are appropriately treated as involving a distribution of preferred stock that is entirely separate from the other transaction. Thus, if all shareholders in an existing corporation contributed assets in a section 351 transaction and took back preferred stock pro rata, the receipt of the preferred stock would be treated as a separate dividend distribution.

PRACTICE PROBLEMS

1. Corp Z declared a dividend of one share of common stock for each share of common stock outstanding. A shareholder could, however, choose instead to receive a security of the corporation with a face amount of $20. No one elected to take the security. On the date treated as the distribution date, Corp Z's common stock was worth $21 and its $20 face amount bonds had a fair market value of $19.50.

What amount, if any, was taxable to a holder of 100 shares of Corp Z common stock as a result of this distribution?

(a) $2,100.

(b) $1,950.

(c) $2,000.

(d)   No amount taxable.

2. Corp X has only common shareholders. The price of its stock has risen to $400 a share. In order to facilitate sales of its stock, it engages in a stock dividend whereby each shareholder receives 7 new shares for every one share already owned.

What are the consequences to a shareholder who held 10 shares with a basis of $40 each?

(a)   Income of $4,000; 80 shares with basis of $50 each.

(b) No income; 80 shares with basis of $5 each.

(c) Income of $3,600; 80 shares with basis of $50 each.

(d) No income; 10 shares with basis of $40 each and 70 shares with basis of zero.

3. Corp X has only common shareholders. The price of its stock has risen to $400 a share. In order to effectively lower its stock price, Corp X distributes 10 shares of Y Corp stock worth $10 each, which it held as an investment, to each holder of 1 share of its stock. What is the effect of this distribution to a shareholder who owns 10 shares with a basis of $40 each?

(a) No income; 10 shares Corp X stock with basis of $30 each and 100 shares Corp Y stock with a basis of $1 each.

(b) Insufficient information provided.

(c) Income of $1,000.

(d) Gain of $600.

4. Corp X has two classes of stock, common and preferred (which is nonconvertible and both limited and preferred as to dividends.) It declares and distributes a dividend of additional common stock worth $2 per share with respect to each share of the common and a dividend of $3 share on the preferred.

The effect of this distribution on the *common* shareholders is:

(a) $2 per share of income.

(b) $2 per share as a section 301 distribution, the ultimate treatment of which depends upon Corp X's e&p.

(c) No taxable income.

(d) Insufficient information; the result will depend upon overlap in ownership between common and preferred.

5. Corp V has two classes of common stock — Class A, which receives annual dividends of cash, and Class B, which receives annual dividends of stock equal in value to the amount of the cash distributed to the other class. A distribution of $100 per share is made with respect to the class A stock, and a corresponding distribution of stock is made with respect to the class B stock. Corp V has e&p sufficient to characterize all distributions made in this year as dividends.

What is the effect on a Class B shareholder who owns 10 shares with a total basis of $500 and receives 10 new shares?

(a) Section 301 distribution of $1,000; basis of $75 in each share.

(b) No income; basis of $25 in each share.

(c) Section 301 distribution of $1,000; basis of $50 each in old shares and $100 each in new.

(d) No income; basis of $50 in old shares and $0 in new shares.

6. Corp W declared and distributed a stock dividend of 5 shares for every 100 shares outstanding. One shareholder who owned only 10 shares received cash of $30 instead, the prorated value of the 0.5 fractional share he would have otherwise received. How will this distribution be taxed to all of the shareholders?

(a) Taxable to all under section 305(b)(2).

(b) Taxable as a redemption to be tested under section 302 to the shareholder receiving cash; nontaxable to others.

(c) Taxable as a section 301 distribution only to the shareholder receiving cash; nontaxable to others.

(d) Taxable to the extent of $30 for every 100 shares held by other shareholders; fully taxable to the shareholder receiving cash.

7. Corp U has two classes of stock outstanding, class A which is regular common, and class B which can be converted into regular common at any time. As each year passes, the ratio for the conversion increases: in the first year, one share of B can be converted into one share of A; in the second year, into 1.05 shares of A, in the third year, into 1.1025 shares, etc. A cash dividend is paid each year on the class A stock. The value of Corp U common stock increases on average about 3% per year. What are the consequences of holding the Class B stock?

(a) Taxable to the extent of the fair market value of the difference between the value of the stock they could have purchased under the prior year conversion rate and such value under the new conversion rate — e.g., the value of .05 shares at the end of the first year.

(b) None, under *Macomber* and the realization requirement, no gain is recognized until sale.

(c) Taxable to the extent of the dividend received by the class A shareholders.

(d) Taxable to the extent of the annual increase in value of the Corp U stock into which their stock can be converted.

8. Ed is one of six equal shareholders and one of 10 employees of Dotcom Co. Dotcom Co was running short of cash, so he agreed to receive 5 additional shares of Dotcom Co instead of cash for his last month's pay. The other shareholders all paid $5000 in exchange for their additional shares. Both before and after the transaction, Dotcom has only common stock outstanding. What are the consequences to Ed of the receipt of this stock?

(a) Not taxable, as distribution of common on common.

(b) Section 301 distribution of $5,000, taxable as dividend to the extent of e&p.

(c) Gain, the amount of which will depend upon Ed's basis in his stock.

(d) Compensation income of $5,000.

9. Sal is about to sell preferred stock that she owns in Corp Z. Under which of the following circumstances will her sale definitely be treated the same as it would be if her stock were common stock, and thus unaffected by the provisions of section 306?

(a)   She was taxed when she received the stock as a distribution with respect to other stock she then held in Corp Z.

(b)   She is selling the stock to Corp Z in connection with its complete liquidation.

(c)   She is selling the stock to another individual, and Corp Z had no earnings and profits when the stock was distributed to her. She received the stock on the initial incorporation of Corp Z.

(d)   She is selling the stock to Corp Z and, although it had earnings and profits when the stock was distributed to her, it now has no earnings and profits.

(e)   She purchased the stock for cash.

(f)   She is selling the stock to Corp Z and will own no other stock in Corp Z (either actually or by attribution) after the transaction.

(g)   She is tendering the stock in exchange for stock of an acquiring corporation in a transaction that will qualify as a reorganization under section 368.

(h)   She received the stock on the initial incorporation of Corp Z.

DISCUSSION PROBLEMS

1.   X Corp has two classes of stock outstanding, with 1,000 shares of common held by 5 shareholders (worth $5 million in the aggregate) and 500 shares of preferred (worth $1 million in the aggregate.) It has $500,000 in earnings and profits.

(a)   The regular annual cash dividend has been paid on the common stock. In the same year, there is a stock dividend on the common, resulting in each outstanding share receiving two additional shares of the same class of common. What result?

(b)   What if the dividend was paid in a new class of stock, with identical economic rights to the existing common but different voting rights?

(c)   What if the dividend was in a new class of stock, with economic rights the same as the existing common except that the first $2 million of liquidation proceeds must be paid to it after the preferred stock's liquidation rights have been satisfied?

(d)   What if there were no preferred outstanding, and X Corp distributed 500 shares of preferred stock on the common (i.e., 100 shares to each of the common shareholders)?

(e)   What if, after two years of mediocre performance in which earnings and profits has increased only by a total of $50,000 and during which no distributions of any sort have been made, shareholder A sells 100 shares of the preferred stock he received in part (d) back to X Corp for $280,000?

(f)   Three more years passed since the redemption in part (e), and shareholder B sold the 100 shares of preferred stock he received in part (d) to an unrelated party. During these three years, Corp X has booked substantial losses, reducing its e&p to $100,000 as of the time of B's sale. But these losses do not accurately reflect the change in the value of Corp X; since Shareholder B sold his preferred stock for $2 million.

(g)   What if X Corp is merged into Y Corp, and in the merger those C Corp shareholders still holding the preferred stock issued in part (d) receive preferred stock in Y Corp? What if they receive common stock of Y Corp?

2.   X Corp has two classes of stock outstanding, common and preferred. The preferred has limited liquidation rights, but participates in growth to the extent that its cumulative dividend increases as the inflation-adjusted market value of the common increases. There has been some contentiousness about the computation of this increase. An agreement has been reached that the old formula will be abandoned and replaced with a right to a distribution of common to the preferred shareholders whenever the market value of the common stock has increased more than 15%. What would be the tax consequence of such an agreement?

3.   Smallco has 100 shares outstanding, held by five shareholders, three of whom (A, B, and C) each own 12% of the stock, and two of whom (E and F) each own 32%. In year 1, Smallco redeems, pro rata, half of A, B, and C's stock. In year 2, it redeems half of E's and F's shares. In year 3, as Smallco prepares to redeem more of A's, B's, and C's stock, E's son, fresh out of law school and handling his father's financial affairs, suggests that this course of action might not be the wisest. Before any of the redemptions, the total worth of the corporation was $1,440,000.

What is E's son anxious about? Under this pattern of redemptions, when and under what theory might each of the shareholders be taxed? *See* §§ 302(b)(2)(D), 305(c).

(a)   If the effect on E and F is a deemed taxable stock distribution in the first year, what is the amount of this deemed distribution?

(b)   If everyone is treated as having received a dividend distribution in the first year (A, B, and C because the serial nature of their actual redemptions transformed them into dividend equivalent distributions, and E and F because the redemption of A, B, C could not be viewed as "isolated redemptions" under 305(c)), what should happen in the second year?

4.   Corp X issues preferred stock with a par value of $100, with a preferential dividend of 1% that is mandatorily redeemable in five years for $150. What result to the redeemed shareholder? To the corporation?

5.   Al received 100 shares of Bigco preferred stock in connection with Bigco's acquisition of Littleco in a section 351 transaction three years ago. This preferred stock had a total value of $5000 at the time Al received it in exchange for common stock that Al had held with a total basis of $1000. Both Bigco and Littleco have historically been very profitable.

According to its original terms, Al had a right to put the preferred stock to Bigco for $65 a share five years after the acquisition unless certain performance contingencies were met in the first two years, in which case Al was entitled to sell to Bigco for $70 a share in the second year.

What is the effect on Al when the contingency is met and he asks to be redeemed in the second year? What if the contingency is not met, and Al asks to be redeemed in the fifth year?

6.   Corp X has two classes of stock outstanding, 200 shares of common and 50 shares of convertible preferred. One share of convertible preferred can be converted into four shares of common for $10. The corporation distributes a stock dividend of one share of additional common on the existing common. What change in the conversion rights of the convertible preferred shareholders must be made to prevent the distribution on the common from being considered an increase in the proportionate interests of the common shareholders? What is the consequence if the preferred shareholders have no right to such a change?

9.2.   RECAPITALIZATIONS

Statutes and Regulations	IRC §§ 354, 356, 368
	Reg. §§ 1.301-1(*l*), 1.368-2(b) (eighth sentence), 1.368-2(e)
Other Primary Authorities	Bazley v. Commissioner, 331 U.S. 737 (1947)
	Rev. Rul. 86-25, 1986-1 C.B. 203

A recapitalization involves a "reshuffling of the capital structure" in a single corporation. Helvering v. Southwest Consol. Corp., 315 U.S. 194 (1942). Such transactions have long been considered within the group of transactions entitled to special nonrecognition treatment as "reorganizations" within the meaning of that term in section 368. In such transactions the shareholders enjoy nonrecognition under section 354 to the extent that they receive stock in exchange for stock with the consequences of receiving other consideration as well determined under section 356. (The tax treatment of reorganizations more generally is considered in Chapter 15 and following.)

In a recapitalization, there will be only one corporation to which the shareholders effectively give up their old stock and receive new stock. Ordinarily, this corporation does nothing but issue its own stock and debt, transactions which would not ordinarily give rise to corporate income, so the status of the transaction as a reorganization is frequently of little consequence to the corporation. Although recapitalizations are not mentioned in section 381, it is generally assumed that a recapitalization will have no effect on the tax attributes of the corporation. The limitations of section 382 can apply, however, if there has been more than a 50% change in stock ownership as defined in that section.

Qualification as a reorganization matters to the shareholders, however, since section 354 may be the only source of nonrecognition for their exchange of shares, and treatment of nonstock interests received is likely to be different under section 356 than if either the rules regarding regular sales and exchanges of stock or the rules regarding distributions of or with respect to stock apply.

9.2.1. Qualification as a Recapitalization

Unlike the other provisions of section 368(a)(1) and Reg. section 1.368-2, neither (a)(1)(E) nor Reg. section 1.368-2(e) provides any language suggesting the general nature of the transactions contemplated. As a somewhat inadequate substitute, the regulation instead provides examples of transactions that will be treated as recapitalizations, as follows:

(1)   a "discharge" of bonds by issuing preferred stock to the bondholders;

(2)   a surrender to a corporation of 25% of its preferred stock and the receipt by the former preferred shareholders of common stock;

(3)   the issuance of preferred stock in exchange for common stock;

(4)   an exchange of outstanding preferred for newly issued common; and

(5)   an exchange of outstanding preferred stock, even when dividends are in arrears, for other stock.

In short, recapitalizations involve exchanges of debt or equity interests in a corporation (or both). Such transactions frequently involve replacement of all of the stock of a corporation, but they need not. It appears that an "exchange" of interests is required, but there are several relatively old authorities that suggest that sufficient changes made in the articles of incorporation regarding the rights inherent in various classes of stock may be treated as a deemed exchange.

In order to qualify as a "reorganization," the capital restructuring must serve some business purpose of the corporation. Reg. § 1.368-1(b). Perhaps surprisingly, the other judicial doctrines upon which reorganization status is usually conditioned (that is, continuity of business enterprise and continuity of shareholder interest) have been held not to apply to recapitalizations. Rev. Rul. 77-415, 1977-2 C.B. 311, *obsoleted by* T.D. 9182, 2005-1 C.B. 713 (promulgating Reg. § 1.368–1(b) (eighth sentence)), first held that there is no continuity of interest requirement in a recapitalization. Conceding a battle that it had lost in the courts on several occasions, the Service ruled that the continuity of interest doctrine should not be applied to reorganizations that are not "mergers or consolidations." That particular ruling was probably not a taxpayer victory. It prevented the creation of original issue discount that would otherwise have allowed the corporation to deduct interest without actual payment. Under the law then in effect, securities issued in a reorganization would not give rise to original issue discount. By ruling that a transaction in which preferred stock was given up in exchange for bonds was a reorganization even though "continuity of proprietary interest" was not maintained, the Service was able to disallow the corporation its desired interest deductions. Despite the fact that significant changes have been made in the law governing the apparent stakes in that ruling, it remains good law. In Rev. Rul. 82-34, 1982-1 C.B. 59, *rendered obsolete by* T.D. 9182, 2005-1 C.B. 713, the Service held that the continuity of business enterprise requirement was also inapplicable, citing little other than Rev. Rul. 77-415. This aspect of recapitalizations was solidified by the 2005 introduction of the eighth sentence of Reg. section 1.368-1(b). More recently, the Treasury has indicated that recapitalizations are not subject to any net-value requirement in respect of the exchanged interest. Prop. Reg. § 1.368-1(b)(1).

A recapitalization need not involve all shareholders of a class of stock — i.e., a shareholder's stock may be exchanged for a different class of stock in a nonrecognition recapitalization while others continue to hold shares of the exchanged class. As discussed below, this aspect of recapitalizations puts considerable pressure on the distinction between transactions which will be honored as exchanges of stock for which nonrecognition will be available, and transactions that enhance the rights of some shareholders in a way that implicates section 305.

9.2.2. Types of Recapitalizations and their Tax Consequences

a. Stock-For-Stock Exchanges

Probably the most common type of recapitalization is one in which some common shareholders have all or a portion of their common stock replaced with preferred stock, so as to "freeze" the value of their ownership interest in the preferred stock and yield future growth and control to younger management. Rev. Rul. 74-269, 1974-1 C.B. 87. It seems clear that recapitalization status will in most such cases prevent gain recognition with respect to the stock exchanged, under section 354.

Preferred stock that is nonqualified preferred stock under section 351(g), however, will be treated as boot under the reorganization provisions unless received in respect of similar stock. § 354(a)(2)(C).

Family Corporations' Use of Section 351(g) Stock

Section 354(a)(2)(C)(ii) provides a special exception from the ordinary taxability of the receipt of section 351(g) stock in reorganizations. If the corporation is a "family corporation" for five years before and three years after the exchange in question, the section 351(g) NQP stock will qualify for nonrecognition just like all other stock. An extension of the statute of limitations, similar to that involved in avoiding family attribution under section 302(c), is required to insure compliance.

Status as a family corporation is tied to the definition provided in section 447, a provision permitting smaller corporations and corporations engaged in farming to use the cash method of accounting. Under section 447(d)(2)(C)(i), 50% of the combined voting power, and 50% of all other classes of stock must be owned by the same family. "Family" for these purposes is very broadly defined. See § 447(e)(1).

Ordinarily, an exchange that would otherwise receive nonrecognition under section 354 that transfers section 351(g) NQP stock for section 351(g) NQP stock will not be taxable. See § 354(a)(2)(C); Reg. § 1.356-6(a)(1). This makes some sense, since the stock given up presumably was already taxed on receipt; only the first receipt of section 351(g) NQP triggers the unfavorable taxable treatment. Exchanges that continue a shareholder's interest at the same modest level of risk should enjoy the same treatment that exchanges of interests that actually were debt securities would have enjoyed under section 354(a)(2).

> *Does stock that avoided taxation under the special rule for recapitalizations of family corporations get this same free pass in a later exchange for section 351(g) NQP stock, say, of a publicly traded issuer? The answer is not entirely clear. Status as "nonqualified preferred stock" under section 351(g)(2) is determined solely with regard to the characteristics of the instrument, and there is no language in section 354(a)(2)(C) or Reg. section 1.356-6(a)(1) further limiting the term based on having actually triggered a tax in the past.*

Nonrecognition on the exchange is not the only issue of consequence in such transactions. Stock-for-stock exchanges can frequently raise questions under the gift tax, if the older generation has received stock worth less than the value that it surrendered, and there are special rules under the transfer tax regime that cover this situation. Furthermore, preferred stock received with respect to common may carry with it a section 306 taint. *See* § 306(c)(1)(B). This will occur when the effect of the transaction is essentially equivalent to a stock dividend, *cf.* Reg. § 1.306-3(d), Ex. 1 (pro rata receipt of preferred stock in a merger), or when the stock given up is section 306 stock, Reg. § 1.306-3(d), Ex. 2 (preferred stock received in recapitalization in exchange for preferred stock will not be section 306 stock unless the stock given up was section 306 stock). A recapitalization may also result in a constructive distribution of stock to which section 305(c) applies.

i.   Basis after Stock-For-Stock Recapitalizations

In a stock-for-stock recapitalization, the shareholder's basis in the stock received is the same as his basis in the stock given up. As is the case with any other reorganization, any blocks of stock acquired at different times or held with different bases will be preserved in the stock received. Thus if a shareholder gives up stock held in two equal blocks of six shares each, one with a total basis of $54 ($9 per share), and the other with a total basis of $108 ($18 per share), for six shares of new stock, the new stock will be held in two blocks of three shares each, one with a basis of $54 ($18 per share) and one with a basis of $108 ($36 per share).

Although this basis allocation seems fairly straightforward, determinations are complicated when shares received are not easy multiples of shares given up. For instance, if the shareholder above receives 3 shares of preferred stock and 12 shares of common stock and there is no other specification of the terms of the exchange, the shareholder will be treated as having received 1½ shares of preferred and 6 shares of common with respect to each block of stock. If the preferred is valued at $1 per share ($3 total) and the common is valued at $.50 ($6 total), the basis of each block will be allocated 1/3 to the 1½ shares of preferred stock and 2/3 to the 6 shares of common. Thus $54 of basis in the first block will be allocated 1/3 (or $18) to 1½ shares of preferred stock (for a basis of $12 per share and $6 per ½ share) and 2/3 (or $36) to the common (or $6 per share). The $108 basis in the second block of shares will similarly be allocated, so that there is one share of preferred with a basis of $24, ½ share of preferred with a basis of $12 and 6 shares of common stock with a basis of $12 per share. How should we think about these two "half shares" of preferred? Both the regulations finalized in 2006 and those proposed in 2009 clearly anticipate that this stock will be treated as having two different "segments," and each segment will continue to be held with a distinct basis (and holding period, where relevant). Prop. Reg. § 1.358-2(b)(3)(ii) states that "if a share . . . is received in exchange for more than one share . . . and such shares . . . were acquired . . . at different prices, the share . . . received shall be divided into segments based on the relative fair market values of the shares . . . surrendered. Each segment shall have a basis determined under the rules of this section." *See* Prop. Reg. § 1.358-2(*i*), Ex. 13; Reg. §§ 1.358-2(a)(2)(i), 1.358-2(c), Ex. 2.

This technique of dividing shares that are in reality one share into distinct segments each with a distinct basis takes on new importance under the regulations proposed in 2009 that require a fictional "recapitalization" in order to reconcile a shareholder's position after a transaction in which stock is deemed issued for the purposes of analyzing the consequences of the transaction, or after a transaction in which basis is not used but the stock to which it attached is no longer held. Such fictional recapitalizations are invoked as the solution to the disappearing basis problem in redemptions recast as distributions under section 302(d), see Prop. Reg. § 1.302-5(a)(2), including those that are so recast under section 304, see Prop. Reg. § 1.304-2(c), Ex. 2 and 3. Consider a shareholder who owns all 100 shares of a corporation in two blocks, one with 75 shares with a total basis of $75 and one with 25 shares with a total basis of $50. When the shareholder sells 20 shares of stock back to the issuing corporation in a transaction that is taxed under section 302(d) as a dividend distribution, the shareholder will hold her 80 remaining shares in two blocks, one of 60 shares with a basis of $75 and one of 20 shares with a basis of $50. This result is obtained by assuming a fictional recapitalization in which all shares were given up in exchange for 4/5 of a new share. Prop. Reg. § 1.302-5(e), Ex. 1. (This calculation was made unrealistically simple because the deemed exchange ratio in the recapitalization resulted in a whole number of shares in each block. Much more commonly, the deemed exchange ratio will result in fractional shares, which must be re-aggregated to reflect the actual holding. If, for instance, the shareholder in the preceding example had held 100 shares and redeemed 50, the fictional recapitalization would have involved receiving half of a share in exchange for each of the 100 shares given up, resulting in one block of 37 shares with a basis of $2 each, one block of 12 shares with a basis of $4 each, and one share with a segment with a basis of $1 and a second segment with a basis of $2.)

Such a fictional recapitalization will also be invoked when stock in a reorganization is deemed to have been issued when such issuance would have been a meaningless gesture. Prop. Reg. § 1.358-2(d) & (i) Exs. 9, 10 (no stock issued in a transaction deemed to be a reorganization described in section 368(a)(1)(D) involving single blocks of Target and Acquirer, resulting in two blocks of Acquirer stock).

ii.   Stock-For-Debt and Debt-For-Stock Exchanges

Recapitalizations include not only exchanges in which shareholders become more senior (or junior) with respect to other shareholders, but also transactions in which shareholders become debt holders or debt holders become shareholders. So long as there is a recapitalization, such debt exchanges are nonrecognition transactions to the extent they satisfy the nonrecognition provisions of section 354.

A threshold requirement for debt exchanges to qualify under section 354 is categorization as a "security."

Definition of "Security"

Generally speaking, securities are negotiable instruments that permit investment in enterprises for purposes of making a profit. See, e.g., SEC v. W. J. Howey Co., 328 U.S. 293 (1946) (setting forth a three-part test for investment contracts treated as securities requiring an investment in a common enterprise with the expectation of making profits primarily from the efforts of others). They may be issued in certificated form or in book-entry or electronic form. They may represent an obligation of the issuer, in the form of debentures, bonds, certificates of deposit, notes or commercial paper, or an equity ownership in the issuer, in the form of stock, certificates of beneficial ownership in a trust, or other equity. Securities may be traded on public exchanges or in dealer-based "over the counter" markets. They are generally fungible, meaning that when "securities" are borrowed, an equivalent security and not necessarily the identical asset must be returned.

"Securities" for purposes of the federal securities laws thus includes many types of instruments, whether debt or equity or something in between. There are a number of provisions with similar definitions in the tax Code. See, e.g., § 1236(c) ("For purposes of this section, the term 'security' means any share of stock in any corporation, certificate of stock or interest in any corporation, note, bond, debenture, or evidence of indebtedness, or any evidence of an interest in or right to subscribe to or purchase any of the foregoing"); § 475(c)(2) (defining securities broadly for mark-to-market purposes but specifically exempting contracts to which section 1256(a) applies from the definition); Rev. Proc. 2004-28 (concluding that the Code provisions related to regulated investment company diversification rules under section 851(b)(3) should be interpreted consistently with the 1940 Investment Company Act in deciding whether to treat repurchase agreements as securities); § 351(e)(1) providing an explicit (and broad) list of items to be "treated as" securities).

For the purposes of the provisions of sections 354 and 356, however, the meaning of securities is limited to debt instruments. Such instruments will generally include a right to be paid at least a sum certain, at a certain maturity date, and with a return that is relatively predictable, and therefore readily identifiable as interest. Debt securities are distinguished from other types of debt by their duration and by the nature of the security involved.

If security holders become stockholders, the exchange is covered under section 354. But if there was unpaid accrued interest on the debt, section 354(a)(2)(B) will spoil nonrecognition to the extent of the interest. This amount will not be treated as boot under section 356, but instead as ordinary income. *See* § 354(a)(3)(B) (cross reference to section 61).

If old stockholders receive stock and some securities and the transaction is honored as a recapitalization, section 354(a)(2) will treat as boot the fair market value of the excess principal amount. A pro rata exchange of stock for stock and bonds, however, may fail to qualify as a recapitalization. *See* Bazley v. Commissioner, 331 U.S. 737 (1947) (applying substance over form principles to treat a pro rata exchange of old common for new common and debt, in form a recapitalization reorganization, as a dividend distribution). (Note that the current taxation of dividends at the preferential capital gains rate takes much of the bite out of the consequences of falling under *Bazley*.)

If a stockholder receives only securities in exchange for stock, section 354 will not apply. *See* § 354(a)(2)(A) (making section 354(a)(1)'s nonrecognition provision inapplicable when and to the extent that securities are received in greater principal amount than given up). This seems unquestionably the correct approach when the effect is pro rata and the exchanging stockholder continues to have an interest in the stock of the issuer; indeed, Reg. section 1.301-1(*l*) could be invoked to treat the exchange as a separate transaction directly taxable as a dividend. If the dividend-like effect is not so obvious, the transaction will be governed by the ordinary redemption rules. *See* Reg. § 1.354-1(d) Ex. 3 and Rev. Rul. 77-415, 1977-2 C.B. 311. The application of the redemption rules can produce a fully taxable exchange (including the recognition of losses) in some cases — i.e., when the stockholder owns no other stock or when a meaningful reduction in his stockholding has resulted. On the other hand, it can result in dividend treatment of the full value of the securities received in some situations in which continuing interests are held. In this context, the denial of section 354 treatment means at least that the exchanging stockholder will not have the benefit of the boot-within-gain limitation of section 356, and that if differences emerge after the decision in *Clark* between the tests for dividend equivalency under section 356 and those under section 302, any advantages under section 356 will not be available.

Contrasting Section 356 with Section 302

Under the longstanding IRS position in Rev. Rul. 77-415, a shareholder who gives up stock and receives only securities in a recapitalization is not taxed under sections 354 and 356, but instead under section 302. Although it is not entirely clear, the logic of this position — that section 356 can apply only if an exchange covered by section 354 has occurred — should apply both to situations in which the shareholder owns no other stock (the situation in the ruling) and the situation in which the shareholder owns other stock that is not involved in the recapitalization.

Given that under the Clark *case, the character of boot gain will essentially be governed by section 302, how much difference can this position make? The answer is "lots."*

Suppose a shareholder holds common stock that amounts to 20% of the stock of the issuing corporation. In a recapitalization, the shareholder gives up three-quarters of his stock (an amount that constituted 15% of the common stock before the transaction) in exchange for securities with a face and fair market value of $100,000. All of the other shareholders exchange some of their old class of common for several different classes of common, so after the transaction our shareholder owns 5.8% (5/(100-15)) of the common stock.

Under Rev. Rul. 77-415, this transaction will be treated as a redemption, to be honored as a sale or exchange under the standards of section 302(b). If the shareholder had a basis of $20,000 in his original holding, he will have a gain of $85,000 ($100,000-(3/4*$20,000)). If the shareholder had a basis of $200,000 in his original holding, he will have a loss of $50,000 ($100,000-(3/4*$200,000)). He would hold the shares of his remaining stock with a basis of $50,000.

> *Now contrast the result if this shareholder had given up all of his old stock, and received back new common stock and securities in the same proportions as above. Section 356 would now apply, since "section 354 . . . would apply . . . but for the fact that . . . the property received consists not only of property permitted by section 354 . . . to be received without the recognition of gain but also of other property." Under section 356(a)(1), gain would be triggered to the extent of boot and characterized under section 356(b), but no loss could be recognized under 356(c). Thus, if the shareholder had a basis of $20,000 in his original holding, he would recognize gain of $100,000. (If he received $100,000 worth of securities above in exchange for 3/4 of his interest, his entire interest must be worth roughly $133,000. Since he has at least $100,000 gain in his overall holding, the entire fair market value of the excess securities will trigger gain; he will hold the stock he receives with a basis of $20,000 ($20,000 plus $100,000 minus $100,000). If the shareholder had a basis of $200,000 in his original stock holding, he will not recognize his loss, but will hold his new stock interest with a basis of $100,000 and the securities with a basis of $100,000.*
>
> *Given the starkness of this result, can the corporation and the shareholder negotiate for a better result, simply by making it clear that 3/4 of the shareholder's old stock interest was exchanged for securities and ¼ for the new stock interest? In that case, the shareholder with a $200,000 basis could recognize a $50,000 loss on the exchange in which he received "only" securities, and hold his new stock with a basis of $50,000.*
>
> *Conventional wisdom among tax practitioners prior to the advent of the January 2009 proposed regulations would probably have been a straightforward "no." Under the regulations proposed under section 358 in January of 2009, however, such "specifications of the terms of the exchange" may be possible if the specification is "economically reasonable" and the overall result is not essentially equivalent to a dividend. (One might question whether specification can be economically reasonable when it is solely tax motivated.)*

b. Debt-For-Debt Exchanges

If security holders remain security holders but take securities with different terms, the transaction is probably considered part of a recapitalization and therefore nonrecognition is available under section 354, except to the extent of the fair market value of any excess principal amount. There is little authority on the point, because for many years the IRS simply treated such changes in terms of securities as "mere refinancings" that were not taxable events. Since *Cottage Sav. Ass'n v. Commissioner*, 499 U.S. 554 (1991), and the related *"Cottage Savings* regulations" in Reg. section 1.1001-3 governing debt modifications, there is general agreement that the standards for changes in terms that will be treated as realization events with respect to debt are lower, and the importance of qualifying as a reorganization is therefore more important.

Note that recapitalization status, and the nonrecognition and income characterization it brings with it, generally only benefit the shareholders and security holders, not the corporation.

c. Corporate Consequences of Exchanges in Which Securities and Other Debt are Retired

A corporation that buys back its debt for less than the adjusted issue price will have cancellation of indebtedness income. If the principal of the new debt is greater than its issue price, new debt will also be subject to the original issue discount regime under sections 1271 and following. For example, a corporation that repurchases old debt with a face amount of $1,000 (and holder basis of $1,000) and a value of $900 with new debt with a face amount of $950 and a value of $900 will have cancellation of indebtedness income of $100 ($1,000 adjusted issue price of old debt minus $900 issue price of new debt) and the new debt will be issued with $50 of original issue discount ($950 stated redemption price at maturity minus $900 issue price).

Similarly, a retirement premium in respect of the repurchase of the old debt may be matched by issue premium on the new debt. (As suggested in the discussion of the history of the lack of a continuity of interest requirement in recapitalizations, this represents a significant change in the law. The relevant rules have only been stable for the last decade, after a series of relatively technical statutory changes.)

9.2.3. Potential Overlap With Other Types of Transactions

The regulations include some relatively stark examples of the apparent overlap between recapitalizations that are taxed as reorganizations and other transactions. Why, for instance, is the second item in Reg. section 1.368-2(e), involving a receipt by preferred shareholders of common stock in exchange for their preferred, a recapitalization in which the shareholders are not subject to taxation on their exchange of stock rather than a taxable redemption of the preferred stock? Here, the answer seems relatively straightforward: section 317(b) defines a redemption as an acquisition by a corporation of "its stock from a shareholder *in exchange for property*" (emphasis added), and section 317(a) excludes the transferring corporation's own stock from the definition of property. Thus, the use of stock as consideration by the issuing corporation makes section 302 inapplicable, and section 368(a)(1)(E) applies instead.

The apparent overlap of recapitalizations with stock dividends taxable under section 305 is less easily dealt with. Look again at the second example in Reg. § 1.368-2(e). Why isn't the receipt of common in exchange for preferred by preferred shareholders viewed as an increase in their proportionate interest and subject to tax as a stock dividend under section 305(c) (or even perhaps section 305(b)(4))? A similar conclusion is reached in example 2 of Reg. § 1.305-5(d). And what about the third situation in Reg. section 1.368-2(e), setting forth in more general terms the transaction described in Reg. section 1.305-3(e), Ex. 12, involving a typical "freezing" of equity interests on the retirement of a major shareholder? Why is there no scrutiny of these transactions under section 305(c)? After all, the statutory language specifically includes recapitalizations in the list of transactions that should trigger taxation for shareholders whose interests are increased. As noted in the discussion of section 305, Treasury exercised its discretion in promulgating regulations under section 305(c) by limiting constructive distributions in transactions that would otherwise be recapitalizations to those that are pursuant to a plan to periodically increase a shareholder's proportionate interest or that involve an exchange of preferred shares with dividends in arrears for other stock that results in an increase in the preferred shareholder's proportionate interest. Reg. § 1.305-7(c)(1). This regulatory position limiting the applicability of section 305(c) in recapitalizations is consistent with the legislative history of section 305(b), although Treasury seems to have exercised its discretion in ways that decidedly favor the taxpayer.

The fact that the receipt of preferred stock in a recapitalization will not ordinarily result in a deemed distribution under section 305(c) does not prevent the application of section 305(c) based on the terms of the stock. If the stock has an excess redemption premium as described in the last sentence of section 305(c) and Reg. section 1.305-5(b), section 305(c) will apply.

There is also a less troubling overlap between the transactions to which section 1036 applies and recapitalizations. Section 1036 provides for a tax-free exchange of common for common or preferred for preferred of the same issuer. The regulations under section 1036 make it clear that a transaction in which the exchange occurs because of a restructuring of the issuing corporation will be both a section 1036 exchange and a section 368(a)(1)(E) recapitalization. Reg. § 1.1036-1(a). Section 1036 also applies by its terms to transactions between shareholders, without the participation of the issuing corporation.

9.2.4. Other Issues

a. Convertible Interests

It is generally assumed that when a shareholder exercises an option to convert stock into another class of stock, or a convertible debt into stock, there is no recognition of gain or loss. Sometimes this result has been justified as simply the maturing of the rights embodied in the instrument, giving rise to nontaxable receipt. It has also been justified by considering the transaction — even though it might have involved a unilateral action on the part of shareholders — as a recapitalization. In most circumstances, the theory will not make a difference. In the case of preferred received in respect of common, however, the theory will determine which of the section 306 tests will be applied to determine whether the preferred stock carries the section 306 taint. If the "maturing rights" approach applies, section 306(c)(1)(C) will apply. In contrast, if the transaction is treated as a recapitalization, section 306(c)(1)(B) will apply.

b. Recapitalizations in Connection with Other Transactions

The Service has ruled that a recapitalization may be present, and thus nonrecognition available, when interests are restructured in anticipation of other transactions. For instance, a subsidiary may be recapitalized in order to obtain "control" for the purposes of transactions in which control is required, such as liquidations under section 332 or spinoffs under section 355. Rev. Rul. 69-407, 1969-2 C.B. 50 (a parent owning stock representing 70% of the vote caused the subsidiary to recapitalize so that the parent held 80% of the vote). Recapitalization may also facilitate qualification as a reorganization under section 368(a)(1)(B). *See* Rev. Rul. 76-223, 1976-1 C.B. 103 (a recapitalization immediately prior to a section 368(a)(1)(B) reorganization extended the vote to previously nonvoting preferred, to avoid the need to acquire any such stock).

PRACTICE PROBLEMS

Assume that there is a corporate business purpose for all of the transactions outlined in these practice problems.

1.   Common for Common. A and B each own 100 shares of common stock of X Corp. A exchanges all of her common stock (which has a fair market value of $1 million and is held with a basis of $0.1 million) for a different class of common stock that includes some extraordinary governance rights, but is of equal fair market value. What result to A?

(a)   Gain on taxable sale of common of $.9 million.

(b)   Taxable stock dividend upon receipt of common.

(c)   Nontaxable exchange under section 354.

(d)   Boot gain of $.9 million, to be characterized under section 356.

2.   Common for Preferred. A and B each own 100 shares of common stock of X Corp. A exchanges all of her common stock (which has a fair market value of $1 million and is held with a basis of $0.1 million) for a preferred stock of equal fair market value. The preferred stock includes no special redemption rights and the dividends on it depend on corporate performance. What result to A?

(a)   Gain on taxable sale of common of $.9 million.

(b)   Taxable stock dividend upon receipt of preferred of $1 million under 305(b)(1).

(c)   Nontaxable exchange under section 354.

(d)   Boot gain of $.9 million, to be characterized under section 356.

3.   Common for Preferred. A and B each own 100 shares of common stock of X Corp. A exchanges all of her common stock (which has a fair market value of $1 million and is held with a basis of $0.1 million) for preferred stock of equal fair market value. The preferred stock has dividend rights that are designed to mimic the interest paid on the corporation's bonds. What result to A?

(a)   Gain on taxable sale of common of $.9 million.

(b)   Taxable stock dividend upon receipt of preferred.

(c)   Nontaxable exchange under section 354.

(d)   Boot gain of $.9 million, to be characterized under section 356.

4.   Preferred for Common. A and B each own 100 shares of common stock of X Corp and 100 shares of preferred. A exchanges all of her preferred stock (which has

a fair market value of $1 million and is held with a basis of $0.1 million) for more common stock. What result to A?

(a)   Gain on taxable sale of preferred of $0.9 million.

(b)   Taxable stock dividend upon receipt.

(c)   Nontaxable exchange under section 354.

(d)   Boot gain of $0.9 million, to be characterized under section 356.

5.   Preferred for Preferred. A and B each own 100 shares of common stock of X Corp and 100 shares of preferred. A exchanges all of her preferred stock (which has a fair market value of $1 million and is held with a basis of $0.1 million) for a different class of preferred stock. Neither the preferred stock given up nor the preferred stock received includes any special redemption rights and the dividends on the new preferred depend on corporate performance. What result to A?

(a)   Gain on taxable sale of preferred of $0.9 million.

(b)   Taxable stock dividend upon receipt of preferred.

(c)   Nontaxable exchange under section 354.

(d)   Boot gain of $0.9 million, to be characterized under section 356.

6.   Preferred for Preferred. A and B each own 100 shares of common stock of X Corp and 100 shares of preferred. A exchanges all of her preferred stock (which has a fair market value of $1 million and is held with a basis of $0.1 million) for a different class of preferred stock. Both the preferred stock given up and the preferred stock received have special redemption rights and the dividends on both do not depend on corporate performance. What result to A?

(a)   Gain on taxable sale of preferred of $0.9 million.

(b)   Taxable stock dividend upon receipt of preferred.

(c)   Nontaxable exchange under section 354.

(d)   Boot gain of $0.9 million, to be characterized under section 356.

7.   Preferred for Common. A and B each own 100 shares of common stock of X Corp. A also owns 100 shares of preferred. A exchanges all of her preferred stock (which has a fair market value of $1 million and is held with a basis of $0.1 million) for common stock. The old preferred stock had substantial dividend arrearages, and thus the fair market value of the common stock received was greater than the liquidation preference on the old preferred. What result to A?

(a)   Gain on taxable sale of preferred of $0.9 million.

(b)   Taxable stock dividend, in part, upon receipt of common.

(c)   Nontaxable exchange under section 354.

(d)   Boot gain of $0.9 million, to be characterized under section 356.

8.   Preferred for Common and Cash. A and B each own 100 shares of common stock of X Corp and 100 shares of preferred. The preferred stock was received in

a recapitalization five years earlier, in exchange for common stock. A exchanges all of her preferred stock (which has a fair market value of $1 million and is held with a basis of $0.1 million) for $0.8 million of common and $0.1 million of cash. What result to A?

(a)   Gain on taxable sale of preferred of $0.9 million.

(b)   Taxable stock dividend upon receipt of common and cash.

(c)   Nontaxable exchange under section 354.

(d)   Boot gain of $0.9 million, to be characterized under section 356.

(e)   Insufficient facts.

9.   Common for securities. A and B each own 100 shares of common stock of X Corp. A exchanges half of her common stock (which has a fair market value of $0.5 million and is held with a basis of $50,000) for a different class of common stock that includes some extraordinary governance rights as well as securities with a face amount and fair market value of $0.4 million. What result to A?

(a)   Gain on taxable sale of common of $0.9 million.

(b)   Taxable stock dividend upon receipt of securities.

(c)   Nontaxable exchange under section 354.

(d)   Boot gain of $0.4 million, to be characterized under section 356.

10.   In anticipation of a public offering, the preferred shareholders and the securities holders of Success Co both exchanged their interests for common stock. In this transaction, Success Co in effect bought back securities with a principal amount (and adjusted issue price) of $1 million for common stock worth $0.9 million. What result to Success Co and the securities holders?

(a)   Loss of $0.1 million recognized by securities holders, cancellation of indebtedness income of $0.1 million to Success.

(b)   Nonrecognition to security holders, cancellation of indebtedness income of $0.1 million to Success.

(c)   Nonrecognition to both security holders and to Success.

(d)   Loss of $0.1 million to securities holders, no immediate effect on Success.

DISCUSSION PROBLEMS

1.   Max Corp, which currently has only one class of stock owned equally by five related shareholders (father and four children) and is worth $1,000,000, exchanges its outstanding common stock for new voting common worth $800,000 and new nonvoting common worth $200,000. One shareholder received all of the nonvoting common and the other four shareholders received voting common. The shareholder receiving nonvoting common is the patriarch of the firm who is gradually withdrawing from participation in its direction. At the time of the exchange, Max Corp had $500,000 of accumulated earnings and profits. Can Max Corp represent to its shareholders that this transaction is nontaxable? How does this compare to a

redemption of half of the patriarch's shares as a means of reducing his control?

2.   X Corp currently has two classes of stock, common and preferred, both with the economic rights normally associated with these classes of stock. The preferred stock was all issued on the initial incorporation of X Corp. X Corp plans to engage in a recapitalization primarily in order to clarify certain voting rights. A new class of common has been issued in exchange for all of the outstanding common, and a new class of preferred has been issued in exchange for all of the outstanding preferred stock, with the same stated liquidation rights except that the preferred's liquidation rights have been increased to the same extent that dividends were in arrears on the old preferred stock and the rights thereto eliminated.

(a)   Can X Corp represent to its shareholders that this transaction will be nontaxable?

(b)   Can X Corp assure its preferred shareholders that the stock they receive will not be section 306 stock?

3.   Y Corp has outstanding 1000 shares of common stock and 1000 shares of preferred stock and 1000 bonds with a principal amount of $1200 each. Each corporate interest is currently worth $1 million (the interest rate payable on the bonds is well below current market), and there is no accrued interest or dividend arrearage.

In a recapitalization, all of the preferred shareholders become common shareholders. For half of Y Corp's common shareholders, their $500,000 worth of the common stock is replaced pro rata by a new class of common and $500,000 worth of newly issued securities; for the other half, their $500,000 worth is replaced solely by the new class of common. The old securities holders receive new securities worth $1 million (the same class of securities as that received by some of the old common shareholders). Because the interest rates on the bonds are issued at market, however, the principal amount of the new securities issued to the common shareholders is $500,000 and the principal amount issued to the old bond holders is $1,000,000.

(a)   What is the effect of this transaction on:

(i)   the common who take common and bonds?

(ii)   The common who take only common?

(iii)   The bondholders who take only bonds?

(iv)   The corporation?

(b)   What if Y Corp had issued common stock to the bondholders?

4.   You are striving mightily to do some tax planning for a client, and much depends upon how much taxable income and gains he had this year. At the very last minute, with apologies for not have realized it might matter, he reports to you that he gave up preferred stock worth $500,000 which he had held with a basis of $50,000 and received in exchange a new class of preferred stock in the same corporation. His interest represents about 5% of the value of the corporation. What else do you need to know before you know enough about how to characterize this transaction to

proceed with your planning? In what order should you ask the questions? What else might you need to know if he also received cash of $100,000? If he had received only common stock?

SUBCHAPTER S AND ENTITY CHOICE

Chapter 10

INTRODUCTION TO SUBCHAPTER S

Statutes and Regulations	IRC §§ 1361(a), (b)(1); 1362(a), (b)(1), (c), (d) (heading only), (f); 1363 (omit (d)); 1366(a), (b), (c),(d); 1367; 1368(a), (b)
	Reg. § 1.1361-1(l); 1.1366-1, -2; 1.1367-1; 1.1368-1
Other Primary Authorities	Maloof v. Comm'r, 456 F.3d 645 (6th Cir. 2006)
	Taproot Admin. Servs. v. Comm'r, 133 T.C. 202 (2009)

Subchapter S allows certain qualified corporations to elect out of the classical tax system. Before 1996 (when LLCs were first granted the ability to "check the box" and receive partnership treatment), this election was the only way to achieve both limited liability and pass-through treatment for shareholders.

A corporation that elects subchapter S status is not itself taxed on its income; its income is passed through to its shareholders, just as the income of a partnership is passed through to the partners. In many other respects, however, it is taxed more like a regular corporation than a partnership; indeed, most of the provisions of subchapter C apply to it. For instance, gain is recognized to the corporation when appreciated property is distributed to shareholders, nonrecognition to shareholders for transfers in exchange for stock is conditioned on meeting the requirements of section 351, and gain or loss is recognized on a liquidation.

10.1. ELIGIBILITY FOR SUBCHAPTER S STATUS

Most of the limitations on eligibility and corporate capital structure are aimed at keeping the pass-through as simple and straightforward as possible. The most important include the restriction of the corporate structure to a single class of stock (which means that all stock shares equally in both earnings and liquidation value) and to natural persons or entities that cannot easily be tiered in such a way as to effectuate special allocations.

Only domestic "small business corporations" as defined in section 1361(b) can elect to be pass-through entities under subchapter C. Such corporations must

- Not have more than one class of stock

- Not have more than 100 shareholders (counting family members as one shareholder)

- Not have a nonresident alien as a shareholder (because the income allocated to such a taxpayer would likely never be subject to US tax)

- Not have as shareholders persons who are not individuals (that is, are not human) unless those shareholders are any of the following:

    o S corporations themselves which own 100% of the stock of the subject corporation

    o Grantor trusts whose beneficiaries are treated as the owners of trust assets

    o Decedent's trusts set up as grantor trusts, or by will, for two years after death

    o Voting trusts

    o A small business trust as defined in section 1361(e)

    o A qualified subchapter S trust as defined in section 1361(d)(3) (only one beneficiary), or

    o Certain tax exempt organizations

- Not be one of certain types of "ineligible" corporations, including most banks and insurance companies, which are subject to special income tax regimes.

The election to be subject to pass-through under subchapter S is actually not made by the corporation, but by its shareholders. All of its shareholders must join in the election, since it results in the inclusion in income of amounts on which the shareholders would not otherwise be taxed.

Subsections 1361(c)(4) and (5) and Reg. section 1.1361-1(l) make it clear that it is the economic features of stock, not the corporate governance features, that control whether there is more than one class of stock. However, the statute itself provides that the one-class-of-stock rule will nevertheless not be violated if interests that are issued as "straight debt" are subject to reclassification as equity for the purposes of determining the deductibility of interest to shareholders.

Counting Family Members

A husband and wife (and their estates) are treated as one shareholder. Additionally, all "members of a family (and their estates) are so treated. § 1361(c)(1)(A). The tests for membership in a family, and thus the determination of the number of shareholders based on counting all family members as one, are not entirely intuitive. Under Reg. § 1.1361-1(e)(3)'s interpretation of the statute, a snapshot is taken at the first relevant date of those owning stock in the S corporation. From this snapshot, the family patriarchs are identified: anyone six generations or less above anyone currently owning stock is potentially such a patriarch. Anyone who is a lineal descendant of this patriarch is a member of the same family as the patriarch. (There is some chance that the S corporation will have fewer shareholders under this test than everyone thinks, since not everyone knows who their fifth cousins are, but since most S corporation shareholders actually know how each of them came to be shareholders, there should not be too many surprises here. Luckily, there is no adverse consequence to having too few shareholders — only to having too many.) After this snapshot is taken, lineal descendents of those counted as family members within the snapshot will be family members, as will any other lineal descendent of the patriarch who acquires stock later.

There is no continued counting of generations after the snapshot is taken, and thus no worry that the number of families involved increases as new generations are born or older generations die off. The snapshot is taken for existing shareholders in S corporations existing in 2004 in that year; for those becoming shareholders in pre-existing S corporations on the date they first own stock; for later-formed S corporations, on the date the election is made, or when there is a new shareholder not a member of a family in which she would already be counted, for that shareholder's family only.

10.1.1.　Terminations of S Corporation Status

An election to be taxed as an S corporation can be terminated in three ways: first, by an express revocation, under section 1362(d)(1); second, by issuing stock that violates the one class of stock rule or by permitting a nonqualifying shareholder to own any of its stock, under section 1362(d)(2); and finally, if the S corporation has ever been a C corporation and still has earnings and profits, by accumulating too much passive income, under section 1362(d)(3).

Although all existing shareholders must consent before a Subchapter S election is effective, the transfer of stock to a qualifying shareholder will not terminate the old election or require a new one, unless transfer resulted in more than 100 shareholders.

10.2.　TAXATION OF S CORPORATIONS AND SHAREHOLDERS

10.2.1.　Passthrough of Items of Income and Deduction

Although an S corporation must compute its income and file a return, it is not generally taxed on its own income. (In very limited circumstances, it may be taxed on certain types of income, as noted below.) Instead, under section 1366, items of its income are passed through to shareholders and taken into account by them as if the items had been realized by them. Those items — including charitable contributions, capital gains, tax-exempt income, and foreign taxes — that might have an effect on the shareholder's calculation of income are passed through item-by-item. *See* § 1366(a)(1)(A), (B).

The means of allocating income to shareholders are far simpler in S corporations than the corresponding rules for partnerships. This is the intended result of the "one class of stock" limitation — each share of that one class must, by definition, be entitled to the same proportion of income and loss as every other share.

The greatest complications in the allocation of income arise as a result of the sale of shares during the taxable year. In a year in which no shares change hands, the calculation is easy: each shareholder takes into his income his share, on a pro rata basis, of the corporation's income. In years in which shares change hands but no shareholder is terminated, section 1377 requires that each pass-through item be allocated to each day of the year, and then allocated to each shareholder according to the number of shares held on that day. In a year in which a shareholder is terminated, section 1377(a)(2) allows an election (by the corporation and all affected shareholders) to treat the S corporation's year as ending with the termination, with a new short year ending at the end of the corporation's regular year.

As discussed further below, losses are allocated to individual shareholders as of the end of each taxable year. If the losses and deductions to be taken into account exceed the shareholder's basis in the corporate stock (plus, where relevant, the shareholder's basis in debt of the corporation to the shareholder), the excess is treated as incurred by the corporation and *allocated to this shareholder* to be used in the next year. § 1366(d)(1)–(2). They become, in effect, a tax attribute of this shareholder that is available indefinitely but cannot be claimed by anyone else. As in partnerships, such allocated losses may also be further subject to the loss limitations in section 465, dealing with amounts at risk, and section 469, dealing with passive activity losses.

10.2.2. Effect of Pass-Through on Basis

a. Items of Income

When items of income are passed through, the shareholder's basis in her stock is increased under section 1367(a). This treatment is frequently explained as treating the shareholders as if they had received distributions of income and recontributed them. This is true as far as it goes — but remember that the corporation may have income that will be passed through, even if it has no cash to distribute. As is the case in a partnership, this mechanism takes account of the absence of an entity-level tax by creating a record of the amount that the shareholder can receive from the S corporation without additional taxation. Accordingly, items of income received tax-free by the corporation will nonetheless increase basis, allowing this value to be distributed without losing the exemption.

b.   Items of Loss

Items of loss are similarly passed through, reducing basis. The shareholder may only claim the benefit of such items to the extent of his stock basis (and his basis in debt the corporation owes him) under section 1366(d). As a technical matter, these two records of the shareholder's investment in the corporation are kept separately. Basis in stock is reduced before basis in debt is reduced, and basis in debt is restored by gain recognition and contributions before basis in stock is restored. *See* § 1367(b)(2). This ordering limits the circumstances in which a lender/shareholder may have a basis in the corporation's debt to him that is lower than its face amount (a situation in which the ordinary rule that a lender does not have income on the return of principal would not apply).

The idea behind this limitation on debt-as-basis is that only these amounts represent losses that the shareholder will actually incur. Expenses and losses of the corporation can exceed the sum of the owners' bases in stock, and therefore cannot be used by the shareholders in the taxable year in which they arise because the use of debt proceeds by the corporation may result in the accrual of deductions and losses. Under subchapter S, the fact that this debt will not necessarily be repaid by the shareholders results in their inability to use the deductions except to offset their income from the corporation.

Comparing Debt as Basis in Subchapter S and Subchapter K

Under section 1366(d), an S corporation shareholder may only use the amount the shareholder has actually made available as loan proceeds to the corporation as basis available to support the pass-through of losses. This basis determination is simpler than in the similar determination for partners in a partnership, because section 752 in effect provides that all debt owed by the partnership is allocated to partners' tax accounts as if it were money already contributed by them. The subchapter S corporation scheme presumes that the shareholders will not have to pay on the corporation's liabilities, because the corporation affords limited liability. (This presumption will hold even if the shareholders guarantee the debt.) The subchapter K scheme presumes the opposite, that is, that all partners may be called upon to pay the recourse debts of the partnership. The difference between these two sets of rules made more sense when entities taxed under subchapter K could not easily offer limited liability to their owners and before the rise of nonrecourse debt. Under subchapter K, there should always be enough allocated liability, in the aggregate, to support the deduction of all items accrued by the corporation, if there have been no special allocations. The limits of section 1366(d) are therefore much more likely to defer the benefit of the pass-through of losses than are the corresponding limits in subchapter K.

Furthermore, only actual loans to the corporation from the shareholder count: a shareholder in an S corporation is not in any better position to deduct items that are passed through because he has guaranteed a debt of the corporation. In that case, there is no benefit to the shareholder until he actually pays on the guarantee, at which point he will have a basis increase under section 1366(d). In general, this is a sensible rule, since one debt should give rise to basis in only one taxpayer. The problem here is that the corporate debtor is not the only taxpayer that needs basis before the deduction can actually produce a tax benefit. Therefore, if a lender insists on individual shareholder guarantees of debt to a corporation, it may be more beneficial overall to have the shareholders borrow personally and relend to the corporation, which may then guarantee the loan, rather than the other way around.

When a shareholder is unable to use deductions because of the section 1366(d) limitation, the items carry forward to the next taxable year. They are personal to the shareholder; that is, they are to be taken into account only by the shareholder to whom they were originally allocated. *See* § 1366(d)(2)–(3).

10.2.3. Effect of Distributions

a. General Rules

Distributions of cash or other property can be received by shareholders without tax to the extent of their basis in their stock under section 1368(b)(1). (Basis in debt cannot be used to offset distributions: it is reserved for the return of debt principal.) As one should expect, such distributions reduce the shareholder's basis down to, but not below, zero. Accordingly, only distributions in excess of basis trigger income, which will be characterized as gain from a capital asset under section 1368(b)(2).

Note that the rules in section 1368 regarding the effect of distributions only apply to distributions that would otherwise be taxed under section 301. If the transaction is a section 302 redemption treated as a sale or exchange under section 1001 (or recast as such a redemption), the result will be different: the basis available to offset gain will be only the basis of the stock actually given up. In other words, the regular rules of subchapter C apply where those rules are not made inapplicable by, or inconsistent with, specific subchapter S provisions. *See* § 1371(a).

Distributions of property will trigger gain, but not loss, to the corporation, under the ordinary rules of section 311. The recognized gain will pass through to shareholders under section 1366. The distributee shareholder will have a fair market value basis in the distributed property (and will reduce the basis of her shares by the same amount). (The subchapter C rules governing liquidating distributions apply similarly to S corporations and their shareholders. Liquidating distributions under sections 331 and 336 therefore may result in loss or gain recognition to S corporations, and such distributions to shareholders are received in a taxable exchange for their stock, so that either loss or gain may be recognized if the shareholder has a basis in his stock that is greater or less than his ratable share of the corporation's assets.)

Sections 1366(d)(1)(A) and 1368(d) (flush language) rather cryptically direct that basis increases under 1367(a)(1) resulting from the pass-through of items of income will take place before the effect of a distribution is calculated, but that the reductions under 1367(a)(2) resulting from the pass-through of items of loss will not. *See also* Reg. § 1.1367-1(f) (indicating the ordering rule for adjustments to basis as increases followed by distributions followed by nondeductible, noncapitalizable expenses, followed by losses and deductions). This ordering rule tends to avoid gain as a result of distributions at the cost of suspending losses. The overall effect is the avoidance of character mismatches. (A shareholder may elect to take losses and deductions into account before nondeductible, noncapitalizable expenses, under

Reg. section 1.1367-1(g), but must then apply that rule for all future years unless the Commissioner permits otherwise.)

Note that sections 1366 and 1367 distinguish the treatment of the items of income that are separately passed through because they may affect the shareholder's own tax calculation from "nonseparately computed items." Thus, in any given taxable year, the shareholder can have both an item of gain and income that is passed through and increases basis under section 1367(a)(1) and an item of loss and deduction that is passed through and reduces basis under section 1367(a)(2). These two groups of items are not netted for the purposes of the ordering rule. For example, if the S corporation has both $3000 of net long term capital gain (a separately allocated item) and $1000 of current operating losses and distributes $2500, the shareholder's basis will be increased by $3000, decreased by $2500 with no section 1368 gain, and then decreased by $500 (the allowable portion of the operating loss) to zero, with the remaining $500 of the operating loss suspended. In the next year, if the S corporation has $1600 of operating income and distributes $900, the shareholder's basis will be increased by $1600, decreased by the $900 distribution with no section 1368 gain, and then further decreased by the $500 carry forward of the operating loss from the prior year.

Ownership of Multiple Blocks of Stock

The regulations clearly anticipate that blocks of stock acquired in an S corporation at different times and therefore held with different bases will, in general, be accounted for separately. Nonetheless, increases and decreases in basis are determined and allocated to all shares pro rata on a per share, per day basis. Reg. § 1.1367-1(b)(2), (c)(3). If the amount attributable to a share reduces its basis to zero, the excess is allocated proportionately to all remaining shares to reduce their bases. Reg. § 1.1367-1(c)(3) (second sentence).

---

b.   Allocations as Wages Subject to Employment Taxes

A shareholder of an S corporation may under state law also be an employee of the corporation. But there is no incentive to be paid as an employee rather than as a shareholder, since receipt of wages will be ordinary income and subject to employment taxes. What if an S corporation shareholder who is an employee of the corporation simply fails to take a salary at all? The Service asserts the authority to characterize an appropriate portion of the shareholder's distributive share as wages, subject to employment taxes.

Note that section 1372 treats an S corporation as a partnership for fringe-benefit purposes and all shareholders who own more than 2% as partners. Accordingly, those shareholders are not eligible for the exclusion ordinarily provided for employee fringe benefits. If the corporation does pay such benefits, those payments will be treated as compensation — the corporation must deduct these amounts as compensation and report them as such on the shareholder's W2, which, of course, the shareholder must include as ordinary income.

10.3.   ENTITY OWNERSHIP OF S CORPORATIONS

10.3.1.   S Corporations as Controlling Shareholders

Although the rule has not always been so, S corporations may now freely own stock of other entities. If an S corporation owns all of the stock of another corporation that is entitled to make the S election, the parent S corporation may elect to have the subsidiary S corporation (often called a "Q Sub") disregarded for tax purposes. *See* § 1361(b)(3).

The results of this election are very similar to the results obtained by electing to have a wholly owned LLC taxed as a disregarded entity. The parent S corporation is deemed for tax purposes to own all of the assets (and incur all of the liabilities) of the Q Sub. The items of income and deduction of the Q Sub are treated as such items of the parent S corporation.

At the time the election is made, the subsidiary is deemed to have liquidated. In most situations, this deemed liquidation will have the effect of an actual liquidation under section 332.

The transfer of any of the stock of a Q Sub will terminate the election. The mechanism for the restoration of the Q Sub to recognized corporate status is set forth in section 1361(b)(3)(C)(ii), which provides that the sale of stock will be treated as a sale of an undivided interest in the assets of the Q Sub, followed by the acquisition of these assets by a new corporation in a transaction to which section 351 applies. Thus the selling S corporation recognizes gain only on the portion of the assets deemed to have been transferred. (This 2006 change to the statute has not yet been reflected in the applicable regulations. *See* Reg. § 1.1361-5(b) ex. 1.)

10.3.2.   Other Entities as S Corporation Shareholders

Certain types of simple trusts have long been allowed as S shareholders. Grantor trusts that themselves cannot have multiple classes of stock, as described in section 1361(c)(2)(A)(i), and "qualified subchapter S trusts" with one beneficiary, which are treated as the same as grantor trusts under section 1361(d), are appropriate as S corporation shareholders because the trust income will be passed through to the beneficiary in straightforward ways that do not defeat the point of the one-class-of-stock rule. Voting trusts, permitted under section 1361(c)(2)(A)(iv), similarly do not defeat the one-class-of-stock rule. The statute also recognizes that it is necessary to account for the reality that individual S shareholders may die leaving a grantor trust holding the stock, and thus it permits trusts as shareholders for a two-year period under section 1361(c)(2)(A)(ii) (trust created before death) or section 1361(c)(2)(A)(iii) (trust created by will upon death).

"Electing small business trusts" were added to the list of eligible shareholders in 1996 to facilitate the use of S corporations in estate planning. § 1361(c)(1)(A)(v). Unlike the other trusts that may be S shareholders, these trusts will be taxed on the S income passed through to them. § 641(c).

Exempt organizations, including both pension plans exempt under section 401(a) and exempt entities under section 501(c)(3), were added to the list of permissible shareholders in 1997. Under special rules, such entities (except for ESOPs, see section 512) will be required to take into account as unrelated business taxable income (UBTI) all pass-through items of income and loss and all gains on the subchapter S corporation's stock itself.

> **Complications when ESOPs Are S Corporation Shareholders**
>
> *The possibility that an ESOP can be an S corporation shareholder has created some problems. First, there is tension between the ESOP beneficiaries' right to a distribution of the assets held by the ESOP and the S corporation's desire not to have its stock end up in the hands of ineligible shareholders such as IRAs. Second, the fact that the ESOP (unlike other exempt entities) avoids UBTI treatment on the S corporation income has proven an impetus for innovative tax advisers to develop strategies that divert the right to the ultimate economic benefit away from the ESOP while leaving the income allocation with the ESOP. Such transactions were largely frustrated by the enactment of section 409(p). See Rev. Rul. 2004-4, 2004-1 C.B. 414..*

10.4. EFFECTS OF PRIOR STATUS AS A SUBCHAPTER C CORPORATION

When an existing subchapter C corporation elects to be treated as a subchapter S corporation, there will be lingering effects on the S corporation of the prior C corporation's attributes, both in terms of its earnings and profits and its treatment of built-in gains upon conversion.

10.4.1. Effect of C Corporation Earnings and Profits

To the extent that the corporation had earnings and profits as a C corporation, the distribution of those earnings and profits will be treated as a dividend. Section 1368(c)(2). The ordering rules in section 1368(c) ensure, however, that dividend treatment will occur only after the distribution of all of the earnings accumulated during S corporation status (called the "accumulated adjustments account" or "AAA", as defined in section 1368(e)(1)). This mechanism is unambiguously pro taxpayer, given that there will by definition be no corporate shareholders wanting to claim a dividends-received deduction. *See* § 1368(c), (e).

10.4.2. Effect of Built-In Gains

The S corporation will itself be taxable under certain circumstances on the "built-in gains" present in the C corporation at the time of conversion. Only the net gain position of the C corporation at the time of the S election is subject to this tax, and this special tax is imposed only on such gains that are recognized during the first ten years after the change to S status. Congress tinkered with this already (overly?) generous rule in 2009, temporarily shortening the gain recognition period to seven years for corporations that had elected to be S corporations before 2004, presumably hoping that the additional tax break would provide more liquidity for these entities.

As easy as it may be to have an intuition about how this provision operates, its implementation is somewhat complicated. Most of the difficulty stems from the fact that the provision includes as "built-in" gains not just easily identified gains and losses associated with particular assets held as of the time of the election, but also "items . . . properly taken into account during the recognition period but . . . attributable to periods" before the election, and from the fact that there is no simple correlation made between the net unrealized built-in gain and the items that will be included as recognized built-in gain.

The net unrealized built-in gain is determined using the overall value of the entity (including goodwill) that would be treated as the amount realized on a sale of all of its assets. Reg. § 1.1374-3. This hypothetical amount realized is then reduced by liabilities that would give rise to basis or deduction when paid, and further reduced by the total of the corporation's basis in its assets. (Additional adjustments may be made for section 481 items and for built-in losses that would be disallowed under section 382 on an actual sale of assets.) This amount will be the maximum amount subject to the section 1374 tax.

Each year, items of income and loss must be examined to determine whether they are items attributable to the years before the subchapter S election. Reg. section 1.1374-4 takes a relatively straightforward approach. First, gain or loss on particular assets is included to the extent that it existed on the date of the election. For items of income and expense, only those items that an accrual basis taxpayer (unconstrained by the limitations of the economic performance rules in section 461(h)) would have accrued before the election are treated as "built-in."

10.5. OTHER SPECIAL SUBCHAPTER S PROVISIONS

There are a number of other provisions throughout the Code that interrelate with the subchapter S election. A variety of these are discussed in this section. Others will be discussed in later chapters.

10.5.1. Check-The-Box Entities and Subchapter S

Although all of the relevant authorities to date are private letter rulings, it appears that any entity that is taxable as a corporation for federal income tax purposes may elect to be taxed under subchapter S. Thus an LLC that has elected to be taxed as an association, or a partnership taxable as an association, will both be eligible.

10.5.2. Availability of Section 338(h)(10) Election

The income generated by a corporation subject to subchapter S is only taxed at one level. Consistent with this, the regulations under section 338(h)(10), which are considered in more detail elsewhere, provide that shareholders of a subchapter S corporation can join with their buyer to elect under section 338(h)(10) to treat a sale of stock by shareholders as if it were a sale of assets by the corporation, followed by a liquidation of the corporation. Under such an election, the measure (because asset basis is used) and character of gain will be different (and likely less favorable to the S corporation shareholders), but the purchaser will own a corporation whose assets' bases reflect the consideration paid.

10.5.3.   Installment Reporting in S Corporation Liquidations

Like the shareholders of a C corporation, S corporation shareholders who receive in complete liquidation an installment note acquired by the corporation prior to liquidation ordinarily treat payments under the note as receipt of payment for the stock and thus defer the related gain recognition with respect to their corporate stock. § 453(h)(1)(A).

The results are not as favorable to the shareholder as it might at first appear, however, because of the way in which the installment sale affects the S corporation shareholder's ability to use her stock basis. Section 453(h)(2) covers distributions in liquidation that take place over more than one taxable year. In that case, basis that is allocated to property received in a prior-year liquidating distribution may be reallocated upon the occurrence of the succeeding-year liquidating distribution, so that the stock basis is appropriately allocated to all of the liquidation property. This provision prevents the corporation and shareholders from timing the receipt of a note compared to other property among the liquidating distributions in a way that provides frontloaded basis to the other property.

For instance, suppose A holds all of the stock of S corporation (S) with a basis of $100; and S has a piece of land worth $120 held with a basis of $50, and cash of $80. S sells the land for an installment note to be paid in two years and liquidates. A will ultimately receive value of $200 and must allocate the $100 in stock basis between the note and the cash as follows: 3/5 (or $60) to the installment note and 2/5 ($40) to the cash. Thus the receipt of cash will produce immediate gain of 40; and half of each installment payment will be gain (characterized as gain on the sale of the land). If A had kept S in existence, distributed the cash, and then distributed the note proceeds as they came in, A could have used $80 of her $100 of basis to offset the receipt of the cash, leaving $20 of basis to be applied against the receipt of payments on the note and thereby deferring inclusion of income.

There is no mechanism that allows a special increase in the inside basis in the assets held by the corporation when stock in an S corporation is sold at a gain. (There is such a provision, section 743, that allows electing owners such an inside basis change when partnership interests are sold.) As a result, a new S corporation shareholder is likely to have a loss upon liquidation, resulting from the pass-through of corporate gain that was not yet realized at the time she purchased the stock, but was realized by the corporation before it was liquidated. For instance, suppose an S corporation with two shareholders owns an asset with a fair market value of $100 and a basis of $10. If a new shareholder buys half of the stock, she will pay $50. If the asset is sold, and the proceeds then distributed in liquidation, she will have $45 of gain allocated to her, increasing her stock basis to $95, but she will receive only $50 in the liquidation, producing a loss of $45, which will not always be available to offset the gain.

Entity Comparison Chart

		Subchapter C	Subchapter S	Subchapter K
Comparison of Regimes for Entity Taxation		entity incorporated under general corporate law; any entity with publicly traded interests	100 SH, domestic not regulated, ind. SH, single class of stock	non-corporate organization, including LLC, UPA, ULPA so long as not publicly traded
		separate entity for all purposes (except corp. subsidiaries), double taxed	separate entity for computing income, no nonrecognition on taking assets out, single taxed	rarely treated as truly separate entity; merely an accounting device
Contributions	entity:	nonrecognition (118 and 1032)		nontaxable (721)
	owner:	nonrecognition possible (351); tax characteristics of contribution can be commingled (but 336(d))		nontaxable (721) and; but "strings" remain connecting original contributor (e.g., 704(c))
Liquidations	entity:	taxable 336 (except 337)		nontaxable 731(b)
	owner:	taxable 331 (except 332)		nontaxable 731(a); except cash and marketable securities, then nontaxable only to extent of basis in p'ship; basis in p'ship becomes basis in assets distributed, 732(b)
Distributions	entity:	gain but no loss if property distributed; no deduction		nontaxable 731(b)
	owner:	dividend to extent of e&p; return of cap. and cap. gain	reduce basis in stock, then gain; 301 if previously a C corp only after S corp earnings distributed	nontaxable 731(a); except cash and marketable securities, then nontaxable only to extent of basis in p'ship; p'ship's basis becomes ptner's basis, 732(a)
Income	entity:	computed and paid at corporate level	computed at entity level, but as if ind., many items passed through as separately computed items	computed at entity level, but as if ind., many items passed through as separately computed items
	owner:	no effect (except presence of e&p)	pro rata allocation only; losses to extent of stock basis and corp-to-SH debt only	special allocations permitted if substantial economic effect; losses used up to entire p'ship basis, including p'ship debt allocable

change in owners	entity	no effect (except 382)	no effect (except 382), unless no longer qualified as subs	
	owner	sale of single asset	sale of single asset	may have gain treated as if individual assets sold (751) may produce deemed distributions if change in share of partnership debt (752)
entity restructuring			can be nontaxable under arcane but well established rules of section 368	patterns of taxability on "mergers" and similar transactions still unclear

PRACTICE PROBLEMS

These practice problems are based on two general sets of facts, with a number of questions exploring variations of those facts.

In all cases, if a question asks how the result would be different, compare the results in the question with those obtained on the facts in the immediately prior question.

For questions 1-10, unless the question states otherwise, assume the following facts:

A and B are individuals owning 40% and 60%, respectively, of the 100 total shares of stock of Smallco, a corporation that is qualified to be, and for which an effective election has been made to be, a corporation taxed under subchapter S. They each have a total basis of $60 in their stock: A has a basis of $1.50 per share, and B has a basis of $1 per share.

1.   Smallco has operating income of $100 in year one, no other items of income and expense, and no distributions or contributions are made. What result to A?

(a)   No income, basis increase of $40 to $100.

(b)   Income of $40, basis increase of $40 to $100.

(c)   Income of $10, basis reduced to $10.

(d)   No income, no effect on basis.

2.   Instead, Smallco has operating losses of $80 in year one, no other items of income and expense, and no distributions or contributions are made. What result to A?

(a)   No deduction, no effect on basis.

(b)   No deduction, basis increase of $32 to $92.

(c)   Deduction of $32, basis decrease of $32 to $28.

(d)   Deduction of $32, no effect on basis.

3.   How would the result be different if A had also lent $60 to Smallco?

(a)   No difference.

(b)   Deduction of $32, stock basis reduced by $16 to $44, debt basis reduced by $16 to $44.

(c)   Deduction of $32, debt basis reduced by $32 to $28, no change in stock basis.

(d)   Deduction of $62.50, reduction of stock basis by $18.75 and debt basis by $18.75.

4.   Instead, Smallco has operating losses of $180 in year one, no other items of income and expense, and no distributions or contributions are made. What result to A, assuming no loans from A to Smallco?

(a)   Deduction of $72, capital gain of $12, basis reduced by $72, increased by $12 to zero.

(b)   Deduction of $60, basis reduced to zero, suspended losses of $12 personal to A.

(c)   Deduction of $60, basis reduced to zero, Smallco carryover loss of $12 to next year.

5.   What result if instead the loss of $180 were the result of a disposition of property contributed by B, which B held with a basis of $200 and which had a fair market value of $20 at the time of the contribution?

(a)   All loss allocated to B, who has loss of $60 and suspended loss of $120.

(b)   No difference.

(c)   Loss of $60 to A, loss of $60 to B, and a suspended loss of $60 to B.

6.   How would the result to A differ if, in addition to having a loss of $180, Smallco had borrowed $100 on a nonrecourse basis?

(a)   No difference.

(b)   Deduction of $72 and basis reduction of $72 (from $100 to $28).

(c)   Deduction of $72 and basis reduction to zero, with a gain of $12.

7.   Assume Smallco had operating income of $100 in year one, and no items of income and expense in year 2. A distribution of $30 to each shareholder was made in year 2. What result to A for the distribution?

(a)   Basis reduction of $30.

(b)   Income of $30.

(c)   Not enough facts given.

(d)   Income of $30 and basis reduction of $30.

8.   Instead, Smallco has operating losses of $80 in year 1, and no other items of income and expense in year 2. A distribution of $30 is made to each shareholder in year 2. What result to A for the distribution?

(a)   Basis reduction to -$2.

(b)   Basis reduction to zero, gain of $2.

(c)   Income of $30.

(d)   Gain of $30.

9.   Smallco has operating income of $100 in year 1, and no other items of income and expense. A distribution of $75 is made to A in year 1. What result to A?

(a)   Basis reduction of $60 to zero and gain of $15; basis restored to $40 by income passed through.

(b)   Basis increased by $40 to $100 as a result of income, decreased by $75 as result of distribution.

(c)   Income of $75, no effect on basis.

10.   Smallco has operating losses of $80 in year 1, and no other items of income and expense in year 1. A distribution of $30 is made to each shareholder in year 1. What result to A?

(a) $32 of loss passed through, basis reduction of $32 as a result of this; basis reduction of $28 and gain of $2 on distribution.

(b)   Basis reduction of $32 as a result of the loss; gain of $30 as a result of the distribution.

(c)   Insufficient facts.

(d)   Basis reduction of $30 as a result of the distribution; loss passed through of $30, suspended loss of $2.

For questions 11–15, assume the following facts unless otherwise stated:

OldC is a corporation that made a valid election late in 2003 to be taxed under subchapter S. It previously operated as a corporation taxable under subchapter C and had $600,000 in accumulated e&p as of the time of the election. E and F are its only shareholders and each owns 50%.

OldC had $200,000 of net income in 2004. Assume there is no additional income in 2005.

E has a basis of $110,000 in her shares, and has been a shareholder since OldC was incorporated. F has a basis of $400,000 in his shares, which he purchased in 2003. (Note that both of these basis figures take into account the income passed-through in 2004.)

At the time of the election, OldC held three assets, parcel 1 with a basis of $10,000 and a fair market value of $510,000, parcel 2 with a basis of $100,000 and a fair market value of $150,000 and parcel 3 with a basis of $400,000 and a fair market value of $200,000.

11.   What result if $40,000 each is distributed to E and F in 2005?

(a) $10,000 will be governed by section 301, resulting in dividend of $10,000 and no effect on basis; $30,000 will result in a basis reduction of $30,000.

(b)   No income and a reduction of basis of $40,000 to each.

(c) $10,000 will be governed by section 301, resulting in dividend of $10,000 and an increase in basis of $10,000; $30,000 will result in a basis reduction of $30,000.

(d) $40,000 to each will be a dividend under section 301.

12.   What result if $150,000 each is distributed to E and F in 2005?

(a)   Each shareholder will have $100,000 of basis reduction; and the remaining $50,000 of his distribution will be governed by section 301 and will result in a dividend of $50,000.

(b)   F will have no income and basis reduction of $150,000; E will have basis reduction of $110,000, with capital gain of $40,000.

(c) $200,000 of the total distribution will be governed by section 301 and result in dividend of $100,000 to E and $100,000 to F.

(d) $150,000 of the total distribution will be dividend under section 301 and have no effect on basis, and $50,000 will reduce basis.

13.   What would be the result if OldC had had no income in 2004, and had made a distribution of $30,000 to each in 2005?

(a) $30,000 of dividend income to E and $30,000 of basis reduction to F.

(b) $30,000 of dividend income to E and $30,000 of return of capital to F.

(c) $30,000 of dividend income to both E and F.

(d) $30,000 of basis reduction to both E and F.

14.   What if in 2007, OldC sells parcel 1 for $510,000?

(a) $300,000 of gain subject to tax under section 1374.

(b)   gain of $500,000, passed through to E only under section 1366; $300,000 of gain subject to tax under section 1374.

(c)   gain of $500,000, passed through to E and F under section 1366; $500,000 of gain subject to tax under section 1374.

(d)   gain of $500,000, passed through to E and F under section 1366; $350,000 of gain subject to tax under section 1374.

15.   How much gain will be subject to tax under section 1374 in 2007 if OldC sells parcel 2 for $200,000 and has not sold parcel 1?

(a) $100,000.

(b) $50,000.

(c)   Cannot tell without knowing the value of OldC in 2007.

DISCUSSION PROBLEM

Individuals A, B, and C form XYZ Corp. and several months later make an election to have it taxed as an S corporation. A contributes Blackacre with adjusted basis of $600 and fair market value of $1,000 in exchange for 100 shares of XYZ Corp. B contributes inventory with adjusted basis of $2,000 and fair market value of $1,000 in exchange for 100 shares of XYZ Corp. C contributes cash of $100 and services worth $900 (all of which is properly capitalized by XYZ Corp.) in exchange for 100 shares of XYZ Corp.

(a)　Is the election effective?

(b)　How are A, B, and C taxed on their contributions? Assuming no other items of income, gain, deduction or loss, what is the result for XYZ and how is that reflected to shareholders?

(c)　What if C is obligated to offer her stock for sale first to B? What if C is obligated to vote her stock in accordance with B's directions?

(d)　Assume the same facts as in item (b). What if C wanted to take back preferred stock worth $100, so that he would be assured of getting his cash investment back if the business failed? What if he insisted on taking back a debt instrument?

(e)　Assume the same facts as in item (b), except that instead of Blackacre, A held two assets, one (which XYZ was likely to sell relatively soon) with a basis of $1500 and a fair market value of $1000, and one (which XYZ was unlikely ever to sell) with a basis of $0 and a fair market value of $500. What result? In such a case, how should B and C react if A insists on receiving something more than 100 shares?

(f)　Assume the same facts as in item (b). In the year following incorporation, XYZ Corp sells half of Blackacre for $1800. What result?

(g)　Assume the same situation as item (f). XYZ Corp also sells all of the inventory in the same year for $700. What result?

(h)　Assume the same facts as in item (g). XYZ Corp distributes $900 to each of the shareholders in the same year. What result? What result if the distribution were not made until the following year?

(i)　Would the result be different in item (h) if XYZ had borrowed $2100 on a nonrecourse basis to buy another parcel of real estate? On a recourse basis? If A, B, and C had guaranteed the debt?

(j)　Would the result in item (h) be different if A had loaned $500 to the corporation?

(k)　Assume the same facts as in item (f) — that is, that half of Blackacre has been sold. What result if, in a later year, XYZ distributes the other half of Blackacre to A, B, and C? Distributes all of the assets it then holds to A, B, and C, except $50 cash?

Chapter 11

CHOICE OF ENTITY AND CAPITAL STRUCTURE REVISITED

Statutes and Regulations	IRC §§ 7701(a)(2), (3),(4), (7), (8); 7704; 385, 351(g), Skim §§ 163(l), 163(j)
	Reg. §§ 301.7701-1, -2, -3, note -4; 1.7704-1
Other Primary Authorities	Commissioner v. Bollinger, 485 U.S. 340 (1988)

So far, we have assumed that all of the entities discussed were subject to corporate tax, with certain electing eligible corporations entitled to pass-through of income under subchapter S.

Throughout the relevant history of the income tax, the decision about type of entity (and, consequently, type of tax regime) that would best serve a particular business has been influenced by a variety of factors, both tax and non-tax.

Among the more prominent non-tax factors have been:

- The availability of limited liability;

- The availability of perpetual life and free transferability of interest;

- The certainty of the package of default legal rights involved;

- The limits on the type of interests potential equity investors are willing to hold;

- The limits on the type of income that potential tax exempt equity investors can or are willing to receive;

- The need to offer employees equity interests as incentives;

- The habits and expertise (and therefore fees) of those planning for the entity; and

- The state fees associated with the form chosen.

Among the more prominent tax considerations have been:

- The relative tax rates for individuals and corporations (including differences in progressivity);

- The availability of certain tax-preferred fringe benefits, especially retirement plans;

- The extent to which payroll taxes will be applied to returns to effort, returns to equity, and combinations thereof;

- The ability to avoid an entity-level tax on all or almost all of the income (e.g., the ability to draw off earnings as salary or interest and the ability to avoid gain on distributions);

- The ease with which the entity can be restructured when the corporate form is considered necessary (e.g., for an IPO, acquisition, or other nontaxable exit strategy);

- The extent to which the most desirable exit strategy is likely to include a taxable transaction in which a fair market value basis in assets after the founders' exit is possible with only a single level of tax; and

- The desire of foreign investors to receive returns through transactions honored as sales.

Perhaps surprisingly, the Code contains no useful definition of "corporation" or any clear indication of what entities are to be taxed under subchapter C. Section 7701(a)(3) indicates that the term "corporation" "includes associations, joint stock companies, and insurance companies," but nothing defines "association." It has generally been taken to mean that the existence of a corporate charter is not determinative of status as a "corporation" for the purposes of the Internal Revenue Code generally and subchapter C more specifically. Ordinarily, the determination is an all-encompassing one: if an entity is classified as a "corporation," it will be a corporation for all purposes and the basic corporate tax scheme requiring both entity and shareholder levels of taxation brings with it the recognition of gain on liquidation, the attention to distributions of earnings and profits, and the availability of reorganization provisions, etc., unless a particular special provision applies.

A number of significant changes in the legal landscape have led to varying planning strategies based on these factors, and to changes in the standards according to which the Service attempts to classify entities.

The earliest authorities on the nature of a corporation involved efforts by the government to classify entities as "associations" taxed as corporations despite their state-law status as trusts. In the leading case, *Morrissey v. Commissioner*, 296 U.S. 344 (1935), the Supreme Court indicated that the most significant factors to be considered in determining status as a corporation were associates, an objective to carry on a business and divide the profits, the continuity of life of the enterprise, centralized management, limited liability, the free transferability of interests, and the holding of property in the name of the entity.

The incentives of the government to force corporate status upon, or to deny corporate status to, business entities have changed over time. The earliest efforts on the part of the government to include trusts within the reach of the corporate tax were undertaken to ensure that the corporate tax base was not eroded as a result of the use of other forms of doing business. For much of the history of the corporate tax, however, corporate status was actually preferable: because individual rates were substantially higher than corporate rates, the overall burden was less. Lower corporate rates made it likely that shareholders would allow corporate assets to accumulate (avoiding the shareholder-level of tax) and be reinvested, regardless of whether it made sense for those assets to continue to be held by the corporation. How could lower rates make up for the fact that corporate profits would be taxed when distributed to the shareholders? As we saw in the introduction to the corporate tax base in the first unit, the burden of the two layers of tax was substantially reduced by two facts: (i) distributions to shareholders could be delayed indefinitely and (ii) even when a distribution was made, the corporate level of taxation on appreciated assets or the value represented by them could be avoided, prior to the repeal of *General Utilities*, if the transaction was carefully structured. The view that these "corporate pocketbooks" were inappropriately avoiding shareholder-level tax led Congress to enact the accumulated earnings tax and the personal holding company tax.

For the most part, these tensions did not put too much pressure on the standards for determining when subchapter C would apply. But beginning sometime in the late 1950s, corporate status became desirable to secure certain fringe benefits, including tax-preferred retirement savings, since a partner in a partnership could not be considered an employee of the partnership eligible for such fringes. Former Reg. section 301.7701-2 revamped the *Morrissey* criteria to make it harder for an entity to claim qualification as a corporation. During much of this era, professionals were not allowed to operate with corporate charters, and the hybrid professional corporate form was not yet invented. Professionals seeking to divert their income into tax-preferred retirement savings therefore had to form entities designed to "fail" under these regulations in order to achieve their goals. Under these regulations, only those factors found exclusively in corporations were counted (dropping out associates and the objective of carrying on a business), and only if an entity had more corporate characteristics than not would corporate status be obtained.

The anti-corporate-status slant of these regulations became outmoded as the availability of tax-preferred retirement plans without corporate status became easier, and, even more important, as the taxation of partnerships evolved. This evolution involved the emergence of the rules that allowed the pass-through to partners of deductions generated by basis resulting from nonrecourse debt and the resulting spread of financing through nonrecourse debt. This pattern of taxation, particularly when combined with cost recovery deductions that clearly allowed basis recovery over a shorter period than debt retirement, led to the proliferation of entities claiming unincorporated status but structured so as to be marketable nonetheless to passive investors. Much hairsplitting was done as the Service tried to keep up with taxpayers' efforts to, for instance, create limited partnerships the general partners of which were undercapitalized corporations. The enactment of the at-risk rules and especially the passive activity loss rules made some of these structures less attractive, but did not relieve all of the pressure on the standards in the regulations for classifying noncorporate entities as associations taxable under subchapter C.

Into this environment entered creative tax advisors who, not content with structuring custom-made entities for clients and then securing the blessing of the Service that they be taxed as partnerships, took it upon themselves to convince several state legislatures to pass new legislation enabling the grant of charters to entities, called "limited liability companies," that would, if the default provisions were followed, be treated as pass-through entities. After several years of issuing rulings blessing these new forms and watching similar state laws proliferate, the

Service announced in Notice 95-14 that it was studying the possibility of allowing pass-through treatment to noncorporate entities on an entirely elective basis. The resulting "check-the-box" regulations were proposed in 1996 and adopted in 1997. T.D. 8697, 1997-1 C.B. 215 (finalizing Reg. §§ 301.7701-1, -2 and -3).

11.1. CHECK-THE-BOX REGULATIONS

Under the "check-the-box" regulations, certain entities can only be corporations while others may elect to be associations taxed as corporations. Included within the tax meaning of "corporation" that may not elect their status are business entities organized under any statute that "describes or refers to the entity as a corporation, body corporate, or body politic," and any joint-stock company, as well as all insurance companies and banks. Reg. § 301.7701-2(b).

The most significant provision in the "check-the-box" regulations provides that those domestic "eligible entities" that are not classified under the regulations as corporations may elect their status. Reg. § 301.7701-3(a) (referencing the corporate classification set out in Reg. § 301.7701-2). Although such eligible entities are most commonly organized under state LLC laws, eligible entities include virtually any type of non-corporate entity recognized under state law, including general partnerships, limited partnerships, and business trusts. If such an entity has more than one member, it may choose to be an association (and thus taxed as a corporation) or a partnership. If it has only one member, it may choose to be an association (and thus taxed as a corporation) or to be disregarded entirely for federal tax purposes.

In essence, these rules require an affirmative election for an eligible entity that is not a per se corporation to be treated as a corporation for tax purposes. If no election is made, newly formed eligible domestic entities will be taxed as partnerships if they have more than one owner. Reg. § 301.7701-3(b)(1)(i). The default rule for almost all non-corporate business entities with a single owner is to be entirely disregarded. Reg. § 301.7701-2(c)(2), 301.7701-3(b)(1)(ii). Thus, even though such entities may serve to limit the exposure of the owning corporation's liabilities associated with the owned entity's activities, the tax consequences of the two can be commingled.

11.1.1. The Election

The entity classification election must be made on Form 8832 and signed by all who are owners at the time the election is made. Any election that is retroactive, or that changes the status of an existing entity, must be signed by all affected owners. Reg. § 301.7701-3(c)(2). Once made, a new election cannot be made without the permission of the Service until 60 months have passed. This once-in-five-year limitation, however, does not apply to limit the ability to elect away from the default treatment (partnership or disregarded) of a newly formed eligible entity. It may also be waived by the Service if the entity changes ownership. Reg. § 301.7701-3(c)(1)(iv).

11.1.2. Changing Status

a. By Election

Many eligible entities elect to be taxed as partnerships when they are first formed and leave this election unchanged throughout their existence. The regulations, however, contemplate that an eligible entity currently taxed under subchapter C can elect to be taxed as a partnership. In such cases, the election produces the same result as if the corporation had liquidated in a section 331/336 transaction (when there is no controlling corporate shareholder) or in a section 332/337 transaction (when there is a controlling corporate shareholder), followed by contribution of the assets to a partnership. Reg. § 301.7701-3(g)(1)(ii) and (iii). The election to go from subchapter C to subchapter K will be treated as the adoption of the plan of liquidation required by section 332. Reg. § 301.7701-3(g)(2)(ii).

The election to go from subchapter K to subchapter C will be treated as though the partnership transferred its assets in exchange for equity interests in the corporation and then liquidated by distributing the stock to the partners (now shareholders). This asset transfer will ordinarily be governed by section 351, unless the "immediately after" test is not satisfied because of a commitment to transfer interests in the entity. Reg. § 301.7701-3(g)(1)(i) and (f) Ex. 4.

b. By Change in Ownership

An existing eligible entity that is subject to subchapter K will become disregarded automatically when its ownership is reduced to a single member. A disregarded entity will become a partnership when some of its interests are sold, resulting in multiple members. Reg. § 301.7701-3(f).

11.2. PUBLICLY TRADED PARTNERSHIPS

Another outgrowth of the pre-1986 tax shelter era was the enactment of section 7704, making any entity taxable as a corporation if it is "publicly traded" within the meaning of that statute. Although these statutory provisions were in place before the check-the-box regulations, the combination of the two sets of provisions is now a regime in which pass-through status is available for any entity not chartered under a state's regular corporation law *unless* that entity must create a market in its interests so that it can seek to raise capital in the public markets. Despite the fact that this result appears to be grounded in economic reasoning, in that publicly traded entities may enjoy a benefit or may be structured in such a way that makes corporate-level taxation appropriate, this rationale has only relatively recently emerged as the justification for the scope of the corporate tax regime.

Section 7704(b) defines "publicly traded" as either (i) "traded on an established securities market" (which Reg. section 1.7704-1(b) specifies as including a regulated exchange, or an exchange that would be regulated if the volume of transactions were sufficient or if it were operated in the US, as well as a "regional or local exchange" or an "interdealer quotation system that regularly disseminates firm buy or sell quotations by identified brokers," leaving the latter two terms undefined) or

(ii) "traded on a secondary market or the substantial equivalent thereof." Interests will neither be treated as traded on an established securities market nor readily tradable in a secondary market unless the entity itself participates in establishing the market, or facilitates the market by automatically redeeming shares traded or including buyers on such markets automatically as partners. Reg. § 1.7704-1(d). The regulations further reduce the chances that an entity will inadvertently become a "publicly traded partnership" by listing the types of transactions in which a partnership can participate without risk of being deemed to have "made a market" in its own interests. Reg. § 1.7704-1(e), (f) and (g). Many more transactions are blessed than one might have thought, given the statutory language. For instance, a partnership may provide a matching service through which potential buyers are matched with potential sellers, so long as posted prices are not binding quotes and actual transfers are delayed at least 45 days from the date information about the seller was first provided, and not more than 10% of the entity's interests are traded in any one taxable year. Reg. § 1.7704-1(g). Private placements are permitted, but, again the regulation rather generously allows any placements that do not require SEC registration and result in fewer than 100 partners. Reg. § 1.7704-1(h).

There is an exception in section 7704 that allows entities that are publicly traded, but which have at least 90% of their income from investments, to remain taxable as partnerships.

11.3. NOMINEE ENTITIES

There remains the possibility, under judicial doctrines unaffected by the check-the-box regulations, that even entities that are organized under regular state incorporation laws can be disregarded under the appropriate circumstances. In general, this doctrine can be invoked when the corporation can be treated as acting only as the nominee or agent of another taxpayer, rather than as acting on its own behalf, with respect to a particular activity or property. Thus the tax consequences of the activity or property are attributed to the other taxpayer, not to the nominee corporation. *See* Commissioner v. Bollinger, 485 U.S. 340 (1988).

11.4. ENTITY CLASSIFICATION, CAPITAL STRUCTURE, AND THE DEBT-EQUITY DISTINCTION

When an entity needs funding, its investors have, at least in the abstract, a choice of whether to participate through holdings that are treated as ownership (equity) interests or as debt. Although some notable finance theory suggests that the mix of equity and debt interests should make no difference in the overall cost of capital to the corporation, in the real world there are differences that cannot be ignored.

One of the most significant is the difference for tax purposes. The essence of the fact that corporations are taxable entities is that all corporate earnings should be taxed to the corporation as earned and any distributions out of those after-tax earnings should be taxed to the shareholders as distributed, without a deduction for the distribution. This rule is reinforced by the presumption in section 316 that distributions on equity are presumed to be out of any corporate earnings available and the provisions in section 302 that transform transactions that are ostensibly in the form of a return of capital into dividend distributions.

The treatment of payments on debt interests is very different: interest is deductible to the corporation, and principal can be repaid out of corporate earnings without tax to the lender. And there is no rule that transforms repayment of debt principal into payment of earnings, so long as the debt is honored as debt, even when the lender is also a shareholder. The corporation and its investors have more control over the timing of returns of principal when debt is used.

Given these differences, the stakes in establishing the corporate structure can be fairly high. But do not forget that these stakes have long been less than they might be because of the dividends-received deduction enjoyed by corporate investors, and they are further reduced so long as dividends are treated as net capital gains (subject to a 15% rate) for individual shareholders. But neither of these provisions alone eliminates the fact that the corporation is a taxpayer separate from its shareholders, so both past and present decisions about corporate structure remain important. Although many of the largest public corporations (many of which were established before there were viable choices for raising capital without public trading in their shares) in recent years have paid very little federal income tax, this result cannot be obtained without significant tax planning efforts.

Despite these stakes, there is no definition of "debt" or "equity" in the Code. There is a general understanding that debt involves a fixed date for repayment and a limit on the rate of return, while equity involves a share of all earnings. Traces of these standards are set out in various places in the Code and regulations — e.g., the straight debt safe harbor in the subchapter S rules in Reg. section 1.1361-1(*l*)(5); the criteria that will make preferred stock "nonqualified" under section 351(g); the limitations on interest deductions in subsections 163(j) and (l). None of these provisions purports to provide an all-purpose definition. It is also generally understood that debt interests are senior to all equity interests, and only equity interests share in the governance of the corporation under ordinary circumstances. But with the development of derivatives and "financial engineering," it is very easy to structure interests that are "hybrid" — that is, that have some of the features of debt (for instance, a fixed time for repayment) but also some of the features of equity (for instance, an interest rate that is contingent on corporate earnings, or the right to be "repaid" principal by taking stock according to a formula that results in a lower than fair market price for the stock).

For most of the history of the income tax, the courts have played a substantial role in defining the nature of an investor's interest in a corporation. The judicial standards, however, are far from determinative. Among the factors courts have considered are the following:

(1)   The presence of an unconditional promise to pay a fixed amount;

(2)   The subordination of the interest to interests of other holders;

(3)   The presence of a fixed maturity date;

(4)   The provision for a fixed interest rate;

(5)   The ratio of debt to equity in the corporation (that is, whether the corporation is "thinly" capitalized);

(6)   The convertibility of interests into equity;

(7)   The relationship between debt holders and equity holders;

(8)   The name given to the certificates evidencing the indebtedness;

(9)   The anticipated (and actual) source of principal payment;

(10)   The nature of the right to enforce payments of principal and interest;

(11)   Participation in management;

(12)   The intent of the parties;

(13)   The source of the interest payments;

(14)   The ability of the corporation to obtain loans from outside lending institutions and the terms on which such loans would be made;

(15)   The extent of the funds used to acquire capital assets; and

(16)   The actual pattern of repayment on the due date or to seek a postponement.

In section 385, Congress gave Treasury the authority to promulgate regulations establishing definitively the distinction between debt and equity. The language of the Code section itself indicates Congress' acceptance of the relevance of the first seven factors above. Despite several promptings from Congress, and several false starts in proposed and later withdrawn regulations, no such regulations have ever been effective.

It appears that these efforts faltered on two fronts: first, every rule that reinforced the corporate level of tax when individual shareholders were involved by treating putative debt as equity gave an extended reach to the situations in which corporate shareholders could use the dividends-received deduction to limit their tax liability; and second, efforts to identify a core "debt" element in all hybrid instruments that could appropriately be taxed under debt standards proved incredibly complex.

Shortly after it indicated that it would not pursue the finalization of regulations under section 385, the Service issued Notice 94-47, 1994-1 C.B. 357, providing some guidance regarding the debt-equity distinction. This notice, however, is focused on the variations that are likely to arise when corporations attempt to avoid regulatory restrictions on debt while nevertheless obtaining an interest deduction; it may not be directly applicable in other contexts.

Over the last decade, Congress has responded to the problems posed in distinguishing debt from equity by seemingly abandoning the notion that the two can be distinguished in some clear conceptual way that reasonably derives all consequences to issuers and holders based on the debt-equity classification. Instead, it has chosen to address particular consequences relating to particular troublesome contexts. It has, for instance, limited the deductibility of interest under subsections 163(j) and (l), and denied some of the consequences of stock treatment to preferred stock that is too close to debt through section 351(g). This "pigeon-holing" of different interests with specialized statutory provisions governing their treatment is sometimes effective at limiting particular abuses, but almost always also lends itself to a new kind of tax arbitrage as the different tax regimes are subject to further financial manipulation.

PRACTICE PROBLEMS

Problems 1–6: True or False?

1.   An entity that can offer all of its participants limited liability must be taxed as a corporation.

2.   Tax law will always follow corporate law: if there is an entity for state law purposes, the tax law will always honor it.

3.   A publicly traded partnership can have pass-through treatment as long as there are no special allocations either for tax or economic purposes.

4.   An entity that would otherwise be taxed as a partnership may elect to be taxed under subchapter C.

5.   An asset generating an income stream will always provide a greater overall yield if it is not contributed to a corporation but is left in the hands of an individual or a partnership.

6.   When a shareholder lends to a 100% owned corporation, the debt will be treated as a contribution to capital, the amount of the loan proceeds will be added to the basis of her stock, and any repayment will be taxed as a dividend.

7.   Nothing Company LLC, has two equal individual members and has been taxed since its creation as a C corporation. It holds an asset with a basis of $20 and a fair market value of $50. If it elects under the section 7701 regs to be taxed under subchapter K, what is the result to it?

(a)   Gain of $30, basis of $50 in asset after election.

(b)   No gain or loss, basis of $20 in asset after election.

(c)   No gain or loss, basis of $50 in asset after election.

(d)   Gain of $30; basis of $20 in asset after election.

8.   Nothing Company LLC, is 90% owned by Big Co. and 10% owned by Big Co.'s sole shareholder. Both companies have been taxed since their creation as C corporations, and Nothing holds an asset with a basis of $20 and a fair market value of $50. If Nothing elects to be taxed under subchapter K, what is the result to it?

(a)   Gain of $50, asset basis of $50 after transaction.

(b)   No gain or loss, basis remains $20.

(c)   Gain of $30, asset basis of $50 after the transaction.

(d)   Gain of $3, basis of $23 after the transaction.

9.   In the previous problem, what result if Big Co buys the stock of Nothing Company LLC held by its sole shareholder, and now owns 100% of Nothing?

(a)   Gain of $30 and Nothing remains subject to taxation under subchapter K.

(b)   Gain of $30 to Nothing, and for tax purposes, Big Co. is treated as the taxpayer with respect to all of Nothing's activities.

(c)   No gain to Nothing and for tax purposes, Big Co. is treated as the taxpayer with respect to all of Nothing's activities.

DISCUSSION PROBLEM

Fred has owned an auto body shop in his own name for several years. The rather casual income statements he has prepared in prior years suggest that he has, if accounted for on the cash basis, profits of about $80,000 per year, before paying himself at all.

In a typical prior year, Fred withdrew about $65,000 in each year to meet his current living expenses, and set aside $15,000 for future investment in the business. How should these profits and withdrawals have been reported for income tax purposes?

Fred's suppliers have said they are giving him better credit terms because of the presence of these reserve funds, but he is not sure how much difference they actually make. He has accumulated about $90,000. He currently thinks that he will look for a location at which to expand his business and will use most of the funds for that.

For non-tax reasons suggested by his insurance agent and his banker, Fred is contemplating changing the form in which he does business. Fred understands the simple corporate form, since his brother-in-law operates his business through a corporation. (He has heard that he ought also to be considering using a limited liability company or a partnership, but he wants first to understand completely the tax consequences of the form he knows best.) He knows, for instance, that distributions of dividends will trigger an income tax on the recipient, but he has watched his brother-in-law pay himself a salary without paying much of a dividend now for years.

(a)   What are the consequences if Fred chooses to incorporate under his state's general corporation law? If Fred has no income other than the auto body shop income, could using this standard state corporate form offer any possible tax advantage? Would anything be different if Fred were a lawyer involved in a solo practice?

(b)   Will the corporate form be as attractive if Fred's profits are expected to as much as triple in the next three years as a result of a contract that he has entered into with an insurance company?

(c)   Will the corporate form be as attractive if the insurance company expects Fred to make investments of more than $300,000 in new equipment that will be entitled to immediate expensing under a special investment incentive provision? [Note: this special investment incentive was made up for this problem, but many such provisions have existed in the real world, and influenced the decision about form.]

(d)   Will the corporate form be as attractive if the insurance company will fund much of the improvements, but will do so only by purchasing preferred stock, which will be redeemable at the insurance company's election in six years?

(e)   Fred may soon inherit a considerable sum from a great aunt, which will generate about $300,000 per year in income from sources not related to the auto body shop. Under these circumstances would the corporate form offer any advantage?

(f)   He could liquidate the inheritance and use the funds to obtain a new location in his own name. He could also use the funds set aside within the incorporated business to develop the new location. What are the potential advantages and disadvantages of each approach? If Fred's bankers and creditors insist that the assets related to the new location be held by the same corporate entity as the old business? What if they must be held in a corporation, but not necessarily the same corporation?

(g)   If there are no other constraints, should he make the funds available as equity contributions or as loans?

(h)   What advantage might there be in lending part of the inheritance to the corporation to meet its working capital needs? In leaving out of the corporation the building and land at which his business is located?

(i)   Fred is also considering expanding his business to include sponsoring entrants in demolition derbies. His buddies have convinced him that he should be concerned about the tort exposure this might entail. What tax considerations should be taken into account in the decision whether to have a separately incorporated entity, and what the relationship between the two corporations should be? (Others are worrying about the business and general legal consequences of this proposal.) Should he own the demo derby operation directly, or should it be a subsidiary operation of the main business? What are the consequences of changing his mind with respect to the form he uses for this aspect of the business?

(j)   If Fred decides to incorporate, should he make an election to be taxed under Subchapter S?

(k)   If Fred incorporates and does not elect Sub S immediately, what complications arise should he decide to do so in the future?

(l)   If Fred decides not to incorporate but to organize as an LLC, can he make a "check-the-box" election? How will the LLC be taxed if he does?

(m)   How might the answers to all of the above questions change if Fred has a "silent partner" who will invest $100,000 in the business but will not actively participate in it?

(n)   How might the answers to all of the above questions change if Fred has a key employee to whom Fred would like to offer an equity interest, but the employee is not likely to be able to accumulate much cash in the near future?

(o) How might the answers to all of the above questions change if there is a nationally known corporation that is reported to be interested in buying up successful small auto body shops in exchange for its own stock?

TAXABLE ACQUISITIONS AND SECTION 338

Chapter 12

GENERAL RULES FOR TAXABLE ACQUISITIONS

Statutes and Regulations	IRC §§ 1060; skim § 197 Reg. §§ 1.1060-1(a), (b)(1)-(4), (c)(1)-(4); 1.338-1(a), -2 (definitions as needed), -6, -7(a)-(b); skim Reg. § 1.338-4, -5.
Other Primary Authorities	Enbridge Energy Co. v. United States, 553 F. Supp. 2d 716 (S.D. Tex. 2008), *aff'd*, 2009 U.S. App. LEXIS 24713 (5th Cir., Nov. 10, 2009)

When an ongoing business is conducted by a corporation, a potential buyer of the business has a choice to negotiate to buy the stock or to buy the assets of the corporation. Many factors other than tax considerations will affect this choice (including the need to avoid the liabilities of the old business as much as possible or, pulling in the opposite direction, the need to avoid transfer taxes for each individual asset, renewal of licenses and the physical documentation frequently required in the transfer of assets), but the corporate income tax considerations are usually significant.

In general, if stock is acquired, gain or loss is recognized only on the stock interest — measured by the difference between the shareholder's basis in the stock and the consideration received. When the entity is a corporation, the purchase of its stock will have very little effect on the tax treatment of the corporation's income. There are two significant exceptions to this general rule: first, when an election is made under section 338 to have the transaction treated as a purchase of assets even though its form is a purchase of stock, discussed in Chapter 13 below, and second, when carryover losses and certain excess credits and built-in losses are limited after a change in the ownership as a result of sections 382, 383, and 384.

When an ongoing business is conducted by an individual or when a potential buyer wants to purchase something less than all of the assets of a corporation, there is no similar choice: the purchase must be treated as a purchase of assets. Under well-established doctrines, purchases of going businesses that are not accomplished through the purchase of interests in an entity are treated as separate purchases of the various individual assets owned by the business, both tangible and intangible. Williams v. McGowan, 152 F.2d 570 (2d Cir. 1945). The total amount of consideration received by the seller must be allocated among the individual assets, both for purposes of computing the seller's gain and for purposes of computing the buyer's basis.

12.1. TAXABLE ASSET ACQUISITIONS

Section 1060 and the regulations thereunder (along with regulations promulgated under section 338, discussed further below) provide the rules that apply when the assets of a business are acquired. The approach is essentially the same whether assets are acquired from a corporation, an individual, or some other entity, whenever there is a taxable acquisition of "assets which constitute a trade or business." Reg. section 1.1060-1(b)(2) provides two alternative tests for the existence of a trade or business: the test set forth under section 355 as a necessary criterion for a tax-free spin-off, and the (probably more inclusive) test of whether "goodwill or going concern value could under any circumstances attach to such group" of assets. "Goodwill" is defined as "the value . . . attributable to the expectancy of continued customer patronage." "Going concern value" is defined as including "the value attributable to the ability . . . to continue functioning . . . without interruption notwithstanding a change in ownership."

Under section 1060(a), if the buyer and the seller agree to an allocation of the purchase price, this allocation is binding on the parties (but not on the Service). Under the regulations, a taxpayer may possibly argue against the agreed allocation only upon a showing of mistake, undue influence or fraud. Reg. § 1.1060-1(c)(4). Even without an agreement about allocation, both the buyer and the seller are obligated to report their own allocations of the purchase price to the Service.

12.1.1. Seller's Side Concerns

What are the stakes of this allocation on the corporate seller's side? Sellers generally will prefer to allocate more of the purchase price to high-basis assets and less to low-basis assets, in order to limit gain recognition. Furthermore, although all gain will be subject to tax, all of the gain resulting from the sale of the various assets of the business will not be subject to tax in the same way. Under section 1245, tangible personal property that has been subject to cost recovery will produce gain that is treated as ordinary income to the extent that it recaptures cost recovery deductions, and such recapture gain will not be eligible for installment sale treatment by the seller. Under section 1250, gains on depreciable real property that has been held long term are generally not subject to recapture (except to the extent of "additional depreciation" from pre-1987 methods that recovered costs more quickly than under today's straight-line method). Nonetheless, corporate sellers are subject to a special rule under section 291 that recaptures a portion of the amount that would be recaptured if section 1245 applied instead of section 1250. Furthermore, some business property gains and losses will be included in the taxpayer-favorable section 1231 calculation, whereby an overall net gain will result in the section 1231 items being treated as long-term capital items, while an overall net loss will result in section 1231 items retaining their ordinary character. Other assets will give rise only to capital gains or capital losses (subject to the "basketing" provision in section 1211 that permits them to be used only to offset capital gains). Recall that there is no special capital gain rate available to corporations.

12.1.2. Buyer's Side Concerns

What are the consequences on the buyer's side? Buyers will be interested in allocating purchase price to those assets that permit the most and the most rapid basis recovery. In general, this motivation will result in a buyer's incentive to allocate as much as plausible to tangible personal property, for which relatively fast (3 to 10 years) cost recovery is allowed, and as little as plausible to land, which is likely to be retained indefinitely and which is not treated as depreciable property. Until the adoption of section 197 in 1991, this concern also led buyers to try to avoid allocation of any of the purchase price to goodwill or other intangibles for which no cost recovery at all might be allowed, and to try to develop justifications for the amortization of many assets closely related to goodwill, like customer lists, for which they might be able to establish a useful life. Section 197 now allows the amortization of most purchased intangibles over a 15-year life. Although the statutory provisions appear to be very elaborate on first glance, most of the verbiage is intended to leave in place the amortization or cost recovery that would have been allowed under prior law, whether that cost recovery is faster or slower than 15 years.

An asset purchase will ordinarily leave the tax attributes of the selling corporation, such as losses, earnings and profits, and any special accounting methods, with the selling corporation. The buyer will not acquire any of the net operating losses of the selling corporation and will not be bound by the selling corporation's accounting methods in respect of the acquired assets.

12.1.3. Initial Allocation under Section 1060

The regulations under sections 1060 and 338(b)(5) direct that the "residual method" described in Reg. sections 1.338-6 (for initial allocations) and 1.338-7 (for redetermination of basis to reflect a later change in purchase price) must be followed in allocating the purchase price among the assets. In general, the residual method allocates to each asset, *to the extent possible*, a portion of the purchase price equal to but not exceeding its fair market value, with any residual amount allocated to goodwill and going concern value. It may seem obvious that no asset should be allocated a portion of the purchase price in excess of its fair market value, but this rule was necessitated when taxpayers argued, in deals where a "premium" was paid in excess of the individual assets' fair market values, that a portion of the premium should be allocated to each asset. Under that approach, assets could have a basis higher than fair market value, resulting in either losses on disposition or higher cost recovery deductions.

The section 1060 and section 338 regulations also dictate a priority according to which the purchase price should be allocated to various classes of assets in the event that there is a shortfall at the time of the acquisition — that is, when the purchase price is insufficient to provide aggregate basis equal to the aggregate fair market value of all of the purchased assets. This shortfall can result when the buyer is obligated to make certain kinds of contingent payments in the future or has assumed certain types of liabilities as part of the consideration paid, as discussed below. Under general tax principles, the buyer's basis does not include debt assumption or other types of promised future payments if those payments are not fixed at the time of purchase.

In general, the rank of assets in this priority order reflects the likelihood that the purchaser will engage in a transaction in which the lack of basis assigned to a class of assets would result in artificial income to the purchaser. Under these rules, the purchase price (and, ultimately, basis) is allocated under Reg. § 1.338-6(b) to assets in the following order (i.e., first to Class I, then to Class II, etc.):

Class I	cash and deposit accounts;
Class II	actively traded interests in personal property including publicly traded stock and government securities, certificates of deposit, and foreign currency;
Class III	accounts receivable and any other assets that taxpayers mark to market under their regular accounting methods for those assets;
Class IV	inventory;
Class V	equipment, land and buildings, and any other asset not included in other classes;
Class VI	intangibles other than going concern value and goodwill, and finally;
Class VII	going concern value and goodwill.

For taxpayers who are not involved in trading financial assets (that is, taxpayers for whom most of the items in categories II and III are not important), this list simplifies to a fairly predictable priority of purchase price allocation to cash and cash equivalents, accounts receivable, inventory, depreciable plant and equipment, intangibles, and, finally, going concern value and goodwill.

For example, suppose a purchaser paid $12,500 for a business that included 4 assets with identifiable values as follows:

Certificates of deposit	$1000
Inventory	3000
Equipment	4000
Customer list	1000

Each group of assets would be allocated basis in accordance with the values above, and the "residual" $3500 of the purchase price would be allocated to goodwill, creating a basis in goodwill that would be amortizable under section 197 over a 15-year period.

If the consideration currently paid had been only $8500 (e.g., because the purchaser is liable under the agreement or under applicable state law for a tort judgment expected to be $4000), the purchaser would obtain an aggregate basis at the outset of only $8500. That basis would be allocated as follows:

Certificates of deposit	$1000
Inventory	3000
Equipment	4000
Customer list	500

Installment Sales: Interaction of Sections 1060, 453, 453A, and 279

Section 453 allows gain on a sale of assets to be taken into account when the seller receives payment rather than when the assets are transferred. A ratable portion of the gain realized is recognized with each payment. There are, however, several important issues for sellers to consider in respect of an installment sale of assets.

Sales for notes that are payable on demand or readily tradable are not eligible for installment treatment. § 453(f)(4). Gain will also be triggered to the extent the buyer's debt is sold or pledged.

In an installment sale (whether or not there is some cash up front), the entire purchase price (note and cash) would be allocated under the section 1060 residual method as discussed in the main text. To the extent a portion of the installment debt is allocated to assets that are ineligible for installment sales accounting under section 453 (e.g., inventory or dealer dispositions), the seller would treat the note as a cash payment and no installment accounting would be permitted for those assets. Moreover, to the extent the seller is required to recognize depreciation recapture under sections 1245 or 1250, that gain will be recognized and only the excess gain not subject to recapture will be taken into account under the installment method. § 453(i)(1).

Furthermore, the benefit of an installment sale may be severely limited by section 453A, which imposes interest on the deferred tax liability. The section applies generally to installment sales in a taxable year in which the face amount of the outstanding obligations that arose during, and are outstanding as of the close of, that taxable year exceeds $5 million. The provision also imposes pledging restrictions on any installment obligation arising from a disposition of property for which the sales price exceeds $150,000. See § 453A(a)(2), (b)(1), and (d).

Finally, in the case of a corporate purchaser using debt to purchase assets of another corporation (or the stock of another corporation, in certain situations), section 279 may disallow the purchaser's interest deduction. The section applies to interest paid or incurred on "corporate acquisition indebtedness" to the extent it exceeds $5 million (reduced by certain other acquisition interest amounts). The section applies to debt when the following conditions are satisfied:

• The debt is used to acquire at least two-thirds (by value) of the trade or business assets (excluding cash on hand) of another corporation;

• The debt is subordinated to the claims of trade creditors generally or expressly subordinated to any substantial amount of unsecured debt of the corporation;

• The debt is convertible (directly or indirectly) into the issuing corporation's stock or part of an investment unit which includes an option to acquire stock; and

• The issuing corporation has a debt/equity ratio greater than 2 to 1 or its projected earnings do not exceed 3 times the annual interest payment required.

12.1.4. The Effect of Later Payments on Basis and Amount Realized

If additional payments are made to the seller, or on the seller's behalf, that were not included in the calculation of the purchaser's basis at the time of the acquisition, the additional amount results in an increased basis through an allocation process under Reg. section 1.338-7(b). In effect, the additional amount creates new basis that is added to the adjusted bases of the acquired assets using the original allocation schedule. The additional payments will be allocated first to the highest class to which the original purchase price allocation was less than the aggregate fair market value of the assets in that category, and then any excess additional payments will "fill up" each next higher category until exhausted. The resulting new basis amounts will apparently be recovered over the *remaining* recovery period of the assets involved, according to the rules by which recovery periods were established initially. If a purchased asset is no longer held by the purchaser, the amount may be taken into account as if it were additional basis of that asset at the time of the disposition, generally creating or increasing a loss under the principles of *Arrowsmith v. Commissioner*, 344 U.S. 6 (1952). *See* Reg. § 1.338-7(e), Ex. 1.

Suppose, in the example in Section 12.1.3, above, that a final tort judgment of $5000 was paid in the tenth year after the purchase. At that point in time, $500 of new basis would be allocated to the customer list (because it was the only category for which the original allocation was smaller than the fair market value), and the remaining $4,500 of the additional payment would be allocated to goodwill. Both amounts would be recoverable over the remaining 5 years of the original section 197 amortization period. (Note that the residual class of goodwill is not capped by some estimate of overall value as of the time of the purchase. As a consequence, the fact that the purchaser paid $5,000 when it expected to pay only $4000 is not taken into account through identification of an interest or loss component.)

The treatment of the seller as a result of later payments is governed by the general tax accounting rules applicable to the seller, with fewer issues specifically dealt with in regulations. If later payments are contemplated at the time of the initial sale, much of the seller's gain will be reported on the installment method unless the seller elects out, so long as the consideration received is debt that is neither readily tradable nor payable on demand. Gain related to certain types of assets, however, may never be reported on the installment method, for instance, section 1245 gain, gain on inventory and other property held for sale to customers, and gain on marketable securities. (For most sales of going businesses, interest will be payable on the deferred tax liability under section 453A.)

In general, an accrual basis taxpayer not reporting on the installment method will be required to accrue the present value of contingent payments to be made by the buyer; ordinarily, the buyer will not be able to include such amounts in basis until they are actually paid. Hence the seller may in some circumstances at the time of the sale accrue amounts realized before the buyer is allowed basis.

The effect of later payments that are different in amount from those taken into account at the time of sale is not always easy to discern. Many such amounts that involve payments to third parties on behalf of the seller, however, will be eliminated from the seller's income in the year of payment because their payment would have given rise to a deduction to the seller.

12.2. TAXABLE STOCK ACQUISITIONS

An acquisition of a business accomplished through an acquisition of stock will be taxable to the shareholders, unless the consideration used is the stock of an acquiring corporation and the transaction otherwise satisfies the requirements for a tax-free reorganization under section 368. The somewhat complex rules for this determination are better examined in connection with the rules governing corporate reorganizations in Chapter 15, below. In general, however, any acquisition in which shareholders of the Target, in the aggregate, receive more than 60% of the consideration for their stock as cash will be taxable to the shareholders.

Acquisitions of stock for cash or any other consideration other than the stock of the acquiring corporation produce gain or loss to the shareholders. Except to the extent outlined below regarding the potential disallowance of certain loss and credit carryovers when there is a change in control or unless the section 338 election discussed below is made, the acquisition will have no tax effect on Target. Thus in many situations, Target's asset bases, tax accounting methods, and other tax attributes (except loss and credit carryovers) will be unaffected by a change in ownership. The buyer's consideration will become its basis in the Target stock. The creation of basis in stock rather than assets is a result that buyers frequently will want to avoid if at all possible, since they are more likely to benefit early on from Target's basis recovery on its assets than from using their basis in a disposition of Target stock. A "step-up" in basis, however, is only available after recognition of the built-in gain with which Target holds its assets, a price that frequently neither buyer nor seller will be willing to pay.

Shareholders are treated no differently whether all of the Target stock is sold in one transaction (such as in response to a tender offer to the public shareholders of Target) or whether blocks of Target stock are sold by individuals. The same result will obtain in even more complicated transactions, such as a transaction in which a purchasing corporation (Purchaser) makes a tender offer to buy Target stock for cash, and then causes a taxable merger of Target into one of Purchaser's subsidiaries. Individual shareholders who have held Target stock for more than a year will have long-term capital gains and losses, resulting in gains that are taxed at favorable rates and losses that are subject to limitation under section 1211, in that they may be used only to offset capital gains and the first $3,000 of other income each year.

There is no accounting made in the treatment of the selling shareholder for the amounts that would have been dividends had the Target distributed its earnings and profits before the sale. Indeed, it is fairly well established that even if a corporation does make a distribution in redemption of the stock of a shareholder in connection with a sale of all of its stock, the shareholder will enjoy capital gains treatment as if all the stock had been sold without regard for the usual section 302 tests for distinguishing dividends from sales. Zenz v. Quinlivan, 213 F.2d 914 (6th Cir. 1954); Rev. Rul. 75-447, 1975-2 C.B. 113. Such distributions can be useful when the Target has earnings and profits that the buyer views as unattractive, or when the Target simply has a large amount of liquid assets that the buyer isn't interested in buying (perhaps because financing the purchase of liquid assets doesn't make sense to the buyer). Corporate shareholders, on the other hand, will ordinarily prefer that pre-sale distributions not be integrated with the sale so that they may be treated as dividends eligible for the dividends-received deduction under section 243, as was possible in *Litton Indus. v. Commissioner*, 89 T.C. 1086 (1987). The basis-reducing provisions of section 1059, however, will in many transactions eliminate the benefit of the section 243 deduction.

12.2.1. Sales of Stock in "Qualified Small Businesses"

Section 1202 provides for the exclusion of 50% of the gain realized on the sale of stock in certain small corporations, up to $10 million in gain per shareholder per corporate issuer. In general, the corporation must never have had gross assets valued at more than $50 million, and it must conduct an active business in which 80% of its assets are used. The seller must be the original owner of such stock on issuance. Stock of corporations engaged in certain types of business, including medical practice, law, athletics, farming, and the operation of hotels and restaurants, is excluded from these provisions.

12.2.2. Loss of Tax Attributes upon a Change of Control

Sections 382 and 383, in very general terms, provide that whenever more than 50% of the stock of a corporation is transferred within a year into new hands (and those "new hands" are one or more shareholders who each own more than 5% of the stock), certain tax attributes of the corporation will be reduced. Most important, section 382 limits the use of losses of the Target: in each year after a qualifying ownership change, the Target will only be allowed to use losses equal to a percentage of its value as of the time of the ownership change.

The purpose of this provision is to ensure that when control of a corporation is transferred tax losses continue to be usable only to the extent that they would have been used by the loss-generating corporation before the change. The tax losses will in theory be worth roughly the same to the corporation after the transaction as before, and the selling shareholders will enjoy (through the increase in consideration they receive as a result of the preservation of this tax benefit) some of the economic benefit of the tax losses their corporation has incurred. Not surprisingly, given this underlying purpose, the loss limitation provisions apply in essentially the same way to both taxable and nontaxable changes of ownership. These limitations on the use of losses are explored more fully in Chapter 14.

12.2.3. Transfers of Assets Disguised By Creation of a Corporation

Since the tax consequences to the seller of stock are different from, and in general more attractive than, those resulting from a sale of assets, why would shareholders not simply convert all asset holdings to stock holdings before the transfer by contributing the assets to be sold to newly created corporations? One would think this process would be even more desirable if the consideration may be stock of the acquiring corporation and therefore tax-free reorganization treatment may be available. (Note that much of what follows disregards the tax incentive on the part of many buyers to buy assets rather than stock so that their basis reflects the consideration paid.)

It is fairly clear that the new-corporation strategy will not work if the incorporating transaction is done for no valid business purpose and is close in time to the anticipated sale: the owner of the assets cannot simply transfer the assets to a new corporation before selling or transferring the new corporate stock because the Service will ignore the transitory holding of those assets in corporate solution and treat the shareholder as if the corporation had never existed. *Cf.* Rev. Rul. 70-140, 1970-1 C.B. 73 (ruling that even when assets were contributed to a pre-existing corporation owned by the seller, the transaction would be treated as a transfer of assets, not a nontaxable transfer of stock, to the ultimate buyer.) The possibility of being denied sale of stock treatment upon a disposition of a business is one of the reasons business owners may be advised to incorporate when it would otherwise seem disadvantageous on initial formation of a business.

12.3. SALES OF STOCK FOLLOWED BY SALES OF ASSETS

The ink was barely dry on the repeal of *General Utilities* before tax shelter planners realized that this change would create such great tension between the seller's desire to sell stock and the buyer's desire to buy assets that there would be a market for acquisition structures through which both sides could claim the result desired. The gimmick is popularly known as a "Midco transaction," and involves the interposition of an intermediate entity between the old owner of the stock of Target and the taxpayer that seeks to acquire Target's assets. The role of this intermediate entity is to buy the stock and sell the assets of Target, while somehow avoiding or absorbing the gain associated with the asset sale. Some Midcos may have carryover losses that they hope can be used against this gain (but section 384 will be an obstacle here, unless Midco is willing to hold on for five years); some Midcos may be effectively tax exempt and therefore liquidate Target and sell its assets while claiming no tax on either step (section 337(b)(2) should prevent this, but some entities including Native American corporations may claim that they are immune from federal taxes on the sale in a way that does not implicate section 337(b)(2)).

Many of the simplest of these transactions may be challenged with a simple application of the step transaction doctrine — that is, if it can be shown that Midco would not have purchased the stock if Acquirer had not already agreed to buy the assets, could not have done so without the financing this prearrangement allowed, and bore no economic risk associated with its holding of the Target stock. (The district court in *Enbridge Energy v. United States*, 553 F. Supp. 2d 716 (S.D. Tex. 2008) thought that was such a case and granted the government's motion for summary judgment.) But other transactions more carefully planned and involving either a more substantial economic role for Midco or an unwitting Seller may not be so readily attacked. The Service has attempted in a series of notices, beginning with Notice 2001-16, 2001-1 C.B. 730 and most recently Notice 2008-20, 2008-1 C.B. 406, to delineate the characteristics of such transactions that identify them as listed transactions subject to special reporting and ethical considerations.

Chapter 13

SECTION 338 AND STOCK ACQUISITIONS TREATED AS ASSET ACQUISITIONS

Statutes and Regulations	IRC § 338(a), (b) (skim), (d)(3), (g), (h)(10) Reg. §§ 1.1060-1(a), (b)(1)-(4), (c)(1)-(4); 1.338-1(a), -2 (definitions as needed), -6, -7(a)-(b); skim Reg. § 1.338-4, -5
Other Primary Authorities	Rev. Rul. 90-95, 1990-2 C.B. 67 FSA 200122007

13.1. PURCHASES OF CONTROLLING STOCK WITH A SECTION 338(a) ELECTION

A corporate Purchaser who acquires stock interests representing control of a Target corporation in taxable transactions occurring within a single twelve-month period may elect to treat the transaction as if assets, rather than stock, had been acquired. Control for these purposes is the section 1504(a) definition — 80% of the total voting power of the corporation and 80% of the total value of the stock. The election results in an increase to fair market value in the basis of the Target corporation's assets, in effect allowing asset basis credit for the consideration used by the Purchaser in buying the stock. This "step-up" in basis comes at a great price — the deemed sale of assets requires the recognition of gain and loss with respect to *all* of the corporation's assets. Because the cost recovery allowed on this basis increase will almost never produce a tax benefit greater than the tax triggered by the election, the election allowed by section 338(a) is rarely of much interest. A section 338(a) election will make sense only in the relatively rare cases in which, for instance, a Target has large expiring net operating losses that cannot otherwise be used, has large unrecognized losses that will be triggered, or is a foreign corporation not subject to U.S. tax at all. Otherwise, the cost of the future tax benefit inherent in the basis step-up is tax at the shareholder level (as a result of the sale of the shareholders' stock) and at the corporate level (as a result of the election), a cost that simply is not worth the benefit.

Why is there such an elaborate Code section for an election that it rarely makes any sense to make? There are three answers. First, when section 338 was first enacted before the repeal of *General Utilities*, it produced very desirable results. There were several situations, including both the liquidation of a corporation and the sale of assets in anticipation of a liquidation as described in former section 337, in which a corporation could dispose of its assets without recognizing very much of its gain. (Certain elements of corporate gain, including recapture of cost recovery, were not avoided.) The election in section 338 deemed such a sale in anticipation of a liquidation to have occurred, and therefore frequently had significant consequences only for the buyer. It is only a slight overstatement to say that under this regime the step-up in basis of the corporate assets was essentially tax-free to the corporation. The only tax, therefore, was the tax to the shareholders on their sale of stock: that cost was likely to be relatively low in cases in which shareholders had purchased their stock recently and thus had a relatively high basis, and would in any event likely be a tax on capital gain rather than ordinary income. Section 336 dealing with liquidations has since been amended to require the recognition of gain in corporate liquidations, and the rules in former section 337 limiting the gain recognized in sales in anticipation of liquidation are gone. (The consequences of the election under section 338 are no longer tied to the tax treatment of liquidations.)

Second, the original section 338 replaced former section 334(b)(2), which in turn codified the result in *Kimbell-Diamond Milling Co. v. Comm'r*, 14 T.C. 74, *aff'd per curiam*, 342 U.S. 827 (1951). Under *Kimbell-Diamond*, a corporation was deemed to have purchased Target assets, rather than Target stock, if the Target corporation was liquidated immediately after the purchase. The idea was that the Purchaser should end up in the same place it would have been had it simply purchased assets — that is, with a fair market value basis in the assets. In the litigated case, it was the government that sought this recharacterization of the transaction, because the total amount paid by the buyer was less than the aggregate basis with which the selling corporation held the assets. An attempt was made to regularize the *Kimbell-Diamond* result in former section 334(b)(2), but the results were far from satisfactory. When section 338 was enacted, the legislative history indicated a clear intent completely to replace the old *Kimbell-Diamond*/§ 334(b)(2) regime by providing the section 338 election as the only route by which a purchase of stock would be treated as a purchase of assets. The Service has accepted this pre-emptive effect of section 338 in its rulings, but with some nuance regarding the possibility of characterization of a multi-step transaction (e.g., a qualified stock purchase followed by a liquidation or upstream merger) as a reorganization or as a taxable asset acquisition. See the discussion of Reg. section 1.338-3(c)(1) and Rev. Ruls. 90-95 and 2001-46 in Section 13.3, below.

Third, although the election under section 338(a) is rarely attractive, a related election under section 338(h)(10) remains very attractive when the Target stock is being sold out of an affiliated group to a corporate Purchaser. Under this provision, a controlling parent of Target may agree with the Purchaser to treat a sale of Target stock as if Target sold its assets and then liquidated into the controlling parent. Much of the law developed under the main section 338 election applies with respect to these section 338(h)(10) elections. *See* Section 13.2, below.

13.1.1. Qualified Purchases

The general section 338(a) election (which must be made in accordance with the election provision in 338(g) and is sometimes referred to as a section 338(g) election) is available only to corporate Purchasers. Under section 338(d)(3), section 1504(a)(2) control of Target must be "purchased" in a taxable transaction or in a series of taxable transactions that occur within 1 year. "Purchase" is defined in section 338(h)(3) as an acquisition of Target stock in which the Purchaser's Target stock basis is not determined at all by reference to the basis of the stock transferor, the stock is not acquired in a transaction in which the transferor fails to recognize the entire gain or loss, and the stock is not acquired from a person whose ownership would be attributed to the Purchaser under section 318.

13.1.2.   Tax Consequences of the Section 338(a)/(g) Election

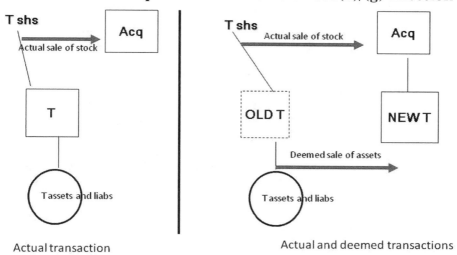

Actual transaction   Actual and deemed transactions

**Effect of 338(a)/(g) election by Acquirer
Deemed sale of assets in addition to actual sale of stock**

When an election is made under section 338(a), there is a deemed sale of *all* of Target's assets from an imaginary "Old Target" to an imaginary "New Target" (even if the Purchaser does not acquire all of the Target stock). Although this sale is conceptually a sale that occurs after the stock purchase by Purchaser (and therefore the income tax liability is clearly not Seller's, see Reg. § 1.338-10), the NOLs and capital loss carryovers of Target (if any exist) are available to offset the gains so recognized.

This sale is deemed to have taken place, according to Reg. section 1.338-4, at a deemed sale price determined by reference to the total amount realized by the sellers of Target stock, the Aggregate Deemed Sales Price (ADSP). New Target's basis, the Adjusted Grossed-up Basis (AGUB), is similarly determined, under Reg. section 1.338-5, by reference to the consideration paid.

When Purchaser buys all of the stock of Target in one transaction with no contingent consideration and no significant acquisition costs are incurred, the ADSP and the AGUB are close to the same and relatively easy to determine. Although the formulas are not the same, both formulas are aimed at achieving an approximation of the fair market value of all of the assets of Target, based on the consideration for the stock that was actually sold. Both because of the common-law doctrines that might lead to differences between a seller's amount realized and the buyer's basis in any sale, and because of the peculiar circumstances under which the deemed sales involved in section 338 elections take place, these amounts will frequently be different.

a. ADSP as Computed Under Reg. Section 1.338-4

The ADSP takes into account all of the consideration received by the seller, without reducing for any amount that the seller might be entitled to defer under installment sale accounting. Reg. § 1.338-4(c)(1). Under general tax principles, this means that the seller will include in the amount realized the expected value of payments that are uncertain.

When less than all of the stock is recently purchased, this ADSP is "grossed up" to an amount that comes closer to the aggregate fair market value of all of the Target assets than if only the amount realized on the amount of stock actually sold were used. Therefore, if the Purchaser acquires only 80% of the stock of Target for $80,000, the ADSP used to compute the gain on the assets of Target will be grossed up to $100,000 (i.e., $80,000/.8). Any selling costs such as brokerage commissions are then *subtracted* in arriving at the grossed up amount realized and the liabilities of Old Target are then added to arrive at ADSP. The object is to ensure that the Target corporation recognizes all of the built-in gains and losses on its assets, assuming that the price of the purchased Target stock corresponds to a proportionate portion of the assets' fair market values.

b. AGUB as Computed Under Reg. Section 1.338-5

The starting point for AGUB is the Purchaser's basis in the stock actually acquired. Under general tax principles, however, the Purchaser's basis will not include any contingent liabilities, or any liabilities that are fixed but subject to tax accounting rules that defer their availability for deduction or basis until economic performance or payment (for instance, under section 461(h) or section 404). These items are, however, likely to have been included in the seller's amount realized under Reg. § 1.338-4, at least to the extent of their expected value. *Compare* Reg. § 1.338-5(b)(2)(iii) Ex. 1 *with* Reg. § 1.338-4(b)(2)(iii) Ex., *and* Reg. § 1.338-5(b)(2)(iii) Ex. 2 *with* Reg. § 1.461-4(d)(5).

This basis amount is grossed up, again to reflect the fact that less than all of the stock may have actually been purchased. This gross-up will increase the New Target's basis to reflect the value of its assets still held indirectly by minority shareholders. However, this gross-up will *not* include any gross-up for the stock held by the Purchaser but acquired before the acquisition date — only the Purchaser's actual basis in this "nonrecently purchased stock" will be used unless the Purchaser makes an election to take that gain into income. Thus, if Purchaser purchased 80% of the Target stock this year for $80,000, but had purchased 5% of the Target stock 10 years ago for $2,000, the grossed up basis for the recently purchased stock would be only $95,000 (i.e., $80,000 * (1-.05)/.8). *See* Reg. § 1.338-5(c). Any acquisition costs would be added to this gross-up calculation to give the grossed up basis in nonrecently purchased Target stock. To determine the entire AGUB, the Purchaser would add the actual basis for the nonrecently purchased stock ($2,000 in our example) to the grossed up basis for the recently purchased stock ($95,000 in our example). The purchaser will also add to this total basis the liabilities of New Target (i.e., all Old Target liabilities, including the tax liability under the section 338 election, that are treated as assumed by New Target).

Thus the AGUB available to allocate as Target's basis in its assets will be reconcilable with the number used as ADSP, but in most situations it will not be the same. It will always be different if either (1) part of the purchase price is contingent and therefore not includible in basis under general tax principles or (2) the Purchaser already owned some Target stock.

c. Allocation of ADSP and AGUB

The rules for allocating the ADSP and the AGUB to Target's assets are the same as those used in actual asset transactions governed by section 1060. Indeed, section 1060 now incorporates by reference these parts of the law developed under section 338.

After a section 338 election, as a result of the fictional sale and resulting gain recognition, New Target is treated as a new taxpayer without most of Old Target's tax history, including its basis or carryover losses. Any unused Target NOLs, credits or e&p accounts disappear as a result of the deemed sale transaction. Accordingly, New Target may make new elections under section 168 and adopt a different taxable year and accounting methods (so long as it satisfies the requirements under sections 441 and 446). New Target does, however, use the same taxpayer identification number as Old Target and the two corporations are treated as the same corporation for various specified Code provisions. For example, a section 338 election is not treated as substituting a new obligor on the debt of Target corporation for purposes of the debt modification rules in Reg. section 1.1001-3. *See* Reg. § 1.338-1(b).

13.2. PURCHASES OF CONTROLLING STOCK FROM A PARENT CORPORATION WITH A SECTION 338(h)(10) ELECTION

If there is a qualified purchase of stock from a corporation that owns at least 80% of the stock of Target, a different election to treat the transaction as a purchase of Target assets rather than stock can be made. Under this election, the parent seller and the buyer *together* agree to treat the transaction as an acquisition of assets rather than stock. The selling parent corporation's basis in its Target stock is ignored, and gain or loss are computed on all of Target's assets, as in the regular section 338(a)/(g) election. Minority shareholders, however, are still treated as selling their Target stock, even when it is included in the qualified stock purchase.

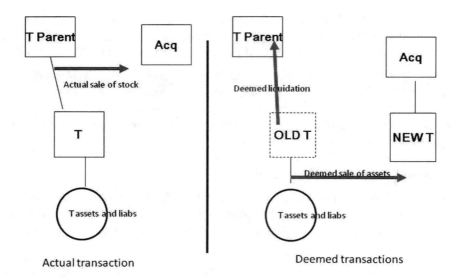

Effect of 338(h)(10) election by T Parent and Acquirer
Deemed sale of assets instead of sale of stock followed by deemed liquidation of T

In contrast to the regular section 338(a)/(g) election which triggers a corporate-level tax *in addition to* a shareholder-level tax, the section 338(h)(10) election triggers a corporate-level tax *instead* of shareholder-level tax. The underlying rationale is that the corporate level *asset gain* recognized by the seller is an adequate predicate for the basis step-up for the buyer, and the corporate level *stock gain* could ordinarily be avoided in any event. This is similar to the justification for the mechanism of the dividends-received deduction and the treatment of section 332 liquidations, which abjure cascading levels of corporate tax in favor of a single corporate-level tax and a shareholder-level tax only when the earnings are paid out to individual shareholders.

Although the problems associated with computing gain and loss after a section 338(h)(10) election are similar to those faced after a section 338(a)/(g) election, the practical consequences are decidedly different: the tax liabilities resulting from the deemed sale become the liabilities of the selling side, not the buying side.

The Code and regulations make clear that the fiction of the deemed sale and liquidation applies while the Target is in the selling group. *See* § 338(h)(10); Reg. § 1.338(h)(10)-1(d)(4). The consequences of an election under section 338(h)(10) are the same as those that would have obtained if the selling parent had in fact caused Target to sell its assets and then liquidated Target. Note that because this fictional liquidation will ordinarily be treated as a section 332 liquidation, Target's remaining tax attributes will survive as attributes of the selling parent corporation under section 381. Thus, for instance, if Target has NOLs that are not entirely absorbed by the gain on the deemed sale of its assets, they are available to offset the future income of the selling parent. Similarly, if the consideration for the purchase of Target stock is an obligation of the type that qualifies for installment reporting, the selling parent may report its gain under the installment method. Reg.

§ 1.338(h)(10)-1(d)(8) (treating Old Target as receiving notes of New Target that are distributed to Old Target's selling shareholder).

Reg. section 1.338(h)(10) tries to block any (perhaps unintended) additional benefits by providing that the (h)(10) election should not "produce a Federal income tax result . . . that would not occur if the parties had actually engaged in the transactions deemed to occur because of [the election]" except as provided for in Reg. section 1.338-1(b)(2).

13.2.1. Availability of the (h)(10) Election to Nonconsolidated Affiliated Corporations and S Corporations

As noted above, the section 338(h)(10) election is premised on the idea that there should be only one level of corporate tax on the sale of a controlling interest in corporate stock in those circumstances in which gain on the assets would have been subject to only one level of tax had the Target corporation sold its assets and liquidated into a controlling parent corporation — i.e., the sale of assets generates the Target corporation tax, and the liquidation in to the controlling parent corporation is tax-free under section 332.

Although the language of section 338(h)(10)(A)(i) itself appears to limit the availability of the section 338(h)(10) election to Targets that have actually been included in the filing of a consolidated return with their selling parent, the flush language in section 338(h)(10)(B) anticipates the extension of the election by regulation to all affiliated groups. Current regulations do permit this election in an affiliated group. Reg. § 1.338(h)(10)-1(b) and (c).

Treasury has extended by regulation the availability of the (h)(10) election even further, to include sales of subchapter S corporations. Reg. § 1.338(h)(10)-1(c). This regulation goes well beyond anything anticipated in the language of section 338 itself, since the Target S corporation is not held by a selling corporate group but rather by various individual S corporation shareholders. The underlying premise of the election regarding whether there should be both corporate- and shareholder-level taxation, however, is satisfied: the liquidation of a Target S corporation would have been taxable, but the items of income resulting would have shown up on the shareholders' return and there would have been only one level of tax.

13.2.2. Proposed Expansion of the Election to Treat Taxable Sales of Stock as Sales of Assets

In August 2008, regulations were proposed that would considerably expand the availability of the mechanism provided by section 338(h)(10). This mechanism — whereby a seller of a controlling interest in stock treats the taxable sale of that stock as a taxable sale by Target of its assets, followed by a liquidation of the sale proceeds — would be expanded to include:

- Transactions that are not sales, so long as they result in the transferee of the stock having a fair market value in that stock (except as a result of the operation of section 1014), including distributions. Thus the regulations speak of *dispositions*, rather than *purchases* of stock. Various types of transfers occurring within a single month are aggregated to determine if there has been a qualified stock disposition.

- Buyers that are not corporations, including individuals.

- Buyers that do not buy controlling interests (so long as a controlling interest is in fact disposed of by the seller). Transfers to several buyers are aggregated to determine whether there has been a qualified stock disposition. Because the disposition transactions include distributions of Target stock, special rules are provided apparently to honor the loss nonrecognition policy of section 311. In any disposition that includes a distribution, losses will be recognized only to the extent that stock was actually sold. Thus if Seller sells 35% of Target stock and distributes 65% of Target stock, only 35% of the loss on each Target asset can be recognized, even though all gain is recognized.

Because there are possibilities for many more owners of Target stock in a transaction that would qualify for the deemed asset sale provided by section 336(e) under these regulations, there are several variations from the provisions in section 338(h)(10) regarding the ways that stock that is not included in the qualified disposition itself is taken into account.

13.3. CATEGORIZING ACQUISITIONS: MULTISTEP TRANSACTIONS INVOLVING LIQUIDATIONS OR MERGERS

13.3.1. Post-Acquisition Liquidations

On occasion, an acquiring corporation that has purchased the stock of Target will want to liquidate Target after the purchase. This will not always be the case, since so long as Target remains intact, the claims of Target creditors will remain claims only against Target assets. A commingling of Target assets with Purchaser assets may result in the exposure of Purchaser assets to Target liabilities.

Prior to the adoption of section 338, both under common-law doctrine and under former section 334(b)(2), such stock-purchase-then-liquidate transactions could, under the right circumstances, result in the transaction being treated as a direct acquisition by Purchaser of Target assets without a corporate-level tax being paid. See the discussion of the *Kimbell-Diamond* doctrine, above. The Service has made it clear that it interprets the legislative history of section 338 as precluding such a recast of a qualified stock purchase and a liquidation, if the integrated transaction would be a taxable asset acquisition rather than a reorganization. *Compare* Rev. Rul. 90-95, 1990-2 C.B. 67, *with* Rev. Rul. 2001-46, 2001-2 C.B. 321. Accordingly, the section 338 election is available in such transactions whether or not an actual liquidation follows the qualified stock purchase.

Therefore, a taxable acquisition of stock followed by the liquidation of Target *with* a section 338 election will result in corporate tax at the Target level and a step-up in basis in the Target assets held by the Purchaser. However, a taxable acquisition of stock followed by the liquidation of Target *without* a section 338 election will be treated as a taxable acquisition of stock followed by a section 332 liquidation (in which Target's basis in its assets will survive without any step-up for the consideration paid for the stock). Such transactions are not likely to be attractive whenever the purchase price paid for Target stock is greater than the aggregate basis of Target in its assets, since Purchaser's basis in Target stock will be destroyed by the liquidation.

The interaction of qualified stock purchases as defined in section 338 and multi-step transactions that may result in transactions that can be recast as nontaxable is considered in the material below on triangular and multi-step reorganizations.

13.3.2.   Taxable Mergers and Taxable Informal Mergers

If a corporation merges into an acquiring corporation, and the consideration used for the transaction is not that which is required to meet the definition of a reorganization (for instance, if the consideration is all cash or includes an insufficient amount of corporate stock to satisfy the continuity of interest requirement or if all of the reorganization requirements for the particular form used are not satisfied), the transaction will be treated as the merging corporation's sale of all of its assets to the acquiring corporation. Although in some areas (for instance, qualifying under section 368(a)(1)(A) as a statutory merger) tax treatment of transactions is dependent upon satisfying state-law requirements, state corporate law never conditions the availability of acquisition techniques upon the tax consequences of the transactions.

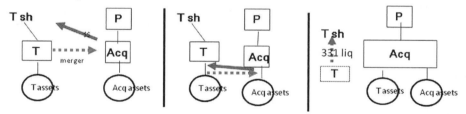

Taxable Forward Cash Merger: Deemed Sale of assets followed by liquidation of T

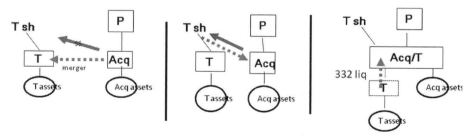

Taxable Reverse Cash Merger: Deemed Sale of T stock followed by liquidation

a. Forward Cash Mergers

If Target is merged into an acquiring corporation or into a subsidiary of the acquiring corporation in a transaction that does not qualify for nonrecognition (for instance, because all cash was used as consideration), the transaction will be treated as an acquisition of assets followed by a liquidation of Target. Rev. Rul. 69-6, 1969-1 C.B. 104. Target will be taxed on the gain on its assets as if it had sold them for cash, and then liquidated. The shareholders of the merged corporation will be taxed based on the difference between the fair market value of the stock in the acquiring corporation that they receive and the cash or other property they receive and their basis in the Target stock disposed of (usually the amount they originally paid for the stock).

When a merger is not subject to nontaxable reorganization treatment and therefore the transaction is treated as a taxable transfer of assets, all of the tax attributes of the Target corporation, including loss carryovers, credit carryovers, and earnings and profits of the acquired corporation, are destroyed.

b. Reverse Subsidiary Cash Mergers

If a transitory subsidiary of an acquiring corporation is merged into Target, the transaction will be treated as a sale of stock by the Target shareholders. They will be taxed as if they had simply sold their stock to the acquiring corporation.

Because the transaction has been deemed to be a taxable acquisition of stock, an election under section 338 to trigger gain on assets and a step-up in basis from this deemed sale may be made. Absent a section 338 election, the Target corporation will not be taxed on its assets and its basis in its assets will remain the same. Although carryover losses will be limited under section 382 just as they would in any sale of stock involving an ownership change, the other tax attributes of Target generally remain intact.

PRACTICE PROBLEMS

True of False?

1. After a taxable acquisition of the assets of a business, all assets will always be held by the purchaser with a basis equal to the fair market value of the assets.

2. A sale of stock will never affect the computation of the tax liability of the Issuing corporation.

3. If an Acquiring corporation pays cash to buy all of the stock of a Target corporation, and then liquidates the Target corporation, the step transaction will apply and the transaction will be treated as a taxable acquisition of assets.

4. If tax is the only determinant and the consideration to be used is cash, then in the case of an acquisition of a business owned by a corporation, a buyer will *ordinarily* prefer an acquisition of assets to an acquisition of stock.

5. When a corporation sells its assets and then liquidates, the only significant income tax involved is computed at the shareholder level. The shareholders must

recognize the difference between their bases in their stock holding and the amount they receive on liquidation.

6. If a corporation sells assets with a combined basis of $500 for a total consideration of $200, it will be able to claim a loss of $300 on its current year's tax return.

7. When all of the stock of a corporation is sold, the old earnings and profits account is wiped out.

DISCUSSION PROBLEM

For all subparts, assume the following information unless otherwise provided. T Corp, a profitable corporation, has the following assets and liabilities:

Assets	Basis	FMV	gain/loss
Cash		$10,000	-
Portfolio of marketable securities	$20,000	30,000	$10,000
Accounts receivable	10,000	10,000	-
Inventory	30,000	200,000	170,000
Equipment ($50,000 § 1245 recapture)	100,000	150,000	50,000
Land	150,000	300,000	150,000
Building (no recapture)	175,000	340,000	165,000
Patent	25,000	60,000	35,000
		1,100,000	*

Liabilities

Bank Loan	200,000

* aggregate gain is meaningless without character

A owns 50 shares of T Corp stock with a basis of $300,000; B owns 40 shares of T Corp stock with a basis of $200,000; and C owns 10 shares of T Corp stock with a basis of $50,000.

The shareholders of T Corp have decided to sell the business to P. Outline the tax considerations in the following alternatives. (Note that you do not have enough information to quantify the amount of tax that will actually be owed as the result of these transactions, and therefore you will not always know the amount that will be available net of tax for further transfers after taxable transactions.) Be sure to consider other steps that may be taken to improve the tax treatment for either the buyer or the seller.

(a) An individual purchaser.

　(i) P, an individual, pays $1 million in cash to T Corp for all its assets and assumes T Corp's bank loan. T Corp then liquidates.

(ii)   What if T Corp's liabilities had included a contingent liability that both parties assessed as the equivalent of a $100,000 bank liability, and the bank liability was only $100,000?

(iii) Suppose instead that P pays $1 million to the shareholders to purchase their stock in T Corp, and T Corp does not liquidate.

(iv)   Suppose P decides to liquidate T Corp.

(v)   What if T Corp had held its assets through Nothing LLC, which since its inception had always been held by T Corp and had made no election regarding its classification for tax purposes. T Corp sold all of its interest in Nothing to P?

(vi)   What if T Corp had held its assets through Nothing LLC, as above, and sold half of its interests in Nothing to P?

(b) A corporate purchaser.

(i)   Same alternatives as above, but suppose P is a corporation (P Corp). Is the choice between an asset purchase and a stock purchase the same for a corporate P?

(ii)   Suppose T Corp has a $700,000 NOL carryover that is about to expire.

(iii) Suppose that P Corp decides to liquidate T Corp.

(iv)   Suppose that P Corp forms an acquisition subsidiary, to which it transfers cash of $1 million, and the acquisition subsidiary is then merged into T Corp in a transaction in which A, B, and C receive only cash.

(v)   Suppose that P Corp forms an acquisition subsidiary, to which it transfers cash of $1 million, and T Corp is then merged into the acquisition subsidiary in a transaction in which A, B, and C receive only cash.

(c) A corporate purchaser and a Target that is an affiliated sub.

(i)   Suppose A, B, and C own the stock of H Corp, the only asset of which is the T Corp stock. H Corp owns all of the stock of T Corp except for a class of privately issued preferred stock that has no voting rights and does not participate in the growth of T Corp. H Corp's basis in the T Corp stock is $200,000. T Corp sells its assets to P Corp (which assumes T Corp's liability) for $1.2 million and then liquidates. H Corp then liquidates.

(ii)   Suppose that prior to any asset sale, T Corp liquidates, and then H Corp liquidates. A, B, and C then sell the former T Corp assets to P Corp for $1.2 million.

(iii) Suppose that rather than an asset sale, P Corp purchases the stock of T Corp from H Corp for $1.2 million.

(iv)   What if T Corp's assets include a wholly owned subsidiary?

(v)   What if T Corp is an S corp, owned by A, B, and C?

Chapter 14

TAX ATTRIBUTES AFTER CORPORATE ACQUISITIONS AND RESTRUCTURINGS

Statutes and Regulations	IRC §§ 381(a), (b)(1) and (2), 382, 384, 269
Other Primary Authorities	none

When the stock of a corporation is transferred among shareholders (in a way that is either taxable or nontaxable to the shareholders), for the most part the corporation will be treated as if nothing happened. Consistent with its treatment by the tax law as a separate taxable entity, the corporation continues to hold its assets with the same basis. Similarly, after reorganization transactions that are treated by the Code as if they involved insufficient change in the nature of the corporation to trigger shareholder gain and corporate gain, the transferred assets are held by the transferee corporation with the same basis as they were held by the transferor corporation. Other corporate tax attributes — including carryover losses and credits, earnings and profits, and accounting methods — also generally survive such transactions. (Recall that none of these attributes will move with the assets when they are transferred in a taxable transaction.)

Although the paragraph above reflects the overall approach of subchapter C, there are a number of particular rules that do affect basis in corporate assets and other tax attributes after significant changes in ownership and corporate restructurings. First, section 381 outlines which attributes survive, and sometimes imposes conditions upon their survival. Second, section 382 limits the ability of a corporation to use carryover losses that would otherwise be available under sections 172 and 1212, and section 384 limits the ability of any corporation to use its excess built-in losses against the built-in gains of another entity. Third, section 269 provides an anti-abuse rule that disallows the use of attributes when a corporation has acquired another corporation "with the principal purpose" of "evasion or avoidance of Federal income tax by securing the benefit of a deduction, credit, or other allowance." (Note that sections 382, 384, and 269 apply both when the restructuring is taxable and when it is nontaxable.)

14.1. SECTION 381

Section 381(a) is the general rule providing for carryover of listed tax attributes in transactions between corporations in which the transferee (often referred to here as Target) has a carryover basis. The statute ties this treatment to section 332, involving the complete liquidation of a controlled subsidiary, and section 361, involving transfers of assets in reorganizations. (It does not include either B reorganizations, because there is no transferee corporation and the Target remains intact, or section 351 transactions, perhaps because the assets transferred need not constitute a business prior to the transfer and thus would not necessarily have a tax history that should survive.) This does not mean, however, that the list of transactions in section 381 comprises all those for which some attributes may carry over or that nothing but basis carries over in all transactions described only in section 351 and in no other reorganization provision. *See, e.g.,* Rev. Rul. 95-74, 1995–2 C.B. 36 (outlining the circumstances in which a corporation may "inherit" the accounting treatment of amount paid with respect to contingent liabilities after a section 351 transaction).

Although section 381 was one of the (albeit limited) attempts to rationalize subchapter C by restating the decisions reached in prior case law, *e.g.,* Commissioner v. Sansome, 60 F.2d 931 (2d Cir. 1932) (holding that a successor corporation after a reorganization inherits the predecessor's earnings and profits), it does not provide an exclusive list of the attributes that will carry over. Section 381(c) lists attributes that are "inherited" by the transferee corporation and outlines some of the limitations on their use, as follows:

(1)   net operating loss carryovers, which carry only to the transferee corporation's taxable years after the transfer ratably by days (with other guidelines for dealing with part years);

(2)   earnings and profits of the transferor, which become the transferee's, but a deficit from the transferor cannot "go around the corner" and reduce past earnings and profits of the transferee (such a deficit can only reduce future transferee earnings and profits);

(3)   capital loss carryovers, with limitations similar to those applicable to net operating loss carryovers;

(4)   the method of accounting of the transferor, unless there is a conflict with the transferee's methods; and

(5)-(26)   various other tax accounting items, including inventory methods, and the tax history that might lead to future taxable recoveries under the tax benefit rule.

The implementation of these limitations is addressed in detail in the regulations. *See* Reg. §§ 1.381(c)(1)-1 through 1.381(c)(26)-1.

14.1.1. NOL Carryovers

Section 381(b) directs that when corporate assets are transferred in most reorganizations, the transferor's taxable year will end with the transfer, and that any post-transfer net operating or net capital losses cannot be carried back to the transferor's prior years. Such losses can only be used to shelter the transferee corporation's income and gains (so they may be carried back to acquiring corporation's pre-acquisition taxable years). (Losses may also be subject to the limitations in sections 382–384.)

The regulations provide that only a single transferee corporation can be the "acquiring" corporation for the purpose of section 381. In cases in which the assets are transferred to more than one corporation, the regulations provide that the corporation that "directly" acquires the assets is the "acquiring corporation," even if none of the assets ultimately reside in that corporation. Reg. § 1.381(a)-1(b)(2).

Section 381(c)(1) and related regulations contain additional specific rules relating to NOL carryovers. A transferor corporation's NOLs are carried first to the taxable year of the acquiring corporation that ends *after* the date of the transfer. The amount of a transferor corporation's NOLs used by acquiring corporation in the first taxable year after the transfer is limited to the taxable income of the acquiring corporation earned in the post-acquisition portion of the year. The regular ordering rules for carrybacks and carryforwards apply, with NOLs from the earliest year, whether of transferor or acquiring, used first.

In addition, in determining the sequencing of the use of transferor corporation NOLs acquired by acquiring corporation and acquiring corporation's own pre-transfer NOLs, a net operating loss of the transferor corporation for a taxable year that ends on or before the end of the loss year of the acquiring corporation is treated as originating in a taxable year prior to that acquiring corporation taxable year and thus would be used before the acquiring corporation's NOL from that taxable year. § 381(c)(1)(C) and Reg. § 1.381(c)(1)-1(e)(2). For example, suppose transferor and acquirer both have an NOL from their 2007 taxable years: the transferor's 2007 NOL will be considered prior to the acquiring corporation's 2007 NOL for carryover purposes. The short year of the transferor corporation ending on the date of the transfer and the taxable year of the acquiring corporation that ends after that date are treated as two separate taxable years to which an NOL of the transferor corporation for any taxable year ending before that date may be carried, but the taxable year of the acquiring corporation for the year of the transfer is treated as only one taxable year for determining carryovers of the acquiring corporation's NOL. *See* Reg. § 1.381(c)(1)-1(e)(3).

Even if a corporation acquires only 80% of the assets of the transferor corporation (for example, an 80% corporate parent in a section 332 liquidation), the acquiring corporation nonetheless acquires 100% of the NOL carryover of the transferor corporation. Reg. § 1.381(c)(1)-1(c)(2). In the case of a chain of acquisition transactions, an acquiring corporation that acquires assets of a corporation that previously acquired the assets of another corporation in a transaction to which section 381(a) applies succeeds to the net operating loss carryovers available to the first acquirer. Reg. § 1.381(c)(1)-1(g).

> **Bercy Industries and the Rule Against Loss Carrybacks**
>
> *Under section 381(b)(3), a corporation acquiring property is not entitled to carry an NOL for a taxable year after the date of the transfer back to a taxable year of the transferor corporation. If the transferor is the profitable company and the acquiring corporation is the loss corporation, that rule prevents the loss corporation from using its NOLs to get a refund from the transferor corporation's earlier profitable years.*
>
> *In* Bercy Industries, Inc. v. Commissioner, *640 F.2d 1058 (9th Cir. 1981), however, a forward triangular merger involved an empty shell as acquiring subsidiary. The court agreed with the taxpayer that section 381(b)(3) did not prevent the surviving corporation from carrying its losses back to the target's pre-acquisition years. In the court's view, to do otherwise would elevate form over substance, since the merger survivor was really the same corporation that generated the income and the policy against having the business that generates the income be allowed to use the losses was not violated.*

14.1.2. Earnings and Profits

The use of Target's earnings and profits by the acquiring corporation is also subject to several detailed rules, for which further guidance is provided in Reg. section 1.381(c)(2)-1. The acquiring corporation succeeds to the earnings and profits (or deficit in earnings and profits) of the transferor corporation. Any earnings and profits changes to the transferor corporation's account that occur after the date of the transfer and before the completion of the overall reorganization are treated as occurring as of the close of the date of the particular transfer. Reg. § 1.381(c)(2)-1(a)(1).

If both corporations have accumulated deficits or both corporations have accumulated earnings, the accumulated deficits or earnings and profits are simply combined upon the close of the transfer. But if one party has an accumulated deficit and the other has accumulated earnings and profits, the accumulated deficit cannot offset the accumulated earnings and profits — it can only be used to offset earnings and profits that are earned after the transfer (the "hovering deficit" rule). In that case, the acquiring corporation is required to maintain separate earnings and profits accounts after the transfer — one for the transferor and one for the acquiring corporation, and the deficit account cannot offset the positive earnings in the earnings account (no matter which corporation originated the deficit account). Reg. § 1.381(c)(2)-1(a)(5).

Furthermore, in computing the accumulated earnings and profits as of the date of the transfer, it will make a difference whether the transfer occurs on the last day of the taxable year of the acquiring corporation. If it does not, the acquiring corporation's current earnings and profits for the taxable year of the transfer will be treated as partly accumulated prior to the transfer, and a transferor accumulated deficit can only be used against the portion of the acquiring corporation's earnings and profits earned *after* the transfer. Reg. § 1.381(c)(2)-1(a)(6). The amount accumulated before the transfer will be equal to the total amount of the "undistributed earnings and profits" of the acquiring corporation for the year of the transfer (without considering the transferor's deficit) times a fraction, the numerator of which is the days in the taxable year preceding the date of the distribution and the denominator of which is the total number of days in the taxable year. The "undistributed earnings and profits" are the current earnings and profits, *reduced by* any distributions made during the taxable year. This rule accordingly takes distributions for the taxable year into account first, then allocates the remaining current earnings and profits after the reduction for distributions between the pre- and post-change periods on a daily basis. Only the post-change earnings and profits can be offset by the transferor corporation's deficit in earnings and profits.

For example, assume an acquiring corporation (Acquiring) has a current earnings and profits account of $50,000 and no accumulated earnings and profits. The transfer occurs on May 31, but Acquiring's taxable year ends June 30. Acquiring also makes a distribution of $20,000 to its shareholders on June 30. The transferor corporation has a deficit of $250,000. Acquiring's undistributed earnings and profits would be $30,000 ($50,000 current earnings and profits, minus the "nimble dividend" distribution of $20,000). Of those profits, therefore, only $2,465 (e.g., $30,000 * 30/365) will be treated as earned after the transfer and only $2,465 of the transferor corporation's deficit can be used to offset Acquiring's earnings and profits in that year, leaving a "hovering deficit" of $247,535. If Acquiring has $10,000 of earnings and profits the next year and again makes a distribution of $20,000 at year end, the distribution will be a dividend (from $10,000 of current earnings and $10,000 of Acquiring corporation's earnings of $27,535). There will remain a hovering deficit of $247,535 as well as accumulated profits of $17,535.

14.2.   SECTION 382

Congress has long been suspect of transactions in which corporations acquire the previously accrued losses of other corporations, in the form of carryovers of net operating losses and capital losses. Although there needs to be some carryover of losses in order to provide an averaging function, losses would be used — in the absence of an appropriate limiting mechanism — to offset totally unrelated income that has been generated by another business using the capital of unrelated shareholders. Further, the allowance of such losses would, in the minds of some, amount to the government's reimbursement to taxpayers for a part of all corporate losses.

What Is the Evil Behind Loss Trafficking?

Two distinct threads of criticism regarding use of one corporation's losses by an acquirer corporation (or a corporation whose shareholders have changed significantly) are often articulated. First, it is asserted that the losses of the old shareholders should not be available to offset the income of strangers to the loss. Section 382 addresses this concern by limiting the extent to which these strangers, who in effect are in a position to pay the old shareholders for the tax shield provided by the losses, can benefit from buying the loss. But these same limits increase the certainty of the amount of loss the strangers can use, and, as a result, the old shareholders who suffered the loss are more likely to benefit from its use.

Second, some tax experts claim that softening the annual accounting rules of tax to permit any loss carryovers inappropriately subsidizes failing businesses. Others acknowledge that a deduction of a loss amounts to a subsidy when it is allowed even though no value has been lost, but disagree with the claim that a loss carryover deduction is always a subsidy. To the extent that losses are in fact only available when the value represented by income that has been previously taxed is lost, they argue, there is no subsidy (except that involved in timing) in fact since the tax benefit involved in the allowance of such a loss can be viewed as a reimbursement of a tax burden previously imposed.

Congress has somewhat more recently become similarly suspicious of transactions that allow acquisition of "built-in losses," that is, transactions in which the carryover bases of the assets transferred substantially exceeds their fair market value. *See* section 362(e) and various relatively new aspects of section 382.

For many years, the predecessor of section 382 simply denied carryovers under certain (but not all) circumstances when loss corporations were acquired. The statutory provision was augmented by older cases, including *Libson Shops v. Koehler*, 353 U.S. 382 (1957), in which the Court held that there could be no commingling of loss carryovers even in a merger of a number of sister corporations owned by the same shareholders and conducting the same business. The continuing validity of these cases in light of the passage of the predecessor of section 382 remained uncertain. Thus there was ambiguity in the way the limitations applied, and there was a general feeling that the transferor and its shareholders (frequently less sophisticated than the acquirer) generally were unable to bargain for any of the value that a sophisticated and well-advised acquirer might enjoy as a result of being able to use these losses.

In order to remedy this situation, Congress in 1986 adopted the current version of section 382, which both expanded the scope of transactions covered by the section and changed the nature of the limitation. The limit is imposed on the rate at which carryover losses may be used: it will depend upon the value of the loss corporation at the time of a significant change in the ownership of the loss corporation's stock (defined in terms of "owner shifts" and "equity structure shifts"). The section 382 limitation thus permits losses to be used at a rate approaching the use that would have been expected had there been no ownership change.

14.2.1.   The Nature of the Section 382 Limitation

Section 382 contains two types of limits on the use of losses after the corporation that incurred the losses experiences an ownership change. The first is somewhat subjective: none of the Target's losses will be usable unless Target "continue[s] the business enterprise" for two years. § 382(c). Exceptions apply for use of Target's losses against section 338 gains that are required to be recognized by Target and certain unrealized built-in gains of Target at the time of the ownership change.

The second limitation is more mechanical. It is intended to ensure that Target's losses are not worth more after the ownership change than they were worth prior to the change. The provision imposes a "section 382 limitation" that sets the rate at which Target's losses can be used. That annual limitation is defined in section 382(b) in terms of the value (as defined in section 382(e)) of the Target (the "old loss corporation" under section 382(k)(2)), multiplied by a dummy interest rate (as defined by section 382(f)). The idea here is that the amount of income that the surviving loss corporation (the "new loss corporation" under section 382(k)(3)) can shelter should be no greater than the income stream that the Target could have produced. The value of the corporation multiplied by an interest rate (albeit a low interest rate) is simply a practical guess about what income stream Target might have produced had there been no transaction. If in any year the limitation amount is not exhausted, the excess is available as an addition to the next year's limitation amount. This mechanism functions the same way whether Target merely continues to exist with a substantial change in ownership or Target disappears into a new corporation that succeeds to Target's losses under section 381 (i.e., through liquidation or a section 361 transfer).

Target's value for these purposes is determined based on the total value of the Target stock immediately before the ownership change. Several anti-abuse rules apply. For example, under section 382(*l*)(1), capital contributions made to increase Target's stock value and thereby artificially inflate the section 382 limitation are disregarded. Under section 382(*l*)(4), the value of a Target with substantial nonbusiness assets immediately after an ownership change will be reduced by those assets' fair market value in excess of their proportional share of Target's debt. For this purpose, nonbusiness assets are defined as investment assets, and those will be considered substantial if they comprise at least 1/3 of Target's assets. Furthermore, although preferred stock is generally disregarded for other determinations under section 382, it is expressly included for purposes of determining the value of Target. *Compare* section 382(e) and Reg. § 1.382-2(a)(3)(i), *with* section 382(k)(6)(A). Section 382(k)(6) also authorizes Treasury to issue regulations that treat warrants, options, and similar interests in Target stock as stock or to treat stock as not stock.

Note that section 382 does not guarantee that the limitation will permit all of Target's losses to be used. The annual cap on the use of losses may be so low that some of Target's losses will expire unused (as they might have done if Target had continued without the ownership change). For example, a corporation with NOL carryovers of $1000 that suffers an ownership change when it has a section 382(c) value of $200 and the specified interest rate is 4% will be able to use a maximum of $8 of the carryover losses per year (assuming it has sufficient income). Those losses can be carried back 2 years and carried forward 20 years, resulting in a maximum of $176 losses that may be used before expiration.

14.2.2. The Nature of the Transactions That Trigger the Limitation

What transactions trigger the operation of the section 382 limitation? Here the statute essentially creates a set of standards for determining when there has been a sufficient change of ownership to justify limiting the carryover losses to the corporation that survives the ownership change. Note that the section applies to any corporation that has undergone a sufficient ownership change, including one that has had nothing more happen to it than changes in the ownership of substantial blocks of its stock and one that merges into a new corporation that succeeds to its attributes. Furthermore, the ownership changes that trigger the section 382 loss limitations can occur as a result of either taxable or nontaxable changes. The statutory language suggests more of a difference between an "ownership change" and an "equity shift" than there actually is.

The goal of the statute is to identify those transactions through which a new group of shareholders would be permitted to enjoy the tax benefit from the losses incurred by the Target when it was owned by the former group of shareholders. The statute defines the triggering event, an "ownership change," as occurring when there is a change in the ownership of Target stock (generally not including for this purpose section 1504(a)(4) stock, see section 382(k)(6)(A)) by "5% shareholders" such that some group of 5% shareholders has experienced an ownership increase of more than 50 percentage points during the "testing period" (defined in section 382(j) as a "3-year period ending on the day of any owner shift involving a 5 percent shareholder or any equity shift"). For example, if A, B, C, D, and E each owns 20% of the stock (by value) of X Corp, there is no ownership change when D buys both A's and B's stock (he has gone from owning 20% to 60%, an ownership change of only 40 percentage points). In contrast, there is an ownership change if D also buys C's stock (he will have gone from 20% to 80%, with a resulting ownership change of 60 percentage points). A series of "owner shifts," all occurring within the 3-year testing period, will be aggregated to determine when an ownership change has occurred. Thus if D bought A's stock in year 1 and B's and C's stock in year 5, there would be no ownership change as a result of the owner shifts, whereas if the second set of sales occurred in year 3, there would be an ownership change at that point.

The challenge faced by the drafters of the statute was to target appropriate shifts of ownership while recognizing that large percentages of stock of publicly traded corporations change hands regularly. Under section 382(g)(4)(A) and the regulations, those shareholders who each own less than 5% throughout the relevant testing period are all treated as one, single, public "5% shareholder." (Under Reg. section 1.382–2T(g)(1)(iv), an individual who owns 5% or more at any time during the testing period is a 5% shareholder even if that individual does not own 5% on the testing date in question.) When Y Corp is owned 20% by the public and 20% each by A, B, C, and D, there can be an infinite number of trades involving public shareholders that are ignored for the purposes of section 382. But any shareholder who ends up owning more than 5% in the testing period will be counted separately.

If, for instance, F owned .01% of the stock of Y Corp until he started buying up Y Corp stock, his activity would not affect the operation of section 382 until he becomes a 5% shareholder (at the point that he owns at least 5% of the stock by value). If F owned 11% after the transactions, and A and B both sold their stock to D, there would be an ownership change: F's increase of 10.99 percentage points, plus D's increase of 40 percentage points creates a total change of more than 50% in ownership by D and F, who are both "5% shareholders" after the transactions are complete. An IPO of a closely held corporation would create a new 5% shareholder made up of any new shareholders who do not hold at least 5% of the newly issued stock. Similarly, a new stock offering by a publicly held corporation will create a new public 5% shareholder, and that public shareholder group will be treated as separate from the prior public 5% shareholder. Reg. § 1.382-2T(e)(1)(iii) ex. 5. Thus there will be circumstances in which groups of public shareholders will be segregated and each group of public shareholders may be considered a single "5% shareholder."

The possibility of an ownership change must be considered any time there has been an owner shift, whether by issuance, redemption or other transfer of stock, or equity structure shift, including reorganizations, that affects the ownership of a 5% shareholder.

Note that section 382(k)(6)(C) directs that percentages of stock ownership are to be determined by value, not by number of shares.

The testing period, set out in section 382(i), is the three-year period before the event being tested, unless there has been a more recent ownership change, in which case the beginning of the testing period is no earlier than the date of the earlier ownership change. The testing period does not begin to run until there is a loss, whether a loss carryforward or a built-in loss, of concern.

Section 382(*l*) includes a number of operating rules, including the use of the section 318 attribution rules in determining ownership. Section 318 is modified, however, to reflect the fact that the goal is not to determine the maximum that any one owner could be treated as controlling (as is the goal when testing redemptions for dividend equivalence) but instead to determine whether there has been a significant change in the identity of those who ultimately have equity interests in the loss corporation. Accordingly, the modifications include treating all family members listed in section 318(a)(1) as one person and not treating attributed stock as owned unless the owner is already a 5% shareholder in respect of actually owned stock.

More significantly (and perhaps confusingly) the rules also attribute ownership of Target stock *from* a corporation or other entity without any minimum ownership threshold. But when ownership shifts are tested, only the ownership of those from which no further attribution is possible is counted. Reg. § 1.382-2T(h)(2). This has the practical result of counting only the changes in ownership of individuals and aggregations of individuals lumped together as public shareholders. Under this approach, for instance, a widely held entity that owns 20% of the Target stock is not itself treated as a 5% shareholder, but its owners together are treated as a public 5% shareholder of Target. In contrast, if the entity were owned 50% by one owner B but were otherwise widely held, its stock would be treated as held by two

5% shareholders — B, who is treated as owning 10% of Target (50% of 20%), and a public group that is treated as owning 10% of Target. *See* Reg. § 1.382-2T(g)(4), Exs. 1, 2. Stock attributed to individuals from entities will not always be considered in determining the total ownership of those individuals under the rather elaborate rules of Reg. subsections 1.382-2T(h)(2) and (j). Stock will not be attributed to entities. § 382(l)(3)(A)(iii) and Reg. § 1.382-2T(h)(3).

Section 382(l)(A)(iv) indicates that options to acquire stock "shall be treated as exercised if such exercise results in an ownership change," unless regulations provide otherwise. Initially, a rather draconian set of regulations provided that all options were to be treated as exercised. Current regulations, however, provide that options are to be treated as exercised if a principal purpose of their issuance was to avoid or ameliorate the impact of section 382's limits and the options *either* (i) give their holders a substantial portion of the attributes of ownership of stock, Reg. section 1.382-4(d)(3) or effective 50% control (as specially defined), Reg. section 1.382-4(d)(4) *or* (ii) facilitate the creation of income within the loss corporation prior to the actual occurrence of an ownership change (otherwise determined), Reg. section 1.382-4(d)(5).

14.2.3. The Effect of Additional Restructuring

Obviously, the value of the loss corporation will depend upon the amount of its losses that can be used, which in turn depend upon the corporation's value on the change date. Although this is circular, the gross-up involved is finite and may be fully accounted for in the relatively low rate of return allowed under section 382(f): for every additional dollar of loss made allowable, there is an increase in value of at most 35 cents, which frees up at most 35 cents time the imputed return rate (say 7%) of allowed limitation, which in turn produces an increase in value of about 2 1/2 cents, etc.

Given the dependency of loss use upon corporate value, there might be an incentive for the owners of the loss corporation to add value immediately before selling, to make more losses available. It is not exactly clear why this would be viewed as nefarious on its face, since that would require a genuine economic commitment. (Of course, if such "stuffing" transactions were legitimate means of increasing loss usage, there would need to be rules to ensure that the contributions were really at risk, etc.) Nevertheless, any such pre-change contributions within two years of the change date are disregarded under section 382(l)(1). Redemptions and other corporate contractions that occur in connection with the ownership change are also taken into account to reduce the value of the loss corporation on which the section 382 limitation will be based.

14.2.4. Built-In Losses and Gains

Carryover losses are only part of the losses economically accruing before the ownership change: unrealized losses can also be more attractive to acquirers of corporate assets and stock than Congress seems to find seemly, while unrealized built-in gains cut the other way. Therefore, section 382(h) expands the scope of the losses limited by section 382(a) to cover built-in losses not yet recognized. These built-in losses, after all, would have become a part of the losses carried over if they had already been recognized at the time of the ownership change.

The section 382(h) expansion does not include all such "built-in" losses: it will apply only to an amount equal to the "net unrealized built-in loss" (if any) at the time of the ownership change. As built-in losses are recognized, they will be subject to the section 382 limitation as if they were a pre-change loss, up to that net amount, to the extent they occur during the 5-year statutory "recognition period." § 382(h)(7).

The provision takes into account the fact that in some types of operations, operating losses will have been recognized and accumulated early, while gains remain unrecognized at the time of the ownership change. Accordingly, if a loss corporation has a net unrealized built-in gain at the time of the ownership change, recognition of a portion of that gain will result in a corresponding *increase* in the section 382 limitation for that taxable year, allowing a greater use of the loss corporation's carryovers.

A loss corporation will either have net built-in gains (NUBIG), under subsections 382(h)(1)(A) and 382(h)(3), which will increase the section 382 limitation if they are recognized within 5 years of the ownership change, or net built-in losses (NUBIL), under subsections 382(h)(1)(B) and 382(h)(3), which will be treated the same as if they were already part of the carryover loss subject to the limitation when they are recognized within five years of the ownership change. A corporation will not have both NUBILs and NUBIGs: as of the date of the ownership change, it will be determined to have one or the other or neither.

The section 382(h) rules are subject to a de minimis threshold test — they will apply only if the net gain or loss position is more than the lesser of 15% of the value of the corporation's assets (not taking into account cash or marketable securities with values not substantially different from their bases) or $10,000,000. In other words, if a corporation's built-in losses are roughly equal to its built-in gains, it will not need to keep track of any of them. But if its built-in gains are sufficiently greater than its losses, when these gains are recognized the section 382 limitation will be increased; if its built-in losses are sufficiently greater than its gains, when recognized they will be subject to the section 382 limitation as if they had been recognized before the ownership change.

If a recognized built-in loss is disallowed because of the limitation, it will carryforward under the regular rules from that year, even though it is treated for limitation purposes as subject to the limitation in the same mechanism as a pre-change loss.

Loss Limits Make the News (and Get the Attention of Congress)

In Notice 2008-83 (Sept. 30, 2008) Treasury announced that the limits of section 382(h) would not apply to deductions in the nature of bad debt deductions or similar losses on loans claimed by banks (as that term is defined in section 581), regardless of the relationship of those deductions to pre-change positions. This startling administrative move was thought by many to be beyond the power of the Treasury.

> *Many in Congress appear to have thought so. Section 1261 of the American Recovery Act of 2009, signed into law in February, provided that "the delegation of authority to the Secretary of the Treasury under Section 382(m) . . . does not authorize the Secretary to provide exemptions or special rules that are restricted to particular industries or classes of taxpayers." The legislation stopped short of entirely revoking the position in the Notice, however, and it appears that for deals in place before January 16, the notice "shall be deemed to have the force and effect of law with respect to any ownership change." The legislation also included several much less significant provisions tinkering with section 382. A summary of the issues involved in the release of Notice 2008–83 can be found in a document prepared for the Counsel to the Treasury Inspector General, dated Nov. 3, 2009, available at 2011 TNT 16–36.*

a.   Tracing Rules

The idea that built-in losses could be just as subject to objectionable trafficking as losses that are already recognized and carried as carryover losses seems simple enough. So does the idea that built-in gains are likely to represent gains that could have been recognized before the ownership change to use up carryover losses without regard to the section 382 limitation, and therefore should be allowed as an increase in the limitation after the ownership change. Section 382(h) targets these two phenomena, at least when the built-in gains or losses represent a substantial part of the value of the loss corporation at the time of the ownership change.

As easy as the concept is to articulate, it presents an enormous challenge to traditional ways of thinking about tax accounting. First, we must figure out whether a corporation has net unrealized gains or losses. Subsections 382(h)(3) and (6)(C) indicate that this is to be done with an aggregate approach; that is, the taxpayer must determine the relationship between the aggregate fair market value of all of the loss corporation's assets and the aggregate basis of all of its assets and other relevant items. This unrealized gain or loss is further reduced by any liabilities that will give rise to a deduction when paid. Although it is not entirely clear, it appears that this adjustment is made according to the estimated amount of the economic burden of these liabilities.

A loss corporation with a NUBIG needs to keep track only of the gains deemed to be "built-in" that are recognized after the change date. A loss corporation with a NUBIL needs to keep track only of the "built-in" losses.

After the ownership change, the taxpayer must identify which recognized gains (or losses) must be treated as "built-in," and which losses and gains have nothing to do with the existing disparity between fair market value and basis on the change date. For gains and losses on individual assets that are subject to sales and exchanges during the recognition period, this determination is relatively straight-forward: under section 382(h)(2), "recognized built-in" gains and losses are those that are reflected in the difference between the fair market value and the basis of the individual assets as of the time of the ownership change. Thus a loss corporation that has assets with a total fair market value of 100 and a total basis of 10, and an unpaid liability of 18 would have a NUBIG of 72 (100-10-18) (ignoring the thresholds for these illustration purposes). As a result, the corporation would be allowed to increase its section 382 limitation by 72 as those assets with unrealized built-in gains were sold and the gain recognized. Conversely, if the assets were held with a basis of 110, it would have a NUBIL of 28 (100-110-18); as it recognizes its built-in losses (again ignoring the thresholds), they would be included in the carryover amount subject to the overall section 382 limitation.

The statute provides what functions essentially as a tracing provision to ensure that corporations do not inappropriately increase the limitation with later-acquired gains or avoid the limitation for pre-change losses. During the recognition period, the losses (or gains) recognized for this purpose are traced to the assets held at the time of the change date. For corporations with NUBIGs, built-in gains recognized during the recognition period count to increase the limitation only if the corporation "establishes" that the loss corporation held the asset before the change and then only to the extent of the built-in gain existing at the time of the change. Section 382(h)(2)(A). Conversely, for corporations with NUBILs, built-in losses recognized during the recognition period will be subject to the limitation unless the corporation can "establish" that the loss asset was not held by the loss corporation before the change date or to the extent that the corporation establishes that the recognized loss exceeds the built-in loss on the change date. Section 382(h)(2)(B).

Section 382(h)(2)(B) (flush language) further provides that cost recovery of any basis amount in excess of the fair market value of the assets at the time of the ownership change will also be treated as a "recognized built-in loss" to the extent that it is claimed in the 5-year recognition period.

Section 382(h)(6) makes it clear, however, that these straightforward measures of gain and loss as of the time of the ownership change are not the only items to which section 382(h) will apply. Items of both income and deduction that "are properly attributable to periods before the change date" can be "built-in."

Regulations have not yet been proposed under section 382(h), and many aspects of its implementation remain unclear. Rev. Proc. 2003-65 provides some insight into the difficulty of such determinations (and also into the pervasive nature of the problem of determining values rather than using adjusted basis of assets and face amounts of accrued liabilities). This revenue procedure provides a choice between two approaches to the identification of built-in losses as they are recognized. One borrows the approach used under section 1374 for determining gain after the shareholders of corporations subject to subchapter C make an election to be taxed under subchapter S. The other measures the difference between the items recognized by the loss corporation and those that would have been recognized if all of the loss corporation's assets had been subject to a taxable sale. (This second approach is called the section 338 approach because of this fiction of a taxable sale. This label can be confusing, however, because in this context adjustments made to reflect the realization of contingencies at other than their expected value are not typically made, even if they would be after a section 338 election.)

Both approaches reach the results outlined above for assets subject to a sale or exchange within the recognition period and for cost recovery attributable to built-in losses. The measure of NUBIG or NUBIL in each asset will limit the amount of recognized built-in gain or loss (including cost recovery) on each asset. Thus suppose a loss corporation with a NUBIL holds an asset with a basis of $300 and a fair market value of $270 as of the change date. When it sells the asset for $220, only $30 of the resulting loss of $80 will be treated as a recognized built-in loss. Similarly, suppose a loss corporation with a NUBIL holds a depreciable asset with a basis of $200 and a fair market value of $120. After the change date it takes $40 of cost recovery with respect to the asset but only $24 would have been available had the asset been purchased for $120 on the change date. Of the $40 of cost recovery actually taken, $16 will be a recognized built-in loss. If the corporation then sells the asset (now with a basis of $160) for $70, $64 of the $90 loss (the $80 unrealized at the change date less the $16 recognized as cost recovery) will be a recognized built-in loss.

Other items under the "section 1374 approach." But accounting for other items that might be thought to relate to the pre-change period can be different depending upon the approach used. Under the section 1374 approach, other items recognized during the 5-year period after the change date are considered "built-in" only if an accrual-basis taxpayer would have taken them into account as of the change date. This rule is applied, however, as if this accrual-basis taxpayer had not been subject to the various limits that require actual payment, such as the economic performance rules of section 461(h). Therefore the only other recognized built-in loss items for accrual basis loss corporations with a NUBIL will be those items subject to these deduction-deferring limits.

Income (as opposed to gain) generated from gain assets will not be treated as attributable to the period before the change date because it would not have been properly accrued before the change date. Thus, suppose a loss corporation with a NUBIG holds a royalty-generating asset with a basis of $30 and a fair market value as of the change date of $75. If it sells the asset within five years for $80, it will have a recognized built-in gain of $45. If it instead holds the asset and collects $25 in royalties, none of this royalty income will be a recognized built-in gain because none of it would be properly accrued before the change date.

Other items under "the section 338 approach." Under the section 338 approach, the corporation compares the items actually recognized and accrued with those that would have been recognized and accrued had a section 338 election been made.

This approach has some perhaps unexpected results for loss corporations with a NUBIG. Recognized built-in gain includes the amount of additional income that would have been sheltered by the cost recovery deductions that would have been available with the step-up in basis that a section 338 election would have created. (This mechanism *increases* the section 382 limitation — in effect, it allows built-in gains to be taken into account even when they remain unrecognized.) Suppose a loss corporation with a NUBIG holds a depreciable asset with a basis of $45 and a fair market value of $120. If in the first post change year, its cost recovery is actually $5, but would have been $40 had a section 338 election been made, the corporation has $35 of recognized built-in gain as of that year.

The deductions resulting from the payment of contingent liabilities will be recognized built-in loss items under the section 338 method. It appears that the amount so treated will be capped at the expected burden of the liability on the change date. Thus if a loss corporation with a NUBIL has a contingent liability estimated at $200 at the change date, but which results in payment of $210, only $200 will be a recognized built-in loss. If the liability results in payment of $30, only $30 will be. (The NUBIL will not be recalculated in either event.) *See* Notice 2003-65, Ex. 14. (The section 1374 approach would not have included this item as a recognized built-in loss, since no contingent item would have been properly accrued before the change date.)

Although it is not certain, it would appear that income received with respect to gain assets will be recognized built-in gain under the section 338 approach. The treatment of other items, including cancellation of indebtedness income (whether or not excluded under section 108) and bad debts, remains unclear.

14.2.5. Using Losses after an Ownership Change

Section 382 only dictates how much of a loss corporation's loss attributes survive an ownership change; it does not affirmatively say whether those losses can be used. As discussed above, under subsections 381(b)(3) and 381(c), they can be used only to offset the future income of the successor corporation, and cannot be used to offset the past income of either of the predecessor corporations.

The challenge is to bring an income stream into juxtaposition with the losses so that there is income to be offset. One way to do this is simply to merge the loss corporation into a profitable corporation, or contribute assets that are expected to generate profits into the loss corporation. (If these steps are undertaken simply to make use of the losses, it is likely that an ownership change will be triggered. Furthermore, the rules for establishing the section 382 limitation make adjustments for such transactions. See, for instance, section 382(*l*)(1), which presumptively excludes from the value of the loss corporation capital contributions made more recently than two years before the ownership change and section 382(*l*)(4), which reduces the value of the loss corporation for the purpose of calculating the limitation if more than one-third of its value is in investment assets.) Even if "new" profits can be generated without adverse effects under these limitations, one still cannot use the losses faster than the old loss corporation (before the merger or the asset contribution) could have used them.

Some observers hoped that the enactment of section 382 would effectively preempt any other doctrine that might be called into play to limit "trafficking in losses." They did not get their wish: section 269 is still on the books. It denies "the benefit of a deduction, credit or other allowance such person would otherwise not enjoy" that is made available as a result of the acquisition of "control of a corporation" or of "property of another corporation" with a transferred basis (that is, in other than a taxable transaction) if the principal purpose of the acquisition was to acquire the benefit. If section 269 applies, *no* carryover or other benefit will survive the acquisition.

14.3. SECTIONS 383 AND 384

Two additional sections may limit the use of carryover attributes. First, section 383 imposes limits on the uses of certain credit carryovers (the general business credit under section 39 and the minimum tax credit under section 53). Credits are limited to an amount determined on the basis of the tax liability attributable to taxable income not in excess of the section 382 limitation.

Section 382 only comes into play when assets or stock of a loss corporation are acquired. Section 384 aims at limiting the availability of the *acquirer's own losses* and other tax attributes to offset built-in gains of an acquired corporation. It applies whether the gain corporation is the subject of an acquisition of stock, or an acquisition of assets (and tax attributes) in a nontaxable acquisition of assets in a reorganization. It does not apply when there was 50% common ownership for at least five years before the acquisition of the gain corporation occurs.

PRACTICE PROBLEMS

Assume the "long term tax-exempt interest rate" referred to in section 382(e) is 4%. Further assume that, unless stated otherwise, there are no "net unrealized built-in losses" or "net unrealized built-in gains" as defined in section 382(h) or 384.

1.   All of the stock of Loss Co is purchased by one individual for $10 million. Before the acquisition, Loss Co had net operating loss carryovers of about $3 million. In the year beginning immediately after the transaction, Loss Co has operating income of $1 million. How much of Loss Co's NOL can be used in that year?

(a)   None

(b) $1 million

(c) $120,000

(d) $400,000

2.   Same facts as in Question (1) except that Loss Co had only $200,000 of operating income in the first year after the transaction, and $550,000 in the second year. How much operating loss can be used in the second year?

(a)   None

(b) $550,000

(c) $400,000

(d) $600,000

3.   Same facts as in Question (1) except that Loss Co had gain of $1.75 million from the sale, immediately after it was acquired, of a large piece of equipment, all of which was section 1245 recapture.

(a) $400,000

(b) $70,000

(c) $1,750,000

(d) $2,150,000

4.   Loss Corp is owned by A, B, C, D, and E, each of whom owns 20% of its stock. A, B, C, and D are E's children. A, D, and E sell their stock to C. Before the acquisition, Loss Co had net operating loss carryovers of about $3 million. In the year beginning immediately after the transaction, Loss Co has operating income of $1 million. How much of Loss Co's NOL can be used in that year?

(a)   None

(b) $1 million

(c) $120,000

(d) $400,000

5.   Loss Corp paid $5 million for the operating assets of Profit Co. In the year after the acquisition, the combined performance of Loss Corp, including the operation of Profit Co's assets, was profit of $500,000, about twice what Loss Corp's highest earnings had ever been historically. Before the acquisition, Loss Corp had net operating loss carryovers totaling about $3 million. How much of those operating losses could Loss Corp use in this first year?

(a) $500,000.

(b)   about $250,000

(c)   insufficient information: amount will depend upon the value of Loss Corp

(d)   none

6.   Loss Corp paid $6 million for the operating assets of Profit Co. The funds were available to Loss Corp because it received the entire amount in contributions in exchange for newly issued stock from 3 new shareholders who each own 20% of Loss Corp after the transaction. In the year after the acquisition, the combined performance of Loss Corp, including Profit Co's operation, was profit of $500,000, about twice what its highest earnings had ever been historically. Before the acquisition, Loss Corp had net operating loss carryovers totaling about $3 million. How much of those operating losses could Loss Corp use in this first year?

(a) $500,000

(b) $400,000

(c)   insufficient information

(d)   none

7.   Loss Corp used its stock to acquire all of the operating assets of Profit Co in a nontaxable merger. After the transaction, the former owners of Profit Co owned 55% of the stock of Loss Corp. In the year after the acquisition, the combined performance of Loss Corp, including operation of Profit Co's assets, was profit of $500,000, about twice what its highest earnings had ever been historically. Before the acquisition, Loss Corp had net operating loss carryovers totaling about $3 million. How much of those operating losses could Loss Corp use in this first year?

(a) $500,000

(b)   about $250,000

(c)   insufficient information: amount will depend upon the value of Loss Corp

(d)   none

DISCUSSION PROBLEMS

Loss Corp, which has carryover losses of $900,000, is wholly owned by Sue. Gain Corp, a profitable corporation with built-in gains, is wholly-owned by Tom. In each of the following alternative transactions, determine whether § 382 or § 384 or both apply and what tax consequences follow. Assume the applicable rate is 4% and that any applicable continuation of business requirement is satisfied.

(a)   Gain Corp purchases all the Loss Corp stock on the last day of both corporations' taxable year for $10,000,000 cash and installment notes and does not make a section 338 election. Loss Corp has $500,000 of income in the first year after the acquisition, $350,000 of income in the second year, and $475,000 of income in the third year.

   (i)   What if shortly after the purchase, Gain Corp causes Loss Corp to issue a dividend equal to 20% of the total price it promised to pay for Loss Corp, and used the dividend to pay on the installment notes held by the former Loss Corp shareholders?

   (ii)   What if, in the original transaction, 9 months before the acquisition, Loss Corp had entered into a public offering, and still had $1 million of the cash proceeds of that offering on hand?

   (iii) What if shortly after a purchase for $10,000,000 Gain Corp causes Loss Corp to sell one of its principal assets for $8,000,000, with very little gain recognized on the asset sale?

   (iv)   What if, in the last hypothetical, virtually all of the $8,000,000 represents gain?

(b)   Gain Corp purchases all the Loss Corp stock for cash and makes the § 338 election.

(c)   Assuming the same facts as above with respect to values and post-acquisition earnings (here, of the combined entity), Loss Corp merges into Gain Corp, and Sue ends up with 65% of the Gain Corp stock.

(d)   Assuming the same facts as above with respect to values and post-acquisition earnings (here, of the combined entity), Loss Corp merges into Gain Corp, and Sue ends up with 40% of the Gain Corp stock.

   (i)   What if Gain had in the prior year also merged with another much smaller loss corporation, Liloss (whose old shareholders now own 10% of Gain) that had a value of $2 million and net operating losses of $60,000?

   (ii)   What if Loss had held patents (the value of which was not easily determined at the time of the merger, but this uncertainty was taken into account at the time of the negotiations over the amount of Gain stock Sue received), and rights related to one of these patents was sold for $2 million six months after the merger? (Assume, in the alternative, that this sale gave rise either to ordinary or capital gain.)

(iii)   What if Loss had held an account receivable for $3 million (on which no write-off had yet been taken) that became entirely worthless in the year after the merger, when its obligor was dissolved after a bankruptcy proceeding?

(e)   Suppose Loss Corp and Gain Corp form L-G, a joint venture partnership. Under the L-G partnership agreement, much of the L-G income is allocated to Loss Corp.

(f)   Loss Corp purchases all the Gain Corp stock for cash and does not elect section 338.

THE IDEA OF A NONTAXABLE REORGANIZATION

Chapter 15

OVERVIEW OF NONTAXABLE REORGANIZATIONS

Statutes and Regulations	IRC §§ 368(a)(1); 354; 356; 358; 361; 362(b)
	Reg. § 1.368-1 (all), 1.368-2(a), (b) & (k)
	Prop. Reg. § 1.368-1(b), (f)(2)
Other Primary Authorities	Rev. Rul. 2000-5, 2000-1 C.B. 436
	John A. Nelson Co. v. Helvering, 296 U.S. 374 (1935)
	Paulsen v. Commissioner, 469 U.S. 131 (1985)
	Honbarrier v. Commissioner, 115 T.C. 300 (2000)

A stock or an asset acquisition can be nontaxable if it is accomplished through steps that come within the statutory definition of a reorganization, as outlined in section 368(a). "Reorganization" is thus a term of art in tax that refers only to those transactions that satisfy the particular requirements of one of the categories set out in section 368(a), rather than to the broader range of restructuring transactions that might be called reorganizations in other contexts. For instance, there is very little connection between the use of the term "reorganization" in bankruptcy and its use in subchapter C.

All of the transactional types in the section 368 definition of reorganization require that a significant portion of the consideration used by the Acquirer consist of stock of the Acquirer or its parent. Beyond that basic similarity, each transaction type has special requirements and generalizations are difficult.

The Service in regulations has summarized the purpose of the reorganization provisions of the Code: "to except from the general rule [of US tax law, that upon the exchange of property, gain or loss must be accounted for if the new property differs in a material particular . . . from the old property] certain specifically described exchanges incident to such readjustments of corporate structures made in one of the particular ways specified . . . , as are required by business exigencies and which effect only a readjustment of continuing interest in property under modified corporate forms." Reg. § 1.368-1(b).

The reorganization provisions generally are relatively easy to justify: without them, there would be a tax cost, sometimes quite significant, to changes in corporate structures. Prior to the statutory grant of nonrecognition to reorganizations, the Supreme Court had ruled that any change in corporate form that substantially changed shareholders' rights could be a realization event, triggering gain both to the shareholders and to the corporation. *See* Cottage Sav. Ass'n v. Commissioner, 499 U.S. 554 (1991) (providing a historical overview of the primary cases in which the Court had dealt with the "realization" concept). Two of these cases are now read to have viewed a change in a corporation's state of incorporation as likely to bring with it changes in the nature of the shareholders' rights sufficient to constitute a realization event and make the exchange of stock taxable, even though the shareholders continue to own very similar interests in a corporation that holds all of the assets of the original corporation. United States v. Phellis, 257 U.S. 156, 173 (1921); Marr v. United States, 268 U.S. 536 (1925).

Many of the detailed requirements of the statute, however, are harder to justify. Indeed, the rules describing the transaction patterns that qualify as reorganizations are among the most arcane in U.S. tax law. The reason lies in the fact that the provisions began as a legislative reaction to the early judicial opinions holding almost all corporate restructuring transactions taxable. Although Congress made it clear early on that it did not think all corporate restructuring transactions were taxable, it left it to the courts to determine most of the standards for distinguishing nontaxable from taxable transactions, intervening only sporadically to redirect the law. The rules for reorganizations thus evolved through a series of interactions among Congress, the courts, and, more recently, the Treasury Department through its regulatory process, with the courts tending to interpret the language of the statute relatively strictly, at the urging of the government. Prior to very recent regulatory changes intended to make the many aspects of reorganization law more coherent, there had been no attempt to rationalize the result of this evolutionary process. As a consequence, there are a number of seemingly arbitrary differences among the patterns of transactions that qualify as reorganizations. Recent regulatory developments have eliminated some of the more arbitrary aspects of reorganization law, but there are limits to the ability of the government to address through regulations complexities stemming from the limitations in explicit statutory language. Indeed, several recent regulations have abandoned prior government and judicial interpretations of the statute that were long considered settled law and now, for instance, allow many more variations in the steps that may be taken before and after a transaction without jeopardizing the tax status of the transaction as a reorganization, particularly in the use of the affiliated group concept (through which the interests of several related corporations can be aggregated and through which indirect ownership can suffice to establish control, further discussed in the unit on consolidated returns) to expand the reach of the statutory provisions.

15.1. THE SOURCES OF THE RULES

Understanding the process by which reorganization rules have developed will help make sense of the rules. Start with the proposition that the statute contains only minimal information about the nature of the transactions anticipated, creating considerable uncertainty about the status of some transactions. Add to this uncertainty the idea that most practitioners tend to be somewhat conservative in planning transactions that rely on these provisions because the stakes — full taxation of shareholders and, in many cases, of corporations — are often quite significant.

The ruling request process has played a significant role in the development of the law regarding nontaxable reorganizations. Once the ruling process has resulted in consistent reactions to a new approach that solves a particular problem, practitioners may use that settled approach and refrain from further innovation. The law on reorganizations is therefore explainable only by reference to this evolution. It would not be too misleading to observe that the patterns of transactions used by practitioners are in many ways like ruts in a dirt road — it's easier to let your wheels ride in them than to take a different route. Nobody (or hardly anybody) tries to design a new pattern of transaction just to see whether the Service will agree that it works, though practitioners may well seize an opportunity to test a more aggressive interpretation when it arises. Hence there are many questions about reorganizations that remain unanswered and that have not been dealt with through amendments to the statutory language.

Another source of complication comes from the fact that the federal income tax rules governing the categorization of transactions as reorganizations are developed by the federal government, while the law governing the underlying transactions is primarily a matter for the states. Although there are many similarities in the state laws governing corporate restructuring transactions, there is no uniform law of corporate mergers or corporate acquisitions that applies in all of the states. Accordingly, the federal income tax rules cannot simply ascribe tax consequences to particular transactions as defined by state law. Further complications arise because the tax rules took on something close to the shape in which they now appear at a time when corporate law regarding mergers was only beginning to be rationalized.

Mastering the rules defining reorganizations is made even more difficult because there are legislative, administrative, and judicial sources of law, all contributing to various aspects of the definitions in a relatively unpredictable way. For instance, the courts created a "continuity of shareholder interest" doctrine, now explicitly required in the regulations, that mandates that the Acquirer in all reorganizations use its stock (or the stock of its parent) as a substantial part of the consideration for the acquisition. Several of the statutory provisions defining reorganizations, however, also include specific requirements regarding the type of consideration that the Acquirer can use, rendering aspects of the continuity of interest doctrine redundant. The difficult interaction of legislative and judicial authority is made worse by statutory amendments — such as those allowing the use of stock of a corporation that controls the Acquirer or those permitting boot in reorganizations involving asset transfers — that have been appended to the pre-existing language without an adequate effort to ensure that the resulting language is fully coherent.

15.2.   THE BASIC PATTERNS OF THE TRANSACTIONS

There are three basic patterns according to which reorganizations involving more than one corporation can occur: (i) acquisitions of the stock of Target (generally thought of as "B" reorganizations because their most straightforward form is set forth in section 368(a)(1)(B)); (ii) acquisitions of the assets of Target ("C" reorgs); and (iii) transactions whereby corporate structures are combined by operation of law ("A" reorgs or statutory mergers). These distinctions are best thought of as ways of characterizing the overall effect of reorganization transactions, not necessarily as explicit steps to be taken to adhere to the statutory requirements.

In considering the possible tax treatment of a particular transaction, its tentative characterization as a particular type of reorganization is merely a first step, because the step transaction doctrine may apply to recast the transaction. Frequently, but not always, the steps according to which an acquisition actually took place will be combined (or stepped together), resulting in recharacterization as an integrated transaction from the first to the last of the steps. In this way, for instance, the transitory existence of a corporation may be ignored; an acquisition of stock followed by a liquidation can be treated as an acquisition of assets; a merger can be treated as an acquisition of stock; and so forth. Understanding the potential for application of the step transaction doctrine requires a close reading of previous announcements of the Service, as well as case law.

In the simplest versions of each of these three basic types of "acquisitive" reorganizations, there will be only one corporation remaining that holds the assets that were transferred without gain recognition, and only one corporation's stock that could be received by Target shareholders in exchange for their Target stock. These acquisitive reorganizations can usually be conceptualized as an exchange (involving a transfer of Target's assets in exchange for the receipt of stock and other property of Acquirer) followed by the re-transfer of the stock and other property received by Target in a distribution to its shareholders. Once Target has transferred its assets to Acquirer in an acquisitive reorganization, it has little role to play other than as a conduit to pass the consideration it received on to its shareholders. In some cases, when merger law is used to effectuate the transaction, these steps may not always be readily apparent, since, for instance, all of the consideration from Acquirer ends up immediately in the hands of Target's shareholders.

These simple reorganization transactions can be complicated, however, by the possibility that they can be accomplished in a "triangular" way — either because the stock that Target shareholders receive is issued by a corporation that controls the Acquirer that obtains Target stock or assets, or because the Target stock or assets are transferred by the Acquirer to another corporation. Authority for such variations is provided in some places by statute and in other places only by regulations.

On the Use of Corporate Stock as Boot

Can a Target shareholder receive only the stock of one corporation if a transaction is to succeed in being a tax-free reorganization? In acquisitive reorganizations (as opposed to divisive reorganizations to which section 355 applies), only the stock of one corporation can be received as consideration entitled to nonrecognition. And, without exception, that stock must be the stock of the Acquirer or the parent of the Acquirer.

What if some stock of some other corporation, whether or not related to Acquirer, is also received? The answer will depend upon the identity of the issuer of the other stock and the nature of the transaction. In the best case, such stock will be simply treated as boot, the same as cash or any other property, and will trigger gain. In the worst case, the receipt of the stock of both the Acquirer and the parent of Acquirer will spoil the reorganization. See, e.g., § 368(a)(2)(D)(i).

Although it may be easiest to see the patterns of reorganizations contained in the statute if one assumes that there is no relationship between "Target" and "Acquirer" before the reorganization, in general the same rules that apply when the corporations involved are totally unrelated will also apply when the corporations are already related in some way. There are, however, a few special statutory rules that apply in some situations involving reorganizations among previously related parties: for instance, section 368(a)(1)(D) applies to the transfer of assets among commonly controlled corporations. There are also some special situations that are addressed in the consolidated return regulations, which may alter the way the reorganization provisions apply within consolidated groups. In still other situations, the presence of pre-existing relationships among the corporations involved will require considerable scrutiny to determine exactly what is being given up and what is being received in exchange before these exchanges can be considered to be within the reorganization, but in the end the general rules will apply.

In addition to these acquisitive reorganizations, there are several other basic patterns of transactions set forth in section 368. Recapitalizations and other "mere changes in form" that involve only one corporation ("E" and "F" reorgs), and bankruptcy restructurings ("G" reorgs) are generally subject to fewer technical conditions. Divisive transactions — a common form of which is popularly called a "spin-off," which may involve one kind of "D" reorg — permit the continuation of a single "Target" corporation in two corporations owned by the former Target shareholders. Divisive transactions are subject to many additional restrictions, mainly found in section 355, and considered in Chapters 23 through 25.

15.3.   CONSEQUENCES TO THE PARTIES IN ACQUISITIVE REORGANIZATIONS

Mastering the reorganization definitions will be facilitated by keeping in mind the goal: achieving a restructuring without triggering a tax to the shareholders who give up their stock in Target in exchange for stock in Acquirer and without triggering a tax to Target on the transfer (if there is one) of its assets to Acquirer. These favorable tax consequences are allowed because the Target shareholders' stock in Acquirer represents, at least in some sense, a continuation of their equity ownership of Target — i.e., in some sense, Acquirer stock is stock of the "same corporation" as Target.

Most of the statutory, judicial, and regulatory rules governing the qualification of a transaction as a "reorganization" involve, in one way or another, concern about whether the "same corporation" has survived. In general, these concerns break down into concerns about whether there has been enough "continuity of interest" (considering the Target shareholders' continuing equity ownership of Target), and enough "continuity of business enterprise" (considering the historic assets or the historic business of the Target corporation). Other possible ways of identifying the "same" corporation — by identity of management or employees, for instance — are not treated as important.

The answers to variants of these two questions — whether shareholder interest has continued, and whether the business enterprise is continued — have taken some strange turns, and have not always been consistent. Among the issues that must be considered in this connection are the following:

- What is the effect of a distribution to Target shareholders immediately before the reorganization transaction?

- What is the effect of Target's disposition of some of its assets immediately before the reorganization transaction?

- What is the effect of prior ownership of Target stock by Acquirer?

- What is the effect of the receipt by Target shareholders of consideration that does not represent any continuation of the economic position reflected in their old Target stock?

- What is the effect of the transfer of Target stock (or assets) to a subsidiary of Acquirer? To several subsidiaries?

- What is the effect of the distribution of Target stock (or assets) to a shareholder or indirect shareholder of Acquirer?

- What is the effect of the use of stock that is issued by the parent or grandparent of Acquirer rather than of the Acquirer itself?

There is no single answer to these questions for all reorganizations, because each of the reorganization descriptions includes slightly different language and the law interpreting this language has frequently evolved relatively independently for each definition. Much of the detail associated with these questions will be discussed in the chapters addressing particular types of reorgs. This chapter provides a comprehensive overview of the tax consequences of acquisitive reorgs generally, followed by a more detailed examination of A reorgs.

15.3.1. Consequences When Stock is the Sole Consideration

In exploring the consequences of acquisitive reorganizations, it makes sense to first explore the simplest of cases — those in which all assets of the Target remain (directly or indirectly) in the hands of Acquirer, and Target shareholders receive only Acquirer stock.

a. Shareholder Consequences

To the extent that shareholders give up stock in a corporation that is a party to a reorganization (Target), and take back stock in a corporation that is a party to a reorganization (Acquirer), they are treated for tax purposes as if nothing happened. The exchange of stock is tax free under section 354. Target shareholders will have a basis in their Acquirer stock that is the same as the basis of their stock in the Target (sometimes called a "substituted" or "exchanged" basis). See §§ 358 and 7701(a)(44). No gain must be recognized, and no loss can be recognized by shareholders in a transaction that qualifies as an exchange within a reorganization. Ordinarily, inability to recognize losses in a reorganization is not a problem: shareholders seeking to trigger a loss can sell their Target stock to anyone other than Acquirer without threatening the status of the transaction as a reorganization.

> **What Transactions Are Part of a Reorganization?**
>
> *Although the presence of "a reorganization" will bring both the Target corporation and its shareholders within the applicable nonrecognition provisions (sections 361 and 354, respectively), Target corporation and its shareholders may be involved in other transactions that are not so governed. If a stock or debt interest in Target is redeemed by Target in a transaction that is not considered part of the reorganization, for example, the interest holder may recognize both gain and loss under section 302 or section 1001.*
>
> *It is not always easy, however, to determine when such transactions will be considered apart from the reorganization. Some such situations were identified long ago, and the consequences are relatively predictable: if a stockholder or a bondholder receives only cash in exchange for all of her interests in Target, neither section 354 nor 356 will apply, and gain or loss will be recognized. Recently promulgated and proposed regulations, discussed below in the consideration of the allocation of boot, offer the possibility that many more exchanges can be considered not to be part of the reorganization, even when the stockholder involved also receives Target stock and thus participates in a transaction that is governed by section 354.*

b.   Corporate Consequences: Target

In asset acquisitions, Target generally exchanges its assets for the Acquirer consideration and then distributes all of the properties received from the Acquirer, as well as any remaining assets retained by Target and not transferred to Acquirer. It either disappears by operation of law (in a merger) or is eventually actually liquidated. In stock acquisitions, Target obviously continues to exist, though it may be subject to limitations on the use of its losses. In a special kind of asset acquisition that resembles a stock acquisition (the "reverse triangular merger"), Target continues to exist but it may hold additional properties received from the merger into it of a subsidiary of Acquirer.

Perhaps because of the role of judicial decisions in the development of the law of reorganizations, transactions that can be tax-free to the shareholders will also be tax-free to the corporations involved, if a transfer of corporate assets has occurred. In an acquisitive reorganization where stock is the only consideration, Target will recognize no gain on any of its assets, either because they were not transferred (either actually or by law) or because the nonrecognition afforded by section 361 applies to both the exchange of assets with Acquirer and the distribution of stock to Target shareholders.

c.   Corporate Consequences: Acquirer

Acquisition of assets. In general, Acquirer will have used its stock and securities to acquire either Target assets or Target stock. The use of such consideration will not result in gain or loss to Acquirer. *See* § 1032. The transferred assets will have the same basis to the Acquirer as they had in Target's hands (sometimes called a "carryover" or "transferred" basis). *See* §§ 362(b), 7701(a)(43). The surviving corporation will also succeed to the Target corporation's tax attributes, subject to the limitations of section 382 and the special operating rules of section 381 relating to the taxable years of the entities involved.

Acquisition of stock. Exchanges of solely Acquirer stock for Target stock are similarly tax-free to the Acquirer. § 1032. Less intuitive are the rules for determining the Acquirer's basis in Target stock. Acquirer takes the stock with the former Target shareholders' aggregate basis. *See* § 362(b). This rule may seem a bit unwieldy, since it requires Acquirer to gather information that may not be easily accessible. However, it is the same rule that would apply if Target shareholders had simply contributed all of their Target stock to Acquirer in exchange for 80% or more of Acquirer stock in a transaction that qualified for nonrecognition treatment under section 351.

15.3.2. Consequences When Non-Stock Consideration Also Used

When the consideration transferred by Acquirer includes other property or money as well as the stock of Acquirer, both shareholders and corporations that are participants in the reorganization face a different set of tax consequences.

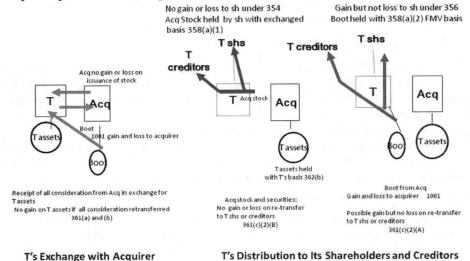

The Taxation of Parties to Reorganizations
General Principles under Sections 354, 358, 361 and 362

a. Shareholder Consequences

In those situations in which non-stock consideration is permitted, shareholders will generally recognize some type of income under the rules of section 356. Recognition makes sense because shareholders have become disinvested in the corporation, to the extent that boot is received. First, their realized gain (or loss) on the relevant exchange will be computed. Second, the gain recognized (if any) will be limited to the sum of the cash and fair market value of any other non-stock consideration received in the exchange. (This is the same approach as that used in section 1031, dealing with like-kind exchanges involving boot.) Third, this gain may be recharacterized as a dividend (rather than gain on a sale of stock) if the shareholder would have had dividend treatment had he arranged for a share repurchase from Acquirer immediately after the reorganization. Commissioner v. Clark, 489 U.S. 726 (1989).

b. Corporate Consequences: Target

Section 361 prescribes the tax consequences for the Target corporation, both on the exchange with Acquirer and the distribution to Target shareholders. The Target corporation is not taxed on the exchange under subsections (a) and (b) of section 361, so long as any boot, here meaning property that is not stock or securities of Acquirer, is distributed to Target shareholders. Section 361(b)(3) provides that transfers to creditors to repay a Target liability in connection with the reorganization will also "purge" Target of the possible exchange consequences of its receipt of boot.

Under section 361(c)(1), Target is generally not taxed on the re-transfer that is its distribution to its shareholders of the consideration it receives from Acquirer, although in limited circumstances it may recognize gain. More specifically, under section 361(c)(2), Target will never recognize gain on the distribution of the stock, securities, and other debt obligations that it receives from Acquirer (defined in the statute as "qualified property"). However, it may recognize gain on its re-transfer of any other consideration from Acquirer, as well as on any of its own property that it distributes to shareholders.

c. Corporate Consequences: Acquirer

The use by Acquirer of non-stock consideration (in those situations in which it is allowed) will trigger the same results to Acquirer that the use of such consideration would outside of the reorganization provisions. When property such as land or the securities of another corporation is used, gain or loss will be triggered on the transfer. Because Acquirer's basis in the Target stock or assets received will be determined under section 362(b) by reference to the transferor's basis in the assets or stock, Acquirer's gain on the non-stock property transferred will *not* increase Acquirer's basis in the acquired assets or stock.

Similarly, and far more significantly, if Acquirer uses cash as part of the consideration for Target's assets or stock in a reorganization, there will be no increase in the basis of the stock or assets it receives in respect of that cash boot.

When Acquirer uses its debt as consideration, it will not recognize gain, although the debt may be treated as boot to those receiving it.

15.4. A REORGS AND JUDICIALLY IMPOSED REORGANIZATION REQUIREMENTS

The oldest and most basic of the reorganization definitions is that of the statutory merger, or "A reorg," so called because it is described (or more accurately, characterized) in section 368(a)(1)(A). The statute simply provides that "a statutory merger or consolidation" is a "reorganization." In a typical A reorg, one corporation

(Target) is essentially absorbed by another corporation (Acquirer) for consideration that is paid to the Target's shareholders — that is, Target's assets and liabilities become assets and liabilities of Acquirer, its stock ceases to exist, and the consideration paid by Acquirer (stock as well as cash and other property, if any) is distributed appropriately to Target shareholders — all by operation of law under the state merger statute. Terms of the deal are approved by the boards of directors of each corporation under the regular corporate charter procedures. State merger statutes typically specify the nature of the shareholder approval that must be obtained prior to the transaction — Target shareholders must approve such transactions because Target will cease to exist — and also describe in some detail the rights of dissenting shareholders, including (in some states) appraisal rights.

> **The Relationship Between State Merger Statutes and Reorganization**
>
> *Although most of the text discusses the merger of one corporation into another, A reorgs also encompass consolidation transactions in which two corporations join together to form a new corporation. The following diagram illustrates a divisive state-law merger transaction (not recognized as an A reorg under the federal income tax definition), a good acquisitive merger transaction, and a consolidation merger transaction.*

Good Type A Reorganization - Statutory Merger

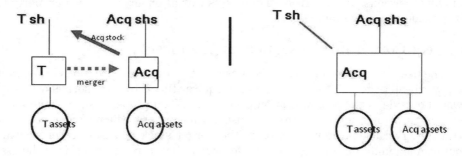

Good Type A Reorganization - Consolidation

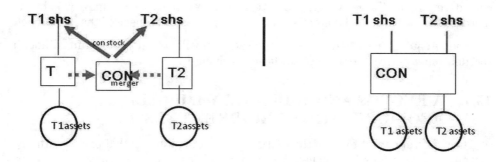

BAD Type A Reorganization – Attempted "Divisive" Merger

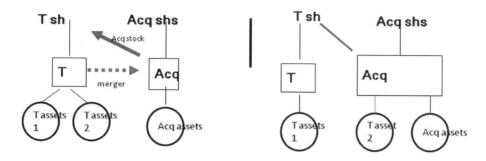

The primary provisions determining the federal income tax consequences of this transaction, and all other reorganizations, are sections 354 and 358 for shareholders; sections 1032 and 362 for the Acquirer; and sections 361 and 358 for Target, as elaborated upon further below. In addition, section 368(b) also indicates which corporations are considered "a party to a reorganization" for purposes of sections 351 through 385 (that is, Part III of Subchapter C). This provision once played a significant role in limiting the ways in which the acquired stock or acquired assets could be retransferred within the Acquirer's affiliated group after the reorganization. That role has been reduced considerably by the development of the continuity of business enterprise regulations in Reg. § 1.368-1(d) and the safe harbor for movements of assets or stock in connection with a reorganization under Reg. § 1.368-2(k). These provisions are discussed in more detail below.

The tax statute contains no additional conditions for qualifying for reorganization treatment, beyond the inference that compliance with a state law definition of "merger" or "consolidation" is required. However, faced with corporate restructurings that involved shareholders whose interests had changed in ways inconsistent with "a continuing interest" in a "modified corporate form," courts , required something more than mere literal compliance with a state merger law. They imposed additional requirements that are now articulated in the regulations: (i) that there be a continuation of the business enterprise of the Target corporation, Reg. § 1.368-1(d); (ii) that there be a continuation of shareholder interest in the Target represented by stock of the Acquirer or its parent, Reg. § 1.368-1(e); and (iii) that there be both a plan of reorganization and a corporate business purpose for the transaction, Reg. § 1.368-1(c) (last three sentences). *Cf.* § 354 (requiring that the transaction be undertaken "in pursuance to a plan of reorganization"); § 361 (same). These judicially invented and administratively adopted requirements are common to all reorganizations. They tend to play a more significant role in determining whether a transaction qualifies as an A reorg because of the lack of other specific conditions for A reorg treatment.

15.4.1. Continuity of Business Enterprise

Under the continuity of business enterprise requirement (sometimes referred to by its acronym, "COBE"), either the historic business of the Target must be continued by the Acquirer or the historic business assets of the Target must be used by the Acquirer. There are few authorities other than the regulations developing the continuity of business enterprise requirement. Reg. § 1.368-1(d) provides that if Target has several lines of business, only one significant business of Target must be continued. The regulation also makes clear that continuing a business that is newly entered into by Target in connection with the plan of reorganization will not be sufficient to satisfy the requirement.

Another aspect of the continuity of business enterprise requirement involves limits on the form through which the Acquirer can conduct the business or businesses of Target, including by creating new subsidiaries or partnerships to which Target's assets or business is transferred.

Note, however, that the COBE requirement does not restrict what Acquirer does with its old business. Acquirer cannot liquidate Target and then merge to acquire the cash and investment assets, nor can Acquirer merge then immediately cash out Target's assets. *See* Reg. § 1.368-1(d)(5) Exs. 3–5. Acquirer can, however, sell its own pre-merger assets for cash prior to the merger and use that cash to expand the acquired Target business. Rev. Rul. 81-25, 1981-2 C.B. 132.

**The Enhanced Role of COBE under the New Post-Reorg
Transfer Provisions in Reg. § 1.368-2(k)**

The regulations promulgated under section 368 now set forth the exclusive method of satisfying the COBE requirement. The regulatory expansion of COBE over the last ten years has been significant. It includes as entities whose assets or activities may satisfy COBE other corporations related to Acquirer. This change was made at least in part to accommodate related expansions of the ways in which Target's assets could be transferred after the reorganization, as described below.

In particular, the regulations have brought into the reorganization area the concept of a "qualified group" (borrowing from section 1504's concept of affiliated groups) while still maintaining the control definition in section 368(c) as the aggregate required linkage (requiring at least 80% of voting power and at least 80% by number of each other class of shares). A qualified group is "one or more chains of corporations connected through stock ownership with the issuing corporation [Acquirer], but only if the issuing corporation owns directly stock meeting the requirements of section 368(c) in at least one other corporation, and stock meeting the requirements of section 368(c) in each of the corporations (except the issuing corporation) is owned directly . . . by one or more of the other corporations." Reg. § 1.368-1(d)(4)(ii). The issuing corporation is viewed as the head of the qualified group. Further, the regulations provide for looking through a partnership of which the group owns section 368(c) control — in spite of the fact that the Code does not provide for section 368(c) to apply "directly or indirectly." Reg. § 1.368-1(d)(4)(iii)(D).

> *As a consequence of the regulation's use of a group concept and the expansion of section 368(c) to include situations in which the requisite ownership is achieved by aggregating the ownership of more than one member of the qualified group, COBE will be satisfied as long as Acquirer can be treated as conducting Target's business (or using Target's historic assets) because the business or assets continue within the qualified group. That is, COBE need not actually be satisfied by the corporation that acquires direct control of Target assets in the reorg, but rather can continue to be satisfied when the qualified group, in the aggregate, retains the requisite continuity of business enterprise. Accordingly, a drop of Target stock into two first-tier subsidiaries of Acquirer, so that Target is owned 50% by each subsidiary, would not defeat COBE, since Acquirer would own stock of the two subsidiaries representing section 368(c) control and the two affiliates own stock of Target in the aggregate representing section 368(c) control.*
>
> *This loosening of the COBE requirement was made in conjunction with a loosening of the limits on any restructuring by Acquirer that involved the assets or stock acquired in the reorganization. Until relatively recently, the limits were thought to be strict on Acquirer's ability to re-transfer either the assets or the stock that it acquired in a reorganization without jeopardizing the status of the entire transaction as a reorganization, and it was especially difficult to anticipate when it was unclear which transfers would be considered part of the reorganization under the step transaction doctrine. Reg. section 1.368-2(k) provides more clearly stated — and more liberal — limits on these re-transfers. Now that many more re-transfers are permitted, COBE plays an enhanced role in determining what kinds of post-reorganization transfers will likely be permitted.*

15.4.2. Continuity of Shareholder Interest

The idea behind nonrecognition treatment for Target shareholders is that, because in the end they own Acquirer stock and Acquirer holds Target stock or assets, the Target shareholders retain something similar to the same economic interests that they held before the transaction, though in a diluted and indirect form. The courts fashioned a continuity of shareholder interest requirement (sometimes referred to by its acronym as the "COSI" requirement or otherwise shortened to "continuity of interest") to capture the idea that retention of too small a continuing interest by Target shareholders should cause a transaction to fail the reorganization requirements. Reg. § 1.368-1(e)(i) states that the purpose of this requirement is "to prevent transactions that resemble sales from qualifying for nonrecognition" and that its essence is "that in substance a substantial part of the value of the proprietary interests in the target corporation be preserved in the reorganization. At the very least, this means that they must receive an equity interest, that is, an interest that gives them a right to the future earnings and/or growth of the corporation."

Through much of its history, questions about the continuity of shareholder interest doctrine were focused on (i) the Target shareholders and the interests they receive, including whether the Target shareholders had acquired their interest in Target very recently (the "historic shareholder" COSI concern), (ii) whether at the conclusion of the reorganization and related transactions the Target shareholders held an interest in Acquirer that was too remote from the Target stock or assets (the "remote shareholder" COSI concern), and (iii) whether the former Target shareholders retained their interest in Acquirer for a sufficient time after the reorganization to credit their interest in Acquirer as continuing their interest in Target (the "post-reorganization" COSI concern).

Developments in the late 1990s, however, clarified that what is really at stake is the nature of the consideration used by Acquirer. Under this more recent approach it does not matter how long the Target shareholders have held their stock prior to the reorganization, as long as enough Acquirer stock is ultimately used; therefore, an Acquirer seeking to secure nonrecognition treatment for Target shareholders need not worry about how much Target stock has traded in the market for cash in anticipation of the reorganization. Reg. § 1.368-1(e)(8) Ex. 1(ii) (adopting the result in *J.E. Seagram Corp. v. Commissioner*, 104 T.C. 75 (1995), as explained in T.D. 8760, 63 FR 4174 (1998)). Similarly, it does not matter how long Target shareholders hold their Acquirer stock after the reorganization, so long as enough Acquirer stock is used and there is no arrangement for former Target shareholders to be directly bought out with Acquirer funds (or by a party that is related to Acquirer). Reg. 1.368-1(e)(8) Ex. 3 (as explained in T.D. 8760, 63 FR 4174 (1998), rejecting the result in *McDonald's Restaurants of Illinois, Inc. v. Commissioner*, 688 F.2d 520 (7th Cir. 1982)). The Service has generously provided that Acquirer's open market buybacks of Acquirer stock in which former Target shareholders may participate will not threaten continuity, even when the goal is to reacquire the same number of shares as were issued to Target shareholders in the reorganization transaction. Rev. Rul. 99-58, 1999-2 C.B. 701. Similarly, it does not matter (for the purposes of determining whether the transaction qualifies as a reorganization) that some shareholders receive no Acquirer stock and are completely cashed out, so long as enough of the aggregate consideration used by Acquirer is stock. *See* Rev. Rul. 66-224, 1966-2 C.B. 114 (holding that all cash to two of four equal shareholders should be treated the same as 50% cash to all shareholders).

There are both quantitative and qualitative considerations relevant to the COSI inquiry. Until recently, there had been considerable uncertainty whether some amount of stock less than 50% would be adequate. In a very short 1935 opinion, the Supreme Court concluded that a continuing shareholder interest of 38% was sufficient. John A. Nelson Co. v. Helvering, 296 U.S. 374, 375 (1935). Most practitioners considered this an outlier opinion and were reluctant to advise clients to undertake transactions with only 38% stock consideration in reliance on that case, because the Service ruling guidelines on the question, first promulgated in Rev. Proc. 77-37, 1977-2 C.B. 568, insisted on a representation that 50% of the consideration would be stock. The recent administrative review of the reorganization provisions seems to have loosened the requirement: the regulations now include examples reflecting the conclusion that a 40% equity stake in Acquirer is sufficient to satisfy the COSI requirement. Reg. § 1.368-1T(e)(2)(v), Ex. 1.

In general, qualitative questions about whether "proprietary interests" have been preserved are determined on an absolute, rather than a relative, basis. Thus, in an older case, continuity of interest in a corporation was not preserved when its shareholders received ten-year bonds in exchange for their stock, even though the corporation's only assets were the right to collect rents on property subject to 900-year leases with the Acquirer. Roebling v. Commissioner, 323 U.S. 773 (1944). More recently, the interests of shareholders in a stock savings and loan were not preserved even though they received the only kind of interest allowed by law when that stock institution merged into a mutual savings and loan. Paulsen v. Commissioner, 469 U.S. 131 (1985).

The limited authorities on the question, furthermore, seem to indicate that qualification as stock for the purposes of the COSI requirement is an all-or nothing matter. If the interest received can be treated as stock, it will count for continuity even if a considerable part of its value comes from debt-like features, including preferential dividends. The amount of the "proprietary interest" continued will not be reduced by the value of the debt features.

15.4.3. Business Considerations

The A reorg is the most flexible in terms of the nature of the consideration that can be offered, since only 40% of the value of Target must be represented by Acquirer shares after the transaction. Not only may cash and other property be used, but also various types of convertible securities, warrants, and other contingent security interests may comprise part of the consideration for the deal.

The A reorganization is also the most flexible in terms of the Target assets that must be transferred to the Acquirer. So long as the continuity of business requirement is satisfied, Target may dispose of assets prior to the merger or Acquirer may dispose of some acquired assets in connection with the merger.

Despite the ease with which the transactions can achieve tax-free reorganization treatment, Target's liabilities frequently make the A reorganization unattractive. All of the Target liabilities are acquired — contingent or fixed, documented or "hidden" (e.g., tort or environmental liabilities). Not only do Target assets remain subject to Target liabilities, but Acquirer's assets are now also directly exposed to them. A subsidiary merger form (often referred to as a triangular merger), through which Target's liabilities will survive as liabilities of the subsidiary rather than Acquirer, mitigates the problem; but Acquirer's assets remain indirectly exposed. Though the subsidiary merger forms, described in subsections 368(a)(2)(D) and (a)(2)(E) and considered below in Chapter 19, may be useful in relieving some of the problems of a direct merger, they have their own additional conditions that sometimes make them inappropriate to the particular situation.

Under state law, a majority (and in some states, a super-majority) of shareholders must approve a merger. Dissenting shareholders will have appraisal rights, but in many states, the existence of these rights may not be sufficiently troublesome to spoil the transaction.

15.4.4. Mergers Involving C Corporations and Disregarded Entities

Certain entities, such as limited liability companies (LLCs) and certain specialized pass-through entities, may be treated as "disregarded entities" when they are controlled by a single owner. Reg. § 1.7701-2(c)(2). As the state law applying to LLCs and other pass-through entities evolves, such entities are far more likely to be able to engage in transactions, authorized when accomplished according to statutory provisions, that resemble the merger transactions available to corporations. These new state-law provisions raise questions about how such transactions are to be taxed: for instance, how should the tax law treat the merger into its sole owner of an entity that is disregarded for tax purposes (i.e., because the tax law views it merely as a division or an extension of the sole owner)?

Key to the understanding of the treatment of mergers with disregarded entities is that a merger under a state statute is necessary, but not sufficient, to satisfy the A reorg requirement. Texas, for example, provides by statute for divisive mergers, whereby the assets of a single corporation may be held by two or more corporations after the merger. In Rev. Rul. 2000-5, 2000-1 C.B. 436, the IRS dealt with this new possibility, ruling that such a divisive merger could not satisfy the A reorg requirement because implicit in the reorganization is the idea that Target shareholders hold only stock of one corporation after the transaction, and only one corporation remains to hold the assets of Target. Regulations finalized in 2006 set out the conditions under which transactions with disregarded entities can be treated as mergers qualifying under section 368(a)(1)(A). These rules reflect the importance of the idea developed in Rev. Rul. 2000-5 that divisive mergers do not qualify under section 368(a)(1)(A) no matter what a particular state law may allow. Accordingly, the merger into an Acquirer of a disregarded entity that holds only some of the assets of a Target corporation cannot qualify as an A reorg, even though nominally there has been a "statutory merger," since Target survives and continues to hold other assets that are not part of the merger transaction. Assets that were formerly held by a single corporation cannot be held by two or more corporations after the merger except as a result of the transfer of Target assets to corporations related to Acquirer in one of the specific drop-down or push-up transactions that are sanctioned by Reg. § 1.368-2(k).

But in those situations in which the transaction can be structured as a merger of a Target corporation into an acquiring LLC, many of the technical restrictions involved in the older reorganization forms can be avoided since these transactions are, for tax purposes, equivalent to a merger into Acquirer. Accordingly, a merger of a Target corporation into a disregarded entity owned by Acquirer will be treated as a merger under section 368(a)(1)(A), but a merger of a disregarded entity of Target into an Acquirer corporation will not qualify. In the latter case, the merger will fail one or both of the requirements that all of the assets and liabilities of the Target be transferred and that Target cease to exist by operation of law. Reg. § 1.368-2(b)(1)(ii)(A), (B); 1.368-2(b)(1)(iii), Ex. 6.

In the language of the regulation, there will be a merger if all of the assets of each member of a combining unit (here, the transferor unit, meaning Target and any disregarded entities it may own) become the assets of one or more members of another combining unit (here, the transferee unit, or Acquirer and any disregarded entities it owns) and each member of the transferor/Target unit ceases its separate legal existence. Reg. § 1.368-2(b)(1)(ii). Thus, if Target corporation T is merged under state law into disregarded entity DE owned by Acquirer, there can be a good merger, since T's assets will be held by DE (and therefore treated as held by Acquirer for tax purposes) and T disappears by operation of the state merger statute. Reg. § 1.368-2(b)(1)(iii), Ex. 2. On the other hand, if DE is owned by T and merges into Acquirer, T will still exist after the transaction, as will Acquirer (now holding DE's assets), so there will be no A reorganization. Reg. § 1.368-2(b)(1)(iii), Ex. 6.

15.4.5. Net Value Considerations

The proposed regulations under section 368 indicate that mergers qualify under section 368(a)(1) only if both Target and Acquirer have a net positive value at the time of the transaction. Prop. Reg. § 1.368-1(b), (f)(2)-(3). Under these rules, the value of the assets of the merged corporation must exceed the liabilities assumed by Acquirer, and the value of the assets of Acquirer must also exceed its liabilities.

Net Value Transactions

The absence of net value in an entity creates special problems throughout in the corporate tax regime. The availability of nontaxable status under the reorganization provisions is no different. Can there be a reorganization if a corporation transfers assets that are encumbered by liabilities, whether fixed or contingent, that may be greater than the value of the assets if they were unencumbered? Is there a reorganization if some shareholders are willing to take back stock in an entity that seems to have no net value because it could not pay its liabilities if all of its assets were sold but the corporation has so far been able to meet its debts as they become due? The technical explanation is that a Target with excess liabilities can make no net transfer of property to an Acquirer, and an insolvent Acquirer has no capacity to engage in genuine business transactions. Compare purported section 351 transactions and purported section 332 liquidations when there is no net value. These questions as well as the underlying questions about how the presence of "net value" should be determined and how it relates to other notions of insolvency are currently under examination by Treasury and the Service.

15.4.6. Use of Parent Stock and Transfers of Assets

The statutory language of section 368(a)(1)(A) is particularly sparse compared to the other reorganization definitions. No mention is made in the statute, in contrast to the description provided in subsections 368(a)(1)(B) and (C), of the use of parent stock or of the possibility of dropping acquired assets into subsidiaries.

Such variations are possible, but consideration of them will be deferred until the discussion of all varieties of "triangular" reorganizations in Chapter 19. It is worth noting that the regulations now deal with these transactions in terms of two distinct issues. The first, under Reg. § 1.368-1(d)(4), is whether the COBE requirement is satisfied. The second, under Reg. § 1.368-2(k), is (i) whether a transfer subsequent to the principal reorganization transaction should be viewed as so integral to the overall transaction that it cannot be considered to be separate from the reorganization and yet so fundamentally change the transaction that it no longer fits the statutory description or instead (ii) whether it should be seen as a reasonable post-reorganization internal restructuring that will not cause the principal reorganization transaction to fail reorganization status, even if the subsequent transaction was inevitable from the outset.

On the one hand, if a transfer causes the transaction to fail the COBE requirement, the transaction cannot qualify as a section 368 reorganization. The

COBE regulations expand the possible drop-downs of Target assets beyond those explicitly permitted in the Code by defining a "qualified group" built on the section 368(c) control definition but otherwise adopting a concept of aggregated entities similar to the definition central to affiliation set forth in section 1504(a). So long as the transfer comes within the requirements as defined in the regulations, it will not fail the COBE requirement, but if it does not come within the regulatory definition, it cannot satisfy the COBE requirement.

On the other hand, the Reg. § 1.368-2(k) provisions for post-reorganization transfers to Acquirer-related parties act as a safe harbor. So long as the transaction comes within its requirements for stock or asset transfers and also satisfies the COBE requirements in Reg. § 1.368-1(d), it will not be considered to fail because of the step transaction doctrine. The regulation essentially blesses distributions so long as they do not result in liquidation or a distribution of all of the acquired Target stock. *See* Reg. § 1.368-2(k)(l)(i). It blesses "other transfers" not described in the distribution rule if all or part of the assets or stock are transferred, so long as the stock transfer does not result in the entity (Target, Acquirer Subsidiary, or Acquirer, as the case may be) ceasing to be a member of the qualified group and so long as that entity does not terminate its corporate existence in connection with the transfer. In both cases, of course, the COBE requirement must be satisfied or the reorg will fail. If the initial steps related to a reorganization satisfy the definitional requirements and the later transfer satisfies the COBE requirement and comes within the safe harbor, the reorganization itself will not be recast but will continue to qualify under section 368. If the post-reorganization transfer does not fall within the Reg. section 1.368-2(k) safe harbor for transfers, however, the purported reorganization transaction itself and the post-reorganization transfer(s) must be reassessed under the step transaction doctrine. As a result, the purported reorganization is likely to fail the definitional requirements for a successful reorganization.

PRACTICE PROBLEMS

Problems 1–6: True or False?

1. In order to meet the common law continuity of interest test required for nonrecognition to be available in a corporate reorganization, all shareholders of the Target corporation must become shareholders of the Acquiring corporation.

2. Virtually all of the reorganization provisions are premised on the idea that if the transaction should be nontaxable to the Target corporation, it should also be nontaxable to the Target shareholders to the extent that they receive Acquirer common stock.

3. Since the repeal of *General Utilities*, a corporation that transfers all of its assets to another corporation will recognize gain with respect to those assets unless section 351 or section 332 applies to the transaction.

4. The judicial doctrine conditioning qualification as a reorganization on the continuity of shareholder interest has been entirely replaced by the express statutory provisions governing the nature of the consideration that can be received by Target shareholders.

5. Section 368(a)(1)(A) and the related sections dealing with the tax treatment of shareholders and corporations involved in the transactions referred to therein provide nonrecognition to all shareholders in any transaction that qualifies under state law as a statutory merger.

6. A Target shareholder can receive readily tradable stock in a corporate reorganization without having to recognize gain on the Target stock given up.

7. Al is a shareholder in Targetco, which is about to be merged into Publico in a transaction in which all Targetco shareholders will receive common stock of Publico. Al purchased his stock, which represents 7% of the stock in Targetco, in 1990 for $5000. He will receive stock of Publico worth $100,000. What will be Al's basis in the Publico stock he receives?

8. Al is a shareholder in Targetco, which is about to be merged into Publico in a transaction in which all Targetco shareholders will receive publicly traded bonds of Publico. Al purchased his stock, which represents 7% of the stock in Targetco, in 1990 for $5000. He will receive bonds of Publico worth $100,000. What will his basis be in the bonds he receives?

9. Al is a shareholder in Targetco, which is about to be merged into Publico in a transaction in which most Targetco shareholders will receive common stock of Publico. Three shareholders, who together owned 15% of the stock, held out and will receive cash instead. Al purchased his stock, which represents 7% of the stock in Targetco, in 1990 for $5000. He will receive stock of Publico worth $100,000. What will be Al's basis in the Publico stock received?

10. Al is a shareholder in Targetco, which is about to be merged into Publico in a transaction in which all Targetco shareholders will receive common stock of Publico. Al purchased his stock, which represents 7% of the stock in Targetco, in 1990 for $5000. He will receive stock of Publico worth $100,000. More than 65% of the shareholders of Targetco have indicated that they are planning to sell their stock in Publico as quickly after they receive it as they can. Al plans to hold onto his stock. What will his basis be?

11. Al is a shareholder in Targetco, which is about to be merged into Publico in a transaction in which all Targetco shareholders will receive common stock of Publico. Al purchased his stock, which represents 7% of the stock in Targetco, in 1990 for $5000. He will receive stock of Publico worth $100,000. After the merger, Publico will drop the assets of Targetco into a subsidiary in a transaction that will qualify under section 351. What is Al's basis in the Publico stock he will receive?

DISCUSSION PROBLEMS

FBS Inc (DBA Fred's Body Shop, Inc.) has 100 shares of common stock and 50 shares of nonvoting preferred stock outstanding. The preferred stock is currently redeemable at a price that today represents roughly 15% of the value of FBS. Acquirer Co., a publicly traded corporation, has made overtures regarding the acquisition of FBS in exchange for its stock. The two companies have agreed that the total value of FBS, including the value represented by the preferred interests, is about $100,000.

1. From the preliminary discussions, it appears that neither the FBS preferred shareholders nor Acquirer have any interest in the preservation of the preferred interest as such. It also appears that the holders of about 40% of the value of FBS will prefer to take all cash rather than to take Acquirer stock. The holders of another 10% of the common stock have liquidity problems such that they will want some cash. The remainder will not agree to any transaction unless it is nontaxable to them. Can this transaction be accomplished consistently with the desires of all four groups of FBS shareholders?

2. Despite having turned up nothing that should be troubling about the way FBS has conducted its business, Acquirer is nervous about a merger of FBS directly into it, due to potential state law liabilities that it would acquire. However, even those shareholders who are willing to take Acquirer stock are not willing to take the stock of a wholly owned subsidiary of Acquirer. Can a transaction be arranged that satisfies both Acquirer's desire that it not become a successor to FBS for state law purposes and the FBS shareholders' demands regarding the consideration they are willing to take?

3. Although Acquirer has never said so in so many words, there are rumors that Acquirer does not plan to continue the auto body business at all, but instead is interested in the land on which one of the shops is located. Should this be of other than sentimental concern to the Target shareholders hoping for nonrecognition treatment?

4. There have been rumors that Acquirer is about to announce a tender offer whereby it hopes to repurchase 10% of its stock in exchange for cash. The timing is likely to be such that the offer will still be open after the acquisition of Target is complete. Other than what it might mean regarding the fair market value of Acquirer stock, should this fact be of concern to the Target shareholders hoping for nonrecognition treatment?

5. Determine whether the following transactions can be treated as reorganizations. You may assume that in all cases the corporations in question are acting pursuant to their state's merger law, and that Target merges into Acquirer, and that there is adequate continuity of business enterprise, with the shareholders taking back the consideration stated:

(a) Each holder of one share of Target common stock (the only stock outstanding) receives $85 cash and $15 worth of Acquirer common stock.

(b) Each holder of one share of Target common stock (the only stock outstanding) receives $35 cash and $65 worth of Acquirer common stock.

(c) Each holder of one share of Target common stock (the only stock outstanding) receives $35 in cash and $65 worth of Acquirer preferred stock, which is limited and preferred as to dividends, does not participate in corporate growth, and bears a cumulative dividend measured by an interest index.

(d) Each holder of one share of Target common stock (the only stock outstanding) receives $35 cash and $65 worth of Acquirer preferred stock, which is limited and preferred as to dividends, does not participate in corporate growth, and is subject to redemption by Acquirer three years from the date of the transaction.

(e)   Each holder of one share of Target common stock (the only stock outstanding) receives $35 in cash and $65 worth of stock of Mega Corp, a corporation that is unrelated to Acquirer, which has been holding the Mega Corp stock as a portfolio investment.

(f)   62% of the holders of Target stock receive nothing but Acquirer stock; 38% receive nothing but cash.

(g)   38% of the holders of Target stock receive nothing but Acquirer stock; 62% receive nothing but cash.

(h)   Each holder of one share of Target common stock (the only stock outstanding) receives $35 in cash and $65 worth of Acquirer common stock. Six months after the transaction, Rival Co., which is unrelated to Acquirer, makes a tender offer for the stock of Acquirer, as a result of which all of the old Target shareholders sell their Acquirer stock.

(i)   Each holder of one share of Target common stock (the only stock outstanding) receives $35 in cash and $65 worth of Acquirer common stock. Six months after the transaction at issue, Rival Co., which recently acquired, in a single private transaction, 80% of Acquirer, makes a tender offer for the rest of the stock of Acquirer, as a result of which all of the old Target shareholders sell their Acquirer stock to Rival Co. for cash.

Chapter 16

BOOT IN REORGANIZATIONS

Statutes and Regulations	IRC §§ 354(a)(2); 356(a), (c), (d), (e), (g); 361
	Reg. §§ 1.354-1; 1.356-1,-2,-3,-5,-6
Other Primary Authorities	Commissioner v. Clark, 489 U.S. 726 (1989)
	Rev. Rul. 68-23, 1968-1 C.B. 144
	Rev. Rul. 78-250, 1978-1 C.B. 83

16.1. TAX CONSEQUENCES OF BOOT

Not all reorganization transactions are conducted using solely Acquirer stock for consideration. Many will involve a substantial amount of non-stock consideration, usually cash but sometimes other properties such as notes (non-security debt obligations) of Acquirer. This Part explores the tax consequences of these boot properties to Target shareholders, Acquirer, and Target and some of the special issues that have arisen in connection with the promulgation of proposed regulations that permit designation of consideration in reorganization transactions.

16.1.1. Consequences to Target Shareholders

Clearly, to the extent that Target shareholders receive boot, they will be outside the nonrecognition protection of section 354. Surprisingly, however, the tax consequences of the boot payment may not always be determined under section 356, the provision that ordinarily applies when other properties are received in addition to those permitted to be received without the recognition of gain. When the shareholder is treated as having given up stock, but receiving only boot, the shareholder will be treated as if he had simply redeemed his stock, and thus recognition of both gain and loss is possible. Under a tracing rule permitting specification of consideration that was included in final regulations promulgated in 2006, and extended in proposed regulations issued in 2009, there is considerably greater possibility that a shareholder will be treated as having participated in such a transaction. The extent of the change effected will depend on whether those regulations are finalized as promulgated. Much of the discussion in this chapter relates, in one way or another, to these regulations and the somewhat controversial opportunity to designate what consideration is received for what items in a reorganization exchange in which such designation is motivated by tax rather than economic consequences.

a. Allocations of Boot in Reorganization Exchanges

Frequently in reorganization transactions, Target shareholders will hold stock of several classes or stock of a single class that was acquired in several blocks. The terms of the reorganization may specify which consideration is received by Target shareholders in exchange for each class or block of Target stock. Under regulations finalized in 2006, such designations of the consideration received for particular shares or blocks of shares will be honored if that designation is economically reasonable. Reg. § 1.356-1(b). If a shareholder holds two classes of stock and the consideration for each class is separately designated, the consequences of the transaction under sections 354, 356, and 358 (or in fact, under section 302) will be determined as if two distinct exchange transactions had taken place as to that shareholder, one with respect to each block of stock. Thus a shareholder with multiple blocks of Target stock could be treated, in exchanges taking place as part of a single reorganization, as having given up some stock only for stock, some stock only for property from the Target corporation (retained cash or other properties), some stock only for Acquirer boot properties, and other stock for both stock and boot. Under the 2006 regulations, the only limitation on such specification is that its terms be "economically reasonable." Without such specification (and perhaps under prior law no such specification would have been honored even if made), any boot received (including Target retained properties distributed in connection with the distribution of Acquirer properties, such as in a C reorg) would be allocated pro rata to all of the stock given up.

Regulations proposed in February 2009 elaborate substantially on the possibility and consequences of such specifications. The government's rationale for these taxpayer-friendly interpretations of the reorganization provisions rests on the idea that each share of stock (or at least each block of stock acquired at a different time or in a distinct transaction) should be treated as a separate unit of property. Implicit in the way the regulations implement this idea is the additional idea that a taxpayer in a reorganization transaction should be able to choose what part of the overall consideration received in the transaction is treated as having been exchanged for each such block of stock in the Target corporation. In these proposals, the Service and Treasury seem to accept that it is appropriate to permit the taxpayer to specify an allocation that allows as much gain as possible to be sheltered by the nonrecognition treatment that comes with being treated as part of a reorganization and yet also allows as much loss as possible to be recognized in the components of the overall transaction that are treated as not part of the reorganization. An approach that allows taxpayers to specify the part of the exchange consideration that is received for particular shares is not a necessary corollary to the treatment of the share as the basic unit of property; in fact, it appears to run counter to a fundamental principle of the federal income tax that a taxpayer should not be permitted to manipulate tax characteristics in order to achieve tax benefits when there is no economic rationale other than tax for the distinctions made.

As this text goes to publication, it is not clear whether the final regulations will endorse this approach to the allocation of boot. Even if this general approach is endorsed, it remains to be seen what content may be given to the requirement that such specified allocations be "economically reasonable." Because specification of consideration to particular shares is likely to be mainly (or quite possibly entirely) tax driven, it is difficult to foresee what allocations would be treated as economically reasonable.

The proposed regulations, however, would limit the ability of a Target share-holder to specify consideration in reorganization transactions to those transactions that are *not* dividend-equivalent. The regulations seem to contemplate that each Target shareholder would have to make an individualized determination of dividend-equivalency based on the overall consideration received in connection with the reorganization in exchange for Target shares. If in the aggregate these exchanges are dividend equivalent under the section 302 analysis, then the specification of particular consideration for particular shares would be disregarded and the consideration would be treated as received pro rata in respect of all of the shareholder's Target shares. If, however, the aggregate exchange were *not* dividend equivalent (i.e., if sections 302(b)/302(a)/1001 would apply), then the specification would be honored if economically reasonable and the shareholder may be able to reduce recognized gain or even recognize losses in connection with the reorganization.

This new approach to the allocation of boot in reorganization transactions under both the 2006 regulations and the 2009 proposed regulations is thus radically different from that traditionally used in transactions under section 351, in which boot is allocated pro rata across all of the properties transferred. *See* Rev. Rul. 68-55, 1968-1 C.B. 140. It is also different from what seems to have been the consensus view of the operation of the reorganization provisions, in which the relevant "exchange" in sections 354 and 356 was considered to be the entire reorganization exchange. If followed to the extent suggested in the proposed regulations and the related preamble, this ability to specify allocations of the consideration received in reorganizations and thereby segregate certain compo-nents of a reorganization into separate exchanges can have rather startling effects.

b. Dividend-within-Gain Rule

If both stock and non-stock consideration is received by Target shareholders in respect of a block of Target shares, section 356(a) provides that the boot will trigger recognition of any realized gain, up to the amount of boot, in much the same way that boot triggers gain in a like-kind exchange under section 1031. Recognition makes sense because shareholders have become disinvested in the corporation to the extent that boot is received. Thus when Target stock is given up in exchange for stock and boot, the shareholder's basis in the Target stock is compared with the value of the stock and boot received to determine the realized gain (if any) on the exchange. That realized gain will be recognized, to the extent of the boot. § 356(a)(1) (flush language) ("gain . . . shall be recognized, but in an amount not in excess of the sum of such money and the fair market value of such other property"). The shareholder's gain is computed on each block of stock separately: basis in a loss block cannot be used to reduce gain on an appreciated block of stock. Rev. Rul. 68-23, 1968-1 C.B. 144. Note that receipt of both stock and boot in respect of a block of shares cannot trigger losses: the boot only triggers gain realized by the shareholder (and cannot create gain in excess of that built into the shares).

The "dividend within gain" rule of section 356(a)(2) will transform this "gain" into a dividend if the exchange has the effect of a dividend. Strangely, section 356(a)(2) expressly incorporates by reference section 318, which provides for constructive ownership of stock held by a related party, but not section 302, which provides the substantive standards for determining dividend equivalence of simple redemptions.

The Oddity of Section 356(a)(1) Dividend-within-Gain

Under section 356(a)(1), when a shareholder in a transaction that would otherwise be governed by section 354 receives not only stock but also boot, that shareholder recognizes "gain" as a result of the exchange, but only to the extent of the boot. As is the case with most nonrecognition provisions, boot will trigger "gain" only to the extent thereof (that is, only gain actually realized on the exchange can be recognized because of the receipt of boot). This "gain" may be recharacterized as a dividend under section 356(a)(2).

The ability to use the basis in the stock given up — even when the transaction has the effect of a dividend — produces results that are anomalous compared to the results elsewhere in subchapter C.

Suppose A forms two corporations, X Co and Y Co by transferring $1000 for 10 shares in both cases. X Co is successful and has plenty of earnings and profits; Y Co has had no earnings and profits. Most of the ways that cash can be withdrawn from X Co will produce dividend treatment with no basis offset: any withdrawal of cash from X Co will be taxed as a dividend; any repurchase of X Co stock by X Co will also be taxed as a dividend under section 302; and the proceeds of any sale of X Co stock to Y Co (or vice versa) will also be taxed as a dividend under section 304, since under that provision, on these facts, there will be no use of basis and the e&p of both corporations will be available. But if A gives up Y Co stock in a reorganization in exchange for X Co stock and cash boot, the amount taken into income will be limited by the overall gain with which A holds the Y Co stock. Suppose that A gives up 1/5 of his stock in Y Co, when it is worth only $100 per share, in exchange for X Co stock worth $100 and $100 cash. Because A has no gain on the Y Co stock, he will recognize no income or gain under section 356(a)(2). A will have succeeded in monetizing his shares without taxation because the dividend-within-gain rule allows the basis to be taken into account first.

This anomaly has long been present within subchapter C. The peculiarities of section 356(a)(2) within subchapter C are easier to understand when one realizes that in 1942, when the predecessor of section 356(a)(2) was adopted, sections equivalent to sections 302 and 304 were not part of the Code.

The Supreme Court in *Commissioner v. Clark*, 489 U.S. 726 (1989), assumed, as have most authorities, that the standards of section 302 are relevant, and are likely the determinative standards for the dividend-equivalence analysis. In that case, the Court considered a sole shareholder in a corporation that received stock and cash in a forward merger. Rejecting the government's position that the transaction should be tested as if the boot had been received from the Target corporation immediately before the transaction, the Court tested the transaction for dividend-equivalence by comparing the actual situation in which the shareholder had received both cash and Acquirer stock to a hypothetical situation in which the shareholder had first received only Acquirer stock and then redeemed a portion of the stock for the cash boot. The cash boot left the shareholder in the same place as he would have been in if he had first received 1.3% of Acquirer and then had Acquirer stock redeemed such that he held 0.92% of Acquirer. Accordingly, the Court allowed the shareholder to characterize his recognized gain as exchange gain rather than dividend income. Rev. Rul. 93-61, 1993-2 C.B. 118, confirms the Service's interpretation of *Clark*.

Because basis has already been taken into account (in determining the amount of gain that may be recharacterized under section 356(a)(2) as a dividend) and because dividends are taxed at the same rate as capital gains under current law, recharacterization of recognized gain as a dividend will have an impact only when the shareholder has capital losses (or, in the case of a corporate shareholder, as to the availability of a dividend-received deduction and the application of section 1059). For individuals, section 1(h)(11) directs that dividends be taxed as if they were capital gains, but neither that section nor the capital gains provision includes them in the capital gains netting calculations.

As always when the question of dividend-equivalence arises, the earnings and profits of the corporation making the distribution are relevant. Section 356(a)(2) notes that the "dividend within gain" rule will apply only to the extent of the distributee's "ratable share" of the undistributed earnings and profits of the corporation. There are two questions here. First, which corporation's earnings and profits should be considered for this rule — Target's or Acquirer's or perhaps the combined Target-Acquirer that exists after the reorganization? Since Target shareholders are exchanging their Target stock for Acquirer stock and since Target is treated in acquisitive reorganizations as a conduit that distributes the Acquirer stock and boot to Target shareholders, it would be reasonable to assume that Target's earnings are the relevant ones. However, the *Clark* case treated the boot distribution as a hypothetical redemption of hypothetical post-reorganization Acquirer stock held by the Target shareholder, as though the Target shareholder had received all stock consideration in the transaction and had then redeemed part of it for the boot. Perhaps the same hypothetical recasting should apply as to the earnings and profits calculation and Acquirer's earnings should be reduced rather than Target's. In that case, it is possible that both the Acquirer and Target earnings would be available, since the hypothetical post-reorganization redemption out of Acquirer is out of the combined corporation.

Second, the provision indicates that "undistributed" earnings and profits of the corporation "accumulated after February 28, 1913" are to be reduced. The meaning of "undistributed" in a context that includes "accumulated" (but without the term "current" familiar from the adjustments to earnings and profits in connection with sections 301, 302, and 304) is not specified. Recall, however, that in accounting for the reduction required for ordinary redemptions the Service ruled that regular distributions take precedence (if there are current earnings and profits, they will be applied first to regular distributions and only if there is an amount remaining will it be added to accumulated earnings and profits to determine the redeemed shares' "ratable share"). Rev. Rul. 74-338, 1974-2 C.B. 101. Here "undistributed" earnings and profits could be read consistently with that position to mean the sum of any current earnings and profits not allocated to distributions taxed under section 301 and deemed to have occurred at the time of the reorganization, plus any accumulated earnings and profits remaining available for distribution as of the time of the reorganization distribution.

Section 1059(e)(1)(B) clarifies that boot recharacterized as a dividend under section 356(a)(2) will be treated as a redemption for the purposes of applying the standards in section 1059(e), treating such transactions as extraordinary dividends without regard to holding period.

**The Recognition of Target Shareholder
Losses in Reorganizations**

When a shareholder holds his Target shares with a loss and receives only boot in exchange for Target stock given up in a reorganization, the shareholder will recognize the loss. It may not be obvious on first reading of the statute, but neither section 354 nor section 356 is applicable unless the shareholder has also received stock in a corporation that is a party to the reorganization. Note, furthermore, that logic requires this result because otherwise the former Target shareholder would end up with basis in boot greater than its fair market value, a result generally reserved for the qualifying property in nonrecognition transactions.

This result also applies when a shareholder receives only those types of consideration that might not always be treated as boot, but nevertheless are not qualifying property. Thus, shareholders who receive only securities in exchange for their Target shares will also be able to recognize any loss in those shares, see Rev. Rul. 77-415, 1977-2 C.B. 311, obsoleted by T.D. 9182, 2005-1 C.B. 713, as will shareholders who receive only stock described in section 351(g) when not in exchange for section 351(g) stock, see §§ 356(e), 354(a)(2)(C).

Under regulations proposed in February 2009, shareholders who can show that they received only boot for a particular block of Target stock would also be entitled to recognize losses on that block of stock, even though they gave up other blocks of Target stock in exchange for Acquirer stock, so long as the designation of consideration to the loss block was economically reasonable and the overall effect of the transaction was not dividend equivalent. See Prop. Reg. § 1.354-1(d).

---

c. Basis of Stock Received by Shareholders

Section 358 governs the basis of the stock and any boot properties received by Target shareholders in a reorganization. Reg. section 1.358-2 provides rules under which the basis and holding periods of stock will be traced in section 354 transactions. Consider, for instance, a shareholder who receives 50 shares of Acquirer stock in exchange for 25 shares of Target stock, one block of 10 Target common shares with a $5 per share basis, and one block of 15 Target common shares with a $8 per share basis. The shareholder will be treated as having received 20 shares of Acquirer stock with a $2.50 per share basis, and 30 shares of Acquirer stock with a $4 per share basis.

Note that the approach used in this regulation is not the same as that ordinarily used in section 351 exchanges. In section 351 exchanges, boot is allocated to all of the property transferred, gain is recognized with respect to all gain property, and the basis taken in the stock received is the basis in the assets transferred plus gain recognized, allocated among all of the stock received to produce an average basis (except to the extent that the assets have a different holding period, in which case every share will, for a short period of time, be segmented to reflect the basis and holding period of the various assets). Suppose a section 351 transferor transferred three assets each worth $100 and with a basis of $50, $70, and $95, respectively, in exchange for class A stock worth $180, class B stock worth $90 and cash of $30. *See* Reg. § 1.358-2(b). $10 of cash would be allocated to each asset, producing $10, $10, and $5 of gain, for a total of $25 of recognized gain. The stock would be held with a total basis of $210 (50+70+95 plus 25 minus 30), allocated ratably to the stock received, so that the class A stock would be held with a basis of $140 and the class B stock with a basis of $70.

Reg. section 1.358-2 allows a different result when consideration is specified in a reorganization exchange. Suppose, for instance, that a Target shareholder held two blocks of Target common stock, each worth $100 and held with bases of $50 and $70, and one block of Target preferred stock also worth $100 held with a basis of $95. Suppose further that the terms of the exchange provided that the Target preferred stock was exchanged for Acquirer class B stock worth $70 and $30 in cash; the common stock was given up in exchange for Acquirer class A stock. Assuming that these terms are economically reasonable, the boot will be treated as received only with respect to the Target preferred stock, and thus only $5 of gain will be recognized, and the Acquirer class B stock will be held with a basis of $70 ($95 plus $5 minus $30). The Target shareholder will hold two distinct blocks of class A stock, one with a basis of $50 and one with a basis of $70.

If, on the other hand, there is no means of determining which consideration was given for which Target stock (or the specification is not "economically reasonable"), the composite approach used for section 351 transactions will apply. Reg. § 1.358-2(c), ex. 4. The result in the problem would be an allocation of cash of $10 to the Target preferred and to each block of the Target common, and therefore a total gain recognized of $25. The Acquirer class A and Acquirer class B stock would be similarly allocated, resulting in three distinct blocks of each class of Acquirer stock for the purposes of determining basis. The Acquirer class A stock (worth $60) and class B stock (worth $30) deemed received in exchange for the Target preferred stock would share basis of $90 of the Target preferred stock ($95 increased by the gain recognized of $5 and reduced by the $10 of boot allocated), resulting in basis of $60 and $30, respectively. The Acquirer class A stock (worth $60) and class B stock (worth $30) deemed received in exchange for the higher basis block of common stock would share basis of $70 ($70 increased by the gain recognized of $10 and reduced by the $10 of boot allocated), resulting in basis of $46.70 and $23.30. The Acquirer class A stock (worth $60) and class B stock (worth $30) deemed received in exchange for the lower basis block of Target common stock would share basis of $50 ($50 increased by the gain recognized of $10 and reduced by the $10 of boot allocated), resulting in basis of about $33.33 and $16.67.

16.1.2. Consequences to Corporations That are Parties to a Reorganization

a. Target

As in bootless reorganizations, Target's tax consequences are determined under section 361. Recall that most acquisitive reorganizations can be conceptualized as first, an exchange (involving a transfer of Target's assets in exchange for stock and other property of Acquirer), and second, the re-transfer of the stock and other property received by Target in a distribution to its shareholders. When boot is received from Acquirer, Target's tax consequences in this exchange are controlled by section 361(b). The distribution by Target of the Acquirer stock and boot as well as of any retained Target assets is governed by section 361(c).

Under section 361(b), Target will not recognize gain on the exchange of its assets for the consideration from Acquirer, so long as this other property (i.e., boot that is neither stock nor securities) is "distributed in pursuance of the plan of reorganization" either to shareholders or creditors. Section 361(b)(1)(B) provides, however, that Target will recognize gain on the exchange of its assets for Acquirer consideration if no such distribution is made. (It is unclear exactly when this language will come into play, since even partial dispositions of the property Target received from Acquirer may threaten the status of the transaction as a reorganization.)

Thus, although in most situations, we will not need to know Target's basis in any of the consideration it receives from Acquirer in exchange for its assets, there are situations in which we might. Target's basis in the Acquirer consideration received in the exchange will be determined under section 358. Its basis in the stock or securities of Acquirer will be an exchanged basis under section 358(a)(1). This is the familiar formula for nonrecognition transactions generally: Target's basis in its transferred assets, minus boot, plus any gain recognized by Target on the exchange. Its basis in the Acquirer boot will be a fair market value basis. §§ 358(a)(2), 358(f) (treating Acquirer boot as other property and not nonrecognition property for this purpose).

Target will not ordinarily recognize gain on the distribution to its shareholders in connection with the reorganization of most of what it has received from Acquirer. § 361(c)(1). Section 361(c)(2), however, limits this general rule of nonrecognition to "qualified property." "Qualified property" is defined to include Acquirer stock (or stock rights) and any form of Acquirer debt (including notes). See § 361(c)(2)(B(ii). It also includes those same interests when issued by Target itself. § 361(c)(2)(C)(i). Note that this "qualified property," which can be re-transferred by Target without gain (even if it has appreciated while Target has held it), includes some types of property that will trigger gain when received by Target's shareholders.

Consideration received by shareholders in the reorganization that is not qualified property can have its origin either in Acquirer or in the Target itself. If the consideration is an unwanted asset retained by Target that has appreciated while held by Target, Target will recognize any gain (but not loss) on the distribution to its shareholders under section 361(c). (As described under the section on allocation of boot, such transactions may require an examination of whether the distribution was in fact a separate redemption of Target shares held by the Target shareholder, rather than part of the reorganization.)

Similarly, Target will recognize any gain (but not loss) under section 361(c) on the distribution to its shareholders of boot property received from Acquirer that is not "qualified property." This provision will tax Target only on any appreciation in such boot properties during the period that Target held the properties, because Target will have acquired those properties in the exchange with a fair market value basis.

Thus, if there is some time between the receipt of the consideration by Target and Target's distribution in liquidation and the consideration that is not "qualified property" has appreciated during this time, Target will be subject to tax on that appreciation under section 361(c)(2). Target would similarly be subject to tax under that provision on the distribution to its shareholders of any of its retained properties, to the extent that those properties have a fair market value in excess of basis. Transfers to creditors of Acquirer stock (and the other types of interests in Acquirer that are defined as "qualified property"), even if appreciated, will not be subject to tax and will be treated as a distribution to Target shareholders under section 361(c)(3). Transfers to creditors of any boot that is not qualified property (or any Target retained assets) will trigger recognition.

Note here that section 361(c)(2) distinguishes among the types of consideration received from Acquirer that we would generally call "boot" (and that will be "boot" under section 356 when received by shareholders). It treats any "obligations" of Acquirer differently from other boot. Gain on these "obligations," because they are included in "qualified property," will not be triggered if re-transferred either to creditors or shareholders. Gain, but not losses, on any other boot transferred to shareholders will be recognized; while both gains and losses on other boot transferred to creditors will be recognized.

Do not be confused by the fact that section 361(b)(3) also contains language directing that transfers to creditors can be viewed as transfers to shareholders. That language only ensures that a transfer to a creditor does not trigger Target gain on the transfer of its assets in its exchange with Acquirer. Its scope (covering all boot) does not affect the more limited special treatment for transfers to creditors in section 361(c)(3).

b.   Acquirer

If the boot consideration has its source in Acquirer, Acquirer will recognize gain or loss on the boot transfer. Although section 1032 provides nonrecognition to Acquirer on exchanges of Acquirer stock for Target stock or assets, there is no general provision granting overall nonrecognition on the Acquirer side of a reorganization. Thus boot transfers by Acquirer will be taxable exchanges under section 1001. For example, see Reg. § 1.358-6(d)(3) Exs. (c) and (d).

The use of boot in a reorganization will not have an effect on Acquirer's basis in the acquired assets or stock, despite the language in section 362(b) that Acquirer's basis will be "increased in the amount of gain recognized to the transferor." This language does not allow Acquirer to increase its basis for gain recognized *by Target shareholders on boot that is distributed to them by Target*; it only allows an increase in Acquirer basis for any gain recognized by the Target corporation itself under section 361(b) on its exchange with Acquirer, since Target is the "transferor" in that exchange. Since Target will recognize gain only in the rare case when it fails to distribute all of the Acquirer consideration to its shareholders, Acquirer generally will get no basis bump up from use of boot.

16.2.   EXCHANGES OF SECURITIES IN REORGANIZATIONS

Although we have considered transactions in which securities were used by Acquirer in a reorganization (that is, statutory mergers under section 368(a)(1)(A)) and looked briefly at some of the definitional provisions of the primary section 368 acquisitive transaction provisions that anticipate their use (in particular, section 361 and section 358(a)(1) as it applies to Target), we have not considered the way such property is treated either as it is issued by Acquiror or as it is received by Target shareholders. As the term is used in the Internal Revenue Code, securities means only debt interests, not equity: it is generally applicable only to debt instruments and not certain forms of obligations such as trade payables and other short-term debt. See the sidebar on the definition of securities in Chapter 9.

For Target shareholders, sections 354(a) and 356(d) provide a special rule according to which securities issued by Target may be exchanged for securities issued by Acquirer (or, apparently, by any corporation that is a party to the reorganization) without the recognition of gain, so long as the principal amount of the securities received is not greater than the principal amount of the securities given up. If there is such an excess principal amount, it will be treated as boot to the extent of its fair market value. Under the regulations, warrants generally are treated as zero-principal amount securities. *See* Reg. § 1.354-1(e), 1.356-3(b).

Target's tax consequences on receipt of securities are determined as usual under section 361. It will have no gain or loss on the exchange of its properties for Acquirer stock and securities, so long as any boot received in the transaction is distributed. § 361(a) and (b). It will have no gain or loss on the distribution of those securities even if they appreciate in Target's hands, because they will be "qualified property." § 361(c).

Acquirer's consequences are less easy to summarize. As an issuer of securities in the transaction, it will have no immediate tax consequences. If the securities are issued at a discount, however, the normal original issue discount rules under section 1271 will apply. As a transferee of the securities of another corporation to which it is not related prior to the transaction, it will be treated as if it received any other asset. As a transferee of its own securities, or the securities of an issuer that is a related party, it will have cancellation of indebtedness interest, subject to the special rules in section 108.

16.3.   SECTION 351(g) NONQUALIFIED PREFERRED STOCK

Section 354(a)(2)(C) provides that nonqualified preferred stock as defined in section 351(g) will not be treated as stock or securities unless it is received in exchange for similarly defined nonqualified preferred stock of Target. This provision does not purport to make such stock "not stock" for purposes of continuity of interest or, if the nonqualified preferred is voting stock, for purposes of satisfying the voting stock requirements of the various reorganization types, but it does mean that shareholders who receive such stock will be treated as receiving boot consideration.

"Nonqualified preferred stock" is defined in section 351 (with respect to both section 351 transactions and section 354 transactions) as "stock which is limited and preferred as to dividends and does not participate in corporate growth to any significant extent" *and* which has any of the special redemption or dividend rights described in section 351(g)(2). In general, preferred stock will be nonqualified preferred stock if its terms are such that it is likely to be redeemed or if it bears a dividend that varies with an index.

Note that the American Jobs Creation Act of 2004 added the following sentence to section 351(g)(3)(A):

> Stock shall not be treated as participating in corporate growth to any significant extent unless there is a real and meaningful likelihood of the shareholder actually participating in the earnings and growth of the corporation.

16.4. WHEN WILL RECEIPT OF SOMETHING OTHER THAN ACQUIRER STOCK BE CONSIDERED BOOT IN A REORG?

What are the consequences when, in connection with a reorganization, Target shareholders acquire something other than the stock of Acquirer (or Acquirer Parent) in the exchange? There is no statutory limit on the amount of such non-stock consideration in some reorganization types (i.e., A reorgs and forward triangular mergers under section 368(a)(2)(D), which are subject only to the common-law continuity of shareholder interest requirement), whereas in others non-stock consideration is either impliedly forbidden (i.e., B reorgs under section 368(a)(1)(B)) or its receipt is subject to fairly strict limitations (i.e., C reorgs under section 368(a)(1)(C) in which if there is any boot, stock worth 80% of the value of all Target's assets must be used; and reverse triangular mergers under section 368(a)(2)(E), in which control must be acquired solely with stock).

The definitional rules described previously all assume the hardest part of what is frequently a difficult factual question: when will transactions in which Target shareholders receive something other than Acquirer stock be counted as part of the reorganization and thus run the risk of spoiling the reorganization because of the limitations on non-stock consideration? When the question is posed this way, it is easy to see that more is at stake than just the straightforward question whether boot can be received under the particular type of reorganization targeted. When, for instance, will a distribution by, or redemption of, Target result in Target no longer owning "substantially all" of its assets, so that a C reorg cannot be used? When will stock retired as a result of Target stock redemptions be treated as no longer outstanding for the purpose of calculating how much stock amounts to "control" for B reorgs and reverse triangular mergers? When will the substitution of the historic shareholders of Target, through sales to either third party non-participants (i.e., "strangers" to the reorg) or corporations that are parties to the reorg spoil the transaction altogether?

Why might Target shareholders end up with something other than Acquirer stock? There are various possible circumstances, but the circumstances themselves do not always provide much of a justification for distinguishing among them in order to determine tax consequences. There are two obvious starting points that might seem to make a difference: either the Target shareholders or Acquirer may have reservations about proceeding with the transaction if all historic shareholders will receive only Acquirer stock.

Starting with Target shareholders, why might they all not end up with Acquirer stock? Some shareholders of a publicly held Target will often want to unload their Target stock (or will be induced to do so by those seeking to buy it) in anticipation of an acquisition of Target. Those shareholders who sell into the market will receive cash. In other situations, some Target shareholders may have rights to be redeemed that are triggered by events leading up to a reorganization. Others may exercise, or threaten to exercise, their dissenter's rights because they think that Acquirer is not offering a fair price. Still others may not object to the price at the current relative prices of Acquirer and Target stock, but may not want to run the risk of taking only Acquirer stock as consideration. Rarely, there may be an asset held by Target that is of such special value to a Target shareholder that the easiest way to account for its value is simply to transfer it to this shareholder. Still more rarely, Target shareholders may insist that a replacement for an asset held by Target and about to be transferred to Acquirer be bought by Acquirer and transferred to Target shareholders.

Acquirer's demands may also result in Target shareholders receiving something other than stock. Acquirer may want Target to shed itself of cash (and, perhaps not so incidentally, of earnings and profits) before the transaction, perhaps to facilitate its financing. Acquirer may simply not want some of the specific assets of Target, and Target shareholders who object to the sale of these assets may end up receiving them in redemption of a part of their interest.

Given these multiple rationales for some non-stock consideration being trans-ferred to Target shareholders, there have been a variety of different rulings covering non-stock transactions, with different outcomes depending upon which particular condition in which particular reorg pattern was at stake. In some situations, such receipts could be ignored because they were the result of a transaction that was not considered to be part of the reorganization itself. For instance, the Service has always been relatively generous in allowing transactions that take place prior to B reorgs to be considered separate from the B reorg itself, in order to allow dissenters to be paid off. But in other contexts, similar connections between pre-reorganization transactions and the reorg itself have led to treatment as an integrated transaction.

Recent announced rulings and regulatory changes have rationalized much of this doctrine. Most significant is the standard embedded in Reg. section 1.368-1(e)(1)(ii). This regulation provides that continuity "is not preserved to the extent that consideration received prior to a potential reorganization, either in a redemption of the target corporation stock, or in a distribution with respect to the target corporation stock, is treated as other property or money received in the exchange for the purposes of section 356, or would be so treated if the target shareholder also had received stock of the issuing corporation in exchange for stock owned by the shareholder in the target corporation." The negative implication of this statement is that only if the non-stock consideration received by Target shareholders is considered boot subject to section 356 will the Target stock that they once held be counted for continuity purposes.

The examples in the regulations make it clear that the primary criterion at play here is the source of the consideration. In example 9, Target redeemed one of its two shareholders entirely for cash and later Acquirer acquired all of the outstanding Target stock from the remaining shareholder in a B reorg. Reg. § 1.368-1(e)(7), Ex. 9. The example states that Acquirer provided none of the funds for the redemption. Even without specifying how large the interest of the redeemed shareholder was, the example concludes that continuity of interest will be tested only by reference to the consideration used by Acquirer in the exchange with the "remaining" shareholder. Because the redemption in example 9 is explicitly stated to have been triggered by the contemplated B reorg yet even so the distribution of Target assets was treated as a separate transaction from the reorganization, it appears that the Service is not likely to use the step transaction doctrine to treat non-stock assets received by Target shareholders as reorganization "boot" subject to section 356 unless the assets can be traced to Acquirer.

In similar fashion, the regulation dealing with reverse subsidiary mergers states that "stock in the surviving corporation [Target] which is surrendered in the transaction . . . in exchange for consideration furnished by the surviving corporation (and not by the controlling corporation or the merged corporation) is considered not to be outstanding immediately before the transaction" for purposes of the control requirement. Reg. section 1.368-2(j)(3)(i). Example 2 illustrates this rule, providing that dissenters' stock will be removed from the denominator for the purpose of determining whether "control" has been acquired when Target (and not Acquirer or Acquirer subsidiary) furnishes the consideration. Reg. § 1.368-2(j)(6), Ex. 2. Similarly, Example 3 of the same regulation states that Target's redemption of preferred stock will remove it from the calculation of "control" for the same purposes (though Target could still fail the "substantially all" test because of the consideration used). Reg. § 1.368-2(j)(6), Ex. 3.

There is some tension between the conclusion that (i) consideration used to redeem Target shareholders will be considered in determining whether a requirement of the reverse merger has been satisfied so that reorg treatment is available, and the further indication that (ii) that same consideration will apparently not be treated as "boot" received in the reorg but rather as a distribution in redemption separate from the reorg. Perhaps the best way to view this apparent contradictory treatment of the consideration is that it serves as a limitation on the amount of Target shareholder stock that can be redeemed separately from the C or reverse merger reorganization, and on the amount of unwanted Target assets that can be withdrawn from the transfer to Acquirer.

The rule announced in Reg. section 1.368-1(e)(1), which essentially eliminates the importance of "historic" shareholders, accords with a number of precedents. The Service had long held, for instance, that there would be no continuity problem in situations in which historic shareholders were eliminated well prior to the reorganization transaction itself. This approach allowed B reorgs to be conducted through tender offers which triggered substantial market sales in the days leading up to the reorganization transaction. The question is whether the disposition by the historic shareholders should be viewed as part of the reorganization. On this point, the Service seems to have borrowed from its longstanding precedent that redemption of some dissenting shareholders by Target prior to a B reorg will not spoil the B reorg, even though Acquirer's payment of the same amount as consideration to those shareholders in the reorganization would have prevented nonrecognition treatment for all Target shareholders.

In any of these cases in which historic shareholders' disposition of Target stock is treated as separate from the reorganization because the value has been provided by Target, the tax consequences of the redemption will be determined under section 302. Similarly, a distribution with respect to stock that occurs in a transaction that is not a part of a reorganization will be taxed under section 301.

PRACTICE PROBLEMS

1.   In a statutory merger of Corp X into Corp Y that met the definitions of a transaction described in section 368(a)(1)(A) and thus was generally granted nonrecognition, Corp X shareholder A received 100 shares of Corp Y common stock worth $500 and $30 cash. By how much was A's income (disregarding character as capital or ordinary) increased?

(a) $530.

(b) $30.

(c)   None.

(d)   Insufficient information provided.

2.   In a statutory merger of Corp X into Corp Y that satisfied the requirements of a transaction described in section 368(a)(1)(A) and thus was generally granted nonrecognition, Corp Y paid all of the legal, accounting and appraisal fees of Corp X, amounting to $50,000. Shareholder A owned 20% of Corp X before the transaction, and 5% of the combined Corp Y after the transaction, an interest which is worth about $1,000,000 both before and after. Another 20% shareholder of Corp X received only cash, about $1,000,000. How much boot must shareholder A take into account in reporting the consequences of this transaction for federal income tax purposes?

(a) $10,000 (20% of $50,000).

(b) $2,500 (5% of $50,000).

(c) $12,500 (25% of $50,000).

(d)   Probably none.

3.   Shareholder B has owned 50% of the stock of Target since it was first incorporated, for which he contributed rights to computer software in which he had no basis. Target has experienced nothing but operating losses since then. Target merged with Acquirer Corp, and B and his fellow shareholder both received 100 shares of Acquirer stock (somewhat optimistically valued at $200,000) and $10,000 in cash. Acquirer Corp was incorporated a little more than a year ago, and has done

nothing since except make acquisitions like this one. What will be the result of the cash received for tax purposes?

(a) $10,000 of gain.

(b) $10,000 of dividend.

(c) Insufficient information: we need to know how much of Acquirer B owns after the transaction.

4. Target merged into Acquirer in a transaction that qualified as a merger described in section 368(a)(1)(A). C held stock of Target with a basis of $10,000 and bonds of Target with a face amount (and fair market value) of $10,000 and a basis of $10,000. C received in the transaction Acquirer stock worth $130,000 and bonds with a face amount (and fair market value) of $20,000. What is the amount of boot received by C in this transaction?

(a) $20,000.

(b) $10,000.

(c) $50,000.

(d) None.

5. In a transaction that qualified as a reorganization under section 368(a)(1)(A), former Target shareholder A received Acquirer stock worth $1,000,000 and a parcel of Target's land worth $1,000,000 that was unwanted by Acquirer and which Target had held with a basis of $100,000. What is the amount of boot received by A?

(a) $100,000.

(b) $2,000,000.

(c) $1,000,000.

(d) None.

6. In question 5 above, what if the land had been subject to a $600,000 mortgage?

(a) $1,000,000.

(b) $400,000.

(c) Insufficient information.

(d) None.

DISCUSSION PROBLEMS

1. Sam, Sal, and Syd are equal shareholders in Target Co, which is about to be merged into Bigger Co. Target Co is worth $9 million, and Bigger Co is worth $15 million. Target Co has more than $4 million in earnings and profits; Bigger Co has more than $6 million. Sam, Sal, and Syd are all willing to take some of the consideration they receive in Bigger Co stock, but not all of it. Sam and Sal are original shareholders of Target and hold their stock with negligible basis. Syd purchased his Target stock two years ago for $2 million. What are the tax results to

the Target shareholders of the following choices of consideration:

(a)   The Target shareholders each receive $2 million in Bigger Co stock and cash of $1 million.

(b)   The Target shareholders each receive $2.5 million in Bigger Co stock and cash of $500,000.

(c)   Sam owns two fifths (40%) of the Bigger Co stock prior to the reorganization. He receives $1 million in Bigger Co stock and cash of $2 million. The other Target shareholders each receive $2 million in Bigger Co stock and cash of $1 million.

(d)   As in part a, except that Target and Acquirer each had earnings and profits of only $1 million.

(e)   As in part a, except that the Target shareholders had agreed among themselves to cause Target to distribute a dividend of $500,000 to each of them, even before negotiations with Bigger Co began.

(f)   As in part b, except that the non-stock consideration received from Bigger is a vacation condo, to replace the one adjacent to the business premises of Target.

(g)   As in part b, except that the non-stock consideration is the vacation condo owned by Target.

(h)   As in part b, except that the non-stock consideration is the right to use the vacation condo owned by Target and acquired by Bigger in the transaction, for one month each year for the next 50 years.

2.   Al owns 1000 shares of Target common stock. He purchased 500 shares of common for $10 a share in 1980 and 500 for $1000 share in 1996. In a statutory merger that is a transaction described in section 368(a)(1)(A), Al receives 3000 shares of Public Co common stock, worth $600,000.

(a)   What is his basis in the Public Co stock he receives?

(b)   What if, instead of 3000 shares of Public Co stock, Al had received 2000 shares of stock (worth $400,000) and $200,000 in cash?

(c)   What if the block of stock purchased in 1996 were preferred stock, also worth $600 per share at the time of the merger, and Al received 1500 shares of Public Co stock (worth $300,000) in exchange for the 1980 common block and $300,000 in cash for the 1996 preferred block?

(d)   What if the block of stock purchased in 1996 were preferred stock, also worth $600 per share at the time of the merger, and Al received 1500 shares of Public Co stock (worth $300,000) in exchange for the 1980 common block and $300,000 worth of newly issued Public Co preferred in exchange for his Target preferred block?

3.   Jed is a shareholder and creditor of Target. He holds Target bonds with a face amount of $5 million and a fair market value of $7 million, and he has a very low basis in his Target stock. Target is about to be merged into Solid Co. Jed is willing

to renegotiate his debt so that he holds bonds of Solid Co, but he does not want to recognize gain on either his stock or his bonds. Can this be accomplished?

Chapter 17

TRANSFERS OF STOCK: "B REORGS"

Statutes and Regulations	IRC § 368(a)(1)(B)
	Reg. § 1.368-2(c)
Other Primary Authorities	Chapman v. Commissioner, 618 F.2d 856
	(1st Cir. 1980)
	Rev. Rul. 72-354, 1972-2 C.B. 216
	Rev. Rul. 67-448, 1967-2 C.B. 144
	Rev. Rul. 79-4, 1979-1 C.B 150
	Rev. Rul. 79-89, 1979-1 C.B.152

17.1. GENERAL

Transfers of stock of Target in exchange for voting stock of Acquirer will qualify under section 368(a)(1)(B) as a reorganization as long as Acquirer directly owns 80% of Target (i.e., 80% of all voting stock and of each class of non-voting stock) after the transaction. The voting stock need not be common stock (voting preferred stock in Acquirer would suffice), but it must be stock. Only voting stock of Acquirer itself, and not its parent, may be used.

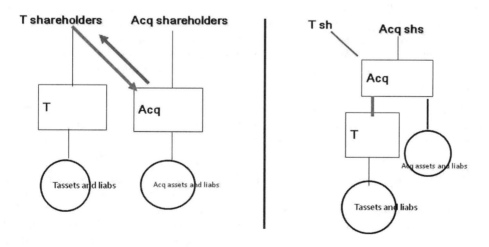

Type B Reorganization – voting stock for stock

No boot property whatsoever, including non-voting stock of Acquirer, is allowed in a B reorg. Consequently, issues arise regarding simultaneous or apparently connected transactions in which Target shareholders receive something other than Acquirer stock for their Target stock. Under various rulings, it is clear that such transactions will be permissible so long as they are not in substance payment by Acquirer of boot to Target shareholders. Some Target shareholders may therefore be redeemed before the transaction. Rev. Rul. 55-440, 1955-2 C.B. 226; *cf.* Reg. § 1.368-1(e)(8) ex. 9. They may also be redeemed through the exercise of dissenters' rights, if the value received by these shareholders is not paid by Acquirer. Rev. Rul. 66-365, 1966-2 C.B. 116. Cash in lieu of fractional shares will not jeopardize the B reorg, so long as it is not negotiated as consideration for the deal; it will be treated as a separate section 302 redemption. Rev. Rul. 66-365, 1966-2 C.B. 116. Finally, an exchange of debt securities (including warrants) that is part of the same plan is treated as a separate exchange from the stock exchange and will also be tax-free to the Target debtholders under section 354, except to the extent there is excess principal received. Rev. Rul. 98-10, 1998-1 C.B. 643.

Acquirer may pay some of the costs of the reorganization transaction that might be considered Target's obligations without being treated as providing non-stock consideration for Target shares, but care must be taken not to provide too much benefit to Target shareholders through such expenditures or condition the exchange of stock on the ancillary benefits being provided by Acquirer to Target shareholders. *Compare* Rev. Rul. 73-54, 1973-1 C.B. 187 (permitting Acquirer to pay directly or assume Target's liabilities for Target's "bona fide reorganization expenses" but not for expenses for shareholder investment planning advice or other legal and accounting expenses of Target shareholders), *and* Rev. Rul. 79-89, 1979-1 C.B. 152 (permitting Acquirer to assume or pay Target debt guaranteed by Target shareholders where the payment was not a condition of the exchange and not part of the consideration for the shareholders' stock), *with* Rev. Rul. 79-4, 1979-1 C.B. 150 (finding B reorg requirements failed when, as a condition for the exchange of stock, Acquirer pays Target debt that is treated as a debt of its guarantor-shareholder). Care must similarly be taken in other situations to ensure that Acquirer is not treated as providing benefits that in fact constitute additional consideration for stock. Loans made by Acquirer to a Target shareholder, covenants not to compete, and purchases of assets owned by a Target shareholders might all be subject to close scrutiny.

As is the case in connection with other reorganizations, there is no requirement that Target shareholders remain Acquirer shareholders. They are free to sell the Acquirer stock they receive into the market. A redemption by Acquirer, on the other hand, is susceptible to scrutiny under the step transaction doctrine.

Note that in the ordinary B reorg, a block of stock constituting control does not need to be acquired in a single transaction or within a certain time frame. The only requirement is that Acquirer have control after the transactions for which nonrecognition is sought. Prior ownership by Acquirer of some Target stock will therefore not necessarily disqualify the transaction for nonrecognition. Reg. § 1.368-2(c). Care must be taken in such "creeping" B reorgs, however, that there be no possibility that an earlier acquisition of Target stock for consideration other than voting stock would be integrated with the current transaction and considered part of the plan of reorganization. So-called "old 'n cold" purchases will not spoil the B reorg, but purchases close in time to the reorganization are likely to be stepped together with the stock-for-stock exchange. Furthermore, the Target stock need not be acquired in a single, simultaneous stock-for-stock transaction. Rather, a series of stock-for-stock exchanges over a relatively short period of time (12 months is mentioned in the regulations) can be stepped together so that the stock held after the series of exchanges is tested for the "control immediately after" requirement. Reg. § 1.368–2(c) (fifth senence). This permits Acquirer to acquire Target stock through a tender offer that extends over a typical period of six months or so.

17.2.   TRANSFERS OF TARGET STOCK (AND ASSETS) SUBSEQUENT TO THE REORGANIZATION

Section 368(a)(2)(C) expressly permits the Acquirer in a B reorg to "drop down" the stock received to a corporation "controlled by" it. This language is a partial legislative reversal of the Supreme Court's decision in *Helvering v. Bashford*, 302 U.S. 454 (1938).

The legislative language could be read as a requirement that only permits a drop down from Acquirer to a subsidiary directly controlled, under section 368(c), by Acquirer, with the result that continuity that is any more "remote" is not good enough. Over time, however, the Service has developed a more expansive administrative position regarding transfers of the stock (or assets) acquired in reorganizations. The regulations now clearly provide that a drop may be down more than one tier, so that the issuing corporation (i.e., the original acquiring corporation) can become a grand-parent or even a great-great-grandparent to the newly acquired Target. *See* Reg. § 1.368-1(d) (clarifying that there is no continuity of business enterprise problem with such a transfer); Reg. § 1.368-2(f), (k) (providing that the reorganization definitions will still be considered satisfied even if these additional steps are taken).

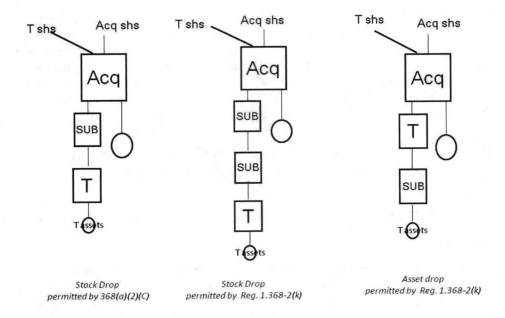

Permitted drops after B reorg

The regulations also describe expanded circumstances in which distributions (sometimes called "push-ups") and other transfers of stock or assets acquired in reorganizations will not threaten the status of the overall transaction as a reorganization. In general, such transfers will be permitted so long as they are made to corporations closely related to the Acquiring corporation and do not result in the actual or de facto liquidation of the Target corporation. (These and other alterations of the basic reorganization patterns are considered more fully in the discussion of triangular mergers.)

17.3.   USE OF PARENT STOCK

The parenthetical in section 368(a)(1)(B) allows a "triangular" B reorg in which Target stock is transferred to a corporation that is controlled by the corporation the stock of which is used as consideration. In plainer terms, Target stock can be transferred to a newly created subsidiary of Acquirer without defeating the reorganization. This parenthetical was made necessary by the decision in *Groman v. Commissioner*, 302 U.S. 82 (1937), in which the Court held that parent stock did not count as stock of a "party to the reorganization." Note that the stock of only one corporation may be used. Reg. § 1.368-2(c).

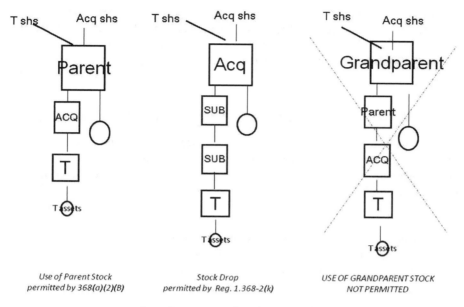

Grandparent stock not permitted

The statute does not allow the transfer of Target stock to a corporation that is not directly owned by Acquirer. Only a controlling parent's stock, not "grandparent" stock, may be used. Many of the adverse consequences of this limitation are mitigated, however, by the ability of Acquirer to "drop" the Target stock into Acquirer subsidiaries or to distribute Target stock. § 368(a)(2)(C); Reg. § 1.368-2(k).

Nor does the statute allow the use of the stock of both Acquirer Parent and Acquirer Sub. Since one or the other will be treated as boot and no boot is allowed in a B reorg, the use of both types of stock will spoil the B reorg. *See* Reg. § 1.368-2(c).

17.4. EFFECT OF PRIOR OWNERSHIP OF TARGET STOCK BY ACQUIRER

The statutory test for a B reorg requires only that Acquirer have control immediately after the transaction: it does not require that Acquirer *acquire* control *in* the transaction. Thus, Acquirer can structure an acquisition of a small minority interest in a corporation it already controls as a B reorg, permitting those minority shareholders to exchange their stock in Target for Acquirer stock in a nonrecognition transaction. *See* Reg. § 1.368-2(c).

Acquirer may not, however, buy some Target stock with cash, and then proceed to acquire other Target stock using its stock as consideration under circumstances in which the two steps will be treated as part of the same overall transaction. If a purported B reorg takes place shortly after a cash purchase, it is likely that the Service will assert that the two transactions should be stepped together, unless Acquirer unconditionally divests itself of the tainted Target stock prior to the reorganization — e.g., through an unconditional sale to a third party. Rev. Rul. 72-354, 1972-2 C.B. 216 (ruling that a "cleansing" sale would be permissible, as was confirmed in *Chapman v. Commissioner*, 618 F.2d 856 (1st Cir. 1980), although in that case Acquirer's right to repurchase the stock disposed of prevented this treatment).

17.5.   RECASTING TRANSACTIONS AS B REORG

In Rev. Rul. 67-448, 1967-2 C.B. 144, the Service held that if Acquirer created a transitory subsidiary that merged into Target in a transaction in which Target shareholders received only Acquirer stock, the transaction would be treated as a good B reorg. So long as the subsidiary was truly "transitory" — that is, it had no historical tax attributes and was created solely as a vehicle for the anticipated transactions, its temporary existence could be ignored. The transaction was characterized by reference solely to its starting point (Target shareholders owning Target stock) and its ending point (Target shareholders holding Acquirer stock and Acquirer owning Target stock), and thus as a B reorg.

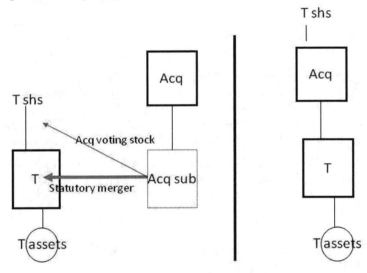

Rev. Rul. 67-448

Merger of a newly created Acq sub *into* T with T surviving and with Acq stock as consideration
Recast as exchange of T stock between T shs and Acq effected through merger

This ruling is of less interest than it was when first announced, since much of the territory it covers is now also covered by section 368(a)(2)(E), which sets for the requirements for the nontaxable reverse subsidiary merger. But statutory restrictions on the reverse subsidiary merger, including the requirement that control be acquired in the reorganization transaction, mean that Rev. Rul. 67-448 and the use of the transitory subsidiary as an acquisition vehicle is not entirely dead letter.

17.6.   BUSINESS CONSIDERATIONS IN B REORGS

The business considerations for B reorgs stem directly from the continuing existence of Target as an intact corporation. Because Target's assets are not transferred to Acquirer, Acquirer is not directly exposed to Target's liabilities. This is especially significant if Target's business or assets is of a type that may have hidden liabilities, such as environmental liabilities. Transaction costs are generally reduced, because the parties need not negotiate an asset-by-asset price allocation and Target's debt can survive the transaction without renegotiation. Similarly, unless Target is subject to specific contractual terms to the contrary, the stock acquisition will not affect its non-assignable contracts, franchises, government permits, and the like.

Ordinarily only Target's shareholders need to approve the transaction, if there is prior authorization for the issuance of Acquirer stock sufficient for the transaction.

17.7.   CONSEQUENCES TO TARGET SHAREHOLDERS AND TARGET

Target shareholders have exchanged their Target stock solely for Acquirer voting stock. This exchange will be afforded nonrecognition under section 354(a). They will hold their Acquirer stock with an exchanged basis determined under section 358 — that is, their basis in their Acquirer stock will be the same as their basis in their Target stock.

Although several classes of Acquirer voting stock — both preferred and common — can be used, many of the questions about allocation of boot and multiple classes of stock will not arise in B reorgs because no boot is allowed. Basis in blocks of stock, however, will be traced under Reg. § 1.358-2(a). Because the transaction involves the transfer of Target's stock by its shareholders, not the transfer of its assets, Target will continue to hold its assets with its old basis unchanged. Section 382 will apply, however, to limit the use of its losses.

The Practice Problems and the Discussion Problems relating to B Reorganizations can be found at the end of Chapter 18.

Chapter 18

TRANSFERS OF ASSETS BY TARGET AND RECEIPT OF ACQUIRER STOCK BY TARGET SHAREHOLDERS: "C REORGS"

Statutes and Regulations	IRC §§ 368(a)(1)(C); 368(a)(2)(G)
	Reg. § 1.368-2(d)
Other Primary Authorities	Rev. Rul. 57-518, 1957-2 C.B. 253
	Rev. Rul. 67-274, 1967-2 C.B. 141
	Rev. Rul. 67-326, 1967-2 C.B. 143
	Rev. Rul. 73-54, 1973-1 C.B. 187
	PLR 200747006
	Rev. Proc. 89-50, 1989-2 C.B. 631

"C reorgs," or transfers of Target assets for Acquirer stock, were first included in the statute when the corporate law in many states did not afford an easy route for a statutory merger. These transactions therefore are sometimes referred to as "practical mergers." Indeed, a practical merger might well have been used to allow a corporation subject to relatively restrictive corporate law to effect a move to a state with more flexible rules for transactions like mergers. A new corporate entity would be created in the more flexible state, the assets of the old corporation would be transferred to the new entity, and the stock of the new corporation would be distributed to the shareholders.

18.1. STATUS AS A C REORGANIZATION

Section 368(a)(1)(C) grants reorganization status to "the acquisition by one corporation, in exchange . . . for . . . its voting stock . . . of substantially all of the properties of another corporation." Although this may seem as if it is a complete definition, and no cross-reference to other requirements is provided in subsection (a)(1)(C), there is an additional statutory limitation in section 368(a)(2)(G). A transaction will not satisfy the "C reorg" definition unless Target distributes all of its assets — both those received from Acquirer and those it did not transfer to Acquirer — pursuant to the plan of reorganization. For this purpose, transfers to creditors in liquidation will be treated as if they were pursuant to the plan of reorganization. The statute thus contemplates that Acquirer will own the bulk of the assets of Target after the completion of the reorganization, and Target will go out of existence.

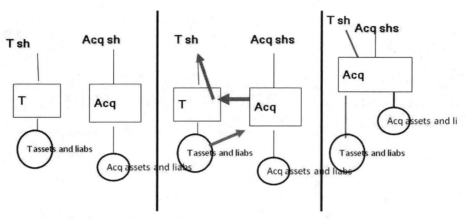

**Type C Reorganization – Voting stock for assets
Practical Merger**

The statute grants authority for government waiver of this liquidation requirement, but it is not clear what circumstances merit such a waiver. The provision furthers the congressional purpose that C reorgs not be divisive. *See* Rev. Rul. 88-48, 1988-1 C.B. 117 (describing the addition of the provision as furthering the congressional aim of preventing divisive use of C reorganizations). When the provision was added to the statute, the General Explanation for the 1984 Act (at 190) stated that waivers should be granted only if the distribution would result in "substantial hardship," and that transactions taking place under a waiver were to be treated for tax purposes for both Target and its shareholders as though the undistributed assets had been distributed and then recontributed to the capital of a new corporation. Rev. Proc. 89-50, 1989-2 C.B. 631, describes one situation when waiver might apply — when the corporate charter itself has value. Under the guidance, the shell corporation must be sold within 12 months after the transfer of its assets to Acquirer, and the shareholders must be treated as if they had in fact received the value inherent in the charter and any other assets that may have been retained to meet any state minimum capital requirement.

18.1.1. Substantially All

For a valid C reorg, the transfer must be of "substantially all of the assets" of Target. In many cases, there may be particular Target assets that Acquirer does not wish to acquire (for instance, a manufacturing facility with environmental problems) or some Target shareholders may insist on distributions of particular Target assets in redemption of their stock in connection with the reorganization, so that the question of whether Target has transferred substantially all of its assets becomes pivotal for qualification as a C reorg. There is only a smattering of case authority or other administrative guidance interpreting this phrase in the context of C reorgs.

In Rev. Proc. 77-37, 1977-2 C.B. 568, the Service provided a bright-line safe harbor based on the percentage of the gross and net value of Target transferred, providing that a transfer of 70% of Target's gross asset value and 90% of Target's net asset value (that is, asset value less liabilities) is adequate. Under this ruling guideline, a corporation with assets of $10 million subject to debt of $5.5 million must transfer at least $7 million gross value of its assets and $4 million worth of net assets. Accordingly, if only $7 million of gross assets were transferred, no more than $3 million of Target debt could be assumed. Now that any assets retained by Target must be distributed to Target shareholders, there appears to be less reason for tax administrators to be concerned about the "substantially all" requirement — any appreciation in retained assets will be subject to tax at the corporate level on the distribution by Target under section 361(c) and the assets will be treated as boot received by the Target shareholders. But there is no authority clearly indicating that "substantially all" will not be read to require more.

Note that the step transaction doctrine may also apply to treat assets that Target disposes of prior to the transfer of assets to Acquirer as part of the denominator in determining what percentage of Target's assets have been transferred to Acquirer. The test will be applied no later than at the time the reorganization plan was put into place, making it harder to strip a Target corporation of substantial unwanted assets and still qualify for C reorg treatment. *Compare* Helvering v. Elkhorn Coal Co., 95 F. 2d 732 (4th Cir. 1937) (finding that a tax-free spin of unwanted assets followed by a purported C reorg of the distributing corporation failed the substantially all test), *with* Rev. Rul. 2003-79, 2003-2 C.B. 80 (ruling that the tax-free spin of wanted assets followed by a C reorg of the newly formed controlled corporation holding those assets will satisfy the substantially all requirement as to the controlled corporation, even though it holds only half of the assets of the distributing corporation).

Key Authorities on "Substantially All"

• *Rev. Proc. 77-37, 1977-2 C.B. 568;*

• *Rev. Rul. 57-518, 1957-2 C.B. 253 (no particular percentage is controlling, but rather depends on nature of properties retained, purpose of retention, and amount; ruling permitted retention of about 30% of assets (cash, receivables, 3% of inventory) in about same amount as liabilities);*

• *Rev. Rul. 88-48, 1988-1 C.B. 117 (sale of 50% of assets, amounting to a distinct business, followed by transfer of proceeds and remaining business adequate);*

• *PLR 7952186 (interpreting section 368(a)(1)(D), assets used to redeem Target shareholders prior to redemption included);*

• *PLR 7952119 (interpreting section 368(a)(1)(D), sales prior to transfer and sales of up to 2% net value after transfer not defeat "substantially all");*

• *Rev. Rul. 78-47, 1978-1 C.B. 113 (in "downstream" transfer of assets to corporation in which transferor held minority interest, transfer of only operating assets satisfied "substantially all");*

• *Rev. Rul. 70-240, 1970-1 C.B. 81 (interpreting section 368(a)(1)(D), continuation by transferee of operating business sufficient despite sale of operating assets and distribution of liquid assets);*

• *Arctic Ice Machine Co. v. Commissioner, 23 B.T.A. 1223 (1931) (interpreting the 1926 Act, 68% of net worth not sufficient when transferor purported to transfer but immediately repurchased its receivables);*

• Commissioner v. First Nat'l Bank, *104 F. 2d 865 (3d Cir. 1939) (interpreting the 1928 Act, 86% of net worth, constituting all operating assets, treated as substantially all, although reorganization status denied for lack of continuity of interest);*

• Schuh Trading Co. v. Commissioner, *95 F.2d 404 (7th Cir. 1938) (interpreting the 1928 Act, include goodwill transferred even when not shown on transferor's books or otherwise separately identified);*

• Moffatt v. Commissioner, *363 F.2d 262 (9th Cir. 1966), cert. denied, 386 U.S. 1016 (1967) (interpreting section 368(a)(1)(D), no particular percentage; following Rev. Rul. 57-518; include employees if valuable asset);*

• Smothers v. United States, *642 F. 2d 894 (5th Cir. 1981) (interpreting section 368(a)(1)(D), necessary operating assets is benchmark for substantially all test; operating assets were only 15% but sufficient);*

• Smith v. Commissioner, *34 B.T.A. 702, nonacq. C. B. XV-2, 46 (1936)* nonacq withdrawn, *1957-2 C.B. 7 253 referenced in Rev. Rul. 57-518 (none of assets retained, which were cash and receivables, were for operating business or for distributions to shareholders);*

• James Armour, Inc. v. Commissioner, *43 T.C. 295 (1964) (66% of assets OK for section 354(b)(1)(B), where all operating assets transferred and only cash and receivables retained);*

• Gross v. Commissioner, *88 F.2d 567 (5th Cir. 1937) (interpreting the 1926 Act, substantially all need not include surplus cash not needed in business that could have been distributed as cash dividend whether predecessor of subsection 368(C) or (D) applied);*

• Pillar Rock Packing Co. v. Commissioner, *90 F.2d 949 (9th Cir. 1937) (retention of 32% of value of company, in form of receivables, fails requirements);*

• Rev. Rul. 74-457, *1974-2 C.B. 122 (cash used to pay regular cash dividend will not be counted in the denominator for the substantially all calculation, unless the distribution occurs after the transfer of the other assets);*

• Rev. Rul. 2003-79, *2003-2 C.B. 80 (corporation newly separated in a 368(a)(1)(D)/ 355 transaction has "substantially all its assets" for purposes of an unrelated later C reorg); and*

• PLR 200621011 *(regular redemptions of a mutual fund are disregarded in the substantially-all analysis, but an extraordinary dividend of 10% paid to a 50% shareholder is considered).*

18.1.2. Boot in a C Reorg

A quick reading of the statute suggests that Acquirer must use as consideration "solely" its own voting stock. The basic provision is modified by the "boot relaxation" rule of section 368(a)(2)(B), which permits some non-stock consideration to be used in a C reorg. The boot relaxation rule is fairly stringent, however, in that it essentially establishes a different standard for continuity of interest when there is boot in a C reorg. Voting stock of Acquirer must be used to acquire at least 80% of the total value of Target. When there is other non-stock consideration, assumed liabilities are counted as part of the consideration in this calculation. Thus, the boot and liabilities assumed, together with any Target assets not transferred to Acquirer (which are also treated as boot paid to the shareholders as part of the reorganization) cannot amount to more than 20% of the fair market value of all of Target's assets. Given the extent to which assets are likely to be encumbered by liabilities in the course of Target's general operations, this "boot relaxation" rule is often of little use in structuring acquisitions. Any liabilities assumed, or any properties that are retained by Target to pay creditors or held back to be distributed to Target shareholders, reduce the amount of cash boot that can be paid by Acquirer.

18.1.3.   Liability Assumption When There is No Boot

What if there is no consideration other than the stock of Acquirer and the assumption of Target liabilities by Acquirer? Does the assumption of liabilities count as consideration paid by Acquirer? In *United States v. Hendler*, 303 U.S. 564 (1938), the government won its argument that liability assumptions in connection with reorganizations, just like liability assumptions in any other asset transfers, should count as consideration received by the transferor whose debt is relieved. As soon as the ink was dry on the court's opinion (and maybe before), the government rued its victory: any prior reorganization involving an asset and liability transfer for which only stock could be used would, under this decision, now be treated as a taxable transaction. If this rule were applied to previously completed transactions, this government victory could have resulted in a stepped up basis for both shareholders and corporations, even if the statute of limitations had passed for reporting gain. Congress therefore undid the effect of the *Hendler* decision with the enactment of section 357(a), which provides that liabilities generally do not count as boot in either section 351 transactions or section 368 reorganizations.

The relationship between this general rule disregarding liabilities and the boot relaxation rule in C reorgs is clarified by additional language in both the definitional and boot relaxation provisions. The C reorg definition indicates that assumed liabilities will be disregarded "in determining whether the exchange is solely for stock." § 368(a)(1)(C). If there is any other non-stock consideration, however, the boot relaxation rule applies. Solely for its calculations, it treats the assumed liabilities as "money paid for the property" of Target. § 368(a)(2)(B).

18.2.   TAX CONSEQUENCES

18.2.1.   Consequences to Target

Because Target actually transfers its assets, the language of section 361 fits comfortably with what has actually happened in the transaction. It anticipates two transfers of assets that must be accounted for: (i) Target's exchange with Acquirer, in which it transfers its assets (and any liabilities) in exchange for Acquirer stock (and any boot) and (ii) Target's distribution to its shareholders, in which it transfers the consideration that it receives from Acquirer, and any retained Target assets, to its shareholders.

Section 361(a) governs the exchange of Target's assets for Acquirer stock. It provides, as expected, that Target will recognize no gain or loss when the consideration is solely Acquirer stock. It also provides nonrecognition to Target on the receipt of Acquirer securities.

Section 361(b) covers Target-Acquirer exchanges in which Target also receives non-stock, non-security boot from Acquirer. It provides that such boot will not trigger gain to Target on the exchange so long as it is distributed to shareholders or, as allowed by section 361(b)(3), to creditors.

Section 361(b)(1)(B) provides that if the boot is not so distributed to shareholders or creditors, its receipt will trigger Target's recognition of any gain realized *on the exchange* (i.e., on the transfer of Target assets to Acquirer). This gain would, apparently, be computed as a sliver of the gain on all of the properties transferred by Target to Acquirer, computed as if Target received a proportionate part of the boot in exchange for each asset. Happily, this scenario appears highly unlikely in the context of a C reorganization, because distribution of "the other property [Target] receives" is required under section 368(a)(2)(G).

Section 361(c) governs the taxation of Target on reorganization distributions to its shareholders. Note section 361(c)(4), which provides that sections 311, 336, and 337 do not apply to such transfers. One of the consequences of this provision is that no losses will be recognized on the distribution, even if they would have been recognized in an ordinary complete liquidation.

The principle rule, set out in section 361(c)(1), appears on first reading to provide for nonrecognition of gain or loss on *any* distribution by Target to its shareholders in connection with the reorganization, since it applies to "any distribution to its shareholders of property." Subsection (c)(2), however, requires Target to recognize gain when it distributes appreciated property that is not "qualified property" to its shareholders. The exception from gain recognition for "qualified property" in section 361(c)(2)(B) covers any stock, stock rights, or obligations of Acquirer received by Target in the exchange. (It also provides nonrecognition for distribution of similar interests in Target.) As a result, Target will not be able to recognize its loss, but will be taxed on its gain, on distributions to shareholders of boot properties other than Acquirer debt that have appreciated while being held by Target as well as on distributions to shareholders of any retained Target assets that are appreciated. The gain will be recognized as though the items of appreciated property were sold to the distributee at their fair market values. Target will have a fair market value basis in the boot properties under section 358(a)(2), with the result that Target is taxable under section 361(c)(2)(A) only on any appreciation incurred while the boot property is held by Target. Such boot appreciation is likely to be insubstantial in most cases, because of the liquidation requirement for a successful C reorg and the unlikelihood of extensive delays between the transfer from Acquirer and the liquidation.

Shareholders will not be the only ones with claims on Target. Indeed, under general state corporate law requirements, no liquidating distributions can be made to Target's shareholders until Target's creditors have been satisfied. Section 368(a)(2)(G) anticipates this by providing that liquidating distributions to creditors of the consideration received from Acquirer will be considered to take place pursuant to the plan of reorganization and thus satisfy the requirement that Target distribute all of the consideration received from Acquirer, as well as its retained properties, in pursuance of the reorganization plan. Section 361(b)(3) ensures that gain is not recognized on Target's exchange with Acquirer if Target transfers boot property to creditors rather than distributing it to Target shareholders, clarifying that whenever gain on its transferred assets can be avoided by Target only by a distribution as required by section 361(b)(1), a distribution to creditors will suffice. Section 361(c)(3) prevents any gain or loss recognition on the re-transfer of Acquirer stock, stock rights, or obligations to creditors, regardless of whether their value has changed since they were received.

Determining that Target is not subject to tax on its realized gain on the exchange with Acquirer or on transfers of qualified property to creditors, however, does not answer all of the questions involved with transfers to creditors in connection with a reorg. Is Target taxed on its realized gain in any properties that it transfers to creditors to repay debts in connection with the reorganization? Can it recognize losses in some cases?

The answer appears to be yes. Neither section 361(b) nor section 361(c) provides nonrecognition for Target's use of non-debt boot to pay creditors: section 361(b) only ensures nonrecognition on Target's exchange with Acquirer, and section 361 simply does not apply to non-debt boot transferred to creditors. Thus, it appears that section 1001 applies as it ordinarily would to tax Target on the gain (or loss) realized on its use of boot (other than Acquirer debt) to pay creditors. That gain would be limited to the appreciation while held by Target, since Target receives a fair market value basis in boot properties. Target would similarly be taxed on use of any of its retained assets to pay creditors.

Finally, it might be worth considering the consequences to Target if it were to dispose of the Acquirer stock, stock rights, securities, or other debt obligations (i.e., the qualified property for purposes of section 361(c)) other than by distributing them to its shareholders or creditors. Assume that there is a legitimate business purpose for such a sale — e.g., because Target's creditors demand cash and refuse to accept Acquirer stock or debt as payment. First, there is no provision that provides for nonrecognition on such a disposition. Therefore, if Target were to sell Acquirer stock, it would recognize gain under the ordinary gain recognition rules. Its basis in the Acquirer stock for these purposes would be a basis derived from its basis in the assets it transferred, according to section 358(a). Second, such a disposition may not be possible without disqualifying the transaction as a C reorg. Target is required to distribute the Acquirer consideration and its retained properties to its shareholders or creditors pursuant to the reorganization plan under section 368(a)(2)(G). Under the literal terms of the statute, such a sale may cause the entire restructuring transaction to fail to qualify as a C reorg, unless a waiver is granted. The legislative history suggests, however, that sales and distributions of the proceeds may count as the required distribution (i.e., that the required liquidation need not be an *in-kind* distribution of the assets themselves).

Consequences to Target under Section 361[6]

	Distributed to Shareholders	Distributed to Creditors	Sold & Proceeds Distributed to Creditors[4]
Acquirer stock			
No change[1] *Appreciated*[2]	No G or L on T's **exchange** with P under § 361(a)/(b)(1)(A)	No G or L on T's **exchange** with P under § 361(a)/(b)(1)(A)	No G or L on T's **exchange** with P under § 361(a)
Depreciated[3]	No G or L to T on **distribution** § 361(c)(3), (c)(1)	No G or L to T on **distribution** § 361(c)(1)	G or L on **disposition:** T has a § 358(a)(1) basis in the stock § 361(c) inapplicable since stock is sold rather than distributed; Cash payment to creditors is not a taxable transaction to T
Acquirer Boot[5]			
No change in value while held by T	No G to T **on exchange** under § 361(b)(1)(A) No L to T **on exchange** under § 361(b)(2) No G or L to T on **distribution** under § 361(c)(2) and § 361(c)(1)	No G to T **on exchange** under § 361(b)(1)(A) and § 361(b)(3) No L to T **on exchange** under § 361(b)(2) No G or L on **use of boot to pay creditors** (a § 1001 disposition) since it has a FMV basis	G to T on **exchange** under § 361(b)(1)(B) No L to T **on exchange** under § 361(b)(2) No G or L on **disposition of the boot** since it has a FMV basis **Cash payment to creditors** is not a taxable transaction to T

	Distributed to Shareholders	Distributed to Creditors	Sold & Proceeds Distributed to Creditors[4]
Appreciated in value while held by T	No G to T **on exchange** under § 361(b)(1)(A)	No G to T **on exchange** under § 361(b)(1)(A) and § 361(b)(3)	G to T on **exchange with P** under § 361(b)(1)(B
	No L to T **on exchange** under § 361(b)(2)	No L **on exchange** under § 361(b)(2)	No L **on exchange** under § 361(b)(2)
	G to T on **distribution** (equal to appreciation while held by T) under § 361(c)(2)(A) and § 361(c)(1)	G is recognized on **use of boot to pay creditors** under § 1001 (to extent of appreciation beyond FMV basis)	G is recognized on **disposition of boot** under § 1001 (to extent of appreciation beyond FMV basis)
		§ 361(c)(1)/§ 361(c)(2) do not apply since boot is distributed to creditors and not to shareholders	**§ 361(c)** does not apply since there is a disposition of the boot to third parties, not a distribution
		§ 361(c)(3) does not apply to treat transfer of boot to creditors as distribution to shareholders; it only covers qualified property	**Cash payment to creditors** is not a taxable transaction to T
Depreciated in value while held by T	No G to T **on exchange** under § 361(b)(1)(A);	No G to T **on exchange** under § 361(b)(1)(A) and § 361(b)(3);	G to T on **exchange with P** under § 361(b)(1)(B)
	No L to T **on exchange** under § 361(b)(2)	No L to T **on exchange** under § 361(b)(2)	No L to T **on exchange** under § 361(b)(2)
	No L to T on **distribution** under § 361(c)(1)	L is recognized on **use of boot to pay creditors** under § 1001 (to extent of depreciation below FMV basis)	L is recognized on **disposition of boot** under § 1001 (to extent of depreciation below FMV basis)
		§ 361(c)(1) does not apply since boot is distributed to creditors and not to shareholders	**§ 361(c)** does not apply since there is a disposition of the boot to third parties, not a distribution
		§ 361(c)(3) does not apply to treat transfer of boot to creditors as distribution to shareholders, it only covers qualified property	**Cash payment to creditors** is not a taxable transaction to T

	Distributed to Shareholders	*Distributed to Creditors*	*Sold & Proceeds Distributed to Creditors*[4]
Retained T Assets			
Appreciated	*(not relevant to whether T has **exchange** gain since not involved in the exchange with P)* G to T on **distribution**, *under § 361(c)(2)*	*G is recognized on* **use of retained assets to pay creditors** *under § 1001* **§ 361(c)(1)** *does not apply since retained properties are distributed to creditors and not shareholders* **§ 361(c)(3)** *does not apply to treat transfer of boot to creditors as distribution to shareholders, it only covers qualified property*	*G is recognized on* **disposition of assets** *under § 1001* **Cash payment to creditors** *is not a taxable transaction to T*
Depreciated	*(not relevant to whether T has **exchange** gain since not involved in the exchange with P)* No L on **distribution** *under § 361(c)(1)*	*L is recognized on* **use of retained assets to pay creditors** *under § 1001* **§ 361(c)(1)** *does not apply since retained properties are distributed to creditors and not shareholders* **§ 361(c)(3)** *does not apply to treat transfer of boot to creditors as distribution to shareholders, it only covers qualified property*	*L is recognized on* **disposition of assets** *under § 1001* **Cash payment to creditors** *is not a taxable transaction to T*

[1] *"no change" means that the item has not changed in value in the time held by Target;*

[2] *"appreciated" means that the item has appreciated while held by Target;*

[3] *"depreciated" means that the item has depreciated while held by Target;*

[4] *"sold and proceeds distributed to creditors" must be part of plan of reorganization and might nevertheless result in disqualification of reorganization.*

[5] *Chart assumes that Acquirer is fully taxable on boot transfers and that the boot is not an Acquirer note (which would complicate the chart since it is boot for the exchange, but qualified property for the distribution).*

[6] *Determination in each box assumes that every other item received in the exchange is distributed to the shareholders pursuant to the reorganization*

18.2.2. Consequences to Acquirer

Acquirer has no gain or loss upon the issuance and exchange of its shares for Target assets under section 1032. It will, however, recognize any gain (or loss) in boot property exchanged or in any property used to repay Target's creditors directly, under ordinary recognition provisions. Acquirer's basis in the Target assets will carry over from Target under section 362(b), and Acquirer will not receive any basis "boost" for its own gain recognition on boot properties. Acquirer will have a tacked holding period in Target's assets determined under section 1223(2).

Acquirer, furthermore, will not increase its basis in Target assets as a result of Target gain under section 361(c)(2)(A), since any such gain is not recognized by Target *on its transfer to Acquirer*. Only in the bizarre and perhaps impossible case in which Target failed the requirements of section 361(b)(1)(A) by failing to distribute the consideration received from Acquirer either to its shareholders or to creditors without failing the distribution requirement of section 368(a)(2)(G) would there be gain of the sort anticipated by the language at the end of the first sentence of section 362(b). (In some other reorganization transactions involving very similar asset transfers, but in which the distribution to shareholders is in accordance with the requirements for a spin-off contained in section 355 rather than with the requirements of section 354, such Target gain (and such Acquirer basis increase) is possible. In such a transaction, there is no requirement that Target distribute everything it receives; to the contrary, there is a requirement Target (usually called "the distributing corporation") distribute everything it receives. In addition, there is a requirement that it remain not just intact but conducting an active business.)

18.2.3. Consequences to Target Shareholders

Target shareholders will recognize neither gains nor losses on their Target stock exchanged solely for Acquirer stock under section 354(a)(1), unless the stock received is nonqualified preferred stock treated as boot under sections 354(a)(2)(C) and 356(e). Target shareholders who receive both stock qualified for nonrecognition and other property will be subject to tax on their gain, to the extent of the boot. Target assets that are retained and distributed to Target shareholders will generally be treated as boot for this purpose, unless the distribution is separate from the reorganization transaction under general tax principles, including the step transaction doctrine. A Target shareholder that receives no Acquirer stock will be taxed under the general redemption provisions in section 302.

Note that Target liabilities assumed by Acquirer will not be treated as boot to Target's shareholders, even though they are treated as boot for purposes of determining whether the C reorg qualifies under the boot relaxation rule. Similarly, those liabilities are disregarded in determining the shareholders' bases under section 358 in their Acquirer stock and other properties received in the reorganization.

18.3. USE OF PARENT STOCK IN TRIANGULAR C REORGS

The parenthetical in section 368(a)(1)(C) allows a transaction in which Target assets are transferred to a corporation that is controlled by the corporation the stock of which is used as consideration. In plainer terms, Target assets can be transferred to a newly created (or preexisting) subsidiary of Acquirer without defeating the reorganization. This parenthetical was made necessary by the decision in *Groman v. Commissioner*, 302 U.S. 82 (1937), in which the Court held that parent stock did not count as stock of a "party to the reorganization."

The statute does not, however, allow the transfer to a corporation that is not directly owned by the Acquirer — i.e., only parent stock, not grandparent stock, may be used. Many of the adverse consequences of this rule can be avoided, however, given the fact that the Target assets, once received by the first-tier subsidiary, can be further "dropped" under section 368(a)(2)(C), Reg. § 1.368-1(d), and Reg. § 1.368-2(k), so that the issuing corporation ultimately is a grandparent or great-grandparent of the corporation that ends up holding Target's assets.

The statute does not explicitly allow the use of stock of both controlling Acquirer parent and controlled Acquirer subsidiary; neither does it disallow the use of related company stock as boot. It therefore appears that a transaction may qualify as a C reorganization if both subsidiary and parent stock is used whenever one of the corporations' stock issuances may be treated as boot (i.e., is provided in small enough amounts to satisfy the boot relaxation rule, taking into consideration liabilities assumed and other boot properties transferred). The regulations, how-ever, indicate that the use of *voting* stock of both Acquirer parent and Acquirer subsidiary, *cannot* satisfy the C reorg requirements, even if not other boot is used as consideration. Reg. § 1.368-2(d)(1). This comports with the language of the statute, which states that a C reorg involves solely voting stock of the parent *or* solely voting stock of the subsidiary.

18.4. POST-REORGANIZATION TRANSFERS OF TARGET ASSETS

Section 368(a)(2)(C) expressly permits the Acquirer in a C reorg to "drop down" the assets received to a corporation "controlled by" it. This language legislatively "reversed" the Supreme Court's decision in *Helvering v. Bashford*, 302 U.S. 454 (1938).

This legislative language could be read as a requirement that only permits a drop down from Acquirer to a subsidiary directly controlled, under section 368(c), by Acquirer, and thus that continuity that is any more "remote" is not good enough. Over time, however, the Service has developed a more expansive administrative position regarding transfers of the assets acquired in reorganizations. The regula-tions now clearly provide that assets may be dropped down more than one tier, so that the Target assets can be dropped several times without threatening the status of the overall transaction as a C reorg. *See* Reg. § 1.368-1(d) (clarifying that there is no continuity of business enterprise problem with such a transfer); Reg. § 1.368-2(f) and (k) (clarifying that the reorganization definitions will still be considered met even if these additional steps are taken).

Thus, in a triangular C reorganization, the Acquirer subsidiary may further transfer Target's assets to its 80%-owned subsidiary, which may also transfer those assets further down to its 80%-owned subsidiary. Reg. § 1.368-2(k)(2), Ex. 1. Transfers of portions of the Target assets to various affiliated corporations are also permitted. Reg. § 1.368-2(k)(1)(ii)(B).

Other transfers, including to Acquirer's or Acquirer subsidiary's shareholders, are also allowed if the provisions of Reg. § 1.368-(1)(d) (concerned with satisfying COBE) and of Reg. § 1.368-2(k) (concerned with the technical requirements of reorgs) are followed. Thus, in a triangular C reorganization, the Acquirer subsidiary may drop some of the Target assets down into its own controlled subsidiary and then distribute the stock of that controlled subsidiary to Acquirer Parent (the issuing corporation in the reorganization). Reg. § 1.368-2(k)(1)(i), (ii), and -2(k)(2), Ex. 3. These "remote continuity" regulations only provide that the subsequent transfers will not spoil the reorganization: they do not dictate the tax treatment of the transfer itself. Their technical requirements are considered more fully in connection with triangular mergers.

Note that there may be a difference in some circumstances between a transfer to an 80%-owned Acquirer subsidiary using Acquirer Parent stock, and a transfer to Acquirer Parent followed by a drop-down to Acquirer subsidiary. Assuming that the former transaction is a C reorganization and does not qualify as a divisive D reorganization, section 361 governs Target's asset transfer, and section 357(c) does not apply. In the latter transaction, section 351 governs Acquirer Parent's drop down and section 357(c) gain recognition does apply.

18.5.   EFFECT OF ACQUIRER'S PRIOR OWNERSHIP OF TARGET STOCK ("CREEPING C REORGS")

Acquirer's prior ownership of Target stock could theoretically cause a problem for C reorg status. In a purported C reorg in which the consideration is solely Acquirer stock, Target will receive Acquirer stock equal to the value of all of its assets, but some of the Acquirer stock will be returned to Acquirer in its capacity as a shareholder of Target upon Target's liquidation. The transfer of Target assets in respect of the Target stock already owned by Acquirer thus could be treated as in substance a liquidating distribution rather than a reorganization exchange. Therefore, if Acquirer's prior ownership of Target was sufficient to defeat the "substantially all" requirement, the putative C reorg would fail.

In *Bausch & Lomb Optical Co. v. Commissioner*, 267 F.2d 75 (1959), the government succeeded in convincing the court that the liquidation interpretation is correct in the context of a putative C reorg in which Acquirer already owned stock in Target and that the assets that Acquirer received should not be treated as having been received in exchange for its own stock. Regulations have now rejected the *Bausch & Lomb* result, providing that transfers of Target's assets in respect of pre-owned Target stock will not destroy C reorg status, so long as the boot relaxation rule is satisfied, considering only boot distributed to non-Acquirer Target shareholders and Target creditors and any assumption of liabilities. Reg. § 1.368-

2(d)(4)(i) (stating that prior ownership will not prevent satisfaction of the "solely for voting stock" requirement, so long as "the sum of the money or other property that is distributed in pursuance of the plan of reorganization to the shareholders of the target corporation other than the acquiring corporation and to the creditors of the target corporation pursuant to section 361(b)(3), and all of the liabilities of the target corporation assumed by the acquiring corporation (including liabilities to which the properties of the target corporation are subject), does not exceed 20 percent of the value of all of the properties of the target corporation"); Reg. § 1.368-2(d)(4)(ii), Ex. 1. An acquisition of Target stock for cash in a transaction that is stepped together with, and treated as part of, the reorganization will be treated, however, as the use of cash consideration for the assets ultimately acquired. Reg. § 1.368-2(d)(4)(i) (third sentence); Reg. § 1.368-2(d)(4)(ii), Ex. 2.

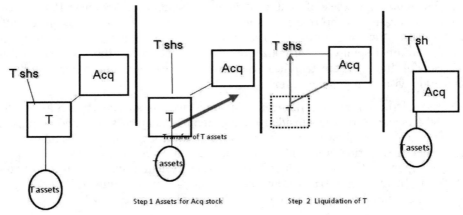

Step 1 Assets for Acq stock   Step 2 Liquidation of T

When Acquirer already owns T stock:
Does Acq receive T assets in exchange for its stock step 1
or in exchange for the T stock it already owns, in step 2
See Reg. 1.368-2(d)(4)

18.6. RECASTING TRANSACTIONS AS C REORGS

In 1967, the A reorg definition in section 368(a)(1) itself did not (as it still does not) include a parenthetical allowing the use of parent stock to accomplish a triangular *merger* transaction, and subsections 368(a)(2)(D) and (E), outlining conditions under which parent stock may be used in connection with A reorgs to achieve subsidiary mergers, had not yet been enacted. Accordingly, the Service issued two rulings in which transactions that had begun as stock acquisitions (and thus began as putative B reorgs) were held not to satisfy the B reorg definition because the acquired corporation went out of existence.

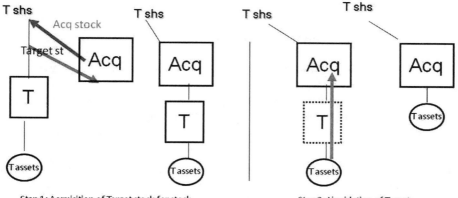

Rev. Rul. 67-274

*stock of Target acquired using Acquirer stock, Target liquidated
tested as an asset acquistion under C reorg definition*

In Rev. Rul. 67-274, 1967-2 C.B. 141, a liquidation of a newly acquired Target in exchange for Acquirer stock was recast as an acquisition of Target assets and tested under the conditions for C reorgs.

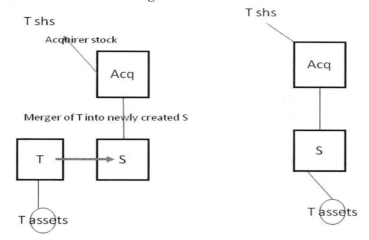

Rev. Rul. 67-326

*merger into new acquirer sub with parent stock treated as acquisition of assets
can be tested as C reorg with Sub as acquirer*

In Rev. Rul. 67-326, 1967-2 C.B. 143, obsoleted by Rev. Rul. 2003-99, a merger of newly acquired Target into a newly created Acquirer subsidiary in a transaction in which Acquirer stock is used as consideration was recast and tested as an acquisition of assets entitled to treatment as a C reorg, so long as the conditions of the C reorg were themselves satisfied. Reliance on this ruling is generally not necessary after the enactment of section 368(a)(2)(D), which provides statutory authorization for some versions of the transactions covered by the ruling.

18.7. BUSINESS CONSIDERATIONS

C reorgs are "asset for stock" deals and thus the economics are very similar to statutory mergers, except that the transfers do not take place by operation of law and there is some flexibility to negotiate which assets or liabilities are transferred. Target shareholders may insist on distributions of some of Target's cash or even its non-operating assets, which may be possible so long as the boot relaxation requirements are satisfied.

Because the transfers of assets do not occur by operation of law as they do in a statutory merger, the parties must in fact execute documents for the transfer of each Target asset and record such transfers appropriately under the applicable local law. Transfer taxes may apply. Thus, a C reorg can involve significant transfer costs, particularly if there are additional distributions or drops planned after the primary restructuring transaction.

One benefit of a C reorg compared to statutory mergers is the increased flexibility regarding liability assumptions. Because a C reorg is an asset acquisition, Acquirer can avoid assuming many or even most of Target's liabilities, if the parties to the reorganization can reach agreement. There may, however, be some liabilities — often contingent or hidden, and in particular for environmental damage and for some consumer torts — that will follow the assets or the line of business and cannot be negotiated away. The law of the jurisdiction under which the liability is defined determines the standards that apply.

In general, only Target's shareholders need to approve the transaction.

18.8. NET VALUE REQUIREMENT AND OTHER LIMITATIONS ON DEBT ENCUMBERING TARGET ASSETS

In 2005, the Treasury and Service undertook a broad regulation project governing the treatment of purported nonrecognition transactions in subchapter C when insolvent companies are involved — i.e., transactions that involve transfers of "no net value." The proposed regulations establish a uniform "net-value" requirement for nonrecognition under sections 351, 332, and 368 and clarify the treatment of creditors in reorganizations for continuity of interest purposes. *See* Notice of Proposed Rule Making, REG 163314-03, 70 F.R. 11903 (Mar. 10, 2005); Prop. Reg. § 1.368-1(b) & (f) (2005) (providing a net-value transfer requirement). Both the assets of Target before the transaction and the stock of Acquirer after the transaction must have a positive net value. Prop. Reg. § 1.368-2(f)(2)(i) confirms that the assumption of liabilities can affect the overall nature of the transaction, even though liabilities will not ordinarily have an impact on a bootless C reorg under the voting stock requirement.

Even before the net value regulations, the regulations contained a limitation on the extent to which Target's assets can be encumbered. *See* Reg. § 1.368-2(d)(1) (last two sentences) (suggesting that too much debt may "so alter the character of the transaction as to place the transaction outside the purposes and assumptions of the reorganization provisions"); Rev. Proc. 77-37 (long providing a "net asset value" gloss on the "substantially all" requirement for ruling requests).

PRACTICE PROBLEMS

True or False?

Unless otherwise specifically stated, assume in all of the problems below that the stock used by Acquirer is "voting stock" as required by the definitional provisions in section 368(a), and that "control" is as defined in section 368(c).

1. A B reorg will never be possible if Acquirer already owns more than 20% of Target stock.

2. As long as there is a chain of control that satisfies section 368(c), if substantially all of the assets of Target are transferred by Target and then Target liquidates, the assets can be transferred directly to an Acquirer that is a fourth or fifth tier subsidiary of the corporation the stock of which is used as the consideration paid to Target for its assets and, the transaction will qualify as a C reorg.

3. If Acquirer uses its stock to acquire all of the stock of Target, and then liquidates Target, the transaction will be a reorganization if the standards of section 368(a)(1)(C) are met.

4. An unlimited amount of boot may be given by Acquirer in a C reorg as long as no liabilities are assumed.

5. As long as Acquirer uses only its stock to acquire 80% of the stock of Target before it acquires any stock for cash, the transaction will qualify as a B reorg.

6. The continuity of shareholder interest standard applicable in statutory mergers requires that more stock be used as consideration in such mergers before they can qualify for reorg treatment than must be used in a C reorg.

7. Acquirer can transfer either assets acquired in a C reorg or stock acquired in a B reorg to a corporation that it controls without spoiling the reorg.

8. Target may not remain as an ongoing entity after a C reorg without express permission.

DISCUSSION PROBLEMS

Fred's AutoBody Inc. (FAB) has developed a parts-tracking software system that will allow it and other body shops to avoid doing business with seamy chop-shop parts dealers. Gaggle, which has a substantial internet presence, believes that this product will have many other uses and has approached the stockholders of FAB to discuss the possibility of some sort of joint venture or acquisition.

The assets on FAB's tax books include land (subject to a $250,000 mortgage), a building, equipment of the sort ordinarily associated with an auto body shop, some far more sophisticated computer equipment than you would ordinarily find at an autobody shop, an antique car that was titled over when the owner couldn't pay his bill, and about $150,000 held in money market and mutual funds. The assets other than the software (which doesn't even show up on FAB's tax books) and goodwill are worth about $1,000,000. FAB still owes $100,000 to its parts supplier (but doesn't ever pay down completely because the parts supplier's terms are very generous) and $50,000 on a bank loan taken out when the roof of the building needed repair.

	basis	fmv
ASSETS		
MM funds		150,000
Land		???
Building		???
Autobody equip		???
Computer equip		???
Antique car		???
SUBTOTAL		1,000,000
Software/Goodwill		???
TOTAL		???
LIABILITIES		
Mortgage on land		-250,000
Account payable to parts supplier		-100,000
Bank loan for roof		-50,000
TOTAL		-400,000

Can FAB avoid tax on the transfer if the following occurs? Can the shareholders of FAB?

1.   The shareholders of FAB transfer all of their stock to Gaggle, and receive in exchange nothing but Gaggle stock worth $3,000,000?

2.   FAB transfers all of its assets to Lil Gaggle, a C corp that is a wholly owned subsidiary of Gaggle, in exchange for Gaggle stock worth $3,000,000, and then FAB liquidates. Lil Gaggle agrees, at the time of the asset transfer, to assume all of FAB's liabilities other than the debt to the parts supplier, which it insists must be paid before the deal closes.

(a)   What is the result if only $2.9 million of Gaggle voting stock is transferred to FAB, along with $100,000 in cash to pay the parts supplier?

(b)   What is the result if only $2.2 million of Gaggle stock is transferred, along with $100,000 of cash to pay the parts supplier, in exchange for all the FAB assets other than the land, which is to be distributed to the FAB shareholders?

3.   What are the results, in either a stock-for-stock or a stock-for-asset transaction, when the additional facts below are considered? (Do not worry about exactly how the shareholders would be taxed if you decide that they will be partially subject to tax.)

(a)   What if all of the stock (or assets) of FAB is (are) transferred, except that 1% of the stock, which is held by Fred, is redeemed in exchange for the car immediately before the other stock for stock or asset for stock transactions?

(b)   What if Fred is the only shareholder, so he simply distributed the car to himself before he transferred his stock (or the Target assets) to Gaggle?

(c)   What if all of the cash held by FAB is distributed to all of FAB's shareholders according to their respective dividend rights prior to a stock for stock transaction?

(d)   What if Fred has guaranteed the bank debt of FAB and the debt is assumed in a transaction planned to be either a B reorg or a C reorg?

(e)   What if Gaggle had lent money to FAB for software development? Buried in the terms of that agreement was a right to convert the debt to stock amounting to 5% of FAB, and Gaggle exercised these rights immediately before the transfer of the other FAB stock (or FAB assets)?

(f)   What if in part (e), above, Fred only owns 10% of the stock of FAB, and unbeknownst to him, Gaggle has obtained options on all of the rest of the stock of FAB from the other shareholders who will, when Gaggle exercises its options, transfer their stock to Gaggle for cash? Only Fred will participate in the proposed exchange of stock for stock and, if the transaction is completed as a C reorg, only Fred will remain a FAB shareholder receiving Gaggle stock as a result. What if Gaggle simply renounces its right to exercise the options? What if Gaggle had exercised these rights 18 months ago?

(g)   What if Gaggle does not plan to use any of the physical assets of FAB and therefore encourages FAB to sell them all before the stock (or asset) transfer? What if Gaggle sells them all immediately after the stock (or asset) transfer?

(h)   What if FAB was not formed until after Gaggle first approached Fred about acquiring the software?

(i)   What if Gaggle forms Lil Gaggle LLC, and FAB is merged into Lil Gaggle LLC?

(j)   What if FAB is actually FAB LLC, 100% owned by FAB Mastershops and formed to facilitate the financing of the software development, and FAB LLC is merged into Gaggle with FAB Mastershops receiving Gaggle stock?

4.   What if, in the stock for stock transaction described in 1 above, Fred is the only shareholder of FAB? He holds two blocks of FAB stock of equal value. One block was acquired when FAB was formed, in exchange for assets that had a basis of about $5000. The other block was acquired for about $1 million when he bought out his partner 3 years ago. What is his basis in the Gaggle stock he receives?

Chapter 19

TRIANGULAR MERGERS

Statutes and Regulations IRC §§ 368(a)(2)(D), 368(a)(2)(E)
Reg. § 1.368-2(b)(2)
Reg. § 1.368-2(j)
Reg. § 1.358-6
Reg. § 1.1032-2
Reg. § 1.368-1(d)
Reg. § 1.368-2(k)
Reg. § 1.338(h)(10)-1(c)(2)

Other Primary Authorities Rev. Rul. 2001-25, 2001-1 C.B. 1291
Rev. Rul. 2001-26, 2001-1 C.B. 1297
Rev. Rul. 2001-46, 2001-2 C.B. 321
Rev. Rul. 2001-24, 2001-1 C.B. 1290
Rev. Rul. 74-564, 1974-2 C.B. 124

19.1. OVERVIEW OF TRIANGULAR MERGERS

The standard A, B, and C reorgs remained unsatisfactory to practitioners even after the extension of the standard patterns through the parentheticals allowing parent stock in B reorgs and in C reorgs (reversing the decision in *Groman v. Commissioner*, 302 U.S. 82 (1937), which held that the parent of Acquirer was not a "party to the reorganization" and that therefore its stock was boot to Target shareholders) and through the ability under section 368(a)(2)(C) to drop Target assets down after A, B, or C reorganizations (reversing the result in *Helvering v. Bashford*, 302 U.S. 454 (1938), which held that a parent corporation did not become a "party to a reorganization" when its actual ownership of Target's assets was only transitory). Most significantly, the advantages of using the provisions of state law to accomplish acquisitions through mergers could not be achieved without Acquirer acquiring Target assets directly, thus exposing all of Acquirer's assets to the potential liabilities of Target. Only in transactions in which assets were actually transferred (C reorgs) or stock was acquired from individual shareholders (B reorgs) could that liability exposure be avoided.

The "self-help" triangular patterns established through Rev. Rul. 67-326, 1967-2 C.B. 143 (allowing a merger into a subsidiary of the corporation that issues stock to Target shareholders to be treated as an acquisition of assets potentially qualifying as a C reorg), and Rev. Rul. 67-448 (allowing a merger into Target by a transitory subsidiary of the corporation that issues stock to Target shareholders to potentially qualify as a B reorg) helped considerably. Under these rulings, taxpayers were allowed to use the step transaction doctrine to their benefit, so that multi-step transactions would be recast according to end results, rather than determining the tax consequences of the transaction based on each step independently. But these rulings did not provide as much flexibility — and certainly not as much certainty — as practitioners wanted in structuring such transactions.

The availability of these newly sanctioned triangular patterns was therefore ratified by the enactment of section 368(a)(2)(D) (forward triangular mergers) and section 368(a)(2)(E) (reverse triangular mergers) in 1968 and 1971 respectively. Although the statute is structured as if the new language merely provides for the use of the stock of the parent in transactions covered by the statutory merger provisions of section 368(a)(1)(A), and although the triangular mergers are frequently referred to as transactions that satisfy section 368(a)(1)(A) "by reason of" subsection 368(a)(2)(D) or (E), the additional conditions render the actual transactions more like C reorgs and B reorgs (respectively) than their self-help predecessors were when first introduced. The patterns in subsections 368(a)(2)(D) and (E) are in some ways more restrictive than their self-help predecessors, but they are in other ways more generous. For instance, in a forward triangular merger, nonstock consideration is permitted, and the stock that must be used need not be voting stock. The changes in the requirements — from the patterns contemplated in the self-help rulings, to those authorized by the statute, to the substantially liberalized patterns now permitted under recent regulations — are typical of the evolution of provisions within subchapter C and entity taxation more generally. This evolution happens to have been in a decidedly pro-taxpayer direction; not all developments under subchapter C have been.

A note on nomenclature: the statute and older authorities focus on which corporation is the "acquiring corporation," whereas newer regulations simply outline transactions involving P (the parent on the acquiring side), S (the subsidiary on the acquiring side, which will usually also be the actual acquirer), and T (the Target). This text will use "Acquirer Parent" to mean the corporation whose stock is used and "Acquirer Sub" to mean the corporation that actually participates in a triangular merger by receiving Target's assets (in the forward merger) or by being merged into Target (in the reverse merger).

In many cases, assuring reorganization treatment is only a part of the challenge in characterizing transactions. It is important to bear in mind that although some transactions may be recast either to qualify as transfers to Acquirer Sub using Acquirer Parent stock, or as transfers directly to a controlling parent, only one corporation can technically be the acquiring corporation. Reg. § 1.381(a)-1(b)(2)(i). There may be substantial stakes involved in determining which corporation is the "acquirer" and therefore which corporation inherits loss and credit carryovers. The regulation provides that the corporation that ultimately acquires all of the assets of Target will be the "acquirer," but if no one corporation retains them all, then the corporation that directly acquires them initially (even if it does not retain *any* of the assets) will be the "acquirer" for the purposes of applying the tax attribute rules of section 381.

19.1.1.   Forward Triangular Mergers under Section 368(a)(2)(D)

Section 368(a)(2)(D) allows the use of Acquirer Parent stock in a statutory merger, so long as no Acquirer Sub stock is used and "substantially all of the assets" of Target are acquired. In the simplest of such transactions, Acquirer Parent creates an Acquirer Sub that will be the formal acquirer in the transaction and Target is merged into Acquirer Sub, with Acquirer Sub surviving. Target shareholders receive Acquirer Parent stock in the transaction. Although the self-help pattern established under Rev. Rul. 67-326 may have required the use of a transitory subsidiary (i.e., a newly created subsidiary that holds no assets other than those that will be transferred to Target shareholders in the transaction), the statutory provision for forward triangular mergers permits transactions that use Acquirer Parent stock as consideration in a merger with an existing Acquirer Sub.

The statute does not specify the amount of stock that must be used in a forward merger, but the transaction must be one that would have qualified under section 368(a)(1)(A) if the merger had been directly into Acquirer Parent. Thus, the relatively liberal judicial continuity of interest standards apply, just as they do in A reorgs. *See* Reg. § 1.368-2(b)(2). This represents another substantial difference between the transactions qualifying under section 368(a)(2)(D) and those granted reorganization status as C reorganizations under Rev. Rul. 67-326.

In a perhaps unexpected twist, however, section 368(a)(2)(D) expressly disallows the use of both Acquirer Sub and Acquirer Parent stock in the same transaction. In other reorganizations in which boot is allowed, the use of the stock of two Acquirer-side related corporations will not always defeat the reorganization so long as the common-law or relevant statutory continuity of interest standard is satisfied, although the stock of one will be boot and will not be counted for continuity purposes. *But see* Reg. § 1.368-2(d)(1) (indicating that use of *voting* stock of both Acquirer Sub and Acquirer Parent in a purported C reorg will disqualify the transaction for C reorg treatment). Although use of stock of the Acquirer Sub disqualifies a forward merger, there are no restrictions (other than COSI) on use of other interests of either Acquirer Parent or Acquirer Sub. Reg. § 1.368-2(b)(2). Reg. § 1.368-2(b)(2) makes it clear that the business purpose and continuity of business enterprise requirements also apply to forward triangular mergers.

The "substantially all of the assets" standard makes the forward triangular merger much like a C reorg followed by a drop of the acquired Target assets under section 368(a)(2)(C) without, of course, the limitations on the amount of boot that can be used under the stringent boot relaxation rule in C reorgs. Administrative rulings have loosened the "substantially all" requirement to permit Target to sell assets prior to and in connection with the merger, so long as it retains the proceeds. *See* Rev. Rul. 2001-25, 2001-1 C.B. 1291 (ruling that the "substantially all" requirement would be satisfied in a forward triangular merger when Target sells half of its unwanted operating assets for cash to an unrelated corporation in a transaction contemplated at the time of the merger, and then retains the sales proceeds). A similar ruling permitted such transactions in the C reorg context. *See* Rev. Rul. 88-48, 1988-1 C.B. 117 (Target's sale of half of its assets to unrelated buyers, and transfer of the sales proceeds as part of the assets in the C reorg).

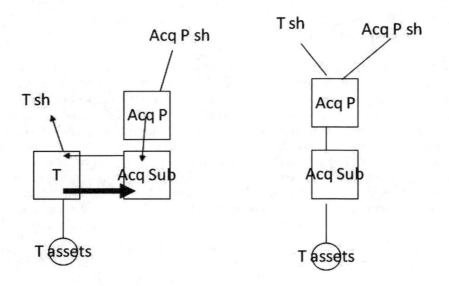

Forward Triangular Merger
Section 368(a)(1)(A) by reason of section 368(a)(2)(D)

19.1.2. Reverse Triangular Mergers under Section 368(a)(2)(E)

Section 368(a)(2)(E) allows the use of the Acquirer Parent stock in a merger of Acquirer Sub into Target, when the Target shareholders give up stock that amounts to control of Target in exchange for Acquirer Parent voting stock. After the transaction, the surviving corporation (Target) must hold substantially all of its own assets as well as substantially all of the assets that the merged corporation (Acquirer Sub) held before the transaction (other than the consideration for the Target stock).

The transaction that is anticipated is one in which Acquirer Sub is merged into Target, leaving Target controlled by Acquirer Parent and Target shareholders owning Acquirer Parent stock. The pattern is essentially the same as that involved in a B reorg, except that the transaction can be accomplished by operation of law under a state merger statute rather than through direct agreements with Target shareholders. The resulting pattern is considerably more useful in one respect than the straight B reorg: boot may be used, so long as enough Acquirer Parent voting stock is used to acquire a controlling interest in Target in the exchange. It is less useful, however, in two significant respects.

First, after the merger is complete, Target must hold "substantially all" of its assets, as well as all of the Acquirer Sub assets other than, as Reg. section 1.368-2(j)(3)(iii) makes clear, the consideration transferred to Target shareholders in the transaction or other assets transferred to Acquirer Sub for use in the transaction (such as to pay dissenting shareholders, creditors, or reorganization expenses). This requirement will not be a problem in the typical case in which a new Acquirer Sub is created for the acquisition. But Acquirer Sub need not be newly created. Thus section 368(a)(2)(E), like section 368(a)(2)(D), goes beyond the patterns allowed by the "self-help" rulings, since Rev. Rul. 67-448 relied on integrating the transaction steps to ignore a newly created transitory subsidiary.

Second, the transaction must involve an exchange of stock amounting to control of Target for Acquirer Parent stock: a transaction in which less than a control amount of Target stock is exchanged for Acquirer Parent stock will not qualify, even if Acquirer Parent actually owns a controlling interest in Target after the transaction because of its pre-existing ownership. Thus, it may be difficult to satisfy the reverse triangular merger's requirement of *acquisition of control in the exchange* when Acquirer Parent already owns a substantial block of Target stock. If the transaction fails to qualify as a reverse triangular merger because of failure to acquire control in the exchange, it may nonetheless qualify for nonrecognition treatment by being recast as a B reorg, if it satisfies the transitory subsidiary rulings. Section 368(a)(2)(E) has been held not to pre-empt the result in Rev. Rul. 67-448. *See* Rev. Rul. 74-564, 1974-2 C.B. 124; Reg. § 1.368-2(j)(6), Exs. 4 and 5 (indicating that the transitory subsidiary analysis may apply to recast a reverse merger that fails because of Acquirer's pre-existing ownership of Target stock). Furthermore, stock that is retired prior to or in connection with the merger transaction using consideration provided by Target will not be counted in determining whether control has been acquired in the exchange. Thus, if Target has 1000 shares before the merger, and 100 are held by dissenters who are cashed out by Target, then only 720 shares (80% of the 900 post redemption shareholders) must be acquired in the merger using Acquirer Parent stock. Reg. § 1.368-2(j)(6), Ex. 2.

Finally, in certain cases it may be possible to treat apparently separate but planned steps in the acquisition of stock as a single integrated transaction that satisfies the acquisition of control requirement. In Rev. Rul. 2001-26, 2001-1 C.B. 1297, based on an analogy with the decision in *J.E. Seagram Corp. v. Commissioner*, 104 T.C. 75 (1995) (treating a tender offer which was a step in a plan that included a forward triangular merger as part of the merger transaction), the Service allowed what appeared to be a failed reverse triangular merger involving acquisition of only about 30% of Target to be integrated with a tender offer in which more than 50% of Target had been acquired by Acquirer Parent in exchange for its stock. The integrated transaction qualified as a reorganization under section 368(a)(2)(E).

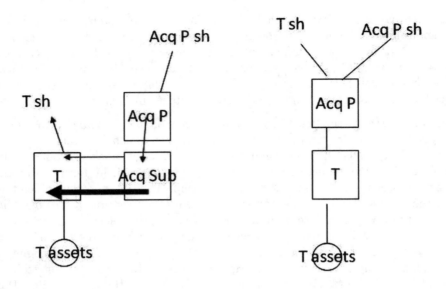

Reverse Triangular Merger
Section 368(a)(1)(A) by reason of section 368(a)(2)(E)

19.1.3. Consequences to the Corporations

For the most part, the consequences to the shareholders and to the parties in triangular mergers are as one would expect. Sections 354 and 356 dictate the measure and character of any Target shareholder gain and the Target shareholder basis in Acquirer stock is determined under section 358. In general, when Target is treated as having transferred assets, section 361 provides nonrecognition for Target and the asset basis for the Acquirer Sub is determined under section 362(b). Because the transactions may involve the use of Acquirer stock by Acquirer Sub, and may involve some deemed transfers among Acquirer side entries, some aspects of the transaction merit closer scrutiny.

19.1.4. Effect of Transfers of Acquirer Parent Stock

Even after the availability of reorganization treatment generally was established, uncertainty existed about the tax consequences of the use of Acquirer Parent stock in triangular mergers. In the most straightforward case, Acquirer Parent would contribute its own stock to Acquirer Sub, which would in turn transfer the stock to Target shareholders by operation of law in the merger. Acquirer Parent would be protected from gain recognition on the issuance of its stock and contribution to Acquirer sub under sections 1032 and 351. Sections 1032 and 118 should likewise prevent any gain recognition to Acquirer Sub on its issuance of stock to Acquirer Parent and on the transfer of Acquirer Parent stock to it. There is no code section, however, that provides similar nonrecognition when a related corporation such as Acquirer Sub uses its parent's stock to acquire Target's assets or stock. To make matters worse, under ordinary tax principles, Acquirer Sub would appear to hold the Acquirer Parent stock with a zero basis, so gain to the full extent of the value of Target might be recognized to Acquirer Sub in the transaction.

This disastrous result (sometimes referred to as the "zero basis" problem) was remedied first administratively by rulings and then in regulations promulgated under section 1032. *See* Rev. Rul. 73-427, 1973-2 C.B. 301 (providing nonrecognition for a subsidiary that was a conduit for the transfer of parent's stock in a failed triangular merger); Reg. § 1.1032-2. The regulation provides the tax consequences for forward triangular mergers, triangular B reorgs, and triangular A reorgs in which Acquirer Parent stock is provided as part of a plan of reorganization to Acquirer Sub or directly to Target shareholders (as may be the case in "parenthetical" C and B reorgs when Acquirer Parent stock is used.) Such transactions in Acquirer Parent stock will be treated as a disposition by the Acquirer Parent of its own stock for the Target assets or stock. Consequently, Acquirer Sub will not have any gain recognition on its use of the transferred Acquirer Parent stock to acquire Target's assets or stock.

This nonrecognition provision under section 1032 only addresses questions related to Acquirer Parent stock made available to Acquirer Sub as part of the plan of reorganization. It does not apply to any other property used by Acquirer Sub as consideration. Thus, if Acquirer Sub used some of its own Acquirer Parent stock (i.e., stock that it did not receive from Acquirer Parent under the reorganization plan), it will recognize the section 1001 gain or loss on its exchange of that stock as consideration in a forward merger or triangular B or C reorganization. Similarly, Acquirer Sub will recognize gain or loss on its transfer of any other asset as consideration. Reg. §§ 1.1032-2(c); 1.358-6(a) and -6(d)(3) Exs. (c) and (e) (referring to section 1001 for gain or loss recognition on use of assets of the controlled corporation in a forward merger).

For reverse triangular mergers, the Acquirer Sub (whether new or pre-existing) acts as a conduit between other parties to the reorganization, merging into Target so that the assets it holds before the merger are held by Target afterwards (other than Acquirer Parent stock that is distributed to Target shareholders and other assets from Acquirer Parent permitted to be distributed without recognition under the regulations). Accordingly, the regulations state that the rule governing Acquirer Sub's disposition of Acquirer Parent stock in reverse triangular mergers is provided by section 361. Reg. § 1.1032-2(b). Acquirer Sub is treated as having exchanged its property, including both newly received and previously held Acquirer Parent stock, to Target shareholders in exchange for Target stock, and as having re-transferred that Target stock to its shareholder, Acquirer Parent, all as anticipated by section 361. Thus, the Acquirer Sub that merges into Target would not recognize any gain or loss on the exchange of Acquirer Parent stock for Target stock in connection with the reorganization or on its distribution of the Target stock to Acquirer Parent in the merger.

19.1.5. Acquirer Parent's Basis in the Surviving Subsidiary Stock

Another important issue for the Acquirer Parent is its basis in the stock in Acquirer Sub (in a forward merger) or in Target (in a reverse merger) after the triangular merger is completed. Administrative guidance again provides an answer to the uncertainties left under the Code.

After a forward triangular merger, Acquirer Parent's basis in the surviving corporation (i.e., Acquirer Sub) is adjusted to produce the result that would have obtained if *first* Target had merged directly into Acquirer Parent, with Acquirer Parent assuming Target liabilities (which would be a section 362(b) basis under the reorganization rules), *followed by* a drop of the Target assets and liabilities down to Acquirer Sub (which would call for a section 358 basis). Reg. § 1.358-6(c)(1) (sometimes called the "over the top and down" rule). The result is a net asset basis — i.e., the rule produces an increase in Acquirer Parent's basis in Acquirer Sub equal to the amount by which the aggregate basis of Target's assets exceeds the liabilities of Target assumed by Acquirer Sub in the transaction. *See* Reg. § 1.358-6(c)(4) Ex. 1. Excess liabilities will not trigger gain, since section 357(c) is inapplicable here.

The rules for Acquirer Parent's basis in Target after a reverse triangular merger are somewhat more complicated. The default rule provides the same "over the top and down" result as would obtain in a forward subsidiary merger — that is, Target's net asset basis is added to Acquirer Parent's pre-existing basis in its merged subsidiary, if any. Reg. § 1.358-6(c)(2). This amount must be proportionately reduced, however, if any Target stock remains in the hands of minority shareholders.

If the reverse subsidiary merger also qualifies as a B reorg (that is, if no consideration other than the stock of Acquirer Parent is used), then Acquirer Parent has the option to elect a basis derived from the basis of the former Target shareholders in their stock (i.e., a transferred basis under section 362(b)). The regulation clarifies that this election is also permitted when the transaction could be recast as a section 351 transaction — that is, when Target shareholders end up controlling Acquirer Parent.

19.1.6. Surviving Subsidiary's Basis in Acquired Assets

In a forward triangular merger, the surviving subsidiary is Acquirer Sub. It will have a basis in the acquired property from Target determined under section 362(b), which governs "property . . . acquired by a corporation in connection with a reorganization." Accordingly, Acquirer Sub will have a transferred basis in Target's assets that is the same as Target's inside basis. There is no possibility of a bump-up from recognized gain, since no gain will be recognized to Target in the merger.

In a reverse triangular merger, the surviving subsidiary is Target. Ordinarily, Target will simply continue its existence with its own assets. But if a pre-existing Acquirer Sub is used for the reverse acquisition rather than the more typical transitory subsidiary, what is the result? It seems clear that neither Acquirer Sub nor Target will recognize gain and loss in the transaction, but it is unclear whether section 361 literally applies. At any rate, Target's basis in the assets acquired from Acquirer Sub should be a transferred basis determined under section 362(b).

19.2.   TRANSFERS BY ACQUIRER AFTER TRIANGULAR MERGERS (AND OTHER REORGANIZATIONS GENERALLY)

19.2.1.   Drops of Acquired Assets or Stock

Section 368(a)(2)(C) has long permitted an Acquirer to drop the stock or the assets acquired in an A, B, or C reorganization to a corporation controlled by Acquirer. This provision was enacted in response to court cases asserting a prohibition against remote continuity of interest. In these cases the courts treated transactions in which the acquired stock or assets were no longer held by the acquiring corporation as failing continuity of interest or as failing reorganization requirements because one of the corporations involved was not a "party to the reorganization." *See, e.g.*, Helvering v. Bashford, 302 U.S. 454 (1938).

The language of section 368(a)(2)(C) itself is very limited, literally allowing drops only of the acquired assets or the acquired stock to a corporation controlled under section 368(c) by the acquiring corporation. This language left open many questions about the potential viability of drops to lower-tier subsidiaries, drops of Target assets after a stock acquisition, and split drops in which the acquired assets or stock were not all contributed to the same lower-tier entity.

The questions involving permissible drops involve fine distinctions in the invocation of the step transaction doctrine and implicate three different requirements for good reorganizations: first, that there be continuity of business enterprise (COBE); second, that the corporations involved could each be considered a "party to the reorganization"; and third, that the transaction itself satisfy the descriptions of the transactions articulated in the statutes, as acquisitions of stock constituting "control" or acquisitions of "substantially all of the assets." Some of these questions were resolved early on by published letter rulings. *See, e.g.*, Rev. Rul. 64-73, 1964-1 C.B. 142 (allowing successive drops after the transactions permitted in section 368(a)(2)(C)); Rev. Rul. 68-261, 1968-1 C.B. 147 (allowing drops of target assets to multiple subsidiaries); Rev. Rul. 72-576, 1972-2 C.B. 217 (concluding that section 368(a)(2)(C) allows drops of target assets after forward mergers).

More recent regulations have substantially reduced the uncertainties about permissible drops after reorganizations. First, COBE can be satisfied even when acquired assets are transferred, so long as those transfers are within an acquirer's "qualified group," as defined in the regulations. Reg. § 1.368-1(d)(4). This regulation only purports to deal with questions regarding the general continuity of business enterprise requirement, and not with the other technical requirements; indeed, it is clear that transactions that may comport with these relaxed COBE requirements may still fail to satisfy the other requirements.

The "issuing corporation" (e.g., Acquirer Parent in a triangular reorganization or Acquirer in a straightforward A reorg) is treated as holding all the businesses and assets held by members of its qualified group. The regulation adopts a definition of qualified group that echoes the definition of an affiliated group in section 1504, except that it relies on section 368(c)'s definition of control (80% vote and 80% of each nonvoting class). Thus, the issuing corporation must directly own stock in at least one corporation that satisfies the section 368(c) control requirement, and stock satisfying that control requirement must be owned, in the aggregate (but not necessarily directly by a single corporation) by other members of the group.

Reg. section 1.368-2(k) helps substantially with some of the other more technical issues relating to the satisfaction of the requirements of particular reorganization transactions. Reg. section 1.368-2(k)(1) generalizes the proposition, implied by many of the earlier specific rulings, that successive drops and partial drops of the assets or stock acquired in A, B, and C reorganizations will not affect the overall characterization of the transaction as a reorganization.

Under these rules, a drop of assets or stock (whether of all or part of the assets or stock acquired) is permitted if the COBE requirements in Reg. section 1.368-1(d) are satisfied and if the transfers also satisfy the additional "other transfer" requirements in Reg. section 1.368-2(k)(1)(ii). In general, a subsequent transfer of assets or stock is permitted so long as it does not result in the termination of the existence of any of the relevant entities. If the subsequent transfer is a transfer of stock, it will be permitted so long as it does not cause the entity in question to no longer be a member of the group, as defined in the COBE regulations. Reg. § 1.368-1(d)(4). Reg. section 1.368-2(f) clarifies that the "party to a reorganization" problem will not exist in those transactions described in Reg. section 1.368-2(k).

Transfers of stock of Acquirer Sub or assets of Target (transferred in the merger to Acquirer Sub) are clearly permitted after forward mergers under section 368(a)(2)(D). Reg. § 1.368-2(k)(2) Ex. 7 (transfer of stock of Acquirer Sub to another member of the Acquirer Parent group); Ex. 8 (transfer of Target assets to a partnership in which Acquirer Sub has a one-third interest). Similarly, drops of Target stock or of Target assets are permitted after reverse triangular mergers under section 368(a)(2)(E).

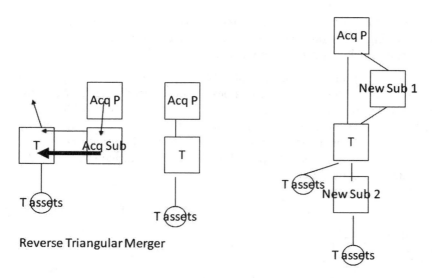

Reverse Triangular Merger

Drops of partial sub stock and of partial T assets

Examples of Permitted Drops under Reg. 1.368-2(k)
Transaction will not be recast under step transaction doctrine

19.2.2. "Push-Ups" of Acquired Assets or Stock

What if, in connection with or after a reorganization, the acquiring side would like to move Target assets or stock "up" within its organization? There are many fewer authorities regarding such transactions, and in general, the possibilities have been considered to be much more limited. For instance, older revenue rulings viewed liquidations of the Target corporation after a B reorganization as tantamount to a C reorganization under the step transaction doctrine, and that would be treated as nontaxable only if the C reorg requirements were satisfied. *See* Rev. Ruls. 67-274, 1967-2 C.B. 141; 72-405, 1972-2 C.B. 217.

However, the 1.368-2(k) regulations now permit a variety of distributions of acquired assets or stock to higher-tier entities. As in the case of "drops" of assets described above, the 1.368-2(k) regulations generally provide that a transaction that otherwise qualifies will not be recharacterized so as to fail to qualify as a reorganization because of a transfer of acquired assets or stock, so long as the COBE requirements are satisfied and the transfers are permitted in the regulations.

Distributions of assets of the Target, acquiring or surviving corporation (or of an interest in an entity received in an exchange for those assets) or of stock of the Target corporation or any combination of stock and assets are permitted, if the following requirements are satisfied: (i) if stock is distributed, the distribution does not cause Target to cease to be a member of the qualified group; and (ii) the distributions do not in the aggregate amount to either (a) sufficient assets to be considered a liquidation of Target, Acquirer (considering only the acquired assets or stock), or surviving (disregarding assets it held prior to the reorganization) or (b) all of the Target stock acquired in the transaction.

Thus, as provided in Example 2 of the 1.368-2(k) regulations, assets acquired in a C reorganization using Acquirer Parent stock may be distributed to Acquirer Parent or, as provided in Example 3, may be dropped into a new subsidiary, the stock of which is distributed to Acquirer Parent. (Note that these regulations do not guarantee that the consequences of the additional step will be those hoped for; they only provide that the additional steps will not affect the characterization of the original reorganization transaction.)

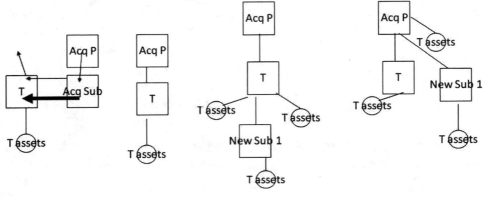

Reverse Triangular Merger   Drop of T assets to New Sub   Distribution of T assets and New Sub stock

Examples of Permitted Distributions under Reg. 1.368-2(k)
Transaction will not be recast under step transaction doctrine

19.3. OTHER PROBLEMS RELATING TO RECHARACTERIZING "MULTI-STEP" REORGANIZATIONS

Transfers of assets by the Acquirer side after the acquisition can create additional problems, involving not just failing to meet the technical requirements of the reorganization definition the transaction was relying upon, but also allowing recharacterization under the step transaction doctrine as a transaction that produces substantially different results. Indeed, such a recharacterization was involved in the case that led to the enactment of section 338, *Kimbell-Diamond Milling Co. v. Comm'r*, 14 T.C. 74 (1950), in which a taxable purchase of stock followed by a liquidation (that would have been nontaxable under sections 332 and 337) was treated as a taxable acquisition of assets.

When Congress enacted section 338, the legislative history indicated that the provision was intended to pre-empt the operation of any nonstatutory doctrine that would recast the purchase of stock as a purchase of assets. The Service confirmed this interpretation of the statute in Rev. Rul. 90-95, 1990-2 C.B. 67, in which it ruled that a taxable acquisition of stock will be treated as a taxable acquisition of assets only if the section 338 election is made. Accordingly, a cash reverse merger that is a "qualified stock purchase" for section 338 purposes cannot be stepped together with an upstream merger or liquidation to produce a taxable asset acquisition. Instead, each transaction will be honored separately. The rationale was that the taxpayer should not be able to use the step transaction doctrine to achieve a cost basis in assets without the toll charge of corporate taxation that would apply if section 338 were elected.

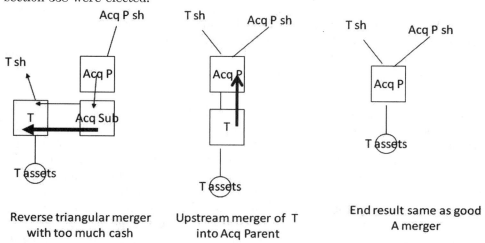

| Reverse triangular merger with too much cash | Upstream merger of T into Acq Parent | End result same as good A merger |

Rev. Rul. 2001-46
Initial taxable steps recast into overall nontaxable transaction

In Rev. Rul. 2001-26, 2001-23 C.B. 1297, however, the Service further developed the interaction of the step transaction doctrine and section 338, concluding that a taxable acquisition of stock should be stepped together with a second ostensible taxable acquisition if integration produces a non-taxable acquisitive reorganization. In the ruling, the first step involved the acquisition of 51% of the Target stock (a failed B reorg that also would not qualify standing alone as a "qualified stock purchase" for section 338 purposes), and the second step involved a stock and cash merger of Acquirer Sub into Target (producing the same end result as a good section 368(a)(2)(E) transaction). Because the consideration for the first step was all stock and for the second step was two-thirds stock, integrating the two steps resulted in a good reverse triangular merger under section 368(a)(2)(E). The Service ruled that the steps should not be treated as two separate taxable transactions, but rather as a single tax-free reverse subsidiary merger.

Shortly thereafter, the Service issued another ruling dealing with the application of the step transaction doctrine in the context of stock acquisitions followed by mergers. In Rev. Rul. 2001-46, 2001-2 C.B. 321, the first step was a reverse subsidiary merger in form that did not qualify under section 368(a)(2)(E) (or as a B reorg) because only 70% of Target stock was acquired for stock, and the second transaction was an upstream merger. If honored as separate transactions under the logic of Rev. Rul. 90-95, there would be a qualified stock purchase without a section 338 election, followed by a section 332 liquidation. On the other hand, integrating the transactions, in accord with Rev. Rul. 67-274 (and Rev. Rul. 2001-26) would result in the overall transaction being characterized as an A reorg. The Service ruled that the transactions must be integrated and no section 338 election would be possible.

Rev. Rul. 2001-46 was not greeted warmly by that part of the bar that would want a taxable acquisition of stock to be treated as such so as to allow an election under section 338(h)(10) (and the resultant step-up in basis of Target assets). The government obliged by adopting Reg. section 1.338(h)(10)-1(c)(2), explicitly "cutting off" the application of the step transaction doctrine when a section 338(h)(10) election is actually made.

The rulings described immediately above all involved situations in which there was enough Acquirer stock used as consideration for Target stock to allow the transactions to qualify as a reorganization if the various transactions involved were all stepped together, but not if the transactions were not stepped together. The ambiguity about the ways in which various acquisition transactions might be recast, and treated as taxable under some analyses and nontaxable under a different analysis, appears in other situations as well. What if an Acquirer uses cash to purchase an 85% interest in Target in what is clearly a good qualified stock purchase, makes no election under section 338, and then causes Target to merge into an Acquirer sub? If the transaction under analysis begins with the cash purchase of the Target stock, there is no continuity, and thus there can be no good statutory merger under section 368(a)(1)(A). If, on the other hand, the transaction under analysis begins with treating the holding of the 85% interest in Target by Acquiring as "old and cold," there is a good statutory merger. Regulations promulgated in 2001 under section 338 view this transaction from two different perspectives, depending on the type of interest at stake. The regulations treat the transaction involving the old Target minority shareholders as beginning with Acquirer's cash purchase of 85% of Target: when that is stepped together with the merger, there is insufficient continuity of interest for these shareholders to be given nonrecognition treatment. For Acquirer, Target and Acquirer Sub, however, the relevant starting point is after the cash acquisition, resulting in a good statutory merger. Reg. § 1.338-3(d). As a result, there is no question but that Acquirer Sub takes Target's assets with a carryover basis under section 362(b).

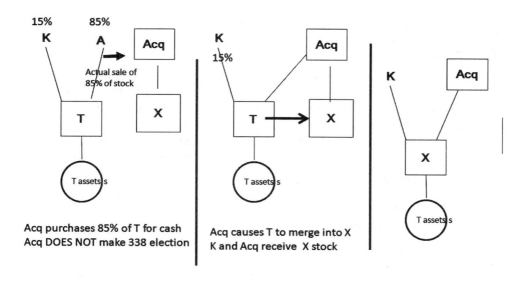

Acq purchases 85% of T for cash
Acq DOES NOT make 338 election

Acq causes T to merge into X
K and Acq receive X stock

Reg. 1.338-3(d)(5)
Acq transaction can be good reorg under A and D;
K's exchange of T stock for X stock is taxed under 1001

The attempt to preserve the preclusive effect of section 338 has led the Service in Rev. Rul. 2008-25, 2008-1 C.B. 986, to adopt a far less intuitive recharacterization of a reverse subsidiary merger. The Service ruled that a liquidation of Target following a reverse subsidiary merger causes the transaction to be treated as a *taxable acquisition of stock* followed by a *section 332 liquidation* because it fails the definitional requirement of section 368(a)(2)(D) that Target retain all of its assets. In other words, unlike the distributions discussed in connection with Reg. section 1.368-2(k) above, the ruling integrates the steps and recharacterizes the transaction because the transfer following the purported reorganization was a liquidation of Target. Unlike the situation in Rev. Rul. 67-274, the recast transaction in Rev. Rul. 2008-25 could not qualify as a C reorg because there was too much boot due to the liabilities associated with the Target assets.

PRACTICE PROBLEMS

Problems 1–3: True or False?

1.   In a transaction that would be described in section 368(a)(2)(D) except for the fact that the stock of both Acquirer and Acquirer Parent are used, the transaction will be taxable to the shareholders but not to the corporation.

2.   A transaction that would be described in section 368(a)(2)(E) except for the fact that Acquirer Parent already owned 25% of Target's stock will be treated as a taxable acquisition of stock, with no consequences to Target except to the extent that section 382 and related sections limit Target's tax attributes as a result of the change in ownership.

3.   Some Target shareholders can remain Target shareholders in a transaction described in section 368(a)(2)(E) but not in a transaction described in section 368(a)(2)(D).

4.   Target (which owns and operates a business adequate to meet the continuity of business enterprise and business purposes tests on which reorganization treatment is premised) holds two assets, each with a fair market value of $50, but with bases of $20 and $200. These assets are transferred to Acquirer Sub in the course of a forward triangular merger which is described in section 368(a)(1)(A) by reason of section 368(a)(2)(D). Acquirer Sub's bases in these assets will be

(a) $20 and $200.

(b) $50 and $50.

(c) $110 and $110 (that is ($20+$200)/2).

(d)   none of the above.

5.   Same facts as in Question 4, except that Acquirer Sub transfers both assets to its newly created and wholly owned subsidiary S-1.

(a) $50 and$ 50.

(b) $20 and $200.

(c) $110 and $110 (that is, ($20+$200)/2).

6.   Same facts as in Question 4, except that Acquirer Sub transfers both assets to Corporation X, a newly created corporation in which, after the transaction, it owns 20%.

(a) $50 and $50.

(b) $20 and $200.

(c) $110 and $110 (that is, (20+200)/2).

(d)   insufficient information.

7.   Same facts as in Question 4, except that Acquirer Sub is merged into Acquirer Parent.

(a) $50 and $50.

(b) $20 and $200.

(c) $110 and $110 (that is, ($20+$200)/2).

DISCUSSION PROBLEMS

Which of the following transactions can you argue should be treated as reorganizations as described in section 368, and thus will involve nontaxable exchanges of stock (or, where relevant, corporate assets for stock) except to the extent that boot is received?

1.   (a) Acquiring Parent forms Acquiring Subsidiary. Target merges into Acquiring Subsidiary, and its shareholders receive Acquiring Parent Stock in exchange for

their Target stock. Immediately thereafter, Acquiring Subsidiary transfers all of Target's assets to a newly formed wholly-owned subsidiary of Acquiring Subsidiary.

(b)   Same as part (a), except that Target shareholders receive about 10% of their consideration in stock of Acquiring Grandparent (which owns 100% of the stock of Acquiring Parent), and about 90% in stock of Acquiring Parent.

(c)   Same as part (a), except that immediately after the merger, Acquiring Subsidiary transfers half of Target's assets to its pre-existing wholly-owned subsidiary, and half to Acquiring Parent.

(d)   Same as part (a), except that immediately after the merger, Target's shareholders contribute the stock of Acquiring Parent that they receive to a newly created corporation, to which they have also contributed cash.

2.   (a) Acquiring Parent forms Acquiring Subsidiary. Acquiring Subsidiary merges into Target, and all of Target's shareholders each receive Acquiring Parent Stock worth a total of $85 and cash of $15 in exchange for their Target stock.

(b)   Same as part (a) (but assuming that voting stock is used), except that Acquiring Subsidiary was created 5 years earlier and has conducted a small business similar to that of Target during those years.

(c)   Same as part (a), except that Acquiring Parent acquired 3% of Target stock in exchange for cash 3 months before the merger negotiations began.

(d)   Same as part (a), except that Acquiring Parent acquired 50% of Target stock as the result of a tender offer made 3 months before the merger negotiations began. In the tender offer, it transferred its own stock to Target shareholders in exchange for their Target stock.

3.   (a) Target is merged into Acquiring Subsidiary in a transaction in which Target shareholders receive Acquiring Parent stock and which qualifies as a merger under section 368(a)(1)(A) by reason of section 368(a)(2)(D). Acquiring Subsidiary is then merged into Acquiring Parent.

(b)   Acquirer acquired 100% of the stock of Target in a tender offer in which 85% of the consideration was its own stock and 15% of the consideration was cash. Unbeknownst to its outside tax counsel, the tender offer would not have been completed if Acquirer had not planned, immediately after its completion, to have Target merge into a 100% controlled subsidiary (that was created for the purpose of the transaction) in order to eliminate Target's corporate charter as quickly as possible. Acquirer's tax department and outside counsel had been counting on making a section 338(a)/(g) election to use the massive carryover losses of Target before they expire. Is this election still available?

4.   Joe claims that boot used by an acquirer in a transaction that qualifies as a merger under section 368(a)(1)(A) by reason of section 368(a)(2)(D) can never increase the basis in the Target assets. Hal claims that it can. Who is correct and why? Hint: in what fundamental transaction will boot that triggers gain produce a basis increase in assets?

Chapter 20

OTHER ACQUISITIVE AND NONDIVISIVE TRANSACTIONS

Statutes and Regulations	IRC §§ 351 revisited, 368(a)(1)(A) & (2)(E) revisited, 368(a)(1)(D), (a)(2)(H)(i), 354(b)(1)
Other Primary Authorities	Rev. Rul. 84-44, 1984-1 C.B. 105
	PLR 201003012
	Kass v. Commissioner, 60 T.C. 218 (1973)
	James Armour, Inc. v. Commissioner, 43 T.C. 295 (1964)
	Warsaw Photographic Associates, Inc. v. Commissioner, 84 T.C. 21 (1985)
	Rev. Rul. 2002-85, 2002-2 C.B. 986
	Rev. Rul. 2007-8, 2007-1 C.B. 469
	Rev. Rul. 2004-83, 2004-2 C.B. 157

20.1. ACQUISITIVE SECTION 351 TRANSACTIONS

Section 351 allows nonrecognition for shareholders' transfers of assets to a corporation when a controlling block of shareholders participate in making such transfers. This is useful not just for the formation of new corporations or for additional contributions by existing shareholders, but also for some transactions in which corporate businesses are combined. The most obvious situation for the use of such an acquisitive section 351 transaction occurs when there are two or more existing businesses some or all of which are already operating as corporations, there are only a limited number of shareholders and other owners, and all of them desire to combine their economic fortunes by combining the businesses. All of the owners simply agree to contribute their stock or assets in a transaction that looks very much like what you would expect if no one had already incorporated. (Note that the limitation on the formation of investment companies in section 351(e) may be relevant in some such transactions.)

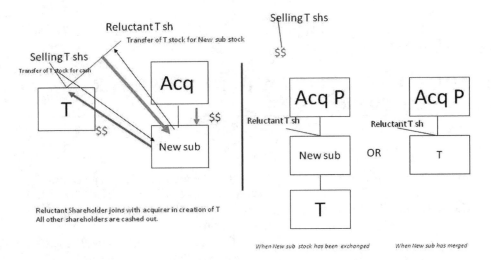

Using Section 351 for Acquisitions

20.1.1.   *"National Starch* Transactions"

Section 351 can also be useful in cases in which some shareholders of a potential Target are reluctant to sell because they do not want to recognize gain on their Target stock but may nonetheless want to diversify their investment (and prefer a fairly liquid investment that could be monetized if necessary). A typical scenario might be an older investor who expects to die relatively soon and does not want to give up the benefit for her heirs of the step-up in basis at death. If a number of shareholders sufficient to satisfy the continuity of interest requirement for an A reorg are willing to continue holding the risks inherent in the existing Target corporation, then a simple A reorg or a forward triangular merger will suffice. Shareholders who are reluctant to sell ("Reluctant Shareholders") can continue with somewhat changed economic risks and no taxable event, except to the extent that they accept boot. But if Reluctant Shareholders represent less than the percentage of Target shareholders necessary for continuity (i.e., 40% or so), can these shareholders in effect have their cake and eat it too by reducing their risk while still participating in a nontaxable transaction? It may be possible, if an Acquirer is willing to accommodate them or if they have enough power to block what they consider an unsatisfactory transaction under state law. *See* Kass v. Commissioner, 60 T.C. 218, *aff'd by court order*, 491 F.2d 749 (3d Cir. 1974), for an interesting example of the plight of such folks when an Acquirer does not want to cooperate.

With a cooperative Acquirer, the goal of a *"National Starch* transaction" is to transfer Target's assets in a nonrecognition transaction, to cash out most of Target's shareholders, but at the same time to permit certain Target shareholders to receive a new equity interest that replaces their former Target holding. Because there is no continuity of interest requirement for nonrecognition under section 351, see Rev. Rul. 84-71, 1984-1 C.B. 106, the percentage of Target shareholders receiving an equity interest in the corporation formed in the transaction can be substantially less than that required for an A reorg.

Shareholders of Acquirer (often a public corporation in these transactions) do not participate in the transaction, so Acquirer cannot be the transferee corporation; instead, the transferee corporation must end up as a lower-tier subsidiary that is controlled by Acquirer but that has the former Target shareholders, the Reluctant Shareholders who receive equity interests, as minority shareholders. But the stock of the parent of a transferor cannot be used in a section 351 transaction, and minority equity interests are often not very appealing. What can be done to make the Target shareholders' minority interest in the lower-tier Acquirer subsidiary more appealing?

Before the enactment of section 351(g), there was a fairly reasonable possibility of satisfying both Reluctant Shareholders (who want a relatively liquid and secure interest that they can receive without tax) and Acquirer (a corporation, often public, that wants to do the acquisition but is not likely to relish having an actively participating minority interest in the acquired corporation remain after the acquisition). Acquirer could transfer to a newly created corporation, Acquirer Sub, sufficient cash to buy out the selling shareholders, in exchange for stock in Acquirer Sub. Reluctant Shareholders could transfer their Target stock to Acquirer Sub in exchange for preferred stock. The preferred stock would have a liquidation preference equal to the agreed-upon value of their Target stock, bear a cumulative preferred dividend, and (probably most important to Reluctant Shareholders) include a right to have the preferred shares redeemed at a convenient time in the future (for instance, shortly after a Reluctant Shareholder's death, and thus a stepped-up basis for the Reluctant Shareholder's heirs). Acquirer Sub could then use the cash to acquire the stock of the selling shareholders. The acquisition could probably be done most expeditiously by means of a third-tier Acquirer Sub that holds the cash and is merged with Target. This cash merger should, under Rev. Rul. 73-427, 1973-2 C.B. 301, be treated as a taxable acquisition by Acquirer Sub of the Target stock. In either case, after the transaction Reluctant Shareholders would hold preferred stock in Acquirer Sub, Acquirer Sub would own all of the stock of Target and whatever other assets are necessary to satisfy Reluctant Shareholders about the risks they are running in holding the redeemable preferred stock of Acquirer Sub.

The enactment of section 351(g) in 1997, apparently in response to the above type of transaction attempted by shareholders of National Starch when it was acquired by INDOPCO, *INDOPCO, Inc. v. Commissioner*, 503 U.S. 79 (1992) (a case more famous for its holding requiring capitalization of acquisition costs) made it considerably harder to fashion an interest in Acquirer Sub suitable for Reluctant Shareholders. In this context, the rationale for section 351(g) may be more convincing than in the non-acquisitive section 351 context. Some stock represents so insignificant a continuing interest in the economic risks of a corporation that its recipient does not deserve nonrecognition, even if its use in a transaction that otherwise qualifies for nonrecognition should not defeat nonrecognition for the corporation or the other shareholders who receive more typical stock interests. If the Reluctant Shareholders' new interests are too thin, they should not be eligible for nonrecognition. This comports with the additional statutory embellishment of the section 351(g) nonqualified preferred concept. For instance, a 2004 amendment modified the language describing what is meant by significant participation in corporate growth. § 351(g)(3)(A). Nonqualified preferred stock is also highly likely not to be considered stock for purposes of the control requirement in section 1504(a)(4).

Sometimes Reluctant Shareholders do not want to hold any interest in Acquirer Sub (which on the above facts was essentially a continuation of Target until Acquirer did something more) but would be willing to receive an interest in Acquirer Parent, especially if Acquirer Parent is publicly traded. This cannot be accomplished in a simple section 351 transaction: Acquirer Sub, not Acquirer Parent, is the transferee; and only the transferee corporation's stock can be received without recognition by transferring shareholders in a section 351 nonrecognition transaction. If Acquirer Parent were to contribute its stock to Acquirer Sub, and Acquirer Sub were to use this stock as the consideration it gives in the section 351 transaction, the Acquirer Parent stock would be boot to the Reluctant Shareholders and section 311 would possibly apply to trigger gain to Acquirer Sub (though the new section 1032 regulations may provide relief in avoiding section 311 gain in appropriate circumstances). Some practitioners argue, nonetheless, that one ought to be able to set the terms of Acquirer Sub stock so that it would include future rights to Acquirer Parent stock, without those rights being treated as separate property rights (and therefore boot to Reluctant Shareholders) or, equally satisfactory in many situations, with those rights being valued at a sufficiently low amount so that any gain triggered would be acceptable to Reluctant Shareholders. In other situations, the Acquirer Sub stock held by the Reluctant Target shareholders may later be exchanged for Acquirer Parent stock in a B reorg, since control need not be acquired in the B reorg.

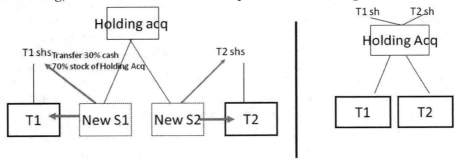

Double Dummy Transaction
making a "failed" rev triang merger nontaxable under § 351

20.2.   "DOUBLE DUMMY" TRANSACTIONS

Although section 351(g) limited the usefulness of the *National Starch* transaction described above as a way to diversify without selling, other acquisitive section 351 transactions remain useful. One such transaction is frequently called the "top hat" or "horizontal double dummy" technique. It usually involves two corporations that must maintain their separate existence yet at the same time want to combine in a way that will allow shareholders to invest in a single entity that combines the risks inherent in each of them. If all shareholders of the separate entities are willing to take stock of the combined entity, then it may be possible for them to join together in a straightforward section 351 transaction in which they form a control group that transfers all of the stock of both entities. Organizing this transaction, especially if the corporations are publicly held, is not an easy task, however.

The solution comes with the use of the "double-dummy." An entirely new corporation that will be a holding company (Holdco) is formed, and Holdco in turn creates two new subsidiaries. These two subsidiaries are each merged into one of the two existing corporations in a reverse subsidiary merger, with the pre-existing public corporations as the survivors. The Holdco (parent) stock is the consideration used in the mergers.

Note that the end result of this transaction is the same as if the shareholders of the existing corporations had directly formed Holdco by transferring to it the stock of both existing corporations in exchange for Holdco stock. In appropriate circumstances, practitioners have found this resemblance sufficient to argue that the double dummy transaction should in fact be treated as a section 351 transaction: the transitory subsidiaries should be ignored, and the transaction should be treated as if the stock of the two pre-existing entities were contributed by their shareholders to Holdco. The Service has agreed with this analysis in many private letter rulings, but there is no precedential guidance upholding this interpretation.

Why is this argument relying on section 351 necessary, rather than simple reliance on the reorganization provisions? In some cases, nonrecognition can be claimed under both sections; in others, there may be technical problems with qualifying under section 368(a)(2)(E). Suppose that the transactions whereby the existing corporations' shareholders give up Target stock and take back Holdco stock would not qualify as a reverse triangular merger because too many shareholders want debt securities of Holdco rather than stock. (Remember that 80% voting stock consideration is required for a successful section 368(a)(1)(A)/368(a)(2)(E) reorganization.) A forward triangular merger might work, but then each Target's corporate entity would be terminated, the corporate law aspects of the transaction could be very different, and the recharacterization of the transaction as a whole becomes more problematic. If the double-dummy transaction is respected as a good section 351 transaction, shareholders who choose to receive Holdco stock will enjoy nonrecognition and the existing Targets will survive. Similarly, a double-dummy transaction that is respected as a section 351 transaction is helpful if there is some question whether the existing corporations will hold "substantially all of their assets" (a requirement of section 368(a)(2)(E), but not of section 351) as a result of asset dispositions before the merger. Finally, the possibility of treating the existing shareholders as transferors in a double-dummy transaction that qualifies as a section 351 transaction opens up the possibility that transferor gain will increase basis in target assets, a result that is not possible without the section 351 recast.

The double-dummy transaction is of less interest now than it was before the 1989 elimination of nonrecognition receipt of securities in a section 351 transaction, since many Target shareholders may prefer to have their Target interest monetized in the deal.

20.3. NONDIVISIVE D REORGANIZATIONS

The language of section 368(a)(1)(D), as further conditioned by section 368(a)(2)(H), anticipates two types of "D reorg" transactions. First, section 368(a)(1)(D) anticipates a "nondivisive" or "acquisitive" transaction, in which there is a transfer of assets to a corporation in exchange for stock of the transferee corporation, which is controlled by the transferor itself (or its shareholders). Under section 354(b), the transferee must acquire substantially all the assets of the transferor, and the transferor corporation must liquidate. Second, section 368(a)(1)(D) anticipates a "divisive" transaction (often referred to as a "spin-off"), in which there is a transfer of assets by a transferor corporation, followed by a distribution of the transferee corporation's stock to the transferor corporation's shareholders, such that the shareholders end up with the stock of both distributing and controlled corporations. This second type of D reorganization is the only one in which the Target shareholders can receive nonrecognition when they end up holding directly the stock of two corporations as a result of the reorganization. Section 355, considered in Chapters 23 through 25, governs nonrecognition for such divisive transactions (generically referred to as "spin-offs").

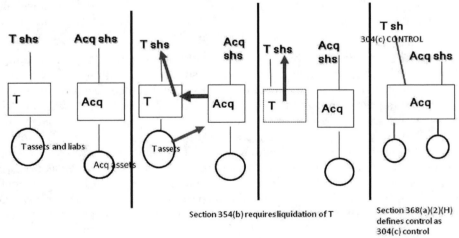

Section 354(b) requires liquidation of T

Section 368(a)(2)(H) defines control as 304(c) control

D Acquisitive Reorg: Asset transfer to controlled corporation
T 's shareholders in control of Acq immediately after

The basic pattern for a nondivisive D reorganization is essentially the same as that for a C reorganization — that is, a transfer of assets in exchange for stock that ends up in the hands of the transferor's shareholders, and a liquidation of the transferor, except that the transferor corporation (Target) shareholders control the transferee corporation (Acquirer) after the transaction. But the technical requirements are much easier to meet. Indeed, as will be made clear in the following discussion, the approach to continuity-of-interest concerns is also entirely different from that in other reorganization definitions. There is, moreover, no limit on the use of boot or any requirement that solely voting stock be used, so long as the requisite control is achieved. The normal control requirement in section 368(c) is altered by section 368(a)(2)(H), which incorporates the far less stringent control rules of section 304 (the code section which potentially transforms sales between affiliated corporations into dividend distributions). The threshold for control and for defining related party is substantially lowered, and the attribution rules of section 318 apply, with modifications specified in section 304(c). Accordingly, the threshold for "control" for nondivisive D transactions is a "50% vote-or-value" test: at least 50% of the aggregate voting power of all classes of stock entitled to vote **or** at least 50% of the aggregate value of all classes of stock. Finally, the "substantially all" requirement in section 354(b) has been interpreted very differently from the ostensibly similar requirement in a C reorg.

Why would there be such a low threshold for reorganization treatment in this context? The answer lies in the fact that, more often than not (at least historically), taxpayers have **not** wanted nonrecognition treatment to apply to them in transactions that fit this nondivisive D pattern. (Indeed, this same motivation may lie behind the conclusion that the net value requirement imposed upon most other nonrecognition provisions in subchapter C was not made applicable to nondivisive D transactions in the 2005 proposed regulations.) To understand this dynamic, consider the context in which the provisions apply: a group of shareholders owns two corporations and transfers most of the assets from one to the other. What might the shareholders be trying to accomplish?

Before the legislative "repeal" of *General Utilities* in 1986, they might have wanted to accomplish an ostensibly *taxable* transfer of assets to provide a step-up in basis. Prior to 1986, a transaction that was effectively taxable only at the shareholder level could nonetheless produce a step-up in corporate basis; that is, the regularly paid price for a step-up in basis was *only* the payment of shareholder tax, since a corporation that liquidated could sell its assets with only limited gain recognition. Suppose the shareholders of a corporation with substantial physical assets wanted to obtain such a step-up in basis to take advantage of newly enacted generous cost recovery provisions. They could try to do so simply by creating a new corporation to which the assets of the old corporation would be sold, perhaps on the installment basis, but which would receive the benefit of the rule in old section 337 that allowed nonrecognition of gain on such a sale when followed by a complete liquidation. (Or they could have achieved the same result by liquidating the old corporation and selling the assets to the new corporation, in that case, taking advantage of the nonrecognition provided by old section 336.) The imposition of reorganization treatment upon such transactions would defeat the desired basis step-up. Even under current law, taxpayers might want to cause a taxable transaction (by creating a transferee corporation and having that corporation buy transferor corporation assets) in order to trigger losses in the assets of the transferor corporation. In each case, those transactions would likely be caught under the net of section 368(a)(1)(D) and treated as reorganizations.

This transaction is nowhere near as desirable now, given that corporate level basis must be paid for by corporate level gain. But even under current law, taxpayers might want to cause a taxable transaction (by creating a transferee corporation and having that corporation purport to buy transferor corporation assets) in order to trigger losses in the assets of the transferor corporation. Or they might want to trigger gain in the transferor's assets in order to take best advantage of expiring loss carryovers. In each case, those transactions would likely be caught under the net of section 368(a)(1)(D) and treated as reorganizations.

On the other hand, there are situations in which taxpayers may want to take advantage of the possibility of a transaction achieving reorganization status. Taxpayers might simply be arranging a transaction to avoid successor treatment for the transferee corporation under state law while nevertheless arranging for the transferee to succeed to the tax attributes of the transferor corporation. *See* Warsaw Photographic Associates, Inc. v. Commissioner, 84 T.C. 21 (1985).

In other situations, shareholders may be attempting to take advantage of the rules regarding corporate liquidations that both allow the use of all of a shareholder's basis in a liquidated corporation as a limit on gain recognized, and ignore the presence of earnings and profits in characterizing such transactions. If shareholders could "liquidate" and then "reincorporate" they would (ignoring corporate level gain for the moment) receive only capital gain treatment on the value received above their basis, and hold stock in a new corporation with no earnings and profits. Reg. § 1.331-1(c) and Reg. § 1.301-1(*l*) might be invoked to treat such transactions as if there had only been a dividend, but in some situations too much has happened to treat the "reincorporated" entity as the identical corporation. Treatment of such a transaction as a D reorganization would deny the shareholders most of the benefits they seek, since gain could be characterized under section 356 as a dividend, and undistributed earnings and profits would remain in the reincorporated entity. Again, since 1986, such transactions ordinarily bring with them unfavorable corporate level gain, limiting the need to stretch the application of a section 368(a)(1)(D)/354 transaction to block such transactions.

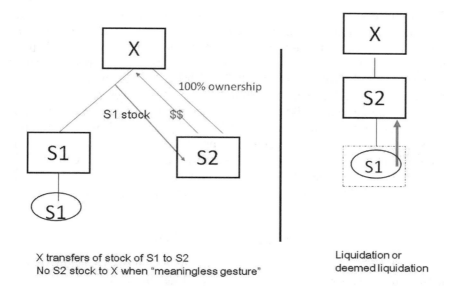

X transfers of stock of S1 to S2
No S2 stock to X when "meaningless gesture"

Liquidation or
deemed liquidation

"All Cash" D Reorganization
through stock transfer followed by liquidation

The "all-cash" D. The requirements of the acquisitive D reorganization have been sufficiently malleable that the IRS has historically taken the position that a transaction can be a D reorganization even when there is only cash and *no* stock actually transferred to the transferor corporation, and the courts have agreed. The government position on these "all-cash" D's was definitively staked out in regulations first proposed in 2006 and finalized in 2009. Reg. § 1.368-2(*l*)(1). This regulation confirms that no stock of the transferee need be actually distributed, despite the language of section 368(a)(1)(D) requiring a section 354 stock distribution, when the transfer of this stock would be a "meaningless gesture" because the stock ownership of the transferee corporation is identical to the stock ownership of the transferor corporation. (The regulations include the notion that stock interests will be treated as identical where the differences are "de minimis".)

Note that section 368(a)(2)(A) directs that if a transaction is both a C reorg and a D reorg (which it will be when substantially all of the assets of Target are transferred and Target is at least as valuable or more valuable than Acquirer), the transaction will be treated as a D reorganization. This provision was apparently enacted to ensure that section 357(c) would apply to these nondivisive transactions to cause gain recognition if liabilities in excess of basis were transferred. In 2004, Congress — apparently bruised from the basis-bumping transactions that led to the enactment of the anti-abuse provision in section 357(d) — amended section 357(c)(1)(B) to limit the application of 357(c) to divisive spinoff transactions — i.e., transactions that are described in section 368(a)(1)(D) by virtue of section 355. The only legislative history for the change is in the Joint Committee on Taxation's General Explanation:

The Congress also believed that it was appropriate to liberalize the treatment of acquisitive reorganizations that are included under section 368(a)(1)(D). The Congress believed that in these cases, the transfer[ee] should be permitted to assume liabilities of the transfer[or] without application of the rules of section 357(c). This is because in an acquisitive reorganization under section 368(a)(1)(D), the transferor must generally transfer substantially all its assets to the acquiring corporation and then go out of existence. Assumption of its liabilities by the acquiring corporation thus does not enrich the transferor corporation, which ceases to exist and whose liability was limited to its assets in any event, by corporate form. The Congress believed that it was appropriate to conform the treatment of acquisitive reorganizations under section 368(a)(1)(D) to that of other acquisitive reorganizations.

PRACTICE PROBLEMS

1. Target Corporation has one 22% shareholder who is reluctant to sell his stock to publicly traded Acquirer. All of the other shareholders are eager and anxious to get the cash that Acquirer is offering. Which of the following transactions will definitely not have a chance of offering the reluctant shareholder nonrecognition, while at the same time offering the reluctant shareholder less risk?

(a) A statutory merger in which all shareholders take Acquirer stock, with promised assistance from Acquirer to help Target shareholders sell into the market next year.

(b) A reverse triangular cash merger in which all the shareholders except Reluctant take Acquirer stock.

(c) A transfer by Reluctant of his stock and by Acquirer of cash to Acquirer sub in exchange for, respectively, preferred stock with cumulative dividends that depend upon the performance of the subsidiary and common stock, followed by a purchase by Acquirer sub of the other 78% from the other shareholders.

(d) A transfer by Reluctant of his stock and by Acquirer of cash to Acquirer sub in exchange for common stock of Acquirer sub that includes within its terms a right to acquire Parent stock in 5 years, followed by a purchase by Acquirer sub of the other 78% from the other shareholders.

2. Which of the rights can be present in preferred stock as defined in section 351(g)(3)(A) without rendering the stock section 351(g) stock?

(a) The issuer is a publicly traded corporation and the holder's heirs have a right to be redeemed at death.

(b) The issuer is not publicly traded and the holder's heirs have a right to be redeemed at death.

(c) The stock bears a cumulative dividend that floats with market interest rates.

(d)   The stock bears a cumulative dividend that depends upon the performance of a stock index.

3.   True/False: A transaction can never be considered a good section 351 transaction unless shareholders engage in a direct exchange with the transferee corporation of shareholder property for transferee corporation stock.

4.   When will a transaction described in section 368(a)(1)(C) always also be described in section 368(a)(1)(D)?

(a)   When less than substantially all of the assets of the Transferor are transferred.

(b)   When the liabilities assumed by the transferee are greater than the basis of the assets transferred.

(c)   When the stock of the Transferee is distributed to the shareholders of the Transferor.

(d)   When the shareholders of the Transferee are also the shareholders of the Transferor.

5.   *True or False:* Because qualification as a D reorganization is always a highly desirable result, the control requirement for a D reorganization is substantially higher than it is in other reorganizations. For good business reasons, she wants to combine their businesses.

6.   Sheryl owns all of the stock of Corp Risky and Corp Solid, both with a basis in her stockholdings much lower than the value of the corporations. Toward that end, she arranges that the following take place: Risky will transfer most of its operating assets to Solid, Solid will transfer cash worth about 10% of the value of Risky to Risky, then Risky will liquidate and transfer the cash and what little remaining assets it has (which it holds with virtually no appreciation) to Sheryl. How is this transaction most likely to be taxed?

(a)   Gain to Risky on 10% of its assets; gain to Sheryl of a little bit more than 10% of her total gain in her Risky stock.

(b)   No gain to Risky on its assets; gain to Sheryl of a little bit more than 10% of her total gain in her Risky stock.

(c)   No gain to Risky on its assets; gain to Sheryl of a little bit more than 10% of her total gain in her Solid stock.

(d)   No gain to Risky; gain taxed as a dividend to Sheryl to the extent of the cash she receives, assuming that her gain in the Risky stock is greater than 10% of the value of Risky assets.

7.   Same as 6, except that the liabilities of Risky associated with the assets it transferred to Solid exceeded Risky's basis in those assets by 500,000.

(a)   Risky will recognize 500,000 of gain.

(b)   Sheryl will recognize 500,000 of gain.

(c)   Sheryl will recognize 500,000 less her basis in Risky stock in gain.

(d)   The excess liabilities will have no effect either on Risky or Sheryl.

8.   Same as 6. What is Solid's basis in the Risky assets it receives?

(a)   Same as Risky's.

(b)   The amount of Sheryl's old basis in her Risky stock is allocated under section 1060 to the Risky assets.

(c)   Fair market value.

(d)   Same as Risky's, increased under section 362 by the "boot gain" recognized by Sheryl.

DISCUSSION PROBLEMS

1.   You were invited to sit in on a meeting with a client, a corporation that seeks to grow by "rolling-up" smaller corporations conducting related businesses. You heard a representative of the client make statements that indicate that he assumes that if more than 60% of target shareholders insist on receiving cash, there is no way to structure a transaction that offers the rest of the shareholders nonrecognition. Was that associate correct?

After having talked with their accountants, they have been led to believe that they can get better tax treatment when they receive the liquid assets of X Corp in a transaction whereby X Corp is liquidated. But they also know that for archaic regulatory reasons, the business of X Corp must be conducted in a form that will be subject to taxation under subchapter C, so they know that they will have to either leave X Corp intact or transfer its operating assets to a new corporation.

What should be the tax consequences of the various alternative proposals they are considering:

(a)   X Corp contributes its operating assets to newly created Y Corp in a transaction that meets the formal requirements of section 351, and retains its liquid assets. X Corp then liquidates, with the liquid assets ending up in the hands of A and B, who then proceed to contribute those assets to a new pass-through entity.

(b)   X Corp is liquidated, and its assets contributed to two new entities owned by A and B: Y Corp (which will in effect take all of the X Corp assets) and Z LLC (which will take all of the liquid assets and invest them). This proposal became far more attractive to A and B when they learned that due to the manner in which some of its contingent receivables were accounted for, X Corp actually holds some assets with a fair market value lower than basis.

(c)   X Corp transfers all of its operating assets to Y Corp, a corporation newly created by A and B, in exchange for a small amount of cash. X Corp then liquidates, leaving Y Corp holding the operating assets of X Corp.

(d)   X Corp transfers all of its operating assets to Y Corp, another operating corporation also owned by A and B, in exchange for an installment note. X Corp then liquidates, distributing to A and B all of its liquid assets and the installment note.

3. X Corp has 4 shareholders, Al, Bev, Cal, and Ed. Al and Bev each own 25% of the corporation, Cal owns 30%, and Ed owns 20%. Ed's lack of interest in innovation is starting to wear on the other shareholders, who are thinking about ways to cash him out.

Although X Corp was very profitable in its early years and has more than $600,000 of earnings and profits, X Corp has had a difficult time lately. First, it has spent more than $500,000 to construct a new widget production line in a new location, only to find out that the equipment simply does not work as promised. Second, it has had trouble distributing its products because of the anti-competitive actions of a rival.

The shareholders of X Corp think its prospects are looking up, however. It recently brought an antitrust suit against its anti-competitive rival, and received this year a payment of $400,000 in settlement of the suit.

X Corp plans to make the best of the bad production line, even though it will have to invest at least $150,000 more before the production line can be operable.

X Corp has the following assets on its tax books:

	Basis	fmv
capitalized new production line & warehouse	400,000	100,000
land at new facility	100,000	100,000
land at the old facility	5,000	10,000
plant and equipment at the old factory	100,000	70,000
raw materials inventory	45,000	50,000
finished goods inventory	20,000	30,000
cash (mostly from antitrust settlement)	400,000	400,000

Your boss has proposed the following transaction:

X Corp should completely liquidate. Each of the shareholders can take $100,000, and a pro rata share of the corporation's operating assets. In the liquidation, the loss on the investment in the production line can be recognized under section 336.

This loss will almost offset the immediate hit of income from the antitrust settlement. The net result (ignoring possible character differences, loss of $330,000 and income of $420,000) will be less in total tax liability for the shareholders and corporation viewed together than if the corporation had not been liquidated.

The shareholders will have capital gain to the extent that the total value that they receive is greater than their basis in their stock under section 331. (Al and Bev inherited their stock relatively recently, so this potential gain is not a great problem for them.) They each would receive about $175,000 in total value, but even for Cal and Ed, with low basis, this amount, taxed as gain realized on their stock, will be entitled to the capital gains preference, and produce a lower tax than the corporate level tax without the loss recognition.

Al, Bev, and Cal should then contribute the new production facility operating assets and $50,000 each to a new corporation, XL Corp. (This would be a section 351 transaction, although no nonrecognition protection would be necessary.) Ed can participate if he insists, but he is not expected to want to, and may assent to essentially being bought out by taking sole ownership of the real estate on which the old plant was located and receiving such other payment from unwanted X assets as can be negotiated.

Your boss has asked you to warn him of any possible tax problems he might have missed. Hint: Compare the interests of each of the shareholders before and after the transaction. What, if anything, is different?

Would it make a difference if Al, Bev, and Cal had created XL first (including promises to fund XL to the extent of $50,000 each), and then XL purchased the new operating assets of X for about $100,000 in XL's notes and the remainder in XL stock, with the notes going to Ed (along with such of the unwanted assets as necessary), and the reminder of the unneeded assets distributed by X to Al, Bev, and Cal?

Chapter 21

DISREGARDED ENTITIES: TRANSITIONS AND COMPLICATIONS

Statutes and Regulations	Reg. § 301.7701-3
	Reg. § 1.368-2(b)

The classification of an entity for federal tax purposes is a matter of federal law and is not definitively determined by the form of the entity under state law. The check-the-box regulations under section 7701 now allow most domestic entities with more than one owner that are not chartered under a state's general incorporation law to elect to be taxed as partnerships, so long as the ownership interests are not publicly traded. Under the regulations, a non-corporate domestic entity that is owned by a single shareholder will be disregarded for federal tax purposes, unless its owner elects for the entity to be classified as an association taxable as a corporation. Such "disregarded entities" may hold assets, engage in business activities, and have their legal forms recognized for state and other federal law purposes; but they will be treated as if they are not entities separate from their owners for federal tax purposes.

21.1. CREATION AND CLASSIFICATION

Although check-the-box elections are frequently made at the time of initial entity formation, they need not be. An election changing the status of an eligible entity can be made at any time, so long as no such election was made in the prior 60 months. Reg. § 301.7701-3(c)(1)(iv). Thus an entity that has a single owner (typically, a domestic limited liability company or "LLC") can switch, by a check-the-box election made on Form 8832, from being taxed as a corporation to being invisible for tax purposes. The election can be retroactive for 75 days or prospective for 12 months. Reg. § 301.7701-3(c)(1)(iii). Similarly, an entity that is disregarded can be changed to an entity taxed as a corporation, merely by checking the box on Form 8832. See Chapter 11 for a more detailed discussion of choice of entity considerations and the development of the check-the-box rules.

21.1.1. Creation of Disregarded Entity

Because the default rule treats a domestic single-member LLC as a disregarded entity separate from its owner, its creation is essentially ignored for most substantive tax purposes. Reg. § 301.7701-3(b)(1). An entity is not deemed to have made an election for the purposes of the 60-month rule when it accepts its default treatment. Reg. § 301.7701-3(f)(4) Ex. 2. Under Rev. Proc. 2002-69, 2002-2 C.B. 831, ordinarily an entity owned by a married couple living in a community property state will be considered to be owned by a single member.

21.1.2.   How Disregarded is a "Disregarded Entity"?

Reg. § 301.7701-3(a) provides in disconcertingly simple language that an eligible domestic entity "can elect its classification for federal tax purposes" and Reg. § 301.7701-3(b)(1)(ii) further provides that a single-member who does not elect otherwise is "disregarded as an entity separate from its owner."

This relatively simple language has produced some interesting puzzles, not all of which have been resolved. Some of these questions involve the interaction of the federal government's rights as a creditor for tax liabilities with state law property and contract rights. These questions have given rise to considerable litigation over the validity and meaning of the regulations under the federal payroll tax scheme; most of these issues have been resolved for liabilities arising after 2007 under Reg. section 301.7701-2(c)(iv) (making a disregarded entity not disregarded for the purposes of payroll obligations). Reg. section 301.7701-2T(c)(iii) provides that a disregarded entity may not always be disregarded if it is a successor by merger to entities that were not disregarded.

Other questions have arisen in the application of the substantive rules of the income tax. For instance, is debt issued by or assumed by a disregarded entity treated as if it were simply a nonrecourse debt of the owner, or as recourse debt of the entity? Only limited answers have emerged: it appears that an election to become disregarded will not by itself be treated as a change in obligor for the purposes of the debt modification rules of Reg. section 1.1001-3, *cf.* PLRs 200315001 and 200630002, because the election will not affect the creditor's rights under state law; the nature of the liability for the purposes of subchapter K will depend upon the situation, *see* Reg. § 1.752-2(k).

21.1.3.   Disregarded Entity to Corporation

If a single-member LLC that is disregarded as an entity separate from its owner elects to be classified as an association taxable as a corporation, the transaction is treated as if the owner of the disregarded entity contributed all of its assets and liabilities to an association in exchange for "stock" of the association. Reg. § 301.7701-3(g)(1)(iv). In other words, the membership interests in the disregarded entity are now treated as though they were issued to the owner in exchange for the assets (and liabilities) held by the LLC and are treated as stock in a corporation. If the single owner remains in section 368(c) control of the entity, the deemed transaction will qualify as a section 351 transaction, and nonrecognition should be available. If at the same time there is a transfer of the interests of the entity such that the original owner does not retain control, the transaction will be taxable under section 1001. *See* Reg. § 301.7701-3(f)(4) Ex. 1.

21.1.4.   Corporation to Disregarded Entity

If a single-member LLC that is classified as an association taxable as a corporation makes an election to be disregarded, the entity is deemed to have distributed all of its assets and liabilities to its single shareholder. Reg. § 301.7701-3(g)(1)(iii). The distribution is governed by sections 331 and 336 when the single member is an individual (and thus gain and loss on both stock and assets will be recognized); and it is governed by section 332 when the single member is a corporation. Reg. § 301.7701-3(g)(2)(ii) provides that the election itself will satisfy the "plan" requirement of section 332.

The ordinary rules for liquidations apply. Thus, if a disregarded entity is insolvent, the deemed liquidation will no longer qualify as a nonrecognition transaction under section 332, which requires a liquidating distribution of property in respect of each class of stock. Loss on the stock, and gain or loss on the disregarded entity's assets, will be triggered. *See* FAA 20040301F; Rev. Rul. 2003-125, 2003-2 C.B. 1243 (worthless stock deduction under section 165(g)(3) for no-net-value liquidation, including insolvent entity's election to be treated as disregarded entity); Prop. Reg. § 1.332-2(b) (nonrecognition liquidation applicable only if recipient corporation receives at least partial payment for each class of stock owned).

21.2.   TRANSACTIONS INVOLVING DISREGARDED ENTITIES

21.2.1.   Simple Transactions

In general, a disregarded entity is merely treated as a pool of assets (and associated liabilities) for the purposes of transactions involving it. A sale of a disregarded entity is treated as a simple sale of assets; a distribution of an ownership interest in a disregarded entity is treated as a distribution of the assets held by the entity; and a termination or liquidation of a disregarded entity under state law is, in general, a nonevent.

A disregarded entity (usually an LLC) may generally issue debt to third parties that is recognized as separate from debt of the owner under state law, with the result that the creditor's remedy will be limited to the entity's assets (assuming the entity's limited liability is respected under state law). For most purposes, therefore, this debt appears to be nonrecourse as to the owner. (Note that under final regulations promulgated under section 752 in 2006 regarding the determination of the extent to which an owner of a disregarded entity bears the economic risk of loss on a partnership liability, an obligation of a disregarded entity to make a payment on a partnership liability under a guarantee or similar arrangement will be taken into account only to the extent of the entity's net value. Reg. § 1.752-2(k).)

21.2.2. Merger Transactions

In many circumstances, entities that qualify as disregarded entities operate under default state laws that are much more like corporate law than like partnership law, including the possibility of short-form mergers. How, then, should their participation in such transactions with corporations that are subject to subchapter C be taxed?

After a period of some uncertainty regarding the federal tax consequences of mergers involving disregarded entities, regulations were finalized in January 2006 governing these transactions. *See* Reg. § 1.368-2(b)(1)(ii). While the general concept of the regulations is easy to grasp, the technical nature of the regulations required the introduction of a new set of terms describing the essence of a merger, as discussed briefly in the initial section on A reorgs. Reg. § 1.368-2(b) defines a "combining entity" as a corporation that is not a disregarded entity and a "combining unit" as a combining entity together with all disregarded entities whose assets are considered owned by the combining entity.

In order for there to be a reorganization involving a disregarded entity, two conditions must be satisfied in addition to the fundamental requirements for A reorgs. The regulations anticipate that there can be more than one transferor unit, and more than one member of transferor and/or transferee units, but the following summary involving only one of each provides a simpler introduction to the concepts.

> All of the assets and liabilities of each member of the combining unit that is a transferor must become the assets and liabilities of the combining unit that is the transferee unit.

> The combining entity that is the transferor must cease its legal operation for all purposes.

Both of these conditions reinforce the notion that transactions that qualify under section 355 provide the only nontaxable way to split a single (for tax purposes) corporation into two (or more) corporations. These conditions contain within them the limitations on the availability of reorganization treatment in transactions involving disregarded entities, as demonstrated by the examples in the regulations.

The merger of a Target corporation into a disregarded entity in exchange for stock of the owner of the entity clearly satisfies these two criteria. The disregarded entity, which is part of the transferee combining unit, becomes the owner of all of Target's assets and liabilities. Target is the transferor combining entity, and its separate legal existence terminates for all purposes. Reg. § 1.368-2(b)(1)(iii), Ex. 2. If Target itself owns one or more disregarded entities, the result would not change: Target is then a "combining unit" and the disregarded entities are merely pools of assets (and liabilities) of Target that are transferred to the transferee unit in the merger.

These rules may facilitate an acquisition in which Acquirer uses an LLC as the acquisition vehicle, frequently more attractive than a traditional forward subsidiary merger with a corporate subsidiary as the acquisition vehicle or other acquisitive structures. Assuming that the Acquirer can rely on the limited liability and corporate governance defaults in the relevant state's LLC law, the Acquirer can use the disregarded entity form of the merger to accomplish the merger within the minimal COBE and COSI continuity standards permitted in an A reorg while enjoying the liability protection and corporate governance implicitly provided by the disregarded entity format (including lack of any required vote by Acquirer shareholders, so long as there is pre-existing authority to issue the stock to be used). *See* Reg. § 1.368-2(b)(1)(iii), Ex. 2 (merger of Target into disregarded LLC of Acquirer, for Acquirer stock); Reg. § 1.368-2(b)(1)(iii), Ex. 8 (Target sale of a division, and distribution of proceeds, prior to merger into Acquirer). If for some reason, it is necessary to have Target merge into an LLC owned by a subsidiary of Acquirer, Acquirer stock — which for some purposes is effectively "grandparent stock" — can be used, so long as the transaction actually satisfies the requirements of section 368(a)(2)(D). *See* Reg. § 1.368-2(b)(1)(iii) Ex. 4 (forward merger of Target into disregarded LLC owned by subsidiary of Acquirer Subsidiary, for Acquirer stock).

In contrast, a merger of a disregarded entity on its own, without the rest of its owner, will not satisfy these criteria. The owner of the disregarded entity is the transferor unit, not the disregarded entity itself. The regulations require that the entire transferor unit transfer all of its assets to the transferee unit. In this example, the owner of the disregarded entity remains intact for tax purposes. This transaction will be treated as the disregarded entity owner's transfer of a group of assets in exchange for stock, which will qualify for nonrecognition treatment only in the very limited case in which the owner holds sufficient stock of Acquirer after the transaction to qualify the transaction for nonrecognition under section 351. Similarly, a reverse subsidiary merger cannot be accomplished using an Acquirer disregarded entity to merge into Target, since the Acquirer, the only candidate for "combining entity" of the "transfer unit" will not cease to exist. Reg. § 1.368-2(b)(1)(iii), Ex. 6.

But disregarded entities in transactions that take the form of reverse subsidiary mergers raise new questions about the application of the step transaction and substance over form doctrines to reorganizations. For example, assume that Acquirer creates a disregarded entity solely to separate a pool of assets to be transferred to Target, and then the Acquirer disregarded entity merges into Target, and only Acquirer stock is used. If such a merger is possible, Target shareholders will hold Acquirer stock and Acquirer will hold Target stock, just as would be the result in a traditional B reorg. Would such a merger of a transitory disregarded entity be entitled to B reorg treatment under the analysis of Rev. Rul. 67-448? If control were present, would the transaction qualify under section 351 as a transfer by Target shareholders of Target stock to Acquirer, followed by a drop of the disregarded entity assets into Target in a subsequent section 351 transaction?

An acquisition of Target's stock for mixed consideration (i.e., consideration that would not qualify for B reorg treatment) followed by Target's conversion into a disregarded LLC will be integrated as an asset acquisition: it will *not* be recast as if there had been a merger with an Acquirer-side LLC. Reg. § 1.368-2(b)(1)(iii), Ex. 9.

Consider now Target's merger into Acquirer's disregarded LLC, with Target shareholders taking back shares in the LLC itself rather than in Acquirer. The disregarded entity loses its disregarded status as a result of the state-law merger, because it has multiple owners. Under the default check-the-box rule, the post-transaction entity is taxed as a partnership. The transaction does not qualify as an A reorg under Reg. section 1.368-2(b)(1)(ii), because Acquirer is not treated as having acquired all of Target's assets. Instead, Acquirer is a partner in a partnership that acquired all of Target's assets. For tax purposes, the transaction is likely treated as if Target had first transferred its assets to a partnership and then liquidated, leaving the Target shareholders holding the partnership interests. This is a miserable result in most cases, because there will be two levels of gain (corporate gain on the distribution of the partnership interests under section 331, and shareholder gain on the liquidating distribution under section 336), with no step-up in the basis of the assets held by the partnership except as otherwise available under the rules of subchapter K.

21.2.3. Creative Tax Engineering Using Disregarded Entities

The availability of mergers into disregarded entities has allowed creative practitioners opportunities for avoiding most of the traditional limitations on obtaining nonrecognition in many situations, or simply assisted in accomplishing desired results in a taxable transaction when an actual sale of assets would be undesirable. Note that these innovative transactions are only of use within affiliated groups (or sometimes when there is a sole individual shareholder), since status as a disregarded entity is dependent upon there being a single owner.

a. Avoidance of Section 311 Gain within an Affiliated Group

Consider an affiliated group with a parent corporation (Parent) and various subsidiaries (Sub, Sub1, Sub2, etc.). Suppose Parent owns Sub, Sub1 owns Sub2. For good business reasons, Parent would prefer to hold Sub2 directly. Sub2 is not eligible for section 355 treatment because its business is too new. Sub1 could simply liquidate, but it is also important that Sub1 remain a distinct legal entity from Parent.

Sub1 forms Sub1-LLC, and merges into it. Sub1-LLC becomes a disregarded entity owned by Parent. Sub1's merger and transformation is treated as a section 332 liquidation of Sub1. All of its assets are treated for tax purposes as if they were owned by Parent. The subsequent actual transfer of Sub2 to Parent is a nonevent for tax purposes.

b. "Phantom Section 338(h)(10) Transactions"

The availability of disregarded entities means that additional alternatives exist for accomplishing a taxable asset sale without the individual transfer of assets. For certain corporate buyers and corporate targets (S corporations, members of a consolidated group), section 338(h)(10) and the regulations thereunder allow the convenience of a transaction that is a transfer of stock in its legal form but a transfer of assets for tax purposes. It appears that the same result can now be obtained far more generally when the applicable state law allows mergers of corporations into single-member LLCs (that are disregarded for tax purposes). The same price — loss of Target stock basis — must be paid for this convenience as is generally involved in a section 338(h)(10) transaction.

Suppose, for instance, that Parent owns all of the outstanding interests in Target. Acquirer wants to buy Target's assets. Transferring them in an actual asset sale will be difficult, however, because of the legalities in effectuating those transactions. If Target forms an LLC into which Target merges, Parent will become the single owner of the LLC and it will be a disregarded entity for tax purposes. The merger of Target into the LLC will be treated for tax purposes as a complete liquidation of Target into Parent, so the transaction will result in Parent being treated as if it owned Target's assets directly, with Target's basis. Acquirer can now buy all of the interests in the new Target LLC, which will be treated for tax purposes as a purchase of the assets of old Target. PLR 9822037.

PRACTICE PROBLEMS

1.	What if disregarded entity ("DE") elects to be taxed as a corporation at a time when it holds an asset with a basis of $10 and a fair market value of $100?

(a)	$90 of gain recognized.

(b)	$90 of gain recognized, but deferred until DE changes its status again.

(c)	No gain or loss recognized.

2.	What if DE transfers an asset with a basis of $10 and a fair market value of $100 to its owner corporation X?

(a)	$90 of gain recognized.

(b)	$90 of gain recognized, but deferred until DE changes its status again.

(c)	No gain or loss recognized.

3.	What is the result if DE merges under state law into a newly formed subsidiary of Acquiring Corp, in a transaction in which its owner corporation X receives Acquiring Corp stock and that would, if DE were a corporation, qualify as a reorganization under subsections 368(a)(1)(A) and 368(a)(2)(D)?

(a)	Normal reorganization treatment — that is, no gain to DE with respect to its assets, no gain to X Corp on its receipt of Acquiring stock in exchange for its interests in DE.

(b)	Gain and loss to X as if X had sold assets directly, no gain or loss to Acquiring on use of its stock.

(c)	Gain and loss to X as if X had sold assets directly, gain or loss to Acquiring on use of its stock.

(d)	Gain and loss to X on its disposal of its interests in DE, no gain or loss to Acquiring on use of its stock.

4.   What is the result if Target Corp is merged under state law into DE, in a transaction in which Target shareholders receive X Corp stock and that would, if DE were a corporation, clearly qualify as a reorganization under section 368(a)(1)(A) as a result of section 368(a)(2)(D)?

   (a)   Normal reorganization treatment — that is, no gain to DE or Target with respect to their assets, no gain to Target shareholders on their receipt of X stock in exchange for Target stock.

   (b)   Gain and loss to X as if X had sold DE's assets directly, no gain or loss to X on use of its stock.

   (c)   Gain and loss to Target on its assets and to its shareholders on their exchange of stock.

   (d)   Gain and loss to X on its interests in DE.

5.   What is the result if Target Corp is merged into DE, which is owned by Acquirer Sub, a 100% owned subsidiary of X Corp, in a transaction in which Target shareholders receive X Corp stock and that would, if Target had merged into Acquirer Sub, qualify as a reorganization under subsections 368(a)(1)(A) and 368(a)(1)(D)?

   (a)   Normal reorganization treatment — that is, no gain to DE or Target with respect to their assets, no gain to Target shareholders on their receipt of X stock in exchange for Target stock, and no gain to X Corp on its use of its stock or on its interests in DE or Acquirer Sub.

   (b)   Gain and loss to Acquirer Sub as if Acquirer Sub had sold DE's assets directly, no gain or loss to X on use of its stock.

   (c)   Gain and loss to Target on its assets and to its shareholders on their exchange of stock.

   (d)   Gain and loss to Acquirer Sub on DE's assets.

6.   What is the result if DE is merged under state law into Target Corp, in a transaction in which Target shareholders receive X Corp stock and that would, if DE were a corporation, qualify as a reorganization under subsections 368(a)(1)(A) and 368(a)(2)(E)?

   (a)   Normal reorganization treatment — that is, no gain to DE or Target with respect to their assets, no gain to Target shareholders on their receipt of X stock in exchange for Target stock, and no gain to X Corp on its issuance of X Corp stock or on its interests in DE.

   (b)   Gain and loss to X as if X had sold DE's assets directly, no gain or loss to X on use of its stock.

   (c)   Gain and loss to Target on its assets and to its shareholders on their exchange of stock.

   (d)   Gain and loss to X on DE's assets.

7.   What is the result if DE is merged under state law into Target Corp, in a transaction in which Target shareholders receive X Corp stock and that would, if

DE were a corporation, qualify as a reorganization under subsections 368(a)(1)(A) and 368(a)(2)(E) except for the fact that Target shareholders received more than 20% of their consideration in cash?

(a)   Normal reorganization treatment — that is, no gain to DE or Target with respect to their assets, no gain to Target shareholders on their receipt of X stock in exchange for Target stock, and no gain to X Corp on its issuance of stock or on its interests in DE.

(b)   Gain and loss to X as if X had sold DE's assets directly, no gain or loss to X on use of its stock.

(c)   Gain and loss to Target on its assets and to its shareholders on their exchange of stock.

(d)   Gain and loss to X on DE's assets.

8.   What is the result if Target Corp is merged under state law into DE, in a transaction in which Target shareholders receive X Corp stock and that would, if DE were a corporation, qualify as a reorganization under subsections 368(a)(1)(A) and 368(a)(2)(D), except for the fact that Target distributed about 40% of its operating assets to its shareholders before the transaction?

(a)   Gain and loss to X as if X had sold DE's assets directly, no gain or loss to X on use of its stock.

(b)   Normal reorganization treatment (apart from the Target distribution of its assets) — that is, no gain to DE or Target with respect to their assets, no gain to X on its use of its stock, no gain or loss to Target shareholders on their receipt of X stock.

(c)   Gain or loss to Target on its assets, gain or loss to Target shareholders on the distribution of operating assets, no gain or loss to X on its use of its stock.

(d)   Gain and loss to X on its interests in DE, no gain or loss to X on use of its stock.

DISCUSSION PROBLEMS

1.   Corp Acq owns LLC1 and LLC2, both of which have always been disregarded entities. It seeks to acquire Corp T and its wholly owned subsidiary, Corp TSub. What is the result if Corp T merges into LLC1 and Corp TSub merges into LLC2, both in exchange for Corp Acq stock, both under the appropriate state merger law?

2.   What if Corp T merges into a disregarded LLC1 and interests in LLC1 are given to the Corp T shareholders in the exchange? What would be the effect if an election to treat LLC1 as a corporation was made immediately before the merger?

Chapter 22

SECTION 368(a)(1)(F) "MERE CHANGES IN FORM"

Statutes and Regulations	Reg. § 1.381(b)-1(a)
	Prop. Reg. § 1.368-2(m)
Other Primary Authorities	Rev. Rul. 96-29, 1996-1 C.B. 50

Much of the law regarding recapitalizations under section 368(a)(1)(E) (discussed in Chapter 9) and F reorgs under section 368(a)(1)(F) (the topic of this Chapter) is somewhat blurry, if not outright obscure. There are several reasons for this, not the least of which is that in many cases the major stakes are not the stakes that are usually involved in reorganizations — nonrecognition to the corporations or to the shareholders involved — but instead some other stake that is less pervasively present in restructuring transactions or, perhaps, is more likely to have been subject to legislative tinkering. Authorities regarding the type of "mere changes in form" anticipated by section 368(a)(1)(F) have considered whether reorganizations that meet another definition as well can enjoy the more favorable treatment that definition would afford for their carryover losses. The resulting push-and-pull of Service and taxpayer positions has rendered the rules more than a little murky.

As in the case of recapitalizations, the difference between this non-acquisitive reorganization transaction and the standard acquisitive transactions described in subsections 368(a)(1)(A), (B), and (C) may be appreciated by simply noting the fact that the regulations now provide that neither the continuity of shareholder interest nor the continuity of business enterprise conditions (nor the net value requirement of Prop. Reg. § 1.368-1(b)(1)) apply in the context of E and F reorganizations. See Reg. § 1.368–1(b) (eighth sentence).

Section 368(a)(1)(F) provides that "a mere change in identity, form or place of reorganization of one corporation, however effected" will be a reorganization, and thus the parties involved can enjoy nonrecognition on any exchanges that may be involved. Despite the fact that something close to this language has been included in the income tax law since nonrecognition was first provided for corporate restructuring transactions, it still has no clear meaning.

For several decades before 1982, taxpayers had an incentive to argue that some transactions that looked more like A or C reorganizations were also section 368(a)(1)(F) reorganizations ("F reorgs"), to enjoy more favorable treatment of carryback losses under section 381. (F reorgs do not cause a termination of Target's taxable year on the transfer date under section 381(b); accordingly, F reorgs also do not use up a year for carrying back losses as do other reorgs.) Taxpayers had made considerable headway in transforming the nature of an F reorganization so that any transaction in which all of a corporation's assets were acquired by a corporation that continued its business and was owned by substantially all of the same shareholders would be an F reorganization.

In 1982, however, Congress added the reference to "one" corporation. The legislative history indicates that the creation of a new corporation, perhaps incorporated under more favorable state law, into which the subject corporation is merged, will not defeat the "one corporation" requirement. This position was confirmed in proposed regulations issued in 2004. Prop. Reg. § 1.368-2(m). Even if a transaction formally involves more than one corporate entity, the transaction can nevertheless qualify as an F reorganization if four conditions are satisfied:

1. All the stock of the resulting corporation, including stock issued before the transfer, must be issued in respect of stock of the transferring corporation (with an exception for issuing a nominal amount of stock to another shareholder).

2. There must be no change in the ownership of the corporation in the transaction, except a change that has no effect other than that of a redemption of less than all the shares of the corporation.

3. The transferring corporation must completely liquidate in the transaction (with an exception for mere retention of nominal assets for the sole purpose of preserving the legal existence of the corporation).

4. The resulting corporation must not hold any property or have any tax attributes (including those specified in section 381(c)) immediately before the transfer (with exception for a nominal amount of assets and the tax attributes related to those, necessary to facilitate the incorporation).

This set of conditions allows various transactions involving corporations with ongoing businesses and empty (although not necessarily new) corporations to be treated as F reorganizations. For instance, a typical "inversion" transaction occurs when an existing corporation becomes a subsidiary of a holding company by merging with its newly created, second-tier subsidiary in a transaction in which its shareholders receive stock of a first-tier subsidiary and the resulting corporation is liquidated. That inversion can be an F reorg if both of the subsidiary corporations are either transitory or have always been completely empty. Similarly, a transaction in which first the stock of one corporation is contributed to an empty corporation that is owned in the same proportion by the same shareholders and then the now-subsidiary corporation is liquidated can be treated as an F reorganization. *See* Prop. Reg. § 1.368-2(m)(5) Ex. 5.

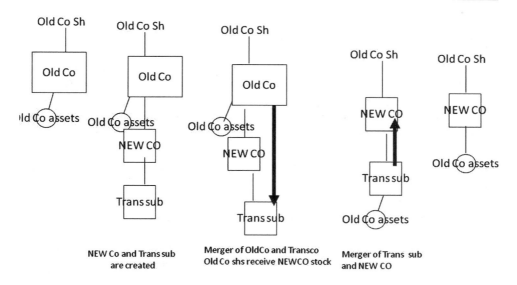

F reorganization "Inversion"
Proposed Reg. 1.368-2(m)
NEW Co and Trans Co must have no tax history

The proposed regulations also include two other ideas which, while arguably consistent with the prior positions of the Service, are nevertheless more controversial. First, they provide that a transaction (or series of transactions) that would otherwise qualify as an F reorg will not fail to so qualify as a result of being combined with other transactions, either before or after or both. Prop. Reg. § 1.368-2(m)(3). For example, this approach would allow a parent corporation that planned to use its stock to make an acquisition by means of a subsidiary merger to restructure in a good F reorg in anticipation of the acquisition without worrying about whether the fact that the Target's old shareholders are getting its stock will defeat the F reorganization. *See* Prop. Reg. § 1.368-2(m)(5) Ex. 7 (in which Parent merges into a newly created corporation chartered in a different state). Although this language restates the position taken in Rev. Rul. 96-29, 1996-1 C.B. 50, it is not entirely clear how much of an exception is actually intended to the initially stated requirement that there be "no change in the ownership" "other than a redemption" of the corporation. Consider the first and seventh examples in Prop. Reg. section 1.368-2(m)(5). In Example 1, the introduction of a new shareholder as a result of a cash contribution defeats F reorg qualification, but in Example 7, the introduction of a new shareholder as a result of a sale of stock by an old shareholder does not. Based on Example 7, however, it is clear that the presence of an F reorganization in the middle of a series of other transactions will not prevent the application of the step transaction to that overall series of events: the step transaction will cause a forward triangular merger to fail when it is followed by a recapitalization that is followed by a redemption of all of the stock issued in the merger.

Second, these regulations treat all distributions of cash or property as unconnected with the F reorganization, and thus as section 301 distributions. Prop. Reg.

§ 1.368-2(m)(4). This reiterates in a strong way the position in Reg. section 1.301-1(*l*). The preamble to these proposed regulations also states that the Service will take the same position with respect to cash received by shareholders in recapitalizations, but asked for comment on whether there should be any exceptions. The proposed regulation extends this idea beyond Reg. § 1.301-1(*l*) by the inclusion of the parenthetical "including in exchange for its shares." This phrase, as the Preamble and the next sentence make clear, is intended to subject all redemption-like transactions to scrutiny under section 302 as if the redemption took place immediately *before* the other steps of the reorganization (rather than after, as would be the case under the traditional reading of the *Clark* case if section 356 applied).

22.1.   F REORGS AND DISREGARDED ENTITIES

Because disregarded entities are "disregarded," reorganization transactions involving them may still qualify as reorganizations involving only single entities. In order for these options to be available, however, there must be a merger statute available for the particular type of entity involved.

22.2.   REORGS AND S CORPS

Because a Q Sub is disregarded for most purposes, the above reasoning applies. Thus, a downstream merger of a parent S Corp into its Q Sub will be an F reorganization. Reg. § 1.1361-5(b)(3) ex. 8. Similarly, in an "inversion" merger, in which a second-tier subsidiary merges into the parent S corporation, with the S shareholders taking back first-tier subsidiary (soon to be parent) stock, if the parent corporation is an S corporation and elects to treat its subsidiary (the old parent) as a Q sub, the transaction will be an F reorganization. Because Q Subs are not disregarded for all purposes, however, there are some practical complications, many of which are discussed in Rev. Rul. 2008-18, 2008-1 C.B. 674.

PRACTICE PROBLEMS

1.   Which of the following could not be characterized as a transaction described in section 368(a)(1)(F)?

(a)   P creates S1. P causes S1 to create S2. P merges into S2, and its shareholders receive stock of S1. S2 is then liquidated.

(b)   P merges into a wholly-owned subsidiary in another state, which it created for the purpose of changing its place of incorporation.

(c)   P merges into a subsidiary of which it bought 100% of the stock 6 years ago.

(d)   P contributes the stock of its wholly-owned subsidiary S1, which it bought five years ago, to a newly created wholly owned subsidiary S2. S1 is then liquidated, with S2 then holding all of the assets of S1 and assuming all of the liabilities of S1.

2.   According to a plan, Acquirer makes a tender offer for the stock of T, in which T shareholders exchange 60% of the stock of T for stock of Acquirer. Acquirer

then causes T to transfer all of its assets to Shellco, which was newly incorporated in another state and which, before this transaction, had only 10 shares of stock outstanding and held by Acquirer. T is liquidated, and its shareholders (its remaining historic shareholders and Acquirer) receive Shellco stock. Newly created Acquirer Sub then merges into Shellco and the shareholders of Shellco take Acquirer stock in exchange for their Shellco stock. How might this series of related transactions be characterized for tax purposes?

(a) A multi-step reverse triangular merger.

(b) A B reorg with an "embedded" F reorg.

(c) A C reorg followed by a B reorg.

(d) All of the above.

3. The shareholders of Oldco create Newco, and then Oldco merges into Newco, with some of the shareholders of Oldco receiving cash and Newco stock, and others receiving only Newco stock. Under the approach of Reg. § 1.368-2(m), this transaction will most likely be characterized as:

(a) A redemption (tested under section 302) of part of Oldco's stock and an F reorg.

(b) An F reorg in which some shareholders receive boot, the consequences of which will be determined under section 356.

(c) A liquidation of all of Oldco (in which all of the Oldco shareholders recognize gain, and Oldco recognized gain on its assets), followed by a contribution of some of its assets to Newco.

(d) A dividend by Oldco followed by an F reorg.

DISCUSSION PROBLEM

X Corp wants to do two things: change its state of incorporation and acquire a group of assets that represent only a small fraction of their current owner's total assets. The assets are, however, currently under the jurisdiction of a state regulatory body. Under current state law, the state regulatory body requires that if a corporation acquires these assets, it must be a corporation incorporated within the state unless a waiver is obtained. X Corp thinks that it may need to close the transaction in which it acquires the assets before it can obtain the waiver.

To try to accomplish this, X Corp engages in the following transactions. It creates a subsidiary in the new jurisdiction, and resolves to merge into that corporation as soon as the waiver is obtained. It then causes the new subsidiary to acquire the assets using X Corp stock as consideration. The merger occurs six months later, when the waiver is granted.

Is this transaction (or any part of it) a reorganization? An F reorganization? Does it matter which type of reorganization it actually is?

Subpart F

DIVISIVE REORGANIZATIONS

Chapter 23

OVERVIEW OF SECTION 355

Statutes and Regulations	IRC §§ 355(a), (b), (c); 356 (especially (b)); 358 (especially (b)(2) and (c))
	Reg. § 1.355-1, -2, -3
	Prop. Reg. § 1.355-3
Other Primary Authorities	Gregory v. Helvering, 293 U.S. 465 (1935)
	Rev. Rul. 2003-79, 2003-2 C.B. 80
	Rev. Rul. 69-407, 1969-2 C.B. 50
	Rev. Rul. 2002-49, 2002-2 C.B. 288

Congress has always been under pressure to provide a means by which corporations can restructure without incurring tax so that the result is two corporations, rather than one. For much of the history of subchapter C, Congress has obliged, but not without the imposition of substantial restrictions, including those now in section 355. Indeed, it is clear that Congress intended section 355 to be the only route to nonrecognition treatment for division of a corporation's existing businesses into more than one corporation whose stock is owned by the corporation's shareholders.

23.1. WHAT EVIL WERE THE SECTION 355 HURDLES CREATED TO PREVENT?

Gregory v. Helvering, 293 U.S. 465 (1935) (illustrated in the accompanying diagram), provides the best understanding of the answer to the question raised in the subtitle. If allowed to restructure in a way that resulted in the creation of two corporations without any restrictions, a corporation whose shareholders sought a dividend could (at least in the world before the legislative repeal of *General Utilities*) simply do as the corporation owned by Mrs. Gregory, the taxpayer in that case, did: incorporate readily marketable assets and transfer the stock of the new corporation to its shareholders. The shareholders could then liquidate the corporation and have access to the marketable assets. The only tax cost to the shareholders would be the preferentially taxed capital gain on the liquidation of the new and transitory corporation (a transaction in which an allocated portion of their old basis would be available), compared to full taxation of a dividend distribution without any basis offset and with no preferential rate. (Note that the use of this technique to avoid dividend treatment is far less interesting when the dividend rate is equal to the capital gains rate.) Before the repeal of *General Utilities*, the corporation could avoid (almost) all gain on its liquidation. Since the repeal of *General Utilities*, the use of this sort of spin-off to isolate assets and bail out earnings is less interesting (but not entirely uninteresting), since any gain on appreciated assets will be taxed at the corporate level on a liquidation.

Section 355 remains an important part of subchapter C nevertheless. This is so not just because of the old concern about dividend avoidance, but because of new concerns about the extent to which corporate restructurings circumvent the principles behind *General Utilities* repeal, broadly interpreted, when they result in shareholders owning the stock of two corporations *so that they can dispose of one of them*. The issue is to what extent a corporation should be allowed to divide its assets in connection with a transaction in which it in effect sells them, without recognizing gain on some or all of them. Congress responded to these concerns through the enactment of subsections 355(d) and 355(e). Since their enactment, the Service has waffled considerably about the strictness with which they should be enforced. The old limitations remain in place nevertheless, and will be considered first, in Chapters 23 and 24. Subsections 355(d) and (e) will be addressed in Chapter 25.

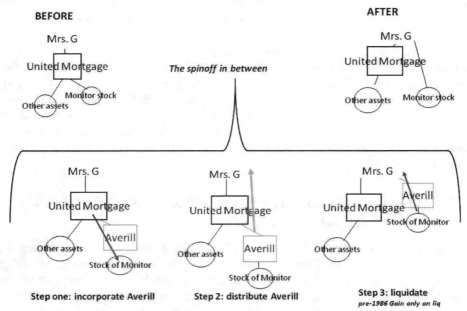

Gregory v. Helvering: Incorporation and Spin of Securities to Mrs. Gregoary

23.2. WHAT TRANSACTIONS ARE CONTEMPLATED BY SECTION 355?

Determining the scope of transactions contemplated by section 355 is not an easy question, because there are actually many variations. First, section 355 is ostensibly just one of the provisions that dictate the terms on which shareholders may receive stock in a nontaxable transaction. Note its placement in the Code between sections 354 and 356. Section 355(a) clearly fits with these provisions, though subsections 355(c), 355(d), and 355(e) are somewhat out of place, because they dictate corporate-level results rather than shareholder-level results.

The transaction contemplated by section 355 is the receipt of stock of a corporation controlled by the corporation in which the shareholder is already an owner. Section 355 thus creates an exception, for distributions of stock in a controlled corporation, to the general rule that stock of other corporations is just "property" when distributed by a corporation to its shareholders.

Section 355 dictates the conditions under which the receipt of the stock of a previously controlled subsidiary of the distributing corporation will be entitled to nonrecognition. The provision applies both when the controlled corporation's stock is received *with respect to* the distributing corporation's stock, *see* § 355(a)(1)(A)(i), and when the controlled corporation's stock is received *in exchange for* the distributing corporation's stock, *see* § 355(a)(1)(A)(ii).

Section 355 accordingly covers transactions which, were it not available (or more importantly, if its requirements are not satisfied), would be taxed as distributions with respect to stock that are likely to be characterized as dividends as well as transactions that would be treated as exchanges for stock and are therefore potentially eligible for redemption treatment. Transactions of the first type are generally called "spin-offs": the shareholders of the distributing corporation (Distributing) receive stock of the controlled corporation (Controlled) in proportion to their interests in Distributing, and continue to own the stock of Distributing after the transaction. Transactions of the second type are generally in the form of "split-offs" in which shareholders receive stock of Controlled in percentages that do not correspond to their interests in Distributing. A typical split-off in a closely held corporation may leave one former Distributing shareholder holding only Controlled stock, having been redeemed out of Distributing, and all of the other shareholders continuing to own the Distributing stock while owning none of the Controlled stock. Transactions of a third type are generally called "split-ups," in which the shareholders receive stock of at least two controlled subsidiaries and the former parent liquidates. Thus, spin-offs bear much in common with ordinary corporate distributions, split-offs resemble (at least for some shareholders) corporate redemptions, and split-ups look like corporate liquidations.

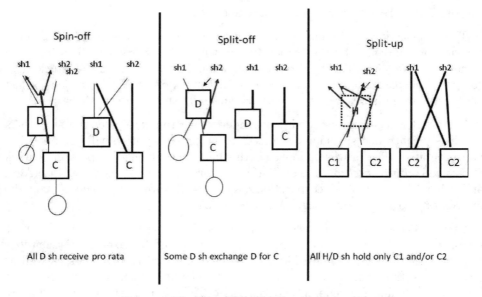

Types of Section 355 Divisive Transactions

The classification of reorganization transactions under these patterns will not generally matter in determining whether the transaction will qualify for nonrecognition under section 355, but the statute does in some particulars treat them differently. The most significant difference in the shareholder-level results lies in how the shareholders will be taxed on any boot they also receive. *Compare* § 356(b) (governing distributions and treating all boot as a section 301 distribution), *with* § 356(a) (governing exchanges).

There is another set of variations on transactions relying on section 355 that will depend upon the steps that Distributing took in preparation for the transaction. If the Controlled corporation whose stock is being distributed is already a subsidiary of Distributing, then the only aspect of the transaction that must be addressed is the treatment of Distributing on the transfer of the Controlled stock. Since section 311 requires the recognition of gain on a distribution to shareholders of property (that is defined as anything but the Distributing corporation's own stock or stock rights), section 355(c) now provides an exception to that rule resulting in nonrecognition on the distribution of the Controlled stock.

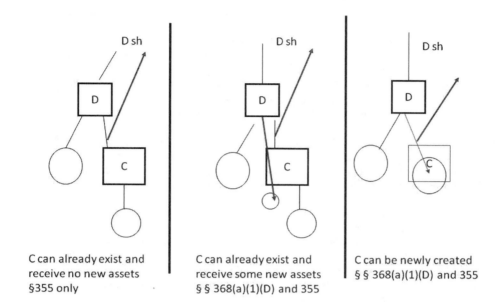

C can already exist and
receive no new assets
§355 only

C can already exist and
receive some new assets
§ § 368(a)(1)(D) and 355

C can be newly created
§ § 368(a)(1)(D) and 355

Use of New or Pre-existing Subsidiary

If Controlled must be created in contemplation of the distribution of its stock, however, its creation is controlled by section 368(a)(1)(D). These are "divisive D" reorganizations. In this type of reorganization, a corporation transfers "a part of its assets to another corporation" and "immediately after the transfer . . . one or more of its shareholders or any combination thereof, is in control of the corporation to which the assets are transferred, but only if, . . . the stock . . . of the corporation to which the assets are transferred [is] distributed in a transaction which qualifies under section . . . 355." The primary tax consequences of these transactions to the transferor/controlling/Distributing corporation will be specified in section 361, the same provision that dictated the treatment of Target in a C reorganization (and the non-divisive D reorg), rather than section 355(c).

Note that transactions through which assets are transferred to a Controlled subsidiary will almost always also qualify for nonrecognition under section 351, if the intended distribution could be ignored for the purposes of "immediately after." *See* § 351(c). Commentators sometimes simply assume this preparatory transaction fits under section 351 and look no further, but with respect to some details (for instance, the treatment of the transferring/controlling/Distributing corporation's earnings and profits), it may be important that it is sections 368(a)(1)(D) and 361, rather than section 351, that apply.

The Many Faces of Section 368(a)(1)(D):
One or Two Surviving Corporations?

A transfer of assets will be described in section 368(a)(1)(D) only if the stock of the transferee corporation is then distributed under circumstances that meet either the conditions of section 354(b) or section 355. Although in both circumstances the shareholders of the transferring corporation end up still indirectly owning all or most of the corporate assets of that corporation, the two involve very different patterns.

When a transaction qualifies under section 354(b) (a non-divisive D), the corporation must transfer "substantially all" of its assets to the controlled corporation and then liquidate. Only one corporation remains. Thus, the simplest non-divisive D reorg results in the Distributing corporation transmuting itself into the Controlled corporation, which is its corporate successor. Non-divisive D reorgs can also be used acquisitively: that is, in a transaction that resembles a C reorganization, the assets of the transferring corporation are transferred to another corporation, but relative sizes (or previous overlap of ownership) of the corporations are such that the shareholders of the transferring corporation take back sufficient stock in the transferee corporation that they have a controlling interest in the nominal acquiring corporation. In other words, in an acquisitive D reorg, the Distributing corporation ends up controlling Acquirer.

Some nondivisive D reorganizations involve very little actual change in the nature of the corporate structures involved. For instance, one such nondivisive D reorg occurs when the nominal Acquirer is created by the transferring corporation's shareholders to facilitate a restructuring in which Acquirer is just sufficiently different from Target that the transaction cannot be considered an F reorganization. All of these nondivisive "D" reorganizations were considered in Chapter 20.

Section 355 thus protects the receipt of the stock of a Controlled corporation in a simple distribution both when the Controlled corporation is pre-existing and no tinkering needs to be done with its assets or capital structure, and when that corporation is newly created (or newly the recipient of a portion of the Distributing corporation's assets) in a reorganization described in section 368(a)(1)(D).

23.3.   BASIC REQUIREMENTS FOR A SECTION 355 TRANSACTION

Nonrecognition to shareholders in a divisive reorganization is available only under certain conditions. These conditions all have to do with preventing the Controlled corporation from being a transitory entity with assets as liquid as the assets that Mrs. Gregory received, or even something less liquid that seems too easily sold. The concept here is similar to what makes preferred stock received as a stock dividend suspect and therefore subject to the section 306 taint. In that case, the section 306 stock represents an interest in a corporation that probably represents a going business, but the interest is so limited that it is too easily sold. Here, the fear is that the stock distributed may be an unlimited interest in something that involves very little economic risk and thus also can be sold too easily.

The statute sets out four tests in section 355(a)(1):

A. The distributing corporation must control the corporation the stock of which is distributed;

B. The transaction must not be principally a device for the distribution of earnings;

C. Both corporations must satisfy the active business test in section 355(b); and

D. The distributing corporation must distribute all of the stock it holds in the distributed corporation, or distribute control under section 368(c) and have approval for what it does retain.

As is the case in most other restructuring transactions for which nontaxable treatment is allowed under subchapter C, the transaction must also satisfy the judicially created business purpose requirement, and probably must also satisfy the judicial continuity of interest requirement. Reg. § 1.355-2(c) sets out the general standards for continuity of interest in section 355 transactions: the old shareholders of Distributing must still own, in the aggregate, interests in both Distributing and Controlled sufficient for continuity. (The applicability of other aspects of the continuity of interest requirement is a bit problematic given the specific language of subsections (d) and (e), and will be considered in connection with those provisions.) The continuity of business enterprise doctrine is not really a consideration, since the statutory active business requirement is so much more stringent.

23.4.   THE ACTIVE BUSINESS REQUIREMENT

Section 355 generally is aimed at ensuring that neither Distributing nor Controlled is something that is too easily sold, making the transaction a device for the distribution of earnings without ordinary dividend taxation. The active business requirement does much of the work in accomplishing this result.

23.4.1.   Active Conduct of a 5-Year Trade or Business

In general terms, section 355(b)(1) requires both Distributing and Controlled to be engaged in the "active conduct of a trade or business," and section 355(b)(2)(B) requires this active business to have been conducted for five years preceding the distribution.

The regulations have traditionally provided a relatively high standard for finding an "active trade or business." Reg. § 1.355-3(b)(2)(ii) provides that these activities must be "a specific group of activities . . . carried on for the purposes of earning income . . . and the activities . . . include every operation that forms a part of, or a step in, the process of earning income or profit." This standard is not easy to apply, however, given the ongoing evolution of American business structures. Under early rulings under this standard, GE Capital would never have been treated as a distinct business, because financing was only an auxiliary function within the business of selling electrical appliances.

Two types of situations present conceptual difficulties, although the regulations attempt to answer some of the more frequently encountered problems. First, when can territorial and other forms of horizontal integration be divided up so that two active businesses exist? Examples in the regulation illustrate permissible divisions of territorially defined operations. Reg. § 1.355-3(c) Exs. 4, 6, 7, 8. Second, when will the separation of vertically integrated processes be treated as resulting in two separate businesses? *See* Reg. § 1.355-3(c) Ex. 9 (allowing the incorporation of a research department), Ex. 10 (allowing the separation of processing functions from selling functions), Ex. 11 (allowing the separation of coal for internal use in steel manufacturing from the steel manufacturing). Further examples illustrate what the focus of the test is supposed to be. Reg. § 1.355-3(c) Ex. 1 (denying two-business status for the separation of manufacturing and sales assets from investment assets), Ex. 2 (denying two-business status for the separation of an actively managed office building from vacant land not yet under development), and Exs. 12 and 13 (both involving the separation of real estate operations from other operations, with different results). The possibility of separating aspects of what is currently conducted as a single business complicates the inquiry, since a determination must be made about whether each separate activity has a sufficiently long life.

The proposed regulations make clear that holding investment properties (including stock or securities) does not constitute the active conduct of a business, and ownership and operation of real estate (including leasing) will not be treated as an active business unless the owner performs significant management and operational services. Prop. Reg. § 1.355-3(b)(2)(iv). There are also special rules regarding the determination whether a partner conducts a business operated by a partnership. Prop. Reg. § 1.355-3(b)(2)(v).

23.4.2. Prohibition under Subsections 355(b)(2)(C) and (D) on Purchase of a Business or Controlling Stock of Corporation Conducting a Business

The statute also includes provisions designed to ensure that the businesses of Distributing and Controlled have been actively conducted by them for the five-year predistribution period or acquired during that period only in nonrecognition transactions. Section 355(b)(2)(C) denies "active business" status to a corporation (and thus, if this is the only business within the corporation, disqualifies the transaction from qualifying as a good divisive reorg) if there is a taxable purchase within the 5-year predistribution period of the business itself (i.e., all the assets that constitute the trade or business). Section 355(b)(2)(D) further denies active trade or business status when there has been a taxable purchase of stock providing control of a corporation conducting the business within this same pre-distribution period. The gist of these two provisions together can loosely be summarized as allowing the acquisition of an active trade or business when Distributing uses its stock for such an acquisition, but not when it uses its assets. *See* Part I.A, Preamble to Proposed Section 355 Regulations, 72 FR 26012, (May 8, 2007).

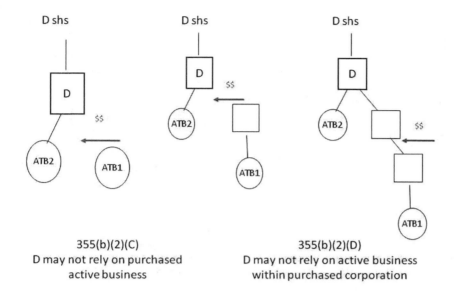

355(b)(2)(C)
D may not rely on purchased
active business

355(b)(2)(D)
D may not rely on active business
within purchased corporation

355(b)(2)(C) and (D) forbidden taxable acquisition of active business

These two provisions, however, only provide that the business acquired (or the business conducted by the corporation over which control was acquired) cannot be relied upon to satisfy the active trade or business requirement. The fact that *Controlled* (that is, the corporation the stock of which is distributed) has participated in such transactions and thereby acquired subsidiaries and businesses that are "too new" will not prevent Distributing's distribution of Controlled from qualification under section 355 so long as Controlled has another, sufficiently aged, active trade or business. The fact that *Distributing* has participated in such taxable acquisitions will not prevent qualification of the distribution of the stock of Controlled under section 355, again so long as there are other sufficiently "aged" active businesses held by Distributing, unless Distributing has acquired *Controlled* itself in a taxable transaction. (As discussed below, some other transactions described in section 355(b)(2)(D), through which a *Distributee* corporation gains control of Distributing may render qualification under section 355 impossible.)

However, subsections 355(b)(2)(C) and (D)(ii) do permit the acquisition of an active trade or business (or the stock of a corporation engaged in an active business) in a *nontaxable* transaction.

Such permitted transactions include transactions whereby Distributing acquires the assets constituting an active trade or business of another corporation through a statutory merger, effectively acquiring assets in exchange for its stock.

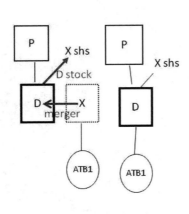

Acquisition by merger using D stock
D may rely on ATB1

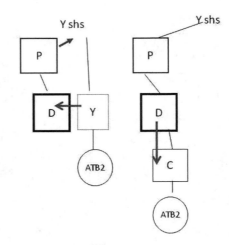

Acquisition by (a)(2)(D) merger with drop
D may rely on ATB2

355(b)(2)(C) nontaxable acquisition of active business
Prop. Reg. 1.355-3(d)(2) ex. 28

Permitted transactions also include the acquisition of control of a *corporation* when the stock of Distributing is used in a nontaxable transaction. § 355(b)(2)(D)(ii); Prop. Reg. § 1.355-3(d)(2) Exs. 43 and 47 (stock of controlled acquired in B reorg).

Although subsections 355(b)(2)(C) and (D) seem to allow reliance on acquired active trades or businesses (or acquired stock of controlled corporations engaged in active trades or businesses) whenever those acquisitions are accomplished through nontaxable transactions, the government has long held some such transactions with suspicion. In some nontaxable transactions Distributing could in fact use its *assets* to acquire active businesses in ways that are inconsistent with the overall purposes of section 355. Accordingly, the government has taken the position that such transactions may not be used to acquire an active business, even if no gain or loss is actually recognized to either party in the transaction through which the corporation engaged in the active business is acquired. Such transactions might involve, for instance, the transfer by Distributing of liquid assets to an unrelated corporation that is conducting an aged active business, in exchange for the stock of the transferee corporation, as a result of which Distributing has section 368(c) control of the previously unrelated corporation. Such a transaction would be nontaxable under section 351, but it would have allowed Distributing to use its assets, rather than its stock, to acquire the business of (and a controlling interest in the stock of) the corporation. *See* Preamble at C.3.b.i.; Prop. Reg. § 1.355-3(d)(2) Exs. 30 and 37.

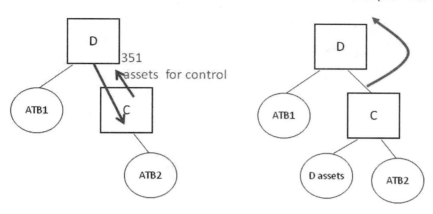

Transfer of assets to be used in ATB2 to previously unrelated C
D may not rely on ATB2 until year 6

355(b)(2)(D)(ii) purpose not met when D uses assets
Prop. Reg. 1.355-3(d)(2) ex. 30

Similarly, if Controlled were to acquire an active trade or business using *its* stock in a merger of a corporation engaged in an active trade or business into Controlled, the transaction would be treated as one in which Distributing acquired the business using its assets (that is, the stock of Controlled) and thus the acquired business could not be relied upon by Controlled. Prop. Reg. § 1.355-3(d)(2) ex. 31.

As described above, section 355(b)(2)(D)(i) has long provided that a business conducted by a corporation purchased by Distributing cannot be relied upon as the active trade or business conducted by Distributing. The transactions that might be used to try to achieve the same end are frequently not straightforward. Thus, section 355(b)(2)(D)(i) (second clause) directs that Distributing cannot acquire such stock "through 1 or more corporations."

For instance, this language blocks the use of nonrecognition transactions involving the stock of newly acquired Controlled corporations that might otherwise appear to be inoffensive nontaxable acquisitions of the type allowed by section 355(b)(2)(D)(ii), when Distributing might be said to "indirectly" acquire control. Thus this language prevents Distributing from purchasing through its wholly-owned Subsidiary all of the stock of Business Co, only to then liquidate both Business Co and Subsidiary in nontaxable section 332 liquidations and claim that it has acquired the active business of Business Co in a nontaxable transaction. Nor can T accomplish a similar result by acquiring the stock of D Co, merging downstream into D, then reincorporating its old active business in a New C Co to be spun-off to the old T shareholders. *See* Prop. Reg. § 1.355-3(d)(2) Ex. 39 (substantially restating the longstanding example in Reg. § 1.355-3(b)(4)).

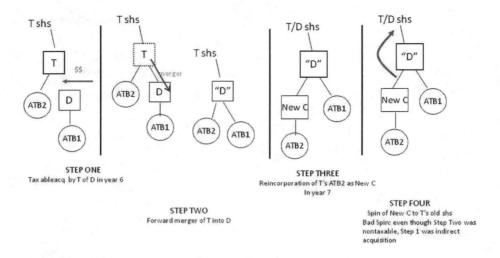

Prohibited "Indirect acquisition of control" in Prop. Reg. 1.355-3(d)(2) ex. 39

23.4.3. Distributee's Acquisition of Control of Distributing

Section 355(b)(2)(D)(i) also includes language perhaps most directly intended to frustrate attempts to arrange indirect sales of Controlled through the acquisition of control of Distributing by Distributee in a taxable transaction followed by the effective redemption of that stock through a section 355 distribution. If allowed, these transactions would permit "a corporation to dispose of an appreciated subsidiary without the proper recognition of gain contrary to the repeal of the *General Utilities* doctrine." Preamble to Section 355 Proposed Regulations, Part C.3.ii. The usefulness of this particular provision in this role has been largely, but not entirely, supplanted by subsections 355(d) and (e).

If Distributee has engaged in a transaction by which it has impermissibly acquired control of Distributing, Distributing will not be considered to be engaged in an active trade or business, regardless of how many businesses it actually is conducting.

Other Problems with Controlled Stock Purchases

Even if an acquisition of stock of a Controlled corporation does not cause the transaction to fail the active business requirement, two other problems will sometimes be present. First, when additional stock of Controlled is acquired in a taxable transaction within the five-year period, this stock may be boot (sometimes called "hot stock") that causes gain recognition both to Distributing on its distribution and to the shareholders on its receipt under section 355(a)(3)(B). This problem is discussed below at Chapter 24, Section 24.3. Second, when 50% or more of the stock of either Distributing or Controlled is held by new controlling shareholders as a result of a section 355 distribution, or as a result of a transaction anticipated at the time of a section 355 distribution, section 355(d) or section 355(e) may apply. When either of these provisions applies, the penalty is Distributing's gain recognition on the distribution of Controlled: these provisions do not result in the transaction's failure to qualify for nonrecognition for shareholders. The "new controlling shareholder" issue will be considered in Chapter 25.

23.4.4. The Concept of a Separate Affiliated Group under Section 355(b)(3) for the Purposes of the Active Trade or Business Requirement

The active trade or business requirement has long included an alternative rule when Distributing is a holding company that is distributing the stock of one or more of its subsidiaries, but that holding company rule has been significantly modified in recent legislation. Two sections were relevant to the former holding company rule. Section 355(b)(1)(B) permitted Distributing to be a holding company that had no assets other than the stock of Controlled corporations that themselves satisfy the active business requirement. Somewhat similarly, the second clause of section 355(b)(2)(A) (now repealed) permitted Distributing to be a holding company if "substantially all of its assets consist[ed] of stock and securities of a corporation controlled by it (immediately after the distribution) which [was] so engaged."

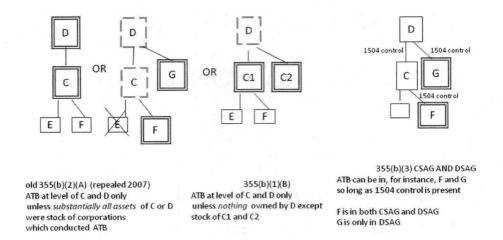

old 355(b)(2)(A) (repealed 2007)
ATB at level of C and D only
unless *substantially all assets* of C or D
were stock of corporations
which conducted ATB

355(b)(1)(B)
ATB at level of C and D only
unless *nothing* owned by D except
stock of C1 and C2

355(b)(3) CSAG AND DSAG
ATB can be in, for instance, F and G
so long as 1504 control is present

F is in both CSAG and DSAG
G is only in DSAG

Where must an active trade or business be held?
The effect of the enactment of 355(b)(3)

The limitations on the availability of holding company treatment under the prior version of the statute, and the requirement that otherwise Distributing and Controlled themselves must be conducting the active businesses relied upon, were somewhat arbitrary. They frequently required considerable pre-spin restructuring to move assets and subsidiaries (that were too new or did not amount to an active business) under other subsidiaries that qualified as conducting active businesses. Accordingly, section 355(b)(3) was added in 2005, with substantial amendments in 2006 and again in 2007, to change the rules applicable for finding active businesses among related corporations. The change was clearly pro-taxpayer — it introduced a look-through rule that allows a corporation to be treated as conducting an active trade or business as long as there is an adequate trade or business anywhere within the affiliated group of corporations below it. This approach eliminates most of the preliminary restructuring that seemed to be required under the old holding company rule. Proposed regulations issued in May 2007 (*before* the final amendment of the statutory provision) provide generally taxpayer-favorable resolutions to most of the questions raised by new section 355(b)(3). Many aspects of them are, however, somewhat controversial.

Section 355(b)(3) introduces the concept of a "Separate Affiliated Group" (SAG). So long as there is a qualifying active business in the appropriate SAG, the corporation at its head will be treated as conducting an active trade or business, regardless of the location of the business within the SAG. This is accomplished through the language that provides that "for the purposes of determining whether a corporation meets the [active business] requirements of paragraph (2)(A), all members of such a corporation's separate affiliated group shall be treated as one corporation." Interpretations of this language by the Service and Treasury suggest that it is appropriate to view, for the purposes of the active business test only, all of the assets of the SAG as owned by the corporation at its head. The concept is very much like that of "disregarded entities," though for a very limited purpose. For instance, Examples 5 and 6 of Prop. Reg. section 1.355-3(d)(2) allow the activities of various members of a SAG to be combined for the purpose of finding a single active business, even though there would be only incomplete "segments" of a business in each of the corporations without the SAG rule. *See also* Prop. Reg. § 1.335-3(b)(1)(ii) (providing that transfers of assets and activities within a SAG will be disregarded, and that a transaction whereby a corporation becomes a subsidiary member of a SAG will be treated as an acquisition of the corporation's *assets*, solely for the purpose of finding an active business).

Both Distributing (at the head of a DSAG) and Controlled (at the head of a CSAG) can be the common parent of a SAG. The SAG is merely the group of corporations underneath the corporation in question that are related to that corporation by vote and value as set forth in section 1504(a) (disregarding in the value determination plain vanilla preferred — i.e., nonvoting, limited, and nonconvertible preferred — as provided in section 1504(a)(4)). For example, if D owns all of the stock of C and of Sub 1, and if C owns all of the stock of Sub 2 and Sub 3, the DSAG includes D, C, Sub 1, Sub 2, and Sub 3; but the CSAG includes only C, Sub 2 and Sub 3. Assuming that all of the stock of C is distributed to D's shareholders, D will have an active business after the spin if either it or Sub 1 has an active business; C will have an active trade or business if any of C or Sub 2 or Sub 3 has an active business. Note that D can be owned by some other corporation, and, for the purposes of some other transaction, be considered part of that corporation's SAG.

Section 355(b)(3) introduced a new layer of complication into the lore of spinoffs because its standard for control adequate to find a SAG is different from the standard used elsewhere in the reorganization provisions and even elsewhere in section 355. These older provisions use the vote and number of shares standard of section 368(c). Therefore, Controlled can be eligible as the object of a spinoff and yet not be part of the DSAG. This strange result stems from the difference between section 368(c) control and section 1504(a) affiliation.

Section 1504(a) Affiliation Compared to Section 386(c) Control

Section 368(c) control requires 80% of the total vote and 80% of the shares of each other (i.e., each nonvoting) class of stock; whereas section 1504(a) affiliation requires 80% of the total vote and 80% of the total value. Is it possible to have one without the other? Yes, both ways.

It is fairly common to have affiliation for section 1504(a) purposes but not control for section 368(c) purposes, because when testing for section 1504(a) affiliation, one ignores "plain vanilla preferred" stock (stock that is nonvoting and limited in both dividend and liquidation rights). Under the Service's longstanding interpretation of section 368(c) in Rev. Rul. 59-259, 1959-2 C.B. 115, section 368(c) control requires 80% of each class of nonvoting stock. The plain vanilla preferred held by outsiders will be ignored for section 1504 purposes, but not for section 368(c) purposes.

*Can section 368(c) control exist without section 1504(a) affiliation? In simple situations, when there is control for section 386(c) purposes, there is likely to also be affiliation for section 1504(a) purposes. Owning 80% of the voting rights and 80% of the stock of each nonvoting class of stock will frequently mean that 80% of the vote and 80% of value are held. But section 368(c) requires only 80% of the combined voting power, not 80% of each class of voting stock. Thus, if voting preferred stock (which is **not** ignored for section 1504(a) purposes) worth more than 20% of the total value but with less than 20% of the vote is held by others, there can be section 368(c) control without section 1504(a) affiliation.*

Other strange results stem from the fact that moving from section 368(c) control to section 1504(a) affiliation can be treated as an acquisition of the assets of Controlled. For instance, suppose Distributing has section 368(c) control of Controlled in year 1, but a class of voting stock with sufficient value remains held by others such that section 368(c) control is present but section 1504 affiliation is not. Both Distributing and Controlled are engaged in separate active businesses. In year 3, Distributing buys all of the other stock of Controlled for cash. Distributing now has section 1504(a) affiliation, and this relationship was acquired in part in a taxable transaction. Controlled is now part of the DSAG, and thus Distributing and all of the corporations under it are treated as one corporation for the purpose of finding an active business. Does this mean that Distributing should be treated as having acquired Controlled's business in year 3 in a taxable transaction, and that therefore Controlled's business cannot be relied upon as an active business because of section 355(b)(2)(C)? The (somewhat controversial) answer in the proposed regulations is yes. *See* Prop. Reg. § 1.355-3(b)(4)(i)(A) (taxable acquisition that brings corporation conducting business into Distributing's SAG during 5-year period treated as a purchase of the business in violation of section 355(b)(2)(C)); Prop. Reg. § 1.355-3(d)(2), Ex. 42 (illustrative example). (If this transaction had occurred, it would not mean that Distributing could not successfully spin off another subsidiary, OldControlled; indeed, Distributing could contribute the stock of Controlled to Oldcontrolled, and spin off OldControlled. After its stock was received by Distributing's shareholders, OldControlled could not spin off Controlled to its (formerly Distributing's) shareholders, since Controlled would be viewed as having been acquired by OldControlled in an impermissible transaction.)

The preamble to the regulations acknowledges that this result derives from treating section 355(b)(2)(C) (dealing with the acquisition of the assets that constitute a business), rather than section 355(b)(2)(D) (dealing with the acquisition of a controlling interest in stock of a corporation that is conducting an active trade or business), as the applicable provision whenever section 1504(a) affiliation is achieved in a taxable transaction. *See* Preamble at A.2; Prop. Reg. § 1.355-3(b)(4)(i)(A). The proposed regulations conclude that moving from section 1504(a) affiliation to section 368(c) control does not create the same problem, since Distributing is treated as owning Controlled's assets and engaged in its business from the point of section 1504(a) control. *See* Prop. Reg. § 1.355-3(d)(2) Ex. 4. This conclusion puts considerable pressure on the plain language of section 355(b)(2)(D), which speaks only of acquiring stock representing control. This look-through rule in the regulations seems to be very strong and not clearly necessary.

Note again that even if there are no active trade or business issues related to the taxable acquisition of a business or of stock, there may be other repercussions related to the distribution of newly acquired Controlled stock. *See* § 355(a)(3)(B) (treating recently purchased Controlled stock as "other property" and "not . . . as stock of" Controlled, both for Distributing under section 355(c) and for its shareholders under section 356). See Chapter 25 for further discussion of this rule and the effect of recent temporary regulations on its impact.

There are advantages as well as disadvantages to applying the SAG concept in testing for taxable acquisitions of businesses under section 355(b)(2)(D). Any corporation in the SAG can be treated as in the business of any other corporation in the same SAG. Prop. Reg. § 1.355-3(d)(2), Ex. 20 demonstrates the increased potential for spins that this provides. Controlled has been a member of Distributing's DSAG for more than the 5-year active business period, so Distributing is treated as engaged in Controlled's business. When Distributing acquires section 1504(a) stock of an unrelated Target that conducts the same business as Controlled, it is treated as a mere expansion of Distributing's existing business. Distributing can spin Controlled (which conducts the business) and retain Target (so Distributing continues to conduct the business). Note that this expansion would appear to permit affiliated groups to do something very close to what the original provision was aimed at deterring — use existing surplus cash to buy a business that makes it possible to spin a surplus business to shareholders.

The proposed regulations appear to go even further in applying this "treat all corporations as one corporation" concept. These regulations treat transfers within a SAG group as nontaxable transactions that will not interfere with the active trade or business requirement — even a transfer for cash from the DSAG to the CSAG. Thus, Distributing can receive cash on the transfer of a business to Controlled or one of its subsidiaries and Controlled can still count this as its active business as long as the business was 5 years old in Distributing's hands. (A similar concept has long been in the regulations. *See* Reg. § 1.355-3(b)(4) (1977 & 1989); 2007-2 C.B. 466, Notice 2007-60.) While this approach seems well within a permissible reading of the statute when the DSAG contains nothing but the CSAG (and therefore each corporation can be deemed to be only a separate division of Distributing), the proposed regulation does not appear to be so limited. It appears to apply when a sister subsidiary of Controlled, which is in the DSAG but not in the CSAG, transfers one of its second-tier subsidiaries to Controlled for cash. *See* Prop. Reg. § 1.355-3(b)(4)(iii)(A); Reg. § 1.355-2T(g)(5) Ex. 4.

23.4.5. Disqualified Investment Corporations

As if the active trade or business requirement in section 355(b) was not enough, a new section 355(g) was enacted in 2006 that has provoked more questions than it answered. It disqualifies from section 355 treatment any Distributing or Controlled if any person (who did not own such an interest prior to the transaction) ends up owning more than 50% of a "disqualified investment corporation." A "disqualified investment corporation" is one that holds more than two-thirds of its assets in relatively passive investments, including the stock of other corporations (but not including stock when an interest greater than 20% is owned).

23.5. THE DEVICE TEST

The device test was intended to prevent the corporate division from merely being a step in a series of transactions designed to bail out earnings and profits through post-spin stock sales or liquidations. It has diminished in importance with the 2003 enactment of legislation temporarily equalizing the tax rate on capital gains and dividends, but it remains an obstacle to some spin transactions.

Exactly what constitutes a "device" is not clear, but the regulations provide needed guidance. The regulations designate certain factors such as pro rata distributions, post-spin sales, and certain aspects of the nature and use of assets as evidence of a device. Reg. § 1.355-2(d)(2). Others such as a strong corporate business purpose, a publicly held Distributing, and distributions to domestic corporate shareholders are designated as evidence that the transaction is not being used as a device. Reg. § 1.355-2(d)(3). In addition, the regulations set out three transactions that "ordinarily do not present the potential for tax avoidance": absence of earnings and profits (defined to include no appreciated property that would cause gain recognition if distributed), section 303(a) transactions, and section 302(a) redemptions. Reg. § 1.355-2(d)(5).

> **Authority Relevant to Finding a Device**
>
> *The regulations provide a series of examples on the device analysis that are useful. Reg. § 1.355-2(d)(4), Exs. (1)–(4). In addition, the following revenue rulings provide further guidance on the "device" analysis:*
>
> • *Rev. Rul. 64-102, 1964-1 C.B. 136 (pre-split transfer to existing subsidiary to equalize values not a device since minority shareholder would have had exchange treatment anyway);*
>
> • *Rev. Rul. 71-383, 1971-2 C.B. 180 (similar where redemption would be "substantially disproportionate");*
>
> • *Rev. Rul. 71-384 (no device where no earnings and profits); obsoleted by 2003-99 after the promulgation of Reg. § 1.355-2(d)(5)(ii) (providing that unrealized appreciation may be surrogate for e&p); Rev. Rul. 86-4, 1986-1 C.B. 174 (investment assets factor in device determination);*
>
> • *Rev. Rul. 73-44, 1973-1 C.B. 182 (transfer of only one of three businesses sufficient to avoid device characterization, since these were operating assets not easily liquidated); clarified by Rev. Rul. 76-54, 1976-1 CB 96, obsoleted by TD 9435, 2009-1 C.B. 333 (promulgating Reg. § 1.355-2T(g) and its modifications to "hot stock" rules);*
>
> • *Rev. Rul. 83-114, 1983-2 C.B. 66 (predistribution capital contribution not a per se device, but must satisfy business purpose requirement).*

The Practice Problems and the Discussion Problems can be found at the end of Chapter 24.

Chapter 24

TAX CONSEQUENCES

24.1. TAXATION OF DISTRIBUTING

Section 355(c) sets out the rules for the treatment of Distributing when the distribution is not part of a reorganization. There are no surprises here: Distributing does not recognize gain on the distribution of the stock and securities of Controlled. Despite the fact that section 355(c) states that sections 311 and 336(a) will not apply, the results of its provisions are the same as if section 311 did apply. Distributing will recognize gain but not loss on the distribution of other property, and there is a super-strong rule for measuring gain on the distribution of excess liability property, similar to that in sections 336(b) and 311(b).

Section 361 sets out the rules for the taxation of Distributing when the section 355 distribution is part of a reorganization (i.e., when Controlled is newly created in a D reorg). Distributing does not recognize gain or loss on the exchange of assets for stock of Controlled under section 361(a)/(b) and it receives nonrecognition treatment on the distribution of Controlled stock to its shareholders under section 361(c). The results are for the most part the same as under section 355(c), although there are a few differences that provide more generous results, as when Controlled is a pre-existing subsidiary.

One such quirk involves the application of section 361(b)(1)(A)'s "boot-purging" rule. In acquisitive reorganization transactions, Acquirer can transfer boot to Target without triggering gain on Target's assets, so long as this boot is re-transferred to shareholders. Section 361(b)(3) extends this rule even further, by allowing transfers to creditors to be treated the same as transfers to shareholders. When applied in the context of divisive reorganizations, this rule allows a newly formed Controlled to transfer cash to Distributing without triggering Distributing's realized gain, if any, on the assets transferred to Controlled, so long as this cash is retransferred to creditors. The last sentence in section 361(b)(3) (added in 2004), however, limits the amount of boot Distributing can receive from Controlled and retransfer to its creditors under the protection of this rule: the boot cannot exceed Distributing's basis in the assets that it has transferred (reduced by any liabilities assumed).

In transactions that include a D reorg, section 312(h), as interpreted in Reg. § 1.312-10(a), provides a special rule for allocating earnings and profits of Distributing to Controlled according to the relative fair market value of the assets transferred and retained. If the transaction does not involve a D reorg, Reg. § 1.312-10(b) provides that Distributing's earnings and profits are reduced by the lower of the amount that would have been allocated had a D reorg taken place or the net worth of Controlled (defined as basis plus cash minus liabilities).

The other tax attributes of Distributing remain with Distributing. If the transaction is a split-up, in which a holding company Distributing must liquidate, the tax history of the liquidated corporation will disappear. If the transaction involves a split-off, however, there may be enough ownership change to trigger the application of the section 382 limitation.

Note that all bets are off with respect to nonrecognition for Distributing if subsection 355(d) or (e) are triggered by certain types of changes in the ownership of Controlled, as discussed in the next section.

24.2. TAXATION OF THE RECIPIENT SHAREHOLDERS

Under the general provisions of section 355, Distributing shareholders receive Controlled stock without recognizing gain or loss. Section 358(c) provides the basis rule for section 355 transactions that are not exchanges; section 358(a) provides the basis rule for those that are. Despite the peculiar formula in section 358(c) (retained Distributing stock is treated as having been exchanged), there are no surprises here. The old basis of Controlled will be allocated by fair market value between the Controlled stock and the Distributing stock held by Distributing's shareholders.

> **Comparing the Application of Section 358 in Section 355**
> **Distribution and Exchange Transactions**
>
> *In a section 355 transaction that is an exchange, section 358(a) applies to determine the basis to the distributee shareholder in the Controlled shares ("property permitted to be received under such section without the recognition of gain or loss"). That will be equal to the basis in the "property exchanged" (Distributing shares) minus the value of "other property" or "money" (i.e., property or cash boot) received plus any gain recognized on the exchange. No surprises there.*
>
> *In a section 355 transaction that is a distribution, section 358(c) applies. It tells us to treat the transaction as though it were an exchange (so we will apply section 358(a)), except that we will treat the shareholder as exchanging Distributing shares and as getting Distributing and Controlled shares (plus any boot) back. Accordingly, the aggregate basis in the Distributing and Controlled shares will equal the old basis in the Distributing shares (the property exchanged) minus the boot plus "any amount which was treated as a dividend" and any gain recognized. In a boot-free spin, the old Distributing basis is simply allocated between Distributing and Controlled in accordance with their relative fair market values. In a spin with boot, the boot will reduce the overall value of Distributing: the boot is likely to be treated as a dividend distribution (since the regular rules in section 301 apply, under section 356(b)). If there is enough e&p so that all is treated as a dividend, the basis effects of the boot (reduction as property received and increase as a result of the dividend) will cancel out and the old Distributing basis will be allocated by fair market value under section 358(b) between Distributing and Controlled. If there is not sufficient e&p in Distributing, then some of the boot will be treated as a return of Distributing basis and, if there is excess beyond that, as gain recognition. Thus the amount of basis available to be allocated between Distributing and Controlled could be considerably less than Distributing's old basis. The regular formula provided in section 358(a) will apply (and now we see why there is a provision for increasing the basis for amounts treated as a distribution of a dividend and for gain recognized that is not treated as a dividend).*

If boot is received in a section 355 transaction that does not involve an exchange, it cannot escape being characterized as a section 301 distribution with respect to stock. *See* § 356(b). If boot is received in a transaction that does involve an exchange, however, the effect on the shareholder will be tested under section 356(a). *See* § 355(a)(4)(A) (cross reference).

Under section 355(a)(3)(A), the excess principal amount rule in section 356(d) will apply to the extent that Controlled securities are received. Not surprisingly, nonqualified preferred stock will also be treated as boot under section 355(a)(3)(D), unless it is received with respect to nonqualified preferred stock.

24.3.   "HOT STOCK"

Section 355(a)(3)(B) sets out a "hot stock" rule that treats the stock of Controlled that is acquired in a taxable transaction differently for both Distributing under section 355(c) and for its shareholders under sections 355(a) and 356. The purpose behind this provision generally is to prevent Distributing from using its earnings to buy the stock of Controlled that had not been necessary to its management of Controlled, so that such stock could be distributed to its shareholders instead of its earnings.

Thus, if this "hot stock" rule applies, Distributing's shareholders will have gain under section 356 and Distributing will have gain on a distribution of appreciated property under section 355(c)(2), to the extent of the appreciation in the purchased stock. For example, if Distributing already has section 368(c) control of Controlled but Controlled is not a member of Distributing's DSAG, the purchase of an additional amount of Controlled stock (still not bringing Controlled into the DSAG) would not spoil the overall transaction as far as qualification as a good section 355 spin; but gain, if any, would be recognized by Distributing on the purchased stock under section 355(c) and that purchased portion of the Controlled stock would be boot to the shareholders. *See* Reg. § 1.355-2T(g)(5) Ex. 1.

This "hot stock" rule will no longer apply in many previously covered situations since the amendment of the active business requirement to treat affiliated groups as a single corporation. Treasury and the Service were given the authority to modify the application of section 355(a)(3)(B) in the context of the SAG active trade or business requirement in order to harmonize the hot stock and SAG rules. Section 355(b)(3)(D). Under somewhat controversial temporary regulations, taxable acquisitions of Controlled stock will not be "hot stock" if this acquisition is made after Controlled has become a member of the DSAG. *See* Reg. § 1.355-2T(g)(5) Ex. 2. Acquisitions that fall short of section 1504 control, and thus leave Controlled outside the DSAG, are still problematic. *See* Reg. § 1.355-2T; T.D. 9435, I.R.B. 2009-4, 333.

24.4. TAXATION OF CONTROLLED

If Controlled is a pre-existing entity, and therefore section 355 applies to the distribution without section 368(A)(1)(D), there is no consequence to Controlled's basis in its assets as a result of the distribution of its stock.

If Controlled is newly created, sections 368(A)(1)(D), 1032, and 362(b) determine the tax consequences. Ordinarily, the transfer by Distributing will also qualify under section 351, in which case Controlled's basis in the transferred assets would be determined under section 362(a). Does the loss limitation provision of section 362(e)(2) apply in this section 362(a)/(b) overlap context? The proposed regulations under section 362(e)(2) take the position that even if a transaction is described in section 362(b) (the provision ordinarily thought applicable), it will be subject to the section 362(e)(2) limit if section 362(a) also applies. Prop. Reg. § 1.362-4(b)(5). A further provision in the proposed regulations avoids the basis reducing effect of section 362(e)(2), however, if, as is ordinarily the case in section 355 transactions, all of the Controlled stock is held after the transaction by those who derive their basis other than from the property contributed to Controlled. Prop. Reg. § 1.362-4(b)(6).

24.5. TAXATION OF RECIPIENT SECURITY HOLDERS

Section 355(a)(1) anticipates that the Controlled stock can be distributed to Distributing's security holders in exchange for their securities without Distributing recognizing gain on the Controlled stock transfer. Note that this language says nothing about the tax treatment of the owners of securities, or the corporation that may have experienced cancellation of indebtedness income, both of whom have engaged in a debt for equity swap.

PRACTICE PROBLEMS

Problems 1–10 do not invoke situations intended to call for the application of subsections 355(d) and (e).

Assume that Distributing owns, and has owned for quite a few years, all of the common stock of Controlled (the only class of stock outstanding), and that this stock is distributed proportionately to the existing shareholders of Distributing in a transaction, and that Controlled and Distributing can be treated as each conducting an active trade or business immediately after the distribution, and that the other requirements of subsections 355(a) and (b) are satisfied. Assume further that subsections 355(d) and (e) are inapplicable. Assume that Distributing has considerable available e&p, unless the facts suggest otherwise.

Controlled is worth a total of $5 million and is held with a basis of $1 million.

Suppose further that A is a shareholder of Distributing who owns 100 shares of stock with a fair market value before the distribution of $5,000 and a basis of $2,000. A receives with respect to his old shares of Distributing 25 shares of Controlled, with a fair market value of $1,500. After the transaction, he holds both the old Distributing shares (the value of which is reduced by the distribution of Controlled) and the Controlled shares.

1.   Assuming all of its shareholders simply continue to hold their Controlled stock, what is the tax effect to Distributing of this distribution to its shareholders?

(a)   Gain of $3,000.

(b)   No gain recognized.

(c)   Gain of $4 million.

(d)   Insufficient information.

2.   What is A's basis in his Controlled stock after the transaction in question 1?

(a) $1,500.

(b) $500.

(c) $600.

(d)   Insufficient information.

3.   On the facts in question 1, what if Distributing (which has always been a very profitable corporation) had also distributed $5 cash with respect to each share of its stock so that A received stock in Controlled worth $1500 and $500 of cash?

(a)   A recognizes $500 of gain.

(b)   A recognizes $2,000 of gain.

(c)   A recognizes $1,500 of gain and $500 of dividend income.

(d)   A has dividend income of $500.

4.   On the facts of question 1 as modified by question 3, what will be A's basis in his Distributing stock after the transaction?

(a)   A's basis in his Distributing stock will be reduced, to about $1,333.

(b)   A's basis in his Distributing stock will be unchanged.

(c)   A's basis in his Distributing stock will be reduced to $1,500.

(d)   A's basis in his Distributing stock will be reduced to $900.

5.   The facts are the same as in question 1, except that A gives up 30 of his old shares of Distributing and receives 25 shares of Controlled, with a fair market value of $1500. After the transaction, he holds 70 of his old Distributing shares (the value of which is reduced by the distribution of Controlled) and the Controlled shares.

Assuming all of its shareholders simply continue to hold their Controlled stock, what is the tax effect to Distributing of this distribution to its shareholders?

(a)   Gain of $1,500.

(b)   Insufficient information.

(c)   No gain or loss.

(d)   Gain of $4 million.

6.   On the same facts as question 5 (section 355 exchange), what is A's basis in the Distributing stock he continues to hold after the transaction?

(a) $2,000.

(b) $1,400.

(c) $3,500.

(d)   Insufficient information.

7.   The same facts apply as in question 5 (a section 355 transaction involving an exchange), except that A exchanges 40 shares of Distributing stock for stock of Controlled worth $1,500 and $500 of cash. Assume other participating shareholders receive only stock of Controlled. Tax consequences for A?

(a) $500 of dividend.

(b) $500 of gain.

(c)   Insufficient information.

(d) $1,200 of gain.

8.   In question 5, what would be the effect if Distributing had not owned the stock of Controlled for several years but instead had incorporated Controlled by transferring one of its active businesses to it before the distribution?

(a)   No change in applicable law or result.

(b)   Gain of $4 million.

(c)   Change in applicable law, but no change likely in result on these facts.

(d)   Deduction of $5 million.

9.   What if, in question 1, all of the stock of Controlled had been purchased 3 years before it was distributed and Distributing's business was not the same as the business of Controlled?

(a)   Gain of $4 million.

(b)   Gain of $5 million.

(c)   No gain or loss.

(d)   Insufficient information.

10.   Which of the following run a risk of not being treated as a division after which there are two active businesses adequate to satisfy the active business requirements of section 355(b)? Your answer need not be limited to a single item, but may include as many as seem appropriate.

(a)   A computer repair business that has operations in Chicago and Milwaukee, dividing by geography.

(b)   A computer software business that owns the strip mall in which it is located, and separates the ownership of the strip mall from the ownership of the software business.

(c)   A computer repair business that handles both hardware installation and data recovery, separating its data recovery operations.

(d)   A computer repair business that has outstanding accounts payable from 10 major corporate clients, separating its collection operations from its repair business.

DISCUSSION PROBLEMS

1.   Tom, Fred, and Jeff jointly run what used to be a very small auto body shop as a corporation, Chop Co. Tom, Fred, and Jeff each owned 300 shares of Chop Co, each with a basis of $10,000.

Slowly but surely over the 12 years that they have been operating, the business has drifted in two directions: Tom has focused on finding insurance companies that want a regular stable of shops to work as partners in accident repair work. Fred and Jeff have instead built relationships with auto dealers and auto supply stores that are likely to send those who want custom alterations on new cars to them.

They have run into a number of problems trying to manage the direction of the business. For instance, some of the potential insurance company partners will lend to auto body shops that want to upgrade certain types of equipment, but these loans tend to come with lots of strings attached. To make matters worse, Fred's uncle is interested in investing in Fred's business, but does not want to watch his investment taken over by Tom's insurance companies. Jeff isn't sure that he wants to invest any more in the businesses at all; indeed, he was hoping that a significant dividend would be declared sometime in the near future.

Their accountant has sent them to you to investigate whether some sort of spin-off or split-off might be appropriate.

What questions do you need answered before you can assure them that they can restructure in a way that will help with their problems without involving adverse tax consequences?

2. Unfortunately, Tom, Fred, and Jeff did not wait for your response before proceeding with a plan something like that originally suggested. They caused Chop Co to create a new corporation, Custom Co, and contributed to it some of the equipment of Chop Co needed for the custom work Fred expects to continue to perform and enough cash to allow Fred to acquire such other equipment as he will need. Chop Co then distributed all of the stock of Custom Co to Fred, who gave up all of his stock in Chop Co. Chop Co distributed $150,000 in its notes to Jeff. As a result, Tom owned all of the stock of Chop Co.

What are the possible results of the transactions described?

3. Fred was concerned that some of his auto dealers would be anxious if Jeff was taken out of the picture too quickly. Therefore, on the creation of Custom Co, a class of preferred stock was created, which Jeff could force to be redeemed at a price to be determined based on the performance of Custom Co. The formula was designed to give Jeff plenty of incentive to stay visibly involved in the business of Custom Co. Jeff received this stock instead of notes when he and Tom gave up all of their stock in Chop Co. Does this issuance of preferred create a problem for the spin?

4. As in Problem 3, except that Chop Co distributed $10,000 in cash to Jeff and Fred at the same time they gave up their stock in Chop Co.

5. As in Problem 3, except that Chop Co distributed $10,000 in cash to Tom, Jeff, and Fred at the time that Jeff and Fred gave up their stock in Chop Co.

6. Assume the same facts as in Problem 1, but that Tom, Jeff, and Fred all wanted to remain involved in both parts of the business. They took the same steps described in Problem 2 above, except that they all received equal portions of the stock of Custom Co. They say that the motivation was to be able to separate the two businesses in order to facilitate discussions both with lenders and with future investors.

For the time being, assume that there have been no commitments made with Tom's insurance company associates, Jeff's auto salespeople, Fred's uncle, or anyone else.

Chapter 25

POST-*GENERAL UTILITIES* ANTI-ABUSE RULES

Statutes and Regulations
IRC §§ 355(d), (e), (f); 368(a)(1)(D); 357(c)(1)
Reg. § 1.355-6, -7

Prior to the repeal of *General Utilities*, well-advised corporations could ordinarily find a way to restructure and sell their businesses without recognizing gain at the corporate level. The combination of old sections 311 (allowing dividends of assets without recognition of corporate level gain and redemptions of stock without recognizing corporate level gain), 336 (allowing liquidation without recognition of corporate gain), and 337 (allowing the sale of assets in anticipation of a complete liquidation of a corporation) allowed many transactions in which corporate assets found their way into the hands of different corporations that were owned by different shareholders with taxes being paid, if at all, only at the shareholder level. Many of these arrangements even allowed a step-up in the basis of corporate assets to fair market value with only shareholder, and not corporate, gain. A good argument could be made that under this regime, the corporate tax base actually only consisted of the ordinary operating income of corporations, and gain on corporate assets rarely was included in that tax base.

When *General Utilities* was legislatively "repealed" in 1986, there was considerable debate about what the larger impact on subchapter C was intended to be. Changes to the language of sections 311 and 336 clearly required corporate gain to be recognized when assets were transferred from corporations to their shareholders. Other changes in the language of subchapter C, in particular new section 355(c) and the revised section 361, clearly spelled out more of the details about when gain would *not* be recognized when assets were distributed or transferred by corporations. But many commentators argued that there was a larger implication behind *General Utilities* repeal — a corporation should not be able to transfer some assets in taxable transactions (thereby triggering losses but not gains) while at the same time transferring other assets in nontaxable transactions (thereby avoiding recognition of gain), and a corporation should not be able to transfer some assets with a carryover basis and other assets with a stepped-up basis.

In the late 1980s and 1990s, therefore, as the Service and Treasury learned of transactions that might be used to effect "bust-ups" of corporations in which corporate assets found their way into the hands of new corporations without complete gain recognition at the corporate level, they successfully asked Congress for legislation to block some such transactions.

Perhaps the most famous of the transactions causing concern were the "mirror" transactions, which were blocked by congressional action in 1987. These controversial transactions involved the formation by a corporation of two subsidiary corporations in consolidation. The subsidiaries would use contributed cash to purchase the stock of Target in a taxable transaction, and cause the liquidation of the Target's assets such that unwanted assets were distributed to one acquiring subsidiary, and wanted assets to another. Under the unamended law controlling consolidated returns, the liquidation would be treated as a section 332 liquidation, and no gain or loss would be recognized. The Acquirer, however, would hold one subsidiary with unwanted assets in a corporation whose stock it held with a fair market value basis. This unwanted subsidiary with its unwanted assets could then be sold to a third party without tax. Amendments to section 337(c) blocked this transaction.

25.1.   SECTION 355(b)(2)(D)

Another anti-bust-up provision was the predecessor of current section 355(b)(2)(D). This confusing subsection (discussed at length above in connection with its role in the determination of the presence of an active trade or business) is aimed at the transaction in which section 368(c) control of Distributing is acquired in a taxable transaction before Distributing implements a section 355 distribution (among other transactions to which it also applies). In such circumstances, a purchasing distributee corporation would end up with two subsidiaries, Distributing and Controlled, that it held with a fair market basis. The distributee corporation could then sell the stock of the corporation that was conducting an unwanted business without recognizing corporate level gain on the underlying assets. It might also make a section 338 election to step up the basis of the other corporation's assets.

Although the premise was not uncontroversial, this technique was thought to violate the spirit of *General Utilities* repeal. The new subsection literally denies active trade or business status to the business of Distributing when control of Distributing is acquired in a taxable purchase by a distributee corporation within 5 years of the distribution, and thereby makes section 355 in its entirety unavailable. Thus the provision denies the possibility of nonrecognition to both Distributing and the distributee shareholder(s).

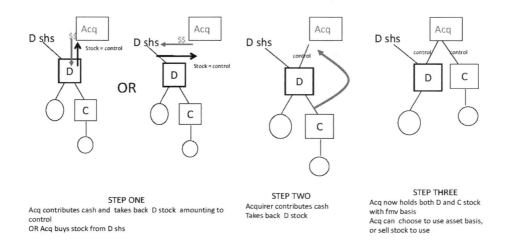

STEP ONE
Acq contributes cash and takes back D stock amounting to control
OR Acq buys stock from D shs

STEP TWO
Acquirer contributes cash
Takes back D stock

STEP THREE
Acq now holds both D and C stock with fmv basis
Acq can choose to use asset basis, or sell stock to use

355(b)(2)(D)(i): the 1987 "mirror" concern

The same result obtains under the section if Distributing acquired, in a taxable transaction, section 368(c) control of a corporation that is conducting the business that Distributing will be treated as conducting after the spin of Controlled. § 355(b)(2)(D)(i) (second clause).

25.2. SECTION 355(d)

The 1990 enactment of section 355(d) further restricted distributee purchases of Distributing and/or Controlled stock prior to the spin. Subsection 355(d) was designed to more generally prevent an intended purchaser of a business owned by Distributing from buying stock in Distributing so that it could "catch" a section 355 distribution of the desired business in incorporated form. The "acquire and spin" provision triggers gain to Distributing in a section 355 transaction if any of the distributee shareholders own either 50% of Distributing or Controlled as a result of having purchased stock in Distributing within 5 years of the section 355 transaction (or, in the case of Controlled, as a result of having purchased stock of Distributing and stock of Controlled within 5 years of the section 355 transaction).

Section 355(d) applies to trigger corporate level gain, for example, when X buys 45% of P stock for cash and P splits off S by redeeming out all of the P stock held by X. As a result of the spin, X obtains a basis in the S stock equal to X's cost for the P stock. Without the limitations in section 355(d), X could eventually sell the S stock at less gain than P would have had, and perhaps with very little shareholder gain on the part of the old P shareholders from which X bought its P stock. (X could also have acquired its P stock directly from P in a stock issue for cash.) A similar result would arise if P split off S by redeeming out all of its historic shareholders, in which case X would own 100% of the smaller P with a cost basis.

Section 355(d) provides a unique test for relevant ownership, defining it in section 355(d)(4) as either combined voting power *or* total value of all classes of stock, with its own aggregation and attribution rules set out in subsections 355(d)(7) and (8). It also includes a special rule in subsection 355(d)(6) that effectively tolls the 5-year period if there are arrangements through which the risks ordinarily associated with stock ownership are "substantially diminished" as a result of options, short sales, or other similar arrangements.

Note that the definition of "purchase" is specific to this subsection. Under section 355(d)(5), it excludes only general nonrecognition transactions. Even part of the stock in a section 351 transaction may be treated as purchased, to the extent received for cash, marketable stock or securities or transferor debt.

Although there is some overlap between the transactions that will be affected by subsections 355(d) and 355(b)(2)(D), the provisions are not redundant. Section 355(d) targets any transaction where a 50% interest in either Controlled or Distributing was acquired either directly by purchase or indirectly by distribution on purchased stock. As a result, section 355(d) can cause the Distributing corporation to recognize gain on the distribution because there is a new 50% shareholder of Controlled or Distributing after the spin, as a consequence of the fact that Controlled or Distributing stock was purchased. Section 355(d) does not depend upon the acquisition of any specific amount of Distributing stock, though a purchase within the 5-year period of a 50% or greater interest (defined as a vote or value test, as noted above) will result in corporate taxation on the distribution of the Controlled stock. Similarly, if a purchaser holds a 50% or greater interest in Controlled after the transaction either because of Controlled stock received in respect of purchased Distributing stock or because of a direct purchase of Controlled stock within the 5-year period or both, the transaction will result in corporate taxation on the distribution of the Controlled stock.

Although section 355(d) results in corporate tax on the distribution, it does not disqualify the section 355 spin. Distributing's shareholders would still receive nonrecognition under section 355(a) (or section 356, as relevant).

In contrast, if section 355(b)(2)(D) applies, it causes the spin to fail as a section 355 transaction because section 368(c) control of a corporation conducting the relevant active trade or business was purchased. That is, acquisition during the five-year period preceding the spin of a section 368(c) controlling interest in Distributing in a taxable transaction (or Distributing's taxable acquisition of a section 368(c) interest in a corporation conducting the trade or business that Distributing is engaged in after the spin) would disqualify the transaction altogether, destroying nonrecognition for both Distributing and the shareholders.

25.3. SECTION 355(e)

Finally, in 1997, Congress addressed the circumstances in which a section 355 transaction might be used to "tee-up" a business so that it could be the subject of an acquisition after its stock was distributed. Even under pre-1986 law, the route to such divestitures was a bit tricky, since the statute has always included a non-device requirement, a few courts had read the "active business" test to require the continued existence of both Distributing and Controlled after the section 355 transaction, and the Service was prepared to argue, at least in some cases, that control tests should be applied *after* the post-spin merger, resulting in a failed spin unless the Distributing shareholders ended up in control of Controlled after the merger.

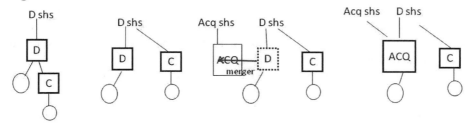

The Morris Trust Transaction
Before the enactment of 355(e)

One pattern of transaction seemed to be possible — the *"Morris Trust"* transaction, named after the case in which a court granted its blessing, *Commissioner v. Morris Trust*, 367 F. 2d 794 (1966), and to which the Service had acquiesced, Rev. Rul. 68-603, 1968-2 C.B. 148. In this transaction, Distributing would be merged with an acquiring corporation after the separation of Distributing and Controlled. Acquirer would now own the wanted assets of Distributing and the old Distributing shareholders would hold the unwanted businesses through their Controlled stock. (The Service had denied spin-off treatment when Controlled, rather than Distributing, was involved in the subsequent merger transaction, using arguments such as the lack of continuing control of Controlled by historic Distributing shareholders. Such a theory would not reach Distributing, however, since it was neither the object of the spin nor the transferee of assets.)

Section 355(e), in a nutshell, triggers gain to Distributing when the section 355 transaction is part of a plan or series of related transactions pursuant to which there is a 50% or greater change in ownership of either Distributing or Controlled. The statute in section 355(e)(2)(A) speaks only of a "plan (or series of transactions) pursuant to which one or more persons acquire directly or indirectly stock representing a 50% or greater interest in the distributing corporation or any controlled corporation." But in every section 355 transaction, there is a plan to have more than 50% of the ownership of Controlled change from Distributing to its shareholders — does this mean that section 355(e) is always triggered? No. The reason lies in the language of section 355(e)(3)(A), especially clauses (ii) and (iv). If a person's ownership in Controlled is obtained "by reason of their ownership in distributing," the acquisition of the interest does not count. Only if strangers to Distributing acquire interests in either Distributing or Controlled can section 355(e) be triggered.

Section 355(e) incorporates most of the technical rules of section 355(d) for determining which acquisitions count as acquisitions by strangers.

The administration of section 355(e) has been a challenge for the Service. One of the reasons seems to lie in the scope of section 355(e), which reaches substantially more broadly than the specific evil Congress was thought to be targeting. The evil, the "monetization" of the value left with Distributing's shareholders, was present in a notorious and well-publicized transaction. The transaction not only separated the two businesses of Distributing and Controlled (with one ending up in the hands of new shareholders), but also separated loan proceeds from the liability to repay those proceeds. When the old shareholders ended up with the corporation that held the loan proceeds, and the new shareholders ended up with the corporation that held the liability, the transaction closely resembled a cash sale. The transaction and variations upon it is discussed further below in connection with the technical details regarding transfers between Distributing and Controlled, and the recent statutory changes affecting them.

The language of section 355(e) was not limited to such transactions, however, and it ostensibly covers all section 355 transactions in which there is a plan, at the time of the distribution, that involves the disposition of enough stock of either Distributing or Controlled such that shareholders other than the historic shareholders of Distributing end up owning more than 50% of the stock of either Distributing or Controlled. And the statute includes a presumption (although not an irrebuttable one) that a plan existed if the requisite acquisition occurred anytime within two years before or two years after the section 355 transaction itself.

Much of the heat regarding section 355(e) was removed in 2002 with the promulgation of regulations (finalized in 2005) outlining when a "plan" would be present and thus trigger gain to Distributing on the distribution of Controlled stock. These rules are substantially pro-taxpayer, at least when compared with the language of the statute or with the earlier proposed regulations.

The regulation promulgated under section 355(e) provides that "the distribution and acquisition can be part of a plan only if there was an agreement, understanding, arrangement or substantial negotiations regarding the acquisition or similar acquisition" during the two-year window specified in the statute. Reg. § 1.355-7(b)(2). This regulation goes on to say that even when there is an agreement regarding an acquisition, the distribution and the acquisition can be considered as not part of a "plan" if there is a substantial business purpose for the section 355 transaction other than a purpose to facilitate the acquisition. The regulation further provides a series of relatively generous safe harbors. Although Examples 1 and 2 indicate that a plan will sometimes be imputed (when, for instance, unwanted assets are spun off or when a public offering is contemplated), the other examples indicate that such imputation is not inevitable even if is it known that the spun-off entity will be an attractive acquisition target. Reg. § 1.355-7(b)(2) Exs. 3 and 4.

There has been a modest degree of simplification as a result of the Service's pronouncement, as directed by the legislative history of the provision, that mergers following a spin-off can involve either Distributing or Controlled, so long as the merger does not run afoul of the "plan" problem following the spin-off. Rev. Rul. 98-27, 1998-1 C.B. 1159; Rev. Rul. 98-44, 1998-2 C.B. 315 (acknowledging generally the effect of the enactment of section 355(e) on earlier published opinions); Rev. Rul. 2003-79, 2003-2 C.B. 80 (essentially obsoleting *Helvering v. Elkhorn Coal Co.*, 95 F.2d 732 (4th Cir. 1937), by holding that the "substantially all" requirement in section 368(a)(1)(C) should be applied to a newly created and spun Controlled as a separate corporation, without reference to the transaction according to which it was created).

25.4. THE BUSINESS PURPOSE TEST

The regulations have always required that section 355 transactions — both the corporate separation and the distribution — be undertaken for a business purpose, and that this purpose be a corporate business purpose rather than a shareholder business purpose. Reg. § 1.355-2(b); Reg. § 1.355-2(b)(3) (requiring a corporate purpose for the distribution). Simple estate planning, for instance, will not suffice, but a rearrangement of the corporation to allow those managing a newly expanding part of the business to invest in, or be compensated by incentive arrangements that involve the stock of, the spun corporation will be an adequate business purpose.

The enactment of section 355(e) caused considerable confusion in the implementation of the business purpose requirement which all section 355 transactions must satisfy. Many of the traditionally satisfactory business purposes involve, whether explicitly or implicitly, making one or both of the corporations more attractive as an acquisition target or as an acquirer of other corporations. Does the presence of such a business purpose imply that there is in fact a plan of the sort that will trigger section 355(e)? The emerging answer, particularly in light of the regulations regarding the presence of a plan, seems to be no.

25.5. THE CONTINUITY OF INTEREST TEST

The regulations have similarly required that section 355 transactions satisfy a continuity of interest test. The traditional approach to this continuity of interest test was that the historic shareholders of Distributing must have an equity interest that represents continuity in both Distributing and Controlled immediately after the transaction. Reg. § 1.355-2(c)(1). This regulation was not amended when the more general continuity of interest provision in Reg. section 1.368-1(e) was amended to focus the doctrine on the extent of the consideration used in the transaction. Thus the continuity of interest requirement in section 355 transactions apparently still has much of the old concern about the continued presence of historic shareholders. There is also substantial overlap between the concerns of subsections 355(d) and 355(e) with the continuity of interest requirement. It appears, however, that the continuity of interest requirement continues in full force. *See* Reg. § 1.355-2(c)(1).

Section 368(a)(2)(H) adds an additional continuity-like factor into the mix:

> For purposes of determining whether a transaction qualifies under paragraph (1)(D) —
>
> . . .
>
> (ii) in the case of a transaction with respect to which the requirements of section 355 (or so much of section 356 as relates to section 355) are met, the fact that the shareholders of the distributing corporation dispose of part or all of the distributed stock, or the fact that the corporation whose stock was distributed issues additional stock, shall not be taken into account.

This provision was added to section 368(a)(2)(H) in connection with the enactment of section 355(e). It essentially lowers the more general control/continuity requirement in the D reorg context from the 80% that might otherwise appear to apply to 50%, the level that triggers section 355(e). (Section 351(c)(2) was also added in 1998, apparently for the same purpose.) Note that this provision may have a downside, in that in transactions in which section 355(e) is failed but the other provisions of section 355 are satisfied, there is little room to argue that Distributing will recognize gain on the assets it transferred to Controlled because of the later acquisitions of Controlled stock. As a result, there will be no basis step-up even though section 355(e) triggers gain to Distributing on the Controlled stock distribution.

25.6. USING SECTION 361'S FLEXIBILITY IN TRANSFERRING BOOT

When Distributing transfers assets in connection with a section 355 distribution, that transfer of assets will ordinarily qualify as a D reorg. The requirements for this reorganization are minimal compared to the other statutory reorganization categories: all that is required (before considering section 355) is a transfer of a part of a transferor corporation's assets in exchange for stock, and a distribution of that stock such that the transferor corporation (or its shareholders) is in control of the transferee corporation.

As the transferor in a reorganization, Distributing's transfer of assets to a Controlled transferee, and its distribution to its shareholders, is governed by section 361 (as well as some provisions of section 355). We saw section 361 as the source of nonrecognition for Target (the transferor) in a C reorganization. Here, Distributing is in the role Target played in a C reorg (the transferor of assets and recipient of stock); Controlled is in the role of Acquirer (the transferee of assets and transferor of stock).

Section 361 includes the idea that the transferor corporation can receive boot from the transferee. Receipt of boot, furthermore, will not trigger gain to the transferor if it is distributed by the transferor to its shareholders or creditors. It is the possibility of Controlled's transfer to Distributing of boot that can be retransferred to Distributing's creditors that practitioners found so appealing in section 361 as amended to reflect *General Utilities* repeal.

To see why this has so much appeal, we need to go back to section 355 transactions more generally. Remember that through a section 355 transaction, Distributing can divide itself in two without tax either to it or to its shareholders. It can also separate recent loan proceeds from the obligation to repay those proceeds, with each in either Distributing or Controlled. It is also possible, so long as the "plan" element predicate to section 355(e) is not present or if there is no substantial gain in Distributing's interests in Controlled, to anticipate an acquisition of either Controlled or Distributing after the section 355 distribution.

This separation of the obligation to repay a debt from the loan proceeds must be done with care, however. If Distributing simply takes out a loan, keeps the proceeds, and transfers the liability to Controlled, section 357 may apply, causing Distributing to recognize its gain on the transferred assets to the extent that the liabilities exceed the aggregate basis of the assets transferred. (This is the same rule Mr.

Peracchi went to such great lengths to avoid.) Thus, one variant of this general approach involves issuing stock — low vote so as not to lose section 368(c) control, but high value so as to generate as much cash as possible — *before* the spin.

But a transfer to Controlled in which Controlled assumes the liability without receiving the proceeds is not the only way to separate the proceeds from the liability. Distributing can take out the loan and contribute the proceeds to Controlled. Then Distributing can be the entity acquired — since the liabilities must end up in the acquired entity. The repayment of the liability is borne by the shareholders of Distributing after the acquisition transaction (which includes strangers to old Distributing), while the proceeds are enjoyed by the shareholders of Controlled (which if nothing else has happened include only the old shareholders of Distributing). If the transaction is to have an effect that approaches a sale, the lender's recourse must be primarily against Distributing after it is merged into Purchaser, and not against Controlled, which now has the loan proceeds and some of the historic assets of Distributing. For various reasons, however, this transaction may not be attractive. Distributing may be a publicly traded entity the stock price of which will be adversely affected by the games with the debt, or it may have publicly traded securities that make additional debt at the Distributing level difficult.

Are there any other choices? Here's where the practitioners found the advantage in section 361(b). If Controlled takes out the loan and transfers the proceeds to Distributing, the proceeds will be boot in the section 368(a)(1)(D) transaction. As a result, the loan proceeds will trigger gain with respect to Distributing's transferred assets, but only if the proceeds are not further distributed either to Distributing's shareholders or its creditors. *See* §§ 361(b)(1) (indicating that boot will trigger gain on the exchange unless it is distributed in pursuance of a plan of reorganization), 361(b)(3) (providing that transfers to creditors will be treated as transfers that are part of the plan of reorganization). This provision makes sense for reorganizations in which the transferor will cease to exist and yet may not have the liquidity to pay its creditors without cash from Acquirer. Although it is not clear that it makes any sense at all in section 355 transactions, it clearly applies by its terms. Thus, Controlled can borrow $10 million, then receive in the reorganization transaction $50 million in assets with a basis of $5 million, and transfer its stock and the $10 million to Distributing. Distributing will have gain with respect to the assets transferred (to the extent of the $10 million of boot) but only if it does not distribute this boot.

The language added to section 361(b)(3) in 2004 limits the ability to use this technique. The value that Controlled can transfer to Distributing without triggering gain is limited to the basis of the assets Distributing transferred to Controlled. This in effect imposes the same limitation on the splitting of liabilities and proceeds under sections 368(a)(1)(D) and 361(b) as section 357(c) imposes on section 351 transactions. There can nonetheless still be substantial benefit in the mechanics of this provision, since Distributing is allowed to apply all of its basis in the transferred assets against the cash so received, rather than just an allocable part.

25.7. RULING POLICY

Rev. Proc. 96-30 sets forth the representations necessary for a private letter ruling confirming that a transaction would qualify under section 355. For many years, the tax bar was reluctant to enter into transactions relying on section 355 without the benefit of such a ruling. In 2003, however, the Service announced a no-ruling policy with respect to some of the more troublesome aspects of the qualifications under section 355 — the business purpose requirement, the non-device requirement, and the presence of a plan under section 355(e). This new policy accords with general Service policy against ruling in situations that are heavily fact-specific. This does not mean that the Service will not give rulings on section 355 transactions, and plenty of rulings appear to be in the pipeline, but they are only available when other issues are presented.

PRACTICE PROBLEMS

True or False?

1.   The presence of a good business purpose will preclude the possibility of a section 355 transaction being characterized as a device for the distribution of earnings and profits.

2.   A business that has been acquired in a reverse triangular reorganization cannot be the object of a section 355 transaction until 5 years after such acquisition.

3.   There will be a good business purpose for a section 355 transaction if Distributing can show that it cannot get credit on the most favorable terms unless it divests itself of the stock of Controlled.

4.   If section 355(d) applies to a section 355 transaction, one need not worry about any of the other restrictions in section 355.

5.   If C Corp's stock was the subject of a section 355 transaction, and if all of the shareholders who received C Corp stock in the section 355 transaction sell that stock 8 months after the section 355 transaction, the corporation that distributed the C Corp stock cannot avoid recognizing gain, if there was any, on the distribution.

6.   If the sole shareholder of a closely held corporation wants to divide the assets held by the corporation so that his children (who have never shown any interest in the activities of the corporation) can inherit relatively equal portions, section 355 clearly provides the means for accomplishing this goal.

7.   A shareholder who receives assets in a distribution with respect to her stock from a profitable corporation (that is, one with e&p) that remains in existence after the distribution will always have dividend treatment on that distribution.

DISCUSSION PROBLEMS

These problems continue from the general fact pattern discussed at the end of Chapter 4.

1.   Six months after the creation of Custom, Fred becomes disabled. His stock interest is purchased for cash by his uncle (who had not prior interest in Custom).

Three months later, his uncle also buys all of Jeff's stock. What are the likely tax consequences and what more might you want to know before you could be certain about the tax consequences?

2. Fred's uncle wants to provide new capital for Custom, and proposes to contribute cash to Custom sufficient to warrant the issuance of nonvoting preferred stock, convertible into common stock, priced to equal to half of the value of Custom at the time it is issued. Also, Tom's insurance company associates want to provide new capital to Chopco, and have proposed to lend $500,000 to Chopco on terms that would result in the lenders holding 51% of the vote of Chopco if the loans fall too far into default. What are the tax consequences to the parties in a purported section 355 transaction distributing Custom stock if either of these plans is implemented? What are the consequences if both plans are implemented?

3. Before the creation of Custom, Chopco purchased with cash the equipment needed for expanding into Custom's side of the business. The cost recovery incentives in the IRC at that time allowed the immediate expensing of the full cost of the equipment. In anticipation of the spinoff, and the cash infusion expected from Fred's uncle, Chopco borrowed against the equipment before it contributed it to Custom. Chopco then used the cash to pay off its creditors.

What if the borrowing against the equipment had taken place essentially at the same time as the creation of Custom, with Custom as the debtor, and the loan proceeds transferred by Custom to Chopco, and then to its creditors?

Part II
FURTHER EXPLORATIONS IN SUBCHAPTER C
TOPICS

ADVANCED TOPICS IN THE NATURE OF DEBT
AND EQUITY

Chapter 26

SECTION 1032 AND SOME SIMPLE TRANSACTIONS INVOLVING A CORPORATION'S OWN STOCK AND STOCK VARIANTS

Statutes and Regulations	IRC §§ 1032, 83
	Reg. § 1.1032-2
	Reg. § 1.1032-3
Other Primary Authorities	Rev. Rul. 2006-2, 2006-1 C.B. 261
	Rev. Rul. 74-503, 1974-2 C.B. 117, *revoked by* Rev. Rul. 2006-2, 2006-1 C.B. 261

We have encountered section 1032 in several different contexts. It is the section that directs that a corporation cannot recognize gain or loss on the issuance of its own stock. This seems the obvious result with respect to newly issued stock: incorporation would be prohibitively expensive if a corporation were required to include as gain all of the value it receives in exchange for its stock on incorporation.

This was not always the rule, however, in other contexts. Stock that had been previously issued, then repurchased, and held as treasury stock actually does have a cost basis to the corporation. Although the government in the earliest days of the income tax took the position that there could be no gain or loss on the issuance of corporate stock, several defeats in court cases prompted it to revise the early regulations to provide that gain or loss could be recognized when a corporation "deal[s] in its own shares as it might in the shares of another corporation." A number of cases concluded that under this language, treasury stock should be treated just the same as any other asset for the purposes of recognizing gain and loss on its transfer.

Of course, once this rule was clearly established, very little gain was ever recognized under it. Why? Suppose a corporation had entered into an agreement in which it was to use its stock to acquire an asset. It held treasury stock, purchased from its shareholders for cash in redemption transactions, and it also had the authority to issue new stock. If the value of the stock had risen since the time of the redemptions, the corporation could simply choose to issue new stock, rather than use the treasury stock, because the use of the treasury stock would trigger gain. Of course, if the stock price had fallen since the redemption, the corporation would use the treasury stock and trigger a loss. To avoid this "whipsaw," Congress enacted the straightforward no gain/no loss provision of section 1032.

26.1.   ISSUING CORPORATION'S USE OF ITS OWN STOCK

Section 1032 provides the issuing corporation with one of the rarest phenomenon in the tax law: unpaid-for basis. The corporation gets a fair market value basis in what it acquires when it uses its stock if the acquisition transaction is a taxable transaction. The corporation takes a basis equal to the transferor's basis in assets under section 362 when the acquisition transaction is a nonrecognition transaction under section 351 or section 368, and takes the transferring shareholders' bases in their stock in a B reorg.

Given the generosity apparently embedded in section 1032 (or at least the understanding behind the pattern of taxation for the transactions in which it seems to apply), what should be its scope? In other words, if its intent should be seen as primarily loss disallowance, how should that affect its scope?

26.2.   SUBSIDIARY'S USE OF PARENT STOCK

26.2.1.   In Section 368 Transactions

When Congress first blessed triangular mergers under subsections 368(a)(2)(D) and (a)(2)(E), there was considerable concern that section 1032 would provide no protection in those transactions in which the parent stock had to be transferred to the merging subsidiary before the merger. The literal language of section 1032 protects only the *issuer's* use of its stock, not anyone else's use of the issuer's stock. The stock of another corporation, even a related corporation, is usually just another asset in the hands of any taxpayer other than the issuing corporation. Without the protection of section 1032, what would prevent the subsidiary from recognizing gain when it used that stock, and would the subsidiary's basis in the parent's stock always be equal to zero? Such a result would defeat the purpose of the new provisions.

The question was a more significant one under these new reorganization provisions than it was under prior law, which permitted the use of parent stock in B and C reorgs, because these newly blessed transactions were more likely, as a matter of the corporate structure, to require the actual transfer of the parent stock to the merging subsidiary, rather than just having one corporation agree to cause the transfer of stock that it need never actually receive.

The Service quickly sent signals that the use of parent stock by the subsidiary would not trigger gain, and it published proposed regulations consistent with those expectations in 1981. There the law remained for more than a decade. Reg. section 1.1032-2 was reproposed in 1994 and finalized in 1995 covering these section 368 nonrecognition transactions.

The regulations under section 1032 only bless the subsidiary's use of parent stock in triangular reorganizations when it receives the stock from the parent "pursuant to the plan of reorganization." Reg. § 1.1032-2(b). The regulations make it clear that if the subsidiary acquired the stock in open market transactions and then used it as consideration in forward, triangular B or triangular C transactions, gain (and presumably loss) will be recognized. Reg. § 1.1032-2(c) and (d) Ex. 2.

Note that this regulation does not apply to reverse triangular mergers, in which the merged subsidiary is protected from gain recognition on both its use of parent stock in exchange for Target stock and its distribution of Target stock to parent (all by operation of law) under section 361, the provision applicable generally to "conduit" corporations in reorganizations that conduct an exchange with a party to the reorganization and then distribute the assets or stock received in the exchange to their shareholders in liquidation. But the regulation does provide authority for the application of section 361 to the subsidiary to eliminate any potential for gain on the use of parent corporation stock. *See* Reg. § 1.1032-2(b) (final sentence) and (c) (final sentence).

26.2.2. In Other Transactions

The generosity with which the Service approached the zero basis problem in triangular reorganizations did not extend to other transactions. In Rev. Rul. 74-503, 1974-2 C.B. 117, the Service concluded that when a parent corporation transferred treasury stock it had repurchased on the market to a subsidiary, the transferee corporation took a zero basis whenever "The transfer of [the parent stock] was not for the purpose of enabling [the subsidiary] to acquire property by the use of such stock." The ruling was silent on the consequences when the transfer was for the purpose of allowing its use as consideration in an anticipated transaction. The Service signaled through private letter rulings that there were some circumstances in which transfers with such an intent would be treated differently (see the discussion of stock as compensation and section 83 below), but there was no generally applicable guidance on the question.

But in 1998 the Service and Treasury issued proposed regulations, which were finalized in 2000 as Reg. § 1.1032-3, which further expanded the scope of the protection of section 1032. These regulations provide for nonrecognition on the use of parent stock even when the transaction is a taxable transaction.

Subsection (c) of the regulation sets out the circumstances in which the expansion of section 1032's nonrecognition rule will apply:

(1) The stock must be acquired in circumstances in which the recipient corporation would take a basis under section 362(a) equal to the issuing corporation's basis if the stock had been some other type of asset. The stock may, however, be acquired "indirectly" from the issuing corporation, so long as the series of transactions by which the stock left the issuer's hands and ended up in the corporation's hands "occur immediately after one another." This provision allows the use of issuing corporation stock by lower-tier corporations. Note that this provision regarding lower tier subsidiaries does not change the rules that limit the ability to use "grandparent stock" in most section 368 transactions. The provision probably anticipates the use of grandparent stock as compensation for employees of lower-tier subs.

(2) The acquiring entity immediately uses the stock it receives to acquire money or property.

(3) The party to which the stock is transferred does not take "a substituted basis" in the stock of the issuing corporation. "Substituted basis" is defined in

section 7701(a)(42) to mean either "transferred basis" (basis determined by reference to the transferor's basis, e.g., under sections 338 and 362) or "exchanged basis" (basis determined by reference to other property held by the taxpayer, e.g., under section 358). In other words, Reg. section 1.1032-3 applies only to transactions which are taxable transactions from the point of view of the recipient of the "issuer's stock."

Why would the regulations condition the applicability of the provision to situations in which there is an "immediate [re]transfer" of the issuer's stock to its ultimate recipient? One answer is probably that this provision minimizes the actual gain or loss that is not taken into account as a result of the broadening of section 1032. The preamble to the final regulations gives a slightly more convoluted answer, one that seems to rely on an extension of the step transaction doctrine in various situations:

> In the cases addressed by the proposed regulations, in which the acquiring corporation exchanges the stock immediately for property owned by a third party, the transaction is indistinguishable from one in which the issuing corporation directly exchanges its stock for the property of the third party (an exchange to which section 1032 would apply) and contributes that property to the acquiring corporation, a transaction whose tax result would be the same as the cash purchase model set forth in the proposed regulations. However, in cases where the acquiring corporation's ownership of the issuing corporation stock is more than transitory, there appears to be no comparable transaction which would generate the same tax consequences as the cash purchase model.

> Implementation of an approach that waives the immediacy requirement would raise administrative and policy concerns. If the acquiring corporation were to be permitted to hold the issuing corporation stock for a period of time, the regulations would have to adopt one of two alternative approaches. Under the first alternative, the regulations would provide that the cash purchase model would be deemed to apply at the time that the stock is contributed to the acquiring corporation, giving the acquiring corporation a fair market value basis in the stock. However, such an approach would raise at least two concerns. First, in the case that the issuing corporation stock is not publicly traded, such an approach would impose administrative burdens requiring a valuation of the stock at a time when there is no related transaction to assist in such valuation. Thus, there is a potential for the stock to be overvalued, with a result of inflating the basis in both the contributed issuing corporation stock and the acquiring corporation stock held by the issuing corporation.

> Second, even if the valuation were accurate, providing for the cash purchase model on the date of the contribution would facilitate selective loss recognition. If the acquiring corporation could receive the stock at a fair market value basis and hold on to it, then if the value of the stock decreased, the subsidiary could sell the stock and recognize a loss. The Treasury and the IRS believe that it is inappropriate to issue regulations facilitating selective loss recognition.

Under the second alternative, the regulations would suspend the operation of the cash purchase model until such time as the acquiring corporation actually disposes of the issuing corporation stock. However, such an approach also would give rise to inappropriate tax results. In addition to precluding gain recognition attributable to the zero basis result, this alternative would allow a subsidiary to avoid recognition of gain attributable to real appreciation in this asset.

Reg. section 1.1032-3 only applies to transactions that are taxable to the ultimate recipient of the issuer's stock. Note that Reg. section 1.1032-2 covers the circumstances in which stock used by other than the issuer in nonrecognition transactions will be covered by section 1032. It extends section 1032 only to reorganizations under section 368.

When stock is used by other than the issuer, in circumstances in which the regulations apply, the taxpayer using the stock will not recognize gain or loss. Reg. § 1.1032-3(b)(1). The taxpayer will be treated as if it purchased the stock for fair market value just before it used it, with cash contributed by the issuing corporation. The regular provisions (section 358 for transfers to corporations) apply to determine the effect of this deemed contribution to the corporation using the issuer's stock; under this rule, the issuer's basis in the corporation using the stock will be increased by the value of the stock it contributed.

The regulation provides an illustration of how this is supposed to work. Y agrees with a third party to buy a truck worth $100 from it, using the stock of its parent, X, as consideration. The transaction has the result that would obtain if (1) X had contributed $100 to Y, (2) Y had used the $100 to buy X stock from X (and therefore Y has a basis of $100 in the X stock), and (3) Y used the stock in which it had a basis of $100 to buy the truck. No gain is recognized by either Y or X. X's basis in Y increases by $100 (that is the result under section 358, under the gloss that says that new stock need not be issued if it would be a meaningless gesture in order for a transaction to qualify as a section 351 transaction.) Y's basis in the truck is $100. Reg. § 1.1032-3(e) Ex. 1.

Example 4 provides a somewhat more realistic fact pattern, in which the issuer's (X) stock will be used as compensation to an employee of the using subsidiary (Y) corporation. Again, a transfer by the issuer of X stock worth $100 will be treated as if the issuing corporation contributed $100 to the using subsidiary (Y), which used the $100 to buy the stock, and then used the stock to compensate the employee. X's basis in Y will be increased by $100, Y will have no gain, and the employee will have $100 of compensation income. Y will have a $100 deduction (or increase to basis in some asset) for compensation for services. Reg. § 1.1032-3(e) Ex. 4.

Note that the overall result of this approach is that the corporation using the issuer's stock takes the property received with the same basis that it would have if the issuer had used its stock in a taxable transaction to acquire the asset from a third party and then contributed the asset to the acquiring corporation in a section 118 transaction.

An issuing corporation may sometimes require its transferee/stock-using subsidiary to make some payment for the stock transferred. In that case, only the excess of fair market value above the payment is treated as contributed to the stock-using subsidiary. Reg. § 1.1032-3(b)(2).

Example 5 demonstrates the result in this case, albeit with the additional complication that the employee pays something less than the fair market value of the stock to the issuing corporation. The employee pays $80 for X stock that has a value of $100, and Y (the using subsidiary) pays an additional $10 to X for the stock. The transaction is recast as if Y had received the employee's payment of $80 and then transferred to X for the X stock the following amounts: the $80 from the employee, its own cash of $10, and $10 that originated in a deemed contribution to Y from X. Y then transfers the X stock it has purchased with $100 to the employee. X's basis in Y is increased by $10 (the amount X is deemed to contribute to Y to make the full fair market value purchase of X stock possible), the employee has compensation income of $20, and Y has a deduction of $20 (the difference between the $80 paid by the employee and the fair market value of the stock). Reg. § 1.1032-3(e) Ex. 5.

a.   Limits of Reg. Section 1.1032-3 in Compensation Situations

The employee benefits bar was not happy with the new regulations, nor was the part of the transactional corporate bar that served high-tech clients. The two groups had related problems with the regulations: the felt need to set aside stock in a parent corporation in anticipation of the use of such stock as compensation for employees of subsidiaries. The "immediately" requirement is difficult to satisfy in these circumstances.

For more than a decade, the Service had been willing to overlook the "zero-basis" problem when parent stock was used by a subsidiary to compensate its employees. But in many circumstances, the stock was not transferred to employees immediately, but was instead held in a "rabbi trust." The rabbi trust, treated as a grantor trust of the corporation that established it and whose income would still be taxed to that corporation, held the stock for the benefit of the employees who would ultimately receive the stock. Under section 83, there was a general understanding that transfers to a rabbi trust would not count as transfers to the employees so long as the assets held by the trusts were subject to the general creditors of the employer. Who was the "employer" in the situation in which the subsidiary was obligated to transfer parent stock? Many had assumed that the subsidiary would be, and so had set up rabbi trusts that were subject to the claims of the subsidiary's (but not the parent's) creditors. They were unhappy with the conclusion, in Example 10 of the section 1032 regulations, that the assets of the trust would also have to be available to the creditors of the parent in order to obtain the desired treatment. (What is the significance of the right of the parent's creditors to the assets of the trust? As long as these creditors have such rights, the transfer from the parent to the subsidiary has not happened. The "immediately" condition is satisfied when the stock is transferred to the employees because only then is it treated as having been transferred by the parent.) Those complainants received half a loaf, however, because the preamble to the final regulations indicated that the Service would not raise the zero basis issue with respect to stock transferred to rabbi trusts that were already set up as grantor trusts of the subsidiary corporation.

Similar arrangements had been contemplated in the high-tech industry, in which employees held rights to stock in their employer. Such employees, however, frequently found themselves becoming employees of subsidiaries that were about to be spun-off. How to protect these employees' right to stock of the parent, when the subsidiary that is their current employer is about to become unrelated to the parent (whose stock may have become very valuable)? There were few completely satisfactory answers to this problem.

Note that when the "immediately" requirement was not satisfied, Rev. Rul. 74-503 would still have applied. This ruling would give both sides a "zero basis" in the stock received when a parent corporation contributes stock to a subsidiary in exchange for more subsidiary stock. This zero basis means that, should the subsidiary later sell the stock of the parent, gain would be recognized on the entire proceeds, even though there would have been no recognized gain if the parent had "sold" the stock itself and contributed the proceeds to the subsidiary. (The question at this point is whether the rules in Reg. section 1.1032-2 for nontaxable transactions and Reg. section 1.1032-3 for taxable transactions, both of which are conditioned upon "immediacy," provide adequate flexibility for taxpayers.)

b. Rev. Rul. 2006-2

In early 2006, however, the Service repudiated some of the substance of Rev. Rul. 74-503, and called into question some of the rest of it. The repudiated part was the statement in the ruling that, when a parent contributed its stock to a subsidiary in exchange for the subsidiary's stock, the parent's basis in the subsidiary stock would be determined under section 362. This position had always seemed a strange application of the applicable statutes: the transferor's basis in a section 351 transaction is ordinarily a substituted basis under section 358, not a carryover basis under section 362. But given the circularity of the transaction, and the fact that a substituted basis when the parent used repurchased treasury stock would result in an end run around section 1032, the section 362 approach and the zero-basis it produced was a pragmatic solution. Rev. Rul. 2006-2 declared that the approach was wrong, but did not provide an alternative solution.

The discussions within the tax bar surrounding Rev. Rul. 2006-2 suggest just how precarious the solutions reached under the existing section 1032 regulations are. These regulations, in general, attempt to finesse the difficult questions regarding the nature of the transactions according to which a subsidiary might acquire its parent's stock. But in doing so, they, at best, create more questions and, at worst, create more opportunities for taxpayers to take advantage of the discontinuities within the rules. The existing regulations, for instance, seem to embrace the idea that when a subsidiary uses cash to buy its parent's stock, the transaction should be treated as a taxable acquisition of an asset and the same as if any other taxpayer had purchased such stock. But this treatment has lent support to the treatment claimed by taxpayers for the "killer B" transaction challenged in 2006-2 C.B. 677, Notice 2006-85. (Some taxpayers contend that the killer B transaction can avoid the result (taxable income to the parent) that would usually obtain when a foreign corporation repatriates income by making a distribution of income to its domestic parent. In these transactions, the foreign subsidiary with the income to be repatriated buys stock from the parent in a transaction that is asserted to be a taxable transaction, and then uses the stock as consideration in a triangular reorganization to acquire a foreign subsidiary held by another domestic subsidiary of Parent. Ordinarily, the acquisition of US assets (like the parent stock) would be a repatriation that triggered US income, but in these transactions, the foreign subsidiary does not retain ownership of the parent stock, so there is no repatriation.) The treatment of these transactions is now outlined in Reg. section 1.367(b)(10), but many fundamental issues regarding the consequences of a subsidiary's acquisition of parent stock remains unanswered.

One way to think about the problem in this kind of transaction is whether the acquisition of the parent stock by the subsidiary in exchange for cash should be treated as a purchase of something of value (as it would be if there were no relationship) that does not represent a replacement of the assets of the subsidiary. Perhaps it should always be viewed as a withdrawal of the assets of the subsidiary, and therefore a section 301 distribution by the subsidiary with respect to the stock of the subsidiary held by the parent. Under this logic, the parent stock is received as a contribution to capital.

Another way to see some of the sources of the problems is to simply ask what it means for a subsidiary corporation to own the stock of a parent corporation. Is it really appropriate to treat that stock as just another asset held by the subsidiary for some purposes, but to take into account the special relationship between the parent and the subsidiary and treat them as a single unit for other purposes?

26.3. TRANSACTIONS INVOLVING RIGHTS TO ACQUIRE STOCK AND OTHER SPECIAL EQUITY INTERESTS

Corporations may issue warrants or options to purchase their stock. Ordinarily, when the owner of an asset writes an option on that asset, the owner does not recognize gain on the receipt of the payment for the option. If the option is exercised, the amount received simply becomes part of the purchase price of the asset, increasing the gain to the seller and the basis to the buyer. If the option is not exercised, the seller has income (and the buyer may have a loss) when the option lapses. Should the same rules apply to a corporation's options on its own stock?

In several rulings, e.g., Rev. Rul. 72-198, 1972-1 C.B. 223 obsoleted by Rev. Rul. 86-9, 1986-1 C.B. 290, the Service held that the lapse of an option to buy stock created gain to the corporation. This ruling was a double-edged sword, however, because it provided authority for corporate issuers to claim losses when they repurchased options for more than they had received at their issue. Recognizing this as a problem similar to the one which led to the original enactment of section 1032, in 1984 Congress added the second sentence to section 1032, denying gain or loss on the lapse of acquisition of an option. (Note that under Rev. Rul. 72-198, the law rather bizarrely provided that a corporation would have no gain or loss if it allowed the option to be exercised and then repurchased the stock, but would have gain or loss if it simply repurchased the option.)

26.4. STOCK ISSUED FOR DEBT

When a corporation "redeems" its debt by transferring stock to the debt holder, no gain or loss is recognized with respect to the stock used. (This is a straightforward application of section 1032.)

If the value of the stock is equal to the face amount (adjusted issue price, for debt that has been restated under the OID rules), there are no consequences to the corporation. If the corporation uses stock that is worth less than the adjusted issue price of the debt in the creditor's hands, however, the corporation can recognize cancellation of indebtedness income. § 108(e)(10).

The transaction will be nontaxable under section 368(a)(1)(E) to the debt holder if the transaction is a recapitalization and the debt is a "security."

26.4.1. Convertible Debt

Convertible debt is a strange beast under the Code — taxed in a much more "traditional" way than some other financial instruments. Although the rights held by the holder of convertible debt can be broken down into two distinct sets — those of debt holders and those of the holders of an option to buy stock, in general we do not bifurcate the owner's interest in this way. Therefore, on issuance of the debt, there is no portion of the purchase price allocated to the option feature. Reg. § 1.1273-2(j). This means that there is less OID and less automatic interest deduction for the issuer. Any premium, on the other hand, is not treated as bond premium (which would reduce future interest deductions). § 171.

When the debt is converted into equity according to its terms, there is no taxable event for either the holder or the issuer, even though there may be a substantial difference between the value of the stock used and the face amount of the debt.

These rules do not apply, however, when the debt is convertible into the stock of a different corporation.

26.5. TRACKING STOCK

Most stock, whether preferred or common, represents an interest in the issuing corporation as a whole. Is it possible to give some shareholders more of an interest in one aspect of a corporation's business than is enjoyed by other shareholders (analogous, perhaps, to special allocations in a partnership)? It certainly is possible if the goals of the corporation can be met by creating a new subsidiary to which a particular business is transferred, and then selling interests in that subsidiary. But such minority interests in subsidiary corporations may not satisfy all of the corporation's goals.

Another solution is "tracking stock," stock issued by the parent that offers its holders a dividend return that depends upon the performance of a particular business, frequently, but not necessarily, incorporated separately.

If tracking stock is honored for tax purposes as stock of the issuer, rather than an interest in the subsidiary whose business is tracked (or as some other less well defined interest in something else), the tax consequences of its use are relatively straightforward. Its distribution to common shareholders will be a distribution of stock under section 305 (and thus tax-free if no other class of stock's interests are impaired), and its distribution by the issuer will be covered by section 1032. Later changes in rights can be treated as recapitalizations that do not involve additional distributions.

But if the tracking stock is treated for tax purposes as stock of the subsidiary, then its distribution by the parent is taxable to both the shareholders and the parent (unless the requirements of section 355 can be met). Changes in rights can be viewed as additional distributions by the parent, and the parent may no longer be treated as "in control" of the subsidiary under sections 368(c) and 1504.

Although Treasury seems to have the authority to issue regulations setting standards for when such "tracking stock" will be treated as stock of the parent, *see* sections 337(d) and 355, it has not done so. It has issued a number of private letter rulings in which the use of tracking stock was an important aspect of the transaction, but all of these rulings involve a *representation by the taxpayer* that the stock will be treated as the stock of the issuing corporation, not a *determination by the government* that it should be so treated.

There have been a number of legislative proposals to render some transactions in which tracking stock is created taxable dividends under section 305, but none have yet been adopted.

PRACTICE PROBLEMS

1.   Corp Z has outstanding 30,000 shares of the same class of stock, held equally by 3 individual shareholders, each of whom paid $100,000 for their shares. Corp Z pays one of the shareholders 700,000 for all of his stock.

What is the consequence of this transaction to Corp Z?

(a)   Deduction from income of 700,000; reduction in e&p of 700,000.

(b)   Loss of 600,000, reduction in e&p of 700,000.

(c)   No gain or loss, reduction in e&p by 1/3.

(d)   No gain or loss, reduction in e&p of 700,000, but not below zero.

2.   Corp Z issues 10,000 new shares of common stock, and transfers this stock to a new shareholder in exchange for a contribution of $500,000. Corp Z has outstanding 30,000 shares of the same class of stock, held equally by 3 shareholders, each of whom paid $100,000 for their shares.

What are the consequences of this transaction to the existing shareholders, and to Corp Z?

(a)   400,000 of gain to each shareholder; 500,000 of gain to the corporation.

(b)   400,000 of gain to each shareholder, 500,000 of income to the corporation.

(c)   No gain to the shareholders, 500,000 of gain to the corporation.

(d)   No income or gain to the corporation, no income or gain to the existing shareholders.

3.   Corp Z transfers 10,000 of common stock to a new shareholder in exchange for a contribution of $500,000. Corp Z acquired the stock used in this transaction from a shareholder who was redeemed by Corp Z for $700,000.

Corp Z has outstanding 30,000 shares of the same class of stock, held equally by 3 shareholders, each of whom paid $100,000 (along with the since redeemed shareholder) for their shares.

What are the consequences to Corp Z and the shareholders?

(a)   No gain or loss to the shareholders, no gain or loss to Corp Z.

(b)   No gain or loss to the shareholders, 100,000 loss to Corp Z.

(c)   No gain or loss to the shareholders, 200,000 loss to Corp Z.

(d)   200,000 loss to the shareholders, no gain or loss to Corp Z.

4.   X Corp, a profitable public company, issues a dividend of one share of newly issued common stock on each of its 1000 shares of preferred stock. The common stock was trading at $100 on the day after the issuance. What is the consequence to X Corp ?

(a)   No income or gain, and no effect on e&p.

(b)   No income or gain, decrease in e&p of 100,000.

(c)   Gain of 100,000, decrease in e&p of 100,000.

(d)   Gain of 100,000, no net effect on e&p.

5.   Corp X transfers 100 of its newly issued shares as compensation to its chief executive officer at a time when the shares are worth $100 a share. What are the tax consequences to the corporation and to the officer?

(a)   No deduction for Corp X, income of 10,000 for officer.

(b)   Deduction of 10,000 for Corp X; income of 10,000 for officer.

(c)   No deduction for Corp X; no income for officer.

(d)   No deduction for Corp X; income of 10,000 for officer.

6.   Corp X transfers 1000 of its newly issued shares to the owner of a small corporation from which it has long purchased supplies at a time when the shares are worth $100 a share. The owner in turn transfers all of the stock in the small corporation to Corp X, for which he has a basis of 20,000.

What is the basis of Corp X and to the owner of the small corporation in the stock they now hold?

(a)   Corp X has a basis of zero in the small corporation stock it just acquired; the owner has a basis of 20,000 in the Corp X stock he just acquired.

(b)   We do not have enough information to determine the Corp X basis in the small corporation stock; the owner has a basis of 20,000 in the Corp X stock he just acquired.

(c)   Corp X has a basis of 100,000 in the small corporation stock it just acquired; the owner has a basis of 100,000 in the Corp X stock he just acquired.

(d)   Corp X has a basis of 20,000 in the small corporation stock it just acquired; the owner has a basis of 20,000 in the Corp X stock he just acquired.

7.   Corp X transfers $40,000 and 100 of its newly issued shares to the owner of a small corporation from which it has long purchased supplies at a time when the shares are worth $100 a share. The owner in turn transfers all of the stock in the small corporation to Corp X.

What are the tax consequences to the Corp X and to the owner of the small corporation?

(a)   Corp X has basis of 50,000 in the stock of the small corporation; the owner of the small corporation will compute gain or loss on his stockholding using an amount realized of 50,000.

(b)   Corp X has a deduction of 50,000; the owner of the small corporation will compute gain or loss on his stockholding using an amount realized of 50,000.

(c)   Corp X has basis of 40,000 in the stock of the small corporation; the owner of the small corporation will compute gain or loss on his stockholding using an amount realized of 40,000.

(d)   Corp X has basis of 40,000 in the stock of the small corporation; the owner of the small corporation will compute gain or loss on his stockholding using an amount realized of 50,000.

8.   Corp X created a new 100% subsidiary Corp Y and transferred 100 of its newly issued shares to it, at a time when the stock was worth $1000 share. Later on the same day, Corp Y merged into a small corporation from which Corp X has long purchased supplies. Its owner received the stock of Corp X in exchange for his stock, which he held with a basis of 20,000.

What are the consequences of this transaction to Corp Y and Corp X?

(a)   X Corp Y has no gain or loss; Corp X has a basis no lower than 20,000 in its stock of the small corporation.

(b)   Corp Y has gain of 100,000; Corp X holds the stock of the small corporation with a basis of 100,000.

(c)   Corp Y has no gain; Corp X has gain of 100,000 and holds the stock of the small corporation with a basis of 100,000.

(d)   Corp Y has no gain; Corp X has no basis in the stock of the small corporation.

9.   Corp X created a new 100% subsidiary Corp Y and transferred 100 of its newly issued shares to it, at a time when the stock was worth $1000 share. Twenty-four months later, a small corporation which had only been organized for about a year, but was failing, merged into Corp Y. Its owner received the 10 shares

of the stock of Corp X in exchange for his stock, which he held with a basis of 20,000.

What are the consequences of the transfer of the Corp X stock by Corp Y?

(a)   Corp Y will have no gain on its use of Corp X stock.

(b)   Corp Y will have 10,000 of gain on its use of Corp X stock.

(c)   Corp Y will have a deduction of 10,000 on its use of the Corp X stock.

(d)   Insufficient information to compute the consequences to Corp Y.

DISCUSSION PROBLEMS

1.   X Corp has three classes of stock outstanding: its common voting stock that is publicly traded, a preferred stock that was privately issued and is held by three other corporations that is convertible into common stock, and a publicly traded preferred stock that is strictly limited as to both dividends and liquidation, which the holders can require redeemed in 2011 or anytime thereafter, and which was issued for cash after both of the other classes of stock were issued.

(a)   The common stock was issued for $20 per share. What are the tax consequence to X Corp if it repurchases 10% of the common for $40 per share? What are the tax consequences to X Corp if it repurchases 10% of the common for $15 per share?

(b)   Assume that X Corp held the stock it repurchased in the two transactions outlined in part a as treasury stock. The stock is now trading at $37 per share. What are the results under the following additional scenarios?

    (i)   X Corp is negotiating the acquisition of a business in a transaction which it expects to be fully taxable, but in which it will use its common stock as consideration. Assuming that there is enough of each block of stock, should X Corp use the stock that it repurchased for $40, the stock that it repurchased for $15, or newly issued stock? What will be X Corp's basis in the business assets that it acquires?

    (ii)   X Corp is negotiating the acquisition of an incorporated business in a transaction which it expects to be nontaxable. It plans to create a subsidiary, to which it will contribute its stock. The subsidiary will then merge into the target corporation, and the shareholders of the target corporation will take X Corp stock. Assuming that there is enough of each block of stock, should X Corp use the stock that it repurchased for $40, the stock that it repurchased for $15, or newly issued stock? What will be X Corp's basis in the interest in target that it will hold after the transaction?

    (iii)   The transaction in part (ii) was never completed, but X Corp did create the subsidiary and contribute 100,000 of its shares of common stock to it. What is the sub's basis in this stock? What is the result if the sub sells the stock to the public? What is the result if the sub simply re-transfers the stock to X Corp, and then X Corp sells the stock to the public?

(iv)   The transaction in part (ii) was never completed, but X Corp did create the subsidiary and contribute $100,000 of its shares of common stock to it. What is the result if the subsidiary now uses this stock to compensate its employees, when the value of the stock is $37 per share? When the value is $50 per share?

(v)   The transaction in part (ii) was never completed, but X Corp did create the subsidiary and contribute $100,000 of its shares of common stock to it. X Corp then sold all of the stock of the subsidiary to a stranger. Three years later, the subsidiary sold the stock of X Corp, which it had continued to hold.

(c)   The privately held convertible preferred was purchased for $10 per share. What are the tax consequences (to both the shareholders and to X Corp) of the conversion of this stock into common stock when the common stock is trading at $37 per share?

(d)   X Corp would like to eliminate the outstanding publicly held preferred stock. To do so, it borrows and uses the loan proceeds to make a tender offer for an earlier retirement of the preferred stock. It successfully buys back 100,000 shares that it issued for $15 per share, for $13 per share or, in the alternative, for $18 per share. What are the tax consequences to the shareholders and to X Corp? What would the consequences have been if the preferred stock had instead been interest-bearing bonds?

(e)   When its common stock is trading for $37 per share, X Corp writes and sells a put right for 1000 shares of its stock. This put gives its buyer the right to require X Corp to buy the stock for $40 per share in 9 months, and the buyer pays X Corp $1000 for this right. In nine months, the stock is trading at $41, so the buyer of the put lets it expire unexercised. What is the result of this transaction to X Corp and the buyer of the put?

2.   Z Corp conducts a leasing business that its investment bankers say is undervalued by the market because its ratios are dragged down by the other businesses conducted by Z Corp. For various business reasons, however, a complete spin-off of the leasing business is not feasible.

Z Corp nevertheless contributes the leasing business to a new subsidiary. It then issues a new class of its own preferred stock in exchange for cash. The dividends to be paid on this stock are determined solely according to a formula based on the performance of the leasing business, and its rights to liquidation are limited to the leasing business assets. What are the consequences of the issuance of this stock?

Chapter 27

TRANSACTIONS INVOLVING DEBT OF RELATED PARTIES

Statutes and Regulations	IRC §§ 165(g); 108(e)(4), (6); 368(a)(1)(G)
	Reg. § 1.108-2
	Prop. Reg. § 1.332-2(b), (e)
Other Primary Authorities	Rev. Rul. 68-602, 1968-2 C.B. 135
	Rev. Rul. 2003-125, 2003-2 C.B. 1243

Suppose a corporation owns a subsidiary that has a viable business, but for various reasons, the subsidiary has a debt load that it simply cannot maintain. The subsidiary's outside creditors are at least moderately willing to cooperate in restructuring the subsidiary, since they may well be better off getting partial payment now, and keeping the subsidiary as a customer on an ongoing basis, than they would be if the subsidiary were simply forced out of business. The subsidiary may also be indebted to its parent, either because the parent initially extended a loan or because the parent bought the subsidiary's debt from its original creditors.

There are various questions that arise in these circumstances of considerable importance in determining the tax consequences of transactions. For example, what will the effect of the relatedness of the parties have on the treatment of transactions involving the debt? What impact will the debt have on transactions involving these related parties?

27.1. RELATED PARTY DEBT PURCHASE

There may be some creditors who will simply need to be paid off, at whatever discount they are willing to accept. If the subsidiary pays off the debt for less than the amount owed, it will have debt discharge income. If the subsidiary is insolvent, section 108 will allow an exclusion of some of these amounts, but at a cost of a reduction in the tax attributes of the subsidiary, including its basis in its assets (to the extent greater than fair market value) and its carryover losses and credits.

Can this situation be improved by having the parent buy the subsidiary's debt from the third parties? Section 108(e)(4) prevents a better result: it requires the subsidiary in that case to be treated as if it had repurchased its debt itself. Debt discharge income is thus recognized by the subsidiary at the time the parent purchases the debt. The debt is treated as reissued with an issue price equal to the amount paid by the parent for the debt, and the difference between this amount and the face amount is original issue discount to both of the parties. *See* Reg. § 1.108-2(g) and Reg. § 1.108-2(g)(4) Exs. 1, 2, and 3.

Note that the regulations under section 108 provide essentially the same result with respect to the recognition of debt discharge income when the order of the acquisition of interests is reversed. Thus, even if the creditor's purchase of the debtor corporation creating the relationship between the creditor parent and the debtor subsidiary occurs *after* the debt is in place, the rules of section 108(e)(4) will apply so long as the creditor purchased the debt *in anticipation of* the later acquisition of the debtor (termed in the regulations an "indirect acquisition" of the debt). Reg. § 1.108-2(c).

The regulations provide two measures for determining the amount of discharge of indebtedness income, depending on the length of time that the creditor held the debt before becoming related to the debtor on the "acquisition date." Reg. § 1.108-2(f)(1) (income is measured by the holder's adjusted basis if holding period is less than or equal to six months); Reg. § 1.108-2(f)(2) (income is measured by the fair market value on acquisition date if holding period is more than six months before acquisition date). Correlative adjustments are made in respect of the deemed issuance: the issue price will be either the holder's adjusted basis or the fair market value, depending on the length of the holding period. Reg. § 1.108-2(g).

Thus, under section 108(e)(4), if the debtor subsidiary has debt with a face amount of $100 that is held by unrelated parties, and the subsidiary's parent corporation buys the debt for $75, the subsidiary will have cancellation of indebtedness income of $25. It will be then be treated as having issued debt with an issue price of $75 and a redemption price of $100, resulting in $25 of OID (generating interest deductions for the subsidiary and income to the parent).

27.2. CONTRIBUTION BY PARENT TO CAPITAL OF SUBSIDIARY

What if some of a subsidiary's debt is owed to the parent? Can the debt simply be forgiven, with the result that the subsidiary is treated as if the parent had made a contribution to capital rather than as having debt discharge income? Yes and no. Section 108(e)(6) provides that "if a debtor corporation acquires its indebtedness from a shareholder as a contribution to capital, section 118 will not apply" but the subsidiary will be treated as having satisfied the indebtedness with an amount of money equal to the shareholder's adjusted basis in the debt.

If the shareholder has always held the debt (or if the shareholder acquired the debt in a transaction in which section 108(e)(4) applied and thus the amount of the debt was reset under the OID rules at that time) the shareholder's basis in the debt should equal the adjusted issue price of the debt, and there should be no cancellation of indebtedness income. *See* Reg. § 1.108-2(g)(4), Ex. 3. But if the shareholder/controlling corporation has written off the debt, the debtor corporation will have cancellation of indebtedness income; that is, the debtor corporation will be treated as if it had satisfied the debt with an amount less than the face amount of the debt. § 108(e)(6) (This fiction applies only to the debtor corporation — there is no fictional payment to the creditor/controlling corporate shareholder.)

27.3. ISSUANCE OF STOCK FOR DEBT

Until the early 1990s, a corporation could ordinarily simply use its own stock to pay its creditors and avoid cancellation of indebtedness income. Such a transaction could occur without a reorganization, since there was a general stock-for-debt exception that had first been articulated in case law and then in 1980 was codified in prior subsections 108(e)(8) and 108(e)(10). In 1993, these provisions were eliminated, and now the debtor corporation will be treated as having paid cash equal to the fair market value of the stock that is transferred.

Outside of bankruptcy, when stock is issued in replacement of debt, it is a taxable event for both the debtor issuing stock and the creditor receiving stock. The debtor can have cancellation of indebtedness income if the debt is satisfied with stock worth less than the face amount/adjusted issue price of the debt. This will likely occur either because market interest rates have risen or because the creditor is giving the debtor a break to keep it alive. This does not mean that there will always be cancellation of indebtedness income when stock is issued to repay debt — only that there is no longer a fudge factor between the face value of the retired debt and the value of the issued stock.

Note that this situation is *not* an exception to the rules under section 1032, even though it will involve the recognition of gain in connection with the issuance of stock. The gain, if any, is cancellation of indebtedness income recognized because the corporation can satisfy the debt for less than the loan proceeds plus interest; it is not gain on the stock that is recognized because the stock has a value greater than the corporation's basis in it. Thus, suppose a corporation holds as treasury stock previously outstanding stock that it repurchased for $45 and that is now trading at $60. It transfers this stock to a creditor that holds the corporation's debt with an adjusted issue price of $83. (Assume that interest is currently paid and that the adjusted issue price is the face value and principal amount.) The debtor corporation will have $23 of cancellation of indebtedness income, *not* $15 of recognized gain on the treasury stock. The creditor can also have income if, under its accounting methods and section 165, it has already written down a part or all of the debt.

27.4. RESTRUCTURING WHEN SUBSIDIARIES APPROACH INSOLVENCY

There is an inherent tension throughout subchapter C regarding the circumstances under which interests in controlled subsidiaries are merely assets held by corporations — triggering gain and loss just like any other asset — and when they are treated as something else. For instance, under sections 332 and 337, controlled subsidiaries can be liquidated, with results substantially similar to those that would have obtained had the subsidiary never been in existence. In such a case, the primary characteristic of the subsidiary holding that was asset-like — the controlling corporation's basis in its stock — disappears. On the other hand, when the parent corporation sells the subsidiary's stock, in most cases it will have gain or loss just as it would on any asset.

This tension translates into a conflict when the subsidiary becomes insolvent. Should the parent corporation be able to claim the loss that is associated with the stockholding or should it be able to take over the subsidiary's assets without a taxable event and inherit the tax attributes? Or should it for some reason be able to claim both? Many of the rules developed in this area are designed to keep the parent corporation from trying to claim both.

Note that the following discussion anticipates situations in which a corporation is arguably insolvent, but yet is not necessarily in bankruptcy or receivership. Subsections 368(a)(1)(G) and 368(a)(3) provide special rules that make certain types of reorganizations possible in this context despite the hurdle the lack of value in existing equity interests might present to the application of the traditional reorganization concepts.

27.4.1. Liquidations of Subsidiaries When Debt is Owed to the Parent

Recall that when a controlled subsidiary liquidates, the parent takes the subsidiary's assets with a carryover basis, inherits the subsidiary's tax attributes, and gets no tax benefit from its basis in the subsidiary stock. Thus a parent faced with a subsidiary approaching insolvency will want liquidation treatment under the right combination of (1) valuable appreciated assets held by the sub, (2) large carryover losses owned by the subsidiary, and (3) low stock basis. Will complete liquidation treatment be available?

a. Solvent Subsidiary

Section 332 is generally available in the case of a solvent subsidiary contemplating liquidation, and section 337(b) anticipates that there may be debt between a parent and a controlled subsidiary. When the subsidiary is solvent, the statute conveniently provides that there is no reason to distinguish between the property that is distributed to the parent with respect to the subsidiary's stock (which under the model set out in sections 332 and 337 as a normative matter should not produce gain or loss) and the property distributed to the parent with respect to debt (which less clearly should not be recognized as a result of the transfer).

b. Insolvent Subsidiary

Section 337 by its own terms applies only when there is a liquidation, and that seems to imply a liquidation of the interest of a shareholder *as a shareholder*. What should happen if there is no return to the parent on its stock — that is, when there is insufficient value in the subsidiary to provide any return at all with respect to the stock held by the parent? The regulations provide that "section 332 applies only to those cases in which the recipient corporation receives at least partial payment for the stock." Reg. § 1.332-2(b).

Thus, if a subsidiary corporation that is actually insolvent liquidates, it appears that there can be no liquidation under section 332. *Commissioner v. Spaulding Bakeries Inc.*, 252 F. 2d 693 (2d Cir. 1958), *aff'g* 27 T.C. 684 (1957), and *H. K. Porter Co. v. Commissioner*, 87 T.C. 689 (1986), both held that if the value of the liquidating subsidiary's assets is not greater than the liquidation preference of the preferred stock, there could be no section 332 liquidation. These cases were taxpayer victories, under facts in which the taxpayer sought a loss on the stock when there were apparently no adverse consequences in terms of either asset gain or destroyed loss carryovers or other tax attributes of the subsidiary. The Service reached a similar conclusion to the courts, on simpler facts. Rev. Rul. 59-296, 1959-2 C.B. 87, *superseded by* Rev. Rul. 2003-125, 2003-2 C.B. 1243. (See below for a discussion of the treatment of the transaction if section 332 does not apply.)

i.   When Will a Subsidiary That Owes Debt to Its Parent Be Treated as Being Insolvent?

But can a subsidiary be insolvent simply as a result of debt to a parent? One answer simply might be that insolvency exists whenever the burden of the debt exceeds the value of the assets, according to the same approach that would be used if the debt were owed to a third party. (See below for further discussion of that standard.) Alternatively, one might think that a different approach should be taken with respect to debt to parent corporations. Such an approach might question whether the debt between the parent and the subsidiary should be honored as debt rather than treated as a kind of equity interest. Note that other issues arise if the interest is treated as equity. For example, should it be treated as equivalent to the interests that are labeled common stock for the purpose of determining whether there has been a return on the stock, and therefore a section 332 liquidation? Or is it more appropriate to treat such debt as some kind of preferred interest that has a claim on all of the assets of the subsidiary, in which case there is still no return on the common and no section 332 liquidation? How relevant is section 385(c)'s prohibition on debtor challenges of the character of its own debt?

ii.   What is the Appropriate Treatment if an Insolvent Subsidiary is Liquidated and Section 332 is Inapplicable?

If insolvency prevents the application of section 332, the liquidation will be a taxable exchange. The parent will recognize loss with respect to its subsidiary stock holding (on which it by definition has received no return). Under the appropriate circumstances, this stock loss will be characterized under section 165(g)(3) as an ordinary loss. The subsidiary will recognize gain or loss with respect to the assets that it transfers in satisfaction of its debts (by definition there will be no assets transferred with respect to its stock). If there is no section 332 liquidation, however, the subsidiary's tax attributes (that is, carryover losses and credits) will not survive.

The Service has essentially incorporated most of the prior authorities on these issues into what are popularly called the "net value regs," a sweeping set of regulations that deny nonrecognition status to any transaction that is premised on the presence of stock, if that stock should be treated as worthless. Prop. Reg. § 1.332-2(b) and 1.332-2(e), ex. 2. Here, nonrecognition is premised on receipt of assets in exchange for a controlling interest in stock: if the subsidiary corporation has no "net value," there can be nothing exchanged for stock.

Note that the scope of the net value regulations is not limited to transactions involving related parties. The circumstances in which there is a "net value" problem, however, are likely ordinarily to involve related parties. (Unrelated parties are unlikely to exchange valuable assets for negative value stock.)

Possible reduction of debt owed by subsidiary. Some parent corporations will be perfectly happy if section 332 does not apply and a loss on stock can be claimed. But what if there is a low stock basis and significant asset appreciation? Can a parent corporation facing this scenario take action to make the subsidiary no longer insolvent — by either cancelling the debt owed by the subsidiary or contributing assets sufficient to cover the debt — with the result that a section 332 liquidation is possible? The Service does not view such actions favorably: it has ruled that the step transaction doctrine would apply to deny effect to an attempt to cancel the debt of the subsidiary to permit a section 332 liquidation. Rev. Rul. 68-602, 1968-2 C.B. 135. It is unclear what actions might be taken to avoid this result, but it may be that the presence of an independent business purpose for the cancellation or contribution, combined with the passage of time, would suffice. In that case, the consequences outlined in section 108(e)(6) will apply, and the subsidiary will recognize discharge income if the parent's basis in the debt is less than its face amount.

Note that even if the step transaction doctrine can be avoided and a subsidiary can be "resuscitated" for the purposes of its liquidation, the parent corporation will need to calibrate its actions to ensure that there are no untoward consequences of its contribution of appreciated assets. This is because the "net value regs" deny nonrecognition under section 351 if the stock *received* by the transferor has no net value. Prop. Reg. § 1.351-1(a)(1)(iii)(B). Thus, the transferor must take care to contribute a sufficient amount so that the stock of the subsidiary clearly does have value as a result of the contributions.

27.4.2.   Reorganization Transactions Involving Subsidiaries Approaching Insolvency

If a corporation approaching insolvency can be successfully merged into another corporation, the acquiring corporation can succeed to the tax attributes, including the carryover losses, of the insolvent corporation.

There are of course a number of questions about such carryover losses in the context of an insolvent or nearly insolvent corporation. For instance, how much can those carryover losses ever be worth, if the corporation is insolvent? Special rules, found in regulations promulgated under section 382(*l*)(6), in many cases allow the value of the corporation to be increased by the stock issued to creditors. It is not clear how the section 382 limitation operates in this context when the special rules are inapplicable. Section 382 might, for example, eliminate all of the NOL, since the subsidiary is worth virtually nothing. But section 382 does not apply to every merger: it only applies when the merger results in an ownership change. Even in those cases in which there has been an ownership change, the built-in gain rules seem to allow the survival of at least a portion of the NOLs of the insolvent subsidiary.

If a merger solution to preserving tax attributes were available, then, it appears that the parent corporation would, at least in some circumstances, have a choice between recognition of its stock loss or retention of the subsidiary's potentially more valuable tax attributes. Not surprisingly, the Service when faced with this issue ruled that an insolvent subsidiary could not be merged into its parent-creditor because the acquiring parent would receive no Target assets *in exchange for* its stock. Rev. Rul. 59-296, 1959-2 C.B.87; *Cf.* Rev. Rul. 70-489, 1970-2 C.B. 53 (appearing to confirm this position), *amplified and superseded, respectively by* Rev. Rul. 2003-125, 2003-2 C.B. 1243.

There seems to be a better argument that an insolvent subsidiary could be involved in a merger with a sister corporation. Several courts have accepted the idea, resisted by the government, that such transactions can be mergers when continuity of shareholder interest is satisfied because of the virtual identity of the shareholders of Target and Acquirer. *See, e.g.*, Norman Scott, Inc. v. Commissioner, 48 T.C. 598 (1967).

There is also a possibility that the transaction could be treated as a nondivisive D reorg. There would be a transfer to an Acquirer, after which the shareholders of the Target controlled Acquirer. As in the other situations with insolvent corporations, however, there remains some question whether stock has been issued by Acquirer in exchange for Target assets and whether that stock has been distributed to the Target's shareholder.

Under proposed net value regulations, mergers, B reorgs, and C reorgs all require net value, but recaps and F reorgs do not. In general, there are two requirements for mergers, B reorgs and C reorgs: (1) there must be a surrender of net value for stock, which means that Target must be solvent and that the amount of liabilities assumed, when combined with the other boot involved, must not exceed the fair market value of the assets transferred and (2) there must be a receipt of net value — i.e., Acquiring generally must be solvent *after* the transaction. An exception to the first requirement is made for nondivisive D reorgs, where the only question is whether Target is solvent, even if there is no value given up for which stock is (or could be deemed to be) transferred back.

Note that the net value approach would leave intact the special rules under which a corporation in bankruptcy or similar proceeding can be a party to a reorganization as defined in section 368(a)(1)(G). The net value regulations in such cases allow any liabilities that are extinguished as a result of the transaction to be ignored. The special rules for reorganizations in connection with bankruptcy provide special approaches to the continuity of interest requirement, in effect treating certain creditors as if they were already shareholders immediately before the reorganization. See Reg. § 1.368–1(e)(6).

There is also the possibility that an attempt by Parent to eliminate the debt of the insolvent subsidiary would be honored here, despite the Service's position in Rev. Rul. 68-602. The Service has honored the contribution (and thus cancellation) of a subsidiary's debt to its parent in the context in which the goal was to avoid the application of section 357(c)'s excess liability rule. Rev. Rul. 78-330, 1978-2 C.B. 147.

27.4.3.　Worthless Subsidiary Stock

Under section 165(g), a parent will be allowed a deduction when stock of a subsidiary becomes worthless. If the stock owned constitutes control under section 1504(a)(2) and more than 90% of the subsidiary's receipts arise from activities other than simply investment activities, this loss will be ordinary.

It may be difficult, however, to establish the year in which the stock actually becomes worthless. Attempts at establishing a realization event through "abandonment" may be equally difficult.

Section 382(g)(4)(D) is intended to eliminate any carryover loss after a worthless stock deduction has been claimed by a 50% owner.

27.4.4.　Liquidation/Reincorporation Problems

If an insolvent or almost insolvent subsidiary liquidates, can its parent claim a loss and yet continue to operate the business?

a.　Solvent (But Close to Insolvent) Subsidiary Liquidation

Several rulings suggest that there is nothing inherently inconsistent between the liquidation or merger of an almost insolvent subsidiary and the continuation of the business of the subsidiary by the parent. Indeed, if qualification as a merger is required, the continuity of business enterprise requirement mandates that either the subsidiary's assets be retained, or the subsidiary's business be continued.

Note that if the subsidiary's assets are re-transferred to another subsidiary of parent, the transaction may not be honored as a liquidation because there will be a deemed reincorporation. Such transactions may, however, be recharacterized as some sort of reorganization. See Rev. Rul. 69-617, 1969-2 C.B. 57; PLR 200250024. If the subsidiary was entirely owned by the parent, the difference between section 332 treatment and the recharacterized treatment will be found in the parent's basis in the transferee subsidiary and the location of any tax attributes that might have been inherited by P if liquidation treatment had been honored.

b.　Insolvent Subsidiary Liquidation

But what if the subsidiary was treated as insolvent and a stock loss was claimed? The parent's continuation of the business of the subsidiary in those circumstances might be viewed as inconsistent with the claimed loss. The Service, however, has ruled that the loss is allowable. See Rev. Rul. 70-489, 1970-2 C.B. 53, *superseded by* Rev. Rul. 2003-125, 2003-2 C.B. 1243 (allowing a worthless stock deduction when an insolvent wholly owned subsidiary checked the box to become disregarded).

27.4.5.　Establishing Net Value, Worthlessness and Insolvency

All of the above discussion assumed that there are well established rules for determining how liabilities should be counted in determining when a corporation is insolvent and whether there is net value. Unfortunately, there is not. See "Definition of Liabilities" and "Amount of Liabilities" in the preamble to the proposed net value regulations. 70 FR 11903, 11905–6. This is an ongoing problem for the income tax, just as valuation issues in general continue to cause problems in determining how Code provisions apply.

PRACTICE PROBLEMS

Assume all corporations are solvent unless indicated otherwise.

1.   Sub has outstanding debt held by third parties with an adjusted issue price of $1,000,000 and a fair market value of $850,000. What is the tax result if Sub repurchases the debt for cash from its holders for its fair market value?

(a)   Income of $150,000 at time debt would have come due

(b)   Income to Sub of $150,000 at time debt is repurchased

(c)   Income to Sub to extent that interest payments on debt are avoided

(d)   No income to Sub

2.   Sub has outstanding debt held by third parties with an adjusted issue price of $1,000,000 and a fair market value of $1,000,000. Sub pays this debt by transferring to the holders of the debt land which it holds with a basis of $600,000. What is the tax result to Sub?

(a)   Gain of $400,000 on the land at the time of the transfer, as if it had sold the land and used the proceeds to pay the debt

(b)   Gain of $400,000 on the land, at the time that the principle amount of the debt would have been due

(c)   Gain of $400,000 on the land, recognized over the original term of the debt

(d)   No gain or other income to Sub

3.   Parent owns all of the stock of Sub. Sub has outstanding debt held by third parties with an issue price of $1,000,000 and a fair market value of $850,000. What is the result if Parent buys all of the outstanding debt of Sub at its fair market value?

(a)   No income to Parent or Sub until payment on debt; $150,000 to Parent on payment

(b)   Income of $150,000 to Parent; debt held with basis/issue price of $1,000,000

(c)   Income of $150,000 to Sub, debt held by Parent with basis/issue price of $850,000

(d)   Loss of $150,000 to Parent

4.   Parent owns all of the stock of Sub with a basis of $100,000. Parent also holds debt of $1,000,000 owed by Sub. According to a plan, Sub liquidates, and Sub transfers cash of $5,000,000 and a piece of land worth $1,000,000 that it holds with a basis of $600,000. What is the result of the liquidation?

(a)   Gain of $400,000 to Sub, gain of $4,900,000 to Parent

(b)   Gain of $400,000 to Sub, no gain or loss to Parent

(c)   No gain to Sub, no gain to Parent

(d)   Insufficient information; Parent's basis in the debt must be known

5.   Parent owns all of the stock of Sub with a basis of $100,000. Parent also holds debt with an adjusted issue price/basis in its hands of $1,000,000 owed by Sub. According to a plan, Sub liquidates, and Sub transfers cash of $500,000 and a piece of land worth $80,000 that it holds with a basis of $30,000. What is the result of this transaction to Parent?

(a)   Stock loss of $100,000 and worthless debt loss of $420,000

(b)   No gain or loss

(c)   Loss on debt of $420,000; no loss on stock

(d)   Loss of $100,000 on stock, no loss on debt

DISCUSSION PROBLEMS

All of the stock of X Corp is owned by three brothers, who own the stock and debt of X Corp equally. X Corp conducts a manufacturing business. At the current time, it has the following assets and liabilities:

Assets:

- depreciable physical assets (its building and its machines) with an adjusted basis of $4 million and a fair market value of $10 million,

- finished goods inventory with a basis and a fair market value of $2 million,

- inventory in process with a basis of $2 million and an uncertain fair market value,

- accounts receivable with a face amount that fluctuates between $700,000 and $1 million, and

- a considerable amount of value as a going business with an established customer base and a skilled workforce.

This value is offset by

- bank debt of $8 million with a variable interest rate, guaranteed by the shareholders of X Corp,

- a recourse loan on its land of $1 million at 5.5%, and a nonrecourse loan of $1 million at 6%, debt to its shareholders of $3 million at 6% (held pro rata),

- debt to an outside individual of $1 million at 4%, and

- debt to trade creditors that fluctuate between $500,000 and $1 million which bears no interest as long as it is paid within 4 weeks.

What are the tax consequences of the following transactions? Assume each question below is in the alternative, not cumulative, unless otherwise specified.

1.   A trade creditor (a closely held corporation owned by an individual who seems to be going through a particularly messy divorce and doesn't want his

business to appear particularly successful at the moment) renegotiates a trade debt so that $200,000 is no longer due, but X Corp contracts to buy from this creditor for 18 months without the significant volume discount that it usually enjoys.

2.   X Corp pays off the recourse loan on its land for $1.2 million.

3.   The three brothers contribute to X Corp the X Corp debt owed to them, at a time when interest rates are at 8%. What else would you need to know in order to provide an answer with numbers to this question?

   (a)   Would the result be any different if the three shareholders took back more common stock?

   (b)   In response to pressure from the bank, the three make equal contributions of their own $250,000 in cash to X Corp, and the total $750,000 in cash is used to pay the outside creditor in full.

   (c)   In the alternative, Al, the oldest of the brothers, buys the debt of $1 million held by the outside individual for $750,000 (that is, Al pays the creditor and acquires the right to be paid himself). What is the result if, six months later, Al contributes this debt to X Corp and takes back preferred stock which is convertible into common stock at Al's option?

4.   Y Corp, a large customer of X Corp is interested in buying X Corp for cash. It buys the debt of X Corp from the outside creditor for $750,000 and then pays the three brothers $7 million each in cash for all of their interests in X Corp. (What else might you want to know before you decided how this second payment should be treated?)

5.   Y Corp is interested in buying X Corp for cash. It buys the debt of X Corp from the outside creditor for $750,000 and then two months later, it pays the three brothers $4 million each in cash for all of their stock of X Corp.

   (a)   Assume the other creditors' debt remains in place, but the guarantees of the brothers are released.

   (b)   Assume the bank debt is renegotiated, that is, the bank debt and its guarantees by the brothers are removed, and replaced with different bank debt at a time when interest rates are at 7%.

6.   Y Corp is interested in acquiring X Corp. It buys the debt of X Corp from the outside creditor for $750,000 and then two months later, when the acquisition transaction closes, it transfers its publicly traded stock to the three brothers in exchange for all of their interests in X Corp.

7.   Y Corp is interested in acquiring X Corp. It creates a subsidiary, S corp, which is merged into X Corp, and transfers its publicly traded voting stock to the three brothers in exchange for their stock interests in X Corp.

8.   Assume for the following scenarios that Y Corp acquired X Corp stock for $12 million total in cash and, in the same transaction, paid off the debt to the brothers and the outside creditor. The bank debt remains essentially the same, and the real estate remains encumbered.

Also assume that two years after its acquisition of X Corp, X Corp's capital structure is still essentially the same, except that under Y Corp's management the finished goods inventory has been reduced down to about $1 million. Y Corp receives notice of litigation involving a product made by X Corp. A quick check of the warranties contained in the acquisition documents, the whereabouts of the brothers, and the discovery of the fact (perhaps not yet known by plaintiff's lawyers) that Y Corp was probably heavily involved in the distribution of the product, reveals that X Corp is likely to be on its own in defending this litigation and in paying any ultimate judgment. Y Corp's lawyers estimate that the potential liability from this litigation could be about $15 million. Is there any tax consequence resulting from this discovery?

(a) Shortly after the discovery of the potential tort liability, Y Corp contributed to X Corp intellectual property in which it had no basis, but which had a fair market value of $3 million.

(b) Y Corp loaned X Corp $5 million to defend the tort litigation. The expenditure seems to have paid off, because the litigation was settled with an obligation to pay only $4 million.

(c) Y Corp wants to liquidate X Corp so that it can hold the land in its own name without triggering gain. What will this depend upon? What will be the consequences if it can?

(d) X Corp's management has been so distracted with the defense of the tort litigation that it has totally lost track of its market and sales are falling off fast. Indeed, it would appear that X Corp should discontinue its business. It looks as if it will have net operating losses greater than its income for the carryback years. Can those stranded losses be salvaged somehow?

(e) X Corp is failing, as in the above problem, but a quick survey reveals that Y Corp's basis in X Corp is likely to be larger than the NOLs X Corp will generate. How can a tax benefit be obtained from this basis?

ADVANCED TOPICS IN ENTITY ORGANIZATION

Chapter 28

A BRIEF INTRODUCTION TO CONSOLIDATED RETURNS

Statutes and Regulations	Reg. §§ 1.1502-13, 1.1502-32, 1.1502-80
	Skim Reg. §§ 1.1502-11, 1.1502-21, 1.1502-15, 1.1502-33, 1.1502-19, 1.1502-36

28.1. ELIGIBILITY AND ELECTION TO FILE CONSOLIDATED RETURNS

A group of domestic corporations that are members of an affiliated group of corporations within the meaning of section 1504 may elect to file consolidated returns as outlined in the regulations. There must be a common parent that owns directly 80% of the voting power and value of another member of the group. The stock of all other members (except the common parent) must be owned 80% by total voting power and 80% by value by one or more members of the affiliated group.

"Stock" for the purposes of this control test does not include preferred stock which is not participating and cannot be converted into common stock. This provision reflects the nature of such preferred stock; the provision may nevertheless lead to unexpected results because an entire class of stock can be created and disposed of without threatening deconsolidation.

28.2. COMPUTATION OF CONSOLIDATED INCOME GENERALLY

Members of a consolidated group compute their separate taxable incomes under ordinary tax accounting rules, except for distributions within the group and those items that involve deferred intercompany items. Separate taxable income also does not include items that are subject to limitations at the group, rather than the member, level (including capital and section 1231 gains and losses, and charitable deductions). The Supreme Court has held that other items, in particular product liability losses, must also be determined on a consolidated basis. United Dominion Indus. v. United States, 532 U.S. 822 (2001). Net income and the net of the separate calculations are then calculated for the group, and the rates under section 11 applied. *See generally* Reg. § 1.1502-11.

NOLs of members of the group that arise while the corporation is a member of the group are allowed to offset the income of other members. This general approach is limited, however, to the extent that a corporation's losses arose in a separate return limitation year. *See* Reg. §§ 1.1502-21, 1.1502-1(f). A separate return limitation year is a year in which the corporation could *not* have participated in a consolidated return. Thus, losses arising within an affiliated group that has not elected to file a consolidated return *can* be used to offset the income of other members of the group, should an election to file a consolidated return be made in a later year to which those losses are carried forward. The limitation on the use of NOLs focuses on the affiliated status of the loss corporation, and not on the corporations whose income is offset. Thus, a loss corporation can acquire a subsidiary, elect to file a consolidated return, and use its losses to offset the income of the subsidiary — all subject, however, to the limitations of sections 269 and 384. A special rule, however, limits the losses available to the resulting combined group when a profitable corporation is merged into the common parent of a loss group. Another special rule applies (when section 382 does not) to limit the availability of the "built-in loss" of a newly acquired member (defined essentially as defined in section 382(h)). Reg. § 1.1502-15.

The earnings and profits of the members are initially determined separately. The earnings of upper-tier members will be increased or decreased to reflect adjustments in lower-tier member's earnings and profits. Reg. § 1.1502-33.

28.3.   INTERCOMPANY TRANSACTIONS

The consolidated return regulations set up a scheme whereby transactions among members of the group are calculated when the transactions occur, but are generally deferred and not taken into account while both parties and the subject of the transaction remain in the group (or until one of the parties enjoys a related tax benefit that triggers recognition for the other party). Thus, if S corporation sells an asset to B corporation, where S and B are members of the same consolidated group, the gain to S generally is taken account when B sells the asset outside the group (or as B takes cost recovery reductions in respect of the item). Thus S does not have to take into account its gain until B engages in a transaction that requires it to use the basis that relates to the gain recognized but not yet taken into account by S.

Although the concept is simple enough, the mechanism for accounting for intercompany transactions is not easy to extract from the regulations. In general, Reg. section 1.1502-13 sets up a system whereby the "amount" and "location" of an item of income or deduction resulting from an intercompany transaction are established by reference to the transferring corporation and are set at the time of the transaction. But the transferring corporation will not take these items into account until the later point in time when there is a "corresponding item" to be taken into account by the transferee corporation with which it is "matched." The timing, character, and source of the item and related items are thus determined with reference to later events and by taking into account the tax characteristics of the transferee corporation. Reg. § 1.1502-13(a)(2).

28.3.1.   The Matching Principle

The regulations (which use examples to demonstrate the general principles outlined above, thus avoiding being overly abstract) designate the transferring corporation by S (as in seller, although the regulations cover far more transactions than just sales) and the transferee corporation by B (as in buyer). Reg. § 1.1502-13(b)(1). The effects on S are referred to as "intercompany items," while the later effects on B are referred to as the "corresponding items." Thus, when S sells appreciated property to B, S's gain is an intercompany item, and B's gain on sale outside the group is a matched "corresponding item." In general, B will take into account its "corresponding items" in accordance with its regular accounting rules. S will take into account its intercompany items when they are matched by B's corresponding items, with appropriate adjustments.

The intercompany item that S will take into account is not completely fixed as of the time at which it first arose. The amount that S will take into account is the amount by which B's corresponding amount differs from the tax item that it would take into account at this later time had S and B been considered parts of the same taxpayer. This fictional amount that would be the tax effect on B if S and B had been the same taxpayer is referred to as the "recomputed corresponding item." S must take into account as gain on its earlier sale the difference between this recomputed corresponding item and B's actual corresponding item. This all works because transfers within units of the same taxpayer in general have no tax effect. This approach essentially looks at the difference between (i) treating the transaction between S and B as if they were separate taxpayers — that is, B has a stepped up basis after a sale, and (ii) treating the sale as if they were the same taxpayer — that is, no step-up in basis. *See* Reg. § 1.1502-13(c)(3). The difference between these two measures of gain will determine the amount of S's intercompany item to be taken into account.

For instance, suppose S sells to B for $100 land with a basis of $70, and B sells this land outside the group 3 years later for $110. S's gain of $30 is an intercompany item, and B's gain of $10 on resale outside the group is a corresponding item. If B had not been a separate taxpayer, there would have been $40 of gain on its sale (since B would have held the property with a basis of $70 rather than $100). Therefore, there is a recomputed corresponding amount of $40. S must take into income an amount to reflect the difference between B's corresponding item of $10 and the recomputed corresponding item of $40. Thus S has $30 of gain and B has $10. Reg. § 1.1502-13(c)(7) Ex. 1.

Suppose S's basis had been $135. On selling to B for $100, S would have an intercompany loss of $35. Had S and B not been separate taxpayers, the basis used to compute the gain on B's sale to the outsider for $110 would have been $135, and B would have had a $25 loss (the recomputed corresponding item). Since B has an actual $10 gain (B's corresponding item), S will take into account a $35 loss (the difference between $10 of gain and $25 of loss) when B sells. *See* Reg. § 1.1502-13(c)(7) Ex. 1(e).

In these simple sale examples, the intercompany item/recomputed corresponding item mechanism seems like a cumbersome way to get to the result that seems most appropriate: S is charged with the gain that arose while the property was in its hands, and B is charged with the gain (or loss) that arose while the property was in its hands, with the timing determined by when B's sale moves the item out of the consolidated group. (These items are not netted until the income computed on each separate corporation's return is combined in consolidation.) And so the apparatus of the regulations seems unnecessary.

The payoff for this cumbersome mechanism comes when we consider other, more complex situations. One set of complications involves corresponding items with more elaborate timing, such as an intercompany contract to build a depreciable asset followed by a use of the asset and cost recovery. Suppose, for instance, that S had drilled a water well, incurring costs of $80, which it then sold to B for $100. S therefore has a $20 "intercompany item," held in suspense until B takes into account its "corresponding items." Assume further that B will take cost recovery by deducting $10 in each of 10 years, beginning in the year after the well is constructed (disregarding half-year conventions). This cost recovery is a "corresponding item." So we need to determine what B's cost recovery would have been if it were in fact the same taxpayer as S. If S and B had been the same taxpayer, the basis would have been the capitalized costs incurred by S of $80 (without including the profit element resulting from S's activities), resulting in only $8 of cost recovery that would be allowed each year. Accordingly, $8 is the "recomputed corresponding item." S must take into account $2 of its gain as its intercompany item in each of the 10 years in which B claims cost recovery of $10. *See* Reg. § 1.1502-13(c)(7) Ex. 7.

Another set of complications arises when the corresponding items relate to transactions that ordinarily would be nonrecognition transactions. Return to the first problem above, based on Ex. 1 of Reg. section 1.1502-13(c)(7). Suppose that B transferred the property to a nonmember in a transaction qualifying for nonrecognition under section 1031. Now, there is no difference between B's "corresponding item" and the "recomputed corresponding item" — whether or not S's transfer to B was merely within a division, there would be no gain or loss. Since there is nothing to reconcile, S need not take any of its intercompany item into account — yet. B's later disposition of the property received in the section 1031 transaction becomes the most likely trigger for the corresponding items. *See* Reg. § 1.1502-13(c)(7), Ex. 1(h), 1.1502-13(j)(1).

Finally, in some circumstances, the intercompany items of gain may end up being excluded entirely, and intercompany items of loss may end up being disallowed permanently, because of the nature of the transaction triggering the corresponding item. *See generally* Reg. § 1.1502-13(c)(6)(i). Thus, if S sells loss property to B, and B then distributes the property in a transaction subject to section 311, S's loss will be permanently disallowed because the entire loss would have been disallowed if B had had S's basis at the time of the section 311 distribution. An intercompany item of gain can similarly be excluded as a result of a subsequent transaction by B, but only if there is no possibility that the basis made available as a result of the original intercompany transaction can ever be used. This permanent destruction of basis is present, for example, in a section 311 situation. Accordingly, if S sells to B for $100 gain property with a basis of $70, and the property then declines in value until B distributes it, at which time it is worth only $90, S will take into account only $20 of its intercompany item. *See* Reg. § 1.1502-13(c)(7), Ex. 1(g). In contrast, basis is not permanently destroyed in a section 332 liquidation: if B had liquidated, it would not have recognized its loss but the basis would survive. S's intercompany item of gain would also survive, awaiting the trigger of a corresponding item in the parent.

28.3.2. The Acceleration Principle

Reg. section 1.1502-13(d) outlines the "acceleration" rule, under which S will be required to take into account its intercompany items whenever it will no longer be possible to match these intercompany items with B's corresponding items. In general, this will occur when either S or B leaves the group. S's intercompany items can also be triggered if the asset in question leaves the group in a transaction that would ordinarily be a nonrecognition transaction.

28.4. BASIS AND EXCESS LOSS ACCOUNTS

The basis (previously called the investment account) with which a parent corporation holds the stock of a subsidiary corporation is adjusted as the subsidiary recognizes income and loss. Reg. § 1.1502-32. In many (but not all) respects, these adjustments are the same as those made by a shareholder in a subchapter S corporation or a partner in a partnership. The goal is to "treat P and S as a single entity so that consolidated taxable income reflects the group's income." Thus gain recognized by a subsidiary will increase the parent's basis, so that there would not be an additional item of gain should the subsidiary stock be sold. (Note that prior versions of the regulations adjusted investment accounts according to lower-tier members' earnings and profits — an approach that was abandoned in 1994.)

One special feature of consolidation is that a parent's basis in a subsidiary held in consolidation *can effectively go negative*, through the mechanism of an "excess loss account." (This is one of the few places in which the Code allows negative basis rather than triggering immediate gain.) When a subsidiary held with an excess loss account is sold or transferred in a transaction that would otherwise be nontaxable, the parent will realize gain to the extent of the account. Reg. § 1.1502-19. An excess loss account is eliminated without tax cost, however, in a liquidation to which section 332 applies.

Another difference is that an investment adjustment will not be taken into account in basis until a subsidiary's item of income or loss is actually absorbed by the group. For instance, the investment adjustment associated with items that are represented by a net operating loss will not be made until the loss is absorbed into consolidated income — i.e., used to offset income. The result is that in any transaction that would be thought of, outside consolidation, as involving only one recognition event, there are potentially three events of interest in a consolidated group: (i) the regular taxable event that gives rise to an item of income or deduction, (ii) if the transaction involves another member of the group, the time at which that item will be matched with its corresponding item, and (iii) the time at which the item is absorbed by the group and results in an adjustment to the parent's basis in the subsidiary.

The investment adjustment is "straight-up" like those in subchapter S, rather than subject to the sort of tracing rules used in subchapter K. For example, suppose a subsidiary has assets worth $100,000 and 90 shares of the subsidiary stock is held by one member of the group P with a basis of $50 per share. Another member of the group contributes property worth $10,000 with a basis of zero in exchange for 10 shares. If that property increases in value to $20,000 and is sold, the entire $10,000 of gain on the sale is allocated pro rata among all of the shares. P's basis is thus increased to $109,000 and the other member's to $1000, even though the property had $10,000 of pre-contribution gain, all attributable to the other member, at the time it was contributed.

28.4.1. Loss Disallowance Rule

Unfortunately, there are many situations in which the goal of the basis adjustment system cannot easily be met. Indeed, these rules only work well in the relatively trivial case in which a subsidiary is created by a contribution of cash so that there is no difference between the subsidiary's basis in its assets, the parent's basis in the subsidiary stock, and the fair market value of the assets held by the subsidiary, and all changes in value are immediately reflected in taxable events. In any other circumstance (i.e., almost any real world situation), the built-in gain or loss involved wreaks havoc because it can result in duplicated or artificial items of gain or loss.

Take, for instance, the case in which P pays $500 for the stock of S, which holds assets worth $500 with a basis of $100. When S sells those assets outside the group, it recognizes $400 of gain and has cash of $500. The normal operation of the basis adjustments results in P's holding S with a basis of $900 ($500 plus $400 of gain). If P were to sell the S stock at this point for $500, P would recognize $400 of loss. If the character of S's gain and P's loss are the same, S's gain will in effect be eliminated in consolidation. Because of the disparity between "inside basis" and "outside basis" when the stock of S was acquired, a sale of the asset followed by a sale of the stock would, without more, result in the elimination of the inside gain, and this would, under most ways of thinking about it, defeat the principles motivating the repeal of *General Utilities* that require inclusion of all gain resulting from asset appreciation.

The loss disallowance rule of old Reg. section 1.1502-20 was adopted to correct this situation. It rather heavy-handedly disallowed most losses on the sale of subsidiary stock in consolidation. The 1502-20 regulation mechanism was defined broadly enough to disallow a loss when a parent corporation bought assets at their fair market value and contributed them to a consolidated subsidiary, the assets declined in value without a tax loss being triggered, and the stock of the subsidiary was then sold. Although there was a real economic loss here, the operation of the 1502-20 regulations would have kept this loss from being taken into account until the assets themselves were sold. This was essentially the fact pattern in *Rite Aid Corp. v. United States*, 255 F.3d 1357 (Fed. Cir. 2001), in which the Federal Circuit held that the application of the 1502-20 regulation loss disallowance rule in this case was beyond the regulatory authority of Treasury under section 1502, because it denied to corporations in consolidation a tax treatment to which they would have been entitled outside of consolidation.

After several false starts, temporary regulations were issued and finalized covering some of the issues, in which taxpayers were allowed considerable flexibility in adopting positions in the situations covered under the old regulation. Meanwhile, Treasury was successful in securing from Congress, in new language at the end of section 1502, affirmation of the scope of its power to alter the ordinary operation of subchapter C within the consolidated return context.

A comprehensive new scheme for handling noneconomic and duplicated losses recognized in connection with the disposition of member stock was finalized in 2008, primarily by the introduction of Reg. section 1.1502-36. These regulations, fifty-five pages in the Federal Register, are not for the faint of heart and can only be summarized here. The general approach is to attempt to identify the various components of the basis in the particular block of stock that would otherwise be sold for a loss, and to reduce the basis in that stock *only* by the amount that reflects noneconomic or duplicative loss with respect to that block of stock. The regulations thus disallow only those elements of loss that do not represent economic losses. To the extent that member stock is still sold at a loss after the application of these reductions, additional adjustments must be made to avoid duplication of losses.

The first step is the redetermination of the selling member's basis under Reg. section 1.1502-36(b) to reduce disparity in the bases of the various members of the group holding stock in the entity the stock of which is being sold. This step essentially reallocates from the selling member's basis to the basis of other stock held within the group those positive basis adjustments that were previously allocated to it, and, if there is still a loss in the stock to be sold, reallocating to it (and away from any other stock still held by other members) any negative adjustments. No basis should be lost as a result of this step — only a peeling away to limit the loss on the stock actually being sold.

If there is still a loss in the stock to be sold, the basis in the stock to be sold is further reduced by any remaining noneconomic loss. Reg. § 1.1502-36(c). The amount of this reduction is generally the "disconformity amount" — that is, the amount by which outside basis (the basis in the stock being sold) exceeds inside basis (including not only asset basis but deferred deductions, loss carryovers and the like). The reduction will not be greater, however, than the net positive investment adjustments not already removed under Reg. § 1.1502-36(b).

If there is still a loss on the stock to be sold, the attributes of the subsidiary (including the consolidated attributes attributable to the subsidiary) are further reduced to avoid the duplication of loss. Reg. § 1.1502-36(d).

28.5. EFFECT OF CONSOLIDATION ON PROVISIONS OF SUBCHAPTER C

In general, Reg. section 1.1502-80(a) directs that the ordinary rules of the Code and subchapter C apply to the extent that the regulations do not change the result. There are, however, some explicit exceptions, including the nonapplicability of sections 304, 357(c), and 1031. *See* Reg. § 1.1502-80(b). (Note that the nonapplicability of section 1031 does not result in gain recognition within the group earlier than would occur if section 1031 were available, but it does keep the group from engaging in swaps in a way that essentially assigns the high basis available to property that is about to be sold outside the group.)

28.5.1. Distributions of Cash

Cash dividends reduce the recipient's basis in the distributing subsidiary. This result neutralizes the benefit of the result in *Litton Industries* in consolidation. Cash dividends also increase the recipient's earnings and profits. The section 243 dividends-received deduction is not applicable. *See* Reg. § 1.1502-13(f)(2)(ii).

28.5.2. Distributions of Property

Section 311 still applies, but the resulting gain will be an intercompany item. Losses (which would be permanently disallowed under section 311 outside consolidation) are similarly treated, but if the deferred item when ultimately taken into account results in a loss, it is disallowed. This rule preserves basis in a way that limits future gain to an amount in excess of the distributing corporation's basis.

28.5.3. Distributions of Subsidiary Stock

Distributions of lower-tier subsidiary stock (T) by an intermediate-level subsidiary (S) to a higher-tier subsidiary (P) under circumstances that would give rise to section 311 gain outside of consolidation will result in an intercompany item for the intermediate subsidiary S, that will be matched, like any other intercompany item, with P's treatment at the time the distributed stock is sold or the distributed entity is deconsolidated.

In determining the recomputed corresponding item in such cases, the analysis requires treating P and S as if they had been a single corporation that was still subject to the consolidated return regulations with respect to their holding of T stock. P would not have had a fair market value basis in the T stock. Any subsequent distribution from T to P would have further reduced the basis that P had in the T stock. Each of these effects would have increased the difference between P's recomputed corresponding item and its actual corresponding item, resulting in gain to S on the ultimate disposition by P of the T stock. *See* Reg. § 1.1502-13(f)(7) Ex. 2.

This result, which is consistent with treating the lower-tier T stock as property in the hands of the higher-level sub S, was not always obtained under prior versions of the regulations. The transaction, arguably permitted, was sometimes called a "bump-and-strip" — bump for the distribution, and strip for the borrowing and distributing done by the lower-tier subsidiary to strip value from the distributed subsidiary before it was sold.

28.5.4. Stock Redemptions

Most stock redemptions within consolidated groups will fail section 302(b) and thus be taxed under sections 302(d) and 301 as distributions.

There is a set of cases, however, in which this will not be the case — when a subsidiary owns stock of a parent. Whether the parent redeems the stock or the subsidiary merely distributes it, the subsidiary will recognize gain on the stock transfer. An issuer's basis in its own stock is eliminated (essentially the same result directed under section 1032 outside of consolidation). Reg. § 1.1502-13(f)(4). With such basis eliminated, there will be no corresponding items of the parent to match with the subsidiary's gain, and therefore the subsidiary will be required to take its gain into account immediately, without the deferral normally permitted for sales between consolidated parties. *See* Reg. § 1.1502-13(f)(7) Ex. 4.

Section 304 will not apply to acquisitions from within the consolidated group. Reg. § 1.502-80(b).

28.5.5.   Reorganizations and Section 351 Transfers

Nonrecognition is available under the ordinary subchapter C rules. Thus, for instance, the transfer of appreciated stock in a B reorg within a consolidated group does not cause the gain to be recognized, and does not result in an intercompany item.

The regulations do, however, change the effect of boot (at least to the extent that the distribution of boot could not have been treated as a separate distribution or redemption in a nonconsolidated reorg). Reg. section 1.1502-13(f)(3) provides that any boot received with respect to an intercompany reorganization will be treated as a distribution separate from the reorganization and therefore will have the effect of a separate transaction occurring immediately after the section 354 distribution involved in the reorganization (or immediately before in the case of a section 355 transaction). *See* Reg. § 1.1502-13(f)(7), Ex. 3.

Section 362(e)(2) will not apply to section 351 transactions within a consolidated group.

Section 357(c) is generally turned off within a consolidated group. Reg. § 1.1502-80(d). Thus, for instance, in a section 351 transaction in which liabilities exceed basis, no immediate gain is triggered under section 357(c); instead, an excess loss account is immediately created.

28.5.6.   Distributions of Subsidiary Stock under Section 355

During the height of its concern with spin-offs that allowed the separation of two businesses prior to the acquisition of one of them by strangers to the original corporation, Congress enacted section 355(f), which seems to indicate that spin-off treatment will be unavailable to set up a subsidiary that will be an acquisition target. The general leniency with which the regulations now deal with the "plan" requirement of section 355(e) similarly reduce the strictures of section 355(f).

28.6.   OWNERSHIP AND CONTROL WITHIN A CONSOLIDATED GROUP

In many situations, the combined ownership of various members of a consolidated group can be used to determine ownership and control of subsidiaries. For instance, Reg. section 1.368-1(d), relating to continuity of business enterprise determinations for dropdowns after reorganizations, treats drops to several affiliated subsidiaries linked by section 368(c) control as if they were to one controlled subsidiary. Similarly, Reg. section 1.368-2(k) permits drops of assets or stock among affiliated corporations, so long as either "substantially all" the assets or control stock is not transferred or, if substantially all assets or control stock is transferred, the transfer is to a section 368(c) controlled corporation and the transferee remains a member of the qualified group (with some special rules for partnerships).

There are, however, some notable exceptions. One is section 337(c), which directs that the ownership attribution rules of the consolidated return regulations do not apply for the purposes of the 80% control test in section 332. This rule prevents "mirror transactions" — in which the acquiring consolidated group would arrange to have two (perhaps newly created for this purpose) members buy all of the Target stock and then cause Target to be liquidated into the purchasing members in a way that separates wanted assets from unwanted assets — that would permit the acquiring consolidated group to position itself to sell stock, if a sale of unwanted assets would produce gain, or to sell assets, if the sale of unwanted assets would produce loss.

PRACTICE PROBLEMS

1. S and B are members of an affiliated group that has elected to file a consolidated return. S holds property with a basis of $10 and a fair market value of $40. In year 1, S sells the property to B for $40. In year 5, B sells the property to a non-member for $75. When and to what extent will these transactions be taken into account in computing the income of S and B, and thus of the consolidated group?

(a)   Gain to S of $30 in year 1; gain to B of $35 in year 5

(b)   Gain of $65 to S in year 5

(c)   Gain to S of $30 in year 5; gain to B of $35 in year 5

(d)   Gain of $65 to B in year 5

2.   What if S's basis had been $52?

(a)   Loss of $12 to A in year 5; gain of $35 to B in year 5

(b)   Loss of $12 to A in year 1; gain of $35 to B in year 5

(c)   Gain of $23 to B in year 5

(d)   Loss of $12 to A in year 5; gain of $23 to B in year 5

3.   S owns undeveloped grazing land that it rents to B for $5000 per month for 5 years. When and in what amount is this transaction taken into account in determining the taxable incomes of S and B, and thus of their consolidated group?

(a)   Income to S of $300,000 at the end of the fifth year.

(b)   Income to S of $300,000 at the end of the fifth year and expense to B of $300,000 at the end of the fifth year.

(c)   Income to S of $300,000 at the end of the fifth year, and expense of $60,000 to B at the end of each year.

(d)   Income of $60,000 to S and deduction of $60,000 to B at the end of each year.

4.   P owns all of the stock of S with a basis/investment account of $100; S in turn owns all of the stock of T with a basis of $50. P, S, and T are members of an affiliated group that has elected to file a consolidated return. T has income of $15. What is the effect of this income on the basis/investment accounts of P in S and S in T?

(a)   Increase to $115 of P's basis in S; increase to $65 of S's basis in T

(b)   Increase to $65 of S's basis in T

(c)   Increase to $155 of P's basis in S

(d)   No change in any basis

5.   P owns all of the stock of S with a basis/investment account of $100; S in turn owns all of the stock of T with a basis of $65. P, S, and T are members of an affiliated group that has elected to file a consolidated return. T had income of $15 in the prior year. T has no income but distributes a dividend of $8 in year 2.

(a)   S has income of $8 that is taken into account in year 2. This income in turn increases P's basis in its S stock.

(b)   S has income of $8 and T has income of $ 8.

(c)   S has dividend income of $8, subject to the 100% dividends received deduction.

(d)   S has no income, but reduces its investment account/basis in T by $8. P makes no adjustments to its basis in S in year 2.

DISCUSSION PROBLEMS

1.   What is the P Corp group's consolidated taxable income in the year in which the group, consisting of P Corp and its three wholly owned subsidiaries X Corp, Y Corp, and Z Corp, having the following items of income and loss:

	X	Y	Z
Ordinary business income (loss)	$300	($80)	$40
§ 1231 gains (loss)	80	40	(40)
Capital gains (loss)	20	40	(100)
§ 170 contributions	(60)		

2.   What are the tax consequences of the following transactions?

(a)   P Corp leases computer software from X Corp, paying an annual $300 royalty.

(b)   P Corp pays interest of $60 to Y Corp on an intercorporate loan. Assume that under their respective methods of accounting, this $60 of interest would properly be taken into account in this year.

(c)   In year 1, P Corp. sells land with a basis of $300 and a fair market value of $400 to Z Corp. Z Corp. resells the land in year 2 to an unrelated party for $650.

(d)   Suppose in (c) that Z Corp. sells the property on the installment method and the note pays regular periodic interest. Under the note, a payment of $325 is made in year 3 and a payment of $325 is made in year 4.

(e)   Suppose in (c) that the property sold to Z Corp. is depreciable property that Z Corp. uses in its trade or business. Z Corp. depreciates the property using a straight-line method over 10 years.

3.   Discuss the tax consequences of the following situations.

(a)   P Corp owns all the stock of X Corp, with which it files a consolidated return. P Corp's basis in the X Corp stock is $100. In year 1, X Corp earns $30 and makes no distribution. In year 2, X Corp earns $20 and makes a $50 distribution to P Corp.

(b)   Suppose in (a) that in year 1, P Corp earns $200 and X Corp. has a net operating loss of $160. In year 2, P Corp earns $100 and X Corp suffers a $140 loss. P Corp sells its X Corp stock in year 3 for $60.

(c)   P Corp, parent of a group already filing a consolidated return, buys all of the stock of S Corp for $200, but it does not want all of the assets of S Corp. It sells Asset A, held by S Corp with a basis of $10, for $100; and it distributes to itself Asset B, held with a basis and a fair market value of $100. It then sells S Corp, which now holds only the proceeds of the sale of asset A.

(d)   P Corp is the parent of a group filing a consolidated return in which X Corp is a member. X Corp was formed 5 years ago by a contribution of cash of $10,000. The non-depreciable assets it purchased with that cash are now worth $2000. X Corp has engaged in no other economic activity during these five years. P Corp sells X Corp for $2,000 to A Corp.

4.   What is the consequence to P Corp if a section 338(h)(10) election is made? What is the consequence to PCorp if a section 338(h)(10) election is not made?

TABLE OF CASES

[References are to chapters or pages.]

[References are to chapters or pages.]

TABLE OF STATUTES

[References are to chapters or sections.]

[References are to chapters or sections.]

[References are to chapters or sections.]

[References are to chapters or sections.]

[References are to chapters or sections.]

[References are to chapters or sections.]

[References are to chapters or sections.]

INVESTMENT COMPANY ACT OF 1940

TAX REFORM ACT OF 1997

TREASURY REGULATIONS (Treas. Reg.)

[References are to chapters or sections.]

[References are to chapters or sections.]

[References are to chapters or sections.]

PROPOSED TREASURY REGULATIONS (Prop. Treas. Reg.)

TABLE OF SECONDARY AUTHORITIES

[References are to chapters or sections.]

[References are to chapters or sections.]

[References are to chapters or sections.]

TECHNICAL ADVICE MEMORANDA (T.A.M.)

WEBSITES

INDEX

[References are to sections.]

A

ACCUMULATED EARNINGS TAX
Generally . . . 1.5.2

ACQUISITIONS
Asset acquisitions (See ASSET ACQUISITIONS)
Distributee's acquisition of control of distributing . . . 23.4.3
Stock acquisitions
    Asset acquisitions, as (See ASSET ACQUISITIONS, subhead: Stock acquisitions as)
    Taxable stock acquisitions (See TAXABLE STOCK ACQUISITIONS)
Taxable asset acquisitions (See TAXABLE ASSET ACQUISITIONS)
Taxable stock acquisitions (See TAXABLE STOCK ACQUISITIONS)
Tax attributes (See TAX ATTRIBUTES AFTER CORPORATE ACQUISITIONS AND RESTRUCTURINGS)

ACQUISITIVE REORGANIZATIONS (See NONTAXABLE REORGANIZATIONS, subhead: Acquisitive reorganizations, consequences of)

ACQUISITIVE TRANSACTIONS
Generally . . . 20.1
National Starch transactions . . . 20.1.1

ACTIVE TRADE OR BUSINESS REQUIREMENT
Generally . . . 23.4
Conduct of 5-year . . . 23.4.1
Disqualified investment corporations . . . 23.4.5
Distributee's acquisition of control of distributing . . . 23.4.3
Purchase of business or controlling stock of corporation conducting business . . . 23.4.2
Separate affiliated group . . . 23.4.4

ADJUSTED GROSSED-UP BASIS (AGUB)
Allocation of . . . 13.1.2.c
Reg. Section 1.338-5, computed under . . . 13.1.2.b

ADSP (See AGGREGATE DEEMED SALES PRICE (ADSP))

AFFILIATED GROUP
Avoidance of Section 311 gain within . . . 21.2.3.a
Separate affiliated group . . . 23.4.4

AGGREGATE DEEMED SALES PRICE (ADSP)
Allocation of . . . 13.1.2.c
Reg. Section 1.338-4, computed under . . . 13.1.2.a

AGUB (See ADJUSTED GROSSED-UP BASIS (AGUB))

ALTERNATIVE MINIMUM TAX
Generally . . . 1.5.1

AMOUNT REALIZED
Later payments effect on . . . 12.1.4

A REORGANIZATIONS
Assets, transfers of . . . 15.4.6
Business considerations . . . 15.4.3
C corporations, mergers involving . . . 15.4.4
Continuity of business enterprise . . . 15.4.1
Continuity of shareholder interest . . . 15.4.2
Disregarded entities, mergers with . . . 15.4.4
Judicially imposed reorganization requirements . . . 15.4
Mergers
    C corporations . . . 15.4.4
    Disregarded entities . . . 15.4.4
Net value considerations . . . 15.4.5
Parent stock, use of . . . 15.4.6
Receipt of something other than acquirer stock be considered boot . . . 16.4

ASSET ACQUISITIONS
Stock acquisitions as
    Post-acquisition liquidations . . . 13.3.1
    Purchases of controlling stock (See PURCHASES OF CONTROLLING STOCK)
    Taxable informal mergers (See TAXABLE MERGERS AND TAXABLE INFORMAL MERGERS)
    Taxable mergers (See TAXABLE MERGERS AND TAXABLE INFORMAL MERGERS)
Taxable asset acquisitions (See TAXABLE ASSET ACQUISITIONS)

ATTRIBUTION
Generally . . . 7.2
Entities, from . . . 7.2.2
Entities, to . . . 7.2.3
Family members, from . . . 7.2.1
Options, of . . . 7.2.4
Reattribution . . . 7.2.5

B

BASIS
Acquirer parent's in surviving subsidiary stock . . . 19.1.5
Acquiring's basis in issuing shares . . . 8.2.2.b.iv
Assets, corporate transferee's . . . 4.2.1
Consolidated returns
    Generally . . . 28.4
    Loss disallowance rule . . . 28.4.1
Corporate transferee's in assets . . . 4.2.1
In exchange for stock . . . 3.1.4; 3.2.2.c
Issuing shares, acquiring's basis in . . . 8.2.2.b.iv
Later payments effect on . . . 12.1.4
Redemption taxed as dividend, shareholder of . . . 7.6.1.a
Retained stock, transferor's basis in . . . 8.2.2.b.ii
Stock-for-stock recapitalizations, after . . . 9.2.2.a.i
Surviving subsidiary's in acquired assets . . . 19.1.6

I-1

[References are to sections.]

[References are to sections.]

[References are to sections.]

[References are to sections.]

[References are to sections.]

S

SALES OF ASSETS
Sales of stock followed by . . . 12.3
Taxable sales of assets, taxable sales of stock as . . . 13.2.2
Taxable sales of stock as taxable sales of assets . . . 13.2.2

SALES OF STOCK
Qualified small businesses . . . 12.2.1
Sales of assets, followed by . . . 12.3
Special rates on . . . 1.6
Taxable sales of assets, taxable sales of stock as . . . 13.2.2
Taxable sales of stock as taxable sales of assets . . . 13.2.2

S CORPORATIONS AND SHAREHOLDERS
Check-the-box entities . . . 10.5.1
Distributions, effect of
    Employment taxes, allocations as wages subject to . . . 10.2.3.b
    General rules . . . 10.2.3.a
    Wages subject to employment taxes, allocations as . . . 10.2.3.b
Eligibility for . . . 10.1
Entity ownership
    Controlling shareholders, S corporations as . . . 10.3.1
    Other entities as S corporation shareholders . . . 10.3.2
Installment reporting in liquidations . . . 10.5.3
Other special provisions . . . 10.5
Passthrough
    Basis, effect on
        Income, items of . . . 10.2.2.a
        Loss, items of . . . 10.2.2.b
    Deduction, items of . . . 10.2.1
    Income, items of
        Generally . . . 10.2.1
        Basis, effect on . . . 10.2.2.a
Section 338(h)(10) election, availability of . . . 10.5.2; 13.2.1
Section 368(a)(1)(F) mere changes in form . . . 22.2
Terminations of . . . 10.1.1

SECTION 302 REDEMPTIONS
Corporation's perspective . . . 7.5
Distribution treatment, consequences of
    Generally . . . 8.2.2.b
    Acquiring's basis in issuing shares . . . 8.2.2.b.iv
    Earnings and profits . . . 8.2.2.b.i
    Issuing shares, acquiring's basis in . . . 8.2.2.b.iv
    Retained stock, transferor's basis in . . . 8.2.2.b.ii
    Section 1059 apply . . . 8.2.2.b.iii
    Transferor's basis in retained stock . . . 8.2.2.b.ii
Exchange treatment, consequences of . . . 8.2.2.a
Partial liquidations . . . 7.5

SECTION 302 REDEMPTIONS—Cont.
Sale under . . . 8.2.2
Section 318, stock ownership attribution under (See ATTRIBUTION)
Serial redemptions . . . 7.4
Shareholder's perspective
    Complete terminations . . . 7.3.3
    Not essentially equivalent to a dividend standard . . . 7.3.1
    Substantially disproportionate standard . . . 7.3.2
Statutory provisions, apply . . . 7.1.
Step transactions . . . 7.4
Stock ownership attribution under Section 318 (See ATTRIBUTION)
Tax consequences
    Corporation, to . . . 7.6.2
    Shareholder, to
        Generally . . . 7.6.1
        Basis of redemption taxed as dividend . . . 7.6.1.a
        Extraordinary dividends for corporate shareholder . . . 7.6.1.b
Zenz case . . . 7.4

SECTION 303 REDEMPTIONS
Generally . . . 7.7

SECTION 304 REDEMPTIONS
Acquiring corporation receives stock . . . 8.2.3
Covered transactions . . . 8.2.1
Mechanics of . . . 8.2
Rationale of . . . 8.1

SECTION 336 LIQUIDATIONS (See LIQUIDATIONS)

SECTION 338 (See ASSET ACQUISITIONS, subhead: Stock acquisitions as)

SECTION 351
Acquisitive transactions
    Generally . . . 20.1
    National Starch transactions . . . 20.1.1
C corporation provisions, consolidation on . . . 28.5.5
Liability assumptions (See LIABILITY ASSUMPTIONS)
Transfers of property to corporations under (See TRANSFERS OF PROPERTY TO CORPORATIONS UNDER SECTION 351)

SECTION 355
Active trade or business requirement (See ACTIVE TRADE OR BUSINESS REQUIREMENT)
Basic requirements . . . 23.3
Contemplated by . . . 23.2
Device test . . . 23.5
Hurdles created to prevent . . . 23.1
Subsidiary stock distributions under . . . 28.5.6

SECTION 368(a)(1)(F) MERE CHANGES IN FORM
Disregarded entities . . . 22.1
F reorganizations . . . 22.1

[References are to sections.]

[References are to sections.]